AGENTS OF CHANGE

Agents of Change

American Jews and the
Transformation of Israeli Judaism

Adam S. Ferziger

NEW YORK UNIVERSITY PRESS

New York

NEW YORK UNIVERSITY PRESS
New York
www.nyupress.org

Library of Congress Cataloging-in-Publication Data
Names: Ferziger, Adam S., author.
Title: Agents of change : American Jews and the transformation of Israeli Judaism / Adam S. Ferziger.
Other titles: American Jews and the transformation of Israeli Judaism
Description: New York : New York University Press, [2025] | Includes bibliographical references and index.
Identifiers: LCCN 2024039897 (print) | LCCN 2024039898 (ebook) | ISBN 9781479817542 (hardback) | ISBN 9781479817559 (ebook) | ISBN 9781479817573 (ebook other)
Subjects: LCSH: Israel–Civilization–American influences. | Jews–United States–Emigration and immigration–20th century. | United States–Civilization–Israeli influences. | Orthodox Judaism–Israel.
Classification: LCC DS132 .F47 2025 (print) | LCC DS132 (ebook) | DDC 956.9405—dc23/eng/20241213
LC record available at https://lccn.loc.gov/2024039897
LC ebook record available at https://lccn.loc.gov/2024039898

This book is printed on acid-free paper, and its binding materials are chosen for strength and durability. We strive to use environmentally responsible suppliers and materials to the greatest extent possible in publishing our books.

The manufacturer's authorized representative in the EU for product safety is Mare Nostrum Group B.V., Mauritskade 21D, 1091 GC Amsterdam, The Netherlands. Email: gpsr@mare-nostrum.co.uk.

Manufactured in the United States of America

10 9 8 7 6 5 4 3 2 1

Also available as an ebook

לילדינו היקרים ולכל בני דורם בישראל, שהתייצבו בעת צרה, בתקווה

שמאמציהם יביאו לעתיד טוב יותר.

To our dear children and their entire generation in Israel, who stepped up at the most challenging of times, with the hope that their efforts will have agency for positive change.

CONTENTS

PART THREE: HOMELAND AND BEYOND

What were the chances? A prime minister and a president who were both offspring of Anglo immigrants. That was the reality in Israel from mid-2021 through mid-2022. And it was more than just parentage. Naftali Bennett and Isaac Herzog each spent critical periods of their early development living in North America, immersed in its Jewish cultural and religious life.

President Herzog's overall approval continued unabated into 2024, past the brutal Hamas attacks on Israel of October 7, 2023. Bennett—the first practicing Orthodox Jew to serve as Israel's prime minister—on the other hand, was already out of office by June 2022, even as he appeared to be positioning himself for a return in the coming years. Yet one issue that stood out during their period of overlap was their common effort to support and encourage the more moderate local religious forces within Israel that have gained momentum, especially over the previous two decades. This endeavor included exploring ways to engage non-Orthodox groups and their rabbis and leaders, loosening the religious establishment's monopoly over kosher food supervision, and advancing less rigid approaches to conversion.

At a time when American Jews are divided regarding their opinions on Israel, the Anglo/American pedigrees of these two individuals, their personal exposures to American Jewish life, and the way these manifested in practice are worthy of reflection.

President Isaac "Bougie" Herzog's position as scion to Israeli royalty is well-known. His father, Chaim Herzog, was himself the sixth president of Israel. Chaim Herzog's eloquent English speeches when he served as ambassador to the UN reflected his upbringing in Ireland—where Isaac's grandfather and eponym had been chief rabbi. Arriving in British Palestine in 1936 after completing secondary school in Dublin, Chaim studied in the Hebron Yeshiva in Jerusalem and fought in the Haganah (the pre-state Zionist military organization) before attending law school in London and serving in the British army during World War II. He only returned to Palestine in 1947, at nearly thirty years old, and then met his wife, Aura, who had immigrated after gaining advanced academic degrees in South Africa. By 1950 they were back on the road, when Chaim was stationed in Washington, DC, as the Israel Defense Forces (IDF) military attaché.

Not only was Isaac "Bougie" Herzog born in 1960 to a home of "new immigrants," he spent his high school years in New York during his father's ambassadorship. He was graduated in 1977 from the renowned Modern Orthodox Ramaz School on Manhattan's Upper East Side, where he was elected vice president of the student government and also worked with his classmates as a counselor at the Religious Zionist summer camp Massad.

Rabbi Haskel Lookstein, the longtime Ramaz principal and rabbi of its mother institution, Kehilath Jeshurun (KJ), reminisced that, throughout his Manhattan years, Bougie would accompany his father to synagogue each Sabbath morning, where he would encounter the congregation's moderate and inclusive Orthodox approach to Judaism. Notably, Lookstein himself was challenged in 2016 by the Israeli chief rabbinate, due to his leniencies in regard to Orthodox conversion, before his authority was eventually recognized.

Former prime minister Naftali Bennett's American parents arrived in Israel in 1967 and settled in Haifa, where he was born. Yet like the Herzog family, for mostly professional reasons, the Bennetts returned numerous times to North America for extended periods. When Naftali was a toddler the family lived in San Francisco. He spent his preschool years in Montreal, where his father worked for the Technion-Israel Institute of Technology, and the family began its road to religious observance. They relocated one more time to New Jersey, where Naftali attended Jewish day school until the age of ten. After returning to Israel, the Bennetts' American immigrant credentials were further solidified through his mother's long-time role as director of the northern branch of the Association of Americans and Canadians in Israel (AACI).

Like Herzog, Bennett had an early adult stint in the United States as well. After serving as an officer in top IDF commando units and completing his studies at the Hebrew University in Jerusalem, he moved to New York with his wife, Gilat. There he developed a successful high-tech start-up venture, while she worked as a dessert chef in some of the city's top restaurants.

Profiles of Bennett's wife, who grew up in a secular home, have fixated on the degree to which she shares his religious commitments. In one interview, she described how she began to feel a personal connection to religion during their time in New York, when she attended a "beginner's minyan" at a local Orthodox synagogue that was dedicated to introducing traditional rituals and ideas to those possessing limited familiarity with them. That congregation was none other than Lookstein's KJ, the same one that Isaac Herzog had attended with his father throughout his high school years. Indeed, upon coming back to Israel, the Bennetts apparently felt most contented settling in a community with a strong American immigrant Orthodox contingent and found their comfort zone in Ra'anana, north of Tel Aviv.

Similar to Bougie and Bennett, Israel's longest-serving prime minister, Benjamin (Bibi) Netanyahu, also spent formative years in the United States. Biographers have noted, however, that Bibi's family was far more isolated from local Jewish life than were his younger fellow Israeli statesmen.

This book explores the emergence of moderate directions in Israeli religious life that have begun to come to fruition in the twenty-first century and the key role in their development played by a cadre of American immigrants to Israel who arrived during the 1960s through the early 1980s. It focuses on religious figures and phenomena rather than political figures such as Herzog or Bennett. But the biographical components shared by two of Israel's central state personalities echo key elements that are at the foundation of this volume. As we will see, it was the American religious figures' native Israeli students and protégés who adjusted the novel and ostensibly foreign approaches of their immigrant mentors to local realities and cultural norms, enabling these outlooks to gain a footing in Israeli life. Along with Herzog's and Bennett's models, then, the activities of these students of the immigrant figures testify to a transnational process in which fresh ideas that came from abroad were refined and reformulated by a second generation in ways that could resonate with the local environment. Relatedly, we will also explore the bidirectional quality of key religious trends that first percolated within Israel but have subsequently gained entrée into American Jewish religious life. In the book's conclusion, we will consider what impact the burgeoning

Israeli moderate religious direction might have on the ongoing relationship between Israeli and American Jewries.

* * *

On October 7, 2023, Gaza-based Hamas terrorists mercilessly murdered and tortured over twelve hundred Israeli infants, children, youths, and adults of all ages in horrific ways. They also kidnapped over two hundred human beings, Israeli citizens as well as other foreign nationals, and held them hostage—murdering additional persons—while allowing no human contact with the outside world, including the Red Cross. Thousands of others—including many of the families of the hostages—lost their homes, all their possessions and sources of income, and faced living as transients for months if not years to come. The pain and shock were raw, as was the intense sadness and concern for all innocent people killed or injured as a result of the war instigated by Hamas's atrocities. Closer to home, loved ones and their peers were forced into active duty to protect their fellow Israelis and prevent such massacres from taking place in the future. In the wake of these events, there was a dangerous rise in public acts of hatred, insensitivity, and harassment toward Jews worldwide.

One central premise of this book, substantiated further by the Hamas attacks of October 7, 2023, and the responses to them, is to deflate the idea that the relationship of American Jews to Israeli society has retreated from the critical role it played for the last half-century. The strong and diverse reactions of American Jews from every position on the ideological and political spectrum to the horror and its aftermath have only heightened the importance of delving deeply into the roots, evolution, and burgeoning trends of this ongoing and dynamic interface.

Having experienced firsthand and examined copiously this interaction for nearly forty years, there is no question that, even when not saying so explicitly, I am fully aware that I am part of the story. That personal element is contained within my voice. As I have indicated in previous works, my goal, and what I see as the aim of every responsible historian, is not to lay claim to an absolute, empirical certainty. Rather, it is to present an account and interpretation of past and contemporary human events and phenomena that is predicated on rigorous tools and evidence, one that offers readers—be they trained academics or people deeply interested and invested in the subject—a compelling and illuminating understanding.

ABBREVIATIONS

BIU—Bar-Ilan University

IDF—Israel Defense Forces

HUC-JIR—Hebrew Union College-Jewish Institute of Religion

HUC—Hebrew Union College

ISMO—Israeli Moderate Orthodox [Judaism/Jews]/Orthodoxy

JTA—Jewish Telegraphic Agency

JTS—Jewish Theological Seminary

MK—Member of Knesset (Israel's parliament)

MO—Modern Orthodox [Judaism/Jews]/Orthodoxy

OTS—Ohr Torah Stone Institutions

RZ—Religion Zionist/Zionism

SHI—Shalom Hartman Institute

TMZ—Torah MiTzion Movement

YHE—Yeshivat Har Etzion

YU—Yeshiva University

Introduction

Cultural Agents, Transnationalism, and Americanization

"Some people thought that we were being very reckless. We were not just coming to the land of Israel, we were coming to a hole in the ground. . . . But we were determined."[1] On July 7, 1971, Rabbi Dr. Aharon Lichtenstein, his wife, Dr. Tova Lichtenstein, and their five children, all under the age of eleven, immigrated to Israel from New York. The decision to uproot their family had not been an easy one. On a personal level, it required leaving Tova's father, Rabbi Dr. Joseph B. Soloveitchik, who was not in favor of their plans, four years after her mother had passed away. From a professional perspective, it meant sacrificing their burgeoning American careers, including Aharon Lichtenstein's role as a senior rabbinic figure and titular heir to his father-in-law at Yeshiva University (henceforth YU).[2] Soloveitchik was the preeminent Talmudist and theologian of American Modern Orthodox (henceforth MO) Judaism, the Jewish religious movement that seeks to integrate traditional commitment and active engagement with broader society and culture, and the central religious personality at its banner institution, YU.[3] Instead, the son-in-law accepted the position of co-head at Yeshivat Har Etzion (henceforth YHE). At the time, YHE was a fledgling Israeli *Hesder* program, in which students combine Torah studies with army service. It was established in 1968 in the Gush Etzion Bloc south of Jerusalem, and in 1971 was still housed in temporary structures.[4]

Over fifty years later, YHE is thriving, with more than five thousand alumni in Israel and worldwide, nearly five hundred current full-time male students, a sister school with over two hundred women engaged in advanced learning, an affiliated teacher's college with thousands of matriculants that grants both bachelor's and master's degrees in a range of subjects, and a prolific publishing arm. The organization sustains two campuses adjacent to its original setting with multiple permanent buildings, as well as significant activity in a historic building located in the center of Jerusalem. Scores of graduates are themselves founders or heads of influential educational and religious institutions in Israel and throughout the globe, and many others have gained prominence as social activists and scholars in the academy, as well as in politics, law, medicine, high tech, finance, and industry. Yet when Aharon Lichtenstein, who passed away in 2015, reflected a few years before his death on his impact on Israeli society, he acknowledged some achievements but was decidedly ambivalent: "I experience frustration with regard to my position within the Israeli public scene . . . I think mine has been a moderating voice, in certain respects a positive one; but, by and large, the religious Zionist community has, I think, been taken over, politically and sociologically, by people who have misguided values, and that is not a good feeling . . . I am, politically speaking, almost a lone wolf . . . it pains me . . . I am pained for our society."[5]

Had he lived until October 2021, Lichtenstein might have been more encouraged by skullcap-wearing Naftali Bennett's political coalition, predicated on a partnership between middle-of-the-road Jewish figures from religious and secular backgrounds, together with an Arab party. Then again, by November 2022, he would have witnessed the decisive electoral comeback of Benjamin Netanyahu and the distinctly right-wing government that he built together with five exclusively religious parties. Suffice it to say, from a political perspective it is hard to deflect Lichtenstein's melancholy estimation.

Indeed, his "lone wolf" status was not limited to the political sphere. During much of his Israeli career, few within his adopted cultural and social habitat—the Religious Zionist (henceforth RZ) sector, whose diverse spectrum is characterized by integration of traditional observance and identification with the modern State of Israel—could fully grasp the idea of an illustrious Torah scholar with a Harvard PhD in English literature and an accompanying clean-shaven college professorial look. Nor did the majority resonate with his promotion of a version of Orthodox Judaism that celebrates the merits of learning from non-Jewish literary and philosophical sources, as well as from Jews of all stripes, and encourages advanced women's Torah study.[6]

Yet measured through developments within Israeli religious life, and particularly the RZ segment, during the first quarter of the twenty-first century, a major change has transpired. Alongside the outlook associated with the acclaimed Merkaz ha-Rav yeshiva—whose adherents have advanced a version of Zionism that focuses on its redemptive/messianic elements and have gravitated toward more strict approaches to religious observance and social values—and its offshoots that had long prevailed, an alternative and more varied Israeli religious culture emerged. Within this environment, the voices of the spiritual and intellectual heirs of Lichtenstein and of fellow American Orthodox figures who arrived during the same period have gained far greater stature. Their innovative positions have found extensive expression in areas that have been at the center of Orthodox debates since the late twentieth century, including the role of women in religious and public life, LGBTQs, interactions with non-Orthodox denominations and nonobservant Jews, religious leadership and the authority of the state rabbinate, religious conversion, perceptions of Jewish experience outside Israel, and attitudes toward academic Jewish studies—including Biblical criticism.

I refer to this phenomenon as Israeli Moderate Orthodoxy (henceforth IsMO). IsMO is not a formal movement in the organizational sense, and by no means is it a monolithic one. Rather, IsMO is a spectrum of key institutions, communities, and personalities that has developed geographic strongholds and attracted viable constituencies. In the process, the overall landscape of Israeli Judaism has evolved such that, even among those who identify strongly with other camps, one can discern more diversity.

To be sure, the phenomenon as presented here is not the precinct of the majority of religiously observant Israelis—the Haredi, non-Zionist/traditionalist Orthodox is the fastest growing segment—and neither has IsMO gained the required political clout to secure significant changes in the country's religious bureaucracy.[7] It is also a predominantly Ashkenazic (Jews of Eastern, Central, or Western European origin) trend that shares commonalities with but differs from the *Masorti* (traditionalist) identities of Mizrahi/Sephardic Israelis (Jews who for the most part came from the Muslim lands of North Africa and the Middle East).[8] It bears pointing out, nonetheless, that while there are numerous towns and Jewish settlements particularly in the periphery of the country whose populations remain predominantly Mizrahi, the overall trend among the Israeli population—including within the RZ spectrum—is toward increased marriages between different Jewish groups, resulting in a blurring of ethno-cultural lines.

This book charts and analyzes key aspects of the burgeoning moderate religious direction in Israeli life and the historical process through which it arose. While this endeavor certainly entails acknowledging multiple figures and factors that contributed to the rise of this trend, the focus is on exploring the American backdrop, the ways in which IsMO resulted from the processing of American ideas, and how it continues to interface with contemporary American Jewish religious life. The core assertion of the book is that a small cadre of American immigrants who arrived in Israel from the mid-1960s through the early 1980s and established or led a range of educational institutions for men and women planted critical seeds for transformations that came to fruition during the early twenty-first century. These American immigrants were, each in their own way, cultural agents who laid ideological and institutional foundations for an Israeli moderate religious stream.

The choice of the adjective "moderate" rather than "modern" is intended to emphasize, on one hand, that IsMO is not simply a transplant of American Modern Orthodoxy, but a novel religious trend that draws from the latter but is sui generis to Israeli realities. On the other hand, in contemporary academic writing, as forged in the works of my late teacher Jacob Katz and the many scholars impacted by his model, the term "modern" does not necessarily imply a more temperate or less zealous religious direction. On the contrary, he and others influenced by his outlook defined all Jewish Orthodoxies as "modern." They all reflect novel ways Jewish religious groups have responded to their evolving historical circumstances since the late eighteenth century and the various degrees to which they reinvented themselves as a result—be their reactions more open or alternatively more rejectionist toward their surroundings.[9]

Alongside Lichtenstein, other major personalities in the pioneering cohort of agents of change whose influence we will discuss in this book include the following, with their year of immigration in parenthesis: Rabbi Dr. Chaim Brovender (1965), who started Michlelet Bruria (today Midreshet Lindenbaum), the first women's institute to feature Talmud study; Rabbi Dr. Daniel Tropper (1969), who established the Gesher organization that focuses on Israeli societal discourse, particularly religious-secular relations; Rabbi Dr. David Hartman (1971), the creator of the pluralistic-oriented Shalom Hartman Institute; Rabbanit Malka Bina (1967) and Rabbanit Chana Henkin (1972), the founders of MaTa"N and Nishmat respectively, two groundbreaking frameworks for advanced women's Torah study and religious leadership; Rabbi Dr. Nachum Rabinovitch (1982), a scholar and expert in Jewish law who headed Yeshivat Birkat Moshe in Ma'ale Adumim (east of Jerusalem), an advanced Torah academy whose students (like YHE) are part of the Hesder study/army framework, for over four decades; and Rabbi Dr. Shlomo (Steven) Riskin (1983), the leader of the Ohr Torah Stone (henceforth OTS) educational network—which runs multiple schools, advanced study Torah institutes, and religious leadership training programs throughout Israel—and former chief rabbi of Efrat.

Among these American immigrant pioneers of IsMO, there was plenty of ideological and political variety and even vociferous disagreements. Despite these differences, all of them may be located along the IsMO spectrum. Like Lichtenstein, for the most part this entire coterie of pioneers and core elements of their approaches were initially peripheral to mainstream Israeli religious life. No doubt, they experienced success in cultivating critical masses of students who were inspired by their teachings. But, as we will see, the vital means by which their ideas gained broader traction was through their institutions and their locally born and younger immigrant protégés, who translated and adjusted their credos and outlooks into "homegrown" terms. Put differently, a "recalibration" process transpired that facilitated the refinement and amendment of concepts and positions that can be traced to twentieth-century American Modern Orthodox Judaism through ongoing interaction with Israelis and their native contexts.

Yet this is not simply a one-directional story. The influence of this burgeoning trend has been felt in North America as well. This is due, in part, to the thousands of college-age and postgraduate students who spend intensive "gap years" in Israel-based religious institutions, many founded and headed by the figures discussed in this book or by their disciples, and who upon return serve as conduits for the novel religious perspectives to which they were exposed. In fact, a growing number of Americans who find the moderate worldview appealing choose to pursue their advanced religious training and professional certification in Israeli institutions before setting out on careers as religious leaders in America. Moreover, many of the figures nurtured in the key training grounds of IsMO are themselves children of English-speaking immigrants who travel regularly to North America to lecture in various communities. In parallel, the unprecedented role of digital media and communication has facilitated dissemination of ideas to an international audience. A transnational community of moderate Orthodoxy has thus arisen whose central actors bounce back and forth between its hubs.

Two Israel Prize winners and immigrants from the UK, pathbreaking educator Prof. Alice Shalvi (1926–2023) and world-renowned Talmudist Rabbi Prof. Daniel Sperber (b. 1940), made seminal contributions to IsMO's evolution as well. They both played key roles in the advancement of women's religious education and leadership, and Sperber's approach to Jewish jurisprudence has provided a legal foundation for numerous innovations in ritual, family, and personal status law. Shalvi, who moved to Israel in 1949, headed the Pelech Experimental Religious High School for Girls from 1975 until 1990. Over the course of her career, she gravitated closer to the Israeli *Masorti*/Conservative movement, which differs fundamentally with Orthodoxy on a number of key issues of religious law and theology, and served as rector of its Schechter Institute in Jerusalem.[10] From the time of his permanent settlement in Israel during the early 1970s, Sperber was a central academic figure at Bar-Ilan University (henceforth BIU), serving in the 1980s as dean of the Faculty of Jewish Studies, and toward the end of his tenure as president of the university's Institute for Advanced Torah Studies. He was also involved, among others, in the establishment of the Beit Morasha Institute and Beit Midrash Harel, two Jerusalem-based inventive frameworks for higher Torah learning that cultivate religious leadership among men and women.[11] There are certainly compelling reasons to include both of them among the featured pioneers. However, this book focuses at its core on those whose exposures to American Modern Orthodoxy were critical to their early personal developments. Nevertheless, students and followers of Shalvi and Sperber no doubt carried their influence back to America or on to other Israel-based initiatives, which impacted the type of cross-fertilization discussed in this book.

Professor Tamar Ross (b. 1938) is an American-born figure who similarly had considerable impact on the evolution of IsMO but on whom I do not focus. Ross was born in the United States and moved to Israel at the age of eighteen together with her parents. She taught at Midreshet Bruria/Lindenbaum for over forty years, an advanced institute for women's Torah study in Jerusalem. In the course of this period, she earned a PhD in Jewish thought from the Hebrew University in Jerusalem and had a distinguished career as a professor at BIU. Ross is an expert in the nineteenth-century Lithuanian Mussar movement, which focused on the relationship between ethical behavior and religious growth, and the thought of Rabbi Abraham Isaac Kook (1865–1935), the mystical/metaphysical thinker and religious authority who set forth a redemptive/messianic interpretation of Zionism's role in Jewish history, but her most influential role has been through her writings on Judaism and gender.[12] Indeed, she is considered the foremost theologian of Orthodox feminism, and her book *Expanding the Palace of the Torah* (2004) remains the most rigorous treatment of the subject.[13] A Hebrew translation appeared in 2007.[14] Through her teaching and writing she has certainly affected many students and built a large following both in Israel and abroad. Nonetheless, whereas her primary concentration was on scholarship and actual in-class teaching, the nuclear group at the center of this book are all American immigrants who certainly taught and wrote but dedicated much of their efforts to building and leading Israel-based educational institutions.

* * *

Combining history with thick examinations of lived religious experience, this book engages the interfaces, commonalities, and distinctions between American and Israeli Judaisms through the lens of religious history and transnational studies. It is the first full-length book dedicated to such an examination since the publication of Charles Liebman and Steven Cohen's *Two Worlds of Judaism* in 1990.[15] That work, as its title attests, emphasized core differences that characterize religious life in the world's two largest concentrations of Jews. In particular, the authors accentuated religio-legal rigidity and particularism as core traits of Israeli Judaism that diverged from the voluntarism and universalism that marked American Judaism. They did observe indications of a nascent Israeli moderate religious camp but acknowledged that "it is only in the last three or four years that the position of the religious

moderates has found expression in print, in public lectures, and organizational forums." Yet insightfully (and likely inspired by the authors'
own personal hopes), they allowed that the moderate positions "may
yet prove important in defining how Israeli Jews interpret their religious
tradition."[16]

While showcasing the rise of a budding strand of Israeli Judaism that
has drawn limited scholarly attention,[17] and the key role of American
Jews in its advance, this book's goal is to contribute to broader understanding of the complex relationship between American and Israeli Jewish societies.[18] The past decade witnessed a plethora of publications that
bemoan the distancing of the "Jerusalem and Babylon" of these times.[19]
In parallel, a monograph appeared in Hebrew in 2019 that proclaims that
world Jewry increasingly revolves around the sovereign Israel.[20] These
volumes focus on political perceptions and conflicts, as well as on the
alienation of non-Orthodox Jews from Israel's state-sponsored religious
bureaucracy.

I do not aim to debate these appraisals directly. Nor do I underestimate the degree to which political differences—be they the government's
approach to Palestinians or for a growing vocal minority the very notion
of a Jewish national state—impact upon American Jewish perceptions of
Israel. Rather, I highlight an alternative avenue for addressing the American Jewry–Israel dynamic through the lens of religion, and identify a
stratum marked by vigorous reciprocal connections, arguably stronger
ones than in the past. As cultural linguist Omri Asscher asserted in
2020, "there is more to homeland-diaspora relations than foreign policy
and politics . . . Israeli and American Jewries have historically found
meaning in their collectivity through religion and culture no less than
through political and organizational activity."[21] Among Asscher's contemporary examples that buttress this point, he includes "the influence
of American religious feminism on Israeli religious institutions" and
"the growing number of American yeshiva students who spend a gap
year in Israel in religious Zionist or Haredi yeshivas, and of Reform and
Conservative rabbis who study for a year in Jerusalem."[22] By pursuing
the alternative path that does not focus primarily on politics, I challenge the
totality of the "we stand divided" or "we are not one" approaches. This
book thus offers a fresh but more complex view of the global Jewish
landscape. The intricacies of this dynamic are analyzed in detail in the

conclusion, with the help of recently developed conceptual rubrics that facilitate recommendations that I put forward for the future.

American Modern Orthodox Judaism

Modern Orthodox Judaism is a rubric used to describe a wide spectrum of Jewish individuals, communal institutions, and thinkers rooted in North America who seek to integrate allegiance to traditional Jewish practice and beliefs with appreciation for secular education, scientific knowledge, universal values, and affirmative participation in general society and culture. Avid support for political Zionism and the State of Israel, connectedness to the wider Jewish population, and to various degrees appreciation for women's roles within the religious realm are trademarks of this Jewish sector.[23] Much scholarly discussion has been dedicated toward identifying the unique characteristics of MO Jews, their religious milieus, their theological outlooks and worldviews, and how all of these have evolved over time.[24] What is unequivocal is that Joseph B. Soloveitchik is widely acknowledged as its most important ideologue and intellectual leader—this despite the fact that he expressed ambivalence regarding the term MO itself. During his over four-decade career at YU, he taught thousands of students, including five of the figures highlighted in this volume, and his lectures and publications reached much further. Although strong precedents for MO Judaism may be discerned in the mid-nineteenth century, both in Central and Western Europe—such as German neo-Orthodoxy—and in North America itself, its emergence as an identifiable religious stream may be deemed an early twentieth-century phenomenon.[25] From the outset of that period onward, its institutional homes were to be found in "Americanized" organizations such as YU, the Young Israel synagogue movement, the Orthodox Union (OU) of synagogues, the Rabbinical Council of America (RCA), and numerous full-time "day schools" that combined religious and general studies. While the term Modern Orthodox is used most extensively in reference to North American Jews, it is sometimes applied to similar groupings in other countries as well.

Within the North American context, MO Judaism had historically been compared with Conservative Judaism to its left, due to their positive orientations toward general culture and American society and their common recognitions of halakhah (Jewish law), as the foundation for Jewish life—notwithstanding theological arguments over the source of legal authority and mechanisms for change. In point of fact, during their nascent decades there was considerable overlap of constituencies and the boundaries between them were often unclear. From the mid-twentieth century, however, issues regarding women in particular, such as the *mehizah* separation between sexes during prayer and ordination of women rabbis, along with the general lack of halakhic observance among lay Conservative Jews, sharpened divisions.[26]

On the other side of the spectrum, the MO are differentiated from the gamut of Haredi Orthodox Jews (plural, Haredim—literally, "those who tremble at the word of God" [Isaiah 66, 2]), who emphasize strict observance and demarcation of strong social and cultural boundaries. Their ostensibly involuntary entrance into America Jewish life accorded with the arrival of Holocaust-era refugees from Central and Eastern European who were intent on reconstituting the obliterated *yeshivot* (religious academies) and Hasidic courts that hitherto anchored their worldviews.[27]

In the past two decades, scholars have documented significant divides within the MO orbit, with some adopting more liberal postures once associated with non-Orthodox denominations—particularly regarding gender—while others gravitate toward the Haredi stance. Simultaneously, especially within the non-Hasidic Haredi segment, alienation from the State of Israel and staunch opposition to higher secular education have declined.[28] Thus, distinctions between the more conservative MO factions and the less zealous Haredi population are increasingly blurred.[29]

The figures at the center of this book immigrated to Israel in the 1960s, 1970s, and early 1980s and sought to integrate into its RZ sector. Although some received parts of their educations in Haredi-oriented institutions, they all had strong roots in American MO Judaism.

Israeli Religious Zionism

The term "Religious Zionist" (in Hebrew, *zioni dati*; also referred to as National Religious—*dati-leumi*) can be applied today to a wide range of Israeli Orthodox Jews and institutions that view the State of Israel as a

religiously meaningful phenomenon. RZ parents encourage their chil
dren to be partners in Israeli society, which minimally demands gaining
an elementary and secondary school secular education and fulfilling
their obligations to the country alongside their fellow Israeli young
adults either in the army or through national service (*sherut leumi*—
principally for females).[30]

Like its American MO counterparts, the RZ sector stands in contrast
to the broad variety of religious streams and sects grouped under the
title Haredim. These comprise an assortment of "Ashkenazic" constituencies with strong roots in European Orthodoxies, including multiple
Hasidic courts that trace their origins to greater Poland and Hungary
and Lithuanian-style groups who look to prominent yeshiva heads
for guidance, as well as a growing contingent of "Sephardic" or Mizrahi (Eastern) Jews whose ancestors immigrated for the most part from
Muslim lands. Notwithstanding manifold internal ideological and cultural distinctions, the Haredim share a fundamental suspicion regarding
secular ideals and institutions and their destructive effects on religious
commitment and values. Relatedly, they perceive Zionism and the State
of Israel as purely secular endeavors that are, at best, bereft of any positive religious meaning, if not demonic forces intent on undermining traditional Judaism. As a result, in practice they severely limit the exposure
of school-age children to secular learning, and labor to gain broad-based
exemptions of their young adults from Israeli military and national service. To a great degree due to Israel's mandatory military service, Israeli
Haredim tend to be more emphatic than their American parallels in setting clear boundaries between themselves and the rest of society. That
said, in response to a variety of novel political and economic factors,
even in Israel the twenty-first century has witnessed greater Haredi willingness to countenance advanced secular education and integration into
the general workforce than had been the case beforehand.[31]

As to the historical emergence of the RZ segment, although many
observant Jews were inspired by the proto-Zionist movements that arose
in the last three decades of the nineteenth century and some prominent
rabbis expressed their support, most traditionalist authorities initially
opposed the nascent Zionist movement. By 1897, a few rabbinical figures attended the first Zionist Congress held in Basel, and in 1902, the
Mizrahi RZ movement was established. Over time it founded branches

throughout the Jewish world, including North America. Within pre-state Palestine during the interwar period, the Ha-Poel Mizrachi sub-stream was involved in launching religious settlements as well as schools and youth movements that represented its followers, and prior to the creation of the State of Israel in 1948, RZ political parties arose that later joined the coalitions led by the Labor Zionists, the socialist/secular political stream headed by Prime Minister David Ben-Gurion and his successors. That said, the majority of RZ constituents were urban dwellers who were not part of the vanguard of Zionist settlement, military, or political leadership.[32]

Notably, the first generation of RZ parliamentarians in the State of Israel, who served primarily through the National Religious Party (NRP), directed their political capital primarily toward addressing the specific needs of their electorates. They facilitated the establishment of their own educational system, and together with the Haredi parties, they pushed through legislation that guaranteed the maintenance of Orthodox policies regarding matters of personal identity (birth, marriage, burial, and conversion), provision and supervision of kosher food, religious standards within the public square (Sabbath and holidays) and grounding of the legal authority of the state-sponsored rabbinate. Insofar as defense and foreign policy were concerned, they generally supported the policies of the ruling party, if not staking out positions that were more dovish than those of their secularist cohorts.[33]

Here it is important to point out that, during those early years, one of the key wellsprings for ideological leadership of Israeli RZ, especially through its Bnei Akiva youth organization, was the Religious Kibbutz movement that united the kibbutz religious collective settlements. It put forward a socialist worldview that asserted the positive synthesis between religion and modern life and embraced reasoned leniency regarding religious law and observance.[34] While some of its outstanding products continued to advance these outlooks, from 1967 onward the Religious Kibbutz movement gradually lost its principal role within RZ and was seen as something of an anomaly that was marginal in relation to the new mainstream that ascended.[35] To be sure, figures nurtured in the Religious Kibbutz movement were associated with some of the key institutions at the focus of this book, and there are ideational continuities that can be identified within emergent contemporary IsMO.

Nonetheless, I maintain that the twenty-first-century phenomenon is distinct and that the American "cultural agents" were a critical force in facilitating its development.[36]

A number of scholars of Jewish thought have, in fact, concentrated on comparisons between MO Judaism and RZ, highlighting individual religious experience, the centrality of synagogue life, universalism, and appreciation for secular learning as foundations of the MO weltanschauung. These stand in opposition to RZ's Kook-inspired metaphysical orientation and stress on the teleological character of collective Jewish engagement and observance, along with the far more palpable roles of nationalism and messianism.[37] The two parallel, but distinct, Orthodox approaches are often framed through the differences between the two most profound and influential figures in each camp, Soloveitchik for American MO Judaism and Rabbi Abraham Isaac Kook (1865–1935),[38] along with his son Rabbi Zvi Yehuda Kook (1891–1982), for Israeli RZ.[39]

The RZ elite that arose in the late 1960s was inspired by the Kookian theosophical interpretation of the State of Israel that highlights its role in the redemptive process, and as such the inherent holiness of its seemingly secular endeavor and those who steer it.[40] Adherents to this outlook, often referred to as the Merkaz ha-Rav camp after the yeshiva founded by Abraham Isaac Kook and subsequently led by his son, attained commanding positions within all levels of RZ education, the rabbinate, and its youth movements, especially through their roles in the post–1967 war settlement movement.[41] Although the Merkaz Ha-Rav approach justifies working together with nonobservant Jews for the advancement of the state, in the twenty-first century an ideological substratum popularly known as the *Kav* (line or stance), which is highly critical of Western society, views academic discourse with great suspicion, and is militant in its opposition to feminism and LGBTQ recognition, gained considerable sway.[42] Another popular term applied to some of those associated with the Kav group, but with others as well who are not necessarily as activist on social and political issues, is *Harda"l*—the word itself actually means "mustard" in Hebrew, but its acronymic explication is *Haredi-Leumi* (Haredi Nationalist). This nomenclature expresses a combination of the strict Orthodox standards generally associated with the non-Zionist Haredim, along with allegiance to the State of Israel and its role in rehabilitating the national homeland.[43]

This book, then, brings to the fore a competing, Israeli moderate religious trend to the Kav/Harda"l worldview, which exhibits elements rooted in the once more central approach to RZ life of the Religious Kibbutz movement,[44] but which gained crucial inspiration from individuals nurtured within American MO Judaism. The personalities and institutions that fit this new rubric do not necessarily reject Kook's redemptive understanding of RZ or the settlement movement, but prominent moderate figures have articulated alternative theological bases for their identification with the State of Israel and its core character. Moreover, the integration of their religious values with their engagement with Israeli social and cultural life that marks their worldview differs fundamentally from that of Merkaz ha-Rav and its offshoots.

Transnationalism, Globalization, and Americanization

As noted, the pioneering cultural agents of contemporary IsMO at the center of this book were nurtured on North American soil, but their Israeli-born students played focal roles in translating key themes and adjusting them effectively in the spirit of their own native Israeli culture. This process by which core ideals with roots abroad gained footing within Israeli society acquires greater lucidity through the works of scholars in the fields of transnationalism, globalization, and Americanization.

The dramatic increase in global connectivity that characterized the late twentieth and early twenty-first centuries, and consequent recognition of forces beyond the nation-state and locality that impact on citizens, resulted in rising interest in transnational perspectives. There are multiple definitions of this term. The *Merriam-Webster* dictionary explains "transnational" as "extending or going beyond national boundaries."[45] The *Oxford English Dictionary* infers the political and economic aspects of the term, "[. . .] extending or having interests extending beyond national bounds or frontiers; multinational."[46] In this book the focus is directed toward cultural, religious, and social manifestations, although the links to political and economic ones cannot be severed.

Within the Jewish realm, communications researcher Jeremy Stolow stands out in highlighting the completely "deterritorialized imaginary" of the Haredi Orthodox Agudat Yisrael movement, the worldwide organization of non-Zionist Orthodox Jewry founded in 1912, whose vision is predicated on an assertively "translocal spatial framework" that substitutes for the geographically based Israeli nation-state.[47] Alternatively, others have focused on the transnational character of specific local immigrant groups or populations. Political scientist Judit Bokser Liwerant, for example, has asserted that "Latin American Jews have been marked by the unique features of transnationalism."[48] Citing the work of political economist Sanjeev Khagram and sociologist Peggy Levitt, she puts forward the following depiction: "transnationalism stresses that flows of interactions and relationships continue to be developed notwithstanding the presence of international borders. . . . It points to new and complex patterns of interaction and network building; of social groups and collective identities."[49] Homing in on the impact of Israeli origins and culture on the "Diasporas" that have arisen outside the country over the past seventy-five years, sociologist of language and ethnicity Eliezer Ben-Rephael disputes Stolow, distinguishing between "a transnational orientation" and "an international horizon," the former indicating "a commitment that concretizes . . . the principle of 'dual homeness.'"[50] As to Israel, sociologist Larissa Remennick has devoted considerable attention to the transnational character of immigrants from the regions of the former Soviet Union. Among her insights is the degree to which members of the second generation—who maintain good Russian-language skills—sustain the transnational networks and cultural ties nurtured by their immigrant parents.[51] This discernment has utility in exploring the students of the pioneers of IsMO, many of whom are themselves children of native English speakers.

In comparison to Russian speakers, much less scholarship has been written about American immigrants to Israel, and even less that adopts a transnational perspective. Indeed, to date the most comprehensive monograph on American *aliyah* (the Hebrew term for Jewish immigration to Israel, but literally defined as "going up"; *olim is the plural noun for those undertaking or who undertook aliyah*), appeared in 1989.[52] A relatively new and valuable exception that is predicated on a transnational historical perspective is historian Sara Yael Hirschhorn's *City on a Hilltop*, published in 2017.[53]

Hirschhorn's book focuses on a collection of Jews who came of age in America during the 1960s, subsequently moved to Israel, and chose to live in the territories captured in 1967. Hirschhorn explores the lives of these people and how liberal and progressive worldviews that her subjects internalized as young adults interfaced with and informed, seemingly counterintuitively, their settler ideologies and lifestyles. In the process, she also addresses areas of impact of the American immigrants upon the settler movement. Although some played profound roles in related events, in contrast to those featured in the current book, there is little sense that the Americans were an identifiable cohort that was central to the overall evolution of the settlements and their core supporting casts. Moreover, unlike those at the foundation of this book, for the most part the persons described by Hirschhorn were not institution builders who cultivated a next generation of local followers, nor would the vast majority be characterized as religious moderates. Nonetheless, there is one key player—Shlomo (Steven) Riskin—who features prominently in both works. While Riskin certainly would not be considered a militant settler leader, the very fact that he straddles the line between right-wing activism and moderate religiosity demonstrates the limitations of the political realm as the sole basis for perceiving the core directions of Israeli society.[54]

Like Hirschhorn's work, historian Ava Kahn's 2014 study of the American founders of kibbutz settlements during the 1940s and the 1970s emphasizes the transnational quality of their endeavors. The author notes the American-inspired pluralistic approach to religion in some of the frameworks established by graduates of the Young Judea movement. Unlike most of the "Israeli" kibbutzim, which were more homogeneous, the American founders of Ketura (Arava region) and Gezer (northwest of Jerusalem) created environments in which both religiously committed and secular Jews could partner together and live side by side.[55] Notwithstanding their non-Orthodox approaches, these attempts to institutionalize a moderate approach to religion draw parallels with the Orthodox cultural of agents and the educational bases that they founded which are at the center of this book. Ketura, in particular, has embraced the role of disseminating its worldview through its own educational facility, the Arava Institute.[56] Its impact on those who spent time there as young adults is palpable. There are a few relatively small but vocal groups throughout Israel, such as the pluralistic-oriented Havurat Tel Aviv community, that are populated by its graduates.[57]

A more recent article that engages directly with a key element of IsMO from a transnational perspective is religious studies researcher Ellie Ash's "Observant Feminism across Borders: The Transnational Origins of Partnership Minyanim," published in 2022. The author analyzes the simultaneous emergence in the early twenty-first century among Orthodox Jews in Israel and the United States of "partnership minyanim" (prayer collectives). The traditional Jewish practice is for only men to conduct most rituals. The novel partnership groups facilitate opportunities for women within public prayer, such as serving as the public reader of the weekly Bible portion as well as leading certain sections of the prayer service. The founding participants were men and women committed to an Orthodox understanding of Jewish law, who based their innovations on new interpretations put forward by a small group of rabbis that included some highly respected figures.[58]

Ash concentrates on the connections between two pioneering congregations, one in Jerusalem and one in Manhattan, and the ways in which they manifest the "transnational network" of Orthodox feminists that arose in the late twentieth century. She demonstrates both how each setting drew from the other, as well as the ways in which locality influenced areas in which their paths diverged. Referencing the preliminary studies that led to the decision to develop her work, she points to my own initial explorations of the subject: "[My] findings are generally consistent with Ferziger's analysis. This article adds detail to his broad description of intellectual exchange."[59]

Two adjacent fields to transnationalism studies—globalization studies and Americanization studies—concentrate on the way products, symbols, artistic creations, and trends gain pervasive acceptance and influence throughout the world. The roots of these various commodities are to be found in Western countries, and more often than not in the United States.[60] Such transfers, which have accelerated dramatically through internet technology and social media, propagate shared experience and common language among diverse geographic regions, and facilitate economic and educational opportunities.[61] At the same time, this proliferation is often perceived disparagingly as a form of economic and cultural imperialism that undermines local and indigenous expression.[62]

The phenomenon identified in this book, in which figures and ideas with strong American roots gained footing within Israeli religious life, can be perceived as a form of Americanization. In fact, in seeking to delegitimize the moderate religious worldview, some opponents of aspects of this approach have made just such a claim.[63] That said, as has been emphasized, my understanding is that while the pioneering cultural agents were crucial to the process, the flowering of IsMO in the early twenty-first century reflects a more complex process in which the outlooks modeled initially by the American teachers were then absorbed and reconfigured by their Israeli-born and young immigrant students and followers. Here I have found the scholarship of social scientist Mel Van Elteren to be particularly instructive in elucidating my observations.

In his book *Americanism and Americanization: A Critical History of Domestic and Global Influence*, which appeared in 2006, Van Elteren sought to navigate two conflicting trends.[64] For many years, works on Americanization fixated on the ways American products have been adopted and gained power over other societies. More recently, a contrasting approach arose that gives far more credence to local receptions and the way they transform the concepts into something new, what is sometimes referred to as "transculturation" or the "creolization" effect.[65] The author's aim is to posit an analytical reading that recognizes the way locality influences imported forms, without ignoring the core American elements that remain embedded within the novel phenomenon.[66] Such an approach is especially fruitful in accounting for the cross-fertilizing process by which the novel American-inspired products that emerge in foreign locales then gain resonance within American settings as well.

In a 2011 study, "Cultural Globalizations and Transnational Flow of Things American," Van Elteren expanded upon how cultural symbols and ideas whose initial gestation was in America evolve through their dissemination in other locales. He attested that "[e]ach local setting provides its own appropriation and reworking of global products and symbols, thus encouraging difference, otherness, diversity and variety."[67] Moreover, "[i]n this process of appropriation they give new meaning to the borrowed element." Applied to the current discussion, after moving to Israel, the American pioneers like Lichtenstein and his cohorts disseminated religious ideals and intellectual perspectives that they internalized from the American atmosphere in which they were nurtured. But their Israeli students and followers did not only draw from their teachings, they arose in a different environment and "appropriated and reworked" the American "products and symbols" in fresh ways that opened up vistas for novel directions in Israeli religious life.

This process of "creative appropriation" was, no doubt, nourished by numerous local factors, including the lack in Israel of the denominational clashes that characterized twentieth-century North American Judaism, as well as the twenty-first-century popularization within RZ of mystical outlooks more easily in conversation with postmodern hermeneutical thinking than the more binary modernist perspectives of their mentors. One of the decisive features of the innovative process was the fluid social environment that increasingly came to characterize sectors of Israeli religious society. Without formally detaching from their RZ roots, many children who grew up in observant homes have become far more acculturated within broader Israeli society than were their parents and certainly their grandparents.[68] Indeed, the term *ba-rezef* (on the continuum/spectrum) has entered popular vocabulary as a description of the wide variety of individuals that identify with their RZ roots. They range from the meticulous elites to those who nominally maintain observant lifestyles to a growing constituency that does not necessarily feel obligated by Jewish law but still sees itself as far more connected to the RZ community than to more avowedly secular frameworks.[69] In this dynamic atmosphere, Israeli students continue to assimilate religious teachings and engage with these views in fresh ways, a process that has led some to pursue paths that stretch the theological and religio-legal boundaries that their mentors had labored to maintain.

Elteren asserted that the process of transnational reworking of culture is not one-directional. That is, once an idea or symbol has been digested and reformed in a new environment, globalized conditions facilitate smooth portals for their reentry into their original local contexts. At this point, the reformulated conceptualizations become influential agents for cultural change that impact the frameworks of their initial emergence.[70] With regard to Orthodox Judaism, then, at this juncture the most dramatic and theologically provocative activity is clearly taking place within the Israeli milieu. While this book highlights such transformations within Israeli religious life and the American immigrants who inspired them, it homes in as well to areas in which reworked forms emanating from Israel are also impacting the American Jewish religious environment.

* * *

The rise of IsMO and the critical role of a cohort of American immigrants in its emergence is presented in this volume through a series of historical and cultural case studies that focus on seminal aspects of this late twentieth- and early twenty-first-century development. Taken together, this book offers the first rigorous account and analysis of a sui generis transnational development within contemporary Judaism with critical implications both for the future of Israeli Judaism and its relationship to other Jewish communities worldwide, especially the largest one in North America.

The bulk of the book is split into three main sections. The first, titled "American Milieus and Israeli Careers," focuses on the main cultural agents as well as key perspectives from the American Jewish frameworks in which they were nurtured. These discussions provide critical ideological backdrops for the subsequent Israel-based events along with affording novel perspectives on the relationship between American Orthodoxy, Zionism, and Israel during the twentieth century. There is also a discussion of two well-known American Orthodox figures, Rabbi Meir Kahane and Rabbi Shlomo Carlebach, who moved to Israel during the same period as the agents of change on whom this book focuses, and why they are not included among the key pioneers of IsMO. The discussion of Carlebach, in particular, highlights novel aspects of the contemporary Israeli religious landscape, such as the emergence of Zionist "Neo-Hasidism."

The second section, "Dimensions of Israeli Moderate Judaism," addresses distinct aspects of IsMO, and also includes a chapter, coauthored with my former graduate student Dr. Einat Libel-Hass, that illustrates the growth of a parallel "glocalized" setting within a Tel Aviv–based Reform congregation.

The final section, "Homeland and Beyond," moves past Israel's borders, concentrating on the dissemination of IsMO through emissaries to American communities and the ways their experiences have manifested upon their return to Israel, as well as discussing a novel direction in Orthodox feminism in which digital religion facilitates robust interfaces between Israel-based RZ frameworks and interested parties throughout the globe.

The book concludes with an exploration of the question: What impact can IsMO have on the ongoing relations between Israeli and American Jewries? There is also an appendix that includes a selected list of alumni of the pioneer-founded institutions who have influenced Israeli religious life.

PART ONE

American Milieus and Israeli Careers

1

Roots

Ben-Gurion at Yeshiva University, March 1960

Introduction[1]

On March 8, 1960, Prime Minister David Ben-Gurion's chartered EL AL airplane landed in Boston, the opening leg of a sixteen-day expedition that would include meetings and events in Washington, DC, New York, and London, as well as some rest and relaxation in Oxford, UK. His first trip to the United States in nearly a decade, the official purpose was to receive an honorary degree from Brandeis, the private university founded by American Jews the same year the State of Israel was established. The convocation was actually a pretext to facilitate discussions with US government leaders despite the lack of an official state invitation.[2]

This initial impetus notwithstanding, the campus aspect of Ben-Gurion's journey turned out to be more than a single cosmetic performance. In addition to the leadoff Brandeis occasion, he chose to bookend his US stay with New York appearances on March 16 at the Conservative-associated Jewish Theological Seminary (JTS), the Orthodox-affiliated Yeshiva University (YU), and the Reform movement's Hebrew Union College–Jewish Institute of Religion (HUC-JIR).[3] At all four institutions he delivered major addresses.

Not only do these visits provide fresh insights into Ben-Gurion's approach to American Jewry and its various denominational streams, they highlight the respective responses of the audiences to him and the ideals that he put forward. As a result, they offer a glimpse into how students at these central institutions of American Jewish religious life perceived Zionism, Israel, and especially the prospect of immigration.

In targeting these encounters, a critical observation by historian Jonathan Sarna regarding the early stages in the State of Israel's relationship with American Jewry is especially instructive. Noting one monograph's nearly exclusive concentration on the top level of the American Jewish establishment, he asserted: "focusing . . . on the 'upper crust' fails to recount the subtle ways through which Israel, during the first decade of its existence, slowly began to permeate the homes, schools, and religious lives of ordinary American Jews."[4]

What will become clear in the following discussion is Ben-Gurion's acute desire to strengthen his relationship with one of these alternative sources of American Jewish commitment, young adults, and the responses that these overtures received. A vital witness to these events was Elie Wiesel, Holocaust survivor, author, and future Nobel laureate, and at the time the New York correspondent for Israel's *Yedioth Aharonoth* daily. Summing up the appearances at the rabbinical seminaries, he remarked admiringly, "Had Ben-Gurion come to the United States, not for diplomatic talks but purely to ignite fire in the hearts of the Jewish youth, we would have said *dayeinu* [it would have been enough]."[5]

The materials scrutinized below attest that although Ben-Gurion's patent negation of the Diaspora and emphasis on immigration had long engendered intense conflicts with the American Jewish establishment and led him to temper these positions when dealing with top-level leaders, he still sought to attract the younger cohort to key elements of his core ideals. Furthermore, his hands-on promotion of one-year Israel study programs for college age youth illustrates an aspect of his thinking that to date has not received sufficient attention. At the same time, they raise the prospect that his ideological antagonism and instinctive ambivalence toward traditionalist religious beliefs and culture undermined his appreciation for the deep resonance of his message to the American Orthodox students. Ironically, it was this sector that embraced his study in Israel vision most vociferously and, in turn, from the late 1960s onward became the vanguard of American aliyah.

Ben-Gurion and American Jewry

Ben-Gurion's personal familiarity with American Jewry began in 1915, at the age of twenty-eight, when he arrived there after being expelled from Ottoman Palestine. He lived in New York for three years, where he sought to impact local Zionist circles, and traveled extensively to Jewish communities throughout the country recruiting young Jews to support the Zionist movement and move to Palestine. He also met and married his wife, Paula, who had come from Minsk a few years earlier, and he coauthored two popular works on the early Zionist pioneers and the history of the Land of Israel.[6]

Ben-Gurion made multiple sojourns to the United States in the 1930s and throughout World War II, including one in 1941–1942 for close to a year. By then a central leader of the world Zionist movement, he advocated for a strong political alignment with the United States government, which in his estimation was crucial toward achieving an independent Jewish state. In parallel, "the objectives of these extended visits" included, according to historian Michael Brown, "firming up the will of American Jews, debilitated, he feared, by life in the Diaspora; unifying American Jewry behind the yishuv; and cementing his own alliances within Zionism."[7]

Cultivating American Jewish support demanded, among other tactics, sensitivity to internal American Jewish politics, navigating complex relations with figures like influential Zionist leader Rabbi Abba Hillel Silver, and allaying the deep fears of many regarding accusations of dual loyalty. The efforts of Ben-Gurion and others eventually bore fruit.[8] To be sure, a unique brand of "Americanized" Zionism had developed and grown in influence throughout the course of the previous half-century, but key leaders and organizations and lay constituencies had remained non-Zionist, and some were unequivocally anti-Zionist.[9] In the wake of the Holocaust and especially after the War of Independence in 1948, support for Israel gained a far broader consensus.[10] This connection to Israel took shape during the 1950s as a core element of American Jewish identity, manifesting itself not only in times of crisis but through its steady entrance into Jews' collective consciousness.[11] This was especially so for the MO student constituency at YU.

In parallel with achievement of the initial goal of establishing the state, however, the sharp disparities that had long existed between Ben-Gurion's fundamental perception of world Jewry and those of American communal leaders came to a head. For those at the helm of American life, including key figures at YU, Zionism meant supporting the state philanthropically and politically, and strengthening local Jewish commitment through inspiration from its pioneering Hebrew culture and military bravery.[12] To the founding prime minister, by contrast, even the most congenial Diaspora environment was by definition a foreign and unstable territory in which Jews endured abnormal bifurcated lives. Only in Israel, the authentic homeland, could they realize their healthy and rightful individual and collective existences, and fulfill the modern rendition of the Biblical prophets' historic messianic visions. Thus, in principle, commitment to Zionism meant joining the state-building efforts through aliyah—immigration and permanent settlement.[13]

Zionist and non-Zionist American collaborators alike could not countenance Ben-Gurion's forthright "negation of the exile" and intrusion into local matters, most provocatively through highlighting Israel's centrality to all Jews and public calls for massive aliyah.[14] This tension came to a head in the summer of 1950, when Jacob Blaustein, head of the powerful American Jewish Committee (AJC), conditioned his organization's ongoing support for Israel's political agenda on the government refraining from interfering with internal American Jewish affairs and desisting from headlining the nascent state's preeminence through forthright campaigning for mass immigration. Notably, just one year earlier, at the meeting of the World Zionist Organization executive that took place as part of the first Israel Independence Day since the declaration of the state, Ben-Gurion had concluded his opening address with a seeming ultimatum toward Israel's supporters abroad: "Declarative Zionism has been emptied of content. . . . The critical test is immigration and settlement. . . . Today there is no viability to Zionism that is not pioneering—and the participation which is demanded from you in the building of the State is an active personal one."[15] Yet rather than lose Blaustein and the AJC as a crucial diplomatic and philanthropic asset, the prime minister signed off on a mutually accepted "exchange of letters" in which each side affirmed the boundaries of Israeli and American Jewish engagements with their respective constituencies.[16]

In the following years, despite protests from his American allies, Ben-Gurion returned periodically to blanket ideological statements regarding the failings of Diaspora life. At other times, the alternative tactic articulated in response to Blaustein received concrete expression. In these instances, rather than disparaging American Jewry's current realities, he appealed to their pioneering spirit and the intellectual resources that they stood to offer. While both approaches received expression during his March 1960 American tour, most striking are those instances when his principal outlook came across as he directed his charisma and verbal virtuosity toward convincing religiously committed American Jewish youth to move to Israel permanently. His choice of which of these approaches to utilize at his various venues offers a window into his perceptions of each American religious constituency. The audiences and institutional responses, in turn, deepen appreciation for the multiple strands of attitudes toward Israel developing at that time among American Jewry's denominational streams.

His opening appearance at Brandeis projects a Ben-Gurion quite in sync with the Blaustein interchange. Toward the end of his trip, as exhibited in his New York speeches, especially those at JTS and YU, he found a comfort zone. This was due both to the ability of his student audiences to comprehend his preferred public-speaking language, Hebrew, and to their overall admiration for his core messages.

Hebrew Union College–Jewish Institute of Religion (HUC-JIR)

Of his three visits to religious centers for higher learning on March 16, 1960, it was at HUC-JIR that Ben-Gurion appeared most concerned not to ruffle feathers, but also where he ultimately could not hold back from expressing frustration and disappointment. His dissatisfaction stemmed from the composition of the crowd.

Speaking in his strongly accented but intelligible English, Ben-Gurion distanced himself from the denominational fractures that characterized American Jewish life: "Well I don't know to which section I belong, perhaps to none. . . . I am just a Jew. I am a Jew without an adjective."[17] Sensitive to the Reform movement's internal tensions surrounding Zionism, he expressed sentiments consistent with his 1950 commitment to Blaustein: "I cannot expect, although I would like it with all my heart, all the Jews from all over the world to come to us, but I know that you prefer, and I say this without any complaint, you prefer to remain where you are, and I wish you the greatest happiness in your life here."[18].

Ben-Gurion's main thrust, however, was to encourage HUC-JIR students to spend a year studying in Israel (on the Jerusalem campus whose construction had by then begun) with the hope that some would choose to play a more direct role in the development of his country.[19] Referring

to the mass of immigrants from Muslim countries without secular qualifications that had arrived recently in Israel, Ben-Gurion specified the
importance of recruiting highly educated people from the West to "lift
up our *olim*." Such efforts, he maintained, would reflect the ethos that his
developing country shared with the United States:[20]

> [T]his country was built with the same spiritual power as we are building
> Israel; with the power of pioneering . . . I am sure there must be amongst
> the best youth in American Jewry, among whom the spirit of creative
> pioneering, of dedication for a great historic purpose is still alive. There-
> fore [. . .] you will fail in your educational work if you will not succeed
> in instilling, if not in all your students, at least in the best of them, that
> pioneering spirit which will find that outlet [. . .] in Israel . . . each student
> should study at least one year in Jerusalem. But if not all of them, the best
> of them . . .[21]

The 1960 trip was not the first time that Ben-Gurion raised the idea
of recruiting American students to spend a year of study in Israel. However, it was during this trip, with its emphasis on campus visits, that this
theme stood front and center. That said, his prior articulations sharpen
appreciation for distinctions between his presentation at HUC and those
at JTS and YU. Previously, in the course of his 1949 opening address to
the World Zionist Organization, Ben-Gurion declared, "we must plant
in the hearts of every Jewish student that, in addition to their five or six
years of college education, they should study for at least a year at the
Hebrew University in Jerusalem. Such study will expand their horizons
and enrich their spirits." Yet in contrast to his "post-Blaustein exchange"
HUC discussion, in 1949 he added emphatically and optimistically that
"[s]ome of these students will remain in the Land."[22] As will become
clear, Ben-Gurion's presentations at JTS and YU were far more direct
regarding his hopes that study in Israel would eventuate permanent
settlement.

While omitting any intention to promote immigration, Ben-Gurion's
1960 HUC speech made clear that his goal was to encourage American Jewish students to spend time studying in Israel. Thus, even the
warm reception and large forum that was provided could not prevent
Ben-Gurion from expressing exasperation at the absence of the main

audience that he sought to target with his words. At the outset of his presentation, he clarified with whom he aimed to connect. Despite his tight schedule and diplomatic necessities, he could not leave the country without having the opportunity to "meet Jews, at least young Jews." He remarked somewhat sarcastically, "I will only say to you, and especially then to those students, although I am not sure whether we have your students here. Have you? . . . Then there are not so many. But to all those who came . . ."[23]

This spontaneous interlude signposted an overall strategy that motivated Ben-Gurion's campus visits. Even if his behavior was never fully compliant with the Blaustein interchange, he had gravitated toward recognition that American Jewish leaders, the Reform-oriented ones in particular, were highly allergic to his core perception of the Israel-Diaspora dynamic.[24] Still holding out hope, he distinguished between the establishment, on one hand, and the younger generation that he sought to draw toward his vision, on the other. Thus, the absence of a critical mass of this student demographic at the HUC-JIR event undercut its ultimate value in his eyes.[25]

Jewish Theological Seminary (JTS)

Starting with the language of discourse and the makeup of the audience, one cannot overemphasize the contrast between the HUC-JIR assembly and the raucous event that took place earlier that day at the uptown Morningside Heights campus of JTS. Not only did Ben-Gurion deliver his entire thirty-six-minute JTS talk in Hebrew, but the student representative who opened the gathering also presented a fluid, American-accented but Israeli "Sephardi"–pronounced greeting and presentation in Hebrew on behalf of his fellow degree candidates. This included the traditional blessing when meeting a human king as well as the *sheheheyanu* benediction in praise for reaching an auspicious moment.[26] The celebrated Talmudist and former Jerusalemite professor Saul Lieberman awarded a gift in the name of the institution and offered his concluding comments as well in fluent Israeli Hebrew. Even JTS chancellor Louis Finkelstein, known to be openly ambivalent regarding political Zionism, spoke his few public words in Hebrew.[27] Most of all, the audio recording testifies to the young audience's high level of comprehension, expressed through immediate and enthusiastic applause for Ben-Gurion's declarations, as well as the ongoing spontaneous laughter in response to his chatty witticisms.[28]

The seasoned popular leader, who began his visit with a tour of the renowned JTS Library, sensed the warmth and approachability effused by the group. Uninhibited either in his passion or the clarity of his message, he began by emphasizing briefly the importance of the Hebrew language and the necessity for any true Jewish scholar or religious authority to spend at least a year studying in Israel.[29]

Quickly he got to his main point: "Young men and young women, we need you in Israel, to settle with us, to live with us, to create with us, to suffer with us, and if unfortunately necessary, to fight with us."[30] He explained that, inasmuch as he believed in the legitimacy of Diaspora Jewish life at least materially and intellectually, "rooted Jewish living is impossible if it is not nourished by Jewish independence."[31]

In support of this position he presented an extensive discourse on the core distinctions between the completeness of sovereign Jewish existence and the bifurcated experience of exile, even for the most committed Jew in the most beneficent foreign environment: "You eat bread from wheat that you did not plant, did not reap, flour that you did not bake . . . live in houses that you did not build . . . we live in one domain . . . our Judaism and our humanity are one and the same."[32] He even asserted his confidence that not only did the noted faculty member Mordecai M. Kaplan—whose civilizational approach to Judaism was deeply influenced by Zionist thought—agree with much of what he was saying, but even Finkelstein and most of those sitting in the room did as well.[33]

Beyond the fundamental dichotomy between Diaspora and sovereign homeland existence, Ben-Gurion raised the Holocaust as another compelling reason why American Jews needed to come to Israel. Not due to fears of a recurrence or rise in antisemitism on American soil, but rather, because the Nazis had destroyed Eastern European Jewry. Out of this population the synthesis of historic Jewish messianic yearnings and modern national ideals that yielded a concrete vision of return arose, as well as most of the actual pioneers who structured the practical foundation for the Jewish state.[34] Once again, he lamented that the 1.5 million Jews who had arrived in Israel since its founding were not these people. They were battered remnants from Nazi atrocities along with penniless immigrants from Asia and Africa who had lived ghettoized lives without progressive education and technological skills.[35]

Flaunting his Eurocentric/Western orientation, he appealed to the best of the educated American Jewish youth to replace those lost and join the outstanding younger generation born and bred in Israel. Together they could help the recent arrivals from Asia and Africa acquire the professional and cultural tools to thrive, and in the process prevent the nascent society from sliding into "Levantinism," thus continuing the project begun by Zionism's Eastern European founding fathers.[36] Therefore, he concluded, for those in the audience—that he was sure existed—for whom Israel's total Jewish environment resonated and who were inspired by its pioneering ethos and the importance of the venture, the only response was to make their permanent homes in Israel.[37]

The audio recording of this encounter reveals a natural chemistry between Ben-Gurion and the JTS student body. Not only did the attendees understand his Hebrew, they were clearly aware of the subtleties of Israeli current events and political intrigues, interested in what he had to say, and reacted enthusiastically en masse. As Elie Wiesel reported after witnessing the JTS gathering: "On rare occasions does such a personal connection develop between Ben-Gurion and his listeners, as did yesterday. The students responded to every suggestion and allusion, clapped applause at every idea, and periodically broke out in loud fits of laughter in response to his wisecracks."[38]

At the very end, after Finkelstein closed the ceremony by presenting him with a gold medal pin, Ben-Gurion could not resist turning to the crowd one final time and exclaiming, "If I may beseech you, anyone who is willing to settle in the Land of Israel, I encourage you to do so."[39] This final gesture certainly reflected the overall receptiveness of his listeners to his presentation. Nonetheless, it may have also indicated his acknowledgment of the dissonance between the profound collective fervor of this constituency and the actual likelihood that many would heed his call. As Wiesel registered perceptively, when earlier in the speech Ben-Gurion asked the over four hundred people in attendance how many planned to come on aliyah, just thirty raised their hands.[40]

Notwithstanding his possible disappointment with the immediate impact of his speech, Ben-Gurion's performance was dramatically different from the HUC presentation later the same day. At the HUC gathering, made up primarily of Reform dignitaries, he remained relatively consistent with the parameters set out in the 1950 Blaustein exchange. This was not the case at JTS, where in front of hundreds of students, he reverted to his core worldview that focused on the preeminence of Israel in comparison to Jewish life in exile and encouragement of Diaspora Jews to realize this ideal in practice. This reflected the youthful composition of the audience and the positive energy that came forth. It also points to his perception of the distinctions between the different denominations.

Yeshiva University (YU)

Immediately after his JTS visit, Ben-Gurion traveled further uptown to the Washington Heights campus of YU. Two thousand people, most of them students, filled the cavernous Lamport Auditorium and greeted Israel's founding prime minister with a thunderous singing of *Hatikvah*, Israel's national anthem.[41] As the Labor Zionist prime minister approached the rostrum, a large black satin yarmulkah situated obtusely atop his curly white locks, the institution's two foremost figures—Rabbi Dr. Samuel Belkin, the university president, and Rabbi Dr. Joseph B. Soloveitchik, the celebrated Talmudic authority and theologian—sat behind him on the stage.[42]

Here too, Ben-Gurion spoke in Hebrew and the attendees expressed their thorough understanding through periodic laughs and handclapping. Yet unlike at JTS, at least initially, the Israeli leader appeared to distance himself intentionally from the setting. In retrospect, this disconnect was anticipated in Belkin's welcoming words.

A renowned rabbinic scholar and classicist in his own right, the product of East European yeshivot and holder of a Brown University PhD, Belkin was effusive in his introduction.[43] He declared that while many esteemed rabbis, statesmen, and scholars had paid visits to the campus, none had garnered the excitement and celebration of the Israeli prime minister. Furthermore, he asserted that one could not be an upstanding religious Jew without a deep appreciation for the Land of Israel.[44] These sentences, however, were uttered with a strong Ashkenazi pronunciation and accent that indicated a European "exilic" rather than Zionist-oriented identity. Thus, as opposed to the "Zionized" language at JTS, Belkin's oration adumbrated audibly the rooted "traditionalist" aspects of the YU Orthodox environment, where male students studied Talmud under the tutelage of devout and for the most part non–secularly educated Lithuanian-style rabbis until midafternoon, before beginning their secular college classes. This was further emphasized by Belkin's avowal that truly loyal Jews must be committed to "the holiness of the Torah and the handed-down understanding of our forefathers [*masores avos*]."[45]

Ben-Gurion reacted initially with ambivalence and at times combative language, paying formal respect to his hosts while highlighting his and Israel's departure from the long-held assumptions of pious Jews. After nearly a minute of sustained applause, he began with a subtle ridicule of the name of the institution, which he suggested stemmed from "a bad custom that has become rooted here."[46] According to correct grammatical Hebrew, he claimed, it should have been called "Universitat ha-Yeshiva" rather than "Yeshiva University." That, of course, would have placed the secular element ahead of the parochial one, and it would have also added the letter *taf* at the end of the word "Universita"—the letter for which the distinction between Israeli and Ashkenazi pronunciations is most evident (*ta* vs. *sa*). Moreover, Ben-Gurion related that while singing Hatikvah, he could not help but focus on the last sentence, "to be a free nation in our Land." "I know," he shared in a melancholy tone, "about which Land you were singing, or at least to which one the song refers, and I assume you know too. I want to believe that these were not just empty words, although in truth I have my doubts."[47] At his immediate pause, the vast crowd remained eerily silent.

Beyond his instinctual ambivalence toward the Diaspora countenance of traditionalist Orthodoxy,[48] Ben-Gurion's discomfort and ambivalence may have been spurred by hearing that there had been controversy within YU regarding his visit. As reported by a contemporary source, pressure had been exerted upon the YU leadership by rabbinical figures aimed at thwarting the invitation.[49]

Continuing his moderately confrontational tone, Ben-Gurion detailed the grave military challenges faced by his country that drove him to engineer a personal meeting with President Eisenhower, and he related that whatever the results of this diplomacy, he knew that there was still no reason to panic. Citing the Psalmist, he reassured his Orthodox Jewish audience with a resonant passage, "*Hinei lo yanum ve-lo yishan shomer Yisrael* [Behold, He that guards Israel neither slumbers nor

Figure 1.1. Prime Minister of Israel David Ben-Gurion, with a yarmulkah on his head, faces the YU students while Rabbi Dr. Soloveitchik and President Belkin listen from on stage, March 16, 1960. Courtesy of the YU Archives.

sleeps]" (121:4).[50] But after enthusiastic clapping, an individual shouted out: "Mr. Prime Minister, to which guard are you referring, to the IDF or to the Holy One Blessed be He?" The heckler was silenced and removed quickly, but Ben-Gurion saw fit to answer honestly: "If for many, the 'Guardian of Israel' is 'He who sits on High,' my intent was to those who stand watch in the army camps of the Israel Defense Forces."[51] Continuing his emphasis on the human role as opposed to dependence on the Divine, and in the process pushing back at Belkin's emphasis on the Land of Israel rather than the State of Israel, he proclaimed that "[w]e, the government of Israel, not the government of the Land of Israel, there is a difference between them, for those who understand among you . . . and please don't perceive this as blasphemy, we have taken upon ourselves to fix or finish, that which the Holy One Blessed Be He chose for some reason not to complete."[52]

Eventually, after presenting his own personal trajectory—from Russian/Polish shtetl schoolboy to agricultural day laborer in early twentieth-century Palestine to leadership of the emergent State of Israel—Ben-Gurion returned to the themes he had raised at JTS and would touch upon later at HUC. He expanded upon the dual impact of the downfall of East European Jewry and the massive immigration from Asia and North Africa on the economic and cultural makeup of his country. This was followed by a passionate portrayal of the need for educated and skilled young American Jews to come to Israel. To this end, he shared his efforts to attain a firm commitment on the part of YU's leadership to allow students to spend one of their four college years in Israel, which drew additional enthusiastic applause. This was a theme that spoke directly to an internal conflict within YU at that time.

Sensing the opportunity to inspire a core constituency as he spoke, he concluded by specifying his key listener targets:

> To the outstanding, the daring, the pioneers, among you . . . I want to share the hidden subversion in my proposal . . . certainly a year in the Land will benefit you and American Jewry . . . but I have a scheme, many of those who shall come to Israel will not return and will remain there. This is what I intended to share with you this morning, everyone should come for at least a year, the best of you for eternity.[53]

The recording indicates that the ovations of the crowd were no less spirited regarding the "permanent settlement scheme" proposal than they were in respect to the "year in Israel." Conspicuously, by the time he completed his appearance, Ben-Gurion's ambivalence and discomfort seem to have given way to a recognition that there was great potential in the demonstrative YU student body, if not in the parochial foundations and management of the institution. According to a witness, as he left the rostrum Ben-Gurion acknowledged to Soloveitchik that "[y]outh like this I have yet to see outside Israel."[54]

YU Student Reactions

It is hard to gauge whether or not this final more upbeat impression outweighed Ben-Gurion's initial instinctive discomfort vis-à-vis YU's

Figure 1.2. Ben-Gurion sitting between Soloveitchik and Belkin, YU, March 16, 1960. Courtesy of the YU Archives.

Orthodox environment and impulse to joust with its religious ethos. What is certain is the overwhelmingly positive response of the student body to his appearance, not only during the event itself, but through a number of articles that appeared subsequently in the edition of the student weekly, *The Commentator*, that covered it. The lead headline was "B-G Stresses Study in Israel to Overflow Crowd at YU." The item that followed emphasized that, despite numerous Orthodox concerns over the status of Jewish law in the State of Israel, little of these feelings were evident during the visit. On the contrary, these specific disagreements were suspended by the sheer magnitude of the moment, which was described as the largest audience outside of Israel ever addressed by the statesman in the Hebrew language; "Ben-Gurion was coming to yeshiva, and no welcome was too great for the Prime Minister of Israel."[55]

As to the content of his speech, what was admired in particular was his focus on studying in Israel during college, and even his "plot" to convince people to stay forever was cited with clear appreciation. If any criticisms and doubts were raised in the paper, they were leveled at the YU administration. The student spokesmen were disappointed that few of their peers were invited to the private reception for Ben-Gurion that took place after his lecture.[56]

So appreciative was the newspaper's editorial board of the encounter with Ben-Gurion that they saw fit to print an "open letter" thanking him for his visit and articulating what it meant to the YU student body as Orthodox Jews. The promise of the event, they asserted, was certainly reflected in the forthright advancement of study in Israel as a key element that needed to be added to their educational menu. Yet its symbolic elements, as well as its long-term possibilities, were no less profound:

> Your visit to our School [sic] was one of the most memorable experiences of our lives. . . . Please do not feel we are patronizing when we say that you looked comfortable under the yarmulke you wore. Your act of respect made many of us, for the moment, forget our differences with your party's religious policies. . . . But we were most impressed with the content of your speech. Your ringing appeal for study in Israel showed us that you recognized the important role consigned to our Orthodox youth in Israel's future. We, too, feel that the traditional Jewish student, bred by Torah-true parents and teachers in the concept of *Ha'aretz Hakedosha* [the Holy Land], will provide Israel with its strongest support. Many of us are planning to study in Israel before we settle down. Some of us will linger after our studies, as you yourself predicted.[57]

Three elements jump out from this passage articulated by YU's student newspaper. First, a strong attachment of those who wrote it to Israel and its charismatic founding leader. Second, a clear demonstration that Ben-Gurion targeted a ripe constituency when he deviated from the Blaustein script and shared his true aim, to inspire young Americans to settle in Israel. Finally, a deep desire to deemphasize conflict and advance a vision for the state that integrated Orthodox Jews and their religious values rather than combatting them. Their perception that the yarmulkah sat comfortably on Ben-Gurion's head and effused respect for the values of the institution expressed this sentiment viscerally, if naively.[58]

The byline for the lead *Commentator* article, and likely author of the editorial board's "Open Letter" as well, was the paper's associate editor and YU senior Steven (Shlomo) Riskin. A smaller item on the front page of the same edition announced "Steve Riskin Voted '60 Valedictorian." There readers could learn that this Brooklyn-born cerebral humanities major had compiled a 3.87 GPA while being enrolled simultaneously in the rabbinical ordination program (RIETS), serving as editor in chief of *The Masmid*, the senior yearbook, and competing for three years on the varsity debating team. Riskin actually fulfilled his promise, and within a few years became one of the most popular and revolutionary Orthodox rabbinical and educational figures in America.[59]

Especially relevant to the current discussion is that in 1983, at the height of his Diaspora career, Riskin immigrated to Israel. There, he once again rose to prominence, first as a founder and chief rabbi of Efrat, among the largest settlements in the country, which is situated in the Etzion Bloc, just south of Jerusalem.[60] In parallel, he built the Ohr Torah Stone institutions (henceforth OTS), one of the biggest RZ educational networks in Israel, which has championed a moderate approach that celebrates the synthesis of traditional and secular knowledge, and promotes broadening the scope of advanced Torah studies for youth who come from abroad for a year or two and for Jewish women. It is also a key player in training and sending many Israeli emissaries to communities throughout the world.[61] In the course of his move from the apex of American Jewish life to a driving local force behind key institutions in Israeli religious society, Riskin emerged as an IsMO pioneer.

Aliyah, Religious Zionism, and YU

Ben-Gurion and Riskin's March 1960 crossing of paths provides a framework for analyzing that which arises from the comparison of the Israeli prime minister's visits to the three rabbinical seminaries, and especially those at JTS and YU. On multiple levels, the events had much in common. In all cases his aim was to engage the student body. At JTS and YU, he drew the crowds that he desired; at HUC, less so. All the same, in each of the three instances the responses of those present were exceedingly positive, at JTS and YU one might even say ecstatic. Although it is hard to produce clear evidence of the direct effect of his words on these audiences, as sociologist Chaim Waxman has demonstrated, it was this cohort that was the source of the increased amounts of American Jewish immigrants to Israel throughout the 1960s, and especially the big jump in the years immediately after the 1967 war.[62]

Yet it is not just the number of immigrants that evolved throughout the 1960s and into the early 1970s, but their religious affiliations as well. As Waxman attested, while the majority of the pre-state American immigrants were motivated by classical Zionist ideals, the rising numbers after 1960 and especially post-1967 were denominationally affiliated and integrated strong religious motivations as well. Moreover, despite representing less than 15 percent of the United States Jewish population, the unequivocally largest religious sector among the immigrants to Israel were the Orthodox. During the early 1960s, 34 percent reported that they were Orthodox, 24 percent were affiliated with Conservative Judaism, while 7 percent were Reform. Immediately after 1967 the Orthodox number rose to 42 percent, but steadied at closer to 37 percent, whereas from 1967 to 1971 the Conservative segment peaked at about 29 percent while the Reform reached 14 percent.[63]

Here, then, the intersection—or to some degree the clash—between Ben-Gurion, on one side, and Riskin and his YU comrades on the other, is telling. Based both on his behavior and the nuances of his content, Ben-Gurion appeared to see the students of the Conservative movement as the most natural targets for aliyah promotion. This perception could be substantiated by the movement's Zionist credentials: despite a few prominent dissenters, from its earliest rise Conservative Judaism had adopted the Zionist cause and the modern Hebrew language as core values. For that matter, as sociologist Marshall Sklare's groundbreaking study from just a few years before Ben-Gurion's 1960 visit explained, its core constituency stemmed from second- and third-generation Jews who came from his Eastern European milieu, and whose Jewish identities were characterized by respect for tradition, but minimal personal observance.[64] In 1960 this stream was on the verge of eclipsing Reform as the largest Jewish religious denomination. Thus, Ben-Gurion's unapologetic full-throttled appeal to the JTS gathering reflected both his personal comfort level and his reasonable estimation that it was the youth from this framework that had the most potential to show receptiveness to his message and facilitate a fundamental change in the American Jewish Zionist ethos.

To be sure, as the immigration statistics above show, his recognition of the centrality of Israel for Conservative Jews, especially the elite group that attended JTS, was not completely off target. And indeed, this group has impacted aspects of Israeli culture, especially academics and organizational life far beyond its numbers.[65] At the same time, Ben-Gurion's unequivocal warmth in the Conservative setting stood in sharp contrast with the ambivalence with which he related to the denominational group that ended up being most dominant in the forthcoming rise in aliyah—Modern Orthodoxy as represented by Riskin's YU classmates.

Did this reflect Ben-Gurion's awareness that his visit had been opposed by some of the institution's rabbinical heads? Was he simply uncomfortable in the Orthodox setting and annoyed that he was coerced into wearing a yarmulkah on stage? Was his perception of American Orthodoxy also predicated on Sklare's 1955 study in which he famously declared that "the history of their movement can be written in terms of a case study of institutional decay?"[66] Did he actually think that he could cajole this mass of Orthodox students to move to Israel by explicating before them his own choice of the merits of a human-centered Zionist ethos as an ideal substitute for well-worn Orthodox traditionalism? Or was his ambivalence a derivative of the complex relationship that he had with the National Religious Party in Israel, whose leaders had a close connection with those within the YU community who were at the forefront of the American Mizrachi–Religious Zionist organization?[67] What is apparent is that Ben-Gurion may have misjudged the deep connections of YU and its student body to Zionism and the State of Israel.

YU and Israel: Deep Roots and Pragmatic Tensions

In parallel to the traditionalist orientation of YU's Talmudic instructors, from the initial stages of its existence RZ, the Hebrew language, and subsequently the State of Israel were central areas of focus at this institution. In fact, there was strong support for political Zionism and appreciation for Theodore Herzl among the European-trained old guard of the American Orthodox rabbinate in the first decades of the twentieth century, even as they did not hesitate to express criticism when they felt it deserving.[68]

More dramatically, in 1922, due to family-related financial issues that caused YU's founding president, Rabbi Dr. Bernard Revel, to take a leave, the leader of the American Mizrachi (RZ) organization, Rabbi Meir Berlin (Bar-Ilan), was appointed head of the early version of YU—then referred to as the "Talmudic Academy."[69] Although his tenure lasted less than a year, during that brief period he succeeded in merging the Teacher's Institute (TI) that had been founded by his organization five years earlier with the Talmudic Academy. The alternative track to intensive traditional Talmudic studies that was inaugurated offered a gamut of courses in Jewish studies and pedagogy that were taught in Hebrew by a staff of academically trained and religiously observant scholars who were united in their dedication to Zionism. By 1934 there were 130 students enrolled in its classes.[70] Thus, at this early stage in YU's history, RZ had gained a strong footing within the institution.[71]

TI remained a separate division of YU until 1966, when it morphed into an undergraduate Jewish studies framework known as Erna Michael College (EMC) and later Isaac Breur College (IBC).[72] It also paved the way for the establishment of the Bernard Revel Graduate School (BRGS), where more advanced Jewish scholarship is taught and cultivated. Throughout TI's history all classes were taught in Hebrew, and the student yearbooks and newspapers appeared in Hebrew as well.

From 1924 until 1954, the dean of TI was Dr. Pinchas Churgin, an Eastern European–born yeshiva product, who had settled with his parents in Mandatory Palestine during his teen years, then earned a PhD degree in Semitics from Yale. An RZ activist throughout his adult life, in 1949 Churgin was elected president of the American Mizrachi movement. In 1955 he left YU and moved to Israel, where he served as the founding president of Bar-Ilan University (henceforth BIU, named after Rabbi Meir Berlin/Bar-Ilan), the religious-sponsored academic institution initiated by Mizrachi supporters in the United States in cooperation with Israel-based RZ leaders. Churgin and his cohorts envisioned an Israeli liberal arts institution that would share much in common with YU.[73] In fact, a strong relationship existed between the two Orthodox schools of higher learning during Bar-Ilan's first years and continued after Churgin's untimely death in 1957, under the orchestration of Rabbi Joseph Lookstein (Rabbi Haskel Lookstein's father) of KJ and YU who served as Churgin's initial replacement. Over time Bar-Ilan evolved into an Israeli-style research university structured more like European academic settings, albeit with principal Jewish and religious studies components, and a sizable religious student population.[74]

As to the Bernard Revel Graduate School, from the mid-1950s it was home to the Israel Institute, a joint project with the Jewish Agency. According to a 1956 memorandum, a series of graduate offerings would be taught "relating to . . . the tie of Israel and Diaspora and the role which Israel occupies in our Halachah and general Torah culture."[75] In practice, the course catalogue featured over fifteen classes and seminars, including "History of Zionism," "The Jewish Nation," "Political and Social Institutions of Israel," "Israeli Law," and "The Ethnology of Israel." Students were encouraged to write theses and dissertations on related topics. This framework, which also opened its classes to the wider public, was headed and orchestrated by another prominent rabbi-scholar and RZ activist with roots in Mandatory Palestine, YU professor of Rabbinics and veteran TI faculty member, Dr. Samuel K. Mirsky.[76]

But YU's Zionist moorings were not limited to its more academic-oriented wings. Soloveitchik—whose ancestors and relatives were fiercely anti-Zionist and who was initially affiliated with the Agudath Israel organization favored by most of his traditionalist Orthodox colleagues—came out publicly as a Mizrachi supporter and leader in the 1940s and had demonstrated Zionist sympathies even beforehand.[77] Famously, the speech that he delivered at YU on Israel Independence Day in 1956, where he set out his theological understanding of post-Holocaust Jewish life and the State of Israel in particular, became an RZ manifesto and was adopted as part of the core curriculum in Israel's state religious schools.[78] Together with his clear identification with the Zionist enterprise, Soloveitchik was forthright in his critique of internal developments within the new Jewish state, especially regarding the government's approach to religious issues and the overall development of religious life under sovereign circumstances.[79]

All the same, the tensions regarding YU and Israel that Ben-Gurion's 1960 visit brought to a fore related less to the complexities of the Israeli environment than to how identification with Israel manifested itself in practice within this educational bastion of American Modern Orthodoxy. In 1950, a program known as the "TI Israel Study Plan" had been inaugurated, which enabled YU students to spend their junior year studying in Israel. Over sixty of them participated during the next eight years, attending classes at the Hebrew University in Jerusalem as well as in the Jewish Agency's teacher training center. However, in the fall of 1958, President Belkin decided to discontinue the trips. As he put it in an interview: "our teachers are as good as any in Israel. College education should not be disrupted by a leave of absence." He noted that individual students would still be permitted to leave college to go to Israel, "but only at their own risk."[80]

This decision caused great consternation among the student body. Under the headline "Aliyah," a *Commentator* editorial protested, "One would imagine that, fortunate as the present generation is to be living at the first time in 1,900 years that the Jews have had a state in Israel, Yeshiva would enable its students to take full advantage of the opportunities offered to the Orthodox Jew of studying and sojourning there. This, however, is unfortunately not the case." As to Belkin's concern that the year abroad would interfere with achieving a solid YU college education, the editors opined that such an attitude "negates the role Israel plays in Jewish life today . . . students should . . . be encouraged to go to Israel during their college years because . . . Israel awakens in the student a profound sense of his status as a Jew and equips him with *better* tools for attacking problems of the American *galut*." The article ends with a plea, "We ask the administration to gravely reconsider their decision and its inevitable consequences. They must realize that counter to their prevailing trend in deemphasizing Israel, only by sponsoring such study trips to our homeland can the interests of Yeshiva University and Judaism be best served."[81]

To be sure, there is no mention in this 1958 edition of the student publication of Israel study as a first step toward settlement there. Rather, the program is presented as beneficial to local American Jewish life. Nonetheless, unlike Belkin, who demonstrated little if any appreciation for what an Israel experience could mean to an American Orthodox Jew, this interchange reinforces the impression that, ten years after the establishment of the state, it was part and parcel of the Jewish foundation of YU's student body. For the majority this increasingly Israel-infused

Orthodox Jewish identity remained an ideological or inspirational back-drop rather than a practical goal for their own futures. Yet, as noted, in subsequent years actual settlement became a realistic vision for a growing minority.[82]

The generational division between Belkin and the students expressed in 1958 seemingly foretells Ben-Gurion's focus during his campus visits two years later on connecting with the younger cohort, whom he sensed correctly would resonate more with his proposals. Indeed, the report in *The Commentator* on his 1960 visit makes clear that the issue of spending a year of study in Israel still had not been resolved. In fact, the student publication expressed deep concern as to whether the university would have the "foresight" to enable this aspect of Ben-Gurion's plan to actually come to fruition."[83]

Study in Israel—An Enduring and Ironic Legacy

Ben-Gurion's 1960 vision for masses of American Jewish undergraduates to study in Israel for at least a year eventually became reality, and even his "plot" to convince some to settle permanently bore some fruit. It would certainly be inaccurate to credit him exclusively with this achievement. Yet his efforts drew considerable attention to the idea of dedicated Israel study programs, sparking American Jewish youth to take this path and challenging the heads of Jewish institutions to facilitate their requests, in due course creating an entire educational "industry."[84] It is thus important to recognize Ben-Gurion's poignant role in the evolution of what has become one of the central vehicles for nurturing deep connections between Diaspora Jews and Israel.[85]

In point of fact, throughout much of the twentieth century a sprinkling of American students made their way to the Holy Land, primarily young men who studied in traditionalist yeshivot. During the 1950s, as the YU story attests, some more formal initiatives began to take shape.[86] The numbers increased very gradually throughout the 1960s, but the major turning point was the mid-1970s.[87] From that juncture onward, thousands arrived on a yearly basis. By then Israel's three largest universities had dedicated overseas student frameworks, with some of the classes taught in English. This was the stage when multiple post–high school "gap year" programs began to flourish. All of the major Jewish denominations, as well as the range of Zionist youth movements, sponsored their own frameworks, but nothing compared in magnitude and impact to the eventual proliferation of institutions both for men and women that serviced a wide spectrum of American Orthodox Jews. The "Israel yeshiva/seminary year"—which was buttressed by YU's ultimate decision to offer full accreditation[88]—became so de rigueur for this constituency that a 1997 doctoral dissertation reported 90 percent participation among MO high school graduates.[89] One principal actually opined, "there are graduates who report that their parents are forcing them to go to Israel for the year against their will and there are high schools who use the number of their graduates who go to Israel as part of their publicity campaigns for prospective students."[90]

The Orthodox products of the study in Israel concept initially broadcasted on center stage by Ben-Gurion in 1960 have anchored American aliyah from the 1980s onward.[91] Coming of age during the last decades of the twentieth century under the leadership of Shlomo (Steven) Riskin's generation, they became key partners not only in the development of Efrat and the Etzion Bloc, but of numerous Jerusalem neighborhoods, as well as the renewal of Beit Shemesh west of the Judean Hills, and the embourgeoisement of Ra'anana in the Sharon area and in the central city of Modi'in. Indeed, in 2002 the Nefesh b'Nefesh (NBN) aliyah organization was cofounded by an MO rabbi who studied in one of these Israeli yeshiva programs. Due in part to its close contacts with the core Orthodox feeder population, by 2008 an agreement was reached with the Israeli government whereby NBN would serve as the official "one stop shop" for escorting all North Americans regardless of their religious affiliations through the immigration process.[92]

Of course, apart these significant trends and even with more recent increases, viewed in light of American Jewry's over five million strong population, American aliyah is still a "boutique" endeavor that draws primarily from those with the highest levels of Jewish education and affiliation. Even among the self-identifying RZs who spent a year or more of study in Israel, it remains the precinct of an albeit highly influential but nevertheless numerically minor subsegment.[93]

Together with Ben-Gurion's legacy, then, also lie multiple ironies. For one, his own prejudices may have undermined prospects to buttress his core vision further. In addition, while it did not create a mass movement, the study in Israel experience was arguably the crucial factor both in cementing the axiomatic political support of MO for Israel and in transforming aliyah among its adherents from a respected but daunting act to a viable choice. Herein lies one of the foundations for the overwhelming Orthodox dominance of American aliyah from the 1980s onward—a reality that stands in contrast to Ben-Gurion's desired scenario.

The rising role of aliyah as an MO ideal provided a natural constituency for the IsMO pioneers who arrived on the eve of this acceleration. American gap year students who attended the institutions of the pioneers were inspired to make Israel their permanent home. Simultaneously, those who studied in these institutions guided by the "agents of change" were led to understand that doing so did not demand abandoning a synthetic religious worldview for the more binary one that dominated the Israeli religious scene.

Cumulative Impact

Pioneers and Their Institutions

Introduction

The phenomenon of the influence of the American immigrant "agents of change" manifests three coinciding circumstances: the confluence of the arrival of eight key figures to Israel during a relatively short period, the cumulative effect of their diverse but overlapping educational initiatives upon their local Israeli disciples, and the transmission by their younger cohorts of their understandings to their own constituencies. The eight men and women discussed here as pioneers were nurtured in an array of North American locations and in homes and schools of varying levels of religious commitment and ideological orientation. All but Rabbi Dr. Nachum Rabinovitch completed at least one YU degree, and five of the men studied intensively with Soloveitchik and earned YU rabbinical ordination.[1] Beyond their North American Orthodox backgrounds, what they all had in common was their immigration as adults to Israel during the mid-1960s through the early 1980s, and their leading roles in local RZ-oriented educational frameworks that targeted collegiate-age populations and in some cases additional constituencies as well.

Within these contexts they introduced religious worldviews and intellectual approaches that were grounded in their prior exposures and that differed from Israeli Judaism's dominant approaches. The recipients of their ideas were both Israelis and learners who came from abroad, quite a few of whom became religious leaders, educators, scholars, public activists, and involved community members. For many, the ideas they internalized during their studies were foundational to their own endeavors, even as they processed and reformulated them through their own lenses and experiences.

The interfaces of the Israelis—for whom these outlooks were most novel—with the pioneers and their institutions were transformative. The students were challenged to adjust and recalibrate the fresh ideas they had encountered to their own cultural milieus and social orientations. In time, this "transnational flow" played a crucial role in facilitating the novelties in Israeli religious life that have come to fruition in the twenty-first century.[2]

The Game Changer: Rabbi Dr. Aharon Lichtenstein (1933–2015)

Rabbi Dr. Aharon Lichtenstein was born in Paris in 1933. At the age of seven he lived for half a year with his family in a refugee camp under the Vichy regime, before escaping to America. His father, the son of a ritual slaughterer, grew up in Germany and may be termed a traditionalist Orthodox *maskil* (enlightened Jew). Yechiel Lichtenstein earned a PhD in French literature but devoted his life to Jewish education, first at the Orthodox teacher's seminary in Wurzburg, then at the Ecole Maimonide in Paris, and throughout most of his American career as a Jewish studies teacher at two of YU's affiliated high schools, Brooklyn Talmudic Academy (BTA) for men and Central for women. Aharon Lichtenstein's mother stemmed from Lithuanian yeshiva culture royalty, the daughter of one of the administrators of the famed "Telz yeshiva," whose family lived on the campus itself. She was a learned woman who published articles in Torah journals during her youth.[3] As the son put it in an autobiographical statement, "Our Hebrew-speaking home was an interesting blend of East and West . . . everything revolved around Torah living, in one sense or another."[4]

After stints in Baltimore and Chicago, the family settled in Brooklyn, and despite the father's professional affiliations, the prodigious son was enrolled in the more traditionalist (Haredi) "Yeshiva Rabbi Chaim Berlin." There he was mentored by the younger brother of his future father-in-law, Rabbi Aaron Soloveitchik,[5] and came under the influence of the powerful yeshiva head and a central ideologue of the post-Holocaust renaissance of Lithuanian Orthodox culture in America, Rabbi Yitzchak Hutner.[6] Lichtenstein attested throughout his life that these two figures had a profound impact on him, particularly regarding issues of faith and moral fortitude. He also confessed his serious consideration at a certain point of pursuing advanced Talmud studies in the burgeoning bastion of American Haredi culture, Beth Medrash Govoha of Lakewood, New Jersey. In the end, he felt that Joseph Soloveitchik's creativity would be more beneficial to his development as a Talmudist.[7]

In 1949, at the age of sixteen, he arrived at YU, where he devoted the next years to studying Talmud intensively under the tutelage of its master teacher, Joseph Soloveitchik, while also earning a college degree. After being granted rabbinical ordination by the YU-affiliated Rabbi Isaac Elchanan Theological Seminary (RIETS), in 1953 he took an unusual turn when he applied and was accepted to the PhD program in English literature at Harvard University.[8] Throughout his time there, Lichtenstein continued to study Talmud with Soloveitchik at his Boston home, which was the latter's main residence. During this period Lichtenstein met his teacher's daughter, Tova (Soloveitchik) Lichtenstein, whom he would later marry in 1961.[9]

In 1957, the newly minted Harvard doctor returned to New York and taught English literature at YU's Stern College for Women, while continuing to study and present the review classes of his future father-in-law's Talmud lectures on the men's campus. Within a few years, he was made head of the *kollel* (fellowship program) for advanced rabbinical students and in 1963 he received an appointment as a full-time RIETS instructor. Throughout the 1960s his reputation grew as a preeminent Talmud scholar and heir apparent to his father-in-law. Lichtenstein's integration of multiple worlds was reflected in his intellectual oeuvre, in his religious comportment, and in a moral proclivity that led him to publish a number of seminal essays and support student activism for both Jewish and humanitarian causes.[10]

In the spring of 1966 an ideological controversy arose between Lichtenstein and another prominent young scholar at YU, Rabbi Dr. Irving "Yitz" Greenberg. The latter was also a product of a Brooklyn-based traditionalist yeshiva who had attended college and then achieved a Harvard PhD (in history). Greenberg was then appointed professor at YU and served simultaneously as a pulpit rabbi in a growing adjacent community. Both figures were extremely popular among the YU student body, who saw them as exceptional role models for the synthetic Torah u-Madda (Torah and Science) ideal championed by the institution. Beyond their formal duties, they were both involved in various initiatives aimed at enriching the religious and intellectual lives of the collegiate generation and from time to time participated together in various programs.[11] However, in an article that Lichtenstein penned in response, he took exception to the progressive views of Greenberg expressed in an interview with *The Commentator*. From Lichtenstein's perspective, Greenberg had demonstrated openness to higher Biblical criticism, nonmarital sexual activity, and engagement with non-Orthodox religious streams that deviated from accepted religious standards. Significantly, in numerous cases in which Greenberg and Lichtenstein differed, a generation later some of Lichtenstein's own students articulated views reminiscent of those of Greenberg. This ideational development exemplifies how perspectives that arose in North America were recalibrated by those who received them in Israel.[12]

In 1971, Lichtenstein chose an independent direction when he and his wife and five children (a sixth was born in Jerusalem) moved to Israel after accepting the invitation of Rabbi Yehudah Amital to serve as coleader of YHE. Inasmuch as Lichtenstein remained affiliated officially with YU through his position as principal lecturer at its Gruss Institute in Jerusalem, it was in the context of his primary role as head of an Israeli RZ yeshiva that he opened original vistas within Orthodoxy. As seen, for many years Lichtenstein was considered an outlier by the dominant voices of Israeli RZ, and his yeshiva had a distinctly unconventional reputation. Yet it is not only within the Israeli milieu that Lichtenstein's voice diverged from the consensus. The more conservative approaches that became dominant within YU's rabbinical leadership since his departure did not necessarily reflect his.[13] Indeed, be it vis-à-vis the prevailing RZ yeshiva milieu or the YU environment, Lichtenstein did not necessarily follow the "company line," and as will become clear, and some of his most prolific students would qualify as "avant-garde."[14]

It is imperative to emphasize why Lichtenstein's arrival was such a critical moment in the emergence of IsMO. At base, he was undeniably an extraordinary Torah scholar with a superb rabbinical pedigree, who was nurtured by and maintained relationships with some of the leading traditionalist authorities of the time. His own Talmudic lectures charted new analytic directions within the same conceptual approach as Lithuanian-style Haredi and RZ yeshivot in Israel and throughout the world.[15] Thus, in contrast to other likeminded figures, regardless of one's

Figure 2.1. Rabbi Dr. Aharon Lichtenstein studying the Talmud in the original *beit midrash* (study hall) of YHE soon after his 1971 arrival in Israel. Courtesy of YHE.

opinion of his ideological positions and policies, it was harder to simply dismiss him as insufficiently grounded in core sources of religious knowledge and commitment.

There are intriguing parallels that can be drawn between his father-in-law's role as a "legitimator" of MO and RZ in North America during the mid-twentieth century and that played by Lichtenstein in the gestation of an alternative religious ambiance in Israel during the late twentieth and early twenty-first centuries.[16] Like Soloveitchik, Lichtenstein's main occupation was serving as a yeshiva head and lecturer who taught and cultivated thousands of students over the course of his over forty years as co-leader of YHE. Many of its graduates, like the MO disciples of Soloveitchik in North America, went on to establish or lead new institutions in other parts of Israel and throughout the world or serve in a variety of other capacities that impacted the religious life of their surroundings. And as with Soloveitchik's students, while these disciples drew deeply from their mentor, they did not necessarily maintain strict obedience to the parameters that he set out.[17]

Yet in seeking to understand Lichtenstein's place within Israeli Judaism, there are additional factors that deserve consideration. His partnership with Amital was crucial, both through the yeshiva they built and beyond. Amital was a recognized leader within RZ spheres. A Hungarian/Rumanian–born (Oradea) Holocaust survivor and alumnus of the famed Yeshivat Hebron in Jerusalem whose wife descended from Lithuanian royalty (the Meltzer family),[18] he served in the IDF in the 1948 War of Independence. During his youth in Europe he had been drawn to Kook's redemptive Zionism, and his theological writings after the War of 1967 inspired the Gush Emunim ideological movement that spearheaded the settlement of the territories captured during the 1967 "Six-Day War." In parallel, Amital was one of the founding fathers of the Hesder yeshiva movement. Yet throughout his career he distinguished himself from his RZ milieu through his unconventional thinking. Despite his initial embrace of the redemptive settlement ideology, beginning in the 1980s he departed from the dominant RZ political stance, partnering in the founding of the Meimad moderate religious political party—which offered an alternative to the (by then) decidedly right-wing stance of the veteran NRP—and serving as a minister in the Labor-led coalition of Prime Minister Shimon Peres.[19] As a yeshiva head, he

Figure 2.2. Rabbis Lichtenstein and Amital in the 1980s. Photo by Menachem Klein, courtesy of YHE.

encouraged independent reflection on the part of his students, famously exhorting them not to be "Little Amitals."[20]

Perhaps the most profound example of Amital's commitment to "out-of-the-box" initiatives was his effort to recruit Lichtenstein to serve as co-head of YHE soon after its founding. To be sure, the latter's Talmudic prowess and rabbinic pedigree were certain to draw top students from Israel and abroad and enhance the reputation of the institution. Yet this plan demanded sharing stewardship with a person who hailed from a conspicuously distinct background and possessed a noticeably different personal temperament. For his Israeli students who were used to a relatively monolithic rabbinical model, Amital challenged them to embrace a clean-shaven, tweed-wearing figure with a non-Israeli accent, who was equally comfortable quoting from John Milton and Cardinal Newman as Maimonides and Soloveitchik and did not share the political views of most other RZ rabbis.[21]

If Lichtenstein's background and demeanor were foreign to his Israeli students, his religious outlook as well as his political positions clashed with those of many of his RZ rabbinical colleagues, and he was not shy about expressing his maverick positions. This was especially the case when it came to situations in which he perceived a moral failure on the part of the RZ community or the Israeli government,[22] as well as regarding the strong support he gave to women's advanced Torah study.[23] While these stances certainly caused conflict and likely alienated many, they also clarified the singularity of Lichtenstein's path for those who were exposed to it.[24]

The inventory of Lichtenstein's YHE Israeli students is long.[25] Numerous of Lichtenstein's children have also gained prominence within Israeli religious life as well as in America, extending or reframing different aspects of his works and outlook: Rabbi Mosheh Lichtenstein is co-yeshiva head of YHE; Rabbi Yitzchok Lichtenstein is co-head of the Torah Vodaas yeshiva in Brooklyn and a key editor of the rabbinic writings of his Soloveitchik ancestors; Rabbi Mayer Lichtenstein is rabbi of the Ohel Yonah Menachem synagogue in Beit Shemesh and a leading faculty member at Yeshivat Orot Shaul in Tel Aviv (led by Rabbi Yuval Cherlow); Rabbanit Esther (Lichtenstein) Rosenberg is founding head of Beit Midrash Migdal Oz for Women; Rabbi Shai Lichtenstein has served as coeditor of posthumously published collections of his father's writings, and Rabbanit Tonya (Lichtenstein) Mittelman is principal of the Tzvia High School in Sdot Negev.

The Independent Halakhist: Rabbi Dr. Nachum Eliezer Rabinovitch (1928–2020)

Like Aharon Lichtenstein, Rabbi Dr. Nachum Eliezer Rabinovitch was a profound Torah scholar with strong secular credentials whose writings draw on a wide knowledge base, as well as an unequivocally independent thinker and religious authority. He was also invited by the local Israeli founders, Rabbi Yitzhak Shilat and Hayyim Sabato, to lead a fledgling yeshiva that grew to one of the largest Hesder frameworks—Birkat Moshe in Ma'ale Adumim, a large urban settlement (pop. 37,000) just east of Jerusalem along the road to the Dead Sea. Indeed, his arrival in 1982 and subsequent thirty-eight-year tenure in Israel also played a role in legitimizing an alternative RZ approach to the dominant Merkaz ha-Rav one. Yet in the words of Allan Nadler—a former North American student and insightful Jewish studies scholar in his own right—his teacher was "perhaps the most impressive and the least well known" of leading contemporary rabbis.[26]

Rabinovich arrived in Israel at the age of fifty-four, after a rich career as a synagogue rabbi and educator in North America and the United Kingdom.[27] He had been born in a small town in Quebec to Yiddish-speaking Eastern European immigrant parents, and received his advanced Torah education and was granted ordination at the age of twenty by Rabbi Pinchas Hirschsprung (1912–1998). The latter headed the Merkaz ha-Torah Yeshiva in Montreal and served for four decades as the city's chief rabbi. A Galician Torah scholar who had studied in and remained associated with the famed Yeshivas Hakhmei Lublin in Poland until he escaped the Nazi invasion, he arrived in Canada in 1941. Although his career was focused on the particular Jewish religious realm, an interview from 1942 attested that "the culture of Europe has not been foreign to him. . . . The Rabbi had occasion to refer to the writings and doings of such varied worthies as Diogenes, Plato, Spinoza, Heine, Shakespeare, Lessing, and Kant. . . . Nor is he unfamiliar either with the products of Haskala or of the German Yiddishe Wissenschaft."[28]

During his time in Montreal, Rabinovitch also received a bachelor's degree from Sir George Williams University (today part of Concordia University).[29] He then moved to Baltimore, where he did graduate studies in mathematics at Johns Hopkins University, while continuing his advanced Torah learning at the Lithuanian-style Ner Israel Rabbinical College. He was granted an additional ordination by its founding head, Rabbi Yaakov Yitzhak Ruderman, and was married to Ruderman's niece, Rachel Shuchatowitz, in 1951.

From 1951 to 1970, Rabinovitch served as a communal rabbi, for a brief time in Baltimore, then in Charleston, South Carolina—where he established a local Jewish day school and wrote some of his earliest religio-legal responsa[30]—and subsequently in Toronto. In parallel with local and national religious leadership activities and publication on a broad range of contemporary religious issues, he completed a PhD at the University of Toronto in the history of science.[31]

In 1971 he moved to London after being appointed principal of Jews' College. According to a *Jewish Chronicle* article, he was disappointed to discover that "[t]he college had relatively few students, its finances were in poor shape, and the particular type of Torah scholarship he represented was not, at that time, widely appreciated."[32] That said, a small cadre of bright and motivated locals were drawn to him, most notably the late chief rabbi of the United Synagogue, Lord Rabbi Jonathan Sacks, who had at the point just begun to concentrate on advanced Torah studies and later shared: "By the time I came to study with him, I had already studied at Cambridge and Oxford with some of the greatest intellects of the time . . . Rabbi Rabinovitch was more demanding than any of them. . . . For him, intellectual honesty and independence of mind were inseparable from the quest for truth."[33]

In contrast to London, over the course of nearly four decades in Ma'ale Adumim, buttressed by dynamic younger colleagues, hundreds of students from RZ homes were exposed to Rabinovitch's learning and theological outlook. Simultaneously, his published writing was prolific, most prominently his magnum opus, the twenty-three volume *Yad Peshutah* systematic commentary on the entire *Yad ha-Hazakah/Mishneh Torah* (Code of Jewish Law) of Maimonides.

Together with these tomes, Rabinovitch's most enduring legacy would appear to be his intrepid approach to practical Jewish law, which gained expression in his responsa and essays, through the disciples that he trained, and the many beyond his formal pupils that turned to him for guidance on intricate matters of religious law and observance.[34] His unconventional perspective is evident in rulings on manifold topics ranging from Sabbath and festival restrictions in light of new technologies, to personal status issues, to standards of modesty for both women and men.[35] Two notable figures who consulted with him regularly were YHE alumnus and prominent moderate religious leader Rabbi Dr. Benny Lau and his wife, Rabbanit Noa Lau, director of the Jewish law program at Nishmat Institute: "For nearly thirty years, he was our primary address for questions that were beyond our capabilities . . . we would call him and he was approachable, direct, matter of fact, and above all—he didn't retreat from taking responsibility for his ruling. The feeling that 'there is someone to depend upon' is like an anchor for those at the frontline of communities who confront the many challenges of life."[36] Unlike Lichtenstein, who from early on devoted himself to articulating the conceptual underpinnings of the Talmud, Rabinovitch's career was grounded in his years as a communal rabbi and the pragmatic issues that he encountered.

Figure 2.3. Rabbi Dr. Nachum Rabinovich speaking at an ITIM Conversion Conference, with former Soviet Jewish dissident Natan Sharansky at his left and Rabbi Seth Farber, founder and head of ITIM at his right. The audience includes Professor Benny Ish Shalom (founder of Beit Morasha), Rabbi Ya'akov Meidan (current co-leader of YHE), Rabbi Re'em Hacohen (co-leader of Yeshivat Otniel), and Rabbi Yehudah Gilad (co-leader of Yeshivat Ma'ale Gilboa and former MK), all prominent YHE alumni. Courtesy of ITIM.

In 2016, Rabinovitch's willingness to take independent stands finally gained wider publicity when he joined with ITIM, OTS, and Beit Morasha to establish a rabbinical court for conversion known as *Giyur K'Halacha* (literally "conversion according to Jewish law") outside the auspices of Israel's official state rabbinate. Until his passing, he served as its president and foremost authority. In the words of its official website, "Giyur K'Halacha is based on the writings of Rabbi Nahum Rabinovitch."[37] This initiative is a bold and concrete example of IsMO's coming of age and greater sense of legitimacy, both in terms of the approach to this critical and controversial area of Jewish law, and the coalition of bodies that coalesced around it. Here Rabinovitch distinguished himself from Lichtenstein, who rendered lenient rulings to individuals, but was relatively hesitant to challenge accepted norms and sources of authority.

Rabinovitch, then, was unquestionably a critical figure in IsMO's emergence. Yet, as noted at the outset, for the most part his reputation throughout his Israeli career was limited to his direct students and to a coterie of figures who were either Maimonidean specialists or, like the Lau family, learned of his approach and sought him out. His voice within Israeli religious life was certainly less pronounced than that of Lichtenstein. Why so? There is no clear answer; rather a convergence of factors likely came to play: timing—he arrived over a decade after Lichtenstein, when the Israeli RZ scene or at least the learned elites had gained initial exposure to a similar synthetic model that for some was appealing while for others troubling; intellectual style—unlike Lichtenstein, who combined mastery of Lithuanian conceptualization with the human insight of a literary scholar, Rabinovitch was at his base a mathematician and scientific thinker whose analytical work was painstaking and detailed, and did not suffer the decidedly theoretical but at times intellectually cathartic forms of Talmudic study that dominated both Haredi and RZ yeshivot; personality—unlike Lichtenstein, who could come across as introverted on a one-to-one basis, but possessed a dramatic flair in public settings, Rabinovitch had a relatively flat lecture style, but was exceedingly personable and even jocular in smaller happenstances;[38] quiet subversion—while Lichtenstein was more outspoken and therefore drew criticism, Rabinovitch's challenge to prevailing norms came across for most of his career in legal rulings that generally remained within the purview of those close to him; outsider—Rabinovitch was not only somewhat of an anomaly to mainstream Kookian RZ circles, he also was not part of the YU "clique" and the many disciples of Soloveitchik;[39] partners—while his Birkat Moshe partners Shilat and certainly Sabato stood out among RZ rabbis, a well-known scholar and commentator on medieval Jewish thought and an award-winning novelist respectively, they were very young when they recruited Rabinovitch and never became central players within the power structures of RZ and Israeli society along the lines of Amital;[40] mainstream voices—although there has always been diversity among YHE's faculty, at Birkat Moshe the more mainstream Merkaz ha-Rav RZ outlook was much more present in the teachings of key figures than at YHE, and many students responded to those voices more than to Rabinovitch; contentious public statements— although Rabinovitch did not gravitate to the public stage, on a few occasions he expressed opinions, which were picked up by the press, that located him within the far-right political spectrum, as opposed to Lichtenstein, who denounced extremism adamantly and was lauded for his openness to diplomatic compromise.

Rabinovitch's followers sought to demonstrate that these were exceptional statements that did not reflect his overall worldview. Nonetheless, these isolated cases soiled his reputation within the broader Israeli public, including more liberal-minded RZ constituencies, and likely contributed to his marginalization.[41] All the same, Rabinovitch's example (as well as Riskin's, as we will see below) indicates that the correlation often assumed between religio-legal flexibility and respect for personal autonomy, on the one hand, and political liberalism, on the other, does not necessarily come to bear within the Israeli religiously moderate spectrum.

Like Lichtenstein, Rabinovitch nurtured students who have internalized and processed his core approach and can be identified along the spectrum of IsMO. That said, the list of his influential students is notable but shorter, which may in and of itself reflect his more limited reach.

Bridges to Leadership: Rabbi Dr. Daniel Tropper (b. 1942)

As opposed to the rest of the pioneers, who headed formal educational institutions where the core activity was intensive text study, Rabbi Dr. Daniel Tropper focused his career on the informal realm. In 1969, the same year he and his wife, Fayge (neé Landgarten), came on aliyah, he cofounded the Gesher Organization. The title means "bridge" in Hebrew, and the aim was to narrow the gap between observant and nonobservant Israeli youth. To be sure, in the course of over five decades of living in Israel, Tropper's involvements were manifold, ranging from senior government appointments to helping multiple organizations and schools get off the ground to political activism. Yet his contributions were grounded in the vision that he articulated and implemented through Gesher.

Tropper was the eldest of eight children born to parents who lived an observant lifestyle in Brooklyn, New York.[42] He attended the Rabbi Jacob Joseph yeshiva high school and Yeshiva University, where he studied under Soloveitchik and received his bachelor's degree, rabbinical ordination, and a PhD in ancient Jewish history. As Tropper attested, "After my father and mother, Soloveitchik was the figure who was most impactful on my life."[43]

In 1963, he took off a year from his academic pursuits and dedicated himself to full-time Torah studies at Yeshivat Merkaz ha-Rav in Jerusalem. During that time, he was exposed to the deep tensions between religious and secular Jews that marked the burgeoning Israeli society. After his return to the United States, he and other friends who had also spent a study year in Israel came to the realization that Israel would

Figure 2.4. Rabbi Daniel Tropper, founder of Gesher, with Teddy Kollek, legendary mayor of Jerusalem, during the 1980s. Courtesy of Gesher.

benefit from a nongovernmental framework dedicated to improving the situation. While still in the United States they authored a seventeen-page proposal and began to raise funds.[44]

Soon after his immigration to Israel, he and his cohorts connected with a secular Israeli educator and organized the first Gesher Seminar at Kibbutz Kfar Etzion, the same location where YHE had begun just a few years before. Thirty-five high school–age students chose voluntarily to attend the five-day Gesher event, half observant and half not. Their responses were exceedingly positive. Soon enough more seminars were organized during school vacations and holiday weekends with hundreds of participants each year. Tropper noted that he had witnessed similar types of seminars organized by YU and other organizations during his university days. By 1975 the Ministry of Education had drafted Gesher to run seminars on Zionism and Judaism within the state school system and a retreat center, Beit Gesher, was dedicated in the northern city of Safed.[45]

Over the following decades, Gesher evolved into a multifaceted educational service provider, with divisions focused on education and curriculum development, leadership, Diaspora relations, special programs for IDF soldiers, a foundation for media and film that has supported over one hundred productions aimed at addressing multiple facets of Judaism and Israeli life, and more recently a department directed toward connecting Haredi Jews and other Israelis. During the early twenty-first century, much of the activity was run from a large facility that was built in the center of Jerusalem.[46]

In parallel, Tropper took on additional roles, including special advisor to the minister of education, Zevulun Hammer, from 1979 to 1984. In that position he was instrumental in creating the TALI education network of state schools and supplementary programs that offers enrichment in Jewish subjects geared to families that respect tradition but are not necessarily personally observant. Subsequently he spearheaded Keren ha-Kehillot, which supports groups of young RZ families establishing sub-communities primarily in the periphery of the country. He has also been active politically. Together with Amital, with whom he had grown close since the time of his arrival, they established the Meimad party. Tropper returned to involvement with the mainstream RZ Bayit ha-Yehudi party during the period when Naftali Bennett rose to its leadership.

Tropper's core approach to drawing the disparate Jewish sectors of Israel closer relied on emphasizing their common heritage and the Jewish literary canon. He believed from the outset and continues to assert, "what must connect religious and secular Jews is that they are all shareholders in the Jewish tradition . . . when this is recognized a collective Jewish conversation can exist."[47] In addition to Soloveitchik, he credits the decades-long dialogue and friendship he developed with both Amital and Lichtenstein with helping him navigate the many issues that he confronted within Israeli society.

But their relationship went beyond the personal. From the early days of Gesher, students and others associated with YHE made up a significant portion of the counselor/advisor staff at the seminars and events. Indeed, it is through Gesher's role as a cultivator of leadership within the RZ that Tropper's position as a pioneer becomes most pronounced. From the outset of the seminars, it was not just the high school–age participants, but even more so the young adult "advisors" who attended such events on a regular basis, who gained extensive exposure to the broader Israeli population and simultaneously cultivated their own personal leadership skills. Two of the mentors at the inaugural rendition

Figure 2.5. The groundbreaking ceremony for Gesher's Jerusalem center, late 1980s.
From left: Tropper, Minister of Education Zevulun Hammer, Arthur Aeder and
William Goldberg (key supporters from the United States), and Mayor Teddy Kollek.
Courtesy of Gesher.

were Hanan Porat and Yehoshua Weizman. While both went on to
play significant roles in the mainstream RZ camp, neither was afraid to
take on independent positions, especially when it came to strengthening relations with the broader secular population. Porat was one of the
young people who helped found YHE and recruited Amital to lead it.
He was also a key figure in the settlement movement and for a time an
MK. In parallel, he was a teacher, a man of letters, and a social activist
who maintained close personal relationships with his secular political
competitors.[48] Weizman became the head of the Yeshivat Ma'alot in a
town close to the northern border with Lebanon, where he put forward
an original approach to Talmud study that focused on the impact of
the Land of Israel on the rabbinic canon. While he rejected the territorial withdrawal pacts signed by the late prime minister Yitzhak Rabin

in 1993 and 1995 known as the Oslo Accords, as well as the unilateral withdrawal from the Gaza Strip orchestrated by the late prime minister Ariel Sharon, he was adamant in advocating for peaceful resistance and spoke out vehemently against illegal and violent actions against the government that would foment internal conflict. In 1994, he founded an organization called Panim el Panim (face to face) that organizes home visits and "parlor meetings" in which religious and secular Jews engage in discussions related to contemporary Jewish identity.[49] Like so many students and disciples of the pioneers, these figures did not necessarily replicate Tropper's model, but rather their early experiences with Gesher were integrated into their own "Israeli" adaptation.

Talmud for Women: Rabbi Dr. Chaim Brovender (b. 1941)

For an educator best known for his role in advancing Torah study for English-speaking students from around the globe, Rabbi Dr. Chaim Brovender has had a profound impact upon Israeli Judaism. He was born in Brooklyn and attended the Yeshiva of Flatbush, one of the first MO, RZ-oriented, coeducational day schools in the United States.[50] At YU he studied under Soloveitchik, receiving rabbinical ordination, and completing a bachelor's degree in mathematics.[51] He and his wife, Miriam, both of whom had been active in the Bnei Akiva RZ youth movement, immigrated to Israel in 1965 and settled in Jerusalem.[52]

Over the next decade Brovender dedicated himself to Torah study in the Haredi-oriented Itri yeshiva and earned a PhD in Semitic languages at the Hebrew University in Jerusalem. He also began teaching Torah classes in conjunction with Itri's Darchei Noam–Shappel's Institute to the increasing numbers of students and spiritual searchers who were arriving in Jerusalem after the "Six-Day War."[53] By 1976 he had founded Yeshivat Hamivtar, an institution that targeted collegiates and graduates with minimal background in advanced Torah learning.[54] In parallel, he spearheaded the establishment of Michlelet Bruria as a separate institution geared to a similar population of women. As we will see, Rabbanit Malka Bina was deeply involved in the development of both Darchei Noam–Shappel's and the early stages of Michlelet Bruria. While both institutions grew and have produced hundreds of alumni who have themselves made marks on Jewish religious leadership and education in Israel

Figure 2.6. An early Michlelet Bruria Talmud class for women with Rabbi Chaim Brovender. Courtesy of Rabbi Chaim Brovender.

and throughout the world, it is primarily via Michlelet Bruria—still referred to by many simply as "Brovender's"—that its founder served as a pioneer of IsMO.[55]

The critical step was Brovender's commitment to and encouragement of rigorous Talmud study on the part of women. Although a few American Orthodox institutions—including the Yeshiva of Flatbush where he had been a student—had long enabled their female students to gain basic exposure to the central text of rabbinic literature, the idea of a full-time "women's yeshiva" with a *beit midrash* (study hall, like in a traditional men's yeshiva) was unprecedented and considered by many to be controversial.[56] During the same year of its founding, 1976, Soloveitchik famously delivered the opening lecture for the newly inaugurated advanced Talmud program at YU's Stern College for Women,[57] and BIU opened its *midrasha* (Torah study institution; plural, midrashot) for women.[58] While one of the central initial aims of Michlelet Bruria was to engage young adults who were not brought up in Orthodox homes, the unique curriculum increasingly attracted those who came from robust religious environments and arrived possessing strong skill sets.[59] They were eager to gain greater understanding and competency in the Talmud, long considered the apex of classical rabbinical scholarship.[60]

Over time, the women's English-speaking division evolved from a predominantly collegiate and postcollegiate orientation to mainly a gap year program for MO high school graduates.[61] They were eager to learn from the diverse faculty, which included rabbis and women Torah scholars, as well as prolific academic scholars and groundbreaking Orthodox thinkers such as Professor Tamar Ross. In parallel, during the early 1980s, a Hebrew track for Israeli students was introduced as well.[62] The institution as a whole, including the Israeli offerings, expanded dramatically from 1986 when, due to financial challenges, Brovender merged both of his schools with the OTS educational network that had been established by Shlomo (Steven) Riskin, who became co-head. Soon after, the women's branch was renamed Midreshet Lindenbaum. Brovender remained as *rosh yeshiva* (head of the yeshiva) and as dean of OTS and taught both Americans and Israelis for another two decades. In 2007 he departed and concentrated on two other initiatives, ATID (Academy for Torah Initiatives and Directions; the Hebrew word *atid* literally means "future") (founded in 1999), which focuses on cultivating educational leadership, and the WebYeshiva.org (founded in 2007), which tenders a variety of Torah classes to its participants—primarily in English but in other languages as well—via livestream or recorded videos.[63]

Today Midreshet Lindenbaum is a major center for women's Torah learning, with multiple courses of study that service hundreds of women from Israel and around the world on a yearly basis. Many of the programs were begun by Riskin and the professionals that he recruited, but Brovender created the institution and orchestrated its initial gestation. Its base in the Arnona/Talpiyot section of Jerusalem has a dormitory and cafeteria and multiple classrooms and meeting spaces, crowned by a large beit midrash that is comparable in size and function to what can be found in well-established men's yeshivot. The foreign students' division includes gap year studies for both English and Spanish speakers, and for cognitively challenged young women, as well as the International Halakhah Scholars, an advanced framework for a select group of female educators and religious leaders throughout the globe to study the materials required for rabbinical ordination that is conducted via livestream technology. The Israeli division comprises a program for women modeled after the men's Hesder yeshiva in which Torah study periods and army service are integrated over multiple years (there is also subdivision for army volunteers who come from abroad); one-year and three-month post–high school programs for women prior to their army or national service that has three sites, each with distinct characters (Jerusalem, Lod, and Carmiel); post–army/national service study that includes one- and two-year options; a postcollegiate track; and a full-time Institute of Halakhic Leadership that trains highly qualified candidates in Talmud and Jewish law, with a focus on the subjects required for rabbinic ordination, as well as pastoral training, and provides fellowships for its participants throughout their period of study. The graduates of the five-year course are "certified as spiritual leaders and *Morot Hora'ah* authorized to provide direction in matters of *halakha* [Jewish law]" and there is a "director of career development and placement, to strengthen the practical impact . . . by opening doors and making connections so that graduates can acclimate into leadership positions within the religious public realm."[64] In 2014, a volume of Hebrew responsa authored by graduates of the track was published by Midreshet Lindenbaum.[65]

The Institute of Halakhic Leadership (and to a certain degree the International Halakhah Scholars) differs from the rest of the lineup in that it is geared to cultivating women capable of ruling on Jewish legal matters and serving in "rabbinical-like" capacities. Although there is certainly a strong connection, this legal authority direction diverges from the more "conceptual" realm of high-level Torah study that characterized the original Bruria setting as well as most of the courses until this day. Indeed, the launch of multiple institutions for training Orthodox women as religious authorities, both in Israel and the United States, has propelled this issue to center stage due to conflicts over Orthodoxy and feminism in the twenty-first century.[66] Here it should be noted that a crucial step in advancing this adjudicational route took place in Midreshet Lindenbaum during the second decade after its founding.

One of the key instructors and then head of the Israeli program at its early stages was Nurit Fried, a well-regarded veteran Torah studies educator. In 1988 she began a process that led to the establishment in 1991 of the Training Institute for Religious Court Advocates, under the auspices of Midreshet Lindenbaum.[67] The advocate role is similar to that of a

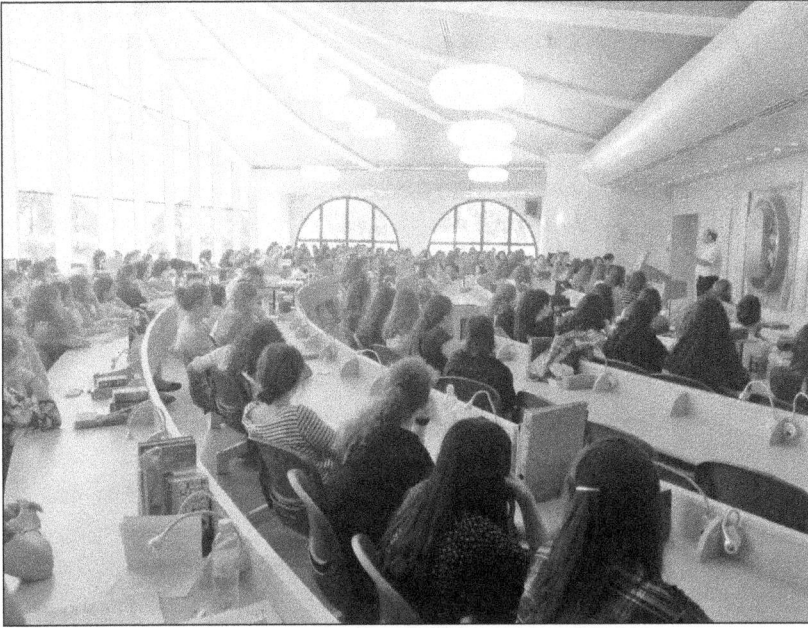

Figure 2.7. The Midreshet Lindenbaum Study Hall. Courtesy of OTS.

lawyer but demands mastery of Jewish divorce and personal status law. Until then only men had served in this capacity. As all divorces of Jewish couples in Israel must proceed through the rabbinical court system, the rising level of women's competency in Jewish law could theoretically enable them to provide those going through this procedure with female professional representation. All the same, the initial graduates were met with considerable opposition from the religious establishment, and full accreditation did not take place until an Israel Supreme Court decision was handed down in 1994. Within the context of the IsMO pioneers, the advent of Brovender's Midreshet Lindenbaum was foundational in the transition from advanced Torah study for women to cultivation of female religious authorities, along with fostering the shifting unique Israeli circumstances that precipitated this evolution.[68]

While Brovender did not initiate all of Midreshet Lindenbaum's programs, they are nonetheless outgrowths of the institution that he originated and shepherded for thirty years. The transnational quality of his contribution, and similarly those of MaTaN and Nishmat, two other educational institutions for women discussed below, differs from those of Lichtenstein, Rabinovitch, and Tropper, and is worthy of particular attention. Lichtenstein, Rabinovitch, and Tropper led frameworks that were established for the local Israeli population, even if some of them developed rich offerings for foreign students as well. In the case of Brovender's institutions, not only did his efforts reflect his American background, but the process by which his innovative approach to advanced women's Torah education entered the Israeli orbit was actually via an English-speaking constituency. By creating a setting for women who had come to Israel and had an interest in high-level study, he set the stage for extending this plane of study to the local Hebrew-speaking population as well. Once adopted by the Israelis, however, the core concept of women studying Talmud morphed into multiple directions,[69] including the connection with army service and the religious court advocates, both of which reflect the unique circumstances of Israeli society.

Brovender's establishment of Michlelet Bruria in 1976 heralded the subsequent emergence of Israel-based Torah institutions for women that placed Talmud and Jewish law at the center of their curriculums.[70] As far as the foreign students were concerned, upon return to their places of origin the experiences of their intellectual and spiritual immersion impacted their surroundings. Some chose to continue to nurture their Torah learning skills and were among the first generation of female Talmud teachers in American Orthodox high schools and communities. Others made their way back to Israel and integrated into the growing mass of female religious leaders and Torah scholars in Israel. Regarding Israelis in particular, Michlelet Bruria/Midreshet Lindenbaum foreshadowed the explosion of a wide variety of post–high school midrashot, some that built on its precedent and others that developed alternative and even defiantly different approaches.[71] Moreover, numerous alumni who spent critical time in its study hall, as well as faculty who began there, went on to dynamic careers as scholars, educators, and leaders.

Gen Women's Learning: Rabbanit Malka Bina, MA (b. 1950)

Rabbanit Malka Bina's initial foray into advanced Torah education was, as noted above, directed toward Jerusalem-based "Anglo" immigrant women. In time, she constructed one of the richest and most widespread

Israeli frameworks for educating woman Torah scholars—both Hebrew and English speakers—with branches throughout the country and programs that have been adopted by American Jewish communities as well.

Bina grew up in the Yiddish-speaking Baltimore home of Rabbi Boruch and Leah Milikowsky and her sole surviving grandparent, her grandmother, all refugees from the Holocaust.[72] Her father, an alumnus of renowned Eastern European yeshivot, was an acclaimed religious high school educator for over four decades at the Talmudical Academy of Baltimore (TA). Notably, while her mother stemmed from a Galician Hasidic family and her father was grounded in his Lithuanian Orthodox roots, a book of memoirs collected from students indicates his openness to women's Torah study, Zionism, academic perspectives, and Jewish enlightenment literature.[73] Their daughter attended the Haredi-oriented Bais Ya'akov school but was also active in the RZ Bnei Akiva youth movement. The careers of two of her siblings also offer evidence for a certain Orthodox eclecticism in their home; one brother is a prominent Israel-based academic Talmudic scholar,[74] while another is an innovative figure within the American Haredi outreach movement to weakly affiliated Jews.[75]

After high school, Malka, the only daughter in the family, studied at Michlalah College for Women in Jerusalem. Her arrival coincided with the triumphant aftermath of the 1967 "Six-Day War." She chose to stay in Israel and complete her bachelor's degree in Jewish studies and education. Soon she met her husband, Aharon—himself the son of a legendary Jerusalem yeshiva high school educator, Rabbi Aryeh Bina.[76] The couple later lived for a brief time in New York, where Malka completed a master's degree in Bible and history at YU's Bernard Revel Graduate School while Aryeh studied with Soloveitchik. Upon their return to Jerusalem, she began her career as a school educator and soon focused on advanced Jewish learning for adult women.

Bina worked with Brovender at Darchei Noam–Shappel's, the outreach-oriented institute affiliated with the Itri yeshiva, and started to teach Talmud to a small group of female students there who expressed interest. She then served as Brovender's deputy at Michlelet Bruria and was instrumental in cultivating a cadre of Jerusalem-based English-speaking women who were eager to participate in concentrated Talmud study, before breaking off and creating her own framework in 1988.[77]

Unlike Bruria/Lindenbaum, which eventually focused almost exclusively on post–high school and university-age students, Bina's original Jerusalem group evolved into the foundation for MaTaN—Midrashah Toranit le-Nashim/Women's Institute for Torah Studies—whose constituency ranges from twelve-year-old bat mitzvah girls to senior citizens, with a strong core of women in their twenties and thirties who have already achieved proficiency in Talmud learning.

The first small beit midrash in the Katamonim section of Jerusalem was later replaced by a multistory dedicated building that houses an array of learning spaces and programs. The offerings at the Jerusalem center comprise full-time and part-time options with concentrations in either Talmud and Jewish law, or Bible, Jewish thought, and Hasidism; specific tracks and fellowships for cultivating female Torah educators; advanced Jewish law cohorts, some with stipends, including a highly selective five-year path equivalent to rabbinical studies whose graduates receive the title *meshivat halakhah*—respondents to religio-legal queries (the MaTaN website includes an interactive link in which its graduates provide answers to practical questions directed to them); and a generous fellowship "created . . . to promote the publication of high-level Torah scholarship by women."[78] In some cases, there are options to earn an MA in conjunction with one of Israel's major universities.

MaTaN has nine affiliated branches throughout Israel. The majority focus on adult education in Hebrew and English, and bat mitzvah preparation classes. The most prolific one is the Sharon center located in Ra'anana, whose founding head, Rabbanit Oshra Koren, is the Israeli-born child of American immigrants and an early alumnus of MaTaN Jerusalem. In addition to orchestrating a rich curriculum of weekly classes in Hebrew and English, a summer session for women from abroad, and a variety of cultural initiatives and events, Koren developed the "Mother-Daughter Bat Mitzvah Program" into a modular course that currently operates in eighty locations in Israel and throughout the world. The Sharon branch also sponsors two-year Jewish law tracks for advanced candidates who are trained to answer queries and offer guidance on practical religio-legal matters.[79] Upon her first exposure in 1993 to a Torah presentation by Koren, Blu Greenberg—a founding figure in Orthodox feminism—shared that "[f]or a brief instant, I find myself thinking Oshra would make a splendid rabbi. And then I think: well,

Figure 2.8. Rabbanit Malka Bina in 2008. Courtesy of MaTaN.

that's exactly what she is. . . . And then: I wonder if Oshra ever thinks of herself that way."[80] Koren is a fruitful example of an early Israeli disciple who further developed a core idea in novel ways that addressed multiple local and worldwide audiences.

Many of the original teachers at MaTaN were male faculty or alumni of YHE and other men's institutions.[81] In fact, Bina asserted that Soloveitchik's and Lichtenstein's unequivocal support for advanced women's learning was critical to her decision to set out on the endeavor and to its widespread acceptance.[82] Today, however, a large proportion of the instructors and program heads are alumni of MaTaN or other institutions that focus on advanced Torah studies for women.[83] Some of these figures also staff the "Shayla Team," which provides practical Jewish law guidance to questioners who can access them through the institution's website.

In the summer of 2021, at the age of seventy-one, Bina announced that she would be stepping away from full-time leadership and taking on the role of president. She appointed Dr. Yael Ziegler, a well-regarded Bible scholar and lecturer who came to Israel as a young adult, as educational director and the founder's daughter Chaya Bina-Katz (a lawyer by professional training) as CEO to jointly head the institution—both are MaTaN veterans. This changing of the guard represented both continuity as well as a new stage in MaTaN's growth and illustrates further the overall theme that is at the center of this book. The official move to a second generation reflects the degree to which MaTaN transformed over the past three decades from a close-knit group of like-minded English-speaking immigrants piloted by a product of American Orthodoxy to an established presence within contemporary Israeli Judaism that has spawned "locally grown" leadership. While the two individuals chosen to move MaTaN forward both also have strong connections to American Jewry, which is critical to ongoing fundraising and promoting international activities, many of the scores of alumni and faculty—especially those who have gained expertise in Talmud and Jewish law—are Israeli born and bred and will continue to digest and recapitulate the outlooks that were foundational to Bina's vision through their local lenses and sensitivities.

MaTaN built on the original steps taken by Brovender in coordination with Bina. It also eventually created more official "rabbinic-like" titles for its graduates along the lines first initiated through the rabbinic court advocates program at Bruria/Lindenbaum, although this was apparently not Bina's original vision.[84] Most profoundly, under Bina's stewardship MaTaN straddled the lines between nurturing elite women Torah scholars capable of functioning as high-level teachers and religious authorities, and expanding rigorous engagement with Torah study toward its becoming a norm for contemporary Jewish women. Not just those with professional or scholarly aspirations, but those of all ages, both adjacent to MaTaN's Jerusalem base and in communities throughout Israel and beyond, are encompassed in this vision. This last geographic step is especially notable, since it testifies to the process by which IsMO has gained traction in communities located outside the Jerusalem corridor.

Spawning a New Form of Authority: Rabbanit Chana Henkin, MA (b. 1946)

In 1990 Rabbanit Chana Henkin and her husband, Rabbi Yehuda Herzl Henkin, founded Nishmat, a manifold "center for advanced Torah study for women" in Jerusalem. From the outset, it provided a beit midrash-style environment and high-level instruction for collegiate-age women to study canonical Jewish sources, including Talmud. Like Bruria and MaTaN, the first cohorts were "Anglo" women. Starting in the mid-1990s, however, a range of Hebrew programs geared to local female populations, such as pre- and post-national service (or army) and a dedicated track for Ethiopian students, were introduced.[85] Through its multiple study tracks and their many alumni, Nishmat has played a substantial role in the evolution of contemporary Jewish women's religious experiences both in Israel and North America. Undoubtedly, its most profound impact has been in the cultivation of a sui generis religious authority figure, the *yoetzet halakhah* (female expert in Jewish family purity law; plural, *yoatzot halakhah*).[86]

A brief look at Henkin's early development provides salient points that came to fruition within her quintessential contribution. Born to an observant family in New York, she was graduated from YU's Central High School and Stern College for Women. At Stern, she recalls being one of the two students out of ninety from her class to register for a course offered in Talmud, which soon became her main intellectual passion. She went on to receive an MA in Talmud from YU's Bernard Revel Graduate School.[87] Throughout her youth, she was active in the Noar Mizrachi RZ movement (which eventually merged with Bnei Akiva), where she met her husband—a young rabbinic scholar and graduate student in sociology of religion at Columbia—who served as secretary-general of the organization. Yehuda was the grandson and close student of Rabbi Yosef Eliyahu Henkin—the renowned New York-based authority of Jewish law famous for his independent rulings, from whom the grandson gained rabbinic ordination.[88]

After brief careers as religious educators in America, in 1972 Chana and Yehuda Henkin immigrated to Israel. They settled in Beit Shean, a northern development town situated close to many veteran secular kibbutzim, whose population was predominantly families of Jews who came from North Africa after 1948. Yehuda was initially a high school teacher and later gained appointment as a regional rabbi under the auspices of the state chief rabbinate. Chana describes dedicating herself to educating the women of the area in the procedures and import of Jewish family purity, and the consequential steep rise in the numbers of those who observed the guidelines.[89] The Henkins lived in Beit Shean for over fifteen years before they moved to Jerusalem and soon thereafter established Nishmat.

The yoatzot program, today known as Keren Ariel, was inaugurated in 1997. The objective is to train women to master the intricate laws of *niddah* that revolve around the female body and reproductive system, including the requirements for ritual purification that are a precondition for marital physical intimacy. With this expertise, they can then serve as resources for those who observe the regulations and seek guidance when facing the myriad issues that arise. The viability of this project is predicated on the emergence of a growing population of Orthodox women with advanced Torah learning skills. Of the eight women in the inaugural class, "[t]he average academic level . . . was midway between M.A. and Ph.D. One woman was a young pediatrician who had taught a *Daf Yomi* (daily Talmud folio) class as a medical student. . . . Another woman taught in the Talmud department at BIU."[90] The "fellows" commit to twenty hours per week of intensive study (two full days of text learning, additional evenings, and special programs) for two years. During this period, they also receive extensive schooling in related topics of physical and mental health, such as fertility, birth control, sexual function, and postpartum challenges. There are regular written tests as well as an all-encompassing final exam before a panel of established authorities. During the outbreak of COVID in 2020, online study was initiated, and it continues. Once the "academic" requirements are fulfilled, the candidates must complete a multimonth internship under the supervision of veteran practitioners before being certified with the title of yoetzet halakhah.[91]

To date, over 160 women have graduated the rigorous training curriculum, including a group that studied in the United States with oversight by the Nishmat Israeli staff.[92] English-speaking alumni have been hired by individual synagogues or consortiums of congregations in various regions of North America. In Israel there are fewer communities that support a dedicated yoetzet position. Rather, some figures integrate this role into broader educational and pastoral ones, while numerous alumni have been hired by Nishmat itself to provide guidance to those women who turn directly to the institution.[93]

Henkin realized from the outset that setting upon a path that generated a cadre of women with extraordinary proficiency in practical Jewish law, previously the exclusive domain of rabbis, would be deemed

Figure 2.9. Nishmat yoatzot halakhah graduation: Rabbanit Chana Henkin is sitting in the middle (with glasses) to the left of her husband, Rabbi Yehudah Henkin.

controversial in the eyes of many Orthodox Jews—even among some who celebrated advanced women's learning. As far back as 1999, she clarified the impetus for her decision to do so nonetheless:

> What prompted me to take this action? Years of work in taharat hamish-pachah (Jewish family purity) and communal leadership made me aware that many observant women will simply not consult a rabbi with an intimate question. . . . All too many women decide the issues for themselves—some stringently, others leniently. Needless to say, unnecessary stringency at the expense of marital harmony, or unwarranted leniency not in accordance with halachah, are both terribly wrong. What happens to a woman trying to conceive who is told by her gynecologist that her conception date falls before her tevillah [immersion] date? What happens to a woman in her 40s who stains repeatedly in mid-cycle and is too self-conscious to consult a rabbi? What happens when a woman wants to know whether her problem is typical and what others do about it? Until now, the answer for most women has been, bite your lip and suffer, or be lax about the halachah.[94]

At the same time, she contended that "women halachic consultants are an evolution, not a revolution."[95] In fact, the program was guided and supervised from the outset by Rabbi Yaakov Warhaftig—a well-respected RZ halakhist—and Rabbi Henkin until his passing in 2020.[96] The granting of the title "yoetzet" (i.e., consultant) further solidifies the impression that the institution is maintaining the traditional formal male/female hierarchy and distinguishes Nishmat from other centers that grant rabbinic-like titles to their woman graduates.[97] Similarly, the explanatory literature asserts that the yoatzot "do not preclude, override or replace the psak (ruling) of any rabbinical authority."[98]

This new female religious leadership role has drawn the attention of academic scholars. They have explored, among other effects, the degree to which the advent of yoatzot expands traditional gender boundaries, or alternatively, ultimately sustains their foundational patriarchy.[99] Other insightful discussions focus on a key element that was introduced soon after the original cohort completed their training—the central role of the internet.[100] Nishmat's multiple websites run in four languages— Hebrew, English, French, and Spanish—and function both as accessible resources (including "TED-like" videos) on Jewish law and women's health, as well as interactive spaces for individuals who seek practical direction on the gamut of *niddah* issues, such as a specialized fertility counseling component.[101] One of the directors of this framework is Dr. Deena Zimmerman, a veteran American immigrant and a pediatrician and public health expert who was graduated from the first cohort and has since authored a comprehensive work on Jewish family law and women's health.[102]

The most ambitious and groundbreaking digital-linked element is the associated "hotline" that was established soon after the first graduating cohort and is today staffed six evenings a week by experienced yoatzot who are available to answer questions by telephone or in writing.[103] These often relate to immediate issues connected to the purification process that will determine whether a couple can resume intimacy after the minimum twelve-day abstinence required by Jewish law. They may also be asked whether there are unusual circumstances, when a leniency can be applied that would shorten the usual standard. It is in this capacity that the yoatzot's activities most directly replace or challenge the classical platform of the male rabbi/halakhic authority.

According to Nishmat's official statistics from 2023, there have been 1,650,000 page views of the website and 400,000 questions have been answered.[104] In a conversation that I had with a yoetzet soon after October 7, 2023, she described a marked rise in the volume of questions, with the majority coming from women soldiers or those whose husbands were on reserve duty.

Supporters celebrate this innovation for enabling women to navigate these complex and personal matters in a sensitive manner that empowers them as bona fide stakeholders in the area of Jewish law most directly connected to them and their bodies. Detractors raise concerns that women are usurping the authority of rabbis and undermining the delicate balance of traditional Jewish communal life that has been sustained through the ages.[105] All the same, a bold example that demonstrates the degree to which yoatzot have been gaining a foothold within MO and are viewed as distinct from other "ordination-like" programs for women arose from a rabbinic decision rendered in 2017 under the auspices of the Orthodox Union (OU), the largest organization of Orthodox synagogues in North America. The main thrust of the ruling was to prohibit women from serving as clergy in member congregations. The eight rabbis who signed the document—seven affiliated with YU—did not include the yoetzet halakhah in the forbidden category, at least tacitly legitimizing it as a women's leadership role that did not compromise core values in their eyes.[106] In fact, in 2022, Nishmat produced an English volume with seventy-seven responsa authored by its graduates that was copublished by the OU Press itself.[107]

Among the growing legion of learned Israeli women, the yoetzet "degree" is not only proof of proficiency in a particular area of practical Jewish law, but for many it has become a type of formal ordination that sanctions them as master teachers and authorities. This comes across in the biographies of numerous lecturers at the various advanced institutions for women's Torah learning, as well as among the membership of organizations such as Beit Hillel for religious leadership that include both rabbis and female figures.[108] Within Nishmat itself, the majority of the main Israeli female educators are graduates of Keren Ariel, including Rabbanit Racheli Sprecher Frankel, a senior lecturer, and Rabbanit Noa Lau, who serves as director of the Keren Ariel program for training yoatzot halakhah.

Whether it is an "evolution" or a "revolution," the Israel-based institution led by American immigrant Chana Henkin since 1990 is responsible for a novel form of women's religious authority. While she remains deeply involved, her heirs are Israel-based alumni who will continue to develop the innovative model in conversation with local realities, others who are Israeli residents but provide guidance for Jews throughout the world who access the website and hotline, and numerous products of Nishmat training who are based in North American communities. Recalling our earlier discussion of transnationalism and Americanization, Nishmat's yoatzot halakhah innovation, which draws from Henkin's American upbringing and sensitivities, illustrates Van Elteren's assertion that the process of transnational reworking of culture is not one-directional. Once an idea or symbol has been digested and reformed in a new environment, globalized conditions facilitate portals for their reentry into their original local contexts. At this point, the reformulated conceptualizations become agents for cultural change that impact the frameworks of their initial emergence.[109]

The Pluralist: Rabbi Professor David Hartman (1931–2013)

All eight North American–born IsMO pioneers discussed in this book have gone against the grain of the Israeli religious establishment in various ways, but Rabbi Professor David Hartman was the figure who most clearly challenged RZ/Orthodox norms. While his Orthodox critics often highlight his deviations, and even those closest to him acknowledge his inconsistencies,[110] through his protégés and the multidimensional Shalom Hartman Institute (named after his father, henceforth SHI), his legacy continues to impact multiple sectors of religious life in Israel as well as North America. Moreover, along with his expansive influence, his Israeli activities remain closely tied to the broader RZ community.

Hartman's early upbringing actually brought him into close contact with the rebuilding postwar "Haredi" world, before he situated himself more formally within North American Modern Orthodoxy. He was born and raised in the Brownsville section of Brooklyn by immigrant parents from British Mandate Palestine whose means were limited; his father would support the family in part by leading High Holiday services with his sons as the accompanying choir. "Duvvy," as he was known,

attended a local Lubavitcher Hasidic–oriented school and the Chaim
Berlin Yeshiva high school headed by Rabbi Isaac Hutner (Lichtenstein
studied there too), where he starred on its basketball team. His reputation as a talented player whose skills were honed on the tough courts
of Brownsville and in the Catskill Mountains summer league led him
to YU in the fall of 1949, where he featured on the YU Maccabees team
along with some of its most legendary hoopsters.[111] Yet after one year, he
abandoned his athletic career and dedicated himself to Talmudic study
at Beth Medrash Govoha in Lakewood, New Jersey.[112]

This yeshiva was founded in 1942 and developed under the leadership
of the Lithuanian refugee Rabbi Aharon Kotler (1892–1962) and later
his son and grandsons into the banner Torah institution of American
Haredi Orthodoxy.[113] Yet in its early years, it included a more eclectic group of students. Among them was the young Shlomo Carlebach,
who eventually left, becoming one of the groundbreaking emissaries of
Lubavitch-Chabad before setting out on an independent path as a rabbi-
songwriter-performer who integrated the folk rock and spirit of the
sixties with Hasidic ideals.[114] According to Hartman, Carlebach's musi-
cal/spiritual talents were even then apparent during late-night piano sessions in Lakewood that visibly moved none other than Kotler himself.[115]

Hartman returned to YU the following year (where he dedicated
himself in the same study hall as Lichtenstein) and soon focused on
the teachings of Soloveitchik.[116] The latter had a seminal influence on
him, at first as an intellectual mentor and role model, and throughout
his life as a point of departure and foil for his increasingly divergent but
never static religious worldview.[117] Professor Lawrence Kaplan, a noted
authority on Soloveitchik,[118] communicated to me a experience that he
has shared publicly before that testifies to the ongoing personal connection between the two, and in which the latter offered a concise appraisal
of his intractable former student:

> In the summer of 1981, I met with the Rav Soloveitchik several times to
> review my draft translation of his book, *Halakhic Man*.[119] One time, as
> I came into the Twersky [his daughter's] home where the "Rav" resided,
> Hartman was just leaving. After he left, the Rav asked me, "Do you know
> him?" "Of course I know him," I replied. "So what do you think of him?"
> the Rav continued . . . I gave an evasive answer, something to the effect of

"he's a great, very dynamic speaker, very controversial." I then fell silent and saw the Rav thinking for a while. Upon reflecting he said [I am citing verbatim]: "He's a searcher. Could use more discipline. I like him."[120]

After ordination in 1954, Hartman accepted a rabbinical pulpit position in the Bronx and enrolled in graduate studies in philosophy at the Jesuit-led Fordham University, while continuing to attend Soloveitchik's Talmud lectures and teaching YU undergraduate Jewish studies courses.[121] From 1960 until his immigration to Israel in 1971 he served as a congregational rabbi in Montreal and earned a PhD in philosophy at McGill University. His reach went beyond his Orthodox synagogue members to college-age Jewish students from the area who flocked to his classes. By that point, he had gained a reputation as an unyielding seeker and religious gadfly who challenged accepted halakhic practices and theological notions. This was punctuated by the colloquium he organized for Jewish theologians that included representatives from all the denominations.[122] Nonetheless, he remained a popular if contentious guest at Orthodox frameworks such as the Yavne student organization, where he was a board member and where Greenberg, Rabbi Dr. Norman Lamm (the future YU president), and then Lichtenstein served consecutively as presidents.[123] He also helped establish a full-time Jewish day school and focused on drawing Jews closer to religious observance.[124]

Arriving in Israel at the age of forty, he taught Jewish philosophy in the Hebrew University in Jerusalem, where he stood out for both his adroitness and passion,[125] as well as at the nondenominational Pardes Institute that opened in 1973 and targeted English-speaking men and women.[126] Gradually, he voiced theological positions that profoundly challenged the boundaries of all versions of contemporary Orthodoxy.[127] In parallel, Hartman began to attract a strong following of native-Hebrew-speaking young people to informal gatherings and classes. The original core group were religiously committed and included some of YHE's most gifted students, who felt frustrated by the theological limitations and dominant ideological trends within the RZ yeshiva world.[128] Over time, he cultivated this collective into a religious avant-garde that counted among its members original thinkers, scholars, and educators. Many remain at the intellectual core of the institution that he founded,

Figure 2.10. Rabbi Dr. David Hartman. Picture by David Rubinger, courtesy of SHI.

which has sprouted multiple schools and programs, and where his son Rabbi Dr. Donniel Hartman is president.

Throughout his over four-decade Israeli career, Hartman navigated between teaching, scholarly and theological writing, and institution building, but there was considerable correlation between them. Describing Hartman's 1978 work, *Joy and Responsibility: Israel, Modernity and the Renewal of Judaism*, the former Stanford professor of modern Jewish thought and later chancellor of the Jewish Theological Seminary, Arnold

Eisen, noted, "Every single article in that collection both teaches and preaches. The learning is marshaled to the cause of moving the reader to accept the challenge of making Judaism come alive in a sovereign State of Israel and a Diaspora where almost every door is opened before Jews. He envisioned halakhah not as a set of dos and don'ts, but as the 'ground for creating a shared spiritual language.'"[129] While on a personal level Hartman remained committed to religious observance, in his last decades his pluralism and alienation from formal Orthodoxy became especially pronounced, as reflected in the titles of his books *A Heart of Many Rooms: Celebrating the Many Voices within Judaism* and *The God Who Hates Lies: Confronting and Rethinking Jewish Tradition*.[130] In time, he also became a favorite commentator on Israeli life for major international media.[131]

From the outset in the 1970s, the SHI stood out among Israel-based frameworks dedicated to rigorous Jewish learning, be they yeshivot or universities, in multiple ways: Like a yeshiva, the main endeavor was "hevrutah"-style, Talmud study between two partners (rather than formal lectures) in a beit midrash setting, but traditional methods and academic tools and resources were integrated together; questions were not deemed too theologically provocative or not sufficiently scientific to be examined; the student body was diverse in their religious backgrounds and lifestyles, although many came from observant homes; women were full participants; in order to neutralize implicit religious hierarchies among the learners, regular prayer services were not held in the main study hall; owing to his knowledge, charisma, and critical role in enabling the "fellows" to dedicate their time, Hartman was certainly the dominant figure, but he did not behave like an authoritative *rosh yeshiva* or a professor who bestows their original interpretations. Rather, his main direct engagements were as a participant in the weekly, often heated group discussions that followed presentations by one of the other figures in the institute.[132]

Key elements that originated at or were employed early on by the SHI have since gained currency within contemporary Israeli religious life. There are multiple study halls that incorporate traditional and academic approaches to Talmud, Bible, and other canonic texts, including Hesder and full-time yeshivot for men,[133] and pluralistic *hevrutah*-style programs established on university campuses.[134] The latter are also

Figure 2.11. The SHI campus in Jerusalem. Picture by Amit Geron, courtesy of SHI.

part of a range of beit midrash frameworks that have sprouted especially since the 1990s throughout the country that are aimed at opening up the "traditional Jewish bookshelf" to all women and men who are interested, without regard to their personal observance.[135] To be sure, as emphasized above, women's study has transformed the landscape of advanced Torah learning on multiple levels, and prominent alumni of the SHI were among the founders of various initiatives to create a more gender-inclusive halakhah-based synagogue, such as Shira Hadasha in Jerusalem, where women lead some of the prayers and chant the weekly Torah portion.[136] Notably, SHI began to operate formally in 1976, the same year Bruria was established by Brovender.[137]

Soon after SHI got off the ground, Hartman also began to organize frameworks for rabbis and lay people from abroad. Today, SHI's multiple-building Jerusalem campus contains within it an array of divisions and schools and runs a range of courses and seminars throughout the country in Hebrew, as well as various offerings for long- and short-term guests. The SHI of North America is headquartered in New York and has expanded dramatically from 2010, with programming hubs in the San Francisco Bay Area, Boston, Chicago, Detroit, Los Angeles,

Washington, DC, Montreal, and Toronto. In addition to core-affiliated advanced fellows who commit to study, perform research, and publish and teach at SHI, there are Israel-based cohorts for training teachers of Jewish content for secular schools and for preparing curricula for studying Israel from abroad, and centers and fellowships focused on gender issues, interfaith relations, Muslim leadership, Judaism and state policy, and journalism. There are also affiliated non-coed high schools geared toward observant young men and women, a mixed-gender gap year program that combines high school graduates from Israel (pre-army) and abroad (pre-collegiate), and a variety of summer institutes for visiting scholars and communal leaders.[138]

One of SHI's most significant projects aimed at impacting Israeli religious life is Rabbanut Yisraelit (Israeli rabbinate), a training body for local religious leaders. It brings together Orthodox, traditional, Conservative, Reform, and secular men and women candidates who already play roles as religious, spiritual, and educational activists. Some possess formal rabbinical ordination from a yeshiva or seminary, and others prior relevant degrees or schooling. It is run in conjunction with Midreshet Oranim, a secular-oriented organization situated south of Haifa, whose motto is "Working to make Judaism accessible, meaningful and relevant for all Jewish Israelis."[139] The two-year curriculum includes study of canonic and modern Jewish texts, pedagogy, communal building and ritual orchestration, counseling, and societal leadership.[140] Those who fulfill the requirements receive ordination.

The heads of the program all grew up in Israel and reflect the pluralistic framing of the endeavor. One is Orthodox rabbi Danny Segel, an alumnus of YHE who previously served the mixed secular-religious settlement of Alon. Another is Rabbi Shai Zarchi, a well-known educator recognized for performing secular weddings that are not under the auspices of the state rabbinate, in which he introduces considerable traditional content. The founder and a central driving force is Rabbi Tamar Elad-Applebaum, who was raised in an RZ home, received ordination from the *Masorti* (Conservative) movement's Schechter Institute, served in Conservative synagogues in America and Israel, and today leads the nondenominational "Land of Israel"–oriented, egalitarian Kehillat Zion in Jerusalem, which portrays its services as[141] an embroidered community of grandparents and children, young and old, diverse families and individuals, Jews and Israelis from all streams and backgrounds, who gather in one prayer of partnership and connections . . . the ingathering of the exiles is not only a physical act of gathering from all corners of the world, but also meant to be an act of gathering the spirit, when all the treasures of the people are gathered together to one prayer woven from endless traditions.[142]

In January 2024, Rabbi Aaron Leibowitz was appointed director of Rabbanut Yisraelit. Born in the United States, Leibowitz immigrated to Israel with his family after high school and was ordained by Riskin and Brovender. Along with leading a Jerusalem congregation, he has gained renown as a religious and local political activist, leading a series of initiatives aimed at reforming kosher food supervision and rabbinical marriage performance in Israel.[143]

As of 2023, Rabbanut Yisraelit had produced three cohorts of fifteen to twenty graduates, and two more were at various stages in the process. To be clear, this is not a typical rabbinical seminary, and the academic and time demands are far less rigorous than those of most ordination tracks of all religious streams. Much of the in-person learning is dedicated to professional development and collective experiences. Yet the long-term potency of the venture is in the Reshet ha-Rabbanut ha-Yisraelit, the growing alumni network that sponsors public events, lectures, and courses yearlong throughout Israel that incorporate the leaders cultivated within the SHI program. The consortium stands out in its combination of religious diversity with a common commitment to working together toward fostering an "Israeli Judaism" with multiple portals that can attract a broad range of local Jews.[144]

As with his fellow IsMO pioneers, Hartman's local heirs have internalized key elements of his worldview that arose within American MO and refined it in multiple directions that address their contexts. Notwithstanding, in June 2023 the SHI announced that Dr. Yehudah Kurtzer, the president of SHI of North America and himself a YHE alumnus, would become co-president with Donniel Hartman of the entire world organization.[145] No doubt the decision was based on Kurtzer's exceptional success as an educator, expanding the SHI brand within North

America, and likely his critical skill set as a fundraiser as well. Yet this turn to an American leader might appear contrary to SHI's Israel-based orientation. At the same time, this move can be perceived as a reflection of the transnational religious process that is producing an alternative to the political realm manifested by the "We Stand Divided" understanding of relations between Israeli and North American Jewries. By connecting both bases, Kurtzer's appointment symbolizes the scenario in which ideas first advanced in North America have evolved through their Israeli encounter, and at this juncture not only return to impact American Jewish life, but actually serve as a critical vehicle for strengthening connections and partnerships between the two centers.

Moderate Incorporated: Rabbi Dr. Shlomo (Steven) Riskin (b. 1940)

Of the eight IsMO pioneers, Rabbi Dr. Shlomo (Steven) Riskin is an exception to the other figures we have discussed in that he did not grow up in a Sabbath observant home, although he was exposed from childhood to his grandmother's deep religious roots. He also attended Orthodox institutions, including YU's BTA high school, which was near his Brooklyn home.[146] At Yeshiva College (YU) he dedicated himself to Talmud and humanities, while simultaneously taking an active role in campus life and leadership. His stretch there overlapped with Brovender and Tropper, who were fellow students, as well as Lichtenstein and Hartman, who were young instructors. Like all of them, he studied with Soloveitchik and sees himself as a lifetime disciple. He attributes considerable influence as well to Rabbi Moshe Besdin, his pedagogical mentor during the time after rabbinical ordination when he began teaching in YU's JSS program for students with minimal Jewish learning backgrounds,[147] along with the preeminent American authority of Jewish law Rabbi Moshe Feinstein, and Rabbi Menachem Mendel Schneerson, the seventh Lubavitcher rebbe and leader of the Chabad movement.[148]

Riskin is also the pioneer figure whose early American-based career has drawn the widest attention, both in scholarly and popular writing. By the time he arrived in Israel in 1983, he had gained a reputation as the religious trailblazer who in his early twenties transformed a small Sabbath prayer gathering with mixed-gender seating on Manhattan's Upper

West Side that self-defined as Conservative. Within a short time after he was brought in as rabbi, it emerged as the prototype urban Orthodox synagogue-center specializing in outreach to nonobservant Jews and creative adult education.[149] Simultaneously, he was a leader in the Soviet Jewry movement, active in the civil rights movement,[150] a popular YU lecturer, and founded boys' and girls' religious high schools that attracted Modern Orthodox families from across North America.[151]

By this time, he stood out among Orthodox rabbis for acknowledging the positive roles that Reform and Conservative religious streams played in strengthening Jewish connections, as well as for his articulation of leniencies on halakhic issues, especially for the sake of defending the rights of women and increasing their roles in religious life. In fact, just before his immigration he earned a PhD from New York University for a dissertation on Jewish divorce law that was later published as a monograph.[152] All the same, unlike Hartman, he was not a pluralist and, despite his relative openness, he was criticized by non-Orthodox figures for staking out clear denominational boundaries.[153] Among the Modern Orthodox, however, his "rock star" status reverberated in his popular nickname, "Stevie Wonder," after the talented soul musician.[154] This stature and its ensuant personal connections, in concert with his visionary qualities and fundraising skills that he fashioned during this period, were critical to his success at creating and sustaining the OTS educational network during the over four decades after he and his family left New York and settled in Israel.

As to Riskin's connection to Israel prior to immigration, recall that he was the editor/writer at *The Commentator*, the YU student newspaper, who lauded Ben-Gurion's YU appearance in front of the packed auditorium of male and female students. Indeed, after serving a few months later as valedictorian at the 1960 undergraduate commencement, Riskin dedicated the following year to study in Israel. Consistent with the YU parochial and academic integration model, he divided his time between Talmudic learning with stints in the prominent Ponovezh (Haredi) yeshiva in Bnei Brak and in the nascent Kerem B'Yavne, which became the first Hesder yeshiva, along with academic studies at the Hebrew University, where he encountered Martin Buber and other Jewish studies luminaries. Toward the end of his stay, Riskin also met his future wife, Vicky, when teaching in a YU-sponsored summer program. While they only moved permanently to Israel over twenty years later, they fostered a connection that was intensified during eight summers that the Riskins and their kids spent at Ein Zurim, a religious kibbutz in the southern Lachish region near Ashkelon.[155]

Those summers turned out to be fortuitous in a very practical way, since it was during one of those visits that Riskin met Moshe Moskowitz (1925–2021), who lived at the nearby Moshav Mas'uot Yitzhak. "Moshko," as he was known, was a veteran local government official and overall mover and shaker. During the course of his long career, he was responsible for the development of some of RZ's most enduring educational institutions and settlements.[156] Moshko invited Riskin to partner with him in establishing Efrat, a new town in the Gush Etzion region, the area south of Jerusalem where Moshko and his family had lived prior to its capture by the Arab Legion in 1948. Since the end of the 1967 war, he had been instrumental in redeveloping the region, serving among others as a driving force in the establishment of YHE and hiring of Amital as head of the yeshiva. Riskin accepted the offer to promote the Efrat initiative and encourage his American followers to purchase homes and settle, and upon immigration to serve as chief rabbi alongside Moshko's role of mayor. For six years prior to their aliyah, Riskin was deeply involved in Efrat, both recruiting potential inhabitants and joining Moshko in lobbying the Israeli government to gain legal and budgetary backing for building the settlement. In 1983, the Riskins moved to Efrat with another seventy to eighty families, some of whom joined them directly from America and others who had come separately, as well as a South African contingent and native-born families. As of 2024, Efrat's population had reached over thirteen thousand residents,[157] 40–50 percent of them English speakers. It remains among the most "upscale" of the West Bank towns, although in recent years it has attracted a more diverse native-Hebrew-speaking religious population. Many are drawn to its "Jerusalem bedroom suburban community" character along with its well-regarded educational institutions, including multiple ones connected to Riskin's OTS network.

In her work on American settlers in the West Bank, Hirschhorn focused on Riskin and Efrat, detailing the process by which he gradually adopted right-wing political views, dismissing the Oslo Peace Accords and supporting (nonviolent) resistance. This evolution in his approach, she suggests, challenges his stature as a "moderate" religious leader. As we will see, his religious and educational activities since his arrival in Israel did not contradict the factual picture that Hirschhorn puts forward. Nonetheless, it underscores the complex landscape of Israeli society when perceived through multiple lenses. Riskin certainly identified increasingly with the political stances of his West Bank neighbors, although he never categorically rejected territorial compromise in an eventual settlement.[158] At the same time, he has also remained outspoken in his opposition to any modicum of violence and has labored to nurture direct discourse with local Muslim clerics. This last focus on "third-party peacemaking" among religious and cultural leaders has gained scholarly attention in recent years, with some commentators offering it as an alternative to the stalled political arena.[159] All the same, as far as his core RZ constituency is concerned, while his political stance would be deemed centrist and certainly not "hard right," the thrust of his core activities locates him in much sharper contrast to the mainstream Merkaz ha-Rav and Kav camps. This divergence is manifest in his more progressive approach to women and gender, relations with non-Orthodox Jews as well as with other religions, the role of religion in Israeli public space,[160] and multiple perspectives connected to Jewish law and theology. So much so that on more than one occasion the state rabbinate sought to prevent the clean-shaven Riskin—who, among other endeavors has appointed women to serve in clergy positions,[161] advocates for greater leniency regarding conversion, acknowledges the Divine in other religions,[162] supports inclusion of gay Jews in Orthodox congregations and the rights of same-sex couples to bring up children,[163] encourages religious women to serve in the army, and campaigns against the policies of rabbinic courts regarding women whose husbands refuse to grant them religious divorces—from remaining in his position as the chief rabbi of Efrat.[164]

Efrat is the physical base and foundation of Riskin's OTS network and where he taught, preached, and modeled an Israel-based communal rabbinate on a daily basis throughout his career, along with publishing regular columns and essays on religious and social issues. But the reach of Riskin and OTS extends far beyond, both within Israel and across the world. Today its offerings include seven junior and senior high schools—three for boys and four for girls—spread throughout the greater Jerusalem area; the entire Midreshet Lindenbaum for Women framework, discussed earlier; a men's Hesder yeshiva (Mahanaim) and the Joseph

and Gwendolyn Straus rabbinical seminary; multiple additional men's ordination tracks and yeshivot including one in the northern town of Carmiel; accessible yeshiva learning opportunities for both men and women
with special needs; a conversion institute for Spanish speakers; a legal aid
organization and hotline for women; several centers for interfaith dialogue and understanding; and six different training courses for emissaries to Jewish communities abroad.[165] The Straus-Amiel program, led by
YHE alumnus Rabbi Eliahu Birnbaum, which trains rabbinic couples to
serve around the globe, has been running since 1999 and as of 2019 had
sent over one thousand of its graduates to countries on six continents.[166]

No doubt, variations on all of these subdivisions exist outside the
OTS network. All the same, in numerous cases Riskin was a forerunner
in introducing these initiatives. But perhaps what is most compelling
about his contribution to IsMO's emergence is the establishment of a
wide-reaching religious and educational conglomerate of sorts. Its main
institutions share a common DNA that is communicated to thousands
of Israeli students on a yearly basis, as well as to hundreds who come
from abroad. Minimally, this is expressed in the types of people chosen
to run the various branches, the key teachers, the curricula, and core
ideals. These were reinforced throughout Riskin's tenure through his
regular encounters with the staff as well as the students. Undoubtedly,
some saw the suit-and-tie-wearing, beardless rabbi as a foreign import,
but they also gained awareness of his accomplishments and storied career of leadership and activism.

By the middle of the second decade of the twenty-first century,
Riskin recognized that he had to groom a successor. However, drawing parallels to the SHI leadership turnover in 2023, the OTS process
illustrates the complexity of stepping into the shoes of an Israel-based
world Jewish leader, especially one whose American roots were critical to his success. In February 2015, OTS announced that Rabbi David
Stav had been appointed co-chancellor and eventual heir to Riskin (then
seventy-four) as its leader.[167] The choice made good sense, since Stav
was a well-regarded locally born RZ rabbinical figure and educator who
was among the founders of and headed the Tzohar rabbinical organization.[168] Like Riskin, Stav had taken strong stands in opposition to the
Haredi-dominated state rabbinate, and they shared a vision of creating
bridges between observant and nonobservant Jews and facilitating more

Figure 2.12. Presentation to Rabbanit Shira Zimmerman of her certification as a "Spiritual Leader and Arbiter of Jewish Law" in Jerusalem by Rabbi Shlomo Riskin and Rabbi Shuki Reich. Courtesy of OTS.

positive religious experiences for the broader Israeli public. In fact, parts of Riskin's "empire" had been built by "acquiring" existing institutions such as Brovender's Bruria and Hamivtar and developing them further. Thus, initially it appeared that a merger with Tzohar was in the making. All said, this was billed as a move that would, in the words of Riskin, "strengthen Modern Orthodoxy and religious Zionism."[169] Or as Stav put it, he hoped to lead "one big movement that will inspire Israeli society."[170]

It is unclear what undermined this plan, but within less than two years, Rabbi Dr. Kenneth (Katriel) Brander was appointed the official successor,[171] and by 2018 he had taken over the reigns of OTS as president and *rosh yeshiva*, with Riskin assuming the title of founder and *rosh yeshiva* and Stav remaining co-chancellor (for a short period). A graduate of four YU schools and student of Soloveitchik in the early 1980s during his last years of teaching at YU, Brander certainly had robust qualifications. In his mid-twenties he took over a struggling synagogue in Boca Raton,

Florida, and transformed it into a thriving Orthodox Jewish center with strong ties to the broader Southern Florida Jewish community.[172] Subsequently, he was hired by YU to create its Center for the Jewish Future and rose to the position of vice president for university and community life. On a more personal level, Brander knew Riskin well from his first pulpit position as assistant rabbi at Lincoln Square Synagogue on Manhattan's Upper West Side, the congregation Riskin founded and led for over twenty years. These qualities and connections may have attracted Riskin and the OTS board, but in order to assume the role, Brander, who was fifty-seven, his wife, Ruchie, and their younger children had to move to Israel. Thus, like SHI and despite its deep footprint and palpable role in Israeli society, OTS chose an heir to its pioneering immigrant founder whose natural habitat was North America.

To date, Brander has demonstrated his commitment to the task, investing effort to connect with his Israeli partners and students, engage Israeli society, and stake out strong positions on key issues of debate, expanding OTS's brand in notable ways.[173] At the same time, it is clear that he is a "foreign import" who still lacks the local credibility of Stav or that accrued by Riskin over four decades, for that matter. Riskin was certainly aware of this challenge but made the decision to nonetheless hand over the reins. This may be attributed to Brander's exceptional skill set, including his critical proven fundraising abilities. That said, his background also facilitates OTS's efforts to build on its now established moderate Israeli base as the source for increasingly impacting world Jewry. This direction was asserted by Brander upon arrival in Israel and subsequently on numerous other occasions: "the goal is to inform the international Jewish community."[174] Returning to the transnational perspective that informs this book, Brander is positioning himself and his institution to intensify the process by which the product that was initiated in North America, then refined and recalibrated in Israel, is reinserted into its original environment and throughout the globe.

Conclusion

The biographical sketches of the eight immigrant pioneers of IsMO have demonstrated the cumulative historical effect of their arrivals between 1965 and 1982 and the establishment of their diverse but overlapping educational initiatives upon their local Israeli disciples and broader Israeli religious life. Before moving forward to advance this understanding further through analysis of specific examples that characterize the departure of the moderate direction from other dominant ones, we will first engage with two influential religious figures who were nurtured by American Orthodox Judaism and immigrated to Israel during the 1970s. Though they each had a significant impact on Israeli life, I have not included them among the central change agents that facilitated IsMO's emergence. Analyzing why will provide further insight into the character of the novel moderate trend and its core ideals.

3

Kahane and Carlebach

Notable but Not Part of the List

Among the North American Orthodox religious figures who immigrated to Israel during the same period as the pioneers, two whom this book does not include in that group stand out for their profound influences on Israeli society: Rabbi Meir Kahane (1932–1990)—the founder of the Jewish Defense League (JDL) in America and leader of the Kach movement in Israel, and Rabbi Shlomo Carlebach (1925–1994)—the New Age Hasidic folk singer preacher who established the Meor (Mevo) Modi'im settlement in central Israel. A brief comparison and exposition of the different reasons each was omitted helps to clarify further the contours of the agents of change who comprise the focus of this book and their relationship to IsMO's emergence.

Kahane and Carlebach were unquestionably radical figures—each in divergent ways. That said, from their childhoods onward both sustained strong connections to American MO Jews, and upon their arrivals in Israel during the 1970s they gained followings within the RZ sector. Contrary to embracing the worldview exemplified by Soloveitchik and his YU cohorts, their highly distinct but occasionally overlapping paths were characterized by respective rejections of the MO synthesis between religious and universal values and culture. These commonalities notwithstanding, within the Israeli RZ spectrum, Kahane exhibited hypernationalist and racist stances that resonated primarily among the fringes of the Kookist camp, whereas Carlebach's New Age Hasidism and certainly his music were actually integrated into all RZ sectors, including core elements of the moderate ones.[1]

Kahane, an American native, attended YU's BTA high school,[2] while the Berlin-born Carlebach stemmed from a storied German Orthodox rabbinic family that embodied the Hirschian Torah with *derekh erez* (modern culture) ideal.[3] Their early adulthoods were nourished, however, through exposure to burgeoning post–World War II American Haredi institutions; Kahane studied for thirteen years at the Mir Yeshiva in Brooklyn, where he received rabbinical ordination (afterward attending NYU Law School), while Carlebach was enrolled in Brooklyn's Yeshivas Torah Voda'ath and Beth Medrash Govoha in Lakewood, before moving to the Lubavitcher Yeshiva and becoming an early devotee and emissary of Chabad Hasidism in America. During his Chabad period, as well as further on in the 1960s, Carlebach worked closely with Rabbi Zalman Schachter-Shalomi (1924–2014), who went on to serve as a founder of Jewish Renewal, an American postdenominational movement that is predicated on Hasidic and mystical teaching.[4] Moving forward, at various points in their American careers both Kahane and Carlebach worked as rabbis of ostensibly MO congregations, but the crucial messages that they communicated and the main frameworks that they cultivated advanced decidedly alternative outlooks.[5]

Kahane, in the words of the late religious thinker Walter Wurtzburger, "[insisted] that to be considered an authentic Jew one must totally reject the entire system of modernity." Thus, "the mere fact that one subscribes to such modern values as democracy and the dignity of human beings is evidence that one has been corrupted."[6] By doing so, one undermined the foundational Jewish values of particularism and survival. This core outlook, which directly contradicted the MO synthesis concept,[7] was reflected in Kahane's approach to the lessons, among others, of the Holocaust, antisemitism, Black-Jewish relations, the persecution of Soviet Jewry, Israel and Zionism, and Arab-Jewish interactions.[8] It was manifested in practice in America through the JDL, which promoted deliberate illegal violence as an effective means to assure that "Never Again" would Jewish blood be spilled in vain.[9]

Carlebach, too, was deeply influenced by the Holocaust, but his focus was on translating the visceral devotion and demonstrative joy rooted in the Hasidic courts and teachings of Eastern Europe into a mentality and lifestyle that would draw all types of contemporary Jews—primarily young ones—toward greater engagement with God and the Torah. While his mixture of mystical storytelling, intense expressions of love for all Jews, and folk-inspired liturgical tunes appealed to searching Jewish youth of the sixties,[10] it challenged the intellectually oriented, refined Judaism that had become a hallmark of the major denominations.[11]

Moreover, his emphasis on the spirit sometimes entailed tolerance of behaviors inconsistent with Jewish law,[12] although he personally remained declaratively committed to conventional halakhic practice.[13] This openhanded posture stood in opposition to the MO predicated on Soloveitchik's ideal construction of law both studied and practiced as foundational to engaging the Divine within the material world.[14]

During the period when they were both part of a common American stage there was a critical difference between the respective dynamics of Kahane and Carlebach in connection to MO Jews. Each figure exhibited decidedly antiestablishment tendencies. Nevertheless, Kahane was perceived almost exclusively through his radical character. Individual MO Jews may have appreciated aspects of his messages, especially defiant young people, but he was a militant provocateur who thrived on his adversarial position vis-à-vis the mainstream leadership and institutions. Regarding Carlebach, on the other hand, even many who were ambivalent in relation to some of his activities and projects appreciated his sincerity and the cathartic qualities of his music—he was invited to perform at middle-of-the-road events, and synagogues began to integrate his tunes into their services.[15] This early divide between Kahane and Carlebach came across vividly through their sizable but highly contrasting roles in the Soviet Jewry movement. Kahane occupied the outside flank that encouraged violence, confronting and provoking even the more activist Jewish players, while Carlebach became a ubiquitous presence at most major demonstrations and his song "Ode Avinu Hai/ Am Yisrael Hai" (Our Father in Heaven still lives, the people of Israel live) was adopted as the unofficial anthem of the movement.[16]

Like his fellow Brooklynites Lichtenstein and Hartman, Kahane immigrated to Israel in 1971; Carlebach—who also spent part of his youth in Brooklyn—put down Israeli roots in 1975. Kahane settled in a Haredi neighborhood in Jerusalem and quickly became involved in national politics through the Kach party that he founded. Among the policies that he advocated were revocation of the citizenship of all Arab residents, immediate annexation of any land under Israeli control, expulsion of the entire populations of villages where an Arab terrorist lived, a legal prohibition of marriage between Jews and non-Jews, and cutting diplomatic relations with Germany and Austria. Despite ongoing efforts to ban his party permanently from running in national elections, in 1984

Kahane won a seat and served for a tumultuous full term in the Israeli legislature before his party was once again banned. In 1987, three years before being assassinated during a trip to New York, Kahane opened a yeshiva in Jerusalem dedicated to spreading his ideas.[17]

Kahane apprehended that he had to restructure his positions to make them both applicable and appealing to Jewish Israelis. To a certain degree he succeeded during his own lifetime in this task. Furthermore, the ideology known popularly as "Kahanism" has been reformulated and adopted by his Israeli followers, including ministers in the Israeli cabinet.[18] Thus, his noninclusion in this book's core group is not due to his lack of impact on Israeli society, although it is felt primarily in the political realm. Rather, while Kahane is certainly a bold example of an American Orthodox immigrant figure from the 1970s who left a mark on Israel, he did so by introducing a worldview that pushed the nationalist religious approach toward its most radical extremes. From this perspective, Kahane had the polar opposite effect from that of the agents of change featured in this book. The latter facilitated the growth of a moderate religious culture that offered an alternative to the mainstream RZ Kookist camp, and certainly stood at the opposite side of the spectrum from those who resonated with Kahane's stances.[19]

Carlebach's relationship to IsMO's emergence is more complex. After numerous visits and performances in Israel during the late 1960s and early 1970s, in 1975 he and a small group of American devotees—the majority of whom grew up in nonobservant Jewish homes—established Moshav Meor Modi'im between Jerusalem and Tel Aviv (originally Mevo Modi'in). Popularly referred to as the "Moshav," its religious leader owned a home there and frequented it throughout the next two decades. Whenever he did so, people thronged there from across the country to experience a "Carlebach Shabbat." The Moshav was a kind of open commune whose character was defined by Carlebach's early disciples. It earned a reputation in Israel as a place for enabling transcendent experiences in an environment imbued with the charisma of Carlebach and others who remained embedded in the American sixties culture. A number of "Carlebach" offshoot musical bands also emerged from its residents and their offspring,[20] but as a local-based "institution" it remained an anomaly that never gained a strong foothold within conventional Israeli religious life.[21]

Nonetheless, Carlebach's influence on twenty-first-century religious trends in Israel and English-speaking countries is palpable. As noted, this had started during his lifetime through his music, which—as is often the case with the creative arts—could be bifurcated from its composer's blemishes and idiosyncrasies.[22] As he grew older and audiences younger, the more conventionally Orthodox ones were less attuned to his avant-garde sides, and the devout temperament of his songs and stories gained preeminence. This evolution was magnified after his death, when a process of sanctification transformed "Reb Shlomo's" life and tales into a renewal of the legacies of the early Hasidic *zaddikim* (righteous persons/leaders).[23] According to popular understandings, these personalities combined unreserved spirituality with profound concern for every Jew and an innate ability to enable even those seemingly furthest away to cleave to the Divine.[24] Before and especially since his passing, a plethora of books have been published in both English and Hebrew that repeat his renditions of classic Hasidic stories, expand upon the novel ones he conceived, share "Reb Shlomo" stories based on his life,[25] and explicate his commentaries on the traditional Jewish canon and liturgy.[26] This corpus has gained a substantial readership within RZ circles.[27] Yet here too there is no clear intersection with IsMO's emergence, as inspired by the activities of the eight pioneers portrayed above.

The more substantive link is through the Israeli role played in the revival of Neo-Hasidism, inspired at least in part by Carlebach. This concept was introduced originally regarding the religious approach advanced by Martin Buber, Hillel Zeitlin, and their European cohorts at the turn of the twentieth century. They mined early Hasidic lore for its spiritual energy, along with its antinomian tendencies,[28] as sources for revitalizing the liberal, non-halakhic-oriented Judaism of their day.[29] Scholars identify several variants of reframing Hasidic themes throughout the century, with the New Age–infused iterations that emerged in the 1960s and Carlebach and his original religious outreach partner Shachter-Shalomi as central examples.[30] Even if Carlebach straddled the line between personal allegiance to Jewish law and tolerance for more individualistic spiritual self-expression, he never left Orthodoxy. However, the tension between the two, combined with the inspirational pathos of his tunes that became the backbone for fresh directions in liturgical devotion, figured centrally in an alternative phenomenon that gained traction within twenty-first-century Israeli RZ circles.[31]

By 2004, ten years after his passing, there were over 114 regular Jewish prayer gatherings worldwide that self-defined as "Carlebach *minyanim*," 64 of them in North America and 48 in Israel. This number, which includes congregations of all denominations and levels of observance, has grown exponentially since then.[32] This is especially so when the scores of "conventional" synagogues around the globe are added that incorporate "Carlebach davening" into their regular schedules. These services are characterized by exuberant singing and dancing to the melodies of Carlebach and often integrate teachings inspired by his ideas and stories as well. Such collective rites are certainly part and parcel of the various concentrations of Carlebach disciples in Meor Modi'im, Jerusalem, Safed, and a sprinkling of yeshivot geared toward American "searchers" who have found their way to Israel.[33] Far less obviously, they have found a place in YU, prominent American Modern Orthodox congregations,[34] and the elite bastions of Soloveitchik-inspired Israeli institutions such as YHE and numerous offshoots that are producing a new generation of local moderate religious leaders.[35]

Carlebach-inspired prayer serves as a core component in a range of advanced Israeli Torah institutions where high-level Talmud study is combined with intense engagement with Hasidic texts and theological orientations that seek to fuse such ideas with RZ outlooks. Counted among them are Yeshivat Otniel and Migdal Oz, which are led respectively by a star disciple of Lichtenstein and his own daughter.[36] These are two exemplary RZ bodies in which ideals such as rigorous Talmudic study, appreciation for secular knowledge, and humanistic approaches to all members of society that were introduced by Lichtenstein and others have been reconstituted by their Israeli receivers and then communicated to their own students. Strikingly, then, in these cases the processing by Israelis of ideas originating in North America has also featured critical elements rooted in Carlebach's legacy.[37]

To some degree in these institutions, but even more so in additional RZ ones that also look positively upon numerous aspects of contemporary culture and ethical ideals (Yeshivat Siah Yitzhak,[38] Yeshivat Mekor Hayyim,[39] and Yeshivat Tekoah,[40] for example), the tension between allegiance to nomian standards and unbridled spiritual expression and personal quests is felt acutely.[41] By no means do any of these RZ institu-tions openly condone nonobservance, but they feature study of Hasidic texts, facilitate multifaceted forms of spiritual self-expression such as meditation and free-form dancing, and encourage lively discourse re-garding the possible impediments of objective technical legal require-ments to engaging the Divine. It is this major phenomenon within Israeli RZ Judaism that offers compelling evidence for including Carlebach—with all his distinctions and even deviations from the rest of the group—among IsMO's pioneers.

Arguably, then, Carlebach epitomizes an American Orthodox im-migrant figure who drew heavily on broader culture, engaged all Jews positively, played a critical role in creating and leading a local Israeli institution with wider impact (the Moshav), and even encouraged in-creased women's participation in Jewish learning and ritual life.[42] Why, then, do I still hesitate to include him among IsMO's pioneers?

First, unlike those featured whose immigration was permanent, Israel was never Carlebach's primary base. He continued to serve as rabbi of the congregation on Manhattan's Upper West Side that was previously led by his father, while spending much of his time touring and perform-ing throughout the world.[43] In fact, his most comprehensive biographer named a chapter of his book "Israel as a Second Home (1980–1994)."[44]

Second, although the sui generis synthesis of Hasidic spirituality and core elements of Modern Orthodoxy within the contemporary Israeli RZ spectrum can be accredited in part to Carlebach, there are additional critical factors only tangentially related to his legacy that underlie these developments. Among them is the increased fixation among RZ Jews with mysticism, which is ostensibly a natural outgrowth of its core role in Kook's theosophically infused writings.[45] A parallel constituent ele-ment is the encounter in the last decades of young religious Israelis with postmodern perspectives, as well as Eastern religions, that contest no-tions of religious truth while buttressing the authenticity of individual experience.[46] This exposure has inspired many to turn to alternative, less rational-oriented religious traditions and texts that are grounded in Hasidism such as the Breslover ideals attributed to Rebbe Nahman of Breslov, the great-grandson of Rabbi Israel ben Eliezer (the "Ba'al Shem Tov"),[47] and those of the Ishbiza dynasty.[48] It has also produced some of the most creative theological writing of this generation, including the works of the late Shagar (Rabbi Shimon Gershon Rosenberg), the cofounder of Yeshivat Siah Yitzhak.[49] The amalgamation of these and additional spiritual modes into RZ culture found linguistic expression in the popular term CHABAKOOK (חבק"וק), which stands for "Chabad, Breslov, Kook, and Carlebach."[50]

A third reason for my ambivalence relates to issues of constituency. Although Carlebach engaged MO and RZ Jews throughout his career, and his impact on them continues to be felt, unlike the other pioneers, he never attended its institutions, nor did he identify clearly with these communities. Moreover, the influence of his music and Hasidic oeuvre can be detected among a far broader spectrum of contemporary Jews. Mention has been made of American New Age Judaism and the Jewish Renewal movement, to which can be added the Conservative and Reform movements as well.[51] On the other side of the spectrum, for Israeli groups that are distant or even antagonistic toward moderate perspectives, including some Haredi streams as well as more anarchistic elements within the RZ gamut such as the "Hilltop youth," Carlebach's legacy is also central.[52] Unlike the eight figures on whom this book focuses, then, it is far more difficult to "claim" Carlebach as an identifiable "member" of the moderate stream.

A final issue that sets Carlebach apart from the core pioneers is the strong assertions of sexual misconduct throughout much of his career. The claims include a variety of levels of harassment of women who were drawn to his charismatic personality, including minors whom he encountered in various public settings. While formal legal charges were never leveled during his lifetime, there is strong evidence from multiple reliable sources.[53] Indeed, his daughter Neshama Carlebach—a talented singer in her own right and protégé of her father's—has acknowledged his deviant behavior in writing. She described an intervention that was initiated by his followers during the 1970s due to his actions, and she apologized to the victims, while emphasizing that for her these did not annul his many profound attributes and contributions.[54]

As a historian, I, too, recognize his strengths and critical role in the evolution of Jewish spiritual life from the second half of the twentieth century and continuing after his death. More specifically, by detailing his Israel footprint I have affirmed that one cannot detach Carlebach the religious persona and his music from IsMO's emergence. That said, the well-documented accounts of his severe delinquency run counter to the centrality of ethics and morality within religious life that is a keystone for the majority of the pioneers. To be sure, inconsistencies can be identified among others as well, but nothing that comes close to the unequivocally problematic deeds of Carlebach. Taken together with the other issues delineated above that distance his model from the rest of the group, my conclusion is that Carlebach is a part of the story of how American immigrants facilitated IsMO's emergence, but he is not one of its foundational figures.

PART TWO

Dimensions of Israeli Moderate Judaism

4

Fragmentary Judaism

The Lichtenstein Approach

It was Purim Eve, 1984, and hundreds of YHE students stoked themselves for the raucous night ahead. The formal chanting of the Book of Esther in the impressive study hall that looks out over a soaring cliff facing toward Jerusalem and the enthusiastic dancing that follows are highlights of the yeshiva calendar.

But first, their revered leader Rabbi Aharon Lichtenstein spoke to them of Queen Esther and her existential quandary: whether to relinquish the comforts of royal anonymity and risk her life to save the Jewish people. In a thundering voice he exclaimed, "Ekhpat o lo ekhpat?" "Do I care or don't I?" Like Esther, he asserted, at some point each person must decide whether they are willing to make the most critical personal sacrifices for the greater good.[1]

Other rabbinic figures might have formulated the predictable segue, preaching the importance of total dedication to Torah study—and justifying the forfeiture of alternative types of fulfilment. To be sure, this was an essential theme at YHE as well. Yet Lichtenstein highlighted a more expansive direction that evening, insisting on reaching out beyond his students' comfort zones. You who are currently absorbed in spiritual and intellectual self-development, he cajoled, should already be cultivating consciousness of the wider Jewish civilization, its challenges, and how willing you are to dedicate yourselves to others. Lest the message be interpreted as patent paternalism, he stressed that foundational to this imperative was the ability to "identify" with those who stood far away from the world of the yeshiva.[2]

This Purim night performance signposted the degree to which grasping how to interface with various Jewish "others"—non-Orthodox, nonobservant, and secular Zionists in particular, as well as active homosexuals and apostates—was foundational to Lichstenstein's overall worldview. By exploring when he began attending to these issues in formal written exposition and how his view developed over the course of his career, we can trace what he shared with and to what extent Lichtenstein departed from those Orthodox authorities over the past two centuries who engaged such topics both from halakhic and ideational perspectives—especially his mentor and father-in-law, Rabbi Joseph B. Soloveitchik (1903–1993), as well as Rabbi Abraham Isaac Kook (1865–1935) and Rabbi Abraham Yeshayah Karelitz (1878–1953, henceforth Hazon Ish). We can also identify correlations or sources of influence for Lichtenstein's engagement with Jewish "others" and assess how they may be distinguished within other central elements of his oeuvre.

Significantly, as we will see, Lichtenstein's core position was distinctive among major Orthodox figures both in Israel and in the United States. Despite his clear disagreement with non-Orthodox and nonobservant Jews on fundamental matters of theology and religious lifestyle, he demonstrated far greater appreciation of and effort to acknowledge positive elements in the positions of other Jews than did his predecessors. And unlike Kook, these evaluations were independent of any specific role for the nonobservant and non-Orthodox in a defined historiosophical redemptive metanarrative.

The Boundaries of the Jewish Fraternity

Lichtenstein, as noted, arrived in Israel with his family in 1971. By then he had studied intensively under the tutelage of Soloveitchik at YU, gained a PhD in English literature from Harvard University, and returned to YU, where he was one of the leading young rabbinical figures during the 1960s.

Throughout his over fifty-year career, the complexities of contemporary Jewish identity and how to relate to those who live alternative paths from Orthodoxy was a recurrent theme in Lichtenstein's written and oral presentations. In fact, the first journal article he ever published is titled "Brother Daniel and the Jewish Fraternity," which appeared in 1963.[3]

Fueled by the controversy then raging over the application for Israeli citizenship under the Law of Return by a Polish Jew who was hidden in a Carmelite monastery during the Holocaust and subsequently became a priest, Lichtenstein examined whether it is possible to actively forfeit one's membership in the Jewish nation.[4] As part of his analysis, he contrasted other "religious deviationists" such as public Sabbath desecraters and those who regularly eat nonkosher food with those who voluntarily adopt a different religion altogether. Lichtenstein demonstrated a keen consciousness of the exceptional ways in which traditional Jewish norms of behavior have been challenged since the emergence of the modern nation-state and the rise of the European enlightenment. While certainly attending to halakhic angles, his discussion moves deliberately beyond the formal legal realm to spotlight broader meanings of Jewish peoplehood.

Lichtenstein was captivated by the implications of the contemporary renaissance of full Jewish sovereignty for defining an essential level of Jewish connection—be it religious or secular. All the same, his conclusion is that the degree of detachment from Jewish collective history and fate implicit in official apostasy undermines any sense of commonality arising from partnership in civil endeavors. Thus, in contrast to all other habitual transgressors and regardless of the Israeli government's actual ruling, he saw no room for one who had adopted another religion to be considered a member of the Jewish "fraternity."[5]

While repudiating a Jewish self that is based purely on political connection, Lichtenstein acknowledged simultaneously that even if religious observance remains the ideal form, positive membership in the Jewish people is not conditioned upon it. This approach locates him within the tolerant camp of Orthodox authorities who differentiate between the meaning of religious deviance in premodern and modern circumstances and in this way defuse much of the sanctions that appear in the Talmud and medieval codes. By no means, however, does he come across as a pluralist. At least regarding the ritual realm, he was consistent with the hierarchical posture initially articulated by nineteenth-century German Orthodox figures that, though evincing greater acceptance, still maintains internal grades that distinguish between the fully observant and those who deviate.[6]

Lichtenstein's minimum expectation of bonding with both the Jewish past and future evokes his mentor Soloveitchik's "covenant of fate," which the latter articulated in 1956 as part of his statement on the theological implications of the Holocaust and official declaration of support for political Zionism.[7] Despite this powerful bond of common history and struggles, Soloveitchik made clear that the higher echelon is reserved for those who also accept the "covenant of destiny" expressed through religious belief and practice.[8] Indeed, Lichtenstein asserts the affinity of his outlook to that of his teacher: "To use a phrase once employed by Soloveitchik, we are a 'community of the committed' and our commitment is not only the source of our chosenness, it is the cause of our being a people at all."[9]

Positive Religious Experience and Values

If Lichtenstein's initial inclusive conceptualization regarding nonobservant Jews drew from Soloveitchik's inventive dichotomy, the more pathbreaking direction that he subsequently articulated can actually be identified through his gradual, nuanced detachment from aspects of his teacher's position. His first literary step in this direction is found in another article that also appeared originally in *Judaism* magazine. Titled "Religion and State: The Case for Interaction," it was published in 1966 and, among other things, entertains more fully some of the notions regarding Jewish political sovereignty and religious life he touched upon in 1963.[10]

In the last section of the article, Lichtenstein digressed from his wide-ranging analysis in order to refute a variety of specific arguments by Israeli philosopher Nathan Rotenstreich for strict separation of the modern Jewish state from historic Judaism. Among them is Orthodox Judaism's obstinate refusal to entertain the idea of "non-Orthodoxy piety." In response, Lichtenstein insisted that "Orthodox Jews recognize that heterodox piety does exist, just as they realize that secularists may lead genuinely ethical lives . . . it would be unwise and immoral to deny the genuine reality of heterodox religious experience . . . heterodox piety may constitute invaluable religious experience, and this consideration is crucial for any intelligent assessment of the individual involved."[11]

Lichtenstein steered away from any equivocation or pluralistic understanding of the assortment of modern Jewish religious trends. At the same time, he affirmed that secular and non-Orthodox Jews possess positive characteristics that are not limited to the realm of common historical survival and fate. In fact, granted the theological heresy of the non-Orthodox, he was more sympathetic to their spiritual quests than to the "Godless" ideological atheism of the secularists.[12] Lichtenstein's words digress dramatically from his own mentor's evaluation of the members of these factions. For, as religion scholar Gerald (Ya'akov) Blidstein emphasized, "Rabbi Soloveitchik . . . finds no legitimacy, spiritual grandeur, or subterranean power in antinomian movements or individuals."[13]

From New York to Jerusalem

Blidstein's contention was made in the context of contrasting Soloveitchik with the mystical-redemptive ideology of the preeminent RZ theologian of the twentieth century, Abraham Isaac Kook. In 1971, Lichtenstein's immigration to Israel intensified his own encounter with Israeli RZ. Together with unambiguous continuities, noteworthy expansions of his approach to Jewish "others" can be discerned from this point forward.

In a 1977 article, "Patterns of Contemporary Jewish *Hizdahut* [identification with]," Lichtenstein opined,

> The possibility of fragmentary Jewishness cannot be dismissed. . . . The traditional Jew may be tempted to limit Jewish self-definition to spiritual commitment while relegating national *hizdahut* to empathy. However, such a view, comfortable as it may sometimes be, is simplistic. It is wrong, logically, because nationality is no less defining than religion; and it is wrong, morally and halakhically, because it understates and undercuts the bonds that link the secular and even the assimilated to his fellows and vice versa.[14]

While still rooted in a relatively strict religion/nation dichotomy, here Lichtenstein broached for the first time the idea of "fragmentary Jewishness" as a positive notion. This conceptualization avoids totalistic definitions of Jewishness. It homes in, rather, on those positive elements that demonstrate commitment to Judaism and form the foundation for connecting Jews to each other. As will be seen, this idea subsequently became a core theme in Lichtenstein's outlook.

In addition, the statement that "nationality is no less defining than religion" would appear to further neutralize the rigidity of the hierarchical dynamic so emphasized in the writings of Soloveitchik and supported—if less stridently—in Lichtenstein's own earlier expositions. Without overly historicizing, it is hard to ignore the fact that such a comment appears six years after Lichtenstein and his family arrived in Israel. The emphasis on "fragmentary" identity along with the improved position of "nationality" suggest an incremental shift from Soloveitchik's stiff distinction between survivalist "exodus from Egypt" and "Sinaitic" destiny toward a more intimate connection between national awakening and spiritual progress. All the same, in the 1977 piece, Lichtenstein also characteristically expresses his ambivalence: "Zionism, along with the rise of the State of Israel, has had negative, as well as positive, results. It has enhanced the affinity of those who might otherwise have become wholly estranged; but by making possible and even encouraging the substitution of national for religious categories, it has diluted the content of Jewish identification for others."[15]

Lichtenstein's 1977 essay contains an additional comment that actually brings to mind Kook's perception of nonobservant Jews—especially those who adopt heretical beliefs: "a Jew may be conscious of his Jewishness and yet reject his patrimony. However, we should not dismiss this level of identification entirely. While full *hizdahut* embraces acceptance as well as awareness, even self-hatred reflects a sense, at times both profound and perverse, of one's roots. Blasphemy, Eliot often contended, is more religious than indifference."[16] The observation that refutation of one's Judaism—not formal apostasy but intellectual or ideological clash—can paradoxically hold within it seeds of deep connection is fundamental to Kook's metaphysical understanding of secularization.[17] Granted, the latter's view is grounded in the principles and metahistorical narrative of Lurianic mysticism. All the same, the language of discourse adopted by Lichtenstein in his initial "Israeli" discussion of nonobservant Jews points toward the more fluid relationship between heterodoxy and Orthodoxy that characterizes Kookian theosophy.[18] This said, there is no indication that Lichtenstein would have suggested, as Kook emphasized, that those who stray from the Torah actually reach insights that are crucial for the development of Judaism, but would have been impossible to attain without the seemingly profane deviation. Indeed, as seen below, subsequently Lichtenstein was adamant in demonstrating the degree to which his position differed from this aspect of Kook's worldview.

Precursor to the Decline in Interdenominational Conflict

By the early 1980s, Lichtenstein had established himself within his new geographic and institutional venues. Rather than concentrating exclusively on these environments, however, his publications and presentations demonstrate his increasing concern for the future of Diaspora Jewry. His ongoing involvement with American rabbinical candidates through his position as head of YU's Gruss Institute in Jerusalem, as well as the rising numbers of students from abroad (particularly English-speaking countries) attending YHE for at least a year, demanded that he address their future challenges as potential leaders. By then as well, the statistics produced by the 1970 National Jewish Population Study (NJPS) of United States Jewry (completed in 1972) were widely familiar, including the unprecedented increase in intermarriage rates to over 30 percent.[19]

In 1984, the same year in which he delivered his impassioned Purim plea to his YHE students to ask themselves "Do I care or don't I?" Lichtenstein published an article titled "Jewish Values in a World of Change: The Role of Jewish Communal Service." There he offered his perspective on setting collective priorities:

> I would assign top priority to the deepening of Jewish identity and commitment. . . . This requires positive content—not necessarily "religious," narrowly speaking, but a clear and conscious call to act and exist as part of the Jewish people . . . Jewish communal service should be primarily oriented . . . to reaching those on the periphery of our world, whose contacts with Jewish education or religious institutions are tangential at best. . . . Coming from an Orthodox rabbi, this may appear to be strange doctrine. But can we responsibly entertain any other?[20]

Viewed in the context of early 1980s American Modern Orthodoxy, it is not especially surprising that one of its brightest products would express deep concern for the spiritual welfare of the broader American

Jewish population. As social scientist Charles Liebman had demonstrated in 1965, unlike the sectarian particularism that characterized post–World War II American Haredi Orthodoxy, the Modern Orthodox had championed a posture of "church-like" inclusivism that supported cooperation with the non-Orthodox on issues of common interest such as the Soviet Jewry movement.[21] Moreover, the mid-twentieth century was the heyday of Modern Orthodox outreach to nonobservant and unaffiliated Jews. YU's Division of Communal Services sponsored Torah Leadership Seminars and its students served as advisors in the OU's National Council of Synagogue Youth (NCSY).[22] YU rabbinical graduates occupied nominally Orthodox pulpits in communities with few observant Jews, and "star" graduates like Shlomo (Steven) Riskin pioneered the outreach-oriented Orthodox synagogue-center.[23]

Yet Lichtenstein's instruction still contains a seemingly unanticipated novel perspective—even for a Modern Orthodox leader. His directive to develop "positive content—not necessarily 'religious,' narrowly speaking," expresses a decidedly nonparochial direction that values a broad scheme of expressions of Jewishness. This position was distinct from the vast majority of the inclusive Modern Orthodox rabbinical activities directed toward the nonobservant, which were aimed at raising the levels of religious observance of the non-Orthodox based on adopting Orthodox ritual norms.

Two years previously, in 1982, Lichtenstein not only acknowledged the importance of adopting an expansive attitude toward what constitutes positive Jewish content, he explicitly included non-Orthodox denominational religious services within this rubric. Writing for a forum on "The State of Orthodoxy," he admonished his compatriots for their triumphalist overfixation on the increasingly evident "resurgence" of American Orthodoxy in light of prior predictions by midcentury social scientists of its demise. Their self-satisfied euphoria, he protested, prevented them from addressing the overall condition of American Jewry: "With intermarriage running close to 50 percent, when studies indicate that three-fourths of our brethren do not enter *any* house of worship *any* day of the year, while the fabric of the Jewish family is impaired . . . can anyone rest content because several thousand *benei Torah* [Orthodox yeshiva students] . . . are now more committed?"[24] Under such circumstances, he argued that it would be wrong to focus on the negative aspects of any Jewish framework—even those religious streams whose theological legitimacy were highly suspect:

> Nor do I share the glee some feel over the prospective demise of the com-petition. Surely, we have many sharp differences with the Conservative and Reform movements. . . . However, we also share many values with them—and this, too, should not be obscured. Their disappearance might strengthen us in some respects but would unquestionably weaken us in others. . . . Can anyone responsibly state that it is better for a marginal Jew in Dallas or Dubuque to lose his religious identity altogether than drive to his temple?[25]

Such an acknowledgment of the intrinsic religious value of non-Orthodox houses of worship would have been an anathema to Soloveit-chik, who referred to them as "Christianized" synagogues that do not justify being characterized as "bona fide Jewish religious institutions."[26] The latter famously advised a young man to stay home rather than ful-fil the commandment of hearing the sounds of the shofar (ram's horn) blowing on Rosh ha-Shana (the Jewish New Year) when in a sanctuary with mixed pews. No doubt Soloveitchik's statements must be under-stood within the heated context of mid-twentieth-century Orthodox–Conservative polemics. All the same, Lichtenstein did not just neutralize the pejorative. He actually buttressed the importance of sustaining non-Orthodox religious institutions.[27] Furthermore, while there is no doubt that Lichtenstein did not support the landmark Conservative responsum from 1950 that permitted congregants to drive to synagogue on the Sab-bath, in the quotation here he expressed appreciation for the pragmatic logic that led to this decision: otherwise most American Jews would not attend synagogue at all.[28]

In 1986, Lichtenstein continued his conciliatory tone in an article for a symposium titled "The State of K'lal Yisrael [the Israelite collec-tive]," further advancing his appreciation for the positive elements of non-Orthodox and nonobservant Jewish expression.[29] Over and above acknowledging the necessity of utilizing less than ideal Jewish com-munal bodies to combat alienation and assimilation, he highlighted the profound spiritual and moral foundation of many within the non-Orthodox camps:

Orthodoxy cannot accord secularists and dissenters the *hekhsher* [kosher certification] they so insistently demand. We can, however, place greater emphasis upon factors which, without denying difference, transcend it; upon confraternity, upon historical and existential ties, upon essential components of a shared moral and spiritual vision, upon elements of both a common faith and a common destiny . . . whatever their deviations, other camps include people genuinely in search of the *Ribbono shel Olam* [the Almighty] . . . secular Jewry, too, harbors moral idealism and a commitment to *Klal Yisrael*. . . . [W]hile we reject leveling compromises, we strive for understanding and respect. This will no doubt seem excessively liberal to some and terribly patronizing to others.[30]

Lichtenstein's affirmation of the constructive impact and sincere spiritual quests of non-Orthodox religious frameworks and individuals did not extend them full theological legitimacy. What it did, rather, is recognize the positive elements in environments and individuals that he considered definitively "fragmentary." To a certain degree his attitude is consistent with his avowal in 1966 that "heterodox piety may constitute invaluable religious experience."[31] Yet here he went beyond "Jamesian" universal categories and identified ideal non-Orthodox religious life with sincere efforts to encounter the particularistic Jewish God, the *Ribbono shel Olam*.[32]

In fact, with full awareness of the theological implications, Lichtenstein even broached the possibility of a unified approach to conversion that would prevent future fissures.[33] This statement was written four years after the Orthodox withdrew from a cooperative conversion framework established in Denver, Colorado, that was recognized by the major American Jewish religious streams.[34] Indeed, Lichtenstein also subsequently testified to the Knesset committee initiated by the late justice minister Ya'akov Ne'eman that led to the creation of a jointly recognized conversion structure in Israel.[35]

Seen in light of developments in later decades, Lichtenstein's statements from the 1980s serve as precursors or attitudinal forerunners to the decreased focus on denominational competition and the "live and let live" atmosphere that largely characterized American Orthodox attitudes toward the non-Orthodox from the late 1990s. As religion scholar

Jack Wertheimer declared in 2005, "Jewish denominations [have] shifted from a public posture of confrontation to one of conciliation."[36] In the early 1980s, however, a very different interdenominational ambiance held sway. Lichtenstein's articulations were put forward in parallel to the Reform movement's acceptance of patrilineal descent as a basis for Jewish identity in 1983 and the Conservative movement's approval of the ordination of woman rabbis in 1986. Notably, while Lichtenstein was expressing appreciation for the positive elements in non-Orthodox synagogue life, other MO-affiliated figures fixated on an impending irrevocable split between the Orthodox and the liberal denominations. As Rabbi Dr. Reuven Bulka proclaimed in 1984, "a cataclysmic split within the North American Jewish community . . . may result in the total renunciation of a significant number within the Jewish community by another group, and the separation-cum-divorce of these two movements into a mainstream Judaism and a new religion."[37]

To be sure, there were additional MO personalities that encouraged cooperation and mutual respect between the movements, but in the 1980s most of Lichtenstein's ideological cohorts were still ensconced in the interdenominational conflicts of the mid-twentieth century exacerbated by the more recent decisions. Norman Lamm, for example, made concerted efforts during his tenure as YU president to avert irreparable divisions between the denominations. Yet only in 2007 did he openly bemoan the confrontational approach toward the non-Orthodox that he had adopted during his previous activity as an Orthodox congregational rabbi:

> When I was in the rabbinate . . . I used to pound the pulpit and storm against Conservative and Reform and secular ideas and practices. In retrospect I think it may have been the wrong approach. . . . The only thing that happened as a result of all these anti-conservative/reform/secular groups is that we have less people davening [praying]. . . . I like the idea of having Conservative day schools and Reform day schools.[38]

Lichtenstein's expression of comparable and even more empathic and somewhat "postdenominational"-oriented views in the 1980s, then, offers additional evidence for the distinctive approach toward nonobservant and non-Orthodox Jews that he nurtured in the course of his career.

Pluralistic Environments and Homosexuality

Lichtenstein's most extensive, and for that matter far-reaching, statements, however, surface toward the end of the first decade and at the beginning of the second decade of the twenty-first century. This was a time when after nearly forty years of a rigorous weekly schedule of multiple high-level Talmud classes and daily involvement in running YHE, health considerations led him to cut down significantly on his teaching and administrative load. It was also a juncture at which Lichtenstein's stature as one of the outstanding Torah scholars of the generation was more readily acknowledged not only among his direct students and followers in Israel and abroad, but throughout the RZ sector—even by ideological critics within this camp. This led to increased interest in exposing the broader public to his singular perspectives.[39]

In 2010, a volume was published by YU's Orthodox Forum with the title *The Relationship of Orthodox Jews with Believing Jews of Other Religious Ideologies and Non-believing Jews*. Along with restating numerous positions, it offers evidence of further evolutions.[40]

On the one hand, Lichtenstein rejected contemporary initiatives to apply leniencies in order to pave the way to recognize weddings performed by non-Orthodox rabbis or the mezuzah parchments written by non-Orthodox scribes.[41] On the other hand, he did not feel that these provisions should undermine a position of respect and appreciation for the valuable work done within non-Orthodox frameworks. As a result, the preemptory moderately "postdenominational" perspective that he initially hinted at in 1982 received more developed expression:

> And does anyone imagine that if every non-Orthodox temple were to shut down forthwith, that on the morrow the membership would flock, en masse, to the nearest *shul* or *shtibel*? If indeed temple attendance and affiliation are waning . . . is there not . . . as much cause for dismay as for gratification?[42] . . . Non-Orthodox movements often provide a modicum of religious guidance, of access to Jewish knowledge and values, of spiritual direction and content. Moreover, they provide it for many beyond

our own pale and reach. In such situations, the contribution to Jewish life is real and meaningful.[43]

This positive evaluation of the role of organized non-Orthodox Jewish life for strengthening Jewish identity led Lichtenstein to suggest that the Orthodox should consider seriously opportunities to assist their counterparts in their meaningful endeavors, "At issue is the advisability of extending assistance—manpower, material, moral, spiritual—to non-Orthodox movements, thus enhancing their stature and entrenching their position within the Jewish world, on the one hand, but also intensifying their commitment to *avodat Hashem* [worship of God], on the other."[44]

Together with counseling careful navigation of such cooperation, Lichtenstein was strident in his repudiation of those within the Orthodox spectrum who emphatically oppose these efforts. "In our world, there are those who subscribe to the thesis that under no circumstances is it permissible or advisable to advance the cause of deviationists. . . . However, I find this view wholly untenable, on moral, national, and, quite frequently, *halakhic* grounds."[45] Extending his "moral" perspective a step further, he revealed areas in which shared "fate" even overrides long held bans against formal ceremonial cooperation. Thus, he was stunned by a student's query concerning a controversy within an American Orthodox synagogue as to the permissibility of participation in a joint communal Holocaust Remembrance Day convocation with non-Orthodox congregations: "Shocked, I responded that, as far as I knew, the Nazis had not differentiated. Could we?"[46]

Not quite as dramatic, but equally controversial within the context of contemporary Orthodoxy, was Lichtenstein's approach toward participation in programs like Limmud. The Limmud Conference model originated in England in 1980 and has proliferated to become an international organization that sponsors as many as eighty conferences per year throughout the world.[47] Such multiday adult seminars are organized by nonsectarian bodies and are predicated on the collective study of sacred texts and presenting the widest gamut of opinions and approaches within contemporary Jewish discourse. The UK event remains the banner program and has since its inception garnered a great deal of controversy, with vociferous calls by prominent religious figures within Anglo-Orthodoxy to boycott it—so much so that throughout his twenty-two-year tenure as chief rabbi, Jonathan Sacks did not attend.[48] Lichtenstein's attitude, in contrast, was that "blanket stonewalling" would be a mistake:

> Ordinarily, regardless of who is holding forth, most of the audience will gain Torah knowledge and spiritual insight. We can, likewise, anticipate a rise in solidarity and fraternity. Moreover, in many such communities, refusal to participate will often be ascribed to a blend of fear, fueled by insecurity, and supercilious arrogance, rather than to pristine insularity; it will be interpreted as an expression of demonization rather than as an assertion of perceived radical incompatibility, and the overall impression will hardly score points for our image. Finally, abstention will leave the entire playing field at the disposal of the heterodox.[49]

It would appear to be no coincidence that Sacks's successor, Chief Rabbi Ephraim Mirvis, an alumnus of YHE who considers himself to be a loyal student of Lichtenstein, chose to break the boycott during his first year of incumbency and spoke at the December 2013 Limmud Conference.[50] He has continued to attend since.[51]

Lichtenstein's independent approach to involvement with the non-Orthodox in religiously charged arenas received keen expression in a March 2013 discussion of the controversies surrounding permission for such groups to pray collectively at Jerusalem's Western Wall (Kotel). The question-and-answer format was documented in a blog initiated by a loyal YHE student, *Pages of Faith: Exploring the Thought of ha-Rav Aharon Lichtenstein*.[52] Lichtenstein encouraged all groups who go there to "come to the Kotel deferentially, reverentially, respecting what the Kotel means to a great many people"; he added, "I would want to maintain halakhic standards; I don't think that having mixed congregations, men and women together, that that's the place to fight it out."[53]

Most troublesome to Lichtenstein, however, were those on both sides who turn this *terra sancta* into a venue either for "political demonstration" or "power struggles." In parallel, he was deeply cognizant of the symbolic importance of the Western Wall to all Jews: "When I'm there, I sometimes see someone with a makeshift yarmulke, standing at the Kotel itself, at the outer wall, crying his heart out, experiencing that which many people more devoted, more halakhically disciplined, perhaps don't feel. I don't think that by challenging the sincerity of Conservative or Reform individuals, or as groups, we gain very much religiously or even, for that matter, politically." Therefore, his practical advice was: "I don't believe . . . that there's so much to be gained by barring people from having access to the Kotel . . . I don't think we should try to have every possible restriction in place in order to manifest and to demonstrate our authority and our power."[54] This would be the case "even if they would have their own *minyanim* [worship quora] and their mode of *tefillah* [prayer]."[55]

Lichtenstein was adamant in maintaining Orthodox standards of Jewish law, but simultaneously he set in place a softer version of the Orthodox Jewish socio-religious hierarchy. Considerable effort was made on his part to accommodate non-Orthodox groups and enable them to experience Judaism's holiest space in a manner that is at least to some degree on their own terms and not those dictated purely by the Orthodox hegemony over Israeli sacred sites. Most profound in this regard was his consent to a clear non-Orthodox presence—apparently including the use of their own prayer books and rituals—as long as men and women remain physically separated during the service.

Issues of gender and sexual identity gain central stage in another installment from the same blog that appeared in April 2013 and addresses Orthodox attitudes toward homosexuality. Lichtenstein fully supported traditional understandings of the Biblical prohibition against male homosexual behavior. At the same time, he argued that this topic underscores an unhealthy double standard that commonly pervades Orthodox Jews. Whereas other sins referred to in the Bible as an abomination (*to'evah*), such as "cheating on weights and measures," are often overlooked or at least easily forgiven, vilification of homosexuals is incessantly supported by the fact that the same term (*to'evah*) is applied in its regard. Similarly, he found it difficult to countenance the fact that today few Orthodox Jews are sensitive to the seriousness of public Sabbath desecration, while at the same time they forcefully and consistently campaign against homosexuals. It is not that he encouraged intolerance toward nonobservant Jews. He simply felt that the pervasive antagonism toward homosexuals was rooted in personal "revulsion" instead of a sincere desire to uphold Jewish law standards. With this in mind he recalled with considerable consternation the "threat" a few years back by a group of Orthodox high schools not to march in New York's Israel Day Parade that ultimately prevented a Jewish gay contingent from participating: "Is it proper, is it fair, and I say this without relenting in our opposition to homosexuality—to decide that all the sins which the whole entire Jewish community has—all of that we can swallow and march with them, with pride and with their flags and everything that they want, but this is the scapegoat."[56]

Lichtenstein felt that historically homosexuality was always treated as a private transgression rather than a communal one. In an age in which the commonness of traditional public sins such as Sabbath desecration or failing to give charity have transformed them into bearable private ones, ironically the opposite makeover has taken place regarding homosexuality. Not only did he protest that this was inconsistent and unfair, but he reflected that, in regard to homosexuality, "as the phenomenon becomes more prevalent, which is unfortunate in itself, but at the personal plane it has become a more common *aveirah* [transgression], it is less of an *aveirah* on the part of the individual."[57] Such a position would, for the most part, neutralize day-to-day sanctions and pave the way for homosexual individuals' acceptance as full-fledged members of the Orthodox community.[58]

The distinctiveness of this assessment of homosexuals is set in bold through comparison to the tone and content of other prominent protégés of Soloveitchik. In December 2009, a public forum was held at YU in which gay students and alumni discussed their personal identity struggles, particularly with being part of the Orthodox community.[59] In response, four prominent YU rabbis publicized a joint statement, the "Torah View of Homosexuality," in which the authors expressed a modicum of appreciation for the challenges faced by Orthodox Jewish men who were attracted to other men, but nonetheless put forward the following blanket statement: "Homosexual behavior is absolutely prohibited and constitutes an abomination. . . . [A]ppropriate sympathy in discreet settings has become conflated with public, celebratory identification of people with an urge for forbidden behavior. In today's *galus* [exile] ssa [same-sex attraction] is not viewed as a challenge of *kevishas hayetzer* [overcoming and taming impulses for forbidden behavior], but rather as a troubling *halacha* lacking in compassion."[60] In the interim years, the approach of YU toward its homosexual students has gained national attention due to the university's unwillingness to grant permission for a gay student club to operate under its auspices.[61]

Ironically, the trajectory of some within the contemporary Haredi outreach world appears closer to Lichtenstein's own direction than that of his YU-affiliated colleagues. As Rabbi Avraham Edelstein, a central figure in worldwide Haredi sponsored outreach, declared in 2013: "We ought to recognize that a significant number of gays are committed to being Torah-observant. Theirs is a great struggle, a struggle we can never presume to understand. . . . Once the Torah prohibits homosexuality, it must be faced as a challenge like any other. Some homosexuals will never overcome their urges. . . . This does not mean that we are asking the gay person to deny his or her essential reality . . . as full-fledged members of the Jewish community, he or she brings some unique sensitivities to the table from which we can all benefit. Not only is it forbidden to discriminate against gays, but we ought to learn from what they have to offer."[62]

In 2010, an independent group of MO rabbis in North America signed a "Statement of Principles" that put forward a more inclusive position than the YU rabbis' declaration from 2009. It was authored by Rabbi Nathaniel Helfgot, a prominent protégé of Lichtenstein.[63] Within the Israeli context, noted YHE alumnus Benny Lau and other moderate figures have articulated more welcoming attitudes toward the gay Orthodox community,[64] including a detailed position paper produced by the Beit Hillel religious leadership organization.[65] In parallel, a figure deeply rooted in the Merkaz ha-Rav world and a highly regarded halakhic authority, Rabbi Eliezer Melamed, has expressed an empathic and welcoming approach toward religiously observant gay men.[66]

Mevakshei Panekha

A final principal source useful to consider in addressing Lichtenstein's approach to Jewish "others" is the book *Mevakshei Panekha*.[67] The volume appeared in 2011 and presents extensive excerpts from a series of conversations/interviews on key topics between rabbi and novelist Haim Sabato and Lichtenstein.[68] They met twenty times over the course of four months. As Lichtenstein did not directly author the passages, there is less of a guarded and deliberately balanced character to this work than those he penned himself or prepared in advance for oral presentation.

The chapter on "relationship to secular Jews" tackles and expands further upon ideas touched upon in Lichtenstein's earlier writings. These include the distinction between his approach and that of major twentieth-century Orthodox rabbinical figures—specifically Kook, Hazon Ish, and Soloveitchik—the basis for his commitment to cooperation with the non-Orthodox, and the concept and significance of "fragmentary Judaism."

The positions of both the Hazon Ish and Kook, declared Lichtenstein forthrightly, were unacceptable to him for they each embody a "judgmental" and "totalistic definition" of an entire population. Regarding the Hazon Ish's portrayal of the nonobservant as an empty wagon or boat,[69] Lichtenstein understood that the pejorative discourse of presenting secular culture as vacant depravity serves the defensive goal of "protecting" the religious public from the attractions of the outside environment. He protested that this description of nonobservant Jewry is simply inaccurate:

> The spiritual and ethical portfolio of portions of this group contains lofty and important matters of significant moral meaning . . . to say "empty wagon" implies that they have nothing, nothing which isn't better that we have. This is something that I believe to be factually false, and I also have no interest in reaching such a situation.[70]

Similarly, though he allowed that Hazon Ish's support of *tinok she-nishbah* (an infant taken captive) as the fitting halakhic category for contemporary nonobservant Jews could be useful for solving certain technical problems such as the prohibition against drinking wine touched by a public Sabbath desecrater, Lichtenstein's concern was with the broader connotations of this terminology. Like the empty wagon, "[i]f we relate to such people as infants taken captive, we do not give them any credit. We do not find any aspect of them deserving of imitation, we assume that there is nothing about them that is spiritually meaningful."[71]

This nomenclature, lamented Lichtenstein moreover, projects an "infantilization of the nonobservant collective as if to declare, 'nebukh' [pathetically], they are not to blame for their situation."[72] From this perspective, Kook's seemingly more beneficent evaluation of the unconscious but constructive role played by secular Zionists in the redemptive process was even more perturbing. For it was essentially saying to them that "you think this and this, but we know that deep inside you there is another world. . . . A day will come when this hidden world will be revealed, when you shall shed a layer of the outer peel."[73] Such expressions infuriated Lichtenstein: "This is how they relate . . . like to an onion that has one peel removed after another. Such engagement is condescending, I would not want to be addressed in this manner and I don't think they [nonobservant Jews] should be related to this way either . . . to me it dwarfs them, it is not the appropriate level of respect for the divine essence in every human being, even if he/she is not exactly as we might like."[74] Lichtenstein further criticized Kook's approach for highlighting the historical and material achievements of nonobservant Jews in matters of politics and power instead of ethics and spirit: "I see no value in humiliating a collective that consists of people whose ideology differs from mine, by saying that they merely serve as a tool in the hands of God."[75]

Lichtenstein's reticence toward "totalistic" perceptions of Jewish others informed his approach to pragmatic issues of cooperation with non-Orthodox leaders and groups as well. As he noted throughout his career, while he recognized the potential pitfalls of working together, he vehemently disagreed with those within Orthodoxy who advocated a sweeping prohibition against such contacts. Rather, each situation needed to be judged according to its respective merits and drawbacks. Adding another element to this measured appraisal, he explained that from an emotional perspective he was incapable of complying with a policy of normative separation from non-Orthodox Jews: "Personally, I would have difficulty totally detaching from the rest of the Jewish people, and maintaining a connection just with my *shtiebl* [small neighborhood prayer hall] and my congregation. We are a family. Today there are very few families in which there are none who have deviated from the path."[76]

The appraisals of Jewish others rendered by his predecessors, he indicated, cannot sustain the connections between the members of such a complex and diverse contemporary Jewish "family." For that matter, they are morally problematic and factually inaccurate. The alternative position that Lichtenstein advanced was to accept and appreciate the reality of "fragmentary Judaism." He had introduced this term in 1977, but in *Mevakshei Panekha*, he presented it as a fundamental principle:

> I think that the proper Jewish-ethical-religious position is to be capable of recognizing and appreciating things that are fragmentary [partial]. . . . I say to my students, if you think of becoming a rabbi, go to the rabbinate with a recognition and appreciation of fragmentary things.[77]

While ideologies are in principle purist and demand full commitment, in reality individual acts of Jewish involvement or expressions of positive connection need to be cherished—even if they will never lead to observance or to provision of support for the interests of the Orthodox. This position is unlike the instrumental orientation of the classical Orthodox outreach model that seeks to bring each participant incrementally to full Sabbath observance. Nor does it possess Chabad's kabbalistic/messianic foundation that places mystical value on each individual Jewish act.[78] At the same time, Lichtenstein stressed that even if he appreciated the ethics and creativity of the secular, as well as the spiritual quests and religious acts of Conservative and Reform Jews, he was by no means an egalitarian pluralist like those who maintain that "[n]o one is perfect . . . they don't keep Shabbat, and we are not careful in other matters."[79] He was absolute in his belief that Orthodox interpretation of Jewish law is the correct one and that upholding an observant lifestyle is the only ideal form of Jewish living. But this did not prevent him from extolling the positive Jewish elements found among others, acknowledging those areas in which these groups and individuals excel beyond his own constituency, and, in turn, encouraging his followers to learn from even their sharpest ideological adversaries.

One Who Learns from All People

Over the past two decades a few analytical pieces have been published that inspect Lichtenstein's overall worldview and draw attention to his deep bond with the nonliberal Christian humanist tradition of seventeenth-century England and its nineteenth-century heirs. Though

Lichtenstein's perceptions of nonobservant Jews were rooted in part in his religious humanism, spotlighting his concept of "fragmentary Judaism" enables a deeper understanding of why he was drawn to Christian sources in the first place and of what allowed him to cleave to these spiritual intellectuals without destabilizing his own religious allegiances.

Unlike the rationalistic doubt and individualistic orientation of the Central and Western European enlightenment, which was inspired by original philosophical thinkers like Bacon, Spinoza, Locke, and Voltaire and gained pervasive influence in these regions during the eighteenth century, the Christian Humanists were infused with a deep sense of absolute religious truth and spiritual devotion. This was combined with a robust ethical conviction and aesthetic sensibility that was conveyed through the literary masterpieces of figures such as Shakespeare, Milton, and Henry More. Lichtenstein's decision during the 1950s to dedicate his doctoral research to More and the Cambridge Platonists is the earliest major evidence of his being drawn to this school of thought. In fact, his choice of Donald Bush as his Harvard mentor—a leading Milton scholar who supported a "Catholic worldview" and was an outspoken critic of the increasingly prevalent modernist school—solidified Lichtenstein's association with this guild.[80]

In contrast to the skepticism of the enlightenment figures, the combination of a strong pull toward God and fundamental morality attracted Lichtenstein to these Christian Humanists. By no means, however, did this attraction undermine his primary commitment to Orthodox Jewish principles of faith, religious practice, and sacred study. On the contrary, according to sociologist of religion Shlomo Fischer, the distinctive position that Lichtenstein advanced was that:

> Jewish particularistic spiritual goals and achievements rest upon universalistic spiritual, cultural and religious achievements: morality, rationality, perfection of character, respect and manners, human sensitivity and understanding, aesthetic sensibility. . . . To the extent that the Jew is more moral, more rational, and the more sensitive and understanding of universal human issues, to that extent, his piety and fear of heaven, his Torah study, the performance of the ethical commandments and his prayer will be richer, deeper and bring him closer to God.[81]

This inclination toward Christian Humanism and alienation from enlightenment skepticism contributes to a more profound grasp of Lichtenstein's approach to nonobservant and non-Orthodox Jews on two levels. For one, as seen above, although Lichtenstein presented a relatively inclusive approach to all Jews, he displayed a more natural connection to religiously oriented Jews, regardless of their denominational affiliation or observance, than to avowedly secular or nationalist atheists. The former, while mistaken in their theological conceptualizations, were fellow partners in the quest for a genuine relationship with the Divine, whereas the atheists pulled themselves out of this sojourn. This bearing stands in contrast to the more common position within Israeli Orthodoxy that secularism is to a certain degree more "neutral"—especially its Zionist formulations—than the "heretical" interpretations of the Reform, for example.[82] Indeed, as Fischer notes, Lichtenstein even raised the prospect that he might feel closer to a non-Jewish religious figure than to a decidedly secularist Jew. Although Lichtenstein rejected this possibility unambiguously and made clear that his bond with other Jews was not predicated exclusively on "spiritual affinity" but also on "physical kinship," the very fact that he theorized about this conflict is telling.[83]

Beyond his affirmation of a minimalist familial "fate" relationship between all Jews, recall that in numerous instances Lichtenstein averred that secular Jews possess vitally positive attributes that are reflected among others in their ethical foundations, creativity, and aesthetic sensibilities. Such a position illustrates a more fundamental symmetry between Lichtenstein's admiration for humanism originating in Gentile spheres and his relationship to Jewish "others." In the same way that Lichtenstein appreciated the unique contributions of non-Jews to the moral and spiritual world without endorsing their entire outlooks, so too he came to regard his Jewish counterparts in a similar way. Like the Christians, for Lichtenstein the non-Orthodox and nonobservant were flawed in their religious understandings and lifestyles. In fact, their defects were far more evident than in the articulations of the Hazon Ish and Kook. The latter two suspended responsibility of the nonobservant for their deviant actions and opinions, and Kook added to this a mystical perception that outward aberrant behaviors conceal a faithful nucleus. Lichtenstein, in contrast, declared unabashedly that these Jewish brethren were downright wrong. He asserted, nonetheless, that this response reflected greater respect for them than the quasi-Lockean tolerance of his predecessors. For Lichtenstein's primary concern or intuition was not to provide halakhic dispensations for people who had made conscious choices. Rather, as in the case of the Christian Humanists, Lichtenstein's focus was on isolating the positive "fragments" that they possessed. The core dynamic of his relationship to all "others" was founded on the inimitable essentials that were manifest in each of them.

Lichtenstein's efforts to ascertain and internalize the positive fragments in others went far beyond strict adherence to the rabbinic maxim "to judge every person favorably" (*Avot* 1:6). These stemmed from his own "self-understanding" of Orthodox Judaism and, for that matter, the human condition in contrast to the perfect God. Put succinctly, his ability to find meaning in the fragmentary was predicated on his rejection of the very concept of "wholeness" or totality within the context of humanity, including the religious tradition to which he was fully committed. This is a core theme that can be identified early on in his writings, but the practical manifestations of this perception played out and evolved over the course of his career, as bookended by the first journal essay he published on a Jewish subject ("Brother Daniel") after returning to YU from Harvard and the 2011 book based on interviews with Sabato.

In 1961 Lichtenstein penned an article, "A Consideration of General Studies from a Torah Point of View," which appeared in the official YU student newspaper, *The Commentator*. In his promotion of the religious legitimacy of studying non-Jewish sources, he lauded the "wisdom of the Gentiles" and described it as "truth." Moreover, Lichtenstein declared that it was imperative for Jews to become familiar with this enterprise, since there are abundant spheres in which the Jewish catalogue is wanting and must build upon the superior non-Jewish creations:

> Nor should we be deterred by the illusion that we can find all we need within our own tradition . . . in many areas, much of the best is of foreign origin . . . to deny that many fields have been better cultivated by non-Jewish rather than Jewish writers is to be stubbornly—unnecessarily—chauvinistic. There is nothing in our medieval poetry to rival Dante and nothing in our modern literature to compare to Kant, and we would do well to admit it. We have our own genius, and we have bent it to the

noblest of pursuits, the development of Torah. But we cannot be expected to do everything.[84]

It is notable that in this passage he did not limit the non-Jewish canon to his seventeenth-century English champions. Together with extolling the illustrious medieval Italian poet and the weighty German liberal thinker, earlier in the same paragraph he speaks of the "ethical idealism of Plato, the passionate fervor of Augustine . . . the visionary grandeur of Milton . . . the lucidity of Aristotle . . . the profundity of Shakespeare . . . the incisiveness of Newman."[85] No doubt Lichtenstein's utmost reverence was reserved for Christian Humanists like Milton and Shakespeare, and their nineteenth-century heir Cardinal Newman.[86] But his capacity to acknowledge the fragmentary—as independently valuable and as a source for advancing imperfect Jewish spiritual endeavors—facilitated his underscoring of the splendor generated even by those such as Augustine, whose influence on Judaism is usually attributed more directly to his "eternal witness" theology, which sustained historic Christian discrimination against Jews for centuries.[87]

On the other chronological pole, Lichtenstein's allegiance to the fragmentary was most clearly articulated in his conversations with Sabato that were published exactly fifty years after his *Commentator* essay. Lichtenstein's fundamental critique of both Kook and the Hazon Ish was for their "totalistic" approach to nonobservant Jews; he declared that recognizing the value of things that are partial or fragmentary was the proper "Jewish-ethical-religious position"; and his vital instruction to his students going into the rabbinate was to "appreciate fragmentary things."

Finally, the manner in which Lichtenstein addressed two seemingly typological deviant "others" from an Orthodox Jewish point of view—apostates and self-identified active homosexuals—also exemplifies the nontotalistic attention to the fragmentary that marked his general orientation, and particularly his approach to "others." In his 1963 discussion of the implications of the "Brother Daniel" case, Lichtenstein argued fervently that ritual apostasy places an individual beyond the boundary of the "Jewish fraternity." All the same, he drew attention to the fragmentary by acknowledging distinctions between types of converts to another religion:

Of course, we should not make the mistake of equating all apostates. There are converts, and there are converts. The Russian student who adopted Christianity in order to gain admission to a university but who remained, as far as he could, socially and emotionally, a Jew is one thing; the social climber who kicks over the traces to enter Christian society with a vengeance is something else entirely. And a monk, fully absorbed in the mainstream monastic order, represents still a further departure. Between a Heine and a Disraeli there lies an immense gap; and between Disraeli and Pablo Christiani still another gap.[88]

All of these figures traversed a crucial border. Even so, at least in some cases, Lichtenstein was still able to discern fragments of Jewish identity. Once again, a half-century later, in his 2013 discussion of homosexuals, Lichtenstein was adamant in acknowledging the halakhic impropriety of their intimate behavior. Yet he protested vehemently against the totalistic inclination of many authorities to define a fellow Jew wholly through this one type of sin.

The Purim evening talk in 1984 described at the outset exemplified presentations Lichtenstein communicated to his YHE students for over forty years. He put forward his perception of a range of Jewish "others" from his Orthodox Jewish vantage point throughout his adult life. His fragmentary view, which dismisses totalistic definitions and focuses on positive elements without losing sight of foundational disagreements, is sui generis and does not follow directly from any of the predominant approaches within twentieth-century Orthodoxy. As he emphasized toward the end of his life, he was quite intentional about passing these ideas on: "if you think of becoming a rabbi, go to the rabbinate with a recognition and appreciation of fragmentary things." His disciples, in turn, internalized these positions and recalibrated them through their local Israeli eyes and then communicated them further through their own formal and informal rabbinic, educational, public, communal, and familial roles.

The following chapters will offer evidence and analysis that highlight ways that Lichtenstein's 1971 arrival in Israel, alongside those of his cohorts, played a crucial role in the rise and increasing impact of IsMO within the Israeli religious landscape.

5

Demonization and the Alternatives

Reform Judaism and the Religious Zionist Rabbinate

A key perception of Emile Durkheim, one of the pioneers of modern sociology, is that the identification of certain behaviors or beliefs as prototypically deviant plays a functional role in the coalescence of society.[1] By highlighting the digression, commonalities among the core group are solidified.[2] Expanding on this theory, Kai Erikson wrote, "The deviant is a person whose activities have moved outside the margins of the group, and when the community calls him to account for that vagrancy it is making a statement about the nature and placement of its boundaries. It is declaring how much variability and diversity can be tolerated within the group before it begins to lose its distinctive shape, its unique identity."[3] If Durkheim called attention to the usefulness of deviance in group building and the need for it to make regular appearances, Erikson came closer to saying that societies often actually look for opportunities to utilize deviance in this manner.[4] Both their works suggest that it is simply easier to define what one is not than it is to articulate an identity in clear, positive terms. By labeling certain people as "outsiders," the rest understand who belongs to the group. That said, Erikson added that deviance is a dynamic category and that, at different stages in the history of a collective or subgroup, activities or ideals once determined to be paradigmatically digressive may be deemed less onerous than in the past.

Building on Durkheim's approach, the late scholar of modern Jewish religious life and thought and my dear friend, David Ellenson, examined a selection of nineteenth-century German Orthodox rabbis who themselves were secularly educated and had adopted a positive attitude toward many aspects of modern culture.[5] Nonetheless, they were adamant in defining certain theological doctrines as well as aesthetic and ritual changes that were adopted by nineteenth-century German Reform as beyond the boundary of authentic Judaism. This they did despite the availability of lenient precedents that permitted such adjustments. Indeed, it was only once these behaviors or attitudes were associated with Reform that they took on symbolic meaning as declarations of departure from accepted religious tenets. Thus, for example, numerous individual premodern synagogues had organs, but after this innovation was adopted universally by Reform it became emblematic of a more fundamental ideological digression from accepted tradition. By highlighting the responses of moderate figures who were open to other aspects of contemporary culture, Ellenson demonstrated that the issues they chose to forbid in their boundary-defining rulings solidified their own association with the broader Orthodox camp, including those who rejected all aspects of modernity.[6]

The Reform movement has made notable but relatively limited inroads into Israeli religious life, and few Israelis are familiar with the details of its worldview. All the same, the label "Reform" is drafted consistently within Orthodox discourse as a tool for demonizing ideological opponents and rendering them outside the margin of normative religious life. Israeli RZ rabbis and organizations have utilized attacks against Reform representatives to solidify their own place within the Orthodox spectrum, while there have been episodes of internal debate within the RZ camp in which the conservative Merkaz ha-Rav/Harda"l ranks have attacked their moderate compatriots. The main claim of the critics is that the religious legal policies and educational approaches of the moderates share much in common with those of the nineteenth-century Reformers. By raising this analogy, the contemporary polemicists distinguish themselves from their colleagues while simultaneously diminishing the distinctions between their own conservative RZ approach and that of the non-Zionist Haredi rabbinate.

Initially, the Israeli RZ moderates themselves labored to show how they differed from the Reform by following the pattern of demonization of the latter. Over time, voices arose that expressed increased appreciation for the positive characteristics of their Reform counterparts. Less foreseeable, a renowned "blue blood" product of the Merkaz ha-Rav-dominant RZ approach has also demonstrated greater openness toward dialogue with Reform figures. While the majority of this camp remains deeply rooted in the demonization outlook, this admittedly lone figure raises the specter of a greater diversity of approaches within his stream as well moving forward.

Historical Precedent

Rabbi Moses Sofer (1762–1839), the Hatam Sofer, was one of the most vociferous opponents of the Reform movement during its initial rise in early nineteenth-century Central Europe.[7] In an 1819 letter, which upon its posthumous publication achieved almost canonic status among Sofer's students and followers,[8] he articulated a sharply adversarial approach to Reform that resonated in much of the subsequent Orthodox discourse on the topic: "If we had the power over them, my opinion would be to separate them from us, we should not give our daughters to their sons and their sons should not be accepted for our daughters so as not to be drawn after them. Their sect should be considered like those of Zadok and Boethus, Anan and Saul, they among themselves and we among ourselves."[9] From Sofer's perspective, Reform was the archenemy of "authentic Judaism." It was a direct threat to the majority of Jews in his day who were still allegiant to observance of the halakhah and traditional customs. Therefore, he sought to delegitimize his contemporary foes by equating them with well-known prior examples of heretical groups. This, in turn, he hoped would dissuade the majority of Jews from associating with the Reformers and adopting their ideology and religious behavior.[10]

Whereas the neo-Orthodox Rabbi Samson Raphael Hirsch (1808–1888) articulated a decidedly more positive attitude toward modern culture than did Sofer, so far as Reform was concerned, his opposition was equally strident. Hirsch never actually proposed prohibiting marriage with Reform Jews, but according to a follower, when the rabbi's strongest financial supporter requested that he perform such a ceremony for his daughter, Hirsch refused.[11] In fact, Ellenson and historian Michael Silber have each demonstrated that in subsequent generations, especially in Hungary, the terms "Reform" and "Reformer" took on an additional role within Orthodoxy. This nomenclature became the designated accusation rendered by zealous voices within internal Orthodox polemics against more moderate Orthodox forces.[12]

Moving to the Western Hemisphere, by the turn of the twentieth century Reform Judaism had established itself as the religion of America's Jewish elite, most of them of Central European origin. Some cooperation did exist between Reform and the predominantly Eastern European Orthodox leaders regarding social welfare and personal freedom issues, insofar as religious affairs and theology were concerned, the gulf between the streams only widened.[13]

Although the idea of an official split has found some outspoken Orthodox proponents, predictions that such a policy would become the majority opinion within American Orthodoxy have not come to fruition during the first decades of the twenty-first century. It would appear that the differences between the two denominations have become so clear that the Orthodox have been relieved of the need to aggressively assert distinctions.[14] In parallel, efforts within Reform to reengage aspects of tradition, combined with American Orthodoxy's increased self-assurance, have actually engendered less confrontational environments for certain types of Orthodox-Reform interactions.[15]

No doubt, instances of direct debates between American Orthodoxy and Reform still persist, especially regarding the status of non-Orthodox conversions. Yet the more likely contemporary polemical scenario is the vituperative application of the "Reform" appellation by Orthodox traditionalists to those within their own stream who promote more liberal ideas and interpretations. Thus, in 2003 a prominent YU Talmudic authority described supporters of Orthodox feminism as following in the path of a series of historical heresies, including the Sadducees, early Christianity, and Reform Judaism.[16]

Reform in Israel and the Israeli Orthodox Rabbinate

Unlike in the United States, since the founding of the state in 1948 Jewish religious life in Israel has been dominated by Orthodoxy.[17] In parallel, the new spirit of nonconfrontation of American Jewish denominational relations has not arrived in Israel. As we have seen, Lichtenstein's approach opens up alternative possibilities, but for the most part, open animus has actually grown since the 1990s in parallel to the modest expansion of the Israeli Conservative and Reform movements.

With the exception of mostly ephemeral efforts by German Jews during the 1930s, the first Israeli Reform and Conservative congregations can date their founding back to the 1950s and 1960s, and both groups began to sprout branches in larger numbers after 1967.[18] But these were almost exclusively to be found among English-speaking immigrants who sought to transfer their familiar religious lifestyles to Israeli soil and generally maintained their distance from mainstream Israeli religious politics.[19]

From the late 1980s the Israeli Conservative (*Masorti*) and Reform (*Yahadut Mitkademet*) movements experienced more substantial growth. In addition to the emergence of congregational branches with sizeable Israeli-born contingents, their Jerusalem-based institutions of higher learning drew locals to their various study programs, including their rabbinical training seminaries. By the twenty-first century these movements were increasingly led by native Israelis or figures who had spent their formative years in Israel.[20] Non-Orthodox rabbis and institutions are not recognized by the state rabbinical bureaucracy, but a rising number of Israelis have chosen to forego official sanction in order to celebrate religious lifecycle events in liberal synagogues and invite Reform and Conservative rabbis to perform their weddings.[21] Yet even as liberal Jewish denominations have gained a modest foothold within Israeli society, for the foreseeable future Orthodoxy will remain the exclusive option for most Israeli Jews.

Nonetheless, from the perspective of the state Orthodox rabbinate, the increased prominence of the Reform and Conservative movements has raised concerns. These have appeared both as a result of Orthodox ideological animosity and because the new options are among the factors that have led to an overall decline in the numbers of people who make use of state-sponsored religious services. Expressions of anxiety on the part of the state rabbinate can be identified from time to time in scathing public statements and in ongoing efforts to prevent non-Orthodox denominations from receiving state funding or from having their representatives sit on local religious councils.[22]

The most explosive source of friction between Orthodoxy and liberal streams remains issues of Jewish identity and the status of non-Orthodox conversions. Regarding Reform or Conservative conversions performed in Israel or abroad, there is no Orthodox debate. All contemporary Orthodox authorities in Israel and throughout the globe reject them.[23]

That being said, to a far greater extent than vis-à-vis Reform, the major battle of the state rabbinate is actually with the non-state-employed Orthodox RZ rabbinate. In this conflict, however, the existence of liberal denominations actually plays a useful role for both parties. In as far as direct challenges to the official rabbinate's domination, the non-state Orthodox rabbinate has been represented most prominently since the mid-1990s by the Tzohar organization, which succeeded in drafting a relatively wide coalition of hundreds of RZ rabbis. Its original goal was to provide free rabbinical services to the broader Israeli population in a more sensitive and attractive way than the official rabbinate—particularly weddings. It has since branched out into the area of kosher supervision.[24] Subsequently, the religious leadership organization Beit Hillel created an additional independent framework to address issues not within the consensus of the Tzohar "big tent."[25]

Unlike the liberal denominations, Tzohar and Beit Hillel's representatives are Orthodox and do not perform weddings without the official approval of the state rabbinate. As Rabbi Yuval Cherlow, an outspoken figure in the IsMO rabbinate and one of the founders of Tzohar, opined in 2005, "As far as I am concerned . . . we are trying to change the rabbinate from within."[26]

Not surprisingly, then, the state rabbinate has long viewed these "upstart" organizations as a serious challenge to its hegemony and has used its leverage as the arbiter of who is sanctioned to perform weddings as a tool for neutralizing independent rabbis. Yet the rabbinate is reluctant to acknowledge that these stricter policies are aimed at Orthodox figures. Rather, the claim is that these measures were enacted to prevent non-Orthodox rabbis from slipping through the cracks and succeeding in gaining halakhic recognition.[27] The unspoken implication is that all liberal rabbis who challenge the state rabbinate's hegemony—be they Reform and Conservative or Orthodox ones—should be subject to intense skepticism. Thus, the existence of non-Orthodox denominations is useful to the state rabbinate, this time in its struggle with its internal Orthodox competitors.

Initially, the Tzohar rabbis acknowledged the potential minefield resulting from their association with liberal non-Orthodox groups and made a point of taking sharp stands against liberal denominations as a way to clarify the great degree to which Tzohar differs from them. From this perspective, Cherlow asserted in 2006: "The claims against the Reform are stronger than those against Christianity and Islam. Despite the fact that the believers in the non-Jewish faiths are enemies and idolaters . . . the Reform Jews are impostors."[28] Indeed, in 1999, Cherlow had taken pains to distinguish between Reform and fresh efforts to introduce greater spirituality and creativity into what appeared to many RZ youth as dry and moribund synagogue life. In an article that was printed in a 2000 edition of the journal *Akdamot*, a publication of the moderate Beit Morasha Institute, Cherlow implored: "How is it feasible to distinguish between holy and profane, between the Reform movement that led to the collapse of the connection between Israel and its Father in Heaven and a call for spiritual renaissance. . . . If the faith renewal will be accompanied by efforts to find favor with the multitudes and to translate the Torah of Israel into the colloquial language of contemporary Israeli culture, it will turn into the Reform movement."[29]

In the spirit of conflict that continues to define the Israeli environment, Rabbi Gilad Kariv, the former director of the Israeli Reform movement and head of its Israel Religious Action Center and subsequently a Labor Party MK, shot back at Cherlow's invectives: "Tzohar believes if they attack us they will increase their status in extreme national-religious groups. They are mistaken. With all due respect for the good intentions of its leadership, and some of the important things it did, Tzohar is nothing more than packaging for the rabbinic establishment and all of its defects and flaws."[30]

In demonizing Reform, Cherlow was being consistent with time-honored Orthodox approaches. As Ellenson emphasized, by highlighting the distinctions between themselves and the Reform movement, the moderate German-Orthodox figures shored up their own Orthodox credentials and deepened their connections to their traditionalist colleagues."[31]

Notwithstanding Cherlow's own early efforts to highlight Reform's deviant status in order to strengthen the bonds of the various strands of Israeli Orthodoxy, subsequently the "Reform" heading was drafted by conservative forces within RZ to combat internal moderate initiatives—with Cherlow himself becoming a principal target of these invectives.

One of the most celebrated of such public polemics took place in the spring of 2009. Rabbi Yehoshua Shapira of Yeshivat Ramat Gan announced before a convention of counselors from the Ezra RZ youth movement that a breach had developed that demanded rending one's garment in mourning. Despite numerous troubles, "the most difficult problem in my eyes is the Neo-Reform movement . . . [which] challenges the Godly nature of the Torah and its continuation in the Oral Law of our day. . . . There is growing within us a new Reform movement— this is my opinion—and it has many of the characteristics of the first Reform. . . . The Neo-Reform movement . . . destabilizes the sanctity of the Jewish home and the sanctity of modesty and purity in the nation of Israel."[32]

Shapira is among the most charismatic and popular leaders of RZ's Harda"l sector, which leans toward legal stringency and social conservatism. In 1994 he established a new yeshiva and nurtured a dynamic urban religious community around it by promoting a brand of Orthodoxy that combines meticulous observance, loyalty to the state due to its position as the "beginning of the redemption," and heightened spirituality. His accusations of "neo-reformism" against the liberal ranks reflect his ongoing project of asserting the "normative" character of his more zealous and punctilious brand of RZ. In doing so he also minimized the differences between his religious approach and that of non-Zionist Haredi society.

Another prominent figure who advances a similar outlook is the ubiquitous Rabbi Shlomo Aviner. Along with heading the Yeshivat Ateret Kohanim in Jerusalem's Muslim Quarter and serving for over thirty years as rabbi in the Beit El Alef settlement, he has recorded hundreds of his many lectures and had them transcribed by an industrious staff. The majority have been uploaded to his yeshiva's website. These form the basis for a series of paperbacks that are distributed through bookstores across the country as well as by representatives in various Zionist yeshivot. For many years, he has also provided a text message service that enables people to send him queries from their cell phones and receive almost immediate responses on any matter of halakhah or general conduct for which they desire guidance. The highlights of these "tweet"-like responsa are published in a bulletin that is distributed each Sabbath in hundreds of RZ-oriented synagogues throughout Israel. Like Shapira, Aviner, too, sees merit in assailing the approach of his moderate RZ ideological adversaries from within by describing them as "Reform."

The impetus for Aviner's criticism was the summer Bible study seminars sponsored by YHE's Herzog College, which attract thousands of attendees annually. Indeed, Cherlow and a good percentage of the founders of Beit Hillel are YHE alumni and present regularly at such events. Among YHE's distinctions is that through its teachers' college it has developed and spread an analytical approach to Bible study that utilizes mainly literary but also archeological and historical tools without compromising on commitment to the Divine authorship of the text. This has become known as the *Tanakh be-govah ha-enayim* (the Bible at eye level) school.

The YHE method, argue the Harda"l leaders, undermines the divine holiness of the Tanakh. Furthermore, by exploring the flaws of the Biblical forefathers and foremothers, it minimizes their greatness and, as a result, the power and truth that emerge from their lives. In line with this position, a more doctrinally conservative Bible study seminar was initiated by the Harda"l rabbinate in the summer of 2012—with Aviner a central advocate—as an alternative to the veteran YHE event. In explaining the need for this program, Aviner emphasized that the problem with the existing highly successful framework was that it was essentially aimed at inculcating in its students "humanistic moral values and fitting conduct." It is simply, then, "an old adversary of which we have been eating its rotten fruit for a few hundred years. For is this not the utterance of the Reform movement, which inscribed upon its banner that the essence of Judaism is universal religious principles and that the rest of the commandments and laws are not appropriate for modern society."[33]

Aviner highlighted the intellectual and spiritual degeneracy that results from the liberal Orthodox Israeli camp,[34] while Shapira underscored the sexual decadence condoned by its leniencies. Interestingly, both these critical dissections are empowered by adopting the strategy identified by John Henderson as common to heresiologists in numerous religions, namely associating the new target with an "already defeated heresy."[35] This is not to say that Reform has disappeared, and as discussed above, the inroads it has made in Israeli society have engendered an aggressive atmosphere, just as Orthodox animus against it has dissipated in the United States in recent years. All the same, it is not the contemporary Reform movement that chiefly concerns the Harda"l rabbis. It is, rather, its nineteenth-century forerunners who pioneered a new worldview that wrested the reins from traditionalist authorities and changed the face of Jewish religious life forever—those the Hatam Sofer compared for posterity to Sadducees, Karaites, and Christians.

A New Moderate Tune

We have seen that the decline in direct Orthodox animus toward Reform that has recently characterized contemporary American Judaism has not, for the most part, been felt in the Israeli environment. Most Israelis are ignorant about Reform and rarely distinguish between it and other liberal branches. Whenever attempts to gain state recognition for Reform do arise, the Orthodox are vigilant in their efforts to protect their nearly exclusive position as the arbiters of Israeli Jewish religious life. In parallel, Reform's historic role in Orthodox eyes as the principal symbol of deviation from Jewish tradition in modern times remains viable. It has been employed by moderate figures like Cherlow as a foil through which comparison lends credence to their own moderate worldviews within Orthodoxy. In direct contrast, the Haredi and more conservative Harda"l rabbis such as Shapira and Aviner have raised the specter of Reform as justification for vilifying those exact innovations for which Cherlow and his cohorts seek legitimacy.

In December 2012 the distinctive Israeli and American Orthodox-Reform dynamics gravitated toward greater confluence. Reacting to a trip to the United States during which he met with Jews from across the religious spectrum, Cherlow penned a letter to his yeshiva students that expressed a transformation in his thinking. In light of the rising rates of intermarriage and detachment of American Jews from active Jewish participation, he felt that the State of Israel should take dramatic steps to neutralize those aspects of Israeli life that alienate American Jews and undermine the state's role as an inspiration for strengthening their Jewish connection. The issue about which he delineated a concrete reevaluation is the Orthodox establishment's attitudes and policies toward non-Orthodox movements, including Reform and its followers.

Insofar as technical halakhah is concerned, he encouraged suspension of rules that prohibit cooperation with non-Orthodox movements and leniency regarding inclusion of Reform Jews in prayer quorums. As to the State of Israel, Cherlow recommended differentiating between codified religious legal standards that are unchallengeable and public policy regarding who is welcomed into Israeli society. Thus, the government should recognize non-Orthodox movements, accept their conversions for citizenship purposes, and provide them funds that will facilitate a more "free market" approach to religious involvement.[36] These shifts, he proposed, could neutralize the growing estrangement of many American Jews from Israel.

To the non-Zionist Orthodox, Cherlow's comments simply gave ammunition for condemning him and his Tzohar partners in typical fashion. In the words of Haredi spokesman Dov Halbertal, "Cherlow and his gang, and the Tzohar rabbis organization, are themselves Reform. They are a greater danger to the Jewish people than the Reform movement."[37] More noteworthy, the Tzohar presidium itself rushed to differentiate Cherlow's views from the association's accepted positions, announcing that it "opposes any official recognition of Reform Judaism by the State of Israel, in terms of conversions or its general way."[38] Such efforts, however, did not appear to placate the Harda"l camp, who subsequently refused to support the candidacy of the Tzohar chairman, David Stav, for Ashkenazi chief rabbi. This ultimately paved the way for the 2013 election of Haredi-oriented Rabbi David Lau to the post.[39]

Did Cherlow's pronouncements set into play a more fundamental reassessment within the moderate circles of Israeli Orthodoxy? It is premature to draw any expansive conclusions. Nonetheless, there are incremental manifestations of change that are worthy of acknowledgment. One is the very fact that a leading figure in the moderate wing of RZ moved toward a model of reconciliation that is closer to the postdenominational dynamic prevalent in the United States. This is especially significant since, as has been emphasized, in the past the same personality did not hesitate to denounce Reform. In the interim, in July 2016 Tzohar convened a special meeting of its Rabbinical Board of Governors to learn more about non-Orthodox movements.[40] Furthermore, in 2021 a prominent moderate figure, Rabbi Ronen Lubitz of Kibbutz Nir Etzion, published a 144-page position paper, *Should We Progress with the*

Streams? Orthodox Judaism and Its Approach to New Denominations and Diaspora Jewry, that explores new ways of engaging non-Orthodox Jews and their movements.[41] Indeed, in July 2023 Cherlow expressed sadness that the section of the Western Wall that is available for public prayers of all denominations is used sparingly, and hoped that Reform Jews would be drawn there "to be blessed, to sanctify God's name, to turn to the Wall in prayer, in their way, their dress, and their honor."[42] This was not a call for reevaluating the consensus Orthodox perception of Reform Judaism from a theological and religio-legal perspective, but it expressed a sense of appreciation for their spiritual engagement that is reminiscent of that of his teacher Aharon Lichtenstein.

An Unlikely Voice of Conciliation

Compared to the changes identified in Cherlow's approach to Reform, which can be seen as aligning with his overall moderate positions regarding multiple controversial issues within the Orthodox and RZ world, an affair that took place in the second half of 2020 points to an internal rift within the Harda"l camp itself.

In June 2020, the weekly *Makor Rishon* newspaper—whose main readership reflects a broad RZ spectrum—organized an international conference, "Am Olam" (nation/world), that brought together Jewish public figures from Israel and the Diaspora. Due to the COVID-19 epidemic, instead of regular sessions in front of a live audience, moderated livestream dialogues were held among representatives from around the globe. All the sessions were recorded and made available through *Makor Rishon*'s website and YouTube link.[43] According to Hagai Segal, the newspaper's editor in chief, the purpose of the event was to "consider what needs to be done to bring the Diaspora closer to Israel."[44] The panel that will likely be remembered best was one that highlighted deep internal fissures within the Israeli Orthodox rabbinate.

The title of the session was "Our Common Purpose: We Are Not Afraid of Dialogue," and it featured Rabbi Eliezer Melamed, head of Yeshivat Har Bracha in Samaria (Northern West Bank), and Rabbi Delphine Horvilleur. Horvilleur was ordained by the Hebrew Union College in Cincinnati—America's oldest institution for training Reform rabbis—and is a leader of the Reform movement in France.[45] The moderator was the historian and author Gil Troy, a professor at McGill University in Montreal who now lives in Jerusalem.[46]

At the time the meeting took place, a public controversy arose. RZ rabbis, mainly Harda"l figures, came out harshly against Melamed's decision to meet with a Reform rabbi.[47] Moreover, six months after the conference itself, Rabbi Yitzhak Yosef, the Sephardic chief rabbi, issued a scathing letter condemning Melamed's actions.[48] Yosef even threatened to excommunicate him if he did not express remorse for his actions. Simultaneously, a petition against meeting with Reform representatives was issued with the signatures of twenty-two RZ rabbis. Here too, most of them belong to the Harda"l camp, but there were also figures not identified with any specific faction. It should be noted that the last document did not explicitly state Melamed's name, but it was clear to all concerned that his actions in June were the impetus for its broadcast.[49]

The rabbinical petition set forth what had been the standard RZ position until then, namely, to avoid direct public engagements with representatives of non-Orthodox movements. On the face of it, then, Melamed's willingness to participate in a public panel with a Reform rabbi was a revolutionary move, precipitating the sharp reactions from colleagues who disagreed with his actions and opinions.

Eliezer Melamed may be termed a "blue blood" heir to the Merkaz ha-Rav legacy. His father is Rabbi Zalman Melamed (b. 1937), who studied and then taught at the yeshiva for more than a decade. In 1978, he founded the Beit El Yeshiva and later the Beit El Bet settlement in the Binyamin region (north of Jerusalem across the Green Line), where he served as rabbi. Eliezer Melamed's mother, Shulamit Melamed (b. 1939), is also a key personality in the settler landscape. She is founder and director of the Arutz Sheva media group, which began with a pirate radio station that gained considerable popularity in the 1980s before being shut down by the government. Today the group operates websites in several languages as well as the weekly *Be-Sheva* newspaper, which is distributed for free via synagogues throughout Israel.[50]

The son, Eliezer Melamed (b. 1961), also studied at Merkaz ha-Rav for six years and taught subsequently at his father's Beit El yeshiva as well. During part of that period he was in charge of the Bnei Akiva youth movement activities in the Old City of Jerusalem. There he orchestrated a complete separation between boys and girls, the first of its kind in the history of the organization. After this change was rejected by the movement's national leaders, he resigned and became founding secretary-general of a new RZ youth association named Ariel, which adopted the strict religious policies advocated by the Harda"l faction. Subsequently he served as secretary of the Rabbinical Council of Judea and Samaria and was very active in opposing the Oslo Accords. He was even suspected of penning a letter that explored interpretations later put into violent practice by Yigal Amir, Israeli prime minister Yitzhak Rabin's assassin in November 1995. Amir justified his actions as necessary from a religious standpoint in order to put a stop to the actions of the man responsible for the concessions made in the Oslo Accords with the Palestinians.[51]

In 1996, Melamed moved with his family to the Har Bracha settlement, which overlooks the city of Nablus. Like his father, he developed a yeshiva as well as a community around it, but he was especially intentional in predicating the settlement on graduates devoted to his religious and educational worldview. During Israel's disengagement from the Gaza Strip in 2005, he ruled that soldiers should refuse orders to evacuate settlements. In response, his institution's status as a Hesder yeshiva that combines army service with study and is entitled to government funding was suspended. Only after his temporary resignation did the Ministry of Defense agree to return the yeshiva to its former standing. Thus, not only does he stem from Merkaz ha-Rav royalty, his early career located him squarely in the more zealous camp.

In parallel, since 2002 his authority throughout the RZ spectrum broadened considerably due to his popular and highly regarded series of religio-legal tomes, *Peninei Halakhah* (Pearls of Jewish Law).[52] The books began as a weekly column on halakhic matters up to date with the realities of the twenty-first century and Israeli life. They are used, in fact, as basic texts in the state religious education system and have become a ubiquitous bar mitzvah/bat mitzvah gift as well. By 2024, twenty volumes had appeared, and over five hundred thousand copies had been sold, including translations into English, Russian, Spanish and French. In light of his accomplishments, Melamed has won several prestigious awards for authorship of Torah literature.[53] Unsurprisingly, until the events of 2020, he was considered the RZ candidate with the greatest chances of being elected Ashkenazi chief rabbi, after three decades in which the position was held by Haredi figures.[54]

Melamed's June 2020 participation alongside a Reform rabbi at a conference broadcast worldwide, therefore, greatly challenged the rabbis who graduated from Merkaz ha-Rav and its splinter institutions, and especially those who espouse a distinctly Harda"l outlook. According to Rabbi Yehoshua Van Dyck, head of the Itamar yeshiva and rabbi of Ramat Magshimim in the Golan Heights, Melamed crossed a red line for anyone considered an Orthodox rabbi: "a consensus existed from the ultra-Orthodox to the most liberal Orthodox . . . to refuse any public meeting with Reform. . . . The Reform movement injures the Torah and the nation of Israel, it is a movement that has caused assimilation, that tried to undermine the centrality of Zion and Jerusalem, that accepted non-Jews [through patrilineal descent]. . . . I studied at the Merkaz ha-Rav yeshiva; this was not the way of its leaders."[55] Rabbi Dror Arie, one of the main activists in the Harda"l/Kav–oriented Noam political movement, was even more adamant when he described the June event as "Melamed's cooperation with the Reformers who are fighting and fought the Torah and Zionism."[56]

In his excellent biographical essay on Melamed published in June 2020, journalist and researcher Yair Sheleg asserted that, along with his deep roots within Merkaz ha-Rav and settler circles, Melamed is an independent figure with a rich track record for trusting his own discretion without feeling obligated to the "party line." Sheleg noted, among others, the warm relationship that was formed between Melamed and Benny Lau. Lau, recall, is a YHE alumnus and leading IsMO figure, and he is also the founder of Project 929, which promotes the study of a daily chapter of the Bible based on the model of the "daf yomi" daily page in the Gemara and tries to unite Jews of all shades of the ideological spectrum around this goal. Sheleg also described the active participation of Melamed and his wife, Inbal, in a series of meetings between rabbis and academics organized by the Israel Democracy Institute. He mentioned as well Melamed's coming to the defense of Shlomo (Steven) Riskin when the chief rabbinate threatened to strip him of his authority to serve as the rabbi of Efrat.[57]

All the same, the harsh attacks against Melamed, and especially the flare-up of the affair six months later, demonstrate that while his autonomous style was known, Israeli Orthodox rabbis could not or did not want to ignore his virtual engagement with the female Reform rabbi from Paris. What in this event caused the Sephardic chief rabbi to return to it about six months after its occurrence and threaten a boycott against Melamed? And what led to the simultaneous publication of a protest letter signed by twenty-two senior RZ rabbis?

A number of commentators saw the late November 2020 attacks on Melamed as the prelude to the struggle for the post of Ashkenazi chief rabbi set to be vacated about a year and a half later. Casting Melamed as a Reformer sympathizer, then, was an indirect way of eliminating his future candidacy.[58] Melamed himself backed up this understanding by making sure to announce afterward that he had no interest in the position. Others pointed to the letter by the Haredi-oriented Yosef as a way to assert his power over the RZ rabbinate.[59]

What seems most clear is that the central impetus was not any real fear that Melamed's meeting would lead to a substantial expansion of Reform Judaism's role in Israel. Rather, as we have seen, despite its relatively "boutique" position in day-to-day Israeli religious life, within RZ internal discourse the Reform has retained its historic status as the symbol of deviation. Thus, any interface with Reform invites the opponents of the moderate wing of RZ to raise this accusation as a black flag that delegitimizes the entire religious ideology of their internal disputants. By acting independently, Melamed, so to speak, went over to the other side of the RZ spectrum. Indeed, this fear that one of their own was gravitating toward perceptions more readily associated with Lichtenstein, Riskin, Benny Lau, and Cherlow, was only buttressed by Melamed's own clear response to his RZ detractors:

> I was amazed to see that in light of the bitter debates with the Reform and Conservative positions, a mistaken opinion developed that the Reform communities and their representatives should be boycotted. When I looked further, I found that there is a campaign of intimidation against those who think that they should not be boycotted. Therefore, although I almost always . . . refrain from participating in meetings and conferences, I made a decision in my heart: the next time I am invited to a meeting with Reform or Conservatives—I will come . . . I did not happen to be there by chance, but with the express intention and the clear sacred duty to maintain good relations among all Jews and their communities.[60]

Melamed did not deny the deep theological gaps between him and his Reform interlocutor and did not underestimate their significance, but in additional comments emphasized the social and national aspects where, in his opinion, there is room for fruitful discussion and perhaps also possibilities for practical cooperation. As he explained: "If we want to strengthen mutual bonds between the parts of our people, representatives of the various communities must meet in friendship and respect . . . regarding Reform and Conservative Jews, after we initially conducted an uncompromising debate with them, we are commanded to look for ways to express brotherhood and our shared destiny, and even learn from all the good in them and their positions . . . the side of drawing closer and love must be stronger than that of argumentation and distancing."[61]

In an effort to delve deeper into the background for the sharp criticism of Melamed, perspectives from gender studies offer a useful analytical tool.

"It's About Gender . . ."

As the critiques of Melamed cited above attest, emphasis was placed on the Reformers as destroyers of religious faith and commitment both past and present, and their responsibility for the assimilation of many Jews. This stance is consistent with the dominant trope regarding Reform in Orthodox internal discourse. But there is an additional element: an influential settler religious figure with an immaculate Merkaz ha-Rav pedigree, and a personal reputation as a pioneer in advancing strict separation between boys and girls within the RZ sphere, met publicly for close to an hour with a woman who today serves as a prominent rabbi in Paris and as an outspoken official leader of the Reform movement in France.

The visual of the event reinforces the sense of an encounter between opposites who nonetheless share something essential in common; a man of close to sixty with a long white beard, wearing the black hat and coat of a rabbinical court judge, appears on the screen adjacent to a woman in her forties with no head covering and dressed in stylish contemporary attire. Yet under both pictures the names are preceded by the title "Rabbi." In fact, the term *Rabbah* that appears in Hebrew further emphasizes the femininity of the French clergyperson. One might surmise that the actual location of each participant—in their respective homes, rather than in the same physical space—would have neutralized the "togetherness" of the event. Perhaps one could even claim that this formally circumvented Orthodox restrictions on public meetings with Reform leaders. On an experiential level, nonetheless, the appearance of just the two of them together with the host "in the livestream room" on screen created a very personal and convivial atmosphere.[62] Despite some obvious disagreements, the conversation itself was conducted with absolute courteousness, even warmth, with a clear sense of mutual respect and an evident desire to learn from each other. In fact, during the discussion it became clear that Melamed and Horvilleur had met previously, during their participation in a conference on world Jewry that took place in Jerusalem in September 2019 under the auspices of the president of the State of Israel.[63]

Melamed's offense, then, was twofold: giving public legitimacy to official representatives of Reform and, perhaps far worse, giving recognition to a woman rabbi. As the first is unlikely to threaten Israeli Orthodoxy in a fundamental way, it is the latter that emerges as the central concern and motivation for his antagonists. This view is reinforced by the fact that gender-related issues are at the center of controversies between the Harda"l/Kav factions and the moderate wing within RZ, most notably concerning issues surrounding female religious leadership and ordination or certification, the status of LGBTs within the Orthodox community, and service of RZ women in the IDF.[64]

To be sure, the crucial role of gender in the Melamed controversy was not stated explicitly by any of the parties involved. Yet a close reading of the public statement signed by twenty-two RZ rabbis against meetings with representatives of the Reform offers persuasive, if not unequivocal, substantiation of this interpretation. The petition cites several verses from the Book of Proverbs to reinforce the gravity of the offense. Notably, these are not Biblical sentences usually found in similar polemical texts:

Regarding such things did Solomon warn in his wisdom: "My son, keep the commandment of thy father, and forsake not the teaching of thy mother. . . . To keep thee from the evil woman, from the smoothness of the alien tongue. . . . Remove thy way far from her, and come not nigh the door of her house." (Proverbs 6, 20–24; 5, 8)

No doubt, these verses can be understood as pointing to a contradiction with fealty to tradition—"the commandment of thy father" and "the teaching of thy mother"—that is expressed according to the signatories by holding meetings with a representative of the Reform movement—"the evil woman" with "alien tongue." But in light of the personalities involved and the contextual backdrop, it is equally reasonable to explicate "the commandment of thy father" and "the teaching of they mother" as alluding to Melamed's parents, both of whom excel in God's laws and Torah. Moreover, the focus on "the evil woman" with an "alien tongue" leads the reader directly to a dangerous French-speaking female. Indeed, the "polysemic" possibilities of these words only buttress the impudence of Melamed's public display.

Conclusion

On March 1, 2021, a ruling of the Israeli Supreme Court was published stating that non-Orthodox converts meet the conditions for immigration under the Law of Return. The reactions from the Orthodox side came quickly. They ranged from extremely harsh attacks to a certain understanding and attempts to explain why the decision does not significantly harm religious values and the status of Jewish law in the State of Israel. Beyond the differences of opinion, a common point emerges that once again illustrates that in the eyes of Orthodox speakers, the issue of the Reform movement and its penetration into Israeli life is marginal in comparison to the function of "anxiety regarding Reform and Reformers" as a way to posture in relation to internal Orthodox debates.

Within two days of the ruling being announced, the Ashkenazi Haredi Yahadut ha-Torah party released an advertisement mocking an American Reform Jewish family that celebrated their dog's bar mitzvah under the title "Bark Mitzvah." All the same, the text attests, the real danger is not the Reformers but the High Court itself: "At the High Court—he's Jewish, and he's also Jewish, and his grandmother was a rabbi, of course he's Jewish. . . . Only Torah Judaism will protect your Judaism and that of your children and your grandchildren."[65] The Sephardic Haredi Shas party also chose to attack, but instead of purely belittling the Reformers, they aimed to stir up the xenophobic and racist feelings of some of the

Israeli public, warning that the High Court's ruling would result in illegal infiltrators from Africa also being able to convert easily.[66]

These reactions echo the trends of demonizing Reform that dominated Orthodox circles throughout the previous two centuries and
stand in contrast to the more conciliatory direction that has developed
in the United States in recent decades. It would appear that the timing
of the publication of the Supreme Court ruling—about a month before
the Knesset elections in April 2021—was the main motive for the con-
demnations. The Haredi parties took advantage of the opportunity to
sharpen their messages with the help of the "satanic symbol" of Reform.

In parallel to the ad campaign, the Hotam movement, which promotes Harda"l positions and especially the defense of traditional family
values from the threats of liberalism, feminism, and LGBTQI, organized a conference that dealt with "changes led by the Reform movement in the State of Israel against the background of the High Court
Ruling." Hotam invited Yehoshua Shapira of Yeshivat Ramat Gan to
be one of the main speakers. He declared that "the Reform movement
invented another, alternative religion, and in this it is much more dangerous than the secular world . . . worse, this attack on Judaism re-
ceives legitimacy from within the religious and Torah world."[67] Shapira
certainly strongly opposes any step that promotes the position of the
Reform movement in Israel, but as demonstrated above in his polemic
regarding the "neo-Reformers," his more focused goal is to critique the
moderate RZ camp.

On the other hand, while Yuval Cherlow and his RZ cohorts insisted
that a secular court does not have the authority to determine the Jewish
legal status of converts, he expressed understanding of the need for the
state to define who is a Jew with regard to the citizenship of immigrants
and their rights. Moreover, he did not attack the Reformers; rather, he
indicated that the Orthodox themselves bear primary responsibility for
the situation in which they have found themselves. Were they to adopt
a more flexible conversion approach, they would be able to extricate
themselves from the conflict with the courts: "If we are wise enough to
open the gates . . . to conversion . . . it is possible that 'from this bitter-
ness, sweetness shall emerge' . . . the Jewish identity of the people of Israel will be strengthened precisely by the 'free market.'"[68] This statement

exemplifies the widening gap that separates Cherlow's IsMO cohort, and pointedly Melamed as well, from the Harda"l camp. It is significant that along with the dominant tenor of demonization, among the RZ rabbis there are those who refuse to boycott the Reformers and even those who show a certain interest in conducting a discourse of mutual respect.

6

Biblical Scholarship and Orthodox Judaism

Between Israel and North America

Contemporary Orthodox rabbis and educators have evinced an increasing degree of acceptance of critical approaches to the Hebrew Bible, including the possibility of multiple authorship.[1] This abandonment of axiomatic theological positions raises broader historical insights that deepen appreciation for the Israeli context of contemporary Orthodox Biblical scholarship and the evolution of IsMO and the role of American immigrants in its development.

The first academic figure to focus on this subject extensively was religion scholar Marc Shapiro, an expert in Jewish law and thought who collected considerable documentation and presented his findings in a rich and meticulously researched article that appeared in 2017.[2] A rigorous chronicler of the theological spectrum of Orthodox Judaism, he posited that this shift toward embracing a critical approach, even to a small degree, was striking, since "[f]or centuries now, traditional Jewish thinkers . . . have regarded as heresy any assertion that portions of the Torah were written at different times by different people."[3] This chapter builds on Shapiro's findings, examining how they play out when considered through the comparative contexts of Jewish life in Israel and the United States.

From Deviation to Mainstream

In 1961, the "Jacobs Affair" created a deep rift within British Jewry's Orthodox United Synagogue organization. Renowned scholar Rabbi Dr. Louis Jacobs was denied the prestigious appointment of head of Jews' College due to his publications in which he contested traditional understandings of the Divine authorship of the Torah. Jacobs eventually left the Jews' College faculty and also disaffiliated from the United

Synagogue, setting up an independent synagogue outside the Orthodox orbit and soon becoming the spiritual leader of England's *Masorti*
movement.[4]

As we saw earlier, five years later, in 1966, a wide-ranging interview
with YU professor Irving "Yitz" Greenberg was published in *The Commentator*, the undergraduate weekly. Greenberg called out MO's flagship institution for its overall unwillingness to confront the intellectual
challenges of the era. One of his core examples was the lack of serious
engagement with the methods and conclusions of modern Biblical criticism. He, therefore, advocated the training of Orthodox experts in this
field. Their entrance into the YU classroom, he contended, was not simply to provide the students with alternatives to the heretical notions arising from the academy. Rather, he sought a synthesis that would admit
the positive and illuminating perceptions of the critics, without eliminating faith in God from the picture: "We should acknowledge a debt
to Bible critics. They have shown that the Torah is not toneless but has
elements in common with the temporal experience of the ancient Near
East. . . . We need to understand Biblical scholarship in order to more
fully understand our own revelation." He indicated further that there is a
broader spectrum of theologically tenable definitions of revelation than
most assume: "what we mean by 'Divine revelation' may be less external
or mechanical than many Jews now think."[5]

In a follow-up letter that was published two weeks later, Greenberg
clarified that he absolutely did not identify with the "liberal" Jewish acceptance of modern scholarship's conclusion, "that Torah is merely the
product of humans."[6] He explained, furthermore, that his comment regarding revelation simply meant that the Torah was received by Moses,
"in a particular time and setting and its images and conceptual material
may be expressed in that language and cultural context."[7] That said, he
reiterated his prior assertion that, despite its secular humanistic bias,
"contemporary Biblical scholarship has enriched our understanding
of the meaning of the *Tanach* [sic],"[8] and that he "anticipates an even
greater enrichment when we develop our own Biblical scholarship by
men who believe that God communicates with man, but who will not
work from an apologetic or stereotyped image."[9] Greenberg expressed
confidence that these efforts would not facilitate the infiltration of heresy into Orthodoxy: "I believe that we can be disciplined enough to

reject conclusions that do not meet our test of validity, when and if, this becomes necessary."[10]

Such reassurances did not assuage the concerns of his critics, including his colleague Aharon Lichtenstein, who penned a sharp rebuke of the content of the interview—including the remarks connected to Biblical studies.[11] Within a few years Greenberg himself drew the irrevocable conclusion that YU was not the place where his intellectual and ideological vision would come to fruition. While he continued to identify as an Orthodox rabbi, he shifted much of his professional focus away from the Modern Orthodox orbit.

No doubt, the British and American controversies of the 1960s each reflected the particularities of their respective local contexts and characters. Yet they also shared common themes, prominent among them being the central role played by Orthodox antagonism toward Biblical criticism. In point of fact, both Jacobs and Greenberg found that there was no room within 1960s Orthodoxy for variants on the consensus approaches to Divine revelation and the historicity of the Biblical account.[12]

Decades later, in the early twenty-first century, esteemed Orthodox rabbis and educators have expressed attitudes regarding the Bible that answer Greenberg's original call, some even going further in their openness to critical approaches than what was deemed "radical" to 1960s Orthodox sensibilities. The key pathbreakers in this phenomenon are Israel-based rabbis and educators identified with the moderate wing of the RZ sector, and prominent among this group are students of Lichtenstein and alumni of YHE. As noted earlier, influential elite figures of the Kav/Harda"l RZ camp, such as rabbis Aviner and Shapira, have been vocal in their opposition to the introduction of any critical scholarship to Bible study.

IsMO and the Bible

Yuval Cherlow, as we have seen, is one of the leaders of the RZ moderate camp. A prized student of YHE and founder of the Tzohar rabbinic organization, Cherlow heads the Yeshivat Amit Orot Shaul in Tel Aviv. He has written openly of his willingness to accept the possibility that multiple verses in the Torah, not just the final passages, were not authored by

Moses—as long as one believes that the Torah itself is of Divine origin.[13] This understanding is in direct contradiction to the eighth principle of belief of Maimonides, which states that "we believe that the entire Torah presently in our possession is the one given to Moses our master (may he rest in peace)."[14] Furthermore, Cherlow does not feel bound to the Bible's historical account on a factual level: "The Torah does not intend to tell us what happened, but what we are to build within ourselves as a result of these events."[15]

Although less controversial than his position on the Pentateuch, Cherlow also does not reject the possibility that the Book of Isaiah was written by more than one author, but nor does he favor this view over the traditional explanations.[16] YHE alumnus Rabbi Aviyah Hacohen, former head of Yeshivat ha-Kibbutz ha-Dati in Ein Zurim, is less equivocal. He is fully convinced of the multiple authorship of Isaiah, and is confounded by the unwillingness of fellow RZ figures who have been exposed to academic perspectives on the subject to acknowledge it. In fact, he has actively encouraged them to reconsider this position. Writing in the journal of the religious-sponsored Efrata College of Education in Jerusalem, Hacohen declared that "the thesis that the book of Isaiah consists of two collections has been tested repeatedly and is well established and credible. . . . Humility is a virtue in many areas; I call for some humility vis-à-vis Bible scholars. Humility toward Bible scholars and acceptance of their views is a value in religious education."[17] Hacohen received a master's degree in Bible from the Hebrew University in Jerusalem but has dedicated his entire career to serving as a religious educator and rabbi, not a professional academic.[18]

Rabbi Chaim Navon is another well-regarded YHE alumnus and a popular columnist and prolific author of works on Jewish thought, law, and society. He teaches at Herzog College and Midreshet Lindenbaum, and served as rabbi of an RZ congregation in the city of Modi'in.[19] Like Cherlow, Navon has written that, with the exception of the Sinaitic revelation, which had to have occurred as presented in the text, he does not assume that the Hebrew Bible necessarily offers a fully accurate historical account. In point of fact, he has no difficulty accepting archeological findings that contradict the Book of Joshua's description of the fall of Jericho's walls, and if historical evidence indicates that camels were not domesticated animals during the period when the stories of the Book of Genesis took place: "Perhaps in truth the Patriarchs did not ride on camels, but on donkeys, or on bulls, or on winged horses. . . . Does this matter to anyone? God, for his own considerations which relate to how the Torah will influence its own and later generations, preferred to write that the Patriarchs rode on camels."[20]

Navon's article appeared in *Alon Shevut*, the official Torah journal of YHE, and received a strong rebuttal from Rabbi Yaakov Meidan, himself a prolific author on Biblical topics, who currently serves as one of the heads of YHE.[21] Yet this did not interfere with Navon being invited to teach in Herzog College and to edit, together with Lichtenstein's son Shai, a book on the Jewish concept of *kedushah* (the sacred) that the YHE leader had nearly completed at the time of his 2015 passing. Navon is also featured regularly at Herzog's annual five-day Tanakh seminar attended by thousands. Indeed, at the 2018 event, a special session took place, "The Correct Meaning of the Biblical Text and the Midrashic Interpretation That Appears in Rabbinic Literature—Parallel Lines or Intersecting Points," in which Navon and Meidan debated their divergent approaches.[22]

An additional, highly respected RZ figure who has expressed openness to critical approaches to the Bible is Rabbi Dr. Yehudah Brandes. Although not an alumnus of YHE, since 2014 he has served as president of YHE's Herzog College. Brandes, who earned his doctorate in Talmud at the Hebrew University in Jerusalem, is certainly a hybrid figure with strong academic qualifications, but he is recognized primarily as an educator and religious thinker who worked for many years in the religious high school system and in Orthodox frameworks for advanced Torah study.[23] In 2015, his article "The Sages and Biblical Criticism" appeared in *Be-Einei E-lohim ve-Adam* (In the eyes of God and man), a collection dedicated to exploring the interface between traditional beliefs and scientific approaches toward the Bible. Basing himself on the overall approach of Maimonides in relation to the metaphorical intentions of numerous Biblical descriptions, the author raises the possibility that "[r]egarding authorship of the Torah as well, one can understand the verses that present Moses as the writer of the Torah in a sense that differs from their literal meaning, but nonetheless without ceasing to be the firm foundation for belief in the Divinity of the Torah."[24]

Rabbi Dr. Amit Kula also did not study in YHE, but along with Cherlow and Brandes, he has long been an active member of the Tzohar association, which seeks to cultivate a more empathetic Israeli rabbinate. He serves as rabbi of the RZ Kibbutz Alumim on the Gaza border (one of the kibbutzim that was overrun by Hamas on October 7, 2023) and is head of the contemporary halakhah think tank of Beit Hillel.[25] In a 2011 Hebrew monograph, Kula argued that it is not essential to believe in the one-time historical event of Sinaitic revelation, nor is it absolutely necessary to accept that there was literally an ancient Near Eastern figure named Abraham the son of Terah who moved from Mesopotamia to Canaan. Rather than focusing on the actual historicity of Biblical text, what is crucial to acknowledge is that it reflects the true word of God.[26] This stance did not prevent Cherlow from publishing a positive review of the book, which ends with the following endorsement: "Those who address both the Torah and the cultural milieu in which they live with integrity, and are searching for a proposal that offers a fresh way of encountering the tension between them . . . will discover that which they desire in this wonderful book by Rav Amit."[27]

Other Israel-based Orthodox figures noted by Shapiro in his article who are willing to contemplate multiple authorship of the Torah, such as James Kugel and Jerome Yehuda Gellman, identify professionally purely as academics, not clergy, and thus do not necessarily reflect an adjustment in the accepted Orthodox religious paradigm.[28] Similarly regarding Tamar Ross, who is known both as an academic and theologian, her writings on a variety of topics are considered radical, and by some to be beyond the pale of normative Orthodox theology.[29] On the other hand, Israeli-born Professor Tova Ganzel is both a qualified academic Bible scholar and a leader in advanced Torah education for women.[30] Representing a religious leadership prototype that is similar to Herzog College's Brandes—with whom she coedited the volume *Be-Einei E-lohim ve-Adam*—Ganzel is the former director of the midrasha, the nonacademic framework located on the BIU campus that provides traditional Torah learning opportunities for female students. She is also a pioneering yoetzet halakhah, who has published rigorous studies of related responsa in Torah journals,[31] and an active member of Beit Hillel.[32] Today she has a full-time academic appointment and is the head of BIU's Basic Jewish Studies Department. In her academic writing and lecturing, Ganzel invokes the "documentary hypothesis" that distinguishes between the Priestly (P) and Deuteronomic (D) elements of the Hebrew Bible. As she concludes in one of her articles, "I have demonstrated here Ezekiel's reliance on Deuteronomic terminology and notions, with which he was familiar as an independent source, for his depiction of idolatry and how he creates a new synthesis by combining them with concepts of impurity from the Priestly literature."[33]

All of the figures featured to this point are highly influential Israeli RZ rabbis and educators that can be categorized as leaders in IsMO and not the Kav/Harda"l faction.[34] Ganzel is the only one who holds a permanent position in a university department. The main focus of most of them, rather, is on disseminating theological ideas, ruling on Jewish law, and inspiring their students.[35] Some have been criticized both orally and in print for supporting what have long been considered to be theologically heterodox ideas. Nonetheless, this has not led to concerted calls for them to repudiate their positions nor has it undermined their authority within their constituencies.

TheTorah.com

The main exception to the Israel-centeredness of Orthodox openness to critical approaches to the Bible is the American-based Project TABS (Torah and Biblical Scholarship). Generally referred to by the name of its website, TheTorah.com, its central goals include: "To make modern biblical scholarship accessible to the broader Jewish community. To integrate the findings of modern biblical scholarship into *torat chayim* (instruction for living). To address the challenges modern biblical scholarship poses to traditional Jewish faith and observance."[36] Toward these ends, it provides introductions to Biblical scholarship for the uninitiated, makes available articles on myriad topics relating to the Hebrew Bible that are predicated on academic research, and archives resources on Biblical theology. It even includes interactive "Ask a Rabbi" and "Ask a Scholar" tools. Although it is an open site that anyone can utilize and includes among its contributors both Jewish scholars from across the religious spectrum and non-Jewish Biblicists as well, its main target group appears to be Orthodox/observant Jews who might be open to scholarly approaches to the Bible or troubled by them. As the editors attest, "we share . . . a conviction that if traditional Judaism is to thrive then it must address biblical criticism."[37]

Such a forthright attitude differs from the type of cautious discussions that characterize the Israeli rabbis and educators highlighted to this point. While the latter entertain conclusions of academic study, they do not profess an active agenda of spreading them widely. To be sure, the TheTorah.com indicates sincere concern for the spiritual welfare of conflicted Orthodox Jews, but it also makes abundantly clear that the exclusive way out of one's theological conundrums is to accept the truths of scientific findings. In arguing for the importance of the TABS project, for example, an article by an Orthodox MIT professor is cited that declares, "To be unwilling to even consider that the Torah might be a composite document is no different in principle from holding firm to the belief that the Earth is stationary and that the sun revolves around it."[38]

This overall outlook of the TheTorah.com reflects the vision of its creators. Two of its main architects are American, university-trained academics (as are most of the TheTorah.com contributors as well) and observant Jews, who have published works predicated on higher Biblical criticism.[39] The founder, who grew up in the UK, stems from a traditionalist/Haredi personal and educational background, and initially worked as a religious outreach specialist with minimally affiliated Jews. After becoming aware of inconsistencies in the Hebrew Bible, he came to the conclusion through independent reading that scientific approaches offered the correct explanations.[40] For all three, then, their acceptance of Biblical scholarship is foundational to their intellectual and religious worldviews.

While English translations of the works of some of the Israeli Orthodox rabbis and educators focused upon here are available at the TheTorah.com, few mainstream North American Orthodox rabbis allow their writings to appear on the site.[41] The conspicuousness of the Israelis is due, primarily, to the energies of the talented, Israel-based editor Zev Farber, who seeks out Hebrew works and translates and posts them. Yet it also supports my contention that most of the noteworthy examples of increased acceptance of aspects of Biblical criticism within contemporary Orthodox Judaism are to be found among Israeli religious figures. These individuals are less encumbered by the demands of denominational declarations of allegiances than are their American counterparts.

The emergence of TheTorah.com does not necessarily indicate a rise in acceptance of critical understandings of the Hebrew Bible by mainstream American Orthodox rabbinical and educational leaders. Rather, it reflects the efforts of a highly motivated, elite cadre of individuals who are both committed to Orthodox interpretation of Jewish law and have fully internalized the dominant exegetical positions of the academy, to facilitate the exposure of others to their approach to the Bible.[42]

Independent of the current upsurge in acceptance of Biblical scholarship among Orthodox religious leaders, what is most interesting about TheTorah.com is that it enables Israelis who know English and Jews who live in English-speaking countries to interface without actual proximity. In contrast, then, to the geographical, political, and cultural foundation of the Israeli/American divide, TheTorah.com exemplifies a flat, virtual platform that skirts physical borders. Such a technologically driven framework possesses significant potential agencies. It will be fascinating to see to what degree one achieves a unique permanent "space" within contemporary Judaism, leading to a more foundational reshuffling of the current territorial partition.[43]

In fact, an initiative launched in the summer of 2018 points to additional globalizing Jewish Bible study platforms with potential to influence the current geographical divide. The Hebrew 929 project was begun in 2014 by Benny Lau. Its goal is to stimulate widespread Jewish exposure to the Bible by assigning the 929 chapters of the Tanakh respectively to individual days. Thus, in the course of less than three years of daily study, one can complete the entire Hebrew Bible. This concept was modeled after the *daf yomi* (literally, "daily folio") program, which leads to completion of the entire Babylonian Talmud over seven and half years and has had a profound influence on the popularization of Talmud study within the Orthodox world.

The original 929 project encourages groups of Hebrew speakers from the entire spectrum of religious and secular orientations to take part and sponsors a website to which scholars from all approaches, including many academics, contribute. The platform shares certain characteristics with TheTorah.com, but it differs in that it is not oriented specifically toward academic perspectives and does not have a declared desire to expose its readers to a particular analytical approach. Rather, it is dedicated toward creating a pluralistic conversation—which means including a wide spectrum of interpretative options from the hypertraditional to the critical academic in its "community of writers."[44]

After a successful completion of the first Hebrew 929 cycle, Lau joined with the late Lord Rabbi Dr. Jonathan Sacks and Rabbi Dr. Adam Mintz, a well-regarded American Modern Orthodox rabbi and scholar,[45] to create an English 929 initiative.[46] This Israel-based venture serves as a unique forum for cross-fructification between traditionalist and academic-oriented voices, and was set up to bring its diverse spectrum of voices to the English-speaking Jewish world. Like the original Hebrew platform, the new English one declares, "The living spirit behind the discourse on 929 is made up of academics, philosophers, writers, artists, public figures and leading personalities from the artistic and creative spheres in Israel, both men and women, who use social networks to post status updates, poetry and images relating to the chapter of the day from a personal point of view."[47]

In light of the 2020/21 COVID-19 pandemic and the move of so much educational and cultural content to the internet, the globalizing directions of TheTorah.com and the new 929 platform grew further. It ought to be recalled that the core of Orthodox rabbis and educators to get involved stem from the IsMO sector. Thus, with or without the distinctions between the TheTorah.com and the phenomenon at the center of the current discussion, the question remains: Why do the Orthodox rabbis and educators that have a greater proclivity toward engaging aspects of higher Biblical criticism emanate from Israel rather than among their American MO counterparts? To delve into this question further, the next section focuses on the dynamics of North American MO and its engagement with academic Bible study, where the situation has certainly changed since Yitz Greenberg's 1966 remarks, but differs, nonetheless, in fundamental ways from the Israeli reality.

North American Bifurcation

North American MO, to a greater degree than Israeli RZ, would appear initially to be the more likely candidate to introduce ideas emanating from the academy into its religious worldview. This religious stream championed the "Torah u-Madda" model of combining commitment to traditional Jewish law and ideals with modern scientific education, especially through its banner institution YU. The latter was led during most of its history by outstanding figures such as rabbis Joseph B. Soloveitchik, Bernard Revel, Samuel Belkin, and Norman Lamm, as well as the most recently chosen president, Ari Berman, who all possessed expertise both in traditional learning and academic disciplines. In parallel, following the precedent of Central European Orthodox forerunners, additional prominent "Rabbi Drs." occupied MO synagogue pulpits throughout much of the twentieth century. In fact, the contemporary scholar who has likely been most instrumental in exposing broader audiences to academic approaches to the Hebrew Bible is James Kugel, an American Orthodox Jew. The author of multiple scholarly studies as well as works like the award-winning *How to Read the Bible* that have succeeded in gaining wide-ranging popular interest,[48] he taught at Harvard for many years and later moved to Israel, where he joined the Bible department at BIU.[49]

YU, as well, has long employed numerous faculty members—including Lichtenstein and Greenberg—that held rabbinic along with academic qualifications, and its curriculum bears out the desire to cultivate students at home in both religious and secular intellectual worlds. Beyond their traditional Talmud concentrations, current YU college students are exposed to academic Judaic studies disciplines—including Bible—as part of their undergraduate course work. Moreover, YU's Bernard Revel Graduate School (BRGS) grants advanced degrees in Jewish history, Jewish philosophy, Talmud, and Bible.[50] The lecturers are Orthodox-practicing, university-trained scholars, many of whom publish regularly in leading academic journals.[51] Some of them have also written on the conflicts between critical approaches to the Bible and Orthodox theology.[52] The result is that aspects of Greenberg's 1960s call for greater consideration of academic Biblical scholarship within YU have been fulfilled.

Yet the YU engagement with Bible differs in substantial ways from the RZ encounter overseas and tenders a lens into distinctions from the Israeli environment. For one, both undergraduate and graduate-level offerings at YU focus on facets of Biblical studies that are less theologically contentious. Even entertaining critical motifs has been attacked by the more conservative elements on campus. There are also advanced courses that deal more directly with issues arising from "higher criticism," but unlike the dominant approach in most university religion and Bible departments, it is difficult to identify a YU academic instructor that presents such positions as correct or theologically acceptable.[53] In fact, well-regarded faculty members have protested vehemently against inviting world-renowned Bible scholars who accept the dominant premises of the academy, including Kugel, to lecture on campus.[54]

More fundamentally, the YU MO model projects a division of powers or authority, rather than an organic integration. Thus, comparable to the United States federal government, YU is not one synthetic organization but a conglomerate whose main campus contains within it a yeshiva—RIETS—and a full program of university studies. No doubt there are multiple overlaps, the most significant one being the fact that on a regular day the same students attend both frameworks. But there are also forthright checks and balances intended to prevent one branch from undermining the independence of the other. In practice, a RIETS/YU rabbinical/graduate student can study Talmud and codes in a traditional study hall from 9:00 a.m. to 2:30 p.m., and then go across the street and attend graduate school classes in Jewish history, philosophy, Talmud, or Bible or sit in the adjacent library and work on his dissertation, before returning at night to official religious space for additional religious enrichment. On both a formal and spatial level, these are two completely separate modes of Jewish intellectual engagement. Truly, in the morning he may hear diatribes against the heretical findings of the scholars, and in the late afternoon he may learn information that contravenes directly the ideals communicated by his religious mentors.

To the undiscerning, the YU divide is camouflaged by various externalities, such as the fact that all but two of the active RIETS advanced Talmud instructors have college degrees and six have doctorates—although only four of them still engage in academic teaching or research. Needless to say, for most of the RIETS senior staff, their early academic exposures are rarely if ever reflected in their Talmudic teaching. More often than not, their familiarity with the college classroom and awareness of the impact of ideas has led them to be especially vigilant in guarding against possible deviations from Orthodox theological standards.[55] Utilizing typologies introduced by sociologist Samuel Heilman, few of the RIETS instructors are "syncretists" who "embrace the modern world." Rather, most sit somewhere between the "tolerators"—who are "entrenched in the traditional Orthodox world," but show greater understanding either in order to attract people to their worldview or due to the sociocultural/

vocational circumstances in which they find themselves—and the "neo-rejectionists,'" who "with the wisdom of former modernists . . . argue that it is not reasonable to live that way." Indeed, regarding the university Bible requirement, Rabbi Herschel Schachter, arguably the most influential figure in RIETS, protested in 2006, "When I was in college, the rabbis taught Tanach (Bible). Now, in recent years, the college has introduced more academic Bible . . . students are stuck taking academic Bible when they want to hear more traditional Tanach [sic]."[56] A few years later, one student published a more detailed diatribe in an official college publication under the unambiguous headline "Shut Down the Bible Department."[57]

On the other side, the faculty members of BRGS and the undergraduate Jewish studies department are professional academics, including leaders in their fields. To the best of my knowledge, all are observant Jews, and at least six have rabbinical ordination, but only one is currently employed by a synagogue.[58] While they are expected to be sensitive to the religious traditions and beliefs of the institution and its student body, they focus exclusively on teaching critical method and exposing their students to the spectrum of academic perspectives.[59] The lack of symmetry between the rabbinical and Jewish studies branches of YU is illustrated by the fact that, during BRGS's over eighty years of existence, Joseph B. Soloveitchik and his son Professor Haym Soloveitchik are among a select few figures who taught in both RIETS and BRGS.[60]

Unlike their counterparts at American Haredi yeshivot, then, YU students are exposed within the same campus in which they study parochial subjects to disciplines and ways of thinking that challenge foundational religious premises.[61] On the other side of the denominational spectrum, the YU experience is distinctive from the training and ideal rabbinical model put forward in Reform, Conservative, and Reconstructionist institutions, where those who guide the candidates through the canon of Jewish traditional literature and law are academically qualified and oriented. The curriculum of the much smaller and more liberal-Orthodox Yeshivat Chovevei Torah (YCT) opens more portals of entry for academic perspectives than that of RIETS. Nonetheless, like YU, YCT's emphasis is unquestionably on the traditional model of Torah study,[62] and its leaders have expressed ambivalence regarding critical perspectives on the Hebrew Bible when espoused by some of its own alumni.[63]

Notably, the study program at YU's Stern College for Women does not delineate as clear boundaries between traditional Jewish learning and academic courses.[64] While some classes in the core Jewish studies curriculum are taught by rabbis and female teachers in a more traditionalist mode, the majority are presented by individuals with advanced academic degrees in the subject.[65] In this light, it is intriguing to witness the evolution of high-level women's Torah study, both in North America and in Israel, and its broader influence on attitudes toward Biblical criticism.

The concurrency of YU's men's advanced educational tracks, then, does not necessarily produce a fluid conversation between traditionalist and academic perspectives.[66] To be sure, some graduates may feel a need to foster a synthetic bond between Torah and secular life[67]—which may actually be manifested in settling in Israel.[68] But others may react to the challenges of integrating both sides by adopting some variation on the rejectionist approach to advanced secular wisdom and culture associated with Haredi Orthodoxy. A more common scenario is that they will carry over the bifurcation they experienced as students into their adult lives, where the divides between their Orthodox Jewish homes and communities, on one side, and secular professional lives, on the other, are more clearly cut.

The 2016 search for a new YU president offered a stark reminder of the predilection toward bifurcation among its American alumni, and the possibilities for greater fluidity that Israel might offer. Seeking an individual who could model the integration of Torah and academic scholarship that stands at the foundation of the institution, the search committee did not find a satisfactory candidate within the North American continent. Eventually they "plucked" Berman out of Gush Etzion, the area just south of Jerusalem that has become a launching ground for a synthetic RZ intellectual environment, and where this highly qualified YU/YHE alumnus had chosen to reroot his family eight years prior.[69]

Israeli Fluidity

In contrast to the bifurcated North American Modern Orthodox environment, in Israel the continuum between academic Biblical studies and more parochial frameworks is less pronounced. This fluidity is reflected in a multitude of forms, some of which were raised by sociologist

Chaim Waxman in a chapter, "Revival of the Bible," that appears in his 2017 monograph, *Social Change and Halakhic Evolution in American Orthodoxy*.[70]

Among the issues put forward by Waxman that I understand as highlighting this fluidity: the deep connection between the Hebrew Bible, the Hebrew language, and the Land of Israel, and relatedly, the long-held Israeli interest in Biblical archeology—which some see as the basis for supporting both religious beliefs and political claims; the high percentage of observant Jewish studies scholars in Israeli universities; the establishment in the mid-twentieth century of a Bible department in the religiously founded BIU that cultivated Orthodox Bible scholars (although in its early decades critical study of the Pentateuch was not part of the curriculum);[71] the regular publication of academic-oriented essays on the Bible in the popular *Mussaf Shabbat* supplement to the Israeli weekly *Makor Rishon*—whose readership is predominantly from the RZ sector;[72] the widespread use among observant Jews of the Jerusalem-based Mossad ha-Rav Kook publishing house's *Da'at Mikra Tanakh* (lavender Bible) series, which integrates aspects of the scientific method[73] and whose contributors include observant Bible professors;[74] and the focus of advanced Israeli RZ education on Kookian mystical thought, along with the more recent widespread interest in certain Hasidic thinkers, which aligns with postmodern approaches to truth that emerged from the academy and facilitate greater halakhic and theological diversity.[75]

Waxman also pointed to the lack in Israel of the denominational struggles that led twentieth-century American Modern Orthodoxy to invoke "faith tests" in order to distinguish between them and the Conservative and Reform movements—who were more open to Biblical criticism.[76] This was one of the central backdrops to the Greenberg and Jacobs controversies of the 1960s. Here too, an aspect of the fluidity of the RZ sector arises that distinguishes it from its North American MO counterpart. Specifically, among the American-born academics, rabbis, and educators who immigrated to Israel—especially in the 1970s and 1980s—are to be found numerous scholars who were nurtured in the Jewish Theological Seminary and other Conservative-affiliated institutions such as the Ramah Camps, the USY youth movement, and various synagogues and schools. Their integration of personal observance with academic and theological approaches not accepted within Orthodoxy was rooted in the critical thinking that characterizes the Conservative movement and its elite institutions.[77] Upon arrival in Israel, some found their religious homes in the Israeli *Masorti* movement,[78] but others chose to attend the far more ubiquitous RZ-oriented synagogues and sent their children to its youth movements and state religious schools. Professionally, some of the academics may have joined the faculty of the Conservative-affiliated Schechter Institute, but others were hired by Israeli universities including the MO/RZ-founded BIU. The net result is that a select cadre of intellectuals and their families that were fully comfortable with critical approaches to the Bible, and had been nurtured in the American Conservative movement, found a space for themselves with the moderate sector of Israeli RZ.

Two other significant examples of Israeli RZ fluidity that are directly connected to Bible study may be added. One is the requirement of Israel's Ministry of Education that secondary school Bible instructors, including those in the religious school system, possess a teacher's license with a specialty in Bible instruction obtained through an academic institution.[79] This means that they must gain exposure to scientific approaches to Bible studies, which may then inform their teaching. This is not necessarily the case among North American Orthodox high school teachers, where Bible is generally considered part of the "religious studies" curriculum (*limudei kodesh*), and for the most part rabbis and woman educators who teach traditional Talmud and parochial classes and have no academic Bible training are the main Bible instructors.

Another Israel-based feature of the growing Orthodox focus on Bible study is the massive expansion in recent decades of high-level woman's Torah study, discussed earlier especially in connection with pioneers Malka Bina, Chaim Brovender, and Chana Henkin. Much attention has been paid to the process that led to the emergence of a new generation of woman religious authorities with expertise in Talmudic law and analytical skills. All the same, unlike men's yeshivot that traditionally focused almost exclusively on Talmud and only recently began to make Tanakh study part of their main curriculum, for women the process was the opposite. Long before Talmud study became acceptable, advanced Bible learning featured prominently in institutions such as Michlalah College for Women in Jerusalem, which was established in 1969.[80] And indeed, while Talmud has gained considerable traction, woman's midrashot (seminaries) often offer the possibility of concentrating on Bible text study or Jewish thought and Hasidism, along with or rather than Talmud.[81] Thus, the proliferation of woman's Torah scholarship may also be expanding the spectrum of what is considered to be core high-level Jewish learning.

As part of a pioneering movement, there is also more openness in woman's study environments to less traditionalist modes of engagement with the text than in male-based environments. In fact, many of the premier woman scholars earned their main qualifications in universities,[82] as opposed to the male yeshiva instructors, some of whom attended university but whose core qualification is Orthodox rabbinical ordination—which was until recently completely unavailable to women and is still a matter of considerable controversy. The result is that the woman's study hall is a less monolithic intellectual environment than the men's beit midrash, where Bible remains secondary to Talmud.[83]

In her comparative study of Orthodox feminism in Israel and the United States, Tamar Ross demonstrated that Israeli Orthodox feminism has exhibited a far greater capacity to explore the theological implications of the feminist critique. Extrapolating to Bible study, the Israeli woman's midrashah cultivates an exceptionally conducive environment for testing the limits of Orthodox theology on multiple fronts or at least encourages the flexibility that facilitates it.[84]

All of these examples support the notion of a relatively fluid interface between academic and parochial approaches to the Bible in Israel, which not only facilitates direct engagement of rabbis and educators with critical scientific perspectives but blurs the lines between them. This contrasts with the more bifurcated nature of American MO involvement. The focus of the remainder of the discussion will be on Lichtenstein and YHE and the role they played in paving the path toward this direction.

Herzog College

In 1962, four years before his published ideological conflict with Yitz Greenberg, Lichtenstein delivered a public lecture at Stern College in which he made abundantly clear that higher Biblical criticism had no place in the intellectual oeuvre of those allegiant to traditional understandings of revelation and Divine authorship. This opinion was echoed in his June 1966 retort to Greenberg in a comment relating directly to the theological implications of Bible study: "I take exception not only to the apparent substance of the original section on revelation, but to the suggestion implied in the juxtaposition of the two adjectives in the statement that 'what we mean by Divine revelation' may be less external or mechanical than Jews now think."[85] On the other hand, a trained scholar of English literature in his own right, in the 1962 address Lichtenstein advocated strongly for the adoption of literary tools developed within the academy as a key to gaining more profound understandings of the characters and religious meanings of the Biblical text: "I propose that we rediscover *kitvei kodesh* [sacred writings] as literature . . . and that in order to deepen our appreciation of them as such, we seek to approach them critically."[86]

By his own later accounting, Lichtenstein never devoted himself personally to teaching or writing this type of Torah analysis—although his oral presentations on the weekly portion often demonstrated a keen literary sensitivity.[87] All the same, in retrospect, the 1962 discourse may be seen as intuiting the new approach to Bible study that was spearheaded from the late 1960s by the faculty and graduates of YHE and its affiliated Herzog College, the Israeli institution co-headed by Lichtenstein.

Lichtenstein arrived in 1971 and joined Amital as co-*rosh yeshiva*. Two years later the educational college was established, with Lichtenstein serving as rector (chief academic officer). Some of the key Bible instructors were recruited by Amital, such as rabbis Mordechai Breuer and Yoel Bin-Nun.[88] They stemmed from the yeshiva milieu, but integrated independently approaches that arose from academic writing. Over time, faculty members were hired who had earned doctoral degrees from Israeli universities and were amalgamated with members of the yeshiva's staff. Today, YHE and Herzog graduates (including women who study separately at the neighboring Migdal Oz campus) serve as Bible instructors throughout Israel, some have gone on to earn doctoral degrees, including renowned lecturers at Israeli university Bible departments.[89] Herzog College's role as a cultural agent is fortified by the fact that it enrolls students not only from YHE and Migdal Oz. It has agreements with numerous RZ yeshivot from around the country, some of which do not necessarily share YHE's religious worldview. It also has a central Jerusalem location that further expands the scope of its exposure through highly popular lectures that are open to the broader public.[90] In addition to its BA and MA degree programs in Bible, Herzog publishes the Bible studies journal *Megadim*, runs the Bible study website hatanakh.com, and sponsors the annual five-day summer Bible seminar/jamboree that attracts thousands of people from Israel and abroad to its rich program of classes, workshops, and Bible-based outings.[91]

Among the featured speakers at the Herzog Seminar are some of the very same rabbis and educators who have demonstrated openness to aspects of higher Biblical criticism—Yehudah Brandes, Yuval Cherlow, Tova Ganzel, and Chaim Navon. On the same 2018 program with them, for example, could be found numerous full-time academic scholars, along with most of the main Talmud instructors at YHE and Migdal Oz.[92] The inclusion of the latter is not surprising, since in parallel to their primary yeshiva and midrasha positions, many of them serve as instructors in Herzog College. This is another stark example of the fluidity of the yeshiva and the academy that marks the moderate camp of Israeli RZ as reflected in its banner institution YHE. Recall, by contrast, the bifurcation in YU indicated by the very few RIETS lecturers who have taught in Yeshiva College or the Bernard Revel Graduate School, and vice versa.

Although it was clearly others—Amital, Breuer, Bin-Nun—who initiated it in practice, the core approach to Biblical interpretation that has become associated with Herzog dovetails to a great degree with the concept put forward by Lichtenstein in 1962. It emphasizes making use of a broad gamut of literary tools to address the text independently or in complement to the exegetical traditions of rabbinic midrash and medieval exegesis. As evidenced by the numerous publications emanating from this circle, however, a variety of stances exist regarding the degree to which academic methods can be drafted. While some have maintained a strict boundary between literary analysis and instruments associated with higher criticism or that take into account historical context, other Herzog scholars have not stuck to such clear distinctions. Among the pioneering instructors, Breuer actually accepted the documentary hypothesis's four-part division of the Pentateuch, but was adamant that this was Divinely orchestrated. Bin-Nun predicated much of his work on reading the Bible in light of modern archeological discoveries.[93] As Rabbi Ezra Bick wrote in the preface to the first in a series of English-language collections of articles authored by Herzog scholars: "Because the understanding of a literary work necessarily requires understanding of external factors in its writing, the studies will incorporate findings from history, archeology, Semitics, and not only literature per se."[94] Recall from the previous chapter that some of the harshest criticism of YHE from the Kav/Harda"l camp has focused on its innovative methodology for studying and teaching the Bible. Anecdotally, a scholar queried a number of RZ women informally as to why they chose to attend the Kav/Harda"l–oriented Bible seminar that was begun as an alternative to the more established Herzog program. One responded that in Herzog the study is not rooted in essential doctrines of Judaism (*sham zeh lo emuni*), while another said outright that they teach "heretical ideas" (*divrei kefirah*).[95]

No doubt Herzog itself does not accept many of the central claims of critical Bible study and has made great efforts to define those tools and insights that are tolerable within the Orthodox worldview. Yet it has created a fluid environment in which the meeting of worlds is constant and distinctions between religious and scientific approaches is much more nuanced.

Bible scholarship that evolved from the institution that Lichtenstein co-headed, then, has actually brought to fruition ideas articulated by Greenberg in his 1966 *Commentator* interview. Critical tools have entered the mainstream of advanced Orthodox learning; a cadre of high-level practitioners of Bible study have emerged that are conscious of the spectrum of academic methods, but highlight one that does not necessarily contradict Orthodox theological principles; and in certain cases, its adherents have demonstrated openness to comprehending the Bible within the historical context in which it originally appeared. To be sure, Lichtenstein himself expressed sharp reservations regarding the potential damage to foundational beliefs that some of these developments portended, but he did not categorically reject them.[96]

Here the role of the incorporation of Lichtenstein into YHE in 1971 needs to be analyzed deftly and with nuance. No doubt Amital was the pioneering figure regarding the emphasis on Bible study; nonetheless, on a number of levels Lichtenstein's personal example was seminal to germinating the environment from which the fluidity evolved. First, his academic stature gave Herzog College legitimacy that did not exist among other yeshiva-connected pedagogical institutions. Second, from the outset and until the last years of his tenure, he served as the rector of Herzog College. As a result, even if he dedicated most of his time to traditional study and teaching and had considerable ambivalence regarding aspects of the educational college, on a formal level he combined the traditional *rosh yeshiva* role with that of a professional academic. Third, although he rarely wrote on Biblical subjects, he was active in publishing on contemporary, historical, and theological topics throughout much of his career. His writing on these subjects has a distinctly formal academic style, with copious footnotes that conditioned his disciples to feel comfortable with critical writing and delivery, and he published his work in academic-style frameworks such as the Rabbinical Council of America's *Tradition* quarterly, the Orthodox Forum series, and the Jason Aronson and Koren/Magid publishing houses.[97] Fourth, although his Talmud lectures were anchored in purely traditionalist understandings of rabbinic literature, they had an academic discipline to their structures, and were predicated on close readings that evoked his training as a literary scholar.

Finally and most importantly, unlike his YU colleagues, Lichtenstein was never a strict bifurcator. His public discourses both within yeshiva settings and outside and his published writings were characterized by continual interspersing of quotations from Jewish religious texts with those of non-Jewish thinkers, philosophers, and theologians, with an especial affinity for Augustine, John Milton, William Shakespeare, Henry More, Cardinal Newman, and C. S. Lewis, among others. Following suit, his entire intellectual oeuvre effused a fluid interplay between the holy and the secular, the Jewish and the Gentile, the yeshiva and the academy. Lichtenstein presented these as all being part of his effort to seek and know God and his world. Although numerous students chose to engage nontraditionalist sources of knowledge and theological perspectives that he decisively shunned, these particulars do not undermine their modeling of his fluid integration example.

In an essay, "Rabbi Aharon Lichtenstein and Academic Talmud Study," published in 2018, Rami Reiner examined a parallel issue to the current discussion.[98] An Israeli who studied in YHE during the 1980s and is today a professor of Rabbinic thought at Ben-Gurion University in the Negev, he focused on Lichtenstein's antagonism toward critical scientific inquiry of the Talmud. Reiner highlighted the complexity of a yeshiva head who celebrated the wisdom that could be gained from those outside the Jewish orbit, yet in certain areas erected formidable boundaries to its application.[99] This analytical perspective shares much in common with a major point made here, for Reiner argues that, despite Lichtenstein's own strong reservations, through Herzog College he actually played a key role in facilitating the introduction of academic Talmud into mainstream RZ Orthodoxy. Due to the interconnections of the arguments, it is worthwhile to include an extended direct citation from Reiner's work, especially as there are echoes of his personal experience as an Israeli student and alumnus of YHE:

> The broad, rich, unique world that Rabbi Lichtenstein brought to YHE coexisted, in those days, with his strong opposition to any whiff of academic Talmud study. Thus, some of Rabbi Lichtenstein's students ultimately continued their search for the truth, but they found it elsewhere, and in different kinds of truth. The driving force was Rabbi Lichtenstein's strength and spirit, but the end result was something far from his spirit, and far from the destinations toward which he strove . . . What happened subsequently? It seems that the history of Herzog College, which is adjacent to, affiliated with, and influenced by YHE, and for which Rabbi Lichtenstein served as rector, shows that sometimes lines that may never intersect can nevertheless grow closer . . . In the early 1990s, as the college steadily grew and developed, prospective teachers of Talmud and halakhah were disqualified one after another as it became clear to Rabbi Lichtenstein, in his capacity as rector, that these teachers had been trained in academic Talmud departments. From that point forward, however . . . the Faculty of Oral Law at Herzog College developed in a different direction, to the point that eventually, every one of its members was the product of research institutions where they had studied Talmud and related disciplines. These facts speak for themselves.[100]

In contrast to Reiner, I do not suggest that Lichtenstein had a more fundamental change of heart at the end of his career and became less equivocal regarding aspects of the academic enterprise that had previously troubled him.[101]

Yet, if the primary goal of Greenberg's 1966 declarations regarding Orthodox Bible study was, in his words, to "develop our own Biblical scholarship by men who believe that God communicates with man," then Lichtenstein was a key figure in advancing this project. Not only those who formally set out upon academic careers in Bible research, but also some of Lichtenstein's most visible rabbinic protégés, have demonstrated their willingness to engage aspects of Bible study that Greenberg encouraged and their mentor rejected.[102] In their underlying aim of integrating a critical orientation with unequivocal allegiance to the Divine origins of the Torah, even when they deviated regarding decisive details from Lichtenstein in crucial matters, it was his fundamental direction that offered them a viable archetype from which to learn.

Conclusion: A Transnational Perspective on Orthodoxy and Bible Study

Van Elteren, as detailed in chapter 1, attested that "[e]ach local setting provides its own appropriation and reworking of global products and symbols, thus encouraging difference, otherness, diversity and variety."[103] Applied to the current discussion, after moving to Israel, Lichtenstein himself persisted to uphold an approach to Bible study that retained influences of the bifurcation-oriented American atmosphere in which he was nurtured. However, his Israeli students related not only to the specifics of his teachings, but to the broader integrative persona that they encountered. Moreover, they arose in a different environment, and some "appropriated and reworked" his "products and symbols" in fresh ways that opened up vistas for possible understandings of the Bible that were not necessarily acceptable to him.

This process of cultural translation was no doubt nourished by numerous factors including the lack in Israel of the denominational clashes that characterized twentieth-century North American Judaism, as well as the twenty-first-century popularization within RZ of the mystical thinkers whose perceptions were more easily in conversation with postmodern hermeneutical thinking. A decisive foundation, however, was the fluid environment that came to characterize the IsMO sector. In this atmosphere, Israeli students of Lichtenstein assimilated his integrative persona and teachings, and engaged with new views and in novel ways a process that led some of them to pursue paths that stretched the boundaries that their mentor had labored to maintain.

Returning to Van Elteren, he asserted that the process of transnational reworking of culture is not one-directional. That is, once an idea or symbol has been digested and reformed in a new environment, globalized conditions facilitate smooth portals for their reentry into their original local contexts. At this point, the reformulated conceptualizations become influential agents for cultural change within the framework of their initial emergence. Insofar as Orthodox Bible scholarship is concerned, at this juncture the most dramatic and theologically provocative activity is clearly taking place within the Israeli RZ milieu. That said, it is not surprising that quite a few of the American Orthodox rabbis and educators that have adopted a broader, academic-oriented toolkit in their Bible teaching and publications are themselves YHE alumni who were influenced deeply by its fluid environment and the individual who personified it.[104]

7

Israeli Religious Leadership

The Role of Academic Education

Leadership figures from Israel's RZ stream have long been challenged to address the complexities of incorporating religious commitment with robust participation in broader society.[1] Nonetheless, until recently, academic studies were extraneous to their professional toolkit. This stands in sharp contrast to the American Orthodox scene in which possession of a bachelor's degree from "an accredited college or university" has long been a requirement for admission to MO's flagship rabbinical school, the Rabbi Isaac Elchanan Theological Seminary,[2] while completion of an MA degree remains a corequisite in some of its training tracks. Thus, it comes as little surprise that of the twenty-eight RIETS main rabbinical faculty, all but two are college graduates and six possess doctoral degrees. Indeed, in the fall of 2021 the lack of a college diploma was raised during a dispute within one well-heeled Manhattan synagogue as justification for disqualifying its talented veteran assistant rabbi from being considered for the senior rabbi position.[3]

Notwithstanding the ongoing disparity from the United States, twenty-first-century Israel has witnessed a marked growth of religious figures who possess academic degrees. Exploring this change offers a unique perspective from which to perceive the interface between academic studies and the emergence of an alternative moderate religious leadership in contemporary Israel—one that counts women among its protagonists.

To facilitate my analysis, I begin by raising certain parallels that associate the disparate cohorts of nineteenth- and early twentieth-century Europe and contemporary Israel, but my aim is not to identify direct links between them. Rather, I seek to provide historical perspective that will serve both as a point of departure and a comparative tool to assist in presenting a brief account of the academically educated rabbi in Israel and characterizing the current generation of degree-holding Israeli Orthodox religious leaders.

Rabbis with Academic Degrees and Their Opponents: Historical Precedent

In 1981, eminent scholar of German Jewry Ismar Schorsch published an article in which he traced the mid-nineteenth-century rise of a new cadre of young personalities whose academic training played a key role in their successful redefinition of the rabbinate, first in Germany and eventually spreading throughout Western and Central Europe and beyond.[4] By the 1840s, German rabbis in most regions had lost their formal authority to impose religious law. For that matter, much of the urbanizing Jewish public had adopted the broader anticlerical attitudes of their non-Jewish neighbors and was becoming increasingly alienated from the old-style rabbi whose main qualification was expertise in Jewish law. By contrast, the novel, revolutionizing rabbinical figures that Schorsch uncovered spoke fluent German and had received university educations that complemented their yeshiva backgrounds.[5]

The majority of the initial groundbreakers had Reformist leanings or gravitated to the moderate "Positive-Historical" circle of Rabbi Zacharias Frankel, but quite a few were avowedly Orthodox. By the second generation, participation in academic studies became a condition for receiving ordination from any of the three newly established German rabbinical seminaries, including the Orthodox one in Berlin.[6]

Schorsch counts at least sixty-one professional rabbis who by 1847 had attained the degree of doctor of philosophy—almost all of them within the previous two decades.[7] He points out that the fundamental concern of the seminaries was that their graduates would be exposed to university-style secular studies and critical thinking. Thus, he includes in the discussion a wide range of rabbis who attended university but did not complete their degrees.[8]

The trendsetters of the 1840s were duly conscious of their departure from long-held models and forged collective ties through synods and conferences at which the pressing issues of the day were debated. Some of the innovators still served as the legally sanctioned *mara de-atra* (local halakhic authority) of their towns or regions. Yet the appeal of these "modern" rabbis to their emancipation-age constituencies, according to Schorsch, was predicated primarily on their scholarly accomplishments and the sophisticated homiletical oratories with which they dazzled their synagogue audiences.

In pre–World War II Eastern Europe, on the other hand, academically trained rabbis were a rarity; the vast majority who did serve were either employed by Reform-oriented congregations or were government-imposed functionaries. Most Orthodox rabbinical authorities were exceedingly wary of such clergymen and endeavored to delegitimize them due both to their supposed ignorance in matters of Jewish law and to the assumption that their souls were "poisoned" through exposure to secular learning.[9]

The most militant stance against the academically trained rabbi was reserved, however, for opposition to attempts to transplant such a model to Mandatory Palestine. This was expressed most dramatically in 1933, soon after the January rise of the Nazi regime. The leaders of the Orthodox Rabbinerseminar in Berlin—including the renowned Lithuanian yeshiva alumnus and rector Rabbi Jehiel Jacob Weinberg—recognized that the future of their institution was imperiled. They put forward a proposal to transfer it to Jerusalem. Despite the extreme circumstances, the most authoritative Lithuanian rabbinical personality of the time, Rabbi Ḥayyim Ozer Grodzenski of Vilna, fought actively to prevent the idea from coming to fruition. The Ashkenazic chief rabbi of Palestine, Abraham Isaac Kook, endeavored to strike a compromise, but after a no-holds-barred campaign in the Orthodox press, the plan was aborted. In the dispatches to his local followers in Palestine, Grodzenski vilified the seminary as a "rabbi factory" that would be "a foreign plant in the vineyard of the House of Israel in the Holy Land, planting there the German culture which has already struck many dead, and we saw what it brought them."[10]

Despite such fierce opposition, there have been a few notable individual rabbinic figures in Israel who did not fit neatly into the dominant "all Torah" model. Most conspicuous was Ashkenazic chief rabbi Isaac Herzog (the grandfather of President Isaac Herzog), who served in the position from 1936 to 1959. All the same, the University of London–credentialed PhD who was "parachuted" in directly from Ireland is actually the exception that proves the rule. The Jerusalem rabbinical old guard tried to prevent his appointment and subsequently treated him as an outsider.[11] Since Herzog, no figure with advanced secular education has been elected to the position, and the only candidate with such background to be considered at all was Soloveitchik, who withdrew during the 1960s when he understood he had little chance of gaining sufficient support.[12]

There have also been a few state-sanctioned rabbis of towns and neighborhoods in large cities, past and present, with bona fide academic credentials,[13] as well as sporadic cases of professional Jewish studies scholars who functioned (often voluntarily) as synagogue rabbis,[14] but they, too, are highly unusual cases that are not reflective of the overall rabbinical environment.[15] To a certain degree, this is reminiscent of the initial prevailing atmosphere in Germany described by Schorsch, where even if there were a few isolated examples in the early nineteenth century of local rabbis with academic exposure, they can be described as anomalies that only testify to their own rarity.

The Israeli Rabbinate

The official framework for rabbinic function in the State of Israel is the chief rabbinate and its representatives throughout the country. Like the European *mara de-atra*, this model is predicated on the idea that all Jews within a given locale make up the constituency of the rabbinical appointee.[16] On a legal level, the Israeli dynamic is secured through the exclusive authority given by the state to the officially appointed rabbinate—at the national, regional, city, town, and neighborhood levels—regarding implementation of personal status law (marriage, divorce, conversion, and burial), as well as the supervision of public religious standards (dietary and sabbatical laws in food establishments, maintenance of the mikveh [ritual bath], the *eiruv* [physical boundary marker defining an area in which public carrying of objects normally prohibited on the Sabbath is permitted], and the halakhic sale of leavened products before Passover).[17]

Beyond the local framework, the rabbinic courts system that is affiliated with the state rabbinate is the main authority regarding adjudication of personal status law (marriage, divorce, conversion, and Jewish burial) for Jews living in Israel and, in some cases, has jurisdiction beyond this area as well. Paradoxically, many of those who occupy state rabbinic positions and seats on rabbinic courts are products of the Haredi (ultra-Orthodox) world who do not necessarily identify with Zionism or the state as reflecting positive developments.[18] This seeming contradiction is primarily economically motivated, as the state-sponsored posts are usually more lucrative than is working as an independent rabbi or yeshiva lecturer.[19]

Parallel to the Israeli state rabbinate, there have always existed alternative Orthodox models. In recent years, as expanded upon below, the concept of a synagogue-based "pulpit" rabbi has gained increased purchase in the RZ sector, although it is still far from the norm. Even so, when such an arrangement is made it is rarely a full-time position. On the contrary, for most synagogue rabbis their communal responsibilities at most supplement their "day job."

The ongoing dearth, until recently, of academically trained Israeli rabbis, even within less cloistered RZ circles, can be attributed in part to the fact that, since the 1970s, the RZ rabbinate has been dominated by the Merkaz ha-Rav yeshiva and its offshoots. This camp, as noted, celebrates working together with nonobservant Jews for the advancement of the state but is far less sanguine in respect to secular learning. Particularly in the twenty-first century, the Kav substrand, which is decidedly critical of Western social and cultural norms and views academic discourse with great suspicion, has gained considerable influence. By contrast, two of the pioneering IsMO figures who headed RZ yeshivot that are not part of the Mercaz ha-Rav milieu have had an especially profound impact on the growing process of academization of Israeli religious leadership, which will be discussed at length below.

New Israeli Religious Leaders and Their Academic Training

To date, then, academic training is by no means a requirement for serving in the Israeli rabbinate on any level and is still far from the norm. Yet, as detailed below, it is gaining traction as part of the broader assertion of a moderate lifestyle within a vocal and recognizable RZ minority and its leadership. Increased academization has been inspired by key figures such as Lichtenstein and Rabinovitch and facilitated by institutions that expose male and female students to higher secular education in a seamless manner. It is evidenced in the rise of three interrelated phenomena: the coalescence of an alternative RZ rabbinate through organizations such as Tzohar and Beit Hillel, the emergence of women as legitimate religious leaders within moderate RZ circles, and the expansion of the synagogue-based rabbinate.

In 2008, I published an article that focused on RZ-oriented organizations that arose in the 1990s and early 2000s, including Tzohar.[20] This rabbinical coalition began out of a sense that the state rabbinate had become, at best, a bureaucratic nightmare; at worst, a misdirected collection of cronies. Rather than facilitating positive connections among the broad spectrum of Israeli Jews to Jewish tradition, the new organizations claimed, the rabbinate was causing greater alienation. As a remedy, Tzohar focused its efforts initially on providing religious services in a user-friendly manner to nonobservant Israeli Jews. My argument was that organizations like Tzohar manifested the rise of an alternative RZ rabbinate that challenged the hegemony of the state rabbinate. They duplicated some of the state rabbinate services but targeted a constituency that had become distanced from the official framework.

In the fifteen years since that article appeared, Tzohar has further established itself and branched out into new areas. In parallel, arguably the most dramatic change in RZ Torah study and leadership is the revolution that has gradually taken place in the involvement and roles of women. As we saw earlier with regard to Bina, Brovender, and Henkin in particular, a new generation of women has arisen for whom rabbinic texts and their methodologies are no longer foreign. Indeed, a growing corps of women have emerged who are committed deeply to Orthodox religious observance and theological principles and are also in possession of advanced expertise in Talmudic study and Jewish jurisprudence.

Recall that the rise of this fresh class of Torah scholars has precipitated the development of original models for female religious leadership as well: the *rosh midrasha* (female head of a women's seminary) and *rosh beit midrash* (female head of a study hall), legal advocates in Israeli rabbinic courts, "halakhic advisors" (yoatzot halakhah) regarding Jewish family law, and (parallel to a few American Orthodox synagogues) "spiritual leaders" in Israeli synagogues have begun to appear. Since 2009, Orthodox training programs for women that teach the exact same curricula as those utilized for achieving rabbinic ordination have sprung up.[21]

The rise in the prominence of women in RZ leadership circles was given concrete expression in 2012, when Beit Hillel was established. Like Tzohar, Beit Hillel protested the intransigence of the state rabbinate, but its focus was on the unwillingness of Israeli rabbis to articulate a more considered approach to religious law. Beit Hillel created a "halakhic think tank" that investigated subjects such as relationships to nonobservant Jews, the halakhic status of LGBT Jews, and the authoritative religious approach to people with physical, mental, and psychological disabilities and published learned position papers that presented lenient rulings. Most dramatically, Beit Hillel defined itself from the outset as a forum for "attentive spiritual leadership" and invited women and men equally—rabbis, yeshiva and midrasha heads, lecturers, halakhic advisors, advocates, and educators—to join at the helm.

Beit Hillel is still perceived by many as an unconventional initiative and has been criticized strongly for its lenient positions, but it would be a mistake to characterize it as a fringe organization. Its activists include highly respected yeshiva lecturers, congregational rabbis, female scholars, and institution builders, and its publications have drawn wide interest. The fact that woman are equal partners testifies to their growing position within contemporary Israeli religious life and highlights the imprudence of limiting a study addressing the new Israeli religious leadership to male rabbis.

Statistical information on Beit Hillel's members and their educational backgrounds offers a very different picture of the role of academics in contemporary Israeli Orthodox religious leadership from that which emerges from the rabbinical establishment. As of August 2021, there were 166 members of Beit Hillel, sixty-six women and one hundred men. These include kibbutz rabbis, synagogue rabbis and *rabbaniyyot*, military chaplains, female religious court advocates, female halakhic advisors, heads of Torah study institutions, lecturers in yeshivot and midrashot, a judge, and a few university lecturers who also serve as congregational rabbis. Seventeen of the women and twenty-five of the men held doctorates, practically an identical percentage. Almost all of the rest were college graduates, and the majority had master's degrees as well.[22]

Tzohar does not publicize or share the names of its members, but a list of the people on its rabbinical governing council appears on its website. The limited information available indicates that here, too, academic training is common, although not quite as universal as in Beit Hillel. Of the thirty-one rabbinical figures that serve on Tzohar's council, at least sixteen have academic degrees—six doctorates, six master's, and four bachelor's.[23] Notably, in 2021 Tzohar took the step of naming two prominent women leaders to its executive board; both hold doctorates and teach in academic institutions.[24]

The biographies of the Beit Hillel members, in particular, offer a picture of diverse academic interests. As one might expect from a group of religious figures and pedagogues, education, Talmud, Bible, and Jewish thought were common academic pursuits, as were helping professions such as social work and mental health counseling—although the latter were more common among the women. Yet there are also quite a few members with advanced degrees in the humanities and social sciences, such as gender studies, media studies, cultural studies, sociology, literature, history, and religion, as well as engineers, computer scientists, and even one member with a Bachelor of Fine Arts from the Bezalel Academy of Art. This list is indicative of a collective that looks at academic credentials as more than a formality necessary in order to gain employment or qualify for various benefits. Like the German rabbinic revolutionaries of the nineteenth century, these religious leaders see academia as an integral part of their intellectual development.

Among the men, there is a strong representation of alumni from YHE, as well as a critical mass of individuals who studied in yeshivot headed by students of Lichtenstein, such as Otniel (Rabbi Re"em HaKohen), Ma'ale Gilboa (Rabbi Yehuda Gilad), Yerucham (Rabbi Eliyahu Blumenzweig, semiretired), and AMIT Orot Shaul (Rabbi Yuval Cherlow). Graduates of Yeshivat Birkat Moshe (Rabinovitch), along with new immigrants ordained by RIETS and Yeshivat Chovevei Torah (YCT), feature prominently as well. Yet there are also notable former students of institutions known to be more religiously conservative, including, among others, Kerem B'Yavneh, Sha'alvim, Hakotel, and even Mercaz ha-Rav.

The women's Talmud and Jewish law educational backgrounds are far more uniform. Almost all made their ways through various programs offered by the four leading Israeli midrashot established for advanced women's Torah study—Midreshet Lindenbaum (Brovinder/Riskin), Matan (Bina), Nishmat (Henkin), and Migdal Oz (Esti Rosenberg, neé Lichtenstein)—with some having studied at the recently reconstituted Beit Morasha. A few participated in advanced traditional Jewish text study through the special program for graduate students at BIU's midrasha, and some of the new immigrants studied after their Israel gap year at New York's Stern College for Women (part of YU), where they enrolled in the Graduate Program in Advanced Talmudic Studies (GPATS), others at Yeshivat Maharat (a New York–based institution for women that grants ordination with the title *Manhiga Hilkhatit Rukhanit Toranit*, a female leader of Jewish law, spirituality, and Torah.

The roles of YHE and its affiliated Migdal Oz in the academization process are especially significant. This is due in great part, as noted, to Lichtenstein's key position as, and personal model of, a religious leader who synthesized secular knowledge within his oeuvre. Today, these two institutions are co-headed and headed, respectively, by his eldest son and eldest daughter, both of whom hold degrees in literature from the Hebrew University of Jerusalem. Moreover, this illustrates the key role of Herzog College in the YHE orbit. It has evolved, as noted, into a far broader academic institution that offers degrees that are officially in education but subspecialize in a range of disciplinary tracks besides classic educational ones, including social sciences and humanities subjects such as geography, communications, and literature; an archeology focus; and MA studies. Most are taught by PhD-credentialed lecturers, some of them professors at Israel's major research institutions. Other yeshivot and midrashot have arrangements that enable their students to pursue degrees at Herzog, thus expanding further its impact upon the evolving RZ leadership. To be sure, many attend the college in order to qualify for government teaching positions and civil servant jobs that demand a college diploma. Yet, as in any such setting, studying in a classroom under qualified academics who are actively involved in research exposes attendees to new vistas, especially those students who have a proclivity for intellectual curiosity.

Alongside the immediate YHE circle, it is instructive to examine the educational training of the senior staffs of the various RZ yeshivot and midrashot as a way to gauge, to some degree, the place of academic study in their collective backgrounds. The following two charts present a snapshot regarding eleven leading yeshivot and six midrashot:[25]

TABLE 7.1. Faculty of RZ Men's Yeshivot (listed in alphabetical order)

Name	Type/ Population	# of senior staff	# with academic degree	# with MA degree	# with PhD degree	Head/s with degrees
Birkat Moshe	Hesder	10	6	1	2	2/3
Ha-Golan	Hesder	14	5	1	1	0/1
Ha-Kotel	Hesder	7	1	0	0	0/1
Har Etzion (YHE)	Hesder	29	24	9	0	2/3
Har ha-Mor	Full-time	10	0	0	0	0/3
Kerem B'Yavneh	Hesder	12	4	0	0	0/2
Ma'ale Gilboa	Shiluv[1]	11	9	3	5	1/3
Mercaz ha-Rav	Full-time	21	0	0	0	0/1
Orot Shaul	Hesder	8	6	4	3	1/2
Otniel	Hesder	15	12	5	1	1/2
Yerucham	Hesder	10	8	2	0	0/1

1 *Shiluv* combines two years of yeshiva study with a full three-year army program.

TABLE 7.2. Faculty of RZ Women's Midrashot

Name	# of senior staff	# with academic degree	# with MA degree	# with PhD degree	Head/s with degrees
Harova	18	0	0	0	0/1
Lindenbaum	23	21	11	4	2/2
Matan	36	34	17	9	1/1
Migdal Oz	26	23	11	6	1/1
Nishmat	9	7	4	1	1/1
Orot Etzion	14	2	0	0	0/1

These tables demonstrate that the RZ advanced Torah study institutions can be divided along the lines of the academic backgrounds of their senior staff. This is patently clear in relation to the women's frameworks, where Orot Etzion and Harova (Israeli program), two institutions inspired by the Mercaz ha-Rav approach, have far fewer academically trained faculty members than the others. A sharp distinction is apparent among the men as well, with YHE and its offshoots figuring prominently among the group with the most college-educated faculty. What emerges is that the positive orientation toward academics among the new Israeli religious leadership has strong roots in the environments in which the figures gained critical exposures to advanced Torah studies.

From a broader historical perspective, the data from the yeshivot and midrashot strengthen the impression that the arrival in Israel of Lichtenstein in 1971 and the immigration of other America MO figures with academic training in the decade before or after who spearheaded the establishment and development of some of these other institutions— Brovender, Bina, Henkin, Riskin, Rabinovitch—was a key factor in the emergence of the new cadre of academically trained religious leadership.

Training and Reception

Returning to the rabbinate that arose in nineteenth-century Germany, Schorsch's article asserts that this phenomenon evolved in response to a collective need of core Jewish constituencies for a novel type of religious leader.[26] This raises the question as to whether contemporary RZ communities are expressing a similar desire for academically trained religious leaders. One set of data, job descriptions advertised and distributed by RZ communal and congregational search committees from across the country, suggests otherwise.[27]

I examined nineteen such documents from a wide range of Israeli geographical locations with diverse socioeconomic environments and RZ orientations. All demanded Orthodox rabbinic ordination, and most specified that the candidates must be unequivocal Zionists. Many also underscored the importance of bridging gaps between diverse memberships and relating to the youth. Some focused on "balancing between conservatism and innovation," as well as the increased consequence of addressing the spiritual needs of women. Others described familiarity with, and ability to communicate, both religious and general knowledge as valuable, but not one mentioned possession of an academic degree or past university attendance. What was stated clearly by almost all was the importance of substantial IDF service—some even stipulating the minimal length of such military experience—as a core requirement for serving as spiritual leader of an RZ community.[28]

The collective focus on military service as reflective of the foundational qualifications for a rabbi is a distinctively Israeli phenomenon that separates Israel from the rest of the Jewish world. On an internal societal level, moreover, this criterion, which emphasizes the integration of a nonparochial national element, distinguishes RZ-oriented communities from their traditionalist Haredi analogues, which idealize purist notions of Torah expertise and devotion. Inasmuch as prominent sectors within the RZ camp have veered toward ideals and practices generally associated with Haredi Orthodoxy, in the eyes of their RZ constituencies, the "army factor" remains an important anchor of identity. Indeed, while in the past, RZ advanced yeshivot hired talented Haredi figures who had not served in the army as Talmud instructors, today this is rarely the case.[29] This army factor sustains a sense of collectivity that prevails across the entire spectrum of the RZ public, as reflected in searches for rabbis in a wide variety of locales.

From this perspective, male army service—not university training—is the Israeli parallel to the role occupied by academics for the nineteenth-century figures presented by Schorsch as having transformed the German rabbinate, regardless of their denominational predilections. It is the common ground that unites the entire spectrum of the RZ sector, from the Kav/Harda"l camp to the IsMO groups, as opposed to Haredi society and its traditionalist rabbinic products.[30]

That said, other ways of analyzing the reception of academically trained religious leaders testify more emphatically to their import. Especially strong concentrations of such rabbis are to be found in certain parts of the country: the Baka, German Colony, and Old Katamon neighborhoods of Jerusalem; the Jerusalem-adjacent Gush Etzion and Beit Shemesh; as well as Ra'anana, Givat Shmuel, and Petah Tikva in the central region (the latter two near BIU). The religious populations in these communities comprise many Israeli-born professionals, Anglo immigrants, academics, and high-tech workers and executives, most with at least one university degree themselves.

The geographical concentration of these figures supports the contention that, parallel to the so-called Harda"lization of vocal elements of the RZ stream, a minority but nonetheless visible constituency is emerging within specific strongholds. This circle does not seek to limit the pursuit of secular knowledge to narrowly practical concerns. Rather, it represents an Israeli Orthodox Judaism that views broad learning and culture positively and appreciates religious leaders who are both familiar with and adept at their integration into Jewish life.

Additional perspective can be gained by noting the central roles played by key university-educated personalities in cutting-edge initiatives that are impacting Jewish life in Israel and beyond. Numerous figures with academic qualifications are expanding the scope of the rabbinic profession beyond the synagogue, the study hall/classroom, and halakhic supervisory and adjudicatory positions. In some cases, there is a direct connection between the individual's studies and his or her pioneering activities, while in others such studies are more in the background. A list of outstanding examples would certainly include, among many others: Rabbi Dr. Benny Lau; Rabbi Dr. Yakov Nagen, an alumnus of YHE and the Hebrew University in Jerusalem, who is a senior instructor in the Otniel yeshiva and heads the OTS's Blickle Institute for Interfaith Dialogue and its Beit Midrash for Judaism and Humanity;[31] Rabbanit Dr. Michal Tikochinsky, an alumnus of Matan and BIU Law School, who is former head of Beit Morasha's advanced women's study program, and current dean of students and lecturer at Herzog College and Migdal Oz;[32] Rabbi Dr. Shaul (Seth) Farber, an alumnus of YHE and the Hebrew University in Jerusalem, who is rabbi of Kehillat Netivot in Ra'anana and founder of ITIM, the Jewish Life Advocacy Center, and in 2018 received a Ministry of Aliyah and Integration Award for Outstanding Contribution to Israeli Society; Rabbanit Michelle Cohen Farber, MA, an alumnus of Midreshet Lindenbaum and BIU, who is founder of HADRAN, an organization dedicated to inspiring women worldwide to study Talmud, in particular the daf yomi seven-and-a-half-year cycle for completion of the entire Babylonian Talmud;[33] and Rabbanit Dr. Rachel Levmore, an alumnus of Michlalah College for Women in Jerusalem and BIU (MA and PhD), who is a legal scholar and director of the Agunah and Get-Refusal Prevention Project of the International Young Israel Movement in Israel and the Jewish Agency, and serves on the Israeli government committee for selection of religious court judges.[34]

The Gender Factor

Of course, the biggest single difference between Schorsch's subjects and those discussed here is that the former were all men. The very fact that women are integrating into Israeli Orthodox religious leadership frameworks reflects a major shift, even as they are clearly a minority and some of the roles that they have occupied remain decidedly avant-garde or controversial even within their own moderate camp. Thus, the high percentage of female religious personalities, advanced teachers, and practitioners who possess advanced academic training invites closer consideration.[35]

Ostensibly, the ubiquity of university credentials among Israeli women religious leaders, even in comparison with their ideologically aligned male counterparts, can be attributed to structures and other pragmatic factors. Young men from RZ families who attend Hesder programs or study full-time in a yeshiva before entering the army are likely to invest many years in advanced Talmudic studies prior to touching academic subjects in a formal manner. Women, by contrast, rarely dedicate more than a year to full-time advanced Torah education before entering the army or national service. Those who partake in extensive learning afterward often do so in dual programs together with college/university studies. For male rabbis whose formative early adult intellectual-spiritual involvements take place primarily within the walls of a yeshiva, then, academic education will more likely be experienced as a complementary and relatively distinct engagement in comparison with their core Torah study. For women, the opposite is often the case. They gain university credentials before or in parallel to achieving a level of religious learning that enables them to serve as leaders. Their academic exposures are not just an additional, supplementary source of knowledge but rather part and parcel of their core intellectual-spiritual training. To be sure, as more "women's yeshivot" that recruit students for full-time advanced Torah study programs after high school are founded, this may change.[36] To date, however, the predominant frameworks of the post–high school years for Israeli RZ men and women lead to divergent paths vis-à-vis academic learning.

Beyond the distinctions between male and female tracks, the need to gain an official title and the status that it provides also contributes to women's more universal academic training. Until recently, rabbinic labels were not available to them, and they are still met with objections and skepticism. An academic degree, especially one that testifies to special expertise, can offer a partial solution for women. This came across in the responses to a set of questions that I sent out to a small sample of Israeli rabbi/*rabbanit* doctors (PhD). Two women made clear that, had rabbinic ordination been a viable and accepted option, they would have been less likely to work toward a doctoral degree. For these women, gaining a recognized university degree was not primarily a way to expand the scope of their intellectual and religious worldviews; it was, rather, a means to achieving a fundamental level of legitimacy as especially knowledgeable religious figures.[37]

As women's religious leadership roles expand, the question arises as to whether their more universal exposure to academic training will be evident in the way that they disseminate Jewish knowledge. An initial indication comes from the respondents—both women and men—to the questionnaire that I distributed. Regardless of their motivations for pursuing the degree, there was agreement as to the immense impact of their doctoral studies on them as religious individuals and on various aspects of their religious leadership roles. Due to intensive exposure to advanced academic research, they felt that they were much more conscious of the need for accuracy, consistency, and grounding what they taught in compelling sources. They also indicated that they had expanded tremendously their "library shelves" of knowledge and exposure to ideas and ways of thinking beyond those that had been available within more traditional learning settings. Moreover, they incorporated these sources into their synagogue sermons and lectures, yeshiva and midrasha classes, and popular religious writing as well. Some spoke passionately about the way their various exposures had come together in a holistic manner such that they could no longer separate the yeshiva and university aspects of their intellectual and spiritual personas. These reactions to advanced university studies could be heard from both women and men, yet in the case of the women the navigation between their parochial and scientific knowledge communities came across more readily as seamless.

Redefinition, Replacement, and Alternatives

Homing in on the role of academic study in the evolution of contemporary Israeli religious leadership, the materials presented here demonstrate that postsecondary university or college training is becoming more common. Possession of academic degrees is especially pronounced among the rising moderate contingents associated with the

Beit Hillel and Tzohar organizations and among the graduates of institutions that are located within the compass of YHE. These frameworks
are the dominant breeding grounds for many of the university-educated
congregational rabbis active in local communities. Rigorous academic
exposures are also something shared by many of the outstanding "rabbi/
rabbanit doctor" personalities who are broadening the scope and direction of Israeli religious leadership from intellectual, social, and legal
perspectives. On this level, a process of redefinition that bears some
similarities to that described by Schorsch is taking place.

All the same, among male rabbis, academic degrees are far from the
norm—certainly in the Haredi sector, but within the more conservative RZ factions as well. Indeed, RZ communities throughout most of
the country—even those with large percentages of members who are
themselves university-educated—will not necessarily expect their rabbis to have gained similar exposures to academic learning. Instead, the
"secular" qualifications that are critical for the male rabbi to possess are
unequivocal Zionism and a record of substantial military service.

The one group of Israeli Orthodox religious leaders for whom university studies are most ubiquitous and, arguably, significant to its emergence is also the least unanimously accepted—namely, women. Yet the
significant inroads women have made have been bolstered by, and in
some cases predicated on, the academic training that they possess. As
noted, their degrees conferred upon them official titles and credentials
at a time when formal parochial designations for women were unavailable or not readily recognized. Their diplomas may not be sufficient for
them to gain employment within the state rabbinate or even as spiritual leaders in most Israeli synagogues, although greater government
accreditation has been granted,[38] but they raise their statures in the
eyes of potential students, parents, and supporters of the institutions in
which they work. Ironically, the fact that a woman has standing within
the secular academic setting also may make it easier for her to gain access to mixed-gender or male audiences that might have been reticent
to learn from a "woman rabbi." In that sense, the academic training may
be seen as playing a subversive role in facilitating entrée into formerly
"protected" venues.[39]

In some cases, moreover, the specific expertise gained by women in
the university or scientific world has been a key to their ability to develop

extraordinarily impactful careers as pioneering religious figures. One outstanding example is Dr. Deena Zimmerman. An American-trained pediatrician and veteran immigrant to Israel. Her strong skill set in advanced Torah learning, together with her medical background, drew her to Nishmat's yoatzot halakhah program during its initial stages. Subsequently, in 2005, she published a book on Jewish family purity law that has gained widespread praise.[40] Today, alongside her medical practice, she is one of the leading authorities on the confluence of women's family law and medicine and serves formally as director of Nishmat's Women's Health and Halacha websites.[41] Through these activities and her general association with Nishmat, the main training ground for yoatzot halakhah worldwide, Zimmerman has emerged as an influential personality in Orthodox religious life, both in Israel and throughout the globe.

Returning to the historical model of German Rabbiner Doktoren, the comparison to their transformative impact on nineteenth-century German Jewry has assisted in clarifying the distinctive contemporary Israeli process. Schorsch asserted that the novel forms of knowledge acquired by the pioneering rabbinical personalities of that era were critical to their successful displacement of the traditional, exclusively yeshiva-trained rabbinate. It is certainly possible that in time academically oriented religious leaders will increasingly gain positions within Israeli state and traditionalist rabbinic frameworks, although this would be a major novelty.

To date, however, a different trend can be discerned in Israel: the rise of a complementary class of religious figures who express their leadership through frameworks outside the state and often beyond the synagogue realm as well. This is by no means a completely unprecedented model. Educators, independent scholars, public activists, and spiritualists have long operated outside the official spaces. The difference in the contemporary situation is that through organizations like Beit Hillel, Tzohar, and a network of post–high school yeshivot and midrashot, as well as certain strategic locales, the alternative religious leadership is both coalescing and cultivating a broader constituency. While this cadre can be identified through multiple common features, the ubiquity of academic training and its expression in the activities of this faction are a bold reflection of that which distinguishes it from Haredi and more conservative (Harda"l) RZ forces.

8

Synagogue and Combat Zone

Two Types of Orthodox Feminism

Two Worlds?

Since the 1960s, American Jewish denominations have been engaging the feminist movement and its religious implications. The Reform rabbinic ordination of Sally Preisand in 1972 was the first on American soil and stands as a landmark moment in the history of religious feminism.[1] The late 1970s witnessed the rise of Orthodox religious feminism and its initial impact on North American Jewish life. From the outset, the fiercest debates between activists and more conservative-oriented rabbinical authorities revolved around efforts to expand the role of women in public ritual. As for Israeli Orthodox Judaism, while advanced Torah study programs grew in parallel to the North American events, significant changes in the parochial landscape only gained prominence in the twenty-first century.[2]

In 2016, an analysis of Orthodox feminism appeared that attributes the relatively recent emergence of more lenient approaches within Israel toward public religious roles for women to the direct influence of pioneering North American counterparts.[3] Yet I contend that, together with considerable interfaces and cross-fructification, the topic of Orthodox feminism also accentuates fundamental distinctions between religious life in Israel and North America. In line with this book's overarching argument, it is the synthesis of elements brought to Israel by Americans with unique local realities and orientations that has facilitated the emergence of an alternative "Israeli" type of religious feminism within the local moderate camp.

Support for the North American stimulus for Israeli Orthodox feminism is to be found in the ongoing growth of schools of higher learning that are training Orthodox women to be Torah scholars. In multiple cases, the founders of these frameworks were American immigrants—including prominent agents of change highlighted here (Bina, Brovender, Hartman, Henkin, Lichtenstein, Riskin) and their disciples. Like their North American counterparts, today some institutions are even offering their strongest pupils study paths that lead to rabbinical ordination or analogous titles. North American immigrants have also played key roles in the Orthodox "partnership" services that originated in Jerusalem in 2002, in which women lead parts of the publicly held prayers and chant the Bible reading.[4] And, of course, the leading theologian of Orthodox feminism is Tamar Ross, who, as noted, immigrated to Israel from the United States at the age of eighteen. The confluence of these developments suggests that, at least as far as Orthodox feminism is concerned, the gap between the "two worlds" is narrowing.[5]

Such a conclusion, however, arises out of an understanding of Jewish life that does not account for the multiple ways that religion manifests itself in Israel. The following analysis highlights a strand of religious feminism that is unique to the Israeli milieu. It reveals critical divergences between these major Jewish populations. That said, it arose within the IsMO sector that internalized and revamped aspects of the American type and then applied it to a distinctly Israeli environment and experience.

In what follows, we will examine and compare two documents that aim to reject the expansion of Orthodox women's role—one from each center. The North American document, which serves here primarily as a foil,[6] is a rabbinical ruling signed by seven rabbis and adopted in 2017 by the Orthodox Union (OU), the largest association of Orthodox synagogues on the continent. It prohibits women from serving as clergy in its member congregations.[7] The Israeli document is a Hebrew booklet regarding gender and the Israel Defense Forces, published in 2018.[8] It is based on lectures delivered by Rabbi Yigal Levinstein, one of the founding heads of the pre-army Torah study academy Bnei David-Eli, better known simply as Mechinat Eli, and a key figure in the Kav/Harda"l RZ sector.

Contrasting these sources homes in on a particular form of Israeli engagement with novel woman's involvements that has not been a focus of studies of religious feminism. Taken together with the more conventional perceptions of expansions of religious roles, this chapter indicates the emergence of two divergent forms of Orthodox religious feminism, albeit with notable overlaps. One has its roots in North America but has since developed a transnational character. The other gains inspiration to a certain degree from North American precedents, but its actual expression is unique to the Israeli sovereign Jewish setting.

The OU Ruling

From one perspective, the OU ruling in 2017 was merely another stage in a series of conflicts over the extent of women's access to religious texts and participation in public rituals that had been brewing for nearly four decades within MO Judaism.[9] These transformations have been spearheaded since the late twentieth century by the Orthodox feminist movement that developed in parallel to the growth of educational frameworks dedicated to expanding the level of women's expertise in traditional Jewish law and literature.[10] The debates address, among other questions, whether women can study and teach Talmud, serve as legal "advisors" regarding the rules of Jewish family purity and as advocates in rabbinical courts, recite the *ketubah* (Jewish marriage writ) under the wedding canopy,[11] conduct their own "women's service,"[12] lead certain rituals in a mixed-gender (with separate seating) public "partnership" prayer setting,[13] and function in authority positions historically reserved for male rabbis.[14]

The OU document, however, is exceptional both in what it sanctions and what it forbids. Veering away from previous negative evaluations of the entire endeavor, the 2017 ruling exclaims:

> some women . . . feel disengaged from their shuls [synagogues] and un-inspired in the synagogue. . . . We recognize that many who are looking for new avenues to increase their shul involvement are motivated by a genuine desire to strengthen their connection with Hashem [God]. . . . Each synagogue should be encouraged to reach out to women to create meaningful ways to involve them in synagogue life. . . . The spiritual growth of our community is dependent upon a steady stream of talented women both serving as role models and teachers, and filling positions of influence.[15]

Thus, the emergence of religiously educated Orthodox women both looking for and able to contribute to spiritual and intellectual elevation is celebrated. This is a sharp departure from prior articulations by numerous authoritative Orthodox rabbis, including those of one of the signees of the OU rule itself, who were far more skeptical regarding both the motivations for and the positive potential of increased women's religious prominence.[16]

At the same time, the OU ruling is adamant that the title "rabbi" and certain tasks portrayed as core clergy roles must be reserved for men only. The main reason to prohibit women clergy, according to the OU document, is because it is not part of the *mesorah*, the handed-down tradition that has been accepted as the consensus approach among halakhah-observant Jews.[17]

In order to clarify the difference between those new female initiatives that are praiseworthy and those that must remain in the hands of men, the ruling presents detailed lists of activities that are permitted for women and those that are absolutely forbidden. The area that emerges as the main sphere of the exclusively male rabbi is "officiating at . . . life-cycle events, . . . sermons, . . . during [prayer] services, . . . leading services."[18]

Seemingly, there is a legalistic rationale behind the decision to focus on synagogue ceremonial ritual roles as the decisive feature of Orthodox clergy and the main basis for prohibiting women from attaining this position. For there remains a consensus among even the most liberal Orthodox authorities that certain aspects of the public prayer service may only be performed by men.[19] Yet the upshot of this position is to concentrate official rabbinical actions almost solely on what takes place in the sanctuary during services and, relatedly, on performance of certain public rituals.

However, since medieval times, if not prior, the predominant mandate of the rabbi was that of a *posek-lamdan*—a legalist-scholar, with little if any official ritual capacity.[20] In fact, the role that modern rabbis began to play within the synagogue was a nineteenth-century variance initiated by German Reform Judaism. Moreover, rather than limiting the scope of the congregational rabbi, the dominant trend within the major denominations of twentieth-century North American Judaism has been an especially expansive job description—lecturer, social worker, chief executive, Hebrew school principal, public activist, among others—that took the figure far beyond the borders of this preserve.[21] By contrast, through the OU ruling the Orthodox rabbi was being redefined as a sanctuary specialist. To be sure, almost all the other tasks outside the sanctuary—teaching, guiding, adjudicating—that were now open to women continued to be fulfilled by male rabbis too. Yet once they were sanctioned by the authorities as legitimately within the domain of female religious leadership as well, they essentially became gender-neutral. Even for the authors of the OU decision who forbade women rabbis, then, the only sphere that remained unconditionally associated with the male rabbi was the synagogue sanctuary during services.[22]

The novel articulation of the Orthodox rabbinate that emerges from the OU ruling, as I have written elsewhere, thus reflects a "sacralization" of this role that, along with clear core distinctions, raises intriguing parallels to the Catholic understanding of the foundational principles of priesthood. This approach is in opposition to the prior American rabbinical ideal that was more analogous to the predominant Protestant perception of the ministry.[23] The decision to locate the crucial boundary between male and female religious leadership within the synagogue sanctuary has important implications for distinguishing between North American and Israeli Jewish religious life.

Mechinat Eli

Along with its outspoken misgivings regarding contemporary secular culture, the Kav camp professes a particularly strong nationalist orientation, which is articulated through its interpretation of the classical Zionist concept of *mamlakhtiyut* (statism), raising the issue of upholding the institutions of the sovereign Jewish government to a pristine religious value.[24] Mechinat Eli was founded in 1988 by two products of the Merkaz ha-Rav yeshiva, rabbis Yigal Levinstein and Eli Sadan. It is grounded in the Kav approach to religion and statehood, and its students are encouraged to gain inspiration from these ideals as they embark upon military service.[25]

This pre-army preparatory/religious study institution for men has cultivated a strong following through its formula of rooting motivation toward rigorous army service in deep spiritual commitment to RZ ideals. Its graduates have reached the upper echelons of the IDF and other security agencies. Its establishment has also spurred the emergence of scores of other such *mechinot* (pre-army academies; singular, *mechina*—literally, "preparation"), both in the religious and in the secular sectors, that have become key feeders to the army's elite units and officers' school.[26] According to the umbrella organization of all the pre-army academies, there are presently twenty-three religious mechinot and thirty-seven "general" ones. The latter are all coeducational, while the religious ones include all-men, all-women, and mixed programs.[27]

Levinstein (b.1957) himself was raised in a family with a markedly secular lifestyle in the southern Israeli resort town of Eilat. After a distinguished military career in the armored corps, in which he rose to the rank of lieutenant colonel, he followed in the footsteps of his air force pilot brother and entered Machon Meir, a Merkaz ha-Rav–oriented Jerusalem yeshiva for newly observant Jews. There he immersed himself in the religious studies and redemptive theology that transformed his own life and ultimately inspired those of his followers as well.[28]

Due to the strong connection and loyalty that Levinstein has cultivated among his many students and alumni—some of whom are themselves today high-ranking IDF officers and well-regarded educators and rabbis—his opinions have force beyond a narrow slice of the RZ camp. During the second decade of the twenty-first century, he became especially outspoken regarding issues related to gender and sexual identity. His pronouncements, particularly those deemed homophobic, have been criticized sharply even by some who deeply respect him.[29] Nonetheless, his overall worldview regarding the relationship between religious values and active participation in the institutions of the state continues to provide an ideological backdrop for many of those who seek to integrate these two realms.[30] In this context, he is one of the most outspoken opponents of RZ women serving in the IDF rather than volunteering for national service, the accepted path until recently.[31]

The Levinstein Booklet

In April 2018, over one hundred thousand copies of a printed booklet titled *Military Agenda?: How Gender Perception Disintegrates the People's Army* were distributed throughout Israel.[32] Based on Levinstein's lectures and edited by two close students, it claims that the current policies of the IDF regarding gender identity undermine its core values and mission.[33] The publication was financed by a prior crowd-sourcing campaign.[34] In parallel to the printed version, dramatic promotional videos[35] and a full-length oral version were uploaded to YouTube.[36]

Specifically, Levinstein attacked the departmental title change of the IDF chief of staff's "Advisor on Topics Relating to Women [acronym: YOHALA"N]" to "Topics Relating to Gender [YOHALA"M]," the issuance of a new protocol regarding women soldiers (the "Command for Integrated Service"), and a document that presents the more fundamental ideational backdrop to these changes.[37]

An official army paper, "From Women to Gender—The Perceptual Basis," was distributed in 2015. It declares that:

> the perception of humanity as divided into two groups (men and women) is imprecise, fixes people in inappropriate patterns, and is an incorrect and inefficient basis for maximizing human resources. . . . The main characteristic (perhaps) of these perceptions and stereotypical gender expectations is that they establish a hierarchical relationship between the sexes, that usually renders superiority to men. . . . The army, in this regard, is an organization whose characteristics emphasize this point.[38]

The practical upshot of this novel approach within the army is to predicate thinking about integration of all soldiers in the army on a recognition of "gendered" biases. The goal is "a strategy and recommendation of practical actions that will achieve a decline in gender inequality . . . and equality of opportunities as expressions of the ethical commitment of the IDF toward those who serve."[39]

The main body of Levinstein's 2018 evaluation is a close reading of the 2015 IDF directive. His crucial argument is that the "transformation" being advanced by the IDF is grounded in radical contemporary feminist discourse that adopts a postmodernist critique of traditional binaries and undermines fundamental values regarding family and male and female roles. According to Levinstein, these are not just vague ideas; rather, he argues that they destabilize the main task of the IDF:

This is not theoretical material from the Gender Studies department in the ivory tower of an academic university. . . . These words are the mistaken worldview today in the IDF! . . . The truth is that the army was not built based on the male typology—the army was built in order to battle our enemies, including those who are very determined to kill us all, and as a result it must place opposite them fighters that can deal with them.[40]

Levinstein concludes his analysis with a clarification and a plea that belies his primary concern. He explains that the topic of women serving in mixed units with religious male soldiers has been a cause of considerable disruption. Thankfully, he opines, the combined efforts of the heads of many yeshivot and mechinot that send their graduates to the IDF led to an arrangement with the army that prevents unnecessary contact.[41] All the same, the new principle that has been established by the IDF has much broader ramifications:

To date, the national religious public dealt mainly with the question of the influence of the Command for Integrated Service on the religious/ observant soldier. But the deeper process is the one identified above, the embedding of an agenda of blurring sexes and identities whose source is the radical school of feminism intent on erasure of identities.[42]

Religious Women in the Israeli Army

Levinstein's denunciation of the IDF gender policies certainly highlights the role of the army as a flashpoint for the Kulturkampf between the worldviews of secular and religious elites. While he is adamant that his complaint stems from concern for all of Israeli society, the most direct target for his extensive dissection of the text is actually his own natural constituency—the RZ camp, where far more women are choosing to serve in the army than ever before.

According to Israeli law, women who declare that they are religiously observant are exempted from mandatory military enlistment. The national service program emerged as a compromise that enabled RZ-oriented draft-age females to serve the country voluntarily through educational, social welfare, public health, and governmental jobs, without obligating themselves to direct military commands, where maintaining their modesty could be challenging. However, over the past decade and a half an increasing number of RZ girls have chosen what was once considered the secular route, active army duty.[43] A 2017 letter produced for the Knesset by its Center for Research and Information testifies that between 2008 and 2015 the number of religious women who enlisted more than doubled from under 1,000 to 2,260, and the figure has continued to grow since.[44] The current rate amounts to close to 25 percent of all RZ female high-school graduates.[45] Additionally, in the past the small minority that did so generally requested to serve in the Educational Corps, where they would work with a primarily female cohort. By contrast, the numbers of religious women that can be found in a broad range of army positions that demand close and ongoing interaction with fellow male soldiers continue to grow, including in advanced intelligence and diplomatic units, a variety of infantry and armament positions, and as field instructors, as well as within elite fighter pilot squadrons. In fact, today a higher percentage of religious women become officers than among those who are defined as secular.[46]

These changes can be attributed to various factors, among them the establishment of an array of RZ mechinot for women that have created female variants on Mechinat Eli's model and encourage their students to explore the wide variety of military jobs that are available to them.[47] Some of the midrashot for women's Torah learning, including Midreshet Lindenbaum and Beit Medrash Migdal Oz, offer study-army programs that draw upon the male Hesder combined yeshiva–army service approach.[48] They also design special tracks for female soldiers to dedicate themselves to enrichment after their release from active duty.[49] Broadly speaking, RZ women's orientation toward enlistment reflects their sense that military service is a foundational act of citizenship and national partnership from which they do not want to be exempted.[50] In contrast to this trend, at Mechinat Eli's own post–high school institution for women, Midreshet Danielle, acceptance is conditioned upon the prospective student's firm commitment to performing national service and not joining the army.[51]

By uncovering what he claims to be the subversive radical agenda of the IDF that seeks to undermine essential concepts of family and sexual identity, then, Levinstein's booklet focuses on the military as a critical

SPECIAL
MOVIE SCREENING

SERVING ON ALL FRONTS

A DOCUMENTARY FILM HIGHLIGHTING THE PARTICIPATION OF OUR STUDENTS AND STAFF IN THE CURRENT STRUGGLE TO DEFEND ISRAEL

MONDAY, JUNE 17TH

MAARIV AT 8:05PM | SCREENING AT 8:30PM

BEIT KNESSET OHEL ARI | 98 RAVUTSKY ST, RA'ANANA

REMARKS FROM RABBI BARUCH WEINTRAUB RA"M AT THE GUSH
RAV OF MEVASER TZION, TEL MOND

Figure 8.1. A poster marking a tribute to religious woman soldiers from Beit Midrash Migdal Oz and male Hesder soldiers from YHE who fought in the IDF during and after the October 7, 2023, massacre. Courtesy of Beit Midrash Migdal Oz.

framework in which the Israeli RZ struggle over feminism plays out. Identification of the RZ sector as the central audience for Levinstein's work is supported not only by examination of the text, but by both anecdotal evidence and recent scholarship on the role of RZ women in the IDF.

My own discovery of the booklet did not take place during an archival visit, the reading of an academic article, or even perusing a newspaper, magazine, or blog. Rather, I noticed a pile of copies on a table in the entrance to the RZ-oriented synagogue that I attended on a Friday evening. They were placed together with the usual array of printed materials on the weekly Torah portion (with ample advertisements for kosher tours and hotels) distributed to the Sabbath-observant congregants who are destined to refrain from surfing the web for the next twenty-five hours. As Jonathan Cohen maintains, such examples of "small media" play central functional roles in cultivating particularistic religious identity within Israeli society.[52] In point of fact, it is clear from the promotional video materials and the process of distribution accompanying the publication of the Levinstein booklet that this sector is the main target in mind.

Relatedly, in a 2018 study of RZ women and the IDF, Elisheva Rosman-Stollman argues that the dramatic rise in the number of religious women serving in the Israeli army has forced the religious establishment to engage an issue that until recently it could simply dismiss as forbidden. Even if there is still considerable opposition among most rabbis and educators, the sheer volume has led an increasing number of them to accommodate and lend support to those "native daughters" who make this choice, and to come to terms with a behavior that was previously shunned. The author sees this as a prime example of a "bottom-up" process of religious change. She concludes, however, with a more expansive suggestion: "women can use military service for ends other than equality while in uniform. . . . As these women join the workforce and the public sphere in Israeli society, it remains to be seen how they will continue to employ this tool in their bargaining with Religious-Zionism . . . and perhaps influence trends that are seen as religious radicalization in Israel."[53]

Levinstein's detailed dissection of IDF gender policy and the accompanying campaign targeting the RZ population are actually indicative of a parallel perception to that of Rosman-Stollman. Yet unlike the cautiously optimistic tenor of the academic article that raises the potential for the army experience to contribute to spiritual existence, Levinstein's gaze is directed toward the specter of its catastrophic effect on religious mores and domestic life. His chief concern, however, is not the potential for the "bottom up" process to advance feminist goals within the parochial sphere—which, to be sure, he would oppose. Rather, his sounding of the alarm conveys his deep apprehension that the issue of gender and army undermines the core religious values of heterosexual marriage and family as societal norms, and essential distinctions between male and female.[54] These are ideals about which there is considerable consensus within the RZ sector, agreement that goes far beyond the confines of the Kav/Harda"l segment.[55] By bearing down on the challenges to these principles inherent to the army's overall approach, he put forward a powerful argument against women's enlistment that would resonate more widely than merely among his core followers. For, as Tamar Katriel has observed, "Through images and practices of masculinity and femininity, and through varying and evolving approaches to citizenship, the experience of military service projects gender . . . identities that penetrate the depths of the social fabric even after military uniforms have been retired."[56] From Levinstein's perspective, then, the most profound challenge of Orthodox feminism is not that it will transform the ritual arena, but that by damaging the bastion of *mamlakhtiyut*—the IDF—it will destabilize the social and civic fabric of RZ life and values.

Bifurcation vs. Sovereignty

There are certainly common elements to expressions of religious feminism and reactions to them in North America and Israel. The most apparent is the fact that, in both geographic regions, prior norms regarding intellectual and ritual participation and authority are being challenged. Yet my corresponding analysis of the OU ruling from 2017 and the Levinstein booklet from 2018 reveals that for Israelis this is just one level of the confrontation, and arguably not the principal one. Levinstein's point-by-point effort to undermine the IDF's overall approach to gender, combined with his extensive campaign aimed at the RZ constituency, place engagement with feminism on a completely different plane. They bring to the fore the intense interface between more devotional manifestations of religious identity and civil life that is unique to the Israeli Jewish climate.[57]

The discussion here indicates that two parallel types of Orthodox feminism are emerging, one whose roots are in North America but has spread beyond, and another one that is unique to Israel. The first one is what is generally thought of when invoking this term, and it centers around what is conventionally considered to be the sacred realm and related issues of observance and Jewish law. The second is a product of the sui generis—insofar as Judaism is concerned—confluence of religion with the public square that has arisen in the sovereign State of Israel and is celebrated in particular by RZ adherents. The degree to which these two forms of religious feminism manifest "two worlds of Judaism" is expressed poignantly in the words of philosophy scholar and feminist theologian Tamar Ross:

> In the Diaspora, Jews can opt to respond to more intrinsic conflicts between their religious and secular lives by constructing an artificial "bubble" of holiness in which they continue to abide by the norms of tradition, cordoned off, as it were, by a myriad of practices designed to create barriers between themselves and their secular surroundings. Though difficult on a cognitive level such bifurcation is still workable where the main business of modernity and the secular values it generates can be left to the Gentiles. Israeli Orthodoxy, by contrast, cannot so easily afford the luxury of distancing itself from its surroundings. Living in a predominantly Jewish state does not lend itself to tolerating dissonance between problematic religious assumptions or halakhic directives and the secular demands of everyday life and current moral standards.[58]

This dichotomy between "bubbles of holiness" versus the role Judaism plays in public "everyday life" is fundamental to the difference between the Jewish spheres in Israeli and North American contexts.

Other than in Israel, the standard condition for Jews in modern times is a divide between private and sectorial religious spheres of existence, on one side, and public space—which is by definition non-Jewish—on the other.[59] Synagogues symbolize principal collective Jewish living spaces, and sanctuaries their cores.[60] This certainly applies to North American

Judaism, where at least until recently synagogue membership—of course completely voluntary and denominationally divided—was the sine qua non for Jewish religious connection.[61]

Inside this structure conflicts over core religious identity that can be avoided outside are sorted out on a regular basis.[62] The synagogue sanctuary is where the most practical and regularly scheduled litmus tests regarding degrees of inclusion and exclusion take place (of course, one-time ceremonies such as marriages and burials are also key moments, but they are isolated events). This is the case for all denominations. In contemporary non-Orthodox synagogues, where gender egalitarianism is the consensus outlook, the need to define the religious status of an individual is directed primarily toward areas such as whether patrilineal Jews and non-Jewish spouses of Jews can count for a quorum, lead services, or be called up to bless the Torah, or whether intermarried Jews can serve as congregational rabbis.[63] Orthodox synagogues are also increasingly addressing some of these circumstances, yet there is considerably greater degree of agreement as to who is a Jew. As to issues of sexual identity and the role of women in particular, as demonstrated above, there is far more intense debate.[64] Thus, the decision of the OU rabbis to draw their red line at redefinition of women's roles in the synagogue sanctuary, is consistent with this communal room's position as the pragmatic arbiter of American Jewish religious identity.

Having said this, the opposite is then true as well. That which takes place beyond the confines of the synagogue sanctuary need not be dictated by core religious tenets. This is so in connection to gender identity issues within civil American life. Although there will likely be correlations between the traditionalist religious views of Jewish individuals and communities and their perceptions of male/female roles in broader society, this is not necessarily the case. The same Orthodox woman for whom it is clear that she has no right to a public role within the synagogue may consider it completely legitimate to develop a career in a field that was until recently male-dominated.[65] This is what is found among the MO, but such a construct is gaining purchase within some Haredi circles as well.[66]

What increasingly distinguishes the MO sector from its Haredi counterparts and is reflected in the OU ruling, however, is the degree to which officially religious positions that serve both mixed male/female audiences can also be divided between those associated with the "male" sanctuary precinct and others that were once part of the male domain but have essentially become gender-neutral. That is, regarding religious studying, teaching, offering guidance, even adjudication, the egalitarian principles of civil society have gained greater acceptance.[67]

Echoing the earlier discussion of Bible scholarship, the best term for describing the condition reflected by the OU decision, then, is bifurcation. Specifically, by insisting that the rabbi in the sanctuary continues to be defined by patriarchal principles, a values-laden boundary was created between the public ritual realm of Orthodox Judaism and every other framework. No doubt, navigation of tensions between secular and religious ideals is endemic to the MO, yet here the division is sharpened. By tolerating certain egalitarian standards in areas of religious life as long as they take place outside the sanctuary, the MO have declared that acclimatizing to societal norms in this area is not by definition antithetical to religious conventions.

To be sure, Orthodox feminists continue to challenge the sanctuary boundary. Nonetheless, to date, even for them there remain aspects of the hallowed precinct in which the patriarchal structure must be maintained.[68] Of course, this MO approach is not accepted by contemporary liberal Jewish denominations, who have adopted egalitarian standards within their sanctuaries—formally erasing distinctions in regard to gender identity between "outside the tent" and inside it.

Ironically, Levinstein's booklet and campaign demonstrate that despite disagreeing vehemently with the specific policies of the liberal movements, he too does not accept a sharp division regarding gender between ritual and other public spaces. His focus on the army highlights the ways that the broader Israeli RZ milieu digresses from MO bifurcation.

In Israel, where public space and institutions are demarcated by the state's Jewish foundations, synagogues play far less central roles in sustaining fundamental Israeli Jewish identity.[69] For Levinstein, in particular, the army is in many ways a more crucial sphere for clarifying the role of women in Judaism than the synagogue. That is, in principle there should be no distinction between the male–female dynamic as played out in the synagogue or in the army. Thus, his opposition to women serving in the army is not merely a matter of maintaining certain standards of modesty, or even ensuring that military operational goals are prioritized. It reflects a holistic religious outlook in which the differences over Orthodox feminism touch on all aspects of public Jewish life in Israel and cannot be sequestered to the ritual or educational realms. The underlying consequence is that the battlefield or the army camp, rather than the synagogue sanctuary, articulates the core struggle over Orthodoxy and feminism in the context of Israeli Judaism.

Conclusion: Transnationalism and Two Worlds of Religious Zionism

Returning to some of the focal "agents of change" introduced earlier, one of the central thrusts of Shlomo Riskin's OTS institutions is his strong advocacy for expanded religious leadership roles for women.[70] Likewise, the pluralistic-oriented SHI founded by David Hartman houses a disproportionate number of RZ staff and fellows that are both North American immigrant families and staunch Orthodox feminist activists. As noted, the four founders of the leading women's institutions for advanced Torah study in the Jerusalem area are all American born. In addition, the two Jerusalem-based egalitarian rabbinical training programs (Harel and Yashrut)[71] are led by North American immigrants. Finally the IsMO religious cultures—including considerable support for Orthodox feminism—that have emerged both in the central Israeli town of Ra'anana and in Jerusalem have strong representations of immigrants from North America. Recall, once again, that the leading Orthodox feminist theologian is Ross, the daughter of an American Orthodox rabbi who grew up in a Modern Orthodox milieu before emigrating with her family to Jerusalem in early adulthood.[72] Taken together, one could suggest, as indicated by Uzan (and Maryles) above, that the ideological bond between the American MO feminists and their Israeli counterparts is a more profound unifying category than the local Israeli RZ rubric.

To be sure, the Israeli settings and personalities listed above have been impacted by key North American figures and exposure to developments within the "bubbles of holiness" across the sea. All the same, after acquiring and digesting these themes, Israelis, some of them second-generation immigrants and many others with minimal connection to North America, have processed them through their own contexts and experiences. They have adjusted—modifying and transforming to meet Israeli realities, expanding and often radicalizing the earlier formulations and agendas.[73]

Moreover, the Israeli interface with the first type of Orthodox feminism has had a profound impact not only on the local environment, but on ongoing developments in North America as well. To cite a few instances: as noted above, partnership *minyanim* that originated in Jerusalem and were first sanctioned by Israel-based rabbis have spread to Jewish communities throughout North America; year after year, Israeli woman's study halls educate side by side hundreds of women desirous of expanding their knowledge and commitment to advanced Torah scholarship with their North American counterparts spending gap years before entering college;[74] most if not all of the female Jewish law consultants on family purity (yoatzot halakhah) that have been employed by North American Modern Orthodox synagogues are alumni of such programs and received their specialized training through the Jerusalem-based Nishmat Institute;[75] this same framework, as detailed, runs a nightly multilingual hotline for women to ask questions to its female experts, with appropriate hours and dedicated phone lines for Israel, United States/Canada, and "other countries";[76] similarly, the vast majority of women training for ordination in the New York–based Yeshivat Maharat, and those serving in clergy-like positions in North American Modern Orthodox synagogues, have spent significant time studying in Israel-based institutions.[77] In fact, among Maharat's most successful graduates are Israeli women who went to New York to gain ordination.[78]

Such mutual cross-fertilization, then, is not one-sided; nor can it be defined any longer as at its core "American." Rather, it exemplifies the transnational perception introduced at the outset of this book that cultural symbols and ideas whose initial gestation was in America evolve through their dissemination in other locales: "Each local setting provides its own appropriation and reworking of global products and symbols, thus encouraging difference, otherness, diversity and variety."[79] Paralleling the discussion of Lichtenstein and Israeli Orthodox Bible scholarship, after spreading from North America to Israel, the first type of Orthodox feminism was encountered by Israelis who "appropriated and reworked" the "products and symbols" in fresh ways that opened up new vistas and understandings that would not necessarily have resulted from the initial North American efforts. This process of cultural translation was no doubt nourished by numerous factors, including the lack in Israel of characteristically North American overarching synagogue and rabbinical organizations that demand organizational conformity from their memberships and the minimal role of liberal denominations.

Once again, the process of transnational reworking of culture is not one-directional. That is, after an idea or symbol has been absorbed and reformed in a new environment, globalized conditions facilitate smooth portals for their reentry into their original local contexts. At this point, the reformulated conceptualizations become influential agents for cultural change within the framework of their initial emergence. This, too, applies to the first type of Orthodox feminism, whose Israel-based "reformulated conceptualizations" have gained considerable traction in their original North American environments.

As to the second type of Orthodox feminism that is so closely entwined with Israeli public space and RZ perceptions of the holiness of Jewish sovereignty, here, too, there are certainly connections to the earlier American developments. Among others is the fact that OTS's Midreshet Lindenbaum and YHE's Beit Midrash Migdal Oz, leading advanced Torah study institutions for women in which very high levels of Talmudic erudition are being achieved, each have integrated programs that enable their students to study and serve in the army, along the lines of but unidentical to male Hesder frameworks.[80] Thus, the first type of Orthodox feminism, to a certain degree, is facilitating the second.

That said, a more profound aspect of the rise of the second type of Orthodox feminism is the emergence of mechinot for RZ women or mixed-gender ones modeled after the Mechinat Eli men's institution pioneered by Levinstein and Sadan. Female mechina students, like their male counterparts in Eli and its offshoots, dedicate themselves to studying traditional texts and examining religious ideals under the guidance of rabbis and female scholars, but they also do regular fitness training, learn hiking, navigation, and survival skills, volunteer with challenged populations, and have special workshops in which they encounter a broad spectrum of Israeli society and culture. In addition, the staff members guide them in the process of enlistment and gaining entry into the various selective army units and maintain contact with them throughout their military service.[81]

Of course the very idea of an RZ women's post-secondary-school Torah institution is part of the overall contemporary revolution in women's Torah study. Yet the focus on pre-military spiritual, physical, and cultural preparation is reflective of the religion/sovereign public sphere synthesis that characterizes the particular Israeli RZ experience and outlook. Inasmuch as elements of this amalgamation can be communicated to their North American Modern Orthodox compatriots, they are not multidirectional. Rather, they highlight the fact that the second form of religious feminism arises from the unique Israeli public religious and everyday life merger, and it is this type that is being challenged most directly by RZ voices such as Levinstein—ironically a founder of the pre-army mechinot.[82]

The centrality of this issue was magnified by the Israeli military response to the Hamas massacre of October 7, 2023, and the war that ensued. Soon after that "Black Sabbath" Day, as Israelis refer to it, numerous media reports highlighted the bravery of scores of female soldiers who engaged in battle with terrorists and saved the lives of countless innocent people. As the war progressed, additional stories appeared of the feats of female IDF combat soldiers. One tragic case was that of Sgt. Rose Lubin, a twenty-one-year-old immigrant from Atlanta, Georgia, who grew up in a Modern Orthodox Jewish home. A month after fending off the Hamas attack at a religious kibbutz on the Gaza border that had adopted her and where she was spending the Simchat Torah holiday, she was stabbed to death by a terrorist during the course of duty in Jerusalem's Old City.[83]

On December 8, 2023, the *Motzash* weekend magazine (which is published as part of the *Makor Rishon* weekly, whose main readership is the RZ sector) featured the story of Lieutenant Hodayah. The twenty-two-year-old officer is pictured on the front cover in full battle gear, including a submachine gun. A black headband around her hair bears witness to her identification as a married RZ woman. She grew up in Efrat, where Riskin is the chief rabbi, and studied at OTS's Neve Hannah religious high school for girls. She has four sisters, one of whom had previously entered the IDF officer's training course. According to Hodayah, the younger sister is exceptionally committed to strict religious standards and is allowed by the army to wear long-skirted uniforms. She also maintained her practice of studying the daily Talmud page "daf yomi" throughout her training. As described in the article, Hodayah commanded a troop of combat soldiers in the artillery corps, while her husband, Elad—they were married in August 2023—served as an officer in the infantry. On October 7, 2023, they were enjoying the Simchat Torah holiday with his parents when the sirens began blaring. They both headed immediately to their units and were actively involved in the fighting. She noted that by enlisting in the artillery division she was following in the footsteps of her grandfather, who had served there during the 1973 "Yom Kippur War."[84]

An anecdotal story offers further evidence of the ubiquity of observant woman soldiers within the IDF and the impact of this reality on religious life. In a conversation that took place about two months after the war began with a veteran yoetzet halakhah who does weekly shifts on the Nishmat hotline, she shared that there had been a major uptick in questions from women regarding the challenges of fulfilling the preconditions for ritual immersion while serving in active duty.

The emergence of this mode of religious feminism and the debates that have ensued have no direct Jewish parallel within the North American Jewish environment, or for that matter anywhere outside of Israel. They exemplify the sui generis elements of IsMO that evolve as the impact of Jewish sovereignty continues to grow and become more evident. If anything, commonalities in discourse among those who oppose such phenomena may be found, for example, within the approaches of Christian groups who battle full-fledged inclusion of women within the American armed forces.[85] Insofar as the internal Jewish plane is concerned, however, it is clear that, while recognizing deep interfaces between Israel and North America facilitated by the agents of change and their students, along with contemporary communications technology and accessible travel, the distinctive political and geographical realities of Israel nevertheless also sustain the religious boundaries between these two centers of Judaism.

"Glocal" Religious Providers

Reform and Conservative Synagogue-Centers in Tel Aviv

COAUTHORED WITH EINAT LIBEL-HASS

The oft-repeated quip attributed to Israel Prize laureate Professor (emeritus) Shlomo Avineri avers, "The synagogue that I do not attend is Orthodox."[1] The implication is that unlike in the United States, where liberal denominations are vital to mainstream Jewish life, in Israel, even those who epitomize Israeli secular culture still see local Reform and Conservative synagogues as professing inauthentic and imported versions of Judaism.[2]

There are, nonetheless, dynamic individual Israeli religious institutions that are challenging these perceptions. One of the leading examples is Beit Daniel, a Reform congregation situated in North Tel Aviv, which is frequented by residents of the city and where well-known public figures, media personalities, and academicians often appear on Jewish holidays and to celebrate personal lifecycle events. Its viability demonstrates that, despite the dominance of Orthodoxy and the political capital drafted by its supporters to undermine the growth of liberal congregations on a national level, novel religious frameworks have emerged that respond to the needs of sectors of Israel's largest urban center. Beit Daniel's achievements may be attributed to the articulation and implementation of a unique "glocalized," consumer-oriented congregational framework that translates and modifies communal and leadership models that arose in the United States to the needs and cultural milieu of the Tel Aviv population. While distinct in matters of theology and the specifics of religious experience from Orthodoxy, the American impact on this liberal Israeli endeavor adds additional perspectives to the transnational elements that adumbrate novel religious directions within multiple corners of contemporary Israeli life.

This chapter examines Beit Daniel's development and foundational characteristics, and its recipe for success within its Israeli urban setting. The institutional structure that emerged there is investigated further through a comparison with another neighboring synagogue, the Conservative/*Masorti* Tiferet Shalom. Both adapted two well-established elements of American Jewish experience and applied them to the Tel Aviv environment. One American model they introduced is the "synagogue-center," a popular multipurpose institution that facilitates collective religious rituals and worship, along with other social, cultural, and educational activities. A second, which often comes hand in hand with the first, is the "rabbi as CEO"—a religious leadership figure who fulfills parochial duties while also being highly engaged in their congregation's administrative and financial affairs.

Along with comparable attempts to combine "imported" and "locally grown" products, Beit Daniel's formula has been more impactful. This feat must be appreciated in the context of broader trends relating to religion in Israeli society since the late twentieth century, along with the particular way Beit Daniel engages Tel Aviv's secular environment. Aside the open and pluralistic ambiance of the city, Tel Aviv is a consumer-driven milieu that is oriented to commodifying products both in the religious and nonreligious spheres. By homing in on these features, Beit Daniel's leadership facilitated a novel Israeli framework that operates as a religious, educational, and cultural service provider for a heterogeneous spectrum of target populations, a "community of communities" grounded on its consumer network.[3]

The data provided in this chapter was collected during four years of ethnographic fieldwork by Dr. Einat Libel-Hass at Beit Daniel and Tiferet Shalom, including numerous participant observations in events ranging from regular Friday and Saturday prayers, through lifecycle rituals and Jewish studies classes, to cultural events, all offered to the general public by the two congregations. Semistructured interviews were also conducted with leaders, congregants, and participants in services.

The Development of Beit Daniel

As we have seen, some Reform frameworks, including the Leo Baeck School in Haifa, predated the establishment of the State of Israel in

1948.[4] Growth into a national movement took place, for the most part, from the 1960s. Even then, the majority of congregations were dominated by first-generation Israelis who arrived from Western countries and their offspring, as well as a smattering of individuals who had been exposed to Reform and Conservative contexts during various temporary and long-term relocations (academics, diplomats and government emissaries, employees of international firms, entrepreneurs).[5] Following this pattern, Beit Daniel was established in 1991 through the merger of two small Tel Aviv Reform congregations whose members were primarily English- and German-speaking immigrants. Yet from the outset the aim of its main backers, the Daniel family (American Jewish industrialists) and the Israeli and World Reform movements (the World Union for Progressive Judaism), was to propagate a stronger Reform presence and interface with a wide spectrum of the Tel Aviv population.[6]

The solid organizational and financial support that was provided from the start enabled Beit Daniel to station itself in its permanent building at a prominent junction at the edge of the Bavli neighborhood in North Tel Aviv. This in itself set a precedent, since it was the earliest instance when a central Israeli municipality allocated land for a Reform congregation.[7] According to Rabbi Meir Azari, the senior religious leader of Beit Daniel from its inception, the establishment of the institution was "a real revolution, since it was the first time that the movement created a truly Israeli-style Reform congregation locally."[8]

Azari (b. 1959) gained initial familiarity with Reform Judaism when as a teenager he attended the Reform-affiliated Leo Baeck High School in Haifa. During those years he was also an active member of Haifa's Or Chadash Reform congregation.[9] He received his BA from the University of Haifa, did graduate work in Jewish history at the Hebrew University in Jerusalem, and was ordained at the Hebrew Union College's Jerusalem branch. By the age of twenty-seven, he was appointed CEO of the Israeli Reform movement.[10] The organizational skills and personal connections that he cultivated during his four years in that position were applied on a congregational level when in 1991 he was chosen to head Beit Daniel. With an Israeli-born rabbi whose mother tongue is Hebrew as leader of its central congregation in the Tel Aviv area, the movement expressed its resolve to dispel the notion that Reform Judaism was purely a foreign transplant.

Learning from America, Learning from Chabad[11]

Beit Daniel was established as a focal point for Reform Jewish activity in the greater Tel Aviv area. The core concept was inspired by the American synagogue-center. Many such American institutions offer a rich recreational program, thus the popular reference to "a shul with a pool."[12] Its sobriquet reflects the efforts by mid-twentieth-century Jewish leaders and activists—most famously articulated by the religious thinker Mordecai M. Kaplan, founder of the Reconstructionist movement—to meet the challenges of their upwardly mobile and suburbanizing second- and third-generation American Jewish constituencies.[13] The key to the formula was to reconfigure the synagogue as an institution that facilitated both religious and social aspects of Jewish life in a way that enabled individuals to decide for themselves where to focus their personal Jewish expression.[14]

Little if any historical precedent for such a synthesis existed in the countries from which the majority of both American and Israeli Jews immigrated.[15] But if in the United States the synagogue has been drafted to strengthen Jewish identity and ethnicity, in Israel it is not perceived as a key place for Jewish social gathering.[16] In point of fact, as noted, the vast majority of Israeli synagogues function primarily as houses of worship and Torah study. Beit Daniel presents a sharp contrast to most of its local parallels. From the outset, its activity model was based on the American synagogue-center, but with an appreciation and sensitivity for the divergent needs and expectations of Israelis. "We developed tools to enable Israelis to enter our synagogue without fear," said Azari, "not just to pray, but for other experiences too that are not confined to those that are between human beings and God."[17]

Indeed, the wide range of cultural and educational activities that Beit Daniel offers illustrates that it is more than a house of worship. At the same time, the various religious services it provides to the wider public reflect the ethical and ideological principles of its progressive brand of Judaism.[18] Yet its founders claim that they did not set out with the intention of resisting Orthodox Judaism openly, but instead wished to provide the Tel Aviv public with an alternative to secularity. Toward this end, they targeted those members of the public in the area who would like to celebrate the Sabbath traditions on Friday nights in some way without the Orthodox rules or theological assumptions. Alongside the aspiration that new members eventually see value in its parochial elements, and following Kaplan's synagogue-center outlook, Beit Daniel's consumer orientation recognizes that each individual needs to have options that will facilitate their form of connecting to the congregation. The result is a dynamic and rich program that is relatively diffuse and characterized by a wide range of constituents and terms of engagement.[19]

The timing of Beit Daniel's establishment was propitious. During the 1990s, the Israeli government narrowed its areas of responsibility pertaining to the provision of educational and welfare services.[20] Nongovernmental organizations (both voluntary and for-profit) sought to fill this void, with Beit Daniel an eager participant. Some local Orthodox frameworks, most actively the Chabad-Lubavitch Hasidic movement that from the late 1950s pioneered Orthodox outreach to the broader Jewish population throughout the world, also recognized this opportunity.[21] In fact, Azari acknowledged that Beit Daniel's activity model shares the organizational rationale of the Chabad approach: "I am not ashamed to admit that I often think about Chabad's activity pattern and its successes. . . . Chabad does excellent fieldwork. . . . Its model says: 'Open the door and let as many people as possible arrive and take part.'"[22] He is quick to emphasize, nevertheless, the vast ideological divide between the organizations, highlighting Beit Daniel's promotion of gender equality and avoidance of missionary work, both sensitive areas with potential to antagonize its key addressees and service consumers.

A Consumer Network Community

"Every day you can go to one activity or another," said a young couple with two small children as they arrived at Beit Daniel to take part in a Hanukkah gathering.[23] On the calendar for December 2002 through January 2003, thirty-six programs appeared. Some were designed for the elderly, others for children, youth, singles, young couples, families, conversion course participants, or immigrants. There were also evening seminars, open to all adults, and cultural events.[24]

During its first year, according to the congregation's records, five thousand people participated in Beit Daniel activities,[25] and larger audiences attended them with each successive year. The estimates in the last two decades are that upward of one hundred thousand people were exposed to the congregation on a yearly basis through lifecycle rituals and study programs. Moreover, from the year 2000, Beit Daniel sought ways to expand its target audiences and directed activities at a larger percentage of the Tel Aviv metropolitan area's over one million residents.[26] One of its most effective initiatives is an ongoing agreement with the Tel Aviv municipality to provide Jewish enhancement programming through the city's formal education system in primary schools and kindergartens. At the same time, the number of consumers of the religious services provided by the congregation—namely conversion courses, bat and bar mitzvah rituals, and marriage ceremonies—increased.[27]

In seeking to understand how Beit Daniel effected a viable model within its Tel Aviv environment, it is crucial to emphasize its distancing from a predominantly membership-driven congregational model— also a staple digression of Chabad frameworks worldwide—from the standard approach. Beit Daniel certainly differs from the prayer- and study-based homogeneity of many Israeli synagogues. Still, it also diverges sharply from the classic Reform or Conservative synagogue-centers abroad in which rabbis or rabbinical staff are hired as primary religious-cultural agents and are accountable exclusively to the congregation that hires them. Individuals join such communities by paying yearly levies or purchasing High Holiday seats. The rabbis are first and foremost employees of the synagogues, and their focus must reflect their principal job of providing religious and cultural content to the formal congregants.[28]

In Israel, by contrast, most basic religious services are supplied by the state—municipal synagogues, local rabbinic authorities, marriage and burial, mikveh (ritualarium), and kosher product supervision. An overdependence on membership dues in order to fund activities would likely have undermined Beit Daniel's institutional vision. Thus, the critical strategic decision of its founders from the beginning was to define their constituency as far wider than full-fledged dues-paying synagogue affiliates. Involvement by the wider populace was solicited instead through a range of specific programming funded by public and private sources, and a fee-for-service model was introduced in which participants are charged for individual programming. The end result is that a significant portion of the Beit Daniel budget is financed by consumers of specific activities, such as lectures, classes, cultural performances, and one-time lifecycle events. Here, once again, we see the notable parallel to the workings of Chabad Houses both in Israel and throughout the world—which draw considerable income from preschools, supplementary education, kosher food provision and supervision, and even pre-Passover matzah baking sessions.[29]

The middle- and upper-class Tel Avivians who are attracted to Beit Daniel are generally willing to pay for its offerings as long as they do not feel pressured into committing to becoming official members or taking on regular congregational responsibilities. Consistent with this consumer orientation, when it comes to bar and bat mitzvahs that take place in the congregation, Beit Daniel works with the families to design a product that meets their personal needs and integrates customs and rituals that stem from individual geographic and ethnic heritages. One prototypically Israeli example came from a family in which the mother is from Yemenite descent and the father of secular Ashkenazic origin. The mother wished to include the priestly blessing (*Birkat Kohanim*) in her son's bar mitzvah ceremony. The problem was that as far back as the nineteenth century, the Reform movement had removed this element of the traditional liturgy from its prayer books, among other passages as well, in order to neutralize what were considered to be bygone and obsolete expressions of internal Jewish hierarchy.[30] Despite this history, the rabbis at Beit Daniel were receptive to the mother's wish and incorporated the ancient prayer into the ceremony. The mother was thrilled to discover that her son could have a bar mitzvah experience that combined Yemenite and Ashkenazic elements of Judaism, as well as both traditional and Reform practices.[31]

Another group that was drawn to Beit Daniel's consumer-oriented, less formalistic approach were young adults who began to participate in congregational activities during their twenties and thirties. When they started frequenting Beit Daniel, they were not willing to become full-fledged members. Instead, they preferred to participate in the various events designed for their age group. They yearned for a Jewish framework that fit the needs of twenty-first-century middle-class secular Israelis who do not wish to commit to a specific congregation. According to one of them, "the Reform movement was user-friendly." He explained that "young adults treat Judaism as they treat the internet, meaning they surf," adding, "online you don't get stuck on a particular website; everybody surfs as long as they want and wherever they want."[32]

This metaphor posits that in a mobile and dynamic society—with pluralistic Tel Aviv as a prime example—there is little need to commit to any single congregation expressing only one type of Judaism, since there is ample opportunity to shift between spaces that offer various versions.[33] Moreover, his words stress that, for his cohort, a congregational membership model that is limited to a specific location and highlights an agreed-upon version of religious faith is undesirable. Instead, searching, picking, and choosing from among a variety of options holds far more appeal. Notably, as they reached their forties, quite a few of these individuals and couples decided to join the existing annual dues-paying membership track.

In the case of Beit Daniel, it would be mistaken to perceive the lack of formal membership as an absolute forfeit of a sense community. Rather, it indicates a reframing of collective construction. The dynamic that has emerged there exemplifies social scientist Manuel Castell's claim that in contemporary complex societies new communities emerge from looser, nongeographically based networks.[34] Various service consumers connected to Beit Daniel form alternative multilocal connections based on shared interests. While the actors are, for the most part, geographically distant from one another, they have chosen to engage Judaism through a specific synagogue-center congregation that facilitates and strengthens their sense of belonging. Thus, Beit Daniel was shaped to be a new kind of Israeli religious congregation that operates alongside the more established local model that primarily serves the residents of a designated neighborhood, "a community of communities."

The Rabbi as CEO

The leadership-driven character of this novel Israeli synagogue-center has been evident from its inception. Upon being hired, Azari's job was defined as that of senior rabbi and CEO of Beit Daniel. The combination of parochial orchestration and organizational involvement was perceived as necessary to address the unique needs of an institution operating both as a formal synagogue and a provider of religious, cultural, and educational services to diverse consumer constituencies. Here a clear confluence can be identified between the impact of American Reform Judaism upon the development of this sui generis Israeli synagogue and the personal biography of its founding rabbi.

Azari shaped his position under the influence of some of the rabbinical examples with which he himself became familiar during his stay in the United States between 1989 and 1991, when his wife served as the Israeli consul general in San Francisco.[35] As Michael Meyer has argued, since the 1960s the role of American synagogue rabbis underwent significant changes. In the past, a rabbi's success was measured primarily by their grand oratorial skills as reflected in their formal sermons. However, since the mid-twentieth century, rabbinical speeches have become shorter and more personal. In the meantime, synagogue committees have attributed greater value not only to a rabbi's spiritual and individual guidance skills, but to their managerial abilities as well.[36]

There are numerous large congregations in major American cities that function along the lines of large businesses; some have upward of fifteen hundred member families, budgets of several million dollars, tens of staff—including assistant rabbis, cantors, youth leaders, Hebrew school teachers, librarians, gift shop workers, cultural and recreational coordinators, caterers, and sometimes even museum curators, as well as a wide variety of lay committees. In many cases, the rabbi or rabbinical team is expected to devote much of their time to the managerial tasks associated with running a large-scale organization. Each case is unique, but as noted earlier, the spectrum of responsibilities may include day-to-day operations, budget building and financial planning, employee hiring and mentoring, fundraising, counseling, ensuring the proper and ongoing functioning of the various committees and subdivisions, and regular meetings with the congregation's executive committee, the Hebrew school faculty, youth groups, the men's club, and the sisterhood, along with counseling and visiting the sick.[37] To be sure, most substantial congregations have a professional administrative workforce as well, but the managerial tasks nevertheless require much of the rabbi's time.

While some rabbis disdain this aspect of their jobs, others perceive their involvement as a key vehicle for keeping their fingers on the pulse and setting the tenor of their congregations.[38]

Azari's rabbinical functions demonstrate clear parallels to those he witnessed in the United States during the late 1980s. Much like the rabbis heading key congregations in the United States, he monitors his congregation's administrative and financial affairs in parallel to addressing spiritual issues, among others. In addition to planning and orchestrating each communal prayer service and individual lifecycle event, and preparing and delivering the sermons, he visits the sick and mourning families. Azari also speaks to numerous congregants on the phone on a daily basis and meets couples who are about to get married or individuals at various stages in the conversion process. Moreover, he is deeply involved in the daily direction of the Beit Daniel kindergarten network, budgeting, fundraising, running of the physical facility, planning special events, public relations, and cultivating connections with the Tel Aviv municipality and other civic bodies.[39]

In sum, his rabbinical activities encompass almost all aspects of the congregation's parochial, programmatic, administrative, and financial affairs. Azari functions not just as a rabbi but also as a CEO, despite the existence of an executive committee, partly comprised of financial professionals, that officially oversees the economic administration of the congregation. Invoking Max Weber's classic typology of different forms of authority, Azari's leadership combines aspects of traditional authority—based on Jewish heritage and values such as respecting rabbis—and rational authority anchored by his role within Beit Daniel's bureaucratic-organizational system.[40]

Outreach Conflict: Members vs. the Rabbi

While the concept of rabbi as CEO has become engrained in the culture of Beit Daniel, other derivative aspects of the synagogue-center have been met with more intense pushback. Chiefly, it is those elements that focus on service provision to specific constituencies that are not made up of regular members or to looser networks of attendees at communal events that have been criticized. In other words, those consumer-oriented functions that have most facilitated the success of this non-Orthodox synagogue within Israel's largest municipality have generated consternation among individuals who remain committed to a more classical congregational structure. These core members sense that their needs and the overall coalescence of the collective are being sacrificed for the sake of peripheral populations.

From early on, for example, the congregation's growing reputation and the hands-on approach of its leadership attracted a vast number of Tel Aviv area families to celebrate the bar/bat mitzvah ceremonies of their children at Beit Daniel. Soon enough, some of the more veteran and active members became dissatisfied, claiming that what had become a weekly occurrence had turned the Saturday morning services into mass events in which they seldom knew the person sitting next to them. By the late 1990s, representatives approached the rabbinical staff with a formal demand not to hold bar mitzvah ceremonies during morning prayers on Sabbath and holidays. Their petition, however, was not accepted. Rather, the rabbi asserted that most regular members attended the Friday night service and not the Saturday morning one.[41] Some lay people indicated that they felt the clerical leadership had overstepped its license.[42]

Those long-time members also objected to prayer innovations introduced to meet the specific needs of bar/bat mitzvah families or other visitors, including shortening the services.[43] One veteran member said: "We come to Beit Daniel, our synagogue, among other reasons because of the prayer style we are used to. Bar mitzvah families are fine with radical prayer innovation . . . but the prayer is also for us, the long-time members, we feel the changes."[44] That said, another affirmed that the top down/rabbi and CEO leadership paradigm that was set into play from the congregation's inception and the benefits that it has accrued are too engrained into the congregational identity to change.[45]

Reflecting, once again, the interplay of American and Israeli environments that characterizes the evolution of Beit Daniel, the tension between core and peripheral groups that arose has many parallels within American communities. So much so that some American Orthodox rabbis and activists have claimed that the only effective way to integrate outreach into the foundational identity of a synagogue is to establish new and independent outlets or branches predicated on engaging the broader Jewish population.[46]

Daniel Centers: American Inspiration and Israeli Political Savvy

In the late 1990s, Beit Daniel set out to establish additional new and separate bases to meet the requirements of specific Tel Aviv sectors and areas. The intention, however, was to maintain them under the auspices of the mother congregation and not to spawn completely distinct entities. Like many of its innovations, the plan for the expansion of Beit Daniel was based partly on the rabbi's familiarity with an American precedent. In this case, it was the Wilshire Boulevard Temple in Los Angeles—a Reform congregation that runs two large spaces simultaneously.[47] During a visit to Southern California, Azari saw that it was not only possible, but under certain circumstances advantageous to cultivate multiple hubs so that each could direct its efforts to different target audiences and address their unique circumstances and needs.[48] In the Israeli case, however, political awareness also played a role in opening up a new avenue for expansion.

Since its 1991 founding, the leaders of Beit Daniel had labored to forge close ties with the Tel Aviv municipality. Over time, this process led to a transformation in the official approach to the presence in the city of Reform congregations. In previous decades, the Reform movement was deemed an unwanted alien import, and had to seek a court order to force the city to provide a parcel of land for a synagogue.[49] By the late 1990s, in contrast, the congregation's desire to grow was welcomed, and Tel Aviv mayor Roni Milo allocated a plot for the construction of a Reform center in Jaffa.[50] The move was not motivated purely by a changed approach to Reform; rather it was rooted in Milo's desire to boost Jaffa's appeal among entrepreneurs, contractors, and investors. Yet the fact that creating a branch of Beit Daniel there was deemed an effective way to help achieve this goal was indicative of the municipality's recognition of the success of the Reform synagogue-center's broad-based educational and cultural activities and ability to address a variety of target audiences.

The Jaffa center became operational in 2007. Its activity model is based on the one employed in the Reform movement's Beit Shmuel in

Jerusalem—a compound of education, culture, and hospitality belonging to the World Union of Progressive Judaism.[51] The Ruth Daniel Center in Jaffa currently includes a guest house,[52] as well as an active Reform congregation headed as of 2020 by Rabbi Binyamin Minich.[53] Since the Jaffa branch's establishment, Beit Daniel was transformed into the Daniel Centers for Progressive Judaism.[54] In December 2010, the Kehillat Halev (congregation of the heart) also joined. This synagogue, which is led by the Brazilian-born Rabbi Rodrigo Baumworcel, is located in central Tel Aviv, in a building whose main function is that of a day center for the elderly, just two blocks from the local Chabad House.[55]

The elements that were foundational to Beit Daniel's effective model—especially its consumer orientation—and the way it has synthesized both American and Israeli elements gain additional clarity and sharpness through comparison with the character and trajectory of the Conservative/*Masorti* congregation Tiferet Shalom.

The Development of Tiferet Shalom

Like the initiators of Beit Daniel, the leaders of Israel's national movement for Conservative Judaism long hoped to position theirs as an ideal religious approach for Israel's non-Orthodox sector.[56] Specifically, they conjectured that Israelis' sympathetic attitude to the traditions and customs of their ancestors—especially those who stemmed from non-Ashkenazic backgrounds—would resonate with the Conservative worldview and ritual environment.[57] To a certain degree, this approach took its cue from the twentieth-century history of the American Conservative movement, which was built on second- and third-generation offspring of East European immigrants to the United States, who found the Reform synagogue alienating and foreign, but were deterred by various elements and demands of Orthodoxy.[58] Similarly, it was hoped that second- and third-generation Israelis could be attracted to the Conservative worldview that respected Jewish law, but highlighted its evolution over time in reaction to changing circumstances.[59] Indeed, the name chosen for the Israeli branch, the *Masorti* (traditional) movement, was intended to highlight this appeal. In practice, there has been some expansion and additional inroads have been made in recent years, especially via the TALI school system that offers religious enrichment within the secular state school system. Yet overall, the *Masorti* branch remains a relatively small, niche religious stream.[60]

Like many non-Orthodox congregations in Israel, in the early 1970s Tiferet Shalom was founded in the North Tel Aviv neighborhood of Ramat Aviv by English speakers seeking a Conservative alternative to the Orthodox status quo synagogue. They aimed to provide their children with a Jewish education reminiscent of what they received in their countries of origin.[61] Tiferet Shalom's core membership expressed a desire to create the kind of Israeli congregation that the national *Masorti* leaders had envisioned. Despite a variety of successful initiatives, for the most part this construct did not materialize.[62]

In the early 2000s, members sought to grow their congregation by making a concerted effort to reach out to the wider public. Toward this goal they hired a full-time rabbi. They chose Rabbi David Lazar, an immigrant from the United States who arrived in Israel during his early adulthood, and whose experience, skill set, and worldview seemed to offer an attractive combination for both the core group and the surrounding Tel Aviv milieu.[63]

Lazar was an IDF army veteran and studied at the RZ Orthodox Kerem be-Yavne yeshiva.[64] He received a BA in Bible from the Hebrew University in Jerusalem, and subsequently gained rabbinical ordination and an MA degree from Jerusalem's Conservative-affiliated Schechter Institute. As rabbi of a Conservative congregation in the Ramot neighborhood of Jerusalem, Lazar had targeted successfully new Israeli-born members to the English-speaking congregation. He also proved to be one of the best fundraisers in the Israeli Conservative movement. Previously, in Ramot, he sought to combine New Age spirituality in the classes and public prayers that he led. Tiferet Shalom's search committee was also aware that Lazar did not feel a need to abide by the typical externals or consensus behaviors that rabbis often adopt. His regular attire was punctuated by T-shirts and flip-flops, he sported an unruly "hippie-ish" long beard, and he was an outspoken activist for LGBTQ rights. Over time, these features caused or at least exacerbated strains with the older and more conventional long-time Tiferet Shalom members.[65]

Like Azari, from the outset Lazar also sought the roles of both rabbi and CEO. He took control of managerial and financial facets of the congregation and narrowed the ability of the membership to oversee his actions. With the Beit Daniel activity model in mind, he emphasized the importance of reaching out to the residents of neighborhoods adjacent to Ramat Aviv: "Beit Daniel showed that geography is not important if you have something to offer."[66] He hoped that adopting Beit Daniel's methods would enable Tiferet Shalom to grow to a similar-sized congregation.

Lazar focused considerable efforts on branding, marketing, and providing content under the auspices of Tiferet Shalom that would expand interest. He introduced musical Friday night services that attracted many young adults and couples with small children, and selected topics for seminars and lectures that spoke to people who were not regular synagogue goers.[67] Such programs, however, were rarely attended by Tiferet Shalom's core congregants. Alongside the outreach activities, other, more traditional classes were offered that appealed to the veteran members. They were often given in English. Again, following the Beit Daniel model, Lazar also tried to reach broader constituencies by presenting special programs in kindergartens and schools, both in Ramat Aviv and beyond. He was careful to steer clear of those in which Beit Daniel was by this time operating.[68]

The outreach efforts produced a marked increase in the number of individuals participating in services. However, for the most part the fresh arrivals only attended Friday night services, while long-time members were more apt to appear at Sabbath morning prayers. This situation emphasized the chasm between the two constituencies, a split that was exacerbated further by the fact that most of the newcomers did not pay membership fees. A category of nonpaying members was established that paralleled to some degree Beit Daniel's nonmember consumers. Yet crucially, Tiferet Shalom never articulated a vision for a service-provider framework along the lines adopted by their Reform neighbors. Indeed, despite Tiferet Shalom's initial policy decision to expand its constituency, which led to the hiring of Lazar, increasingly his outreach efforts met with opposition from the core of strongly committed congregants.[69]

As described above, such issues existed to a certain degree in Beit Daniel as well.[70] Nonetheless, Beit Daniel was founded as a synagogue-center aimed at a diverse Tel Aviv consumer base. It would appear as well that Azari's role from the outset and his prior experience as CEO of the Israeli Reform movement helped him recognize the need to clarify the divisions of power earlier on. He was also adept at sustaining the financial stability that was initially gifted to him. The fact that he had a permanent edifice from which to run his synagogue-center certainly contributed to his ability to do so.

At the beginning of 2009 Rabbi Lazar left Tiferet Shalom. His exit was followed by that of many of the newcomers who had joined after participating in his outreach activities. Soon after, he accepted a rabbinical position in Europe, and eventually returned to his native United States.[71] A new figure was hired by the congregation, but its financial resources had by then further depleted. Still lacking a permanent home, the long-time members' concerns that the ties they had forged would be impeded by outreach activities to multiple target audiences did not dissipate. After two years, he left and established a new congregation in the same vicinity.

A Glocalized Denominational Merger

In July 2020, after a year of discrete negotiations, Tiferet Shalom officially became a branch of the Daniel Centers. This certainly reflected the weakness of the Ramat Aviv synagogue's congregational structure and the difficulty it faced in continuing to operate independently within the *Masorti* movement. With the financial and organizational backbone of Beit Daniel, Tiferet Shalom aimed to be able to concentrate more fully on developing its programming and servicing both for veteran and potential populations. The joining of forces indicated as well that the ideological and theological divergences that led some area residents to turn to the Reform institution in the first place and others to feel more comfortable in the Conservative/*Masorti* setting were more surmountable than in the past.[72]

Mergers between Reform and Conservative synagogues have become common in the United States as well, especially in areas that can no longer sustain multiple houses of worship.[73] The parallel events in Israel, then, bring to the fore the global character of contemporary postideological trends. Since the late twentieth century, scholars of American religion in general, and Judaism in particular, have been describing the increasingly postdenominational tendencies of religious practitioners.[74] Rather than choosing a synagogue based on movement affiliation or fundamental tenets of beliefs and observance, contemporary Jews resonate more with the style and personality of the rabbi, the number of options for individual expression that the congregation offers, the social composition of the collective, and for some, the potential to satisfy their quest for spiritual experience and meaning.[75]

Similar phenomena have been acknowledged in Israel, and the synthesis of Tiferet Shalom into the Daniel Centers highlights the decline in the role of ideology in choosing religious institutions.[76] Yet there are also specific local factors at play in North Tel Aviv that are distinctive to the Israeli context. For nonobservant Israelis, exploring alternative religious options rarely entails abandoning a prior rooted denominational connection. Other than immigrants who grew up in a specific liberal denominational synagogue or were educated in its institutions, few locally born Israelis possess strong movement-based identities. More likely, those who gravitate toward either Reform or Conservative frameworks are motivated primarily by the desire to find a Jewish religious option that is not Orthodox and is unconnected to the state-sponsored clerical apparatus. These Israeli seekers may or may not be conversant in the fine details of the distinctions between Reform and Conservative Jewish theologies and accepted practices. Regardless, the options they choose most probably reflect what is accessible or viable more than the body's specific worldview.

There is also an "Israelizing" quality to the entrance of Tiferet Shalom into the Daniel Centers orbit. It may, in part, indicate a changing of guards from the immigrant founders who came to Israel with more clearly formulated religious identities to their congregational heirs who are simply looking for a functional and vibrant non-Orthodox alternative, with minimal if any concern for franchises and labels. No doubt, this trend undermines the ongoing efforts of the national movements of the liberal streams in Israel to cultivate strong organizational affiliations. This may explain, in part, why serious efforts were made to prevent the negotiations from becoming public knowledge until they were finalized. In the end, Tiferet Shalom's leaders reached the conclusion that they had more to gain by being part of a dynamic non-Orthodox synagogue-center structure than by maintaining their congregation's historic loyalty to the Conservative/*Masorti* movement. Together with its echoes of Israeli disinterest or alienation from strong movement affiliations, the association of Tiferet Shalom with the Daniel Centers celebrates the utility and effectiveness of the service-oriented Israeli synagogue-center rubric that developed in the larger Reform-identified congregation.

Between Global and Local

From the late twentieth century, the founders of both Beit Daniel and Tiferet Shalom focused on establishing the synagogue-center model with which they were familiar from the United States within Israel's secular capital. At first glance, this would appear to have been a misreading of Tel Aviv's religious and social realities. As illustrated at the outset of this chapter through Avineri's quip, when it comes to the popular understanding of what constitutes an authentic Jewish house of worship, even avowedly secular Israelis veer toward a more traditionalist perception. Ephraim Tabory, an Israeli sociologist who immigrated from the United States, has noted somewhat ironically that while Israelis crave certain American name brands, the American identities of liberal religious streams have impeded their growth.[77]

How, then, did the Tel Aviv–based agents of liberal Judaism—particularly the Reform Beit Daniel—succeed over the course of thirty years in rooting their institution within its secular and consumer-driven environment? The foremost ingredient that facilitated their achievements, it would appear, is the commercial/service orientation of their endeavor. To be sure, their core product had an American pedigree, but in Beit Daniel they recognized early on that they had to adjust it to local Israeli tastes and sensibilities.

To draw an analogy from the food industry, numerous prominent American franchises have attempted to enter the Israeli market, some with great success and others with less. No one factor can explain the various examples in their entirety, but some cases are clearer. Despite its enormous appeal in the United States as well as many other countries worldwide, Israelis rejected what was experienced as Starbucks' distinctly American-flavor coffee.[78] On the other hand, while McDonald's Israel has maintained the chain's fundamental concept and symbols, as in other countries, it adjusts its menu regularly to the Israeli consumer's palate.[79]

Applying this distinction to Tel Aviv liberal Judaism, the founders and leaders of Beit Daniel decided that, in order to draw local audiences, it was critical that there be an Israeli essence embedded deeply into the imported American synagogue-center model. This began with their homegrown rabbi and his linguistic and cultural fluency, and filtered down to the types of programming and constituencies that were targeted, the pay-for-service financial structuring, the willingness to create personalized lifecycle events that reflected the multiple Jewish cultures from which the celebrants stemmed, and the ongoing investment in the relationship with the Tel Aviv municipality.

While both Azari and Lazar served as CEO-style rabbis, and centralized their institutional control, Azari displayed sharper political reflexes and people skills. Through these capabilities, he forged close and personal ties with key figures from Israel's academic, business, and cultural worlds. His personal "tool kit" enabled him to harness the politics of the Tel Aviv municipality, the Israeli Reform movement, and congregational factions to advance institutional goals. Azari's collaboration with the city and other organizations also helped him obtain financial resources for Beit Daniel. This capacity to generate revenue outside the traditional channels of congregational income strengthened his position on other fronts as well. More broadly, the pay-per-service paradigm opened up new directions for sustaining the organization. The extraordinary charisma and intellectual and spiritual depth of Lazar, on the other hand, could not compensate for his incapacity to create a workable dynamic for cooperation with his own most devoted congregants, nor to appreciate the nuances of Israeli municipal, governmental, and quasi-governmental agencies. It is telling that an Israeli who was exposed to American models of synagogue life only in adulthood was adept at tweaking them to speak to native Israelis. In parallel, a figure who grew up experiencing the original frameworks was less successful at translating and applying the concepts to his new surroundings.

Conclusion: Tel Aviv, the Rest of Israel, and Beyond

If the Beit Daniel formula has been so successful in Tel Aviv, why has it not been reproduced with similar results in multiple Israeli urban and suburban locales? As illustrated in the comparison to Tiferet Shalom, in part this can be attributed to the unique combination of financial back-bone and effective leadership that characterized the Reform-affiliated institution from the outset. Yet there are additional factors to consider that not only shed further light on the specific case studies addressed above but expand the scope of this discussion toward its broader impli-cations for understanding the trajectory of Judaism in contemporary Israel and beyond.

The achievements of the model that arose at Beit Daniel reflect wider characteristics of twenty-first-century Israeli society, on one hand, and elements that are specific to Tel Aviv's population and culture, on the other. A considerable corpus of scholarship produced since the 1990s has pointed to the inaccuracy of describing Israeli society as split be-tween secular and religious populations.[80] Whether this was ever re-ally the case is subject to debate. What has become clear is that the vast majority of contemporary Israelis do not resonate with the earlier dominant social and cultural Zionist ideologies that put forward a pur-ist Jewish secular nationalism as the preferred, more advanced form of Jewish identity destined to replace the ethnic-church amalgam that had historically prevailed. Rather, together with their bond to the state—where major Jewish holidays are national holidays—most Israelis fit on a spectrum of religious connections which runs from a predominantly secular lifestyle that integrates celebration of major Jewish calendar and lifecycle events to an assortment of traditional Jews who eat kosher, will not eat leavened products on Passover, and may attend synagogue regu-larly, but are not obedient regarding the exactitudes of religious law (in-cluding the Sabbath prohibitions), to the diverse array of Orthodox Jews who relate to the commandments as obligatory. A book by Camil Fuchs and Shmuel Rosner based on a large quantitative study, which will be expanded upon in the conclusion, argues that all three of these strands are part of a novel formulation that has emerged after over seventy years of sovereignty, which the authors refer to as "#IsraeliJudaism."[81]

Along with extensive engagement with core Jewish religious symbols and practices, however, there is also vast and growing resentment toward state-sponsored religious coercion and the chief rabbinate bureaucracy that sustains it. This is by no means a completely new condition,[82] but it has intensified in recent decades.[83] One bold indication of the prolifera-tion of this sentiment is the increasing number of Israelis who identify with the RZ camp and observe Jewish legal restrictions on a personal level but choose nonetheless to get married outside the auspices of the state rabbinate. While such steps are still considered to be somewhat avant-garde within the Orthodox sector, their prevalence is far greater among non-Orthodox Israelis.[84]

Various substitutes have arisen in response to the rising alienation from the state-sponsored religious establishment. For the Orthodox and the large gamut of traditional-oriented Israelis, semiautonomous organizations such as Tzohar, Beit Hillel, and ITIM have emerged that proffer more user-friendly rabbinic services without reneging on fidelity to long-held standards of Jewish law. In some areas, such as conversion and kosher supervision, they have even created independent frameworks that challenge the state monopoly.[85] A cadre of individual Orthodox rabbis also perform weddings according to Orthodox standards without the official sanction of the state rabbinate.[86]

There is, in addition, a vocal minority of Israeli society whose disconnect from Orthodox religious standards and social conventions takes them beyond simple expressions of alienation from the religious establishment. To be sure, a vestige of avid ideological secularists remains, but there is also a contingent of Israeli Jews that seeks out novel and profound ways to express their connection to Judaism outside the conventional Orthodox boundaries. A variety of organizations and social frameworks have emerged to address this constituency. Some, including Alma, Elul, and Mabua/Beit Prat, concentrate primarily on providing intellectual environments and materials that can serve as portals of Jewish engagement for a broad constituency. Others, such as Beit Tefillah Yisraelit in Tel Aviv, numerous prayer groups on secular-oriented kibbutzim and moshavim, and Kehillat Zion in Jerusalem focus on composing and organizing an assortment of prayer and spiritual experiences—the latter integrating strong social action and learning. There are also independent non-Orthodox teachers and spiritual leaders that perform weddings and other religious ceremonies.[87]

To a certain degree, Beit Daniel may be seen as part of this last inclination, or even possibly a forerunner to it. As far back as the early 1990s, both its public prayer offerings and various study and cultural opportunities targeted non-Orthodox Israelis who were interested in introducing Jewish religious content into their lives outside the religious establishment framework. At the same time, Beit Daniel's official Reform identity may be seen as less authentically Israeli as compared to the newer initiatives that do not correlate with the religious divide that dominated parts of Jewish life outside pre-state Palestine and Israel since the nineteenth century.

No doubt, the broader blossoming of alternative Israeli religious initiatives provides context for appreciating Beit Daniel's development and success. Nonetheless, revisiting briefly the particular interplay between its geographic location, its denominational identity, and its organizational structure offers acute insight that highlights the uniqueness of Beit Daniel within the Israeli religious landscape.

As we have seen, the consumer-driven service-provider character of Beit Daniel is a key to its ability to thrive in the diverse environment of Tel Aviv. By enabling multiple constituencies to partake in its offerings without conditioning participation on official membership and its implied coalescence around a defined common collective identity, Beit Daniel was able to reach a variety of local populations—including those seeking religious meaning outside the establishment Orthodox configuration. Indeed, the pay-for-service model means that the same people who utilized Beit Daniel's Jewish products are free to explore other possibilities without any sense of disloyalty to their core institution. This dynamic speaks to the eclectic orientation of many Tel Avivians who would push back against attempts to draw them to exclusive connections with strong and centralized institutions. Yet unlike the various novel intellectual and spiritual enterprises, Beit Daniel is a "full-service shop" that not only provides space for learning, prayer, and cultural experiences, but also has rabbis and religious functionaries who can address specific Jewish lifecycle and identity needs such as weddings, funerals, and conversions for those estranged from or delegitimized by the Orthodox establishment. This combination makes Beit Daniel an address where Tel Avivians can turn to if they need or desire religious engagement.

At the same time, Beit Daniel's official Reform label is less of a stumbling block and even an attraction within the Tel Aviv setting as opposed to other, less cosmopolitan Israeli environments. While Reform may spell heresy or deviation for many Israeli Jews who feel connected to tradition, for a compelling representation of Tel Aviv's diverse inhabitants it projects enlightenment, a willingness to buck the religious bureaucracy, and even a welcome hint of the world beyond the Mediterranean Sea. To be sure, critical masses with similar proclivities can be found in Jerusalem, Haifa, and numerous smaller towns and settlements throughout the country, but Tel Aviv is the epicenter of this cross-section of Israeli society.

Here it should be noted that the ethnic stratification within Israel between Jews whose families came from European countries and those stemming from Asia and Africa that was once self-evident has dissipated dramatically. Nonetheless, descendants of the latter still tend toward greater traditionalism.[88] Thus, it comes as little surprise that the Tel Aviv–based early attendees at Beit Daniel's activities and prayer service were predominantly from "Ashkenazi" homes, or those with at least one parent from this background. Although the percentages have changed over time, Ashkenazim are still clearly in the majority. The strong perception among Jews from Asia and Africa of Orthodox or traditionalist halakhah-based Judaism as the authentic version, regardless of one's personal level of observance, was not initially appreciated by the leaders of the non-Orthodox movements in Israel—especially the *Masorti*-Conservative stream. This led to expectations that a brand of Judaism that respected customs but did not set elitist legal demands would attract the descendants of the immigrants who arrived from Muslim lands after the establishment of the state. To date, the history of religious life in Israel has demonstrated unequivocally that this is rarely the case. A key moment in revealing this point was the rise of the Shas "Sephardic" Haredi political party in the late twentieth century. It draws its voter support not only from those who have adopted a more meticulous level of observance, but from many others who identify with the core ideals without personally adopting the prescriptive observances that come along with them.[89] This loose but quite large Israeli collective established its own set of accepted religious behaviors that are in sync with Orthodox legal interpretation, but focus on a more limited cluster of customs and performances that are internalized mimetically through home and local settings. Some Beit Daniel members, as illustrated above, stem from this upbringing, but not the majority.[90]

Returning to Beit Daniel's adaptation of models first developed in North America, from the 1990s onward, researchers have addressed the changing motivations that draw individuals—especially baby boomers and their offspring—to specific houses of worship and religious communities. Numerous studies have focused on the decline in ideological or theological considerations, and the increased emphasis on personal resonance with specific leaders, the experiential elements, the social and cultural services offered, and the overall ambiance of the setting.[91] In parallel, as pointed out above, the notion of congregational exclusivity and loyalty has lost its power to retain members within the religious spaces to which their families were long devoted.[92] Much of these observations can be applied both to the waning of Tiferet Shalom and the ongoing attraction of Beit Daniel's Tel Aviv synagogue-center as well. The founders of the former were, for the most part, immigrants who grew up in Conservative-oriented congregations abroad and saw their Israeli synagogue as an opportunity to continue along the same lines. Their Israeli-born children likely had a far weaker institutional identity or denominational identity.

To be sure, North America at the turn of the twenty-first century has also witnessed the ongoing rise of more recently established strongly ideological Christian streams, which are often referred to as fundamentalist. Yet along with their emphasis on political and social conservatism, these relative upstarts also follow the same trend as their liberal baby boomer opponents, pushing back against the established religious orders.[93] This too has seeming parallels within Israeli society, especially within various penitent-oriented so-called *ba'al teshuvah* groups and radicalized Hasidic and Neo-Hasidic substreams such as elements within the Breslov orbit.[94]

Parallel to the earlier discussion regarding Orthodox feminism, the comparison with trends in American Jewish religious life ultimately helps sharpen distinctions from their Beit Daniel Tel Aviv counterparts. Inasmuch as Reform or Conservative theology and attitudes toward Jewish law may be thought-provoking for certain Israelis, both the membership-based cohesive congregation and the denominational movement framing are not only foreign to most Israelis, but practically untenable in the country's reality. In the United States, the combination of legal separation of church and state together with the historical role of Protestant denominationalism in the development of American religion provides a natural landscape for the thriving of multiple voluntary religious streams that bring together their constituent congregations.[95] For most Americans, these are the only bodies that provide public prayer and religious services on a regular basis (hospital and army chaplaincies are notable exceptions). In Israel, the government subsidizes the basics—kosher supervision, religious marriage and divorce, ritualariums, burial, and thousands of prayer houses that are open to all at little cost. Thus, more expansive congregational life is a luxury. The Beit Daniel pay-for-service model not only addresses the eclectic character of its Tel Aviv constituency but also takes account of the fact that every Israeli has other options.

This confluence of factors is unique to Beit Daniel's environment and highlights the "boutique" quality of the endeavor. Therefore, its success should not be understood as indicative of a broader advancement of the Reform movement within Israeli society. Most non-Orthodox Israelis who seek religious content outside the standard governments' provisions are not attracted to national religious movements, but to frameworks that give meaning to them personally. Beit Daniel addresses these people in the greater Tel Aviv area, and this is the key to its accomplishments. This does not mean that non-Orthodox congregations cannot or do not succeed in other parts of the country, but far more than in North America, this is fully dependent on these institutions' being grounded in a deep appreciation for the pulse of their prospective constituencies.

This last point sharpens the connection between the liberal congregations and broader cultural phenomena highlighted in this chapter and the bulk of the discussion in this book that concentrates on moderate directions within the RZ spectrum of Israeli Jewish life. Models that emerged in North America have been central to the establishment of all liberal congregations in Israel. Yet Beit Daniel is the liberal framework that has arguably been most effective and is the one most rooted in a transnational process that entailed importation of North American concepts followed by critical adjustments and recalibrations in light of Israeli realities. Understanding this dynamic strengthens this book's central observation that the growth of Israeli moderate Judaism in the twenty-first century is founded on this multistage process—be it the more widespread one within RZ groups identified throughout this work as IsMO, or the local example of liberal Tel Aviv Judaism discussed here.

From Anomaly to Bestseller

The Israeli Reception of Rabbi Lord Jonathan Sacks

The Tragedy of Rabbi Sacks?

Rabbi Lord Jonathan Sacks (1948–2020) was a profound scholar, teacher, and leadership figure who impacted both Jews and non-Jews during the course of his nearly half-century career. In parallel to his official clerical role as chief rabbi of Great Britain's United Synagogue—which earned him both renown and occasionally engendered controversy—his award-winning books and eloquent oral presentations on contemporary Judaism and on the interfaces between religion and culture attracted readers and listeners throughout the English-speaking world. Over time he gained a high standing as a valued public intellectual, moral voice, and defender of Judaism, especially in British society, but across the globe as well. Yet there was one central location on the Jewish map where he was a relatively obscure figure for most of his professional life—the State of Israel.[1]

In 2013, an article about Sacks appeared in a popular Israeli news website that targets RZ readers. At the time, he had just left the chief rabbinate after over twenty years. The piece reported on a local literary launch that he headlined in honor of the Hebrew translation of his book *The Great Partnership: God, Science, and the Search for Meaning.*[2] The columnist praised the volume and its author: "I recommend gaining deep familiarity with the impressive personality of Rabbi Sacks . . . he is a highly knowledgeable intellectual . . . I see the rabbi as an important and critical voice within the mosaic of Jewish voices, that seeks to shake religion from its old-fashioned, exclusionary, and fanatical image."[3]

Despite the Hebrew account's endorsement of Sacks's worldview, the item was headlined "The Tragedy of Rabbi Sacks." This reflected the writer's remorseful perception that, even if four of Sacks's works had by then been translated into Hebrew, the worldview of the Cambridge and Oxford educated religious authority and theologian was foreign to the Israeli environment and could never gain a significant following: "Rabbi Sacks speaks primarily to constituencies that are confronted by liberal and enlightened worldviews. Culturally, he is removed from Israel like the distance between East and West, therefore his talents will only come to fruition in the Diaspora."[4]

Yet I would challenge this assertion on two levels, by both describing a growing Israeli interest in Sacks—foremost within the RZ sector but also significantly among the nonobservant population—that has swelled in the decade since the article was written, and also accounting for this development at least in part as a derivative of the overall evolution of IsMO during the same time period. Seen in parallel to Sacks's increasing popularity among Anglo and North American Jews, his oeuvre may emerge as a core source for transnational conversations between the rising moderate elements within Israeli Jewry and their global counterparts.

Sacks in Israel since 2013

Up until the second decade of the twenty-first century the journalistic description of the limited exposure of Israelis to Sacks's oeuvre would be accurate. A few of his monographs on religion and society were translated and published, primarily by academic presses and think tanks, and a select group of mostly English-speaking immigrants, educators, local intellectuals, and public officials showed interest in him and his worldview. That reality has changed dramatically.

Jumping ahead ten years, the following anecdote was shared with me in August 2023 by a parent whose child had just completed a one-year pre-army mechina. In this particular program, religiously observant and nonobservant Israeli post–high school students dedicate a year to exploring Jewish sources and their meanings for their lives. "The head of the institution proudly informed those in attendance at the end of year ceremony that they had just acquired an extensive Hebrew Sacks library to be circulated amongst all the affiliated programs. One of the parents in our group complained that it would have been better had this been

Figure 10.1. The Hebrew translation of Sacks's book *Morality*, published by Maggid/Koren in 2022.

done at the beginning of the year as it would have saved them money, considering how many books written by Sacks their son asked them to buy through the course of the year!"[5]

This incident illustrates a reality in which Sacks's books have become core texts for religious study, a situation that differs dramatically from the scenario envisioned by the author of the 2013 report. In the interim decade not only has Sacks become a household name for many in Israel, but especially within the RZ spectrum his teachings have gained a status occupied by a select few religious thinkers. His commentary on the Torah portion appears weekly in Hebrew and is available through multiple social media sources,[6] as well as being printed for distribution in hundreds of synagogues throughout the country. Of the twelve of his books that have been translated into Hebrew, eight have appeared since 2013. These include monographs on religion and contemporary society, as well as more popular works on the weekly Torah reading and commentaries on classic Jewish liturgy such as the traditional siddur (prayer book) and the Passover Haggadah.[7] According to Mathew Miller, the head of Koren/Maggid—the publisher responsible for production and distribution of most of the Sacks volumes, both in Hebrew and English (as well as French and Spanish)—while English speakers throughout the world remain their strongest market, the sales of the Hebrew versions are rising at a faster rate. He asserted that Sacks's writings are popular not only in bookstores that sell to a predominantly observant clientele, but in Israeli chains that service diverse populations throughout the country as well.[8]

Indeed, when I attended the annual Shavua ha-Sefer national Hebrew book week fair in June 2023 and reached the Koren/Magid stand in Jerusalem, I was informed by the manager that Sacks books were by far the biggest sellers. Furthermore, a large percentage of the buyers were army/university–age Hebrew speakers in their late teens and twenties. This supported my observation from conversations and visits to homes of young RZ couples that Sacks's works had become ubiquitous and found a place on their bookshelves alongside the canonical twentieth-century tomes of Kook and Soloveitchik, and the nineteenth-century Pentateuchal exegesis of Rabbi Samson Raphael Hirsch (1808–1888).[9]

No doubt, Israeli appreciation for Sacks gained additional momentum after his unfortunate passing at the age of seventy-one in 2020. The overarching theme that emerged from initial reactions was that his voice was unique among contemporary religious personalities and that it was critical that it be heard in Israel. Ido Pachter—the associate editor of Israel's *Makor Rishon* weekly *Mussaf Shabbat* supplement and himself an active moderate RZ rabbi and scholar—referred to Sacks as the "Chief Rabbi of Judaism." Pachter, who asserted that "the past few years proved how important Sacks' voice was for Israeli Jews as well,"[10] went on in 2022 to create a twenty-session podcast dedicated to familiarizing Israelis with Sacks's ideas.[11] Another Hebrew article from 2021 was written by a staff member of the ANU/Diaspora Museum in Tel Aviv and appeared in Israel's *Haaretz* daily, known for its liberal, secular-oriented worldview. It was headlined "A Tree of Life That Was Only Revealed in Israel When It Was Too Late."[12] On the other side of the Israeli religious spectrum, a Hebrew article also from 2021, this one from the independent-minded Haredi publication *Zarikh Iyun*, referred to Sacks as "a light onto the Jews" and applauded him for turning much of his attention in his last years to his Orthodox Jewish audiences. The author and editor in chief encouraged the Haredi world to draw from Sacks's wisdom.[13]

Notably, due to their profound admiration for his worldview, some of the RZ commentators expressed their frustration at Sacks's lack of mastery during his lifetime of Hebrew on a spoken level, such that the rhetorical and homiletical flourish that inspired English-speaking audiences could have touched Israelis more viscerally as well.[14] Others conveyed ambivalence as to their profound attraction to an Orthodox religious thinker who declared himself an unequivocal Zionist and celebrated the transformation in Jewish life catalyzed by Israel's existence, yet perceived much positive in Diaspora Jewish existence.[15]

Since Sacks's passing, institutions and study programs have been established and public events have been held in Israel to honor his memory and examine his worldview, especially in the context of Israeli realities. In September 2021, the Jonathan Sacks–Inquiry and Creativity Religious Primary School was opened in the Gonenim/Katamon section of Jerusalem. All of its students learn about Sacks's ideas during the course of the school year and participate in special activities on the day marking his passing.[16] In 2022–23, a yearlong course on "The Thought and Books of Rabbi Sacks" was taught by Chaim Navon at YHE's Herzog College.[17] In 2021, even Machon Meir, the yeshiva founded by alumni of Merkaz ha-Rav that focuses on nurturing newly observant *baʾalei teshuvah*,[18] featured a series of Bible lectures by Sacks that were translated into Hebrew on its popular website.[19] Echoing the anecdote above regarding the pre-army mechina, in 2023–24 the umbrella group for all these frameworks built a new curriculum based on Sacks's writings and offered stipends to those schools who applied and were chosen to participate.[20]

In as far as advanced intellectual discourse, the second annual "Sacks Conversation" was held in September 2022 at the official residence of the president of Israel. President Isaac Herzog engaged with Dr. Erica Brown, the director of the Sacks-Herenstein Center at Yeshiva University, in a public discussion attended by over one hundred public activists and educators regarding Sacks and his legacy for Israeli Jews.[21] In January 2023, a three-day international academic conference, "Rabbi, Professor, Lord: The Ideas and Influence of Jonathan Sacks," was held at BIU. It brought a large core group of Israeli researchers together with prominent academics and intellectuals from around the world.[22] The event was marked by the announcement of a new university-housed Sacks Institute for Research and Education that would highlight his contribution to political science and philosophy, among other fields.[23] In July 2023, another Sacks intellectual gathering was held in Jerusalem, this one a smaller seminar that drafted twenty-five women and men—rabbis, educators, academics, and public activists—who are committed to Sacks's vision and intent on implanting it further within Israeli religious life.[24]

In parallel with the meeting held at the Israeli president's residence in September 2022, a publicity piece sponsored by the "Rabbi Sacks Legacy Trust" appeared on Ynet.com, Israel's most popular online news outlet and the digital arm of the daily *Yedioth Ahronoth*. Titled "Inspiring: Who Was Rabbi Sacks for You?," it collects reminiscences and insights from a gamut of Israeli public personalities ranging from the secular Esther Hayut, former chief justice of the Israeli Supreme Court to YHE alumnus and leading IsMO figure Benny Lau. Another participant was Miriam Peretz, who immigrated to Israel from Morocco when she was ten years old and became a successful teacher and public school principal in the religious sector. She gained iconic status through her intrepid response to the deaths of two of her sons while serving in the IDF, becoming a national symbol of perseverance and commitment to societal unity.[25] Thus, there is nothing unusual about her presence among a representative group of well-known Israelis impacted by Sacks. What stands out, however, is her description of what caused her to engage his writings more systematically.[26]

The turning point for her was a family debate during a Passover Seder a few years earlier regarding the Biblical account of the Exodus. The specific issue of contention was whether the Israelites behaved properly when they absconded with precious possessions of the Egyptians on the night of their rushed departure.[27] After she questioned the moral fortitude and educational value of the incident, her grandson recommended that she read Sacks's discussion of the relevant passages in order to recognize the necessity of their actions. Sacks examined the Biblical narrative through the psychological role of material restitution in neutralizing long-term feelings of hatred among slaves and other victims, as articulated by leading mental health scholars.[28] Sensing the unapologetic yet emotionally sophisticated quality of this interpretation, Peretz decided to devote time to exploring the teachings of Sacks and has since become a staunch devotee.[29]

Peretz's initial exposure to Sacks, as her portrayal highlights, did not come from a personal encounter with him (she made explicit that she never met him) or attendance at one of his lectures during his lifetime. Rather, it was her Israeli grandson who had read one of the translations of Sacks's books who was the conduit for her subsequent enrichment. This exemplifies, once again, the transition of Sacks from a Diaspora figure with some appeal to limited Israeli audiences to a far more mainstream twenty-first-century source for religious and ethical understanding among a wider spectrum of Israelis.

Patrons, Publishers, and Meaning Makers

Why did Sacks gain so many new Israeli followers and readers since the second decade of the twenty-first century? There is no singular answer that can account for this evolution, but some factors are clear.

First, his own efforts together with those of his loyal and talented staff, especially after leaving the chief rabbinate, to develop his brand and expand his impact in Israel through speaking engagements, Hebrew publications, and social media were extraordinarily impactful. From 2013, no longer burdened with official duties, he spent much more time traveling and set in to play the organized campaign that gained traction posthumously. Since his passing, the Rabbi Sacks Legacy Trust—which is led by family members and key advisors and supporters—has focused on "Israel: The Home of Hope," as one of its "Key Areas of Work."[30] Most of the major educational initiatives, public events, and conferences held in Israel have been orchestrated in coordination with the trust, and it continues to cultivate long-term relationships with a variety of institutions and organizations.

Second, relatedly, was the partnership that he formed with the Koren/Maggid publishing house, which began with his English prayer book and first volume of commentary on the Bible that appeared in 2009 and has expanded to the entire range of Jewish liturgy. From 2013 Koren gained exclusive rights for translation and publication of Sacks's writings, and in the course of the next decade eight more Hebrew tomes appeared, including his highly popular Passover Haggadah and the multiple volumes of Torah commentaries. The Hebrew publications by Koren, which feature literarily excellent translations,[31] were accompanied by a marketing campaign that included live events—some built around public conversations between Sacks and another well-known local personality.[32] To a great degree, then, his popularity within the Hebrew-speaking RZ sector was founded upon the library that Koren created. It is no wonder that Koren/Magid is committed to having all of Sacks's works translated into Hebrew.[33]

Conspicuously, the chairman of the editorial board at Koren/Magid and one of the central people responsible for advancing the Sacks publication program is Reuven (Ronnie) Ziegler. Ziegler is an American alumnus of YHE who immigrated to Israel in the late twentieth century. His first major project was serving as founding editor in chief of the Virtual Beit Midrash (VBM), the framework through which YHE has developed its extensive digital presence. Via his role at Koren/Magid, not only has he been instrumental in bringing Sacks's writings to broader audiences in Israel and worldwide, he has also facilitated the publication of works by numerous key moderate figures, including Lichtenstein, Amital, Chana Henkin, Riskin, Rabinovitch, Benny Lau, and Yuval Cherlow.

Ironically, once Sacks's limitations as Hebrew orator were no longer at issue due to his unfortunate passing, his writings became the nearly exclusive vehicle for communicating his ideas. Under those circumstances, the chasm that may have existed previously between the eloquent English speaker and his Israeli audiences was neutralized by the transformation of his printed Hebrew texts into the exclusive avenue for gaining exposure to his worldview.

Sacks's expanded role in the broader Jewish world was also powered in part by the immense investment that he and his staff made in creating a major online presence. This began before his passing but gained new energy since then. Today, one can watch or listen to scores of videos, podcasts, and recordings, read hundreds of essays and biographical accounts, and access school curriculums and even animated teaching tools.[34] Throughout the initial spread of the COVID pandemic in 2020 and until not long before his death, Sacks continued to connect to his veteran as well as new followers through Zoom and livestream events.[35] This avenue certainly fortified the bond of his natural constituency of Israel-based English speakers with him and his ideas. It also expanded his global presence, and this may have attracted more Israelis. That said, the site contains a limited number of Hebrew items (that go back only to 2016) in comparison to the vast number and variety of English offerings.[36] Thus, to date the main portal of entry for Hebrew speakers into Sacks's oeuvre remains his books and commentaries.

Undoubtedly, then, the increased presence of Sacks within Israeli religious life testifies to the strong correlation between the successful reception of ideas and movements and the effectiveness of the process of marketing and dissemination.[37] Yet the foundation for such a turn is the degree to which the "product" provides value and satisfaction to those who become exposed to it. Here it is useful to examine further the intersection between the Israeli "Sacks phenomenon" and the broader theme of this book.

Had the bulk of Sacks's books appeared and been translated into Hebrew during the late twentieth century, they would likely have gained a readership, but not anything near what occurred during the course of the second and third decades of the twenty-first. The latter, I maintain, resulted from the confluence between the increased availability of Sacks's ideas to the Hebrew-speaking population and the growth during the same period of the IsMO contingent, which sought out or at least resonated with an alternative RZ approach to that identified with the Kook camp. Put differently, the relationship between the appearance of

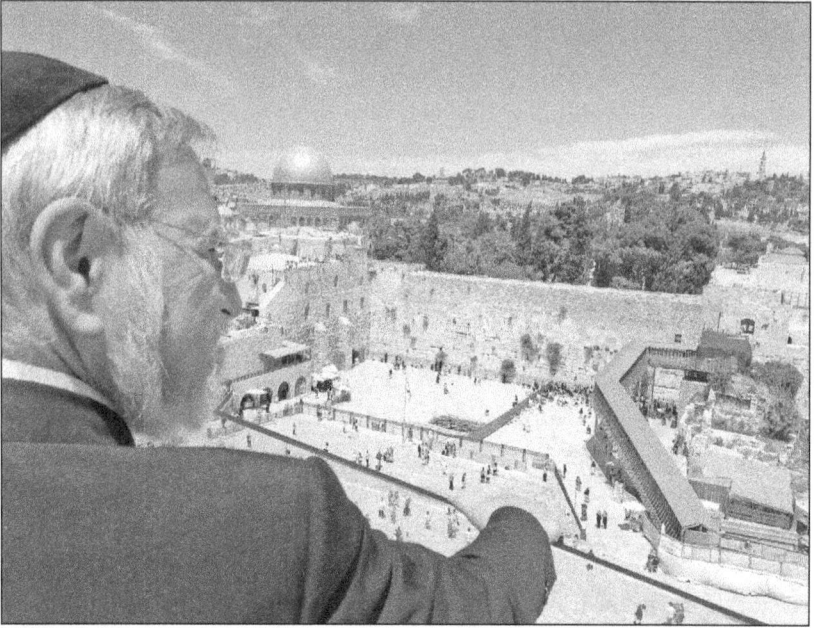

Figure 10.2. Lord Rabbi Sacks in the Old City of Jerusalem looking out on the Western Wall, the Temple Mount, and the Mount of Olives. Courtesy of the Rabbi Sacks Legacy Trust.

the translations and the rise in the stature of Sacks among Israelis is not one-directional. The Koren translations may have opened up this market, but the ongoing demand for his work reflected a readership that gravitated naturally toward his ideas.

In order to flesh this point out more thoroughly, we can focus on the core content of Sacks's teachings and writings. In a July 2019 video message delivered by Sacks to mark the twenty-fifth year since the passing of one his most influential mentors, Rabbi Menachem Mendel Schneerson, the seventh Lubavitcher rebbe, Sacks celebrated a direct link that he uncovered between the rebbe and another hero of his:[38]

> I always sensed a very strong connection between the Rebbe's teaching and the teaching of one of the most influential of all figures in the 20th century, the psychotherapist, the survivor of Auschwitz, . . . Viktor Frankl . . . who developed in his book, *Man's Search for Meaning* a whole

school of psychotherapy, telling people that we have to find our mission in life . . . as a result, I was very moved to discover that the Rebbe sent Viktor Frankl a message in Vienna telling him not to despair. Somehow the Rebbe had gathered that Frankl was despairing of the fact that his whole approach to psychotherapy was not being accepted and was just about to leave Vienna and go to Australia. And it was the Rebbe's encouragement that persuaded him to stay and continue his work. Frankl's work is regarded as one of the most influential of all in the 20th century. And he had a secular equivalent of what the Rebbe was teaching us: We each have a mission in life and we have to fulfil that mission.[39]

As he took up his own mission toward the Jewish people and broader humanity, Sacks was inspired by these figures and gratified to learn that their paths had crossed. Like Schneerson and following Frankl's core insight—which Sacks cited repeatedly throughout his career[40]—over time he increasingly dedicated himself to demonstrating how the Jewish tradition could bring meaning to Jews and non-Jews alike.[41] In so doing, he certainly built on his rigorous academic analytical training but deliberately moved away from the "ivory tower." As he put it in a 2013 interview that appears in a book dedicated to his thought: "I think there's something extremely important which I have tried to practice myself which the English call 'middlebrow.' . . . The real task here is lucidity and simplicity and engaging the reader." Indeed, a comparison between his initial publications through the 1980s and his subsequent writings demonstrates unequivocally that his style changed from a dense scholarly one to a lighter more popular one.[42] As time went on, his production was geared increasingly toward expanding his lay Jewish audiences—prayer books, weekly Torah sheets, etc. These were the tools that would provide or facilitate meaning for a religiously oriented Jewish population.

In emphasizing meaning, Sacks steered away from what could have been a natural direction, charting novel paths in Jewish theology. Rather than reinventing traditional Judaism, Sacks's focus was predominantly on explaining why traditional Judaism provided meaning for twenty-first-century Jews, and to a great degree non-Jews as well. His model of religious thinker as meaning maker stands in contrast, for example, with that of an older contemporary, Rabbi Yitz Greenberg. The latter also began his career as an inspirational congregational rabbi and academic star who was destined to take a lead role in mainstream Modern Orthodoxy for years to come. However, relatively early on Greenberg became immersed in the Holocaust and its theological implications for Jewish beliefs and practices, as well as the relationship of Judaism to other religions. From that point on he put forward novel theological ideas that challenged accepted Orthodox views and led to his being ostracized by some within Orthodoxy. In the course of his career he rose to the highest levels of American Jewish leadership and had many loyal Orthodox followers, but for others his positions were outside the consensus.[43] Notably, the only time Sacks came close to forfeiting his stature within the Orthodox world was when in 2002 he, too, conceptualized seemingly pluralistic perceptions of the "truth" of other religions. As is well known, once he recognized the price he would pay within the Orthodox world, he quickly recanted.[44]

The role of "meaning maker" is a critical element in understanding Sacks's increasing appeal to contemporary Jews. This goes without saying regarding the broader English-speaking world, but applies as well to his Israeli constituencies, most prominently the RZ spectrum.

As noted at various points in this volume, the preeminent religious voices for RZ, especially since the 1960s, have emanated from the Kook school. Kook's theological and legal writings (as well as those of many of his disciples) encompass manifold aspects of religious experience.[45] Yet, with the exception of dedicated yeshiva-trained elites and academics who digest his every word, the core Kookist themes disseminated widely are the mystical sanctity of the entire Biblical Land of Israel, the redemptive underpinnings of modern Zionism and the State of Israel, and the partnership between holy and secular forces that facilitates this esoteric process.[46] Indeed, regarding the latter, some key strands of the contemporary Kook camp have questioned whether their forebear's appreciation for nonobservant Jewish brethren still rings true under current realities.[47] In parallel, there is an intensifying skepticism within contemporary Kook circles toward secular knowledge and a growing assertion of stricter practical application of Jewish law along the lines previously identified with the Haredi communities. All the same, the Kookist focus on redemptive Zionism and holiness of the Land remains a core trope in most RZ educational settings; schools, postsecondary frameworks, and informal youth movement settings.[48]

Kook's persona, spiritual pathos, and innovative understanding of contemporary history and Jewish nationalism have inspired RZ Israelis for over a half a century. However, as highlighted, there have also been a variety of more recent recoils within the RZ spectrum from what is perceived as an overfocus on the Land and a hypercollectivism rooted in religious particularism. These are reflected, no doubt, through variant directions in the postmodern, individualistic-oriented critiques of the late Rabbi Shimon Gershon Rosenberg (Shagar) and others, in tandem with the Neo-Hasidic trends that have gained currency in the twenty-first century.[49] I suggest that the rising interest in Sacks is expressive of another direction in the current RZ search for alternative worldviews.

Sacks presented an Orthodox Judaism that is at once supportive of Zionism and the State of Israel, but not necessarily Land-centric. Moreover, he was openly critical of the intersection between politics and religion that is part and parcel of the Israeli Jewish experience.[50] This position in and of itself is an attractive one for those within the RZ spectrum who are alienated by this dynamic. But even those who are comfortable with mixing religion and politics could find considerable relatable meaning-making material. Much of Sacks's focus is on the contemporary individual, especially moral and interpersonal struggles as well as the pervasive impact of science and technology on the spiritual realm.[51] His position as an intellectual icon and moral leader in broader Western society who posited that Judaism can help make the world a better place certainly added cachet to his stature. Most importantly, Sacks drew from core Jewish texts to promote the consistent "postsecular" message that functioning and producing within broader society and engaging a diverse range of other human beings does not need to be an impediment to one's religious identity and values. On the contrary, the meeting point between one's religious commitment and the scientific and cultural realms can produce a "universalizing particularity" that is especially empowering.[52] The correlation, then, between the new availability of his books in the Hebrew language with the coalescence of the realm of IsMO portrayed in this book produced a boon in interest and attraction to everything "Sacks."

In point of fact, Sacks was far from the first Orthodox thinker to put forward an integrated worldview. To a great extent, he appeared to pattern key aspects of his activities upon the pathbreaking nineteenth-century legacy of Samson Raphael Hirsch and his "Torah im Derekh Erez" approach to synthesizing Torah and modern life.[53] He was also influenced by Soloveitchik and was deeply appreciative of other key Modern Orthodox figures,[54] including Lichtenstein and Rabinovitch,[55] as well as Rabbi Dr. Norman Lamm (1927–2020), the theologian and former president of Yeshiva University.[56] Yet Sacks's focused efforts to speak to the concerns and experiences of his twentieth- and twenty-first-century contemporaries through "lucidity and simplicity and engaging the reader" set him apart from all but possibly Lamm. The latter, like Sacks, was a master of homiletics who honed his communication skills through many years of sermonizing as a congregational rabbi.[57] All the same, Sacks's self-ascribed intentionality of targeting the "middle-brow," along with the novel internet medium that evolved during the height of his career, crystallized his role as a "meaning maker" par excellence for a far wider span of his contemporaries. Once his teachings became available to Israelis in their native tongue, the RZ spectrum was quick to find a central place for his writings among its "Sabbath-day" reading materials.[58]

Conclusion: Canon and Connectivity—Hirsch and Sacks

The comparison between Sacks and Hirsch raises questions regarding Sacks's long-term place in the traditional Jewish literary canon, ones that certainly cannot be fully answered at this juncture, but nonetheless raise additional perspectives on the possible role of Sacks's writing in facilitating novel connections between Jews across the globe.

In her work *Those Who Write for Immortality*, literary scholar H. J. Jackson asserts that inevitably authors possess "a mindset of writing to last."[59] That said, some texts—even when clearly located in a particular historical, cultural, and geographical context—lend themselves more easily to producing ideas with a potential for posterity, while other literary products seem limited by their presentist flavor. At first blush, Sacks appears to be closer to the latter. In the process of engaging his most direct readership with the intention of providing them with meaning, Sacks consciously sacrificed his place within elite philosophical discourse and its attendant long-term intellectual history.

The example of Hirsch indicates a parallel but not necessarily identical scenario. Hirsch was a rabbi in postemancipatory Germany for over half a century. From his earliest work, *Neunzehn Briefe über Judentum/ Igrot Zafun* (*The Nineteen Letters*),[60] which he published anonymously at the age of twenty-eight, Hirsch directed his efforts toward arguing for the ongoing authority of traditional Jewish law and beliefs, and how his contemporaries could find deep meaning in these ideals. Indeed, he claimed that the new "out of the ghetto" circumstances provided opportunities for fulfilling the Torah's original mandate for the people of Israel that had been impossible throughout much of Jewish history. No doubt, his target audiences were his fellow Central and Western European Jews who felt torn between allegiance to long-held religious standards and the promise of full integration into their local societies and cultures. For that matter, his immediate disputants were the leaders of the burgeoning Reform movement, along with those Orthodox who saw value in maintaining formal communal cooperation with them despite their major differences.[61] Notwithstanding, nearly two centuries since he began to publish, his major works have withstood the test of time. This is particularly so regarding his commentary on the Bible,[62] and to a great degree in relation to *The Nineteen Letters* as well as *Horeb*,[63] in which he explicated the meaning of the commandments. Today, many of those who avidly cite Hirsch in their sermons and homilies are unaware of the controversies that he engendered both in his conflict with Reform and vis-à-vis fellow Orthodox colleagues—some of whom felt that his aesthetic changes and German speeches deviated from synagogue norms, while others judged that he had forfeited traditional stances of Jewish solidarity.

Hirsch's best-known work is his commentary on the Bible, which like most of his other primary texts, he wrote in German. One of the main reasons that his books are popular among twenty-first-century Jews is that they have been translated into both English and Hebrew. I suggest that by setting into play the translations of his own literary output into Hebrew, most prominently his commentaries on the Bible, not only did

Sacks intend to influence contemporary Israelis, he recognized that this was the language that would most likely facilitate his "lasting" entry into the traditional Jewish canon. Yet Sacks also intuited that Hirsch's assertively positive evaluation of the need for Jews to integrate distinctly religious and more diverse settings had transformed from a revolutionary nineteenth-century approach to one of the definitive directions of Jewish life moving forward. In this vein, he perceived his role as that of contemporary heir to Hirsch, not necessarily by agreeing with his predecessor on all matters, but because of their shared beliefs that Judaism would thrive when synthesized effectively with insights and revelations that arose independently, along with their fundamental commitments toward making them accessible to their constituencies.

This commonality is expressed succinctly in Sacks's commentary "Without Walls," which discusses the account of the spies sent to scout the Land in the Book of Numbers (chs. 13–17). He explained that when the spies witnessed the local population living behind walled cities, they saw this as a sign of strength and became fearful. This, he maintained, was a grave misunderstanding, for "[p]eople who are strong do not have to live behind defensive walls."[64] Extrapolating to modern times, Sacks set out the three main directions that Jews took when they were given the legal right of citizenship and gained entry into broader society:

> Some were only too keen to assimilate. They were willing to give up key elements of Jewish faith and life, from the dietary laws to belief in the return to Zion. Others, fully aware of the danger to Jewish continuity, retreated into a self-created ghetto. A few—the most famous was Rabbi Samson Raphael Hirsch—managed the delicate balancing act. Jews could be culturally European (Hirsch himself loved German poetry) while remained uncompromising in their religious practice. The synthesis was widely known as Torah im derech eretz [Torah combined with secular culture].[65]

Sacks acknowledged that the persistence through the first half of the twentieth century of virulent antisemitism, and especially the Holocaust, demonstrated that historical animosities do not just disappear, since "people don't change overnight." In his own life, however, the situation had transformed dramatically, such that he felt comfortable stating:

Two centuries ago, segregation and the voluntary ghetto might have been the right response. Jews were not ready for the challenge of Europe and Europe was not ready for the challenge of the Jews. But now is not then. Ours is not the age of the spies but of their descendants, born in freedom. We have had time enough to realize that we can be at home in Western culture without it calling into question Jewish faith or Jewish life. Rabbi Samson Raphael Hirsch's dream—that Jews could become a moral and spiritual influence on the societies of which they are a part—did not come true in his lifetime, but it has in ours.[66]

From this perspective Sacks was building upon the legacy of Hirsch—by now an established member of the traditional canon—and reconstituting it at a time when he perceived even more compelling reasons to assert the integrationist model. As I have argued above, his refitted Hirschian-inspired outlook appealed to the growing constituency of Israeli RZ Jews who were put off by the reawakening of the tendency toward "segregation and ghettos"—be it social or intellectual—within their sector. Here it is worth returning briefly to his dedicated readers outside Israel.

Sacks's predominant audience throughout his career was Jews from across the world—primarily English-speaking ones. Emblematic of his wide appeal are the keen comments in 2018 of the progressive American journalist Peter Beinart, who is both a sharp critic of Israel and a practicing Jew. Since first coming across Sacks's Torah commentary in 2010, he wrote, "his writing has had a deeper impact on my life than any other rabbi's. . . . Since that day, Sacks' words have been a constant presence in my life. I have read, and reread, his books of commentary on the . . . Torah . . . I lead Seders with his Haggadah. I pray from his siddur. I used to watch his lectures at my desk, and now I walk around New York listening to his podcasts."[67]

It would appear that despite clear cultural and political differences, the common draw of moderate RZ Jews and a vast range of English-speaking readers to Sacks's books is that they are predicated on forthright engagement of religion with society and advance the notion that this interface is more meaningful and positive than futile or dangerous. This is a language shared by IsMO and its counterparts throughout the world, even those quite distant from them on political matters. The translation of Sacks's texts to Hebrew has thus not only enabled Israelis who respond to his ideas to gain extensive exposure, it has transformed Sacks's library into a potentially canonic transnational set of texts that can serve as a basis for discourse and debate not focused on the political realm. Again, it is too early in the process to estimate the "lasting" character of his literary production. Nonetheless, this brief foray offers an additional window for appreciating the significance of the translation of Sacks's writings into Hebrew and their long-term potential for fortifying cross-global conversations.

PART THREE

Homeland and Beyond

11

The Digital Sphere

Gender, Talmud, and Israeli Judaism

New Year's Day 2020 saw a crowd of over ninety thousand assemble in freezing temperatures at New Jersey's MetLife Stadium. Rather than the usual football game, they had come for the Siyum ha-Shas of Daf Yomi, the ceremony celebrating study of all 2,711 folios of the Talmud (*Shas*) over the course of a seven-and-a-half-year daily regimen. The nearly five-hour convocation included public prayers, speeches by eminent rabbis, musical performances, and inspirational films. It culminated with recitation of the final passages of the multivolume ancient tome, followed by raucous dancing. Scores of parallel events took place on five other continents, and thousands more joined via livestream.[1]

The daf yomi (literally, "daily page") Talmud-study cycle was conceived nearly a century earlier. Since its inception, the overwhelming majority of partakers were men. While this remains the case, the 2020 festivities marked a watershed when over three thousand attendees came together at a parallel ceremony in Jerusalem for the inaugural Women's Siyum Shas (*siyum*, Hebrew for "completion," here refers to an event marking the finish of formal study of a significant portion of a Jewish religious text).[2]

This chapter engages with what unfolded from that conspicuous January 2020 moment onward. I contend that the emergence of the women's daf yomi trend and the role of digital spaces in this process marks a pivotal juncture in the history of Jewish religious feminism. Moreover, through a comparison between the novel Israel-based women's initiative with a parallel male-dominant American Orthodox one, this chapter introduces a fresh feature of IsMO's transnational character that is manifested in women's daf yomi.

The women's event was spearheaded by Hadran, an Israel-based organization established in 2018 and led by Michelle Cohen Farber, a veteran immigrant from America and religious educator who has been teaching daf yomi since 2013 at her home in Ra'anana, a suburban town north of Tel Aviv.[3] To celebrate the daf yomi milestone, Hadran brought together a coalition of women's learning groups from Israel and around the globe, along with an array of institutions and individuals that are at the forefront of advanced Talmud study for women—thousands in person and more via livestream. The evening's format shared much in common with the MetLife one, but it was orchestrated and led by women, and all but one of the live speakers were women, as were over 90 percent of those who joined. In addition, unlike in New Jersey, the predominant language spoken from the stage was Hebrew and the formal ceremony concluded with a collective rendering of Hatikvah, Israel's national anthem.[4] Of course, it would not have been complete without a recorded video message from Rabbi Lord Jonathan Sacks.

Hadran's innovative posture will come across vividly through a brief rendering of the history of daf yomi, followed by a more detailed presentation of the OU's ALL DAF platform as a contemporary foil. Recall that from the 1970s onward Orthodox female forays into historically male precincts took shape in the expansion of study opportunities for women—especially exposure to Talmud—and organization of ritual settings in which women took more active roles while avoiding explicit rabbinic legal prohibitions. During the late twentieth and early twenty-first centuries, new female religious leadership roles also emerged, along with rigorous training programs.

To all appearances, Hadran's daf yomi initiative is an extension of the less radical study-oriented elements of religious feminism. Yet due to its unique qualities, especially its digital platform, I assert that it diverges in meaningful ways from all tracks of religious feminism to date and puts forth a distinct vision moving forward.

The History of Daf Yomi

From its inception, the daf yomi learning cycle was presented as a means to fortify commitment to Talmud study and connect Orthodox Jews throughout the world.[5] The key founding personality was Rabbi Meir Shapira, a Hasidic Orthodox religious leader, educator, and public activist. He was a principal persona in the Polish branch of Agudath Israel, the organization established in 1912 that amalgamated a broad spectrum of Orthodox Jews throughout the globe whose common denominators were traditional observance and opposition to the Zionist movement.[6] At its first *Kenessiah Gedolah,* or great assembly, in Vienna (1923), Shapira officially launched the daf yomi study program. Emphasizing its global quality, he portrayed a scenario that highlighted why it could facilitate the organization's core goals: "What a great thing! A Jew . . . travels for 15 days from the Land of Israel to America, and each day he learns the daf. When he arrives in America, he enters a study hall in New York and finds Jews learning the very same daf that he studied on that day, and he gladly joins them. Another Jew leaves the States and travels to Brazil or Japan. . . . Could there be greater unity of hearts than this?"[7] In 1931, the first siyum daf yomi was held with great fanfare at the recently opened majestic building of Shapira's yeshiva in Lublin.[8]

After World War II, participation took on an additional "sanctified" level of meaning as a way to connect the learners with the prewar European Judaism and memorialize the millions who had perished at the hands of the Nazis.[9] The siyum ceremonies grew steadily; by 2005 the numbers were calculated to have reached 140,000, and each successive one has exceeded the former.[10] Observers attributed this explosion in popularity to a variety of factors, including the overall expansion of Haredi Orthodoxy and its Talmud-centric male educational system both in Israel and North America.[11] The massive gatherings hailing those who dedicate themselves daily to intensive Torah study also serve as a collective declaration of victory over the "dual threats" of annihilation and assimilation.[12] The trend among high school graduates to spend a gap year in an Israeli yeshiva or seminary contributed new daf yomi learners as well.[13] That said, novel publications and technological innovations since the 1980s also spurred the growth of daf yomi.[14]

Dating back to the 1980s, efforts were made to draft technology as a daf yomi facilitator.[15] Yet the advent of the internet precipitated an explosion in portals and apps. These enable learners worldwide to access the daily page and related audio/video classes and commentaries in multiple languages on computers or handheld devices at their convenience. The protracted time at home during the COVID-19 pandemic and the adoption of live video technologies like Zoom and YouTube Live further bolstered the role of new media.

Here we will focus on two specific portals, ALL DAF and Hadran, which arose along with the cycle that began in January 2020. Each of these novel digital settings addresses (primarily but not exclusively) what can be termed global MO/RZ constituencies, yet they embody distinctive approaches to gender, with profound implications for their visions of its core religious culture.

ALL DAF

ALL DAF is a project of the Orthodox Union, known today simply as the OU, the largest national Orthodox synagogue organization in North America. Established in 1898, initially it brought together congregations that served consciously Americanizing Jews who maintained allegiance to the traditional interpretation of Judaism, and sought out English-speaking, secular-educated rabbis to guide them.[16] Over time, its religious dietary supervision division became the most ubiquitous body of its kind throughout the international kosher food industry.[17] The rising profits from this endeavor have facilitated efforts to strengthen contemporary Orthodoxy through multiple arms, including communal engagement, a national youth movement, college campus representatives, government advocacy, an Israel-based affiliate, and a separate "women's initiative."[18]

To date, the OU has maintained a close relationship with YU as well as with the Rabbinical Council of America (RCA)—the main professional guild for rabbis that serve MO communities—and the vast majority of its member congregations self-define as MO. Its Israeli branch as well services English-speaking immigrants who identify predominantly with the RZ camp. At the same time, OU's kosher standards are accepted by Haredi Jews. Moreover, the representation of graduates from Haredi institutions among its key employees and activists grew considerably in the twenty-first century.[19]

ALL DAF is run in conjunction with OU's Torah department, whose webpage provides links to a wide range of classes that include star male and female lecturers.[20] Available via a website and apps for handheld devices, as of March 2022 ALL DAF's home page featured audio recordings of fourteen different daily daf yomi classes and one filmed for video. In addition, there are over thirty supplementary series for expanded analysis and live broadcasts of a different large local siyum each time a new tractate is completed.[21]

The convenience of the ALL DAF open-access tool had an almost immediate impact, especially when many in-person classes were suspended due to the spread of the COVID-19 pandemic in early 2020. In principle, this seamless availability could also facilitate the growing number of women learners. Yet numerous elements demonstrate that, without being openly exclusionary, it is an unambiguously male-centric framework that targets Orthodox Jewish men forthrightly.

The opening webpage displays pictures of all the core daily Talmud presenters, whose classes can be reached through a simple click. While externals are not necessarily indicative of an individual's specific worldview, the overall impression is of a representative group of Orthodox rabbis, with a clear tilt toward the Haredi streams. They are all wearing dark suits and head coverings, the majority black yarmulkahs, but three don Hasidic-style cylinder hats. Most are bearded, some closely cropped while others with long growths, including the Hasidic figures, whose faces are framed by earlocks (*payot*) on each side. Two others are completely clean-shaven.[22]

Below their portraits there is a link, "About This Speaker," that leads to brief biographies along with descriptions of the style and main qualities of their pedagogic approach. Here the reader learns that of the fourteen lecturers, thirteen are Ashkenazi (of Eastern/Central European origin) men, eight live in the New York area, four in Israel, and one in South Africa. Two received their rabbinical ordination from YU; the rest were educated in Haredi-affiliated yeshivot and appear to continue to identify with one of its various subsectors in the United States or Israel.[23]

The talented individual charged in 2018 with creating ALL DAF is Rabbi Moshe Schwed. Like most of his cohort, he spent much of his early adult life as a full-time fellow (kollel member) in a Haredi yeshiva, in his case, Beth Medrash Govoha in Lakewood, New Jersey, the largest and most influential institution of its kind in the Western Hemisphere, with over seven thousand full-time students.[24] In an August 2020 interview, he shared that "as someone who was in kollel here in Lakewood for many years and never really involved in technology—not even a smartphone user—my skill set coming into this was identifying and producing quality Torah content. But to really understand how people use technology and the best way to lay out the content, I needed an 'education.'"[25] Over the sixteen months that it took to design and produce ALL DAF, Schwed certainly overcame his initial technical knowledge gaps. At the same time, when it comes to substance, ALL DAF offerings seem quite in sync with the content with which he was familiar from the Lakewood yeshiva before being hired by the OU.

As to the daily daf yomi classes themselves, the main language of instruction is English. However, the three Hasidic instructors teach in Yiddish, the colloquial tongue in their circles, which is also often utilized in non-Hasidic haredi yeshivot, but rarely if ever in MO or RZ environments. That there is no Hebrew option is telling. To be sure, the language of the website is English, and its main constituency is residents of English-speaking countries or immigrants to Israel. Yet an effort was made to find presenters in Yiddish, which reflects the fact that addressing the needs of this segment of Orthodoxy was a priority. In all likelihood, most MO subscribers would prefer English instruction as well. Yet many are fluent in Hebrew and might enjoy connecting through the "holy tongue" if such an opportunity were available. Even if the language of instruction is in English, there are distinctive ways to pronounce the Hebrew and Aramaic words of the Talmud text. Other than the one Syrian Sephardic rabbi, all the teachers utilize variations on Ashkenazi accents stemming from Eastern Europe. The overall tenor of ALL DAF, then, gravitates toward a Haredi Orthodox ambiance.[26]

No doubt the ALL DAF team invested considerable efforts to identify an array of talented Talmud scholars who could address a broad Orthodox constituency. From a purely numbers perspective, this makes perfect sense, as the majority of daf yomi learners worldwide are Haredi Ashkenazi males who are most comfortable with the types of teachers and linguistic proclivities that fill the roster (as of November 2020, over forty thousand unique learners had visited the site).[27] Despite being sponsored by the ostensibly MO-affiliated OU, the underlying assumption is that it can serve the widest range of Jews by featuring traditionalist-style teachers and content that is acceptable to both Haredim and MO. Presumably, the opposite is not the case; had either a woman instructor or even decidedly MO or RZ personnel and materials been offered, there stood a risk of alienating the Haredi clientele. Of course, the upshot is that the content excludes key substreams of contemporary Orthodoxy within its pedagogical menu. Most unequivocally, Hebrew speakers, along with a burgeoning group of women who are Talmud scholars or are interested in studying Talmud, are ignored.

The intentionally male orientation of ALL DAF, in parallel to its obscuring of divergences between MO and Haredi men, comes to the fore as well in the various screened presentations of live and recorded events. One example is the only offering that is based on a video upload of a daily class. This particular group meets in Ramat Bat Shemesh, an Israeli urban development with a significant percentage of English-speaking immigrants, predominantly moderate Haredi and RZ oriented. The lecturer is an extraordinarily charismatic middle-aged graduate of well-regarded Haredi yeshivot who left a successful business in the United States to live in Israel. He dedicates much of his time to creating a center that focuses on daf yomi dissemination and produces a variety of study products that are made available online through ALL DAF and other platforms.[28] He also built a very comfortable study hall in which his regular crowd of over seventy attendees, ranging in age from twelve to over eighty, are treated to gourmet coffee and have multiple snack offerings at their disposal. In a filmed interview, he described the clublike atmosphere that he aims to cultivate as being "like a man-cave for Torah."[29]

The siyum events as well reinforce this type of comradery. Upon completion of each tractate, these festive, almost exclusively male gatherings are broadcast live on the site and viewable afterward. At the siyum for Tractate *Eruvin* in November 2020, one of the main speakers was Rabbi Shlomo Schwarzberg from Tom's River near Lakewood, whose daily classes and graphic-enhanced introductions and summaries have gained considerable popularity through ALL DAF.[30] He spoke passionately about the capacity of the platform to bring together Jews of all types and followed this statement by asking why the special prayer text recited at each siyum is written in the plural form: "I believe the reason is because you are not making the siyum by yourself. You are making it with your wife." He went on to explain: "many people here are smiling knowing what their wives do for them so they can learn Torah. Many people watch ALL DAF from work . . . but your wife is taking care of things that help you, you're not making the siyum yourself."[31]

Supportive wives were fêted as well in an article that appeared in the Haredi-oriented *Mishpacha* magazine a few months before the January

2020 siyum, titled "Women of the Daf." The piece begins with a candid explanation: "There's no doubt that daf yomi is a man-centric undertaking, but the Siyum HaShas was an accomplishment celebrated with overflowing hearts on both sides of the mechitzah [synagogue separation between sexes]." The author then shares numerous cases of incredible acts of altruism on the part of these women, including one who went into labor but chose not to disturb her husband's class. Summing up the common sentiments of the different women interviewees, the author writes, "While I expect to hear about all the sacrifices made by daf yomi wives, none of the women I speak to consider it a hardship to take on extra work so their husbands can give their daily shiur. Time and again, I hear how thrilled they are to move mountains so that the untold thousands who commit to learning the daf can have a shiur each and every day."[32]

It would appear that there are two parallel messages that emerge from the "wife who's the real hero of daf yomi" narrative. On one hand, it indicates awareness that for most people who live in contemporary Western society this entire male-centered project is an anomaly—thus, the desire to validate the "holy partnership" upon which daf yomi is built. At the same time, since the mid-twentieth century Haredi Jews have idealized the concept of a kollel (fellowship) couple in which the husband dedicates himself fully to Talmudic study for as many years as possible, receiving a modest stipend, with the wife serving as the main breadwinner. Inasmuch as it is the man who is associated with the formally sanctified task, an entire theology and accompanying rhetoric has developed that glorifies the hallowed character of the wife's ostensibly mundane activities.[33] The "woman who's the real hero of daf yomi" narrative, then, can be viewed as an extension of the kollel couple motif; so to speak, even among those men who have left the study hall and joined the workforce, there is still an opportunity to create a domestic structure that adumbrates the more pristine ideal.

To reiterate, ALL DAF is not a Haredi-sponsored framework. On the contrary, it is a premier product of the OU, the umbrella organization for most American MO synagogues. Thus, the degree to which this extraordinarily rich, digital landscape asserts its male-centeredness and celebrates worldviews that have historically reflected Haredi norms is telling. This is especially so at a time when advanced women's Talmud study has gained widespread MO acceptance, including within circles that oppose extensions of women's opportunities to the ritual and religious leadership realms. Indeed, I offer that ALL DAF's unbridled posture pushes back at the entire notion of expanding roles for women within formerly predominantly male contexts, by emphasizing that Talmud study remains at its foundation a male endeavor.[34] In that sense, ALL DAF may be deemed a reactionary setting that challenges contemporary MO standards. In parallel to fortifying boundaries between MO men and women, ALL DAF simultaneously blurs distinctions between the MO and Haredi-oriented men who are brought together through the platform and its male-centered ambience.

At the alternate side of the contemporary Orthodox daf yomi spectrum sits Hadran, the novel women-centered initiative that was established almost simultaneously with ALL DAF. The two digital platforms have much in common. However, not only does Hadran project a contrasting ideological vision, the predominantly digital dominion through which it operates evinces an inverse effect. Rather than serving as an extension or reinforcement of the traditional male physical spaces of the synagogue sanctuary and the yeshiva study hall, Hadran's digital framing generates a sui generis independent collective female one that does not necessitate any male involvement or validation.

Hadran

Throughout the twentieth century, there were exceptional cases of women who learned Talmud according to the daf yomi cycle. The overall growth of advanced Torah study for women from the last decades, however, inspired many more, including organized local groups, to adopt this practice.[35] In 2017 Harvard- and Cambridge-educated writer/ literary editor and Jerusalem resident Ilana Kurshan raised awareness of women who learn daf yomi considerably when she published a personal memoir.[36] Built on the interplay between the vicissitudes of her personal life and her daily encounter with the Babylonian Talmud, the tome was widely praised and received, among other honors, the prestigious Sami Rohr Literary Prize.[37] In her project "Draw Yomi," completed in 2020, British artist and Orthodox feminist activist Jaqueline Nicholls also applied creative tools to portray her seven-and-a-half-year personal encounter with the daily folio: "I grappled with what was written on the page, and engaged with what, and who, was missing from the Rabbinic discussions."[38] In point of fact, the very decision by Michelle Cohen Farber and her cohorts to orchestrate the first major siyum event arose out of recognition that a critical mass of women daf yomi studiers had emerged.[39]

The coalition that Farber assembled for the globally livestreamed Jerusalem event, with its more than three thousand attendees, echoed Meir Shapira's more expansive conceptualization of daf yomi nearly a century earlier as a vehicle for solidarity among Jews across the planet, this time focusing on the "second sex." Beyond generating this international sorority, it was intended to inspire many more women to participate in the forthcoming cycle. The instrument for this further step was the newly established Hadran organization, which strives to connect women daf yomi learners and classes worldwide.

Hadran's stated goal is "to make Talmud study accessible to Jewish women at all levels . . . in a unique way: by providing a wide range of resources . . . in the voice of women teachers."[40] From the outset of the new daf yomi round in January 2020, the Hadran website facilitated this task by rendering recordings of Farber's daily classes presented in her home available to those who could not attend in person, whether in Israel or abroad. Soon enough, the platform catalogued multiple videoed daf yomi–related programs, expositions, enrichments, and blogs that were taught or orchestrated by women. That said, as with ALL DAF, the spread within weeks of COVID-19, and the periodic debilitating waves of the pandemic, elevated the value of the digital framework profoundly. Indeed, in the case of Hadran it was exceptionally transformative.

After in-person meetings became impossible, Farber began to teach her daf yomi class twice each morning via Zoom, once in Hebrew at 6:15 a.m., and a second time in English at 7:15 a.m. These were broadcast live via the Hadran website,[41] as well as via Facebook[42] and YouTube.[43] In the process, the live digital platform became Hadran's core framework. The main exceptions were tractate siyum events that enabled actual gatherings to take place, although in these cases too, they were "hybrid" experiences in which the majority of participants—and some of the speakers—were located in other parts of the world and joined via Zoom. To be sure, recordings of the classes were sent out almost immediately

Figure 11.1. Pictures from the January 2020 Women's Siyum in Jerusalem featured on the Hadran website. The center photo is of Michelle Cohen Farber, the founder of Hadran, while the left corner one is of Malka Bina, founder of MaTaN and one of the pioneering "agents of change." Courtesy of Hadran.

after they were completed through a WhatsApp group and remained available via multiple media platforms long after they were presented. Notwithstanding, the central live online study session facilitated a novel type of collective daily learning experience; it brought together women (and some men) just starting their day in Israel, Asia, Africa, or Europe with others ending theirs—whether the previous one in North or South America, or the parallel one in Australia or New Zealand.[44]

Like ALL DAF, Hadran's principal engine is its quality content, starting with Farber's pedagogy. An alumnus of Yeshiva of Flatbush in Brooklyn, as a high school student she was drawn to studying Talmud. She went on to attend Midreshet Lindenbaum's Scholars Program. With over twenty years of teaching experience, as well as an MA in Talmud from BIU, her daily classes are spoken either in American-accented English or Israeli "Sephardi"–style Hebrew and integrate traditional interpretations with academic perspectives. The oral presentation is enhanced by brief written summaries of each page and, when deemed necessary, extensive study guides and illustrated sources.[45] In a May 2021 interview, she described why she felt that her classes would fill an existing gap and how she designed her method with this in mind:

> When I went online to see some examples of how people taught a whole daf in 45 minutes, I was surprised to find hundreds of daf yomi shiurim

(lectures) by men but none by women. When listening to the shiurim, it was clear that the average woman who comes with little or no gemara background would have a hard time learning with one of those shiurim, not because they can't learn from a man, but because most of the rabbis teaching assumed the listener had a certain comfort level with basic words and concepts. In addition, the questions that they asked on the gemara or issues they delved into were not necessarily the issues that the women would be interested in pursuing. Also, when a sensitive women's issue arises, many gloss right over it and move on. It was then that I decided that I would record my classes and put them online to be able to offer a class that could appeal to the broader female audience.[46]

As of November 2021, according to statistics provided by the organization, there were sixteen hundred daily listeners to her class, and an additional twenty-five hundred to five thousand individual downloads of tractates that had been completed.[47]

Once one arrives at the Hadran website, a variety of offerings and links are available under the rubric of "Beyond the Daf."[48] Yet, in polar distinction to ALL DAF, the female-centric quality of the platform is celebrated. Some courses that are offered in both English and Hebrew simply reflect the fact that for many women Hadran is their initial gateway to the Talmud. In addition, there are periodic topical guest presentations and ongoing English and Hebrew series, all taught by highly qualified woman scholars and teachers, primarily from Israel, with a few prominent American figures as well. The English options include the daily blog discussion "Talking Talmud" between Anne Gordon, a Jerusalem-based scholar and journalist, and Dr. Yardaena Osband, a pediatrician formerly from New York who immigrated to Israel. There is also a Hebrew video blog titled *Daf mi-she-la-hen* (A page of their own). It features Rabbanit Hamutal Shoval, a former journalist who holds a master's degree in new media and teaches advanced Talmud to women, and Rabbanit Shira Marili Mirvis, the first woman to be appointed as the main religious authority in an Israeli Orthodox synagogue.[49]

Both at "Talking Talmud" and *Daf mi-she-la-hen*, the conversations often gravitate to gendered aspects of the pages studied that week, including exploring how the patriarchy of Talmudic times continues to set the tone for many aspects of Jewish life. As Orthodox Jews, the presenters are committed to traditional Jewish practice and law, but they also acknowledge the many challenges they face as twenty-first-century women who have been brought up to assume their rights to full participation in society. Thus, for example, Tractate *Megilah* declares plainly that women may chant the Torah at a public reading but forbids it because of issues of honor—which is interpreted by traditional commentators as embarrassing those men who are unable to execute this role.[50] The Hebrew duo dedicated their discussion to the conflict between this conclusion and the contemporary reality in which women and men are equals in the workplace and increasingly in the world of Torah study as well. Walking the tightrope between the various approaches within contemporary Orthodoxy, they note that in recent years learned treatises have been published that provide religio-legal justification for women's public Torah public chanting.[51]

Instead of diminishing the impact of Hadran's emergence, the predominantly virtual environment has expanded it. Through the daily classes and supplements, along with the periodic siyum assemblies, a global digital-based women's learning community is being cultivated that integrates accessibility with regular opportunities for direct personal connection. Following the model of the January 2020 gathering, prominent women Torah scholars from around the world—some of them heads of leading institutions for women—are invited to present lectures at the tractate completion occasions,[52] thus cementing the sense that the women daf yomi learners and those who devote themselves full-time to Talmud study are partners in a broader global women's collective. This, too, is reminiscent of the ALL DAF and Agudath Israel daf yomi happenings at which distinguished yeshiva heads and rabbis are invited to share their thoughts and blessings—once again, solidifying the ties between the lay daf yomi network and the elite study halls.

Farber has further nurtured the Hadran women's network by taking periodic trips throughout North America where she addresses audiences in person, including visits to local women's daf yomi groups and their supporters.[53] That these women are part and parcel of a global kinship is emphasized through another component of the website, "Hadran Communities." Listed there with clickable links are the names of nineteen affiliated branches in Israel and twenty-six around the world. Some of these women meet daily in person or virtually, while in other cases

Figure 11.2. Michelle Cohen Farber featured on the cover of *Nashim* magazine, June 2024. Courtesy of Hadran.

the local group complements regular study with Farber through private WhatsApp and Facebook discussions in which members present their own perspectives or relevant materials.[54]

The dedications that are read at the beginning of each session and appear on the digital apparatuses offer an additional lens for discerning the "reception" of Hadran. They echo the sense that women identify with the gendered foundations of the endeavor and perceive it in "communal/global" terms. On December 11, 2021, a woman sponsored the Hadran study in memory of her recently deceased mother, who "loved that I was learning Daf Yomi, and always wished she had been able to learn more in her almost 99 years." A September 17, 2021, listing, also in memory of a woman's mother, offered a similar but sharper articulation: "As a young girl, she begged her father to teach her Gemara [Talmud] so she could expand her knowledge. She would have loved to know that her daughter and daughter-in-law are pursuing that path." That same month a granddaughter noted that "her grandmother . . . often remarked at how much women's learning had grown in her own lifetime. 'I know she'd be thrilled about the Hadran community.'" In August 2021, a daughter who had completed the prior daf yomi cycle asserted proudly that "[o]ur mother succeeded in instilling her love of Torah and Yiddishkeit [traditional Judaism] to her two daughters, both of whom are studying the Daf with Rabbanit Michelle. The Siyum Hashas in January 2020 was one of the highlights of my life and I was overwhelmed to participate in the Hadran [collective prayer] from the audience." Another set of sisters had an interesting discovery: "My youngest sister, who lives in Israel, and I, who live in New York, have just found out this week—after two years!—that both of us have been learning Daf Yomi since the beginning of this cycle, and we can picture our mother asking us to share what we are learning."[55]

Religious Identity, Gender, and Geography

There is no question that Farber, as well as all the teachers and presenters, are either Israel-based women associated with the RZ camp or active in North American MO communities. The same can be said for most of the daily participants as well. According to statistics provided by Hadran, the majority were Orthodox women over forty-five years old,

but there were numerous university students as well as young professionals. Some were studying Talmud for the first time, while others were
experienced learners.[56]

The gender egalitarian consensus of the non-Orthodox streams
would seemingly render obsolete the attraction of a predominantly all-
women's setting. Yet, based on direct communications from site users,
15–20 percent do not identify as Orthodox. This in itself is enlightening,
since it implies that, while daf yomi remains a predominantly Orthodox
male endeavor, it is gaining greater purchase among the non-Orthodox
as well. Indeed, there is evidence from electronic media sources that
from the 2012 cycle, but particularly since 2020, there has been a significant uptick in these sectors.[57] This growing interest, then, can be viewed
as a parallel phenomenon to Hadran; two layers of Jewish society that
were formerly not integral parts of daf yomi culture are simultaneously
taking ownership over this aspect of their religious experiences.[58]

Why do non-Orthodox Jews gravitate to Hadran? Numerous participants expressed that, as opposed to most of the other existing online daf
yomi options that were Haredi-oriented, they were attracted to Farber's
"non-yeshivish" (non-Haredi) style. Furthermore, quite a few correspon-
dents disclosed that they began their daf yomi involvements listening to
other lecturers but were frustrated by the lack of sensitivity to women's
issues.[59] These sentiments dovetail with those of a few men who study
regularly with male teachers but revealed that, when the Talmud addresses gender-related topics, they make a point of turning to Hadran
in order to gain exposure to Farber's perspective. On a pragmatic level,
even if there are many daf yomi portals, none are categorically non-
Orthodox.[60] Under such circumstances, Farber's teaching and Hadran's
overall tenor resonate most closely with Jews who have internalized an
egalitarian Jewish approach.[61]

Together with sharpening distinctions between Hadran and most daf
yomi frameworks, however, the issue of non-Orthodox subscribers also
points to critical areas of commonality with other Orthodox ones. To be
sure, Hadran's presenters are women, and the subjects and range of their
discussions indicate a relatively high degree of openness to diverse approaches. Some even raise challenges to accepted religious norms within
their circles. All the same, in principle both Hadran and ALL DAF can
be described as open-access platforms that project worldviews rooted

within the Orthodox orbit. That non-Orthodox Jews appear to be more comfortable with Hadran does not undermine its core branding and the denominational gatekeeper mechanism reflected in its exclusively Orthodox personnel. Just as ALL DAF's male-orientation facilitates its appeal to a broad spectrum of MO and traditionalist-oriented Orthodox Jews without categorically discounting anyone else who wants to partake, so does Hadran's makeup reflect its focus on a primary constituency of Orthodox women. In both cases, like in an Orthodox synagogue, the non-Orthodox may be invited in, but only on the explicit terms of the sponsoring facility.[62]

The upshot of these shared properties is that beyond portals for disseminating knowledge, both Hadran and ALL DAF function as identity cultivators for alternative approaches within Orthodox Judaism.[63] ALL DAF exemplifies the growing liminality of borders between the more traditionalist factions of MO and primarily the non-Hasidic streams of Haredi Orthodoxy. Its culture is grounded in American-based institutions and key personalities associated with the OU, YU, and various Haredi yeshivot. These groups share a common aversion toward women's entering realms of parochial activity long considered to be male domains. In distinction, Hadran fosters an alternative alliance predicated on women who forthrightly engage the foundational texts of Judaism that were long outside their purview. Likewise, inasmuch as its founder and many key activists are American-born, most are immigrants to Israel whose families have acculturated into the IsMO religious sector through their choice of neighborhoods, education, and fulfillment of mandatory army or national service. Hadran's dual-lingual website, incorporating locally born presenters and targeting multiple audiences, exemplifies the Israeli-American fusion of the entire undertaking.

Both ALL DAF and Hadran, then, may be characterized as containing transnational elements. But in the case of Hadran this aspect is far more pronounced, and the foundational point of its approach is decidedly the Israeli milieu. The comparison between these two novel daf yomi initiatives, then, advances the notion that divergent substreams that arose from twentieth-century American MO have begun to assert their influence on Jewish life in new and creative ways. Pointedly, each are based in one of the two dominant centers of the contemporary Jewish world. The conservative one emanates more directly from the local

American Orthodox communal and institutional structure, whereas the more moderate one is an Israeli-based (IsMO) product that evolved out of the interface of veteran English-speaking American immigrants with local cultural realities.

Hadran, as noted, is part of the broader Orthodox feminist movement that has gradually expanded its impact since the last decades of the twentieth century. Yet it differentiates itself in fundamental ways from other forms of religious feminism that focus on changes to the live ritual sphere as well as in the formal leadership realm. The critical point of distinction is grounded in its digital platform.

Digital Religion and the "Unsynagogue"

Since the 1990s, an entire field of study has arisen to examine the interface between the internet/social media and religion. Due to the fast pace of technological developments, the research is dynamic and constantly evolving.[64] The tragic spread of the COVID-19 pandemic and the mass move to online activities provided boundless additional scenarios to explore.[65] One of the topics that has drawn considerable attention is the nature of online religious experiences and communities. What is their connection to conventional in-person-based practice and institutions? How do digital landscapes reinforce and expand religious knowledge, involvement, and authority? Alternatively, what innovative/subversive potentials characterize online religion, especially in connection to gender, and less conformist frameworks?[66] Relatedly, as handheld devices and apps have become ubiquitous and increasingly the dominant medium of digital engagement, some scholars have questioned the very suitability of an online/offline religion binary and sought new ways to engage the oscillating intersection.[67] Each of these discourses are valuable for deepening the comparison between Hadran and ALL DAF, and especially for discerning the critical role of the digital sphere in facilitating the sui generis path that Hadran is advancing in regard to women and Judaism and transnationality.

Both of the electronic platforms, ALL DAF and Hadran, have multidimensional relationships with in-person religious experience. Initially, Hadran was more clearly framed around a specific daily daf yomi class in a defined physical space—Farber's home. This original structure was built upon a core embodied interaction. ALL DAF, in contrast, was designed from the outset as a "one-stop shop" digital clearinghouse featuring multiple prerecorded daf yomi offerings.[68] Some of the lectures were taught in front of live audiences, but none of them used Zoom or streaming tools to enable simultaneous direct participation, and all but two were exclusively audio presentations.[69]

ALL DAF's focus on reaching a broad constituency through the most current tools raises comparisons to what religion and media scholar Heidi Campbell refers to as the "[digital strategists] who extend and alter their audience via digital platforms . . . modifying communication for a new era."[70] Its prerecorded format produces a one-directional interface with almost no channel for user response. This resonates with the rubric numerous scholars refer to as "religion online," which "presents information . . . via internet transmission"[71]—as opposed to "online religion," where those who join are more actively "doing . . . religion through online channels."[72]

As a powerful vehicle for reinforcing the traditional in-person religious environments and values of its architects and central teachers, ALL DAF recounts as well a second typology articulated by Campbell, the "[d]igital spokesman . . . who harnesses the potential of new media to extend the institutional message."[73] Such "online ambassadors" augment the established base—never challenging its fundamental ideas and mandate, since they "embody the institution to the public"[74] and "are also subject to the legal authority structure it represents."[75]

Due to its entrenched digital foundation, on a technical level ALL DAF was fully geared to meet the socially distanced realities of the pandemic. Conversely, Hadran's centerpiece was forced by COVID circumstances to make a quick switch to a cyber environment. In the process, nonetheless, the reconstituted digital milieu enabled an original type of woman's alternative to traditional male-centered Jewish experience to take form, one that facilitated a more fluid and less binary relationship between virtual and classical religious engagements—so to speak, the rise of a novel "online religious" experience. In her capacity as the main teacher and curator of Hadran, Farber took on a role that is closer to Campell's third typology, the "digital entrepreneur . . . their work transforms . . . [they] become exemplars of innovation, bypassing traditional gatekeepers."[76]

As highlighted, while Farber ceased her regular in-person teaching, through Zoom her daily daf yomi classes remained live, interactive events, only now with many more women in attendance from multiple geographical locations and time zones. Together with the various worldwide local Hadran "chapters," their multiple active social media extensions, and the large-scale siyum gatherings, a collaborative transnational digital religious community arose. Unlike ALL DAF, in this constellation Hadran's prerecorded unidirectional classes and blogs served, not as the main offerings, but as content supplements and cultural enhancements that fortified the women's ambiance of the framework and furthered the sense of community. This may be seen as analogous to activities outside the sanctuary that became staples of "houses of prayer" of numerous religions, especially in the twentieth century.[77]

This association of Hadran with a physical sacred facility is not purely metaphorical. Scholars have advanced the notion that, while certainly distinctive, "emerging technologies provide a sense of a ritual context that is analogous in one way or another to those found offline."[78] To be sure, as opposed to the multitude of churches, synagogues, and mosques that conduct online services, Hadran's formal mandate is study, not public prayer. That said, observers have emphasized the "ritual" character of daf yomi that distinguishes it from classical Talmudic learning. As rabbinics scholar Barry Wimpfheimer explained in his award-winning 2018 tome, *The Talmud: A Biography*,

> The Daf Yomi movement has produced a new religious reality. . . . The Talmud, like the Torah [Hebrew Bible] before it, has become ritualized as a way of marking time . . . just as Jews have been unified over the years by a calendar that includes the ritualized reading of the Torah divided into weekly portions, Jews are now unified by a calendar that includes somewhat ritualized reading of the Talmud divided into daily portions.[79]

Duly aware of the proliferation of online daf yomi sites, he adds, "There is comfort in the regularity of daily study and in the community that surrounds such learning, both in the physical sense (classmates in a Daf Yomi class) and in the virtual sense (people around the world with whom one has kinship because of the shared project)."[80]

This identification of the ritual quality of daf yomi is no doubt correct. Yet there remain critical differences between this characterization as it applies to the majority of male-centered daf yomi environments—be they in person or online—and Hadran's setting. These distinctions set the stage for pinpointing the uniqueness of Hadran. For Orthodox men who engage Talmud study on some level as ritual, at least from the perspective of "calendar" and "performed" reading, their primary ritual space remains the synagogue sanctuary, where the principal activity is prayer not study. Women are certainly permitted by Orthodox Jewish law to join public prayer, but even according to its most liberal authorities, there are significant roles that they are forbidden to play—whether males are present or not.[81] Thus, regarding the Orthodox synagogue sanctuary—the central Jewish ritual environment—there is no debate: it remains a predominantly male domain.[82] As to the beit medrash, here there are less formal restrictions, yet there are still highly regarded figures that question the necessity or even permissibility of women's Talmud study. Recent decades have witnessed the emergence of multiple study halls for women, as well as the expansion of mixed-gender ones, but they remain a small minority in comparison to the hundreds, if not thousands, of men's yeshivot. Indeed, also regarding the women's ones, the religio-legal mandate and final word regarding what is permissible to learn and for which roles women can be trained remains in the hands of men.

Hadran, as a digital space that is grounded in the daily interactive ritual of daf yomi, founded and led by women for women—those men who do partake being the "visitors"—exemplifies a new ritual landscape for women that is completely devoid of male regulation. While it is predicated on the revolution in women's advanced Torah study that began in the late twentieth century, its key characteristics distinguish it from the dominant religious feminist innovations such as women's prayer groups, partnership quorums, and a variety of new religious leadership roles. In all of these cases, ultimately, the women remain situated in male space. By defining its primary location as the digital realm and functioning independent of male supervision, Hadran has generated a new paradigm for religious feminism.[83]

Hadran's regular visual component and extensively advertised public siyum events are among numerous characteristics that distinguish it from another women-orchestrated digital environment that has drawn scholarly attention—blogs. Andrea Lieber highlights the notion expressed by a pioneering blogger that she created "a veiber shul [colloquial Yiddish for women's synagogue/sanctuary]," an "online community [that] is a 'virtual women's section,' playing on the gendered partitioning of the public space of the synagogue."[84] In doing so, Leiber observes, "online presence is not a public presence, but rather represents an expanded private sphere." Hadran may not function within the traditional domains of the men's section of the synagogue or the yeshiva study hall, but it is the opposite of an extension of the private sphere. On the contrary, its autonomous digital space is open access and projects itself outward.

The departure of Hadran from other prior innovations is elucidated further through a comparison to another groundbreaking online framework. As seen earlier, one of the novel women's religious leadership roles that have emerged in the late twentieth century is the yoetzet halakhah (literally, consultant on Jewish law). Nishmat, under the leadership of pioneering "agent of change" Chana Henkin, established its training program that qualifies women to achieve expertise in the legal realm of Jewish family purity.

An ethnographic analysis of Nishmat's online forum by Michal Raucher that appeared in 2015 raises noteworthy parallels to that articulated here regarding Hadran: "we see that the internet has allowed Orthodox Jewish women to enhance their traditional roles. . . . Online, a Yoetzet's unique skill set can be showcased and appreciated. The liminal status of Yoatzot Halacha fits well within the liminal space of the internet and allows for these female legal guides to fill a void in women's observance of Jewish law."[85] Nonetheless, the author points to Nishmat's official communications, emphasizing that graduates are not rabbis and despite their proficiency do not have license to render authoritative rulings. Rather, every recommendation is reviewed by a male rabbinical advisor before being communicated to the questioner. Thus, she observes that "[i]n many ways . . . the Yoatzot are merely an extension of rabbis, an online method of broadcasting rabbinic positions and reaching the female audience that is too embarrassed to turn directly to their rabbis. In this way, yoetzet.org maintains an overarching authority structure within the Orthodox Jewish community."[86]

Instead of the transformative "digital entrepreneur" category suggested above as an apt framing for Hadran, this description is closer to the "digital spokesman" role applied to ALL DAF. The article suggests that, by asserting its formal allegiance to the traditional structure, the fundamental challenge to gender norms implicit in the entire yoetzet enterprise is actually able to proceed with fewer immediate obstacles. Thus, in the long term it may hold within it an especially subversive potency. In the meantime, however, together with its clear "breakthrough" status, it remains rooted in the established authority scheme.

Similar to the yoatzot hotline, Hadran's focus on Jewish learning also does not contest the norms of traditional rabbinical authority directly. In fact, other than some passing remarks related to specific Talmudic passages or in video blog theoretical discussions, it attends minimally to applied Jewish law. Notwithstanding, it is unique in the degree to which its mediated landscape exists as an independent public women's religious space that sustains daily collective ritual and, while emerging from Israel, nurtures both a global network of local chapters and a unified digital community. From this perspective it echoes Mia Löveheim's discussion of the impact of new media on gender and religion: "Mediatization challenges rules and boundaries established by traditional religious authorities primarily concerning women's access to information and their possibility to find platforms to articulate their beliefs as well as connect with other like-minded persons."

Conclusion: Women and the Transnational Sphere of Moderate Israeli Judaism

Earlier we explored the commonalities and distinctions between Orthodox feminism in Israel and in North America, classifying two discrete forms: one that began in the North America, was brought over to Israel, and evolved in critical ways within Israeli settings, and a second that draws on the first but is at its essence sui generis to the sovereign Israeli Jewish environment. The latter is expressed most vividly through religious women's army service. From the perspective of content and core experience, then, Hadran is situated closer to the first category of Israeli Orthodox feminism.

From a geographic perspective, however, it manifests simultaneously a fresh "hybrid" paradigm. The quasi-ritual women's digital space that it facilitates exists independently from either Israel or North America and the male authority and supervision that dominate their Orthodox spheres. As a result, Hadran's transnational character is reflected in the emergence of a novel virtual environment for religious feminism that is less directly moored in either of the centers.

All the same, it was created and is nourished primarily by woman scholars who are themselves rooted in IsMO: women who were trained as Torah scholars in the institutions established or led by key agents of change—Brovender, Bina, Henkin, Lichtenstein, Riskin—who arrived in the mid-twentieth century. Through its digital arena, then, Hadran is displaying an additional layer of IsMO's trajectory. IsMO has certainly influenced North American MO via the hundreds of students who attend its Israel-based Torah institutions each year on gap year programs, as well as the Israeli emissaries—such as the Torah MiTzion fellows—who work within educational and religious frameworks for multiple years. Through Hadran, moreover, IsMO has actually spawned an independent transnational sphere that is grounded in its overall outlook.

Zion and Back

The Torah MiTzion Movement

Jerusalem or Cleveland?

The sights and sounds of the Israeli-style beit midrash were palpable. Young men wearing knitted skullcaps and sandals, many of them bearded, were sitting in twosomes and debating the intricacies of ancient Talmudic texts. The large study hall was lined with books and panels made of Jerusalem stone that were engraved with citations from the works of Rabbi Abraham Isaac Kook. Huge volumes rested upon the tables that separated the pairs, most of them in their twenties. Hebrew-speaking students were engaged in intellectual duels, *tzitzit* fringes spilling out of their untucked shirts, as they engaged canonical texts.

But this wasn't the hills of Jerusalem. I was in Cleveland.

How had this institution sprouted in Middle America? Indeed, how had multiple kollels (post-yeshiva centers for Torah fellows), all predicated on that quintessentially Israel-based model, taken root throughout the world in the course of the early twenty-first century? More broadly, how did the emergence of the Torah MiTzion (TMZ) network, serve as an early indication of a novel global direction within Israeli RZ, and the ways some key figures in this program have, upon their return to Israel, integrated within IsMO.[1]

That day in September 2004 was my first encounter with the beit midrash of the Cleveland Torat Tzion Kollel (Torah of Zion, henceforth CTTK). This institution had been created ten years earlier through the collaborative effort of a local philanthropist and the leaders of YHE.[2] The latter committed to sending senior rabbis to Cleveland for two-year stints, along with a group of post-army students.[3] There they established a study hall in a local day school that served as a base both for advancing their own Talmudic erudition and for educational activities with the student body. In addition, they created an open beit midrash to offer Torah learning opportunities in the evenings and on weekends for the surrounding Orthodox community.[4]

Almost simultaneously, a similar framework was initiated by YHE alumnus Rabbi Jonathan Glass in Cape Town, South Africa.[5] Shortly after, the Torah MiTzion organization was inaugurated in Jerusalem. Under the guidance of founding executive director Ze'ev Schwartz, also a former YHE student,[6] it became a worldwide movement that has reached twenty-eight communities since its inception. Today it encompasses fourteen such RZ kollels, as well as additional affiliated learning centers. They range globally from Moscow to Montevideo and from Melbourne to Memphis. At present, seven are located in North America (seven others operated for over five years), three in Latin America, three in Australia, two in South Africa, and two in Europe.[7] Responding to realities on the ground, two additional components were added during the third decade of TMZ's existence, a program to send women as emissaries[8] and "Lilmod," an online study program that offers real-time partner learning around the world in multiple languages.[9]

This chapter explores the implications of TMZ for the evolution of RZ and the impact its alumni continue to have on Israeli society.[10] TMZ, which was founded and led throughout most of its history by YHE graduates, exemplifies a shift from conceptions that once dominated Israeli Zionism in general and Israeli RZ in particular. This is reflected in its global character, the cooperative Israeli-world Jewry nature of the project, and its approach toward promotion of immigration to Israel.

It is useful to first return to two ideals that long stood at the core of Israeli Zionism's approach to Jewish life outside of Israel, which were touched upon earlier in respect to David Ben-Gurion: *shelilat ha-galut* (negation of the exile) and *shelihut* (sending emissaries). We will examine how TMZ navigates these concepts and why its structure, outlook, and activities represent a modification to the previous paradigms. The chapter also highlights a few key TMZ alumni and how their activities upon their return offer an additional perspective on IsMO.

Shelilat ha-Galut and Shelihut

One of the fundamental motifs of the Zionist rebellion against tradition, with Ben-Gurion a major spokesperson, was its negative perception of Jewish life outside the Land of Israel. Initially, this attitude found its most vehement expression among the antireligious streams of the movement. The exile was the venue where Judaism had lost its historic national character and mutated into a powerless and passive minority lacking the will as well as the skills to take their destiny into their own hands. Religious beliefs that centered on praying for divine intervention had replaced national pride and ingenuity. Obsession with ritual law and practices symbolized the stagnation and abnormality of the ghettoized *galut*, or exile.[11] Naturally, this was an issue that generated a great deal of ambivalence among the RZ, who sought to synthesize the modern political aspirations of Jewish nationalism with rabbinic tradition and authority.[12]

During the late twentieth century *shelilat ha-galut* began to lose credibility among the predominant secular Zionist schools of thought.[13] The distancing of Israelis from this previously held notion can be understood as part of a societal development process that no longer needed the negation of the Diaspora "other" and its religious traditions to sustain a cohesive collective identity. Alternatively, one can view this change as a symptom of a broader sense of ideological malaise[14]—or possibly an example of the influence of post-Zionism, which seeks to detach the State of Israel from its role as a unique homeland for the Jewish people.[15] In the conclusion, I will raise a third possibility.

Concurrent with this secular about-face, the anti-exile position was championed from the late 1960s by the dominant trend in RZ thought and education, the Merkaz ha-Rav school.[16] Abraham Isaac Kook described the *galut* as placing limits on the Torah and the Jewish people (*zimzum* in kabbalistic terms). This stagnant condition is juxtaposed with the boundless spiritual creativity that comes to fruition when the Jewish people live in their natural habitat. It is in the ideology of his students, most prominently his son Zvi Yehuda Kook, as well as their

followers, that negation of the exile actually transformed into demonization. The Land of Israel is the wellspring of holiness, while the *galut* is
the home of the *goyim*, or Gentiles, who despise the Jews. Living beside
them is the seed of Israel's destruction. Thus: "The only true Israel is
redeemed Israel: Israeli sovereignty, Israeli Armed forces, the nation as
an integrated whole and not in Diaspora exiles."[17]

This position was partially a reaction to the Holocaust, which, in
Kook the younger's opinion, was the "absolute negation of a Jewish reality in the exile. . . . The destruction of the exile . . . clarifies substan-
tively . . . that the true existence of the Torah is only in our place—here,
which exists exclusively for us."[18] To be sure, this radical rejection of
galut existence was part of a broader messianic ideology that dominated
mainstream RZ after the Israeli victory in 1967. It focused on expanding the borders and strengthening Jewish sovereignty over all of Biblical
Israel in conjunction with the prophetic promise of ingathering of the
exiles. Not only did a flourishing Jewish exile run counter to the new
redemptive reality, it was also a stumbling block to nurturing an Israeli
population large enough to control the entire Land.[19] The ideology put
forward by the Kook school, as noted, gradually penetrated and eventually set the tone for Israeli RZ both on a political and educational level.

Shelihut

Since its inception in the 1920s, the Jewish Agency has promoted sending out emissaries to Jewish communities across the world as a central
mission of Zionism and the Jewish state. These *shelihim* were involved
in a host of activities ranging from teaching Hebrew and Jewish studies and running youth movements to facilitating clandestine illegal
immigration, providing medical care, and serving as nature counselors
and kitchen workers at Jewish summer camps. From the Zionist and
Israeli perspective, the main aim and justification for this complex and
costly campaign was to convince Jews around the world to immigrate to
Israel—or at least advance this goal indirectly by encouraging them to
visit. This was, of course, consistent with the negative view of the exile
that had long dominated classical Zionist discourse. Religious Zionists,
even those who did not share the extreme antagonism toward the exile

of the Kook school, also viewed generating immigration to Israel as the main goal in working with Jews abroad. As the former NRP figure Moshe Haim Shapiro put it in 1975, "In the Diaspora top priority must be accorded to the encouragement of *aliya* on the part of religious Jews who wish to settle in Eretz Israel."[20] At the same time, the members of the communities throughout the world who hosted the emissaries may have viewed them more as reinforcements for their own local educational needs than as aliyah agents. Particularly since 1948, for the most part they presented the Israelis as authentic Jews who came from the center of the Jewish universe to share some of their pure Jewish identity and spirit with their fractured and assimilation-prone brothers and sisters.

Along with the decline in the *shelilat ha-galut* approach within secular Zionism, alternative perceptions of the Israel-world Jewry relationship have been introduced that filtered down into the *shelihut* enterprise. Rather than the center going to the periphery in order to encourage its inhabitants to return home, new terms like "Jewish peoplehood," "partnership," and *mifgash* (meeting) became the main rationales for sending emissaries, as well as encouraging visits to Israel. The implication of this fresh terminology is that both sides of the Israel-world Jewry axis possess inherent legitimacy and that the relationship is reciprocal. Rather than encouraging the *galut* to join or at least idealize the Zionist collective, each participant has something to learn from the other. Ultimately, the goal is to facilitate the quest of individual Jews throughout the globe—including Israelis—to discover their particular Jewish identity and connection to the Jewish people.[21]

Another position has also been articulated since the 1990s regarding the goal of *shelihut* that seeks to compromise between promotion of aliyah as the only response to the *galut* and the complete removal of the State of Israel from its pedestal above all other Jewish communities. The adherents of what has been termed "New Zionism" want to create a fresh paradigm that recognizes the importance of individual quest and appreciates Jewish life throughout the world. Yet they feel that, ideally and practically speaking, Israel is the cultural and spiritual center of the Jewish people to whom all other communities turn for enrichment and inspiration. To a certain degree this is a reversion to or fulfillment of Ahad

Ha'am's (Asher Ginzburg) vision of cultural Zionism. Unlike almost all other early Zionist ideologues, he sought to downplay the contradiction between the political aims of Zionism and the continuation of Jewish life in exile.[22] The *shelihim* in an age of New Zionism are sent abroad to act as cultural agents who stimulate and reinforce the idea that Israel is the center of Jewish life and the deepest reservoir of Jewish culture and knowledge. Yet in the spirit of partnership, they are also meant to learn through their exposure to other Jews and to strengthen their sense of connection with them. Aliyah is certainly a valuable option, but it is far from the raison d'être for sending *shelihim*.[23]

As part of an examination of which paradigm of emissary service is closest to the model developed by TMZ, it bears noting that the Zionists were not the only Jewish group in the twentieth century that turned *shelihut* into a central aim of their movement. Particularly after the rise of Rabbi Menachem Mendel Schneerson to the helm of the Chabad-Lubavitch hasidic sect in 1951, this Brooklyn-based movement turned *shelihus*—as they pronounce it—into its most hallowed vocation. Rather than promoting a land-centered ideal, however, the *shluchim* of Chabad seek to fulfill their leader's aim of bringing all Jews closer to his vision of God and the Torah by creating religious centers known as Chabad Houses.[24] Chabad is truly a global organization, with over four thousand emissaries serving in sixty countries.[25]

From the late 1980s American Lithuanian-style yeshivot also internalized the *shelihut* ethos and created outreach kollels in North American communities. Similar to TMZ, these frameworks are built around a group of young men and their wives who divide their time between personal daily study in the *kollel beit midrash* and providing Torah learning opportunities and informal programming to local Jews. Yet like Chabad, Israel orientation and aliyah are by no means the educational aims of these organizations. Rather, strengthening connections to Judaism and raising levels of observance are the exclusive goals of these initiatives. Both Chabad *shluchim* and haredi community *kollel jungerleit* (fellows) are encouraged to remain permanently in their postings.[26]

On the surface, then, TMZ shares characteristics with both the Zionist *shelihut* concept and the Chabad/Haredi variants. With an appreciation for the historical changes that have taken place in Israeli approaches to the world Jewry and to *shelihut* since the end of the twentieth century, we will now look more closely at the TMZ approach.

Israeli Perspectives

Haim Zohar was the former Israeli consul in New York and secretary-general of the World Zionist Organization, and later the vice-chairman of TMZ.[27] In 2006, he published an article about TMZ in a collection honoring the centennial of Religious Zionist education. There he asks: "What is our direction? Outreach or inreach? *Aliya*?"[28] His answer is inreach, strengthening the commitment of the "hard-core Jews."[29] As to encouraging aliyah, he states unequivocally that he is against any talk of the subject by the kollel emissaries with the local Jews. Such discussions are ineffective and at best tend to produce immigrants motivated by fear for their personal welfare rather than deep-seated love for the Land of Israel. Mass Western immigration will take place only after the Torah of Israel is planted in the hearts of world Jewry. The practical goal of the kollels, according to Zohar, is to help educate the Jews of the world toward an appreciation of the Torah and Zion as fundamental and interrelated concepts within Judaism.[30] This mission is predicated on full partnership between the emissaries and the local communities, and must be devoid of any sense of superiority or condescension on the part of the Israelis. Broadly speaking, he hoped that Israeli yeshiva graduates teaching the Torah and interacting with Jews from around the globe could create "a world-wide fellowship of those who study in Zionist kollels . . . an ideological-spiritual movement and not a political-organizational one."[31]

This statement by one of the founders and main figures in the TMZ hierarchy shows no hint of the negativism regarding the *galut* that entered mainstream RZ education through the Kook school. Moreover, it significantly downgrades aliyah as the central message of *shelihut*. It encourages, instead, the creation of a global network that is reminiscent of the land-neutral "Jewish Peoplehood" approach to *shelihut* on one hand, and the Haredi Torah–focused community kollel on the other. More likely, however, it can be understood as consistent with the "New Zionism" model of *shelihut* that seeks to balance between a reciprocal Israel-world Jewry relationship and an Ahad Ha'am–like effort to bring forth the fruits of Judaism's cultural and spiritual center to the periphery.

For the most part Zohar's essay is an accurate representation of the tension inherent in the TMZ concept and a reliable expression of the ideological implications that it entails. The TMZ organization and emissaries certainly would like to see more of the Jews with whom they interact immigrating to Israel. Like the outreach activist who is empowered when a previously unaffiliated Jew accepts full halakhic observance, for Israeli Religious Zionists aliyah remains the ultimate confirmation of their ideal. Yet TMZ's main thrust is toward buttressing the identification of Jews with Torah study and the Land of Israel, not encouraging them to uproot their lives. The aliyah imperative, then, has not been renounced, but it has been downgraded significantly.

This interpretation is supported by the official literature published by TMZ and that which appears on the main website of the organization. Consistently, the emphasis is placed on expanding and upgrading the opportunities and level of Torah study taking place in local communities, strengthening Jewish identity and Israel-world Jewry relations, and advancing the "values of RZ."[32] Rarely does the idea of direct promotion of aliyah appear in any of its publications. When it does pop up, it is low on the priority scale, almost hidden.

To offer a number of representative examples: the motto of TMZ that appears on the opening page of its website declares, "Building bridges between Israel and the Diaspora."[33] Its original "Who We Are" section, moreover, makes no mention of aliyah; rather it focuses on what it can contribute to the communities abroad: "Jewish communities around the world face assimilation, weakening of Jewish identity and weakened ties to the State of Israel. There is a dearth of dynamic, idealistic educators who can serve as role models of the successful merging of a deeply religious lifestyle with full integration in modern culture and ideals."[34] Similarly, on the inside cover of a folder that was given out to communities considering opening up a TMZ kollel, as well as to yeshiva students being recruited for *shelihut*, the following aims were listed:

> to transmit the values of RZ by promoting the lofty ideal of Torat Yisrael, Am Yisrael and Eretz Yisrael

[TMZ] stresses the importance of building ties between all Jews and
undertakes to strengthen Jewish identity and unity.

[TMZ] aims to bridge the gap between Israel and Diaspora communities, emphasizing the centrality of Israel, as it is written: "from Zion
the Torah will come forth" . . .

It is notable that the end of the first paragraph is an inverted allusion to
the Mizrachi RZ movement slogan attributed to Rabbi Meir Bar-Ilan:
"Am Yisrael, be-Eretz Yisrael, al pi Torat Yisrael" (the nation of Israel,
in the Land of Israel, according to the Torah of Israel). Whereas in the
original statement the Torah is intended to define the nature of life in
the Land of Israel, here it is the "Torah of the Land" that is being carried
by the emissaries to the nation throughout the world. In addition, as
opposed to the original attempt at combining the three components into
one cohesive whole, here each value can stand independently. Consistent
with this tone, in a letter dated Kislev 5767 (November–December 2006)
former recruitment director Moshe Gadot focused on the idea that
"[t]oday, more than ever, there is great importance to spreading Torah,
and particularly 'Torat Eretz Yisrael' among the Jewish communities that
are struggling with problems of assimilation and problems of Jewish and
religious identity."[35]

The end of Gadot's letter, however, hints that while shelilat ha-galut
of the Kookian sort is clearly nowhere to be found, the classical Zionist
approach to shelihut that focused on promoting aliyah still makes an
appearance. When describing the positive results of the TMZ effort, he
lists the following (in order):

- Batei Midrash [study halls] in the spirit of RZ.
- Many community members have begun to dedicate time to Torah
  study and as a result strengthen their connections to the Torah and
  the nation.
- A growing number of young men and women from the Diaspora
  come and participate in Zionist oriented programs in Israel.
- Families come on exploration and identification trips, and
  Thank God, we are beginning to see the results in aliya to
  the Land.[36]

Clearly the immediate goal is to create bastions of Torah and RZ abroad, but increasing aliyah remains a distant and certainly highly laudable endeavor.

Seventeen years later, in 2023, the revised TMZ website offered an almost identical "vision":

> We believe that the creation of Torah Learning Centers built on the power of deep personal relationships, coupled with Torah learning, can bring Jews closer to each other and thereby rekindle their Jewish iden-tity, foster a love for learning and a commitment to Israel. These centers are staffed by values driven, Israeli, Torah observant shlichim who are able to model a RZ way of life infused with a love for Israel. Through their dedication to learning and a love for others, they form strong re-lationships in their communities and create experiences that allow par-ticipants to experience living a rich Jewish life with Israel at its heart. . . . The participants from these communities are learning Torah, visiting Israel, making Aliyah.[37]

The goal of promoting aliyah is stated openly, but it remains last on the list of priorities.

The classical Zionist approach to *shelihut* has not disappeared com-pletely from TMZ's Religious Zionism. It remains a hallowed goal or a prized achievement, but in practice it has been relegated to a lower level of priority. For one, most Western Jews will not immigrate and therefore concentrating the efforts of the *shelihim* on this aim would be self-defeating. In addition, even if the Israelis want to talk about aliyah, in some cases if the host communities were to know that this was their main purpose they might be less eager to support the programs. Indeed, the former head of the TMZ kollel in Detroit—himself a graduate of a yeshiva headed by a Kookian disciple—was lambasted by some of the local kollel sponsors for focusing too much on aliyah. When time came to replace him, a request was made to send a head emissary with a dif-ferent focus.[38]

These tensions suggest sublimation, rather than a full renounce-ment of efforts to increase immigration. Yet the end result is that TMZ is a banner RZ initiative that has gained a strong footing within world

Jewry since its inception in 1994, in which encouraging aliyah has been formally removed from center stage. This does not contradict the fact, expressed by both its supporters and critics, that its existence in North American communities has raised consciousness regarding aliyah and studying in Israel. What it does say is that this is not its reason for being. Its primary focus is on strengthening the existing religious atmosphere among Jews around the world.

Indeed, a review of questionnaires filled out by TMZ *shelihim* upon return from their period abroad suggests that for most of them encouraging aliyah was not the central focus. Among the five that returned from the Chicago TMZ kollel in 2003, for example, only one wrote that his main goal was to convince local Jews to immigrate. The others spoke primarily in terms of increasing the amount of Torah learning within the community, providing a "Zionist alternative" to the many thriving Haredi community kollels in the area, and doing outreach with the non-affiliated Jewish population in the area. Actually, one of the chief causes of disappointment among the group was that, unlike their initial expectations, the sponsor community wanted them to work almost exclusively with the observant families. Reaching out to more rapidly assimilating Jewish populations, by no means an inherently Zionist endeavor, was not part of their mandate.[39]

It would appear that the role models put forward by the TMZ emissaries certainly inspire individuals to consider immigration to Israel more seriously or at least a term of study. At the same time, TMZ's heightened position and expansion within communities in America, and for that matter throughout the globe, signals an alternative to the classical RZ focus on aliyah. TMZ creates and sustains dynamic enclaves around the world. By doing so it helps to instill a new vitality to communal life outside of Israel—paradoxically one that can make aliyah less of a necessity. When such role models and their teachings are so easily accessible, and without the sacrifices that full-fledged uprooting entails, there is less motivation for taking the more radical step. Individuals will always exist whose commitment to Zionism leads them to move. But among the majority, there is comfort in knowing that one can live in the Diaspora and still interact with Hesder yeshiva graduates and their wives. Taken a step further, in the process of creating this network of

Israeli Torah centers outside the country, TMZ's RZ has buttressed its global, transnational quality.

Two Zionist Yeshivot

Many of the key figures in TMZ, particularly at its initial stages, as pointed out above, were associated with YHE. Along with exposure to Lichtenstein and his protégés, as well as the teachings of his father-in-law, Soloveitchik, the Israeli YHE students experienced directly the ideal of Israeli RZ's contributing to Orthodox communal life through daily interaction with foreign students. YHE runs a large program for young men from North America as well as other English-speaking countries who study Torah for one or two years before returning to their country of origin in order to attend university.

To be sure, YHE is committed to Israel as the ideal place for Jewish existence, but neither disdain nor lack of familiarity with the Diaspora characterize the institution. In fact, one of its major initiatives, the Israel Koschitzky Torat Har Etzion Virtual Beit Midrash (VBM), is an internet-based archive that makes a broad range of lectures and homiletical material available to the English speaking public around the world.[40] It is not surprising, therefore, that products of this orientation would have taken the lead or at least been inclined to the TMZ model of Torah study in service of the world communities.[41]

What is more notable, however, is that while YHE remains the largest feeder school, TMZ did not remain its exclusive project. At least eighteen other Hesder yeshivot, as well as other RZ institutions that are wholly identified with the Kook school, have sent their students as TMZ emissaries.[42] In addition, TMZ received the imprimatur of two of the most authoritative figures in the Kook camp, the late former chief rabbis Mordechai Eliyahu and Avraham Shapira.[43]

Does this mean that the Kook school has abandoned the negation of *galut* that was so vehemently promulgated by its founders? Are these rabbis comfortable with an RZ that deemphasizes territory and focuses on presenting *Torat Eretz Yisrael* (Torah anchored in the Land of Israel) as a foundation for American MO? Scholars have advanced this argument based on literary evidence.[44] I raised this matter directly with

Rabbi Chaim Druckman, the late head of the Bnei Akiva Movement, leader in the Gush Emunim settlement movement and former MK, as well as a strong supporter of TMZ.[45] Druckman felt that TMZ is totally consistent with Kookian ideology. Even if there is minimal direct influence on aliyah, TMZ is crucial for American Jews because it introduces Israel and Zionism into local discourse. To his mind, the alternative for most American Jews is assimilation, while for the Modern Orthodox it is Haredization. Furthermore, he was unconvinced by the conclusion being reached by some communities that Americans are more effective at teaching the Torah. "Torah without *Eretz Yisrael* is not Torah," he said.[46]

Druckman certainly did not acknowledge the global, transnational direction engendered by TMZ. At the same time, he supported the drafting of Israeli yeshiva students to battle assimilation and to buttress Jewish life across the globe. In both cases the value of the people of Israel, without connection to their geographic location, is supreme.

Recognized by them or not, I suggest that prominent representatives of the Kook school have thrown their support behind a project that engenders an alternative perception of the diaspora and of *shelihut* than that expressed by their mid-twentieth-century mentors. The interest on their part in promoting TMZ is particularly illuminating in light of the heavy influence of teachers and graduates of YHE on its development.

The support given by the Kook camp to the TMZ concept can be understood, in part, as exemplifying the upheaval within the RZ camp that arose in the aftermath of the 1995 assassination of Prime Minister Yitzhak Rabin and in response to the 2005 disengagement from the Gaza Strip. After years of focus on settlement as the primary activity of RZ, the abandonment by much of the Israeli Jewish population of this enterprise and its ideals caused at least a partial shift or diversification away from this monolithic path. Many within this population reached the conclusion that "settling the Land" had not engendered "settling in the hearts" of most Israelis. As a result, alternative RZ initiatives began to appear.[47] Another new direction within RZ that has direct parallels with TMZ is the option made available to girls to spend the second year of their national service (*sherut leumi*) as emissaries to Jewish communities abroad.[48]

Returning Rabbis

Since 1994, TMZ has sent 1,582 emissaries to communities throughout the world.[49] One of the biggest challenges for many of them is the return to Israel. This is especially the case for the more successful kollel heads. After investing much effort in learning the surroundings and cultures of their settings abroad, developing close relationships with members of the communities, gaining the confidence of their supporters, and enabling their children to adjust to a foreign environment, couples who run TMZ kollels often have to start all over in Israel. Ideally, these talented individuals seek spaces where they can not only support their households, but hopefully find meaning. This is not simple, as they may discover that, along with the benefits of being close to family and friends, it is hard to reproduce the constant sense of purpose that emissaries often feel. A parallel issue that arises is that, in the course of their time abroad, they learned to appreciate aspects of local communal life that differ from their native Israeli settings. Thus, upon return, they may be eager to introduce innovative ideas garnered abroad to their native Israeli environments.[50]

Notwithstanding these obstacles, there are quite a few TMZ emissaries who have found considerable success in Israel and have even been able to apply elements or approaches to Jewish communal experience that they sampled during their sojourns. In some cases the TMZ experience directly affected where within Israeli religious life the returning figures found themselves after their return. Similar to TMZ, the OTS-affiliated Straus-Amiel Institute headed by YHE alumnus and former chief rabbi of Uruguay, Rabbi Eliahu Birnbaum, specializes in training Israelis to serve as rabbis for communities throughout the world for a few years. Some remain, but most return to Israel. As illustrated in the appendix, its graduates have also drawn from their experiences abroad as they developed their rabbinic careers once back in Israel.[51]

I suggest that this "return" phenomenon illustrates an additional aspect to the transnational character of the burgeoning IsMO. That is, the institutions led by the agents of change produced students who adopted fresh approaches to the Jewish world and toward *shelihut*. This facilitated the cultivation of a cadre of emissaries to Jewish communities abroad who, upon coming home, introduced novel approaches to Israeli life. The result is an ongoing back-and-forth of mutual influence. I will illuminate this issue through a few examples of returning TMZ kollel leaders who occupy a range of positions within the spectrum of IsMO.

Rabbi Mosheh Lichtenstein (b. 1961): The eldest son of Rabbi Dr. Aharon Lichtenstein, after his family immigrated to Israel, he attended the Netiv Meir Yeshiva High School in Jerusalem. He then studied with his grandfather Rabbi Soloveitchik, before completing the YHE Hesder program (serving in the armored tanks corps) and rabbinical ordination, as well as a bachelor's degree in English literature at the Hebrew University in Jerusalem. In 1992 he joined the senior teaching staff of YHE and also taught women in the advanced program at Midreshet Bruriah (Lindenbaum). In 1997, he and his wife, Michal, and family moved to Cleveland, where he served for two years as *rosh kollel* of CTTK. He then returned to YHE, and in 2009 he was chosen as one of the three figures to inherit the helm of the yeshiva after the retirement of the founding figures, his father and Amital. It would be an overstatement to say that TMZ shaped the worldview of a Torah scholar of his stature who is the son and protégé of both his father and grandfather. All the same, not only has Moshe Lichtenstein demonstrated himself to be a worthy heir to his predecessors, he has staked out multiple public positions regarding educational and ideological issues that solidify his role as a leader of the moderate sector.[52] He has been outspoken regarding the importance of respecting the dignity of all human beings, regardless of their faith or ethnic group. Asked in 2016 about the controversial question of whether women could be full-fledged independent halakhic authorities, he fully supported the idea, responding, "I yearn for the day when there will be qualified *poskot* [female adjudicators]."[53]

Rabbi Herzl Hefter (b. 1957): Born in New York, he spent two post–high school gap years at YHE. After graduation from YU he moved to Israel and for the following ten years studied at YHE under Aharon Lichtenstein, before setting out on a career as teacher of Talmud and Jewish law for advanced students. Among others, he trained YU's rabbinical candidates at its Gruss Center in Jerusalem for seventeen years and led the advanced program for women at Midreshet Bruriah (Lindenbaum).

From 1995 to 1997, he was *rosh kollel* of CTTK in Cleveland. In 2013, he founded Beit Midrash Harel in Jerusalem, a coeducational Orthodox rabbinical seminary that gives ordination to both men and women.[54] Hefter has also published widely on Jewish thought—especially on Hasidism and modernity/postmodernity—in both religious and academic frameworks.[55] Through Harel, he has certainly asserted a position that is far more progressive than that of both YHE and TMZ.[56] This in itself exhibits the "second-generation processing" that characterizes the evolution of IsMO.

Rabbi Shai Finkelstein (b. 1976): Born and bred in the Haifa region, he attended the Hesder program at Yeshivat Shaalavim—a more conservative institution than YHE, which also has a highly successful foreign students program—and served in the IDF artillery corps. He received ordination from the Israeli chief rabbinate, and later a BA in Talmud from BIU. In 2000 he moved with his family to Memphis, Tennessee, to serve a two-year stint as *rosh kollel* for its TMZ branch. Due to his success, he was appointed rabbi of the Baron Hirsch Congregation, the largest Orthodox congregation in the area. He remained there until 2016, also earning an MBA from the University of Memphis, at which point he returned to Israel and became the rabbi of Kehillat Nitzanim, in the Baka neighborhood of Jerusalem. Since his arrival, the synagogue has grown exponentially, both in numbers of attendees and congregants, and in the richness of its educational and social welfare programming. Finkelstein is a highly sought-after speaker in Israel and the United States and is the editor of a new Bible commentary endeavor of Koren Publishing House. He is also a PhD candidate in Talmud. In a wide-ranging interview from 2017 in the *Jerusalem Post* headlined "Jerusalem Rabbi Brings Process-Shul Model from Memphis," he focused on the importance of embracing diversity within a communal setting. Finkelstein demonstrated deep appreciation for the challenges faced by LGBTQ Jews and encouraged the expansion of women's roles within religious life without taking an absolute stand in either direction regarding women's ordination.[57]

Two other congregational rabbis serving within walking distance from Finkelstein's synagogue also had stints as TMZ kollel heads. Rabbi Itiel Oron led the Washington, DC, area contingent and upon return in 2019 was installed as Benny Lau's replacement (after eighteen years in the position) at the Ramban Synagogue in the German Colony section.

Rabbi Eitan Ansbacher, rabbi of the Be-Orkha community in the Mekor Hayyim neighborhood, served as a TMZ kollel leader in Montreal.[58]

Rabbi Boaz Genut (b. 1974) grew up in Jerusalem and studied for eleven years at Yeshivat Or Etzion, the Hesder yeshiva founded by Druckman. He served as *rosh kollel* of the TMZ branch in St. Louis, Missouri. In addition to rabbinical ordination, he has a bachelor's degree in education and an MBA. Upon his family's return from *shelihut*, he replaced Schwartz as CEO of TMZ when the latter became the head of World Bnei Akiva.[59] After fourteen years Genut joined the administrative leadership of Tzohar, guiding its major initiatives regarding weddings and development of young rabbinic leadership.[60]

Rabbi Avi Kannai (b. 1969) grew up in Rehovot and studied for nine years at YHE, including the Hesder program, serving in the IDF Paratroopers Brigade. In addition to rabbinical ordination, he is a clinical psychologist with bachelor's and master's degrees from the Hebrew University in Jerusalem. Kannai spent three years as the *rosh kollel* of the TMZ Memphis branch. He is presently the rabbi of the Mitzpe Ramot congregation in Jerusalem and is an active member of Beit Hillel. His life motto is: "True attendance to and acceptance of those who are different without blurring the moral clarity between good and evil."[61]

Rabbi Uri Einhorn (b. 1973) was born and bred in Jerusalem, attended the Hesder program at YHE, and served in the IDF Paratroopers Brigade. From 2002 to 2004, he was *rosh kollel* of the TMZ branch in Cape Town, South Africa. Since 2009 he has served as rabbi of Kfar Shmaryahu, a town adjacent to Herzliyah that is one of the most affluent and secular areas in the country. *Haaretz*, considered the journalistic voice of the Israeli left, ran a highly favorable in-depth interview with him in March 2023 titled "Secular Kfar Shmaryahu Has a Beloved Orthodox Rabbi: What Is the Secret of His Success?"[62] The article highlights his warm relations with all types of local residents and their appreciation for the way that he facilitates religious life in a positive manner. Einhorn was also asked about an incident in 2019 when a group of communal members petitioned to have him removed from his position. His response:

> It was a group of six repentant Jews who no longer live here. . . . They wanted stricter ordinances regarding the Sabbath—closure of the parking

lot adjacent to the synagogue and raising the height of the partition between men's and women's sections. I refused and found myself battling
religious coercion. I am an Orthodox rabbi . . . but I live in a secular
place. My goals are to sanctify God's name in Heaven, to demonstrate the
humane sides of Judaism . . . I don't reprove anyone. In our congregation
there are numerous LGBT couples that attend services with their children, they are dear friends of mine.[63]

Conclusion: *Torat Eretz Yisrael* and the Transportation of Place

The *shelihut* of TMZ differs dramatically from the classical formula that
focused almost exclusively on aliyah. Not only is encouraging immigration to Israel less central, the main focus of activity is actually on
strengthening Jewish life worldwide. As with the Haredi community
outreach kollels, this is done primarily by creating a vibrant beit midrash
that can attract local Jews of multiple ages Torah study and Jewish activity. Without declaring so in words, the very structure and goals of TMZ's
activities in America neutralize any attempt to preserve negation of the
galut as a serious element in the RZ worldview.

Not only has Jewish life abroad gained greater legitimacy through
TMZ, in the process RZ had acquired a new global character. The TMZ
emissaries do not leave their sacred Israeli territory as individuals. They
travel as small collectives called kollels, whose mandate is to cultivate an
RZ atmosphere in a given Jewish community somewhere in the world.
But these Israel-like environments are not created as appendages to the
home territory that will necessarily facilitate the arrival of more Jews.
This may happen in some cases, but it is not the main objective. For the
local communities, the value of the Zionistic spirit of the emissaries lies
primarily in its potential to reinvigorate the local spiritual environment.

Surely the *shelihim* return home and on an individual level reassert
their territorial Zionistic identity. But they are immediately replaced
by others who sustain the Zionist enclaves that were established and
continue the role of nurturing global Judaism with their Zionist spirit.
Indeed, a culture of the Land of Israel has been articulated that exists
independently from the land itself.

* * *

In 2005 the photographers Max Becher and Andrea Robbins opened a new exhibition titled *770*. The two had taken pictures of the Lubavitcher Hasidism's Brooklyn headquarters (770 Eastern Parkway) and of eleven replicas of this building that serve as Chabad centers throughout the world. The display included photos from Brooklyn, Buenos Aires, Haifa, Jerusalem, Los Angeles, Melbourne, Milan, Montreal, New Brunswick, and São Paolo.[64] In the explanatory text that accompanies the exhibition, the artists refer to the phenomenon portrayed through their pictures as the "transportation of Place":

> The primary focus of our work is, what we call, *the transportation of place*—situations in which one limited or isolated place strongly resembles another distant one. . . . Traditional notions of place, in which culture and geographic location neatly coincide, are being challenged.[65]

This, essentially, expresses the feeling that I had that day in September 2004 when I first entered the beit midrash of the CTTK in Cleveland. Right in the middle of America I had come across a study hall whose sounds and sights I identified directly with Israel. As we have seen, this seemingly surreal sensation was indicative of a broader phenomenon. Parallel to Chabad and *770*, TMZ reflects an expansive direction for RZ, from a geocentric movement that encouraged those outside to come in to a global network that is land-centered but emphasizes Judaism's "transnational" character, in which the Torah of the place is being transported to other distant venues. In parallel, as illustrated by the "returning rabbis," they have brought with them a new wave of cultural transmission, as they draw on their experiences and exposure abroad long after they have completed their physical emissary roles and reaffirmed their permanent roots in Israel.

Conclusion

Israelization, American Jewry, and the Bridging Role of Israeli Moderate Orthodoxy

What impact does IsMO's development have on the ongoing relations between Israeli and American Jewries?

In the course of this book, I have portrayed the critical function played by a cadre of American immigrants in the emergence of Israeli Moderate Orthodoxy, tracing core worldviews and ideals that they brought with them; how these were introduced to Israeli society and then assimilated and processed by their Israeli disciples and followers; and the fresh transnational structures and directions (in some cases digital) that have arisen out of this trend. As illustrated at numerous points, this Israeli religious spectrum already plays a critical role for segments of American Orthodoxy. In the following I will assert, moreover, that its existence has significance for broader swaths of American Jewry as well.

This examination is framed through two concepts that have gained traction within academic writing on contemporary Israel in recent years, "Israelization" and "IsraeliJudaism." Each of these terms point to potential ways the phenomenon highlighted here bridges between the two largest centers of the Jewish world. At the same time, they also raise the issue of limitations to IsMO's utility as a bridging factor.

Israelization

Rabbi Elliot Cosgrove is a keen observer of contemporary Jewish life. He serves as spiritual leader of New York's Park Avenue Synagogue, a prominent Manhattan Conservative synagogue with a membership of seventeen hundred families,[1] and is widely considered one of the most respected and influential rabbinical figures in North America.[2] On May 19, 2019, he published an op-ed lamenting the lack of more rigorous religious engagement on the part of most American Jews:

These days, American Jews no longer debate who wrote the Bible. Instead, we argue about Israel. Israel is what brings us together and what
tears us apart. We work to keep our relationship with Israel strong and
are anxiety-ridden at signs of its weakening. We fear for our children's
encounters with anti-Zionism on campus, and we hope that they sign up
for Birthright trips. The labels that delineate our denominations are no
longer based on belief or observance—Orthodox, Conservative, Reform,
Reconstructionist—but on our views about Israel: AIPAC, ZOA, JVP, J-
Street and the rest of the alphabet soup of Israel advocacy. . . . Despite
the fact that we do not live, vote, serve in the military or pay taxes there,
Israel has become the organizing principle and civil religion of American
Jewry. . . . While Jewish sovereignty is a cause for celebration, American
Jews are still seeking to come to terms with this new reality.[3]

Cosgrove's comments reflect the "postdenominational" ambience of
twenty-first-century American Judaism, in which religious movement
labels play less of a role in personal Jewish identification among American
Jews. But as Jack Wertheimer warned in 2005, along with its many blessings, a less contentious environment also brings with it an atmosphere
of complacence.[4] Enter Israel, a topic that increasingly divides American
Jews and in the process elicits considerable passion on all sides.[5]

Cosgrove, nonetheless, decries this focus on Israel debates because he
perceives it as a deflection—a way to avoid addressing core existential
issues:

Clearly, it is easier to take someone to task for their views on Israel than it
is to come face-to-face with the withering of Jewish identity in one's children and grandchildren. If Jews spent less time attacking each other on
Israel and more time building Jewish identity, devoted fewer resources to
supporting the extremes of the Israel debate and more to making Jewish
day school education, camping and synagogue life affordable, American
Jewry would be in better shape, and so would our relationship with Israel.
Why do American Jews talk about Israel so much? Because it is easier
than turning the lens on the endangered condition of our Judaism.[6]

One academic who would agree at least in part with Cosgrove's observation while disagreeing with his conclusion is Yossi Shain. An Israeli

political scientist who held parallel appointments for many years at Tel Aviv University and Georgetown University, he published a book in 2019 that is predicated on the prognosis that Israel is the main Jewish-related issue that concerns American Jews. Yet rather than seeing this as a matter of American Jewish avoidance, Shain put forward a novel theory to explain this development. The book, which was later translated and published in English under the title *The Israeli Century: How the Zionist Revolution Changed History and Reinvented Judaism*,[7] argues that scenarios such as that described by Cosgrove reflect the natural, one might even say deterministic, consequence of what Shain calls the "Israelization" process. In the Israeli century, the theological and ideological debates that once dominated the religious engagements of the American Jew have been upstaged by the transformed conditions of experience associated with the established and rooted Jewish sovereign state.

Shain's "paradigm-changing" thesis challenges the notion that Israel and the Diaspora are, as Liebman and Cohen's 1990 study emphasized, "two worlds of Judaism."[8] Rather, he presents a picture of a Jewish globe with Israel at its center. His core claim is stated on the first page of the book: "Since its establishment in 1948, the State of Israel has gradually situated itself as the most important factor in all areas of worldwide Jewish life. . . . The nation of Israel and Jewish civilization are defined today more than ever through the political, military, and cultural power of the sovereign Jewish state."[9]

Israel's centrality to Jewish life, according to Shain, is reflected in its critical mass of Jews, destined within a few years to outgrow the total Jewish population of the rest of the world, and the diverse, hypercreative, and multicultural Jewish environment that it has facilitated.[10] Israeli academicians, writers, musicians, cinematographers, and "startup-ists" have achieved a global footprint and nourish Jewish pride in communities across the planet.[11]

Shain's is a global vision built around a robust Israeli center. American Jewry is undoubtedly still a rich and powerful "Babylon," but the parallel phenomena of rising Israeli strength and heightened worldwide antisemitism and radical assimilation have made America more peripheral. While no longer predicating its relationship to world Jewry on the hope that they will return home, it is Israel, advances Shain, that to an ever greater degree nourishes its distant kin.

As opposed to North America, where due to assimilatory trends Jewish continuity is becoming tenuous, "[i]t is Israel," says Shain, "where the nation feels rooted and safe in its national identity, that empowers Jews to bring to fruition their global abilities . . . the deep sense that one has a home to return to enables them to traverse and engage the big world with ease and confidence."[12] Thus, the proliferation of expatriate Israelis who have settled in Northern New Jersey, Silicon Valley, Los Angeles, Southern Florida, and Berlin does not indicate a decline in the Zionist ideal. They are a testament, instead, to the fortitude and long-term stability of the Jewish state. These individuals generally maintain close ties with the "mother country." They follow news from "back home" vigilantly and serve as cultural agents who communicate "Israeliness" to their Diaspora brethren. Their successes are Israel's successes.[13]

In point of fact, the swift return of thousands of Israelis living abroad to their reserve units in October 2023, in the wake of the horrific October 7 attacks on Israel by Hamas, supports Shain's understanding of a global Israeli community that continues to perceive Israel as its homeland and center.[14] All the same, Shain's comments regarding safety and security need to be qualified, as it was the grave mistakes of those charged with protecting Israel's citizens, and the initial fears that the attacks precipitated among the broader population, that caused so many of its military reservists to rush home that October.

Israel's own economic prowess, adds Shain, combined with the increasing role of Israelis in North American Jewish life, has neutralized its former dependency on the "rich American uncle." If anything, there is a role reversal in which Israel provides a security blanket, not just on a physical level, for Jewish identity abroad. The preeminent example of this phenomenon is the Birthright (*Taglit*) program. Since its inception in the late 1990s, it has brought over six hundred thousand young adults to Israel for ten days of intensive Israeli and Jewish immersion. In the eyes of Jewish leaders both in Israel and throughout the world, it is considered to be the most successful Jewish educational initiative of the past few decades, and a key to fortifying Diaspora Jewish life.[15] Yet the massive mobilization of American Jews during the October 2023 war in Gaza precipitated by the Hamas attacks tempers some of the certitude with which Shain stresses this aspect of his thesis and points to more reciprocal aspects of the relationship—at least in as far as emergency funding and political lobbying are concerned.

In step with Shain's line of thinking, even the efforts over the past decade to expose Israelis more deeply to the realities of American Jewish life through "reverse Birthright" trips and educational programs are a manifestation of Israel's preeminent place in Jewish life. Rather than a corrective meant to facilitate a more balanced "Jerusalem-Babylon" relationship, following Shain's discourse, these programs reflect the urgency felt by Jews abroad that those at the center appreciate their challenges and unique expressions of Jewish identity.[16]

In the Israeli century, antisemitism has by no means disappeared. On the contrary, there is consensus that the early twenty-first century has witnessed a major uptick in public outbursts of Jew hatred throughout the globe, and not just in European countries whose deeply rooted phobias regarding Jews find strange bedfellows with some elements within Muslim constituencies—ironically themselves the victims of some of the same prejudices. Even in the United States, where Jews have felt especially safe, this is no longer the case, as the two murderous synagogue attacks of 2019 in Pennsylvania and California tragically revealed.[17] Even though at the time that Shain wrote his book these remained isolated and unusual events, the ubiquitous police patrol cars and armed guards along with congregational volunteers in front of most large synagogues gave visual expression to the sea change in the rhythm of contemporary North American Jewish life. No doubt, the dramatic rise in antisemitic attacks and campaigns since October 7, 2023, has only clarified that this dangerous trend is growing dramatically.[18]

Shain is fully aware that there are multiple factors that foster antisemitism. Yet he stresses that the critical distinction between contemporary trends and those of the past is the fusion by so many of anti-Israel attitudes with loathing of Jews. To be sure, non-Jewish anti-Israel activists—as well as Jews who are ambivalent regarding the state if not antagonistic to Zionism—argue that anti-Zionism and antisemitism are dissimilar. All the same, Shain testifies that such distinctions are not borne out given radical Muslim efforts to introduce classical tropes of antisemitism into the discourse of the conflict[19] (and, as figures such as French intellectuals Bernard-Henri Lévy[20] and Alain Finkielkraut have argued,[21] considering other manifestations of public antisemitism throughout the world).[22] Shain thus gives his imprimatur to an expression coined by others, the "Israelization of antisemitism."[23]

Along with the intensification and toleration of antisemitic acts among multiple levels of American society, including academic elites, the events of October 2023 have certainly fortified another Jewish cultural reality that Shain featured in 2019. In parallel to the masses of American Jews who turn to Israel for inspiration and are dedicated to its security and prosperity, a vocal and growing constituency of Diaspora Jews feels alienated from its power and nationalist orientation, especially as reflected in its policies toward Palestinians. For them, explains Shain, Israel's power and ability to inflict injury upon its enemies is the opposite of the universalist, humanitarian, *tikkun olam*–oriented Judaism upon which they were nurtured.[24] Some protest or look for ways to strengthen Israeli groups that advance alternative approaches, and a minority support Boycott, Divesture, and Sanctions (BDS), Jewish Voice for Peace, and other initiatives aimed at punishing Israel for its policies and pressuring it to change them.[25] On this conflict, Shain makes his opinion clear. While certainly opposed to unrestrained force when it can be avoided, in the Niebuhrian debate between sovereignty and humanism, he chooses the former[26]—not due to an all-out rejection of liberal values, but because from his point of view a state cannot function by the same rules as powerless individual Jews living under the control of others.[27]

Yet in his scheme of Israelization, those Jews who are ambivalent about Israel or even adopt stances against the Jewish state are drafted to support his contention. Inasmuch as they voice their distaste or repulsion, it is Israel that drives their passion. Here Shain leans, among others, on the work of Israeli literary scholar Gitit Levy-Paz, who has highlighted the propensity of contemporary American Jewish writers to place Israel and its foibles at the center of their novels.[28] Since 2007, leading literary figures such as Michael Chabon, Nathan Englander, Nicole Krauss, and Jonathan Safran Foer have all published works that grapple with their ambivalence toward the Jewish state, its military power, and its political and religious character. Chabon in particular is outspoken in his reproach of the Israeli government, and he produced a novel, *The Yiddish Policemen's Union*, that renders a counterhistory in which Israel actually never came into existence.[29]

In Shain's eyes, Chabon's "criticism manifests connection."[30] He cites, as well, Englander's own testimony to the obsession with Israel of him and his American Jewish colleagues: "I really don't know what got into us . . . somehow Israel eats away at us. While it is difficult to compare my book to those of other friends in our Jewish mafia . . . among them too, Israel is in the background."[31] Summing up the connection between these Jewish writers and Israelization, Shain declares: "alongside Israeli Hebrew literature, there is also literature being produced in the Diaspora that is characterized by its relationship to Israeli sovereignty. It is not written in Hebrew, nor in the territory of the motherland, but its focus is the Israeli century."[32]

The upshot of Shain's book, then, is that regardless of whether a contemporary Jew identifies with Zionism or not, and even among those who possess deep seated antagonism toward it, what defines the current era—notwithstanding Cosgrove's reticence—is that so much of being Jewish revolves around Israel, thus the "Israelization of Judaism." To be sure, an argument can be made that various critical aspects of contemporary Jewish life are less directly dependent or related to Israel than Shain allows. The globalized nature of the Chabad-Lubavitch movement, for example, raises interesting challenges to Shain's approach. That said, even the evolution of Chabad into a global phenomenon was built on the advent of the State of Israel. Not only did the rise of Rabbi Menachem Mendel Schneerson to the helm in 1951 practically coincide with the establishment of the State of Israel, but much of his revolutionary approach may be understood as aimed at providing a spiritual alternative to the focus on territorial sovereignty and the secular redemptive possibilities that it naturally inspires. His adaptation of military symbols such as those of the Tzivos Hashem—the "Army of God" youth wing, "Mitzvah tanks," and even the unique Chabad male uniform, as well as the training of a crack force of "religious" ambassadors—*shluchim*—are also indicative of a countermovement.[33] Following Shain's focus on conditions and impact rather than agreement or support, and like the American novelists whose ambivalence toward the state actually caused them to "obsess" about the subject and explore alternative models, the rise of Chabad as a global Jewish presence also testifies to the Israel effect.

Furthermore, the ubiquitous Israeli post-army backpackers and adults who are constantly looking for new destinations to conquer are in part responsible for Chabad's expanding global reach in the twenty-first century. In certain major locations, there are actually two dedicated Chabad Houses, one for local families and another purely for Israelis, while in others—particularly in parts of Africa, South America, India, and Southeast Asia—the nearly exclusive clientele are Hebrew speakers.[34] There are also seasonal branches set up by young Chabad *shluchim* in training in parts of New Zealand and other popular extreme sports spots throughout the world.[35] Chabad's role in facilitating Israeli travel is so critical that in some places the centers serve as unofficial consular offices, with the *shliach* and *shlucha* acting as the go-betweens with local governments.[36] This has been especially so at times of natural disasters or when individual Israelis have been endangered or killed. Indeed, Chabad's profound growth since Schneerson's passing is acutely linked in numerous ways to the reality of the sovereign state and the Jewish population that it has produced.

In sum, even if Shain's contention is at times overstated, it challenges all identifying Jews, regardless of where they live and what their attitudes toward Zionism and the State of Israel are, to examine their relationship with the force that most powerfully defines Jewish life in the twenty-first century. It is my contention that the rise and development of IsMO serves as a viable vehicle for navigating this connection.

A Secular Age, an Israeli Age

Charles Taylor's classic 2007 tome, *A Secular Age*, addresses the ongoing academic debate over the degree to which the Western world has become secularized and helps to further elucidate the insight of Shain's analysis. Most previous discussions of the rise of secularism revolved primarily around demonstrating that secular ideals, forces, and institutions in the world were expanding and gaining greater acceptance, while religious ones were declining. The deterministic understanding that secularization was advancing in a linear fashion, typified by books such as Peter Berger's 1979 *The Heretical Imperative*, was challenged by the resurgence of religious fundamentalism that characterized the 1980s and beyond.[37] Thus, Berger himself eventually offered a more nuanced interpretation in light of these upheavals.[38] Taylor, in contrast, is more convinced than ever that the core of contemporary Western civilization is situated in the secular realm. The source for his position, however, is an account of the role of secularism in contemporary society that does not depend on the ups and downs of one side or the other. Rather, the key factor is what he calls "the conditions of belief."[39]

What distinguishes the current era, according to Taylor, is that regardless of one's own personal religious stance, in Western society the point of departure for how to perceive the world is the secular one. That is, on one hand scientific truths and ideal political structures that are completely independent of parochial authority and belief are taken for granted as the normative framework of society. On the other hand, acceptance of religious and spiritual ideals demands digressing from or denying that which is clear-cut and assumed. This situation stands in contradistinction to previous examples, when the opposite was the case. In earlier times, religious principles of belief and practice were the guiding paradigm, and individuals like Spinoza, who challenged these presumptions, were deviants. In the current era, religion has not disappeared, nor for the most part has it been completely dismissed. Yet it is no longer the foundation of authority or truth. It is simply a choice, and far from the obvious one. As Taylor put it:

> the change I want to define and trace is one which takes us from a society in which it was virtually impossible not to believe in God, to one in which faith, even for the staunchest believer, is one human possibility among others. . . . Secularity in this sense is a matter of the whole context of understanding in which our moral, spiritual or religious experience and search takes place. . . . An age or society would then be secular or not, in virtue of the conditions of experience of and search for the spiritual.[40]

Once this "presumption of unbelief" has become dominant, even those who continue to believe staunchly operate, according to Taylor, in a secular milieu.[41]

Unlike Taylor's, Shain's book is not a work of philosophy. Shain is a political scientist and what counts most of all in his work is where the center of power sits. But power, as Shain's tome articulates, is not defined exclusively through military and economic strength, nor through political allegiance. Power also needs to be understood as how a certain body, here the sovereign Jewish state, impacts upon the lives of others—especially Jews.

There is a core analytical perspective that underlies both volumes. In parallel to Taylor's "conditions of belief" and "context of understanding," what characterizes the "Israeli century" is not that the State of Israel is incrementally achieving consensus among all Jews. The main change is that regardless of whether one lives in Israel or not or identifies with the Zionist project or not, Israel has become the central issue around which both Jews and non-Jews worldwide encounter Judaism. Israel is for twenty-first-century Jews what secular constructs are for most Western individuals, the foundational element that frames most other Jewish involvements, ideological positions, political activity, and cultural production.

American Jews and IsMO in an Israeli Age

Shain's paradigm acknowledges that, along with Israel becoming the key "condition of experience" that underlies contemporary Jewish life, there are focal aspects of the sovereign state that exacerbate tensions between the "mothership" and its extensions. This is certainly the case for those who protest Israel's direction in dealing with the Palestinians and ongoing settlement efforts, and even more so for a vocal minority who perceive Israel's very nascence as rooted in colonialism and desire that it morph into a multinational democracy.[42] To be sure, the October 7, 2023, massacre perpetrated by Hamas and the ensuing war initially focused attention almost exclusively on Israel's physical safety and—together with the sharp rise of antisemitic acts in America—may have long-term effects on American Jewish attitudes toward Israel's security needs.[43] But even among those who are overtly supportive of Israel regardless of their political leanings, especially the majority of American Jews who do not identify as Orthodox, there remains deep disaffection.

Much of the resentment is in response to Orthodox control of the state rabbinate and public religious policies regarding marriage, conversion, burial, and funding for non-Orthodox religious streams, along with the sway of Haredi and religious parties over coalition politics and government budgets. This religious discrepancy was illustrated tragically when the chief rabbi of the town of Beit Shean refused to allow the burial of an Israeli young woman murdered during the October 7 Hamas bloodbath in the Jewish section of the municipal cemetery. The father of Alina Palhati, the twenty-three-year-old victim, is Jewish and her brother was converted according to Orthodox law, but she had not completed a conversion program.[44]

According to the prevalent analysis, the phenomenon of rising American Jewish enmity toward core aspects of Israeli life comes under the rubric of "distancing," meaning that there are issues that have contributed to the continually widening gap between American Jews and Israel.[45] Shain's thesis recalibrates the discourse. To be sure, there are areas of sharp disagreement, but he challenges the notion that any contemporary Jew—regardless of their political, religious, or cultural proclivities—can truly distance themselves from Israel, the dominant "condition of experience." Like the inhabitant of a country, state, or city who must respond to the circumstances decided by the ruling group, even when they are not necessarily according to their preferences, the derivative of Shain's model is that the decision that stands before every Jew throughout the world is not if they will engage with Israel, but rather: What will be the nature of their interface?

One viable option for those in disagreement over fundamental issues is to predicate their relationships with Israel purely on criticizing that which is found to be offensive or wrong. A more positive-oriented version would be to take an active role in seeking to advance changes. There are many organizations that are dedicated to this direction, and there are certainly areas where American activism has impacted Israeli society. At a grassroots level this means supporting and joining forces with those in Israel that seek to make foundational changes, be they political, religious, social, or other.

A second, related option is limiting one's dealings with Israel to those frameworks with which one identifies positively. Thus, for non-Orthodox Jews this could mean sustaining the Israeli Conservative (*Masorti*) and Reform (*Mitkademet*) synagogues and movements or, alternatively, contributing to specific academic, educational, health, or social welfare organizations. To be sure, here, too, there is underlying hope for change.

A third direction, which does not necessarily contradict the prior ones but adds critical nuance, is to forge positive and productive associations with personalities and institutions that are more clearly connected to the core sources of religious power or status quo. On one hand, they may not necessarily reflect one's personal religious identity, but on the other, there exist some that are far more conscious and sensitive to moderate voices than other "mainstream" Orthodox groups. The various manifestations of IsMO, as portrayed throughout this book, exemplify such groups. As opposed to those squarely outside the Orthodox orbit, IsMO offers an alternative "insider's voice" that has potential to facilitate change from within.

There is value for American Jews of a broad range of Jewish orientations in building alliances with the gamut of IsMO. While non-Orthodox streams have, as we have seen, made some advances in the twenty-first century, they remain peripheral to the mainstream of Israeli religious life, and there is no indication that this will change. The demographic data points to the ongoing growth of the Haredi population,[46] a reality accompanied by the increasingly similar language used by the Merkaz ha-Rav/Kav/Harda"l camps within the RZ sector and the non-Zionist Haredim regarding religious and social issues. Thus, recognizing that the Orthodox-oriented nature of Israeli religious life and leadership will remain—in Shain's rubric—a key part of the "condition of experience" for the foreseeable future, there is cause for American Jews to cultivate productive relationships with the moderate orbit, which presents the greatest possibilities for productive dialogue and cooperation.

The historical development portrayed in this book strengthens the credence of this contention. IsMO has drawn considerably from the American pioneers who arrived in the mid-twentieth century and the institutions that they shepherded. Indeed, among the many Israeli-born products who have assimilated and processed ideas that they imbibed in these frameworks are children and grandchildren of immigrants from North America, and American Modern Orthodoxy continues to provide key figures who have integrated into IsMO and taken on key roles. Thus, not only is there an ideological backdrop that can draw broader American Jewry into conversation with this Israeli religious spectrum, there are also common roots and cultural continuities that facilitate this relationship.

To further support the book's claim, we can look at two Israeli moderate religious institutions that are active in initiatives that offer models for bridging between Israeli religious realities and American Jews in a variety of ways. By this point, we have explored areas of ongoing exchange between IsMO frameworks and American Jews, including an assortment of gap-year study programs, various aspects of religious feminism including yoatzot halakhah and women's daf yomi, the TMZ movement, various OTS institutions, and shared interest in the writings of Rabbi Dr. Jonathan Sacks. Nonetheless, the notable feature of the following two institutions' outreach is their focus more specifically on crossing points with non-Orthodox Jews from abroad.

ITIM

ITIM ("times," "seasons") is a Jerusalem-based organization that was founded to provide information about religion that would smooth interfaces between nonobservant Jews and the Israeli state rabbinic bureaucracy. It has evolved into a multifaceted structure offering myriad services to a diverse constituency.[47] Its roots can be traced to the year 2000 and an initiative of American immigrant Rabbi Dr. Seth Farber. Farber grew up in the Riverdale section of the Bronx, where he was influenced from a young age by Yitz Greenberg and where he attended the yeshiva high school established by Riskin. He later studied at YHE and earned ordination from YU and a PhD in modern Jewish history from the Hebrew University in Jerusalem. Farber, who is married to the leader of Hadran, Rabbanit Michelle Cohen Farber, is also the rabbi of Kehillat Netivot, a congregation in the central town of Ra'anana that self-describes as "an Orthodox Jewish community that believes in openness, pluralism, acceptance and inclusion of diverse people." Today ITIM has a staff of over twenty-five employees, an annual budget of more than $2 million, and addresses close to five thousand inquiries per year.[48]

Originally supported by the politically liberal religious Meimad movement, ITIM's relatively modest first effort was to prepare explanatory materials regarding Jewish lifecycle events and the procedures involved in interfacing with the state rabbinate. Such brochures were given to secular veteran Israelis, new immigrants, and visitors who were likely to be alienated by the rabbinic bureaucracy. ITIM produced user-friendly booklets with extensive information regarding the historical, philosophical, halakhic, customary, and procedural aspects of a range of Jewish lifecycle events (circumcision, conversion, marriage, divorce, religious ceremonies for women such as *simhat bat* [birth celebration ceremony] and bat mitzvah, and burial and mourning). All were published in Hebrew, English, and Russian, and distributed free of charge by ITIM itself, as well as through various government bodies and as supplements to lifecycle trade magazines. By 2005, over one hundred thousand such resource and instruction collections reached the hands of predominantly nonobservant Jews.[49]

Through its website, ITIM transformed into a cutting-edge religious portal. All the practical information and guidance provided in the brochures were introduced on the Hebrew, English, and Russian versions of the website, but the list of lifecycle events covered was far beyond the print editions. Moreover, the electronic versions offered a wide array of additional services, including a constantly updated list of contact information for religious functionaries and related services (wedding performers, ritual circumcisers, bar and bat mitzvah instructors, marriage counselors, mikvehs, cemeteries, burial societies, local rabbinates); databases for prayers and homiletical ideas for special occasions, as well as for Jewish names; a category titled "Personal Ceremonies" in which people could share their customized rituals in order to help individuals create their own; and an "interactive section" that offered audio clips of religious ceremonies, electronic greeting cards for lifecycle events, and a virtual tour of a mikveh. There was even a "bereavement notice maker" that provided various formulaic and graphic options for announcing the passing of a relative or friend. By 2007, an average of 14,500 people per month were making use of the ITIM website.[50]

ITIM has evolved over time and today focuses on two related areas that are rooted in its original efforts: providing services, information, and personal guidance to individuals—both native Israelis and those who have come from abroad—experiencing lifecycle events in Israel or dealing with bureaucracy related to their religious status (halakhic Jewishness, the validity of marriage and divorce issues, eligibility for religious burial); and advocating in court and government for changes in laws and practices related to the Israeli religious bureaucracy.[51] One of its central efforts is *Giyur K'Halacha*, the independent rabbinic court for conversion created in cooperation with other prominent IsMO-oriented organizations (OTS, Beit Morasha), which was initially headed by prominent "agent of change" the late Nachum Rabinovitch. In 2022, according to an ITIM publication, 20 percent of all Orthodox conversions in Israel were performed through this framework.[52]

ITIM's bridging function also received pronounced expression in 2022 through an international campaign on conversion headlined by a "Love the Convert Shabbat."[53] This role is illustrated no less in its list of key supporters; a broad and diverse range of individuals, organizations, and foundations that represent all types of North American and Israeli Jews.[54]

Shalom Hartman Institute (SHI)

As we have seen, SHI was founded by another key "agent of change," the late David Hartman, a YU-trained rabbi and theologian who immigrated to Israel in 1971 after a successful career in the Montreal MO congregational rabbinate. Over the course of his four-decade-plus Israeli career, he and his institution evolved in a pluralistic direction. All the same, SHI continues to feature core educational programs—including its well-regarded men's and women's high schools and pre-army mechina preparatory year—that are directed toward the RZ constituency. In parallel, its top leadership and many of those in key positions emerged from and remain deeply intertwined with the RZ community in Israel and the MO community in North America. At the same time, it has prioritized programming that engages a diverse range of Jews from abroad with the realities of Israeli religious life.

One of the central examples of this direction is the Rabbinic Torah Study Seminar, which invites rabbis from across the North American rabbinical spectrum to Jerusalem for ten days of intense study and discussion. This is one of SHI's earliest initiatives aimed at connecting with Jewish religious leadership abroad, and it has serviced hundreds of rabbis.[55] The 2022 seminar featured a class titled "Zionism as Loyalty" that was held on July 6, 2022, and led by Dr. Mijal Bitton, a former core SHI faculty member and current research fellow.[56] Bitton is a scholar and educator with deep connections to Israeli Judaism and the leader of an Orthodox congregation in Downtown New York City.[57] In the aftermath of the October 7, 2023, massacre by Hamas, she became an outspoken public advocate for Israel and was a showcased speaker at the rally in support of Israel and against antisemitism held in Washington, DC, on November 14, 2023, attended by close to three hundred thousand people.[58]

SHI later created a complementary summer seminar aimed at lay figures throughout North America called the Community Leadership Program. The 2022 cohort was titled "Aspirational Zionism." Participants were encouraged to "[h]elp shape a constructive dialogue about the future of Zionism for North American Jews."[59] In the summer of 2024, SHI initiated an additional program for Jewish professionals from abroad titled the Wellspring Summit for Educators. The five-day seminar in Jerusalem was conceived as a direct response to changes experienced since October 7, 2023:

> Jewish education and Israel education are at a critical inflection point after the events of October 7, months of the ensuing war, and rising antisemitism in North America. With institutions under constant strain from both external demands and internal pressures, leaders and educators have expressed increasing despair at the prospect of helping their communities find a path through this current moment. . . . The Shalom Hartman Institute is proud to convene the Wellspring Summit for Educators to bring together leaders from across the educational landscape to learn, connect with colleagues, and think creatively and constructively about education during this most difficult time.[60]

Another project, the Hevrutah Gap-Year Program, demands a lengthier commitment and is directed toward younger North American Jews. Like similar frameworks, post–high school students spend their time in Israel studying Jewish texts, along with volunteering and internships. What stands out is that those from abroad are integrated with Israelis of the same age: "North American students live, study, and experience Israel alongside their Israeli counterparts participating in the Israeli Hevruta Pre-Army program. Group dynamics are strengthened through open discourse, participant-led activities, and shared programming."[61]

Both ITIM and SHI exemplify institutions that are part of the IsMO orbit and have created effective vehicles and portals of engagement for a diverse range of Jews from abroad. SHI's programs and overall pluralistic orientation, moreover, highlight the overlap between IsMO, as conceived as a moderate but fundamentally Orthodox phenomenon, and the relatively novel way that the phrase "IsraeliJudaism" has been advanced in recent scholarship. This concept raises additional points that support the bridging possibilities that IsMO offers the non-Orthodox majority of American Jewry, but also highlights limitations.

IsraeliJudaism and American Jews

In the 2018 book *#YahadutYisra'elit*, cowritten by veteran Israeli journalist Shmuel Rosner and the late professor of statistics and pollster Camil Fuchs, the authors argue that over its first seven decades Israel spawned a new type of Judaism that is rooted in statehood. While the majority of Israelis do not self-identify as observant (*dati*), unlike past assumptions that most were definitively "secular," they actually see Jewishness in a religious sense as fundamental to who they are. That is, there is considerable consensus among Israeli Jews regarding endogamy, along with the maintenance of certain religious elements, particularly Sabbath and holiday meals and rituals, and lifecycle ceremonies. To be sure, many chafe at the coercive aspects of Israeli public religion, but in areas where they have complete free choice, the majority integrate religious symbols and practices into their lives on a regular basis.[62]

"For most Jews in Israel," in the words of Rosner and Fuchs, their core identity is:

> Jewishness and Israeliness mixed together into a new formula. There are parts that are exclusive to the observant, and others that are actually emphasized more among the nonobservant. But there is much that is shared by all, or almost all. These are the seeds of a renewed culture, IsraeliJudaism.... A culture in which to be a "good Jew" means both to "uphold holidays, ceremonies, and customs" and "to serve in the IDF" or "to educate toward IDF service."[63]

There are two aspects to their concept of IsraeliJudaism that are relevant to the current discussion. On the one hand, they describe a style of Jewish connection that is traditional and emphasizes positive religious expressions, with neither an obligatory nor a coercive character. On the other hand, there is a strong emphasis on the relationships of religious identity, Jewish sovereignty, and actual "Israeliness." The first aspect of IsraeliJudaism accentuates the value of cementing connections between the broader American Jewish population and IsMO, while the second actually underscores limitations.

From a bridging perspective, along with characterizing the germination of a novel sovereign form of Judaism, Rosner and Fuchs asked how this burgeoning phenomenon relates to the potential growth of Conservative and Reform Judaisms in Israel. The backdrop to this question is that "IsraeliJews" and the liberal denominations share a strong appreciation for a type of religious expression that is devoid of demands for strict conformance. Their answer, based on the statistics that they produced, is that there is some potential for expansion, but for the most part the collective that they described is not seeking an alternative to the Orthodox synagogue and to the overarching Orthodox approach to Jewish law and customs. Rather, what IsraeliJews desire is to pick and choose without outside force, an ability which is interconnected with their sense that performance of traditions reflects their deep-seated connection to their national identity.[64]

Thus, while they crave autonomy on a personal level, the majority of IsraeliJews are still most comfortable with defining the religious standards of the country according to Orthodox guidelines. Many certainly resent the meticulous intervention of religious authorities regarding personal issues such as marriage, divorce, and burial. But even when more options have arisen, the majority still prefer that their personal ritual events and ceremonies be orchestrated according to Orthodox custom.

This IsraeliJewish population is the foundation for the popularity of IsMO-related initiatives begun since the late 1990s, such as the Tzohar rabbis who perform weddings according to Jewish law and in coordination with the state rabbinate but with a sympathetic, user-friendly, and nonmissionizing approach. A more radical approach is taken by an organization called Huppot. Its weddings are all orchestrated by Orthodox rabbis based on traditional standards. However, unlike Tzohar, it caters to couples who refuse to register with the state rabbinate but nonetheless want to be married according to Jewish law.[65] The founder and president of Huppot is Rabbi Aaron Leibowitz, who was ordained by Brovender and Riskin at Yeshivat Hamivtar. Prior to Huppot, Aaron Leibowitz established Hashgahah Pratit, a kosher food supervision framework independent of the state rabbinate that was subsequently merged into the Tzohar organization.[66] Starting from January 2024, Leibowitz was appointed to head the Israeli rabbinate training framework run under the auspices of SHI. In line with the transnational path discussed throughout this book by which American ideas have been processed and reformulated for the Israeli environment, Leibowitz is the son of Rabbi Dr. Yoseph Leibowitz, a former American MO congregational rabbi in Berkeley, California, who immigrated to Israel in the 1980s. In the course of the father's Israeli career, he was both long-time rabbi of a synagogue in the town of Kfar-Sava, in central Israel, that serviced a religiously diverse constituency and a senior lecturer at the pluralistic Pardes Institute in Jerusalem.[67]

Rosner and Fuchs also note that the broad-based attachment of the majority of Israeli Jews to religion is reinforced by a phenomenon referred to in Hebrew as the *rezef*.[68] The term means "continuum" and has been introduced by journalists and scholars to describe the range of lifestyles that can be found among children who grew up in religiously observant homes, RZ ones in particular. If in the past, those who decided to stop leading a fully observant life would adopt a "secular" identity, that is no longer the dominant scenario. Rather, they are more likely to become *datlashi"m*, which is an acronym for *dati'im le-she'avar*—literally, "formerly observant Jews." These are people who are not meticulous in their religious practice but are far from secular and remain deeply connected to the RZ social milieu in which they were nurtured and its fundamental appreciation for Jewish religious customs and values.[69] The rezef of the Israeli RZ collective ranges from the fervently committed to a variety of more eclectic identity types. Most RZ communities and a large percentage of RZ families encompass this diverse assortment.[70] One vivid example is the fact that, among religious settlements that do not allow internal car traffic on Sabbath and certain holidays, it is common to build dedicated parking areas adjacent to their main entrances to accommodate the many offspring who join their families for Sabbath and festival meals.[71]

Another more visceral and tragic illustration relates to the Gaza War that arose after the October 7, 2023, Hamas massacre. Statistically, almost half of the combat soldiers who fell in Gaza were from RZ families. There are multiple explanations for why this was the case, but the relevant nuance here is that in numerous cases the descriptions of the fallen soldiers indicated that they did not necessarily live according to the strictly observant lifestyle of their parents. Nonetheless, they were part of the rezef and were mourned and fêted widely within RZ circles.[72]

To be sure, as noted, particularly among Israelis from Mizrahi/ Sephardi backgrounds, an eclectic approach to the relationship between belief and practice is not a fresh phenomenon. For example, there are abundant families from Mizrahi backgrounds who run a strictly kosher home, celebrate all the holidays and will not cook when forbidden, and are even strict about matters of Jewish family purity (mikveh), but nonetheless drive and perform other acts that are prohibited on the Sabbath. Scholars have coined this group *Masorati'im* (traditionalists), and some claim that they are not simply a less punctilious derivative of Orthodoxy, along the lines of what has been termed "nonobservant Orthodox" among American Jews,[73] but rather that they are a defined group with specific, common forms of religious conduct.[74] For such Israelis, their loose religiosity does not necessarily come with alienation from established Orthodox authority. On the contrary, as is common in many religions, at least on a functional level they distinguish between the laxity tolerated among the lay people and the ideal norms that the rabbinic elite must continue to uphold. From the perspective of Rosner and Fuchs's scenario, what distinguishes contemporary Israeli *Masorati'im* from similar past models, as well as contemporary ones from abroad, is the interlocking of their identities with their connection to the State of Israel and being Israeli.

Notwithstanding the heterogeneous home and ethnic environments that nurture IsraeliJews, from the perspective of the argument in this book, it is significant that the religious institutions and leaders that are in closest ongoing contact with the entire rezef are those within the IsMO network, who likely grew up with or have close relatives and friends who fit into the rubric of IsraeliJudaism. This association certainly opens up the RZ stratum, and particularly those who resonate with IsMO worldviews, to critics who see the assortment of levels of commitment that it produces as a weakness in its overall religious fortitude and the "grave sacrifices" of its overly openminded approach. From another perspective, however, the reality is that IsMO is in a unique position as a religious framework that is organically associated with the phenomenon of

IsraeliJudaism, that which Rosner and Fuchs attest to being the dominant contemporary Israeli Jewish identity. This is due to IsMO's inclusive
orientation and overall appreciation for the many positive values and
cultural contributions that stem from nonparochial environments (for
example, Lichtenstein's concept of "fragmentary Judaism"). Simultaneously, the ties between IsMO and IsraeliJudaism are grounded in the
fact that there are significant familial, social, and cultural connections
and overlaps.

With this understanding of IsraeliJudaism and its close bond with
IsMO in mind, we can return to the potential impact of IsMO on the
relations between American Jews and Israeli religious life and assert the following: The links between American Jews and those Israeli
forces intent on pushing for more fundamental upheavals in the coercive structure of Israeli religious life—including non-Orthodox Israeli
streams—are on many levels a more natural fit. All the same, cultivating
stronger relationships with the range of IsMO institutions and personalities offers unique potential for connecting to the dominant "conditions
of experience" of Israeli society and IsraeliJudaism and partnering in its
ongoing development. Put in more specific terms, the constituents of
Cosgrove's Manhattan synagogue and their cohorts throughout America
for whom Israel is a deep source of passion may find more commonality
with liberal religious movements in Israel, but if they want to engage the
core of Israeli religious life and culture, they will benefit from building
strong relationships with the IsMO orbit as well.

Having said this, the second foundation of IsraeliJudaism as defined
by Rosner and Fuchs, its bond with the state and with what it means to
be an Israeli, simultaneously brings to the fore limitations to the relationship between Israeli and American Judaisms. These limitations were
also magnified by the October 7, 2023, massacre by Hamas and the war
that it precipitated.

Perpendicularity and Proximity

As Rosner and Fuchs maintain, IsraeliJudaism is "Jewishness and Israeliness mixed together into a new formula."[75] In that sense, the lived
realities of sovereign Israeli life produce "conditions of experience"
that have considerable bearing upon all Jews but cannot be duplicated

outside of Israel's borders. This is not an issue of distancing in the sense that scholars have articulated to describe political and ideological alienation. It is, rather, an embedded existential matter.

This actuality was brought home through a post authored by Yehudah Kurtzer, the New York–based co-president of SHI. Kurtzer, himself a YHE alumnus, is deeply committed to Zionism and to Israel's security and prosperity. He is also a liberal thinker and educator with strong pluralist leanings who is not averse to critiquing aspects of Israeli religious and political life and raising tough moral dilemmas. Soon after the October 7, 2023, massacre, he made a solidarity visit to Israel. In a subsequent post he shared his feelings upon learning that Yossi Hershkovitz, a forty-four-year-old YHE alumnus who had served as an educational emissary at the SAR High School in New York where Kurtzer's own children attended, and subsequently was appointed principal of the IsMO-oriented Pelech High School for boys in Jerusalem, had been killed during army duty in Gaza:

> Coming out of Shabbat to read about the death of a beloved Jerusalem educator, principal of a high school, and I'm thinking about parallels and proximities—how those of us who are in the same line of work of Jewish education here in America could never envision being called into military service to defend our country, much less run so courageously into battle the way hundreds of thousands of Israelis did on October 7 . . . my country here has gone to war plenty of times in my lifetime, but I've been safely insulated from it by those wars having been waged on foreign soil, and with an American all-volunteer, all-professional army. *I feel parallel, or adjacent, to the principal of Pelech; but I have no proximity to his choices, and thus maybe, despite the bonds of peoplehood, we are not parallel but perpendicular.*
>
> A beloved Jewish educator killed in battle! How do we confront the magnitude of loss. And we, here, turned about; perpendicular. *We teach Torah here too, maybe a Torah that helps us understand our intertwinedness with the people of Torah over there who do things like leave the classroom and take to the battlefield as twin actions that are in the service of seeking life, and maybe knowing that we will never really get it* [my emphasis].[76]

The fact that Kurtzer is the American-based leader of SHI makes his comments especially poignant. Recall that SHI is an institution headquartered in Jerusalem that was founded by one of the key immigrant "agents of change" who facilitated the rise of IsMO. It is also a framework that has in recent years dramatically expanded its footprint within North America—much to the credit of Kurtzer himself. This international organization exemplifies sovereign-generated Judaism's increasingly prolific role in nourishing its American relatives. Kurtzer's professional raison d'être, then, stands at odds with "distancing" conceptualizations and is rooted instead in the entrenched connectedness articulated through Shain's Israelization.

Nonetheless, Kurtzer pinpointed an existential element that allows for a "perpendicular" meeting between Israeli Jews and their American-based counterparts but prevents the achievement of full nearness: the interwovenness that embodies the Israeli experience as expressed in setting aside one's day-to-day contributions to society when called upon to put one's life on the line for the Jewish state.

These limitations underscore aspects of the lived experience of Israeli Jews that will remain external to American Jews, even to those who are highly sympathetic to Israel and dedicated to interfacing with its multifaceted social and religious culture. They exist in parallel, then, to the vibrant portals of engagement and mutual fructification between American Jews and IsMO that stand at the center of this book.

I will end this study, however, with another no less tragic example, but one that nonetheless buttresses the assertion of IsMO's potentially bridging role among multiple local Israeli constituencies as well as with Jews from North America and beyond. On September 8, 2024, an op-ed blog post appeared in the *Times of Israel* website written by Rabbi Mishael Zion, a prolific Israeli educator who leads the Klausner Congregation in Jerusalem's Arnona neighborhood. His father, Noam Zion, is a veteran American immigrant to Israel and has been a central figure in SHI since its early years.

Just days earlier, the bullet-riddled bodies of six hostages held by Hamas for nearly a year were discovered in a Gaza cave. One of the deceased was Hersh Goldberg-Polin, the child of religiously observant American immigrants who nurtured him in IsMO-type environments in Jerusalem. Portraits of Hersh's face had become ubiquitous symbols of the ongoing captivity of hundreds of Israelis (he was at a music festival on October 7, and his arm was blown off as he tried to prevent a hand grenade from exploding in a shelter crowded with fellow attendees seeking protection). Through his parents' horrific saga and tireless advocacy for their son and his cohorts, and then via descriptions of the funeral and mourning, many Israelis (and others from abroad) were exposed to the moderate, noncoercive, inclusive religious lifestyle of his parents, Jon and Rachel Goldberg-Polin.

Zion, who knew the family well, opened his post by sharing an experience that took place at a work meeting the week of mourning: "'Wait, what type of religious person are you exactly?' the producer asked me when she saw my kippa at the Tel Aviv television studio last week. . . . I answered: 'You've heard of Hersh's parents, Rachel and Jon, from Jerusalem? So I'm religious like them.' And from the look on her face, I immediately felt that she understood."[77]

The author then went on to detail the Goldberg-Polins' form of *Yiddishkeit* (a colloquial Yiddish term that references a warm, homey Jewish religious commitment) that both he and his interlocutor understood implicitly: "It's a Yiddishkeit . . . ethically bound to the infinitely valuable image of God imbued in all humans. . . . A Yiddishkeit of people at home in the world without giving up an ounce of religious commitment, a Yiddishkeit of humility and peace, starkly different from the arrogant religiosity so often portrayed and stereotyped by media and politicians. Theirs is a Yiddishkeit that has existed for years in Israel's byways and neighborhoods and yet has always failed to translate itself to Tel Aviv TV studios or the Israel political eye. And suddenly two parents, our quiet neighbors, became its face and voice . . . ."[78]

ACKNOWLEDGMENTS

I am grateful to a number of colleagues, friends, and relatives who were kind enough to read and remark on the entire manuscript and/or have played especially significant roles in the development of particular aspects of the book: Judy Baumel-Schwartz, Isaac Becker, Shalom Z. Berger, Joshua A. Berman, David Bernstein, Eliahu Birnbaum, Neil Cohen, Ari A. Ferziger, Naomi B. Ferziger, Daniel Goldman, Steven Gotlib, Miriam Herschlag, Jeffrey Sacks, Marc B. Shapiro, Marc Sherman, and Ari Werthenteil.

From my first correspondence with Jennifer Hammer, senior editor at NYU Press, I have been awed by her combination of intellectual precision, professional expertise, and deep human sensitivity. She and the entire NYU staff conducted the process of evaluation, publication approval, revision, copyediting, and production with utmost competence. The critical observations of the anonymous evaluators vastly improved the final product.

In the course of researching and writing this work, I have benefited from generous grants awarded by: the Hadassah-Brandeis Institute at Brandeis University, the Yaschik/Arnold Jewish Studies Program at College of Charleston, the Bildner Center for the Study of Jewish Life at Rutgers University, and the Herbert D. Katz Center for Advanced Judaic Studies at University of Pennsylvania.

Five individuals who continue to impact my academic development profoundly deserve special mention: my doctoral advisor and close colleague, Gershon Bacon; my teacher and late thesis advisor, Jacob Katz; my rabbi and academic mentor, Daniel Sperber; my early supporter and friend Moshael Straus; finally, I mourn the loss of my dear *haver* (comrade) and guide, the late David H. Ellenson, who passed away suddenly in December 2023. He effused a seamless combination of the highest forms of friendliness and human generosity, critical intellectual rigor and creativity, and devotion to family, to Judaism, to Israel, and to the Jewish people.

Bar-Ilan University has been my academic home for over thirty years. There I have had the good fortune to develop relationships with people who took an interest in my work and created an environment of collegiality that enabled me to move forward. Among the numerous individuals affiliated with Bar-Ilan (in addition to those above) who deserve thanks for their encouragement and wise council during the course of preparing this book are: the president, Arye Zaban; the rector, Amnon Albeck; and my fellow faculty members, present and past: Hanoch Ben-Pazi, Kimmy Caplan, Asher Cohen, Yitzhak Conforti, Noah Efron, Shmuel Feiner, Emanuel Friedheim, Judah Galinsky, Tova Ganzel, Uriel Gellman, Yaron Harel, Ari Kahn, Miriam Feldman Kaye, James Kugel, Nissim Leon, Yigal Levin, Aren Maier, David Malkiel, Eli Menaged, Moshe Rosman, Joshua Schwartz, and Jeffrey Woolf. Many of the ideas developed in the following pages were first presented to my graduate students in the Department of Jewish History and Contemporary Jewry. Their questions and suggestions have challenged and inspired me. I am especially proud that my former doctoral student, the talented scholar Dr. Einat Libel-Hass, has coauthored a chapter in this book.

Since 2013, I have been affiliated with the Oxford Centre for Hebrew and Jewish Studies, University of Oxford, both as a senior associate and through my primary role as co-convener of the annual Oxford Summer Institute on Modern and Contemporary Judaism (OSI). Numerous chapters in this book were first presented there, where I was gifted with invaluable feedback. I am thankful to the former president, Martin Goodman, to the current president, Judith Olszowy-Schlanger, to the generous donors to the OSI for their ongoing support of the project, to my co-conveners, Miri Freud-Kandel, Jodi Eichler-Levine, and Hartley Lachter, for their dedication and comradery, and to the scores of participants since the OSI's inception who have helped create a global community of scholars. My OSI partnership with Miri has evolved into a close personal and family friendship, and her keen recommendations have helped me gain appreciation for disciplines and critical perspectives that were beyond my purview.

This book has been enriched considerably through conversations, correspondences, and in many cases the writings of the following colleagues, family members, and friends: Baruch Alster, Brenda Bacon, Shulamith Berger, Sally Berkovits, Avital Ferziger Becker, Sefi Becker, Miriam Bloom, Kenneth Brander, Menachem Butler, Arye Edrei, Zev Eleff, Zvi Erenyi, Michelle Cohen Farber, Shaul (Seth) Farber, Cliff

M. J. Felig, Minna Ferziger Felig, Adi Ferziger, Aviad Ferziger, Ben Zion Ferziger, Chana Reich Ferziger, Dovie Ferziger, Liron Rubin Ferziger, Meira Shulman Ferziger, Jonathan H. Ferziger, Reuven Ferziger, Yoel Ferziger, Yoel Finkelman, Shai Finkelstein, Sylvia Barack Fishman, Daniel Ross Goodman, Fred Gottlieb z"l, Irving "Yitz" Greenberg, Moshe Greenberg, Jeffrey S. Gurock, Harriet J. Hartman, Samuel C. Heilman, Stuie Hershkowitz, Sara Hirschhorn, Ronit Irshai, Lisa Fishbayn Joffe, Alan Jotkowitz, Lawrence Kaplan, Maoz Kahana, Ysoscher Katz, Jerry Lax, Tuvia Lax, Lilach Lev-Ari, Dalia Marx, Michael A. Meyer, Yehudah Mirsky, David N. Myers, Michal Raucher, Uzi Rebhun, Rachelle Rohde, Tamar Ross, Meir Roth z"l, Chen Sabag, Jonathan Sarna, Ted Sasson, Jacob J. Schacter, Zev Schwartz, Yossi Shain, Joshua Shanes, Moshe (Simon) Shoshan, Nancy Sinkoff, Ira Slomowitz, David Sperber, Rose Stair, Shaul Stampfer, Daniel Taub, Brian Thau, Davina Wanderer-Kriel, Chaim I. Waxman, Esther Weinstein, Baruch Weinstein, Tina Weiss, Jack Wertheimer, Steven Weitzman, Yoni Wieder, Emily Winograd, Yaakov Yadgar, Dror Yahav, Reuven Ziegler, Shlomo Zuckier, and Ephraim Zuroff.

I draw strength and wisdom from the lives, ideals, and unconditional love of my mother, Sandra Ferziger Gottlieb, and my late father, Daniel Ferziger z"l, and from my mother-in-law, Bernice Weiss, and late father in-law, David G. Weiss z"l. I feel privileged that the late Dr. Fred Gottlieb entered our family's life.

My wife and loving partner in our joint journey, Dr. Naomi (Weiss) Ferziger, has lived this book at all stages, through unequivocal commitment and emotional sustenance, through ongoing discussions of every aspect of the endeavor, and through listening to or reading multiple versions of each chapter and sharing her critiques and insights, שלי, שלך, שלנו—mine, is yours, is ours.

This book is dedicated to our children, their spouses, and their entire generation of Israeli young adults from every sector of society who "stepped up" on so many levels at the most challenging of times for them and their country. With an optimistic prayer that they may be "agents of change" for good as they move forward in life.

לה' הארץ ומלואה
Jerusalem, Israel
Nissan 5785—April 2025

APPENDIX

Representative Israel-Based Students and Protégés of the American Immigrant Pioneers of IsMO

Note: The lists included here are by no means exhaustive. Nevertheless, the data offers additional evidence of the breadth of influence of the institutions founded and/or headed by the IsMO pioneers and of their roles as "agents of change." Note as well that there are overlaps, as numerous individuals studied in multiple institutions. This is especially so among the women's institutions. I have not necessarily identified individuals with all the locations in which they studied.

RABBI DR. AHARON LICHTENSTEIN/YHE:
Rabbi Michael Abraham—theologian and lecturer, Institute of Advanced Torah Studies, BIU; Mordechai (Moti) Bar-Or—founder of Elul and Kolot, organizations that bring together nonobservant and observant Jews through Torah study; Rabbi Amnon Bazak—author and lecturer in Bible and Talmud, YHE; Rabbi Eliyahu Blumenzweig—founding head of Yeshivat Yeruham; Rabbi Yuval Cherlow, cofounder of the Tzohar Rabbis organization and founding head of Yeshivat Orot Shaul in Tel Aviv; Rabbi Shmuel David—chief rabbi of Hadera, a city in central Israel, and moderate Jewish legal authority; Rabbi Oren Duvdevani—former head of the private kashrut supervision organization Hashgahah Pratit (later integrated into the Tzohar organization), which is challenging the state rabbinate's monopoly; Rabbi Dr. Seth Farber—founding head of ITIM and rabbi of Kehilat Netivot in Ra'anana; Rabbi Yehudah Gilad—rabbi of Kibbutz Lavi, co-head of Yeshivat Ma'ale Gilboa, founding member of the Beit Hillel Organization for Religious Leadership, and former member of Knesset on the Meimad list; Rabbi Dr. Tamir Granot—co-head of Yeshivat Orot Shaul; Rabbi Re'em Ha'Cohen—co-head of Yeshivat Otniel; Prof. Aviad Ha'Cohen—president of Sha'arei Mishpat College, legal activist and writer on Jewish law in the

State of Israel; Prof. Moshe Halbertal—award-winning Jewish philosophy and law scholar at the Hebrew University in Jerusalem and New York
University and core figure at SHI; Rabbi Herzl Hefter—founding head of
Beit Medrash Harel, an egalitarian Orthodox yeshiva that gives ordination to men and women; Stuie Hershkowitz—prominent Jerusalem-based
lawyer, international banker, and communal leader, who served for seven
years as vice president and CEO of the Jerusalem College of Technology
(Machon Lev); Rabbi Prof. Benny Ish-Shalom—Jewish philosophy scholar
and founding head of the Beit Morasha Institute in Jerusalem; Prof. Alan
Jotkowiz—medical doctor/Jewish bioethicist, director, the Ben-Gurion
University Medical School for International Health; Prof. Moshe Koppel—
former mathematician and computer scientist at BIU, author and founding
head of the Kohelet Policy Forum; Rabbi Dr. Benny Lau—rabbinics scholar
and author, former rabbi of the Ramban Synagogue in Jerusalem, and
founding head of the 929 daily Bible program; Professor Yehudah Mirsky—Brandeis University and Jerusalem-based public activist; Rabbi Dr.
Ya'akov Nagen—rabbinics scholar and author, lecturer at Yeshivat Otniel
and director of OTS's Blickle Institute for Interfaith Dialogue and Beit
Midrash for Judaism and Humanity; Rabbi Chaim Navon—former communal rabbi in Modi'in, lecturer at Midreshet Lindenbaum, and columnist;
Rabbi Meir Nehorai—chairman of the Beit Hillel Organization for Reli-
gious Leadership, rabbi of Moshav Massu'ot Yitzhak, and lecturer at Beit
Midrash Migdal Oz; Rabbi Dr. Ariel Picard—former rabbi of Kibbutz She-
luhot, author of multiple texts on Jewish law, and faculty member at the
SHI; Prof. Gideon Sapir—BIU Faculty of Law, senior figure in the Kohelet
Policy Forum; Rabbi Dr. Sharon Shalom—author of a treatise on Ethiopian
Jewish law and custom, first holder of the Chair for the Study of Ethiopian
Jewry at Ono Academic College, and synagogue rabbi in Kiryat Gat; Rabbi
Dr. Avraham Stav—columnist, author of multiple works on Jewish law,
and lecturer in Yeshivat Mahanaim; Jeremy Stavitsky—former principal of
Himmelfarb High School in Jerusalem; Moshe Tur-Paz, former principal
of multiple high schools, former director of education for the Jerusalem
municipality, current member of Knesset for the Yesh Atid party.

RABBI DR. NACHUM RABINOVITCH/YESHIVAT BIRKAT MOSHE
Rabbi Rami Berakhyahu—chief rabbi of the Israel Police Department; Rabbi Meir Fachler—director of Gemara Berura, an institute for

innovation in Talmud study; Dr. Shmuel Faust—literary scholar and associate editor of the *Mussaf Shabbat* section of the weekly *Makor Rishon* newspaper; Rabbi Prof. Dror Fixler—physicist, head of BIU's nanotechnology center, author of articles on Jewish law; Rabbi Uriel Ganzel—rabbi of the settlement Revava and director of the Ethics Center of Tzohar Rabbis; Rabbi Dr. Zahi Hershkowitz—senior lecturer in the Department of Jewish Philosophy at BIU, former synagogue rabbi in Petah Tikvah, and popular lecturer on religious subjects; Rabbi Dr. Ido Pachter—author of works on Jewish law and contemporary Jewish thought, religious activist, editorial board member of *Mussaf Shabbat*, and former communal rabbi in Netanya; Rabbi Prof. Daniel Reisser—scholar of Hasidism and Holocaust theology, chairman of the Department of Jewish Thought, Herzog College; Prof. Arie Reich—scholar of international law, former dean of the faculty of law and current vice rector, BIU; Rabbi Eli Reif—communal rabbi in Modi'in, author of a book on Jewish law for female soldiers; Rabbi Yoni Rosenzweig—communal rabbi in Beit Shemesh, lecturer at Midreshet Lindenbaum, and author of books and articles on contemporary Jewish law; Rabbi Eliyahu Scheinfeld—educator, author of books on parenting, communal rabbi in Jerusalem; Michael (Miki) Scheinfeld—novelist and religious educator; Eliezer "Laizy" Shapira—television producer and director known for the groundbreaking series *Serugim*, which focuses on the religious singles scene in Jerusalem; Prof. Yuval Sinai—faculty of law, Netanya College, former president of Orot College; Dr. Zvi Stampfer—scholar of medieval Jewish manuscripts, head of the research authority at Orot College, popular lecturer on Jewish subjects.

RABBI DR. DANIEL TROPPER/GESHER

Mordechai (Moti) Bar-Or—founder of Elul and Kolot, organizations that bring together nonobservant and observant Jews through Torah study; Rabbi Dr. Adiel Cohen—lecturer, Midreshet Lindenbaum and Beit Berl College; Dr. Tova Ganzel—Bible scholar and former head of the Midrasha for Advanced Torah Study for Women, current head of the Basic Jewish Studies Department, BIU, and one of the first graduates of Nishmat's training program for yoatzot halakhah; Prof. Benjamin Ish-Shalom—founding head of Beit Morashah, a training center for moderate religious leadership, founder of multiple government and

IDF programs for training and supporting candidates for religious conversion, former professor of philosophy, the Hebrew University in Jerusalem, Esther Lapian—lecturer, Seminar ha-Kibbutzim, consultant on Jewish education in Israel and throughout the Jewish world; Shimon Siani—founding head of Yedidim, a national organization focused on underprivileged teenagers and young adults; Inbal Pickholtz Shilo—principal of Meshalev Dor School, a junior and senior high school dedicated to integrating students from diverse religious and social backgrounds; Dr. Hannah Pinhasi—educator, publicist, has played multiple leadership roles at the SHI; Prof. Avinoam Rosenak—scholar of Jewish philosophy and education, the Hebrew University, popular public lecturer; Rabbi Yisrael Samet—rabbi of the *garin torani* (religious core community group) in Lod, head of the *Bereishit* study program for non-observant students at the Institute for Advanced Torah Studies, BIU; Tami Samet—psychologist, member of the Forum Takanah council for addressing sexual abuse among rabbis and religious figures; Yair Sheleg—journalist, author of multiple volumes on Israeli religious life, former fellow at the Israel Democratic Institute, current fellow at SHI; Rabbanit Dr. Leah Vizel—head of the Midrasha for Advanced Torah Study for Women, BIU; Rabbi Dov Zinger—founding head of Yeshivat Mekor Hayyim high school in Gush Etzion.

RABBI DR. CHAIM BROVENDER/MIDRESHET BRURIA/LINDENBAUM

(TITLES USED AS THEY APPEAR ON OFFICIAL PUBLICATIONS; NOTE THAT MANY STUDIED THERE AFTER BROVENDER DEPARTED)
Rabbanit Naomi Adler—Talmud lecturer, Migdal Oz; Rabbi Rahel Berkovits—senior educator at the Pardes Institute and one of the founders of the Shirah Hadashah synagogue in Jerusalem; Rabbanit Naomi Berman—former *rosh beit midrash* (head of the study hall) of Midreshet Lindenbaum; Rabbanit Devorah Evron—head of the Institute for Female Religious Leadership, Midreshet Lindenbaum, campus religious leader, BIU; Rabbanit Michelle Cohen Farber—founder of Hadran; Rabbanit Dr. Chani Frank—yoetzet halakhah, PhD in history of Jewish law, author of religio-legal responsa, lecturer in multiple institutions; Tzippy Hotovely—Israeli ambassador to United Kingdon, former government minister and Knesset member; Rabbanit Racheli Sprecher Frankel—director of the Advanced Halakhah program at MATAN,

lecturer at Nishmat, yoetzet halakhah; Rabbanit Chani Klein—lecturer in multiple institutions, author of religio-legal responsa; Rabbanit Oriya Mevorah—yoetzet halakhah, author of religio-legal responsa and lecturer in multiple institutions, founder of the Afarkeset Institute for the Study of Judaism and Western Culture; Rabbanit Shira Marili Mirvis—sole spiritual leader and halakhic authority for the Shirat Tamar synagogue in Efrat, lecturer in multiple settings; Rabbanit Dina Nagar—lecturer, Migdal Oz; Rabbanit Michal Nagen—founding head of the Zahali Pre-Army Mechina for Religious Women; Rabbanit Hila Naor—director, Ma'aminot be-Madim (support program for women religious soldiers); Professor Vered Noam—former *rosh beit midrash* at Midreshet Lindenbaum, world-renowned scholar of rabbinics and ancient Judaism, Tel Aviv University, the first woman to receive the Israel Prize in Talmud; Rabbanit Bat-El Picard—rabbanit of Yeshurun (largest women's high school in the country); Rabbanit Esti (Lichtenstein) Rosenberg—former *rosh beit midrash* at Midreshet Lindenbaum, founding head of Beit Midrash Migdal Oz; Rabbanit Dr. Jenny Rosenfeld—communal spiritual leader and director of the religious court for financial matters in Efrat; Efrat Shapira Rosenberg—media personality, chairperson of Kolekh (Israeli Orthodox Feminist advocacy organization); Rabbanit Hamutal Shoval—head of the women's study halls in Efrat and Gush Etzion, author of religio-legal responsa, Midreshet Lindenbaum faculty member; Rabbanit Dr. Adina Shtrasberg—author of religio-legal responsa, lecturer in multiple institutions, PhD in Talmud; Rabbanit Shani Taragin—educational director of World Mizrachi, faculty of Midreshet Lindenbaum's Institute for Halakhic Leadership, lecturer in multiple institutions, senior yoetzet halakhah.

RABBANIT MALKA BINA/MATAN

(NOTE THAT THERE IS OVERLAP WITH BRURIA/LINDENBAUM, ALTHOUGH I HAVE SOUGHT TO FOCUS ON ADDITIONAL FIGURES)
Rabbanit Yafit Clymer—pedagogical coordinator of Zahali Pre-Army Program for Women, lecturer in multiple educational venues; Rabbanit Chana Godinger Dreyfus—founding head of Rosh Tzurim (a high-level yeshiva for women); Dr. Tehilla Elitzur—lecturer in Talmud, Herzog College and MaTaN; Rabbanit Carmit Feintuch—synagogue rabbi in Jerusalem and lecturer, Migdal Oz; Rabbanit Shlomit Flint—Talmud

lecturer, Midreshet Be'er in Yeruham and Ashdod; Rabbanit Racheli Sprecher Frankel—head of the Beit Midrash, MaTaN, former dean of students, Nishmat, yoetzet halakhah; Rabbanit Batya Kraus—yoetzet halakhah, head of the advanced Talmud track, MaTaN; Rachel Lifshitz—founding head of Ulpana Emuna for the Arts, lecturer in Talmud, MaTaN Sharon; Rabbanit Esti (Lichtenstein) Rosenberg—former *rosh beit midrash* at Midreshet Lindenbaum, founding head of Beit Midrash Migdal Oz; Rabbanit Bat-Sheva Samet—lecturer, Migdal Oz, religious court advocate; Rabbanit Yael Shimoni—associate head, Yeshivat Drishah, and head of the women's responsa project, Beit Hillel; Dr. Adina Sternberg—lecturer, Bar-Ilan Midrashah for Women; Rabbanit Shani Taragin—codirector of MaTaN, faculty of Midreshet Lindenbaum's Institute for Halakhic Leadership, senior yoetzet halakhah, educational director of World Mizrachi; Dr. Yael Ziegler—Bible scholar, academic director, MaTa"N, lecturer at Herzog College.

RABBANIT CHANA HENKIN/NISHMAT

Yardena (Cope) Bodenheimer—yoetzet halakhah, former director of the Advanced Talmud program at MaTa"N, attorney in the Jewish Law Department of the Israeli Justice Ministry; Dr. Nomi Englard-Sheffer—community yoetzet halakhah in the Greater Modiin area, certified by the chief rabbinate as kashrut supervisor, instructor in Talmud, Basic Jewish Studies, BIU; Rabbanit Racheli Sprecher Frankel (see above); Prof. Tova Ganzel—head of the Basic Jewish Studies Department, former director of the Midrasha for Women, BIU, yoetzet halakhah; Dr. Tirza Y. Kelman—yoetzet halakhah, director of Nishmat's Women's Health and Halacha Hebrew website, academic researcher of halakhah and Jewish ['thought; Rabbanit Dr. Tamar Meir—head of the Literature Department at the Givat Washington College of Education, founder of the women's beit midrash Kulana in Givat-Shmuel, head of women's empowerment projects at Beit Hillel, and author of an award-winning children's book about righteous people among the nations during the Holocaust; Hadassa Klein—yoetzet halakhah, director, yoatzot.org; Noa Lau—yoetzet halakhah, chair of Jewish Law and Coordinator of Keren Ariel at Nishmat, former educator at Pelech School in Jerusalem; Laurie Novick—yoetzet halakhah, director, Deracheha: Women and Mitzvot, YHE; Dr. Deena Zimmerman—pediatrician, yoetzet halakhah, author of multiple works on health and Jewish law, founder of Nishmat's Women's Health and Halacha website.

RABBI DR. DAVID HARTMAN/SHI (ALUMNI AND FELLOWS)
Dr. Orit Avnery—lecturer in Bible and dean of students at Shalem College, director of the Tanakh Initiative and research fellow at SHI, alumnus of MaTa"N and the SHI Rabbanut Yisraelit program, former Bible studies teacher at Pelech High School for Girls and Midreshet Lindenbaum; Tehilla Friedman—alumnus of Midreshet Lindenbaum and Beit Morasha, social and religious feminist activist, former chair of the Ne'emanei Torah va-Avodah movement, former member of Knesset, former advisor to Natan Scharansky, columnist; Dr. Micah Goodman— author of best-selling books on Jewish thought, founder of Mabua–Beit Midrash Yisraeli (formerly known as Beit Prat, a network of houses of Jewish learning for Israeli young adults from across the religious spectrum), voted one of the most influential Jews in the world by multiple publications; Dr. Donniel Hartman—president of SHI, scholar and popular essayist; Prof. Moshe Halbertal—YHE alumnus, award-winning Jewish philosophy and law scholar at the Hebrew University in Jerusalem and New York University, core founding group of SHI; Rabbi Dr. Avital Hochstein—president of Hadar Institute in Israel, received Orthodox rabbinical ordination from Rabbi Daniel Landes and SHI Rabbanut Yisraelit, former head of kollel at the Pardes Institute, a founder of Shirah Hadashah Congregation in Jerusalem; Prof. Ronit Irshai— religious feminist scholar and activist, associate professor and head of the gender studies department at BIU; Yossi Klein-Halevi—award-winning author and columnist; Prof. Menachem Lorberbaum—YHE alumnus, core founding group of SHI and head of the Beit Midrash program, professor of Jewish philosophy at Tel Aviv University; Dr. Chana Pinchasi—founder of the *Heder mi-shelakh* forum for influential female leaders in Israeli society, guide of research teams at the Center for Judaism and the State Policy, former director of SHI's Be'eri School for Teacher Education; Mikhael Manekin—leader of the Faithful Left movement for religious Jews promoting equality through faith, former executive director of Breaking the Silence, an IDF veterans' peace activism group, author; Rabbi Dr. Ariel Picard—YHE alumnus, former rabbi of Kibbutz Sheluhot, author of multiple texts on Jewish law, and faculty

member and former head of the Be'eri educational program at SHI; Dr. Renana Ravitsky Pilzer—former teacher in the Elul Beit Midrash, a founder of Kehilat Shirah Hadashah in Jerusalem, educational director of the SHI Center for Israeli and Jewish Identity and head of the Beit Midrash at its Midrashiya Girls High School, former codirector of its Melamdim School for Teacher Training; Prof. Avi Sagi—professor (emeritus) of philosophy and founder of the cultural studies program at BIU, prolific author on Jewish and general thought, and Jewish law and ethics, academic director of SHI's Military Ethics Research Team and senior research fellow; Rabbi Dani Segal—YHE alumnus, founder of Beit Prat Academy of Leadership, former rabbi of the Alon settlement, codirector of the SHI Rabbanut Yisraelit program, member of Beit Hillel; Yair Sheleg—YHE alumnus, veteran journalist and author, former Israel Democracy Institute fellow; Prof. Avishalom Westreich—associate professor of Jewish law, family law, and jurisprudence at the Law School of the College of Law and Business in Ramat Gan; Noam Zohar—professor (emeritus) of moral and political philosophy, bioethics, BIU; Zvi Zohar—professor (emeritus) of Sephardic law and history and former head of the Rappoport Center for Assimilation Research, BIU, head of the SHI Center for Jewish Law; Mishael Zion—founder of Kehillat Klausner in Jerusalem and founding director of the Mandel Leadership Institute's Program for Leadership in Jewish Culture, author; Noam Zion—core founding group of SHI, prolific author of popular books focused on Jewish family rituals and scholarly works, former head of the SHI Tichon program for North American Jewish educators and teacher in multiple SHI programs.

RABBI SHLOMO (STEVEN) RISKIN/OTS

(ALSO SEE MIDRESHET LINDENBAUM ABOVE; FOR THE MOST PART, THE HAMIVTAR ALUMNI STUDIED UNDER BROVENDER)
Rabbi David Alima (Straus-Amiel Institute)—synagogue rabbi in Modi'in; Rabbi Zvi Alon (Straus-Amiel)—head of Bnei Akiva youth movement, former rabbi of Caesaria; Rabbi Yogav Cohen (Straus-Amiel)—*rosh yeshiva*, Har Bracha High School; Rabbi Roni Diner (Straus-Amiel)—principal, Ner Tamid High School; Rabbi Elad Dokov (Straus-Amiel)—rabbi of the Technion; Rabbi Aryeh Engelman (Straus-Amiel Institute)—synagogue rabbi in Petah Tikvah; Rabbi Itai Fador

(Straus-Amiel)—principal, Jordan Valley Women's High School; Cliff Felig (Hamivtar)—senior partner at Meitar Law, communal lecturer in the development of Jewish law; Rabbi Shimon Felix (Hamivtar)—director emeritus, Bronfman Fellowship; Rabbi Ori Fisch (Straus-Amiel)—communal rabbi in Ma'ale Adumim; Professor Yair Furstenberg (Neve Shmuel High School for Men)—Department of Talmud, the Hebrew University; Dr. Dore Gold z"l (Hamivtar)—former Israeli ambassador to the United Nations; Rabbi Dr. Ahuvia Goren (Mahanayim)—head of the alumni studies program at Yeshivat Mahanayim and scholar of Jewish intellectual history, Van Leer Institute; Professor Yonatan Grossman (Neve Shmuel)—former chairman of the Bible Department, BIU; Rabbi Shlomo Hecht (Straus-Amiel)—synagogue rabbi in Petah Tikvah, former CEO of Beit Hillel; Dvir Kahana (Neve Shmuel)—former CEO, Ministry for Diaspora Affairs; Rabbi Gidon Kaplan (Straus-Amiel)—rabbi, Israel Air Force; Rabbi Tuvia Kaplan (Hamivtar)—*mashgiah ruhani* (spiritual director), Midreshet Lindenbaum; Avishai Kraus (Neve Shmuel)—former deputy CEO of Prime Minister's Office; Michal Lieberman (Neve Hannah High School for Women)—former CEO, Herzl Museum; Sari Meir (Neve Hannah)—head of Europe desk, World Bnei Akiva; Rabbi Chaim Mimren (Straus-Amiel)—principal, Gross High School, Kiryat Gat; Rabbi Ronen Neuwirth ob"m (Straus-Amiel)—founding CEO of Beit Hillel, former synagogue rabbi in Ra'anana, former head Bnei Akiva emissary to North America; Amitai Porat (Neve Shmuel)—head, Alumah Foundation–Youth for Change, former CEO of the Religious Kibbutz movement; Inbal Pickholtz (Neve Hannah)—founding principal, Meshalev Dror secondary school (Meitarim religious/traditional/secular school network); Dr. David Rozenson (Hamivtar)—executive director, Beit Avi Chai; Rabbi Shlomo Sabag (Straus-Amiel)—rabbi, Southern Sharon Regional Council; Rabbi Jeffrey Saks (Hamivtar)—editor, *Tradition* journal, director of research at the Agnon House in Jerusalem, cofounder (with Brovender) of ATID (Academy for Torah Initiatives and Directions in Jewish Education); Rabbi Michael Setbon (Straus-Amiel)—rabbi, Kibbutz Shluhot; Rabbi Yossi Stempler (Straus-Amiel)—rabbi, University of Haifa; Yehiel "Hili" Tropper (Neve Shmuel)—member of Knesset and government minister, veteran senior educator; Moshe "Kinley" Tur-Paz (Neve Shmuel)—member of Knesset, veteran senior educator.

NOTES

INTRODUCTION

1 Lichtenstein, "My Education and Aspirations."

2 Ibid.

3 Gurock, *The Men and Women of Yeshiva*, 132–133, 242–243.

4 Morrison, *The Gush*, 7–44, 69–92. During the 1940s, four Jewish settlements had existed in Gush Etzion. They were captured and destroyed by Arab fighters in May 1948 and absorbed into Jordan. Soon after the June 1967 "Six-Day War," Israel reestablished Jewish presence in the area.

5 Ibid., 5.

6 Sabato, *Mevakshei Panekha*, 9–17. An English version appeared as Sabato, *Seeking His Presence*. For a more analytical discussion of aliyah, with some references to his personal experience, see Lichtenstein, "Diaspora Religious Zionism."

7 The Israeli Haredi sector has also been impacted by North American immigrants. This is a fascinating subject beyond the purview of this book that is deserving of more research. For some relevant starting points see, for example, Caplan, "The Internal Popular Discourse of Israeli Haredi Women."

8 Leon, "The Secular Origins of Mizrahi Traditionalism"; Yadgar, *Secularism and Religion in Jewish-Israeli Politics*.

9 Katz, "Orthodox in Historical Perspective."

10 Shalvi, *Never a Native*; Cottin Pogrebin, "The Famous Israeli You've Never Heard of."

11 Ferziger and Sperber, *Darkhei Daniel*.

12 Irshai, "Tamar Ross: An Intellectual Portrait."

13 Ross, *Expanding the Palace of Torah*.

14 Ross, *Armon ha-Torah mi-Ma'alah*.

15 During the same year, 2000, Yair Sheleg's brief position paper (twenty-two pages), *Hashpa'at ha-Aliyah me-Zefon America*, also appeared.

16 Liebman and Cohen, *Two Worlds of Judaism*, 149. In a brief subsequent piece from 1998, Liebman addressed additional indications of the growing moderacy; see idem, "Modern Orthodoxy in Israel." See also the valuable study by sociologist Shlomo Fischer, "Two Orthodox Cultures," which focuses on differences in the religious characters of RZ and MO.

17 Two veteran Israeli journalists have authored books that offer valuable descriptive accounts of these developments at distinct stages. They focus primarily on internal Israeli historical and sociological factors: Ettinger, *Frayed*; Sheleg,

Ha-Dati'im ha-Hadashim; idem, *Ha-Hut ha-Meshulash*. Historian Kimmy Caplan addressed aspects of the RZ divide in his "Heker ha-Hevrah ha-Yehudit Datit be-Yisrael." Two scholars, Dov Schwartz and his student Ido Pachter, have explored briefly the influence of American MO figures on these developments primarily from the perspective of Jewish thought. See: Schwartz, "Bein Orthodok-siyah Modernit le-Zionut Datit: Behinah Mehudeshet"; Pachter, "Hitpathutah shel ha-Orthodoksiyah ha-Modernit be-Amerika," 330–350. In 2022, *Tradition* maga-zine introduced an online English-language series under the direction of Rabbi Yitzchak Blau known as "Alt-Shift," which examines various trends in Israeli RZ life. See https://traditiononline.org/altshift-series-introduction.

18 See the preface to Ettinger, *Frayed*, xiv, where religion scholar Yehudah Mirsky points to the "valuable point of comparison between these figures and their coun-terparts abroad, especially in the United States."

19 Prominent examples include Alterman, *We Are Not One*; Gordis, *We Stand Di-vided: The Rift Between American Jews and Israel*; Waxman, *Trouble in the Tribe*. For a more optimistic appraisal, see Sasson, *The New American Zionism*.

20 The English version is Shain, *The Israeli Century*. The original version appeared in Hebrew under the title *Ha-Me'ah ha-Yisraelit ve-ha-Yisraelizaziyah shel ha-Yahadut*.

21 Asscher, "The Ben-Gurion–Blaustein 'Understanding' as an Historiographical Yardstick." See also Waxman, "Review: *We Stand Divided*."

22 Asscher, "The Ben-Gurion–Blaustein 'Understanding,'" 44.

23 Grossman, "Decline and Fall: Thoughts on Religious Zionism in America." On the unique characteristics of American MO support for Zionism, see the detailed analysis of Pachter, "Hitpathutah shel ha-Orthodoksiyah ha-Modernit," 337–349.

24 See, for example: Brill, "What Is Modern in Modern Orthodoxy"; Eleff, *Modern Orthodox Judaism*; idem, *Authentically Orthodox*; Gurock, *Orthodox Jews in America*; Waxman, *Social Change and Halakhic Evolution*.

25 Breuer, *Modernity with Tradition*; Eleff, *Who Rules the Synagogue*.

26 Gurock, "The Late Friday Night Orthodox Service"; Sarna, "The Debate over Mixed Seating in the American Synagogue"; Shapiro, *Saul Lieberman and the Orthodox*.

27 On distinctions between substreams of American Orthodoxy, see, for example: Ferziger, *Beyond Sectarianism*; Gurock, "Resistors and Accomodators"; Heilman, *Sliding to the Right*; Liebman, "Orthodoxy in American Jewish Life."

28 Krakowski et al., "The Role of Israel in American Haredi Life"; Baum et al., "Women Pursuing Higher Education in Ultra-Orthodox Society."

29 Ferziger, *Beyond Sectarianism*; Waxman, *Social Change and Halakhic Evolution*, 89–126.

30 Cohen, *Divine Service*. The extended bibliography in Caplan, "Heker ha-Hevrah ha-Yehudit Datit," offers an excellent starting point for scholars working on RZ-related subjects. For alternative approaches to characterizing Israeli Ortho-doxy and RZ, see: Haim Katsman z"l, "The Hyphen Cannot Hold Contemporary

Trends in Religious-Zionism"; Zion-Waldoks, "'Family Resemblance' and Its Discontents."

31 On Haredim in Israel, see the references in https://www.harediresearchgroup.org /bibliography.

32 Luz, *Parallels Meet*; Salmon, *Religious Zionism*, 368–381; Schwartz, *Religious Zionism*, 42–70; Sheleg, *Ha-Hut ha-Meshulash*, chs. 3 and 4.

33 Cohen, *Ha-Tallit ve-ha-Degel*, 110–136.

34 Fishman, *Judaism and Modernization on the Religious Kibbutz*.

35 Schwartz, *Religious Zionism*, 95–104; Sheleg, *Ha-Dati'im ha-Hadashim*, 29–36.

36 The organization Ne'emanei Torah va-Avodah presents its role as continuing to cultivate the values rooted in the Religious Kibbutz movement within contemporary Israeli society; see https://toravoda.org.il; Sheleg, "Shtei Kipot Serugot be-Vitnekh," *Mi-Mashgiah Kashrut le-Nahag ha-Keter*, 57–63.

37 Pachter, "Hitpathutah shel ha-Orthodoksiyah ha-Modernit be-Amerika"; Schwartz, *Religious Zionism*.

38 Mirsky, *Rav Kook*, 557–562.

39 Carmy, "Soloveitchik the Zionist"; Pachter, "Hitpathutah shel ha-Orthodoksiyah ha-Modernit be-Amerika," 330–350; Saks, "Rabbi Soloveitchik Meets Rav Kook," 90–97; Schwartz, *Faith at the Crossroads*, 193–227; idem, *Religious Zionism*, 27–34, 105–114.

40 See the essays collected in Waxman, *Religious Zionism Post Disengagement*.

41 Finkelman, "On the Irrelevance of Religious-Zionism"; Sheleg, *Ha-Dati'im ha-Hadashim*, 36.

42 Fuchs, "The Construction of an Ideological Curriculum."

43 Sheleg, *Ha-Hardal"im*.

44 Sheleg, *Ha-Hut ha-Meshulash*, ch. 10.

45 www.merriam-webster.com.

46 www.oed.com.

47 Stolow, "Transnationalism and the New Religio-politics," 123–124.

48 Liwerant, "Latin-American Jews—A Transnational Diaspora," 351–352.

49 Ibid., 351. See Khagram and Levitt, *The Transnational Studies Reader*, 1–22.

50 Ben-Refael, "Israel-Diaspora Relations," 449. For data on Israeli immigrants to the United States, see Rebhun and Lev Ari, *American Israelis*.

51 Remennick, "Transnational Lifestyles among Russian Israelis," 492–493.

52 Waxman, *American Aliyah*.

53 Hirschhorn, *City on a Hilltop*.

54 Hermann et al., *The National-Religious Sector in Israel 2014*, 36.

55 Kahn, "Transnational Aspirations."

56 Reisinger, *Historical Assessment of the Transformation of Kibbutzim of Israel's Southern Arava*, 25–42.

57 Havurat Tel Aviv, www.havurattelaviv.org.

58 Ash, "Observant Feminism across Borders."

59 Ibid., 158.

60 Kuisel, "The End of Americanization."
61 Sachs, *The Ages of Globalization*, 169–214.
62 Alexander, *The Americanization of Europe*, 432.
63 Aviner, "Ha-Rav Aviner: Shivyon Nashim ve-Gevarim be-Veit ha-Knesset."
64 Van Elteren, *Americanism and Americanization*. See the comparative review: Danielsen, "The American Spirit in Europe Revisited?," 117–126.
65 Van Elteren, *Americanism and Americanization*, 101–124.
66 Ibid., 125–144, 162–178.
67 Van Elteren, "Cultural Globalization and Transnational Flows of Things American," 8.
68 Sheleg, *Ha-Dati'im ha-Hadashim*, 54–63.
69 Engelberg, "Modern Orthodoxy in Post-secular Times," 126–139.
70 Van Elteren, "Cultural Globalization and Transnational Flows of Things American."

CHAPTER 1. ROOTS

1 I am grateful to the following people and institutions for their generous assistance: Shulamith Berger, curator for special collections, and Tina Weiss, head librarian of Hebraica-Judaica, Mendel Gottesman Library, Yeshiva University; Adi Portuguez, head of infrastructure information systems, Michal Laniado, digital archivist, and Ofer Schiff, director, Ben-Gurion Institute for the Study of Israel and Zionism; Dana Herman, director of research and collections, Jacob Rader Marcus Center of the American Jewish Archives; and Jerry Schwartzbard and Ina Cohen, JTS Library. Dr. Fred Gottlieb (ob"m) authored the English translation of the German text. This chapter expands upon the discussion in Adam S. Ferziger, "Ben-Gurion and American Jewish Students at the Cusp of the Sixties: Between Solidarity and Persuasion," *Jewish Quarterly Review* 113, no. 2 (2023): 273–303.
2 Sachar, *Brandeis*, 216–217.
3 JTA, "Ben-Gurion to Visit Jewish Institutes of Higher Learning."
4 Sarna, "Reviewed Works," 169.
5 Wiesel, "Yomo ha-Yehudi shel Ben-Gurion," 2.
6 Shapira, *Ben-Gurion: Father of Modern Israel*, 43–51, 113, 122–130.
7 Brown, *The Israeli-American Connection*, 197–240.
8 Gal, *David Ben-Gurion*; Schiff, *The Downfall of Abba Hillel Silver*.
9 Cohen, *The Americanization of Zionism*; Schiff, "Mabat Aher al ha-Americanizaziah shel ha-Zionut."
10 Shapiro, *From Philanthropy to Activism*.
11 Katz, *Bringing Zion Home*.
12 Segev, "American Zionists' Place in Israel after Statehood," 280–284.
13 Tzahor, "David Ben-Gurion's Attitude toward the Diaspora," 21. On "negation of the exile" (*shelilat ha-golah/galut*), see, for example: Sherzer, "Exporting Israel to the Diaspora: The Attempt to Make Israel's Independence Day into a World-

wide Jewish Holiday"; Shimoni, "The Theory and Practice of Shlilat Hagalut Reconsidered."

14 Tzahor, "David Ben-Gurion's Attitude," 22; Segev, "American Zionists' Place in Israel," 295–302.

15 David Ben-Gurion, "Medinat Yisrael ve-ha-Tenuah ha-Zionit," Opening Session of the World Zionist Congress, May 5, 1949, *Ben-Gurion Archives*–Sde Boker, Item # 241105, 15–16.

16 Ganin, *An Uneasy Relationship*, 81–106; Liebman, "Diaspora Influence on Israel," 271–280; Shiff, "Early American Zionist Responses to the Israeli Demand for *Aliya*." For alternative understandings of the exchange, see: Feldestein, *Ben-Gurion, Zionism and American Jewry*; Shiff et al., "The Ben-Gurion–Blaustein Exchange."

17 JTA, "Ben-Gurion to Visit Jewish Institutes of Higher Learning," 5.

18 Ibid., 9; JTA, "Ben-Gurion Finds American Friendship Deepened; Leaves for London."

19 HUC-JIR, "Mission to Jerusalem."

20 The idea that Zionism shares core values with America was first given expression by some of the early twentieth-century American "converts" to Zionism; see Sarna, "Converts to Zionism in the American Reform Movement," 196–198.

21 Ben-Gurion, "Address at the Hebrew Union College," 10.

22 Ben-Gurion, "Medinat Yisrael ve-ha-Tenuah ha-Zionit," 15–16.

23 Ibid., 5.

24 JTA, "U.S. Zionist Leaders in Counterattack on Ben-Gurion's Assault on Them."

25 Notably, in "Premier Ben-Gurion Comes to Visit," the official HUC-JIR summary of Ben-Gurion's speech, there is no mention of his appeal for students to come to Israel.

26 On the blessing for kings, see *Bavli Berakhot* 51a; *Shulhan Arukh, Orah Hayyim*, 224: 1. The student utilized the form mandated for a non-Jewish/nonannointed king.

27 Gartner, "Conservative Judaism and Zionism," 212–218.

28 https://digitalcollections.jtsa.edu.

29 Ben-Gurion, "Divrei Rosh ha-Memshalah ba-Seminar ha-Theologi ha-Yehudi, New York, New York, March 16, 1960," *Ben-Gurion Archives*–Sde Boker, #86093, 2–3.

30 Ben-Gurion, "Divrei Rosh ha-Memshalah ba-Seminar ha-Theologi ha-Yehudi," 3.

31 Ibid.

32 Ben-Gurion, "Divrei Rosh ha-Memshalah ba-Seminar ha-Theologi ha-Yehudi," 4.

33 On Kaplan, Zionism, and the State of Israel, see, for example, Pianko, *Zionism and the Roads Not Taken*, 95–134.

34 Aronson, "Israel's Security and the Holocaust."

35 Ben-Gurion, "Divrei Rosh ha-Memshalah ba-Seminar ha-Theologi ha-Yehudi," 5.

36 Tal, "David Ben-Gurion's Teleological Westernism."

37 Ben-Gurion, "Divrei Rosh ha-Memshalah ba-Seminar ha-Theologi ha-Yehudi," 6–8.

38 Wiesel, "Yomo ha-Yehudi shel Ben-Gurion."

39 Minute 39.

40 Wiesel, "Yomo ha-Yehudi shel Ben-Gurion."

41 Ibid.

42 Ben-Gurion and Soloveitchik had actually met previously in the latter's hometown of Boston on March 8, the first evening of the trip. Ben-Gurion's diary, *Ben-Gurion Archives*–Sde Boker, Serial no. 217428, offers a few details both as to the content and impression of his partner in conversation: "At eight in the evening Rabbi Soloveitchik came to meet me—a rabbi who graduated from university (in Paris?), an [enlightened] intellectual (*maskil*), an insightful and knowledgeable man. I asked him if there are high quality American youth—that would go and settle in Israel." See Lurie, "Soloveitchik, B-G, Discuss Education."

43 On Belkin, see Stitskin, *Studies in Judaica*.

44 On the roots of American Orthodoxy's relationship with Zionism, see Gurock, "American Orthodox Organizational Support for Zionism, 1880–1930."

45 David Ben-Gurion, "Ha-Nizhiyut shel Am Yisrael," audio recording (Mar. 16, 1960), downloaded from https://www.yutorah.org/search/?teacher=81386. Belkin's introduction does not appear in the seven-page typed transcript of the speech titled "Pegishat Rosh ha-Memshalah im Talmidei 'Yeshiva University' Arzot ha-Berit," available at *Ben-Gurion Archives*–Sde Boker, Serial no. 86095.

46 "Pegishat Rosh ha-Memshalah," 1.

47 Ibid.

48 Zameret and Tlamim, "Ben-Gurion's Private Beliefs and Public Policy."

49 Shurin, "Rosh ha-Memshalah Mar David Ben-Gurion Mevaker be-Yeshiva Universitah," 265–268; *Israelitisches Wochenblatt*, "Ben-Gurion war auch in der Jeschiwah-Universität."

50 "Pegishat Rosh ha-Memshalah," 2.

51 Ibid., 3.

52 Ibid., 4.

53 Ibid., 7.

54 Shurin, "Rosh ha-Memshalah Mar David Ben-Gurion Mevaker be-Yeshiva Universitah," 226.

55 Riskin, "B-G Stresses Study in Israel to Overflow Crowd at YU," 1.

56 Ibid., 1, 3; Persky, "Plainclothesmen."

57 *The Commentator*, "Open Letter."

58 Scholar and former YU student Lawrence Grossman attended Ben-Gurion's next campus speech in 1967. In an email correspondence (June 4, 2020), Grossman shared his recollection that the Israeli statesman began his presentation by lamenting the yarmulkah on his head: "They made me put this on!"

59 Abramson, *A Circle in the Square*.

60 Hirschhorn, *City on a Hilltop*, 25, 98–100, 110–113, 122–139.

61 https://ots.org.il.

62 According to the Israel Bureau of Statistics, between 1950 and 1959, 3,610 American immigrants arrived. From 1960 to 1968, 6,489 came. In 1969 the number ballooned to 5,738, and in 1970 it peaked for that period at 6,882. See Chaim I. Waxman, *American Aliya*, 77–84; Dashefsky and Lazerwitz, "The Role of Religious Identification in North American Migration to Israel," 263–275.

63 By the late 1980s the Orthodox accounted for over 60 percent, and a 2012 study presented the figure of 80 percent among Americans moving to Israel. See Waxman, *American Aliyah*, 98–102; Bayme, "American Orthodox Jews and the State of Israel," 215–231.

64 Sklare, *Conservative Judaism*.

65 Tabory and Lazerwitz, "Americans in the Israeli Reform and Conservative Denominations," 335–347.

66 Sklare, *Conservative Judaism*, 43.

67 Zameret and Tlamim, "Judaism in Israel."

68 Gurock, "American Orthodox Organizational Support for Zionism," 219–234.

69 On the development of the Mizrachi organization in America, see Caplan, "Shorshei ha-Mizrahi be-Amerika"; Lieberman, *Autobiography and Reflections*, 20–38; Salmon, "The Mizrachi Movement in America"; Schwartz, *Religious Zionism*, 105–109.

70 *Beit ha-Midrash le-Morim shel Yeshivat Rabbeinu Yitzhak Elhanan—Toknit Limudim 1934-36*, 6.

71 Gurock, *The Men and Women of Yeshiva*, 67–81, 140.

72 www.yu.edu.

73 Bernstein, "Dr. Pinchos Churgin," 99; Churgin, *Vision and Legacy*; Miller, "Meeting Again (and Again): Reading Pinkhos Churgin's Essay Seventy-Five Years Later."

74 Klein, *Bar-Ilan*.

75 Letter from Rabbi Mordechai Kirshblum to Dr. Bernard Lander (June 21, 1956), YU Archive.

76 Mirsky, "The New Heavens in the New World."

77 Carmy, "Soloveitchik the Zionist"; Farber, "Rabbi Joseph B. Soloveitchik's Early Zionism," 127–130. For citations by Soloveitchik regarding Zionism, see https://mizrachi.org.

78 Soloveitchik, *Kol Dodi Dofek*.

79 Soloveitchik, *Covenant, Community and Commitment*, 163–247.

80 *The Commentator*, "Junior Trips to Israel Ended: School Policy against Leaves." A correspondence between Dr. Bernard Lander, then a dean at YU (later founder of Touro University), and Rabbi Max Kirschblum dated October 13, 1958, and preserved in the YU Archive, indicates that part of the impetus for YU's change of policy was financial.

81 *The Commentator*, "Aliyah."

82 Waxman, "The Centrality of Israel in American Jewish Life." This was written just as the year in Israel phenomenon was beginning to gain traction in Modern Orthodox education.

83 Riskin, "B-G Stresses Study in Israel"; Persky, "Plainclothesmen," 3.

84 For a vivid account of likely the first American university-age delegation to Israel after the establishment of the state, the American Student and Professorial Workshop organized by Professor Abraham I. Katsh of New York University in the summer of 1949, see Baumel-Schwartz, *A Very Special Life*, 145–176. Bernice (Cohen) Schwartz was a participant in a group based in Beit Berl outside Kfar-Sava for six weeks that traveled throughout the country; David Ben-Gurion and his wife Paula visited them on multiple occasions. Previously, I had learned about this initiative through conversations with another one of the original sixty-three delegation members, Dr. Fred Gottlieb.

85 Today most of the programs work in cooperation with the Israeli government through its MASA Israel umbrella organization, www.masaisrael.org.

86 The New York office of the Jewish Agency's Department of Torah Culture and Education in the Diaspora, led by Rabbi Zevi Tabory during the late 1950s, played a key role in promoting the year study programs for observant students. See Waxman, "Looking Backward."

87 On the Yavne Israel Institute spearheaded by Irving (Yitz) Greenberg and involving young figures from the Merkaz Harav Kook yeshiva in Jerusalem who themselves later became major leaders including Chaim Druckman and Zefania Drori, see Kraut, *The Greening of American Orthodox Judaism*, 54–75.

88 www.yu.edu.

89 Berger, "A Year of Study in an Israeli Yeshiva Program," 178; Waxman, "In the End Is It Ideology," 50–67.

90 Goldmintz, "The Post-High School Yeshiva Experience in Israel," 32; Waxman, "A Brief History of Year in Israel Programs," 160–163; Schiff, "The Development of Israel Study Programs."

91 Waxman, *Flipping Out*, 179–182.

92 www.nbn.org.il.

93 Freund, "Up Close with Rabbi Yehoshua Fass." See the parody of Teaneck, New Jersey, which is a fifteen-minute drive from YU and has a thriving Modern Orthodox community, that appeared in 2018: https://i.redd.it/uh5bslonxpf11.jpg.

CHAPTER 2. CUMULATIVE IMPACT

1 Rabinovitch was never affiliated with YU but studied at prestigious North American universities and headed Jews' College (now London School of Jewish Studies), an institution of higher learning that trained rabbis and like YU seeks to integrate academic learning with religious commitment. See Taylor, *Defenders of the Faith*.

2 To be sure, there are other personalities who were impacted by Modern Orthodoxy or parallel phenomena before immigrating and making significant contribu-

tions to Israeli religious society that do not fit the criteria and were not included among the eight pioneers. A partial list would include: Rabbi Dr. Eliezer Berkovits, Rabbi Meir Bar-Ilan, Prof. Pinchas Churgin, Arye Leib Gelman, Rabbi Ze'ev Gold, Prof. Eliezer Goldman, Prof. Emanuel Rackman, and already mentioned, Prof. Tamar Ross, Prof. Alice Shalvi, and Rabbi Prof. Daniel Sperber. Some were primarily products of pre–World War II European Judaism, some never lived in America, some came to Israel before the 1960s or even before 1948, some had abbreviated or partial Israeli careers, and some did not lead institutions or had limited direct interactions with Israeli students. See the discussion of a number of these figures, especially Berkovits, whom the author sees as a forerunner for the changes that took place from the 1980s, in Schwartz, "Bein Orthodoksiyah Modernit le-Zionut Datit."

3 Mittelman, "Women in the Torah World," 73. On advanced Torah study for women in Telz, see Farbstein, *Bnot Ami mi-Telz*.

4 Lichtenstein, "My Education and Aspirations."

5 For alternative biographical accounts, see: Marcus, "The Indomitable Spirit of Rabbi Ahron Soloveichik"; idem, "The Amazing Story of Rav Ahron, ZTL."

6 Goldberg, "Rabbi Isaac Hutner"; Kaplan, "Rabbi Isaac Hutner's 'Daat Torah Perspective' on the Holocaust"; Shalev, "Major Themes in the Biography and Thought of Rabbi Isaac Hutner."

7 Lichtenstein, "My Education and Aspirations."

8 The exact subject of his Harvard studies and their impact on his worldview is expanded upon in detail in the next chapter.

9 Lichtenstein, "My Education and Aspirations"; Zuckier and Carmy, "An Introductory Biographical Sketch of R. Aharon Lichtenstein."

10 For a more extensive discussion of his time in YU, see Ferziger, "'The Road Not Taken' and 'the One Less Traveled.'"

11 Kraut, *The Greening of American Orthodox Judaism*, 49–50.

12 Ferziger, "'The Road Not Taken' and 'the One Less Traveled.'"

13 Ferziger, *Beyond Sectarianism*, 114–129, 211–224.

14 Aspects of Lichtenstein's independent outlook are highlighted in: Brill, "An Ideal Rosh Yeshiva; Fischer, "The Religious Humanism of R. Aharon Lichtenstein"; Jotkowitz, "'I am in the Middle'"; Landes, *Our Roshei Yeshiva*, 35–62; Pachter, "Hitpathutah shel ha-Orthodoksiyah ha-Modernit be-Amerikah," 161–197; Schwartz, "Haguto shel ha-Rav Lichtenstein: Tadmit u-Meziut."

15 Kleinman, "Shitat Limud ha-Gemara ve-Shiurei 'Methodikah Talmudit' shel Ha-Rav Aharon Lichtenstein"; Krumbein, "From Reb Hayyim and the Rav to Shiurei Rav Aharon"; Wolf, "*Hiddush* within the *Beit Midrash*."

16 See Helfgot, "Divrei ha-Rav ve-Divrei ha-Talmid ve-Divrei ha-Rav." This description of Lichtenstein's building upon and departing from his mentor presents an intriguing parallel to the process of Israeli students doing the same in respect to Lichtenstein's worldview.

17 Goodman, *Soloveitchik's Children*; Pachter, "Hitpathutah shel ha-Orthodoksiyah ha-Modernit," 325–329.

18 Finkelman, "Haredi Isolation in Changing Environments," 62–64, 72.

19 Dr. Tova Lichtenstein was also a candidate on the Meimad slate.

20 Brill, "Worlds Destroyed, Worlds Rebuilt; Kahana, "Sippur she-Sham'ati mi-Ha-Rav Yehudah Amital"; Reichner, *By Faith Alone*; Ziegler and Mirsky, "Torah and Humanity in a Time of Rebirth."

21 Amital, "Bino Shenot Dor va-Dor." For a large collection of uncritical but relatively nonhagiographic personal reminiscences in Hebrew by Israeli students from all periods in his tenure at YHE, see "Kobetz Tanhumim," https://etzion .haretzion.org.

22 See, for example: Kahn and Neuman, "A Rabbinic Exchange on the Disengagement"; Lichtenstein, "On the Murder of Prime Minister Yitzhak Rabin z"l"; Lichtenstein et al., "A Rabbinic Exchange on Baruch Goldstein's Funeral."

23 Mittelman, "Woman in the Torah World," 67–80.

24 In noting his impact on burgeoning new religious trends, Schwartz, "Bein Orthodoksiyah Modernit le-Zionut Datit," 228, n. 15, emphasizes "Lichtenstein and his students."

25 Full disclosure: I studied at YHE in 1983–84 and attended Lichtenstein's weekly Talmud class at YU's Gruss Institute in Jerusalem between 1987 and 1989.

26 Nadler, "Maimonides in Ma'ale Adumim."

27 In addition to the biographical sources listed below, see Pachter, "Hitpathutah shel ha-Orthodoksiyah ha-Modernit," 288–290.

28 Klein, "A Great Talmudist: Rabbi Pinchas Hirschprung Interviewed," 4, cited in Robinson, "A Portrait of the Rabbi as a Young Man," 41.

29 *Canadian Jewish News*, "Toronto Meetings," 9.

30 See Rabinovitch, *Shu"t Siah Nahum*, 375–376. The responsum regarding the proper spelling of the name Charleston in a Jewish divorce writ was penned in the summer of 1957.

31 Silberstein, "Personal Autonomy in the Thought of R. Nachum Eliezer Rabinovitch."

32 *Jewish Chronicle*, "Rabbi Dr Nahum Eliezer Rabinovitch."

33 Sacks, "My Teacher: In Memoriam."

34 Rosensweig, "My Rebbe—Rav Nachum Eliezer Rabinovitch"; Pachter, "Hitpathutah shel ha-Orthodoksiyah ha-Modernit be-Amerika," 290–321, 329–330, presents a detailed analysis of Rabinovitch as a religious thinker, arguing that the latter's Maimonidean-inspired approach—which he integrates into both his ideational and legal writings—offers a less bifurcated Modern Orthodox perspective than any of Soloveitchik's students (other than perhaps Hartman), with Lichtenstein serving as a prime foil. Pachter also sees Emanuel Rackman as similarly unique in integrating his moral philosophy with practical Jewish law, and identifies the latter, despite his own admonitions, as distinct from the Soloveitchik's more direct students. Relatedly, see Kaplan, "From Cooperation to Conflict: Rabbi Professor

Emanuel Rackman, Rav Joseph B. Soloveitchik, and the Evolution of American Modern Orthodoxy."

35 Nadler, "Maimonides from Ma'ale Adumim." 40.

36 Lau, "Ha-Koteret Zekan Rabbanei ha-Zionut ha-Datit oseh lo Avel."

37 www.giyur.org.il.

38 Lau, "Ha-Koteret."

39 Pachter, "Yahadut shel Emet: Kavim le-Demuto shel Ha-Rav Nahum Rabinovitch."

40 Somewhat ironically, through the original version of the book, which appeared in 2011 and presented Lichtenstein's core ideas to the broader public in a highly readable Hebrew, Sabato deserves considerable credit for the growth in appreciation for Lichtenstein toward the end of his life and beyond.

41 Nadler, "Maimonides from Ma'ale Adumim."

42 Goldfinger, "Inyan Ishi im Daniel Tropper."

43 Ibid.

44 Interview by Dror Yahav with Dr. Daniel Tropper (via Zoom), Nov. 4, 2022. I am grateful to Dror, who conducted the interview in the context of his doctoral research on RZ and the ba'al teshuvah movement that he is performing under my guidance, for sharing his data with me.

45 Ibid.

46 www.gesherusa.org.

47 Goldfinger, "Inyan Ishi im Daniel Tropper."

48 Klein-Halevi, *Like Dreamers*, 114–264; Rozen, "Bli Galgal Rezervi shel ha-Hevre ha-Zioniim tisha'aru Teku'im"; Sheleg, "Mufkarim."

49 https://yesmalot.co.il.

50 On the commonalities and distinctions between Yeshiva of Flatbush and Ramaz, the Manhattan-based private Jewish day school founded during the same period, see Liebman, "Studying Orthodox Judaism in the United States: A Review Essay," 418–419.

51 On his experience studying with Soloveitchik, listen to the interview from March 5, 2023: https://traditiononline.org.

52 Sofer, "The Human Spirit."

53 www.ohrtorahstone.org.il.

54 See the film *Torat Chaim ve-Ahavat Chesed: A Tribute to Rabbi Chaim Brovender* (2007), https://youtu.be/tbfJCRbE66s?feature=shared.

55 For a rich collection of testimonials by prominent alumni focused on Brovender's strengths and contributions, see https://webyeshiva.org. For another account by a former student that is also laudatory, but nonetheless acknowledges more complexity, see Yanklowitz, "The Growing Legacy of Rabbi Chaim Brovender."

56 The first institution to focus on advanced Torah study for post–high school women was Michlalah College for Women, which was founded by Rabbi Yehudah Cooperman in the mid-1960s. Although initially some Talmud was taught, this path was abandoned quickly, and focus was placed on the Bible

with the use of rabbinic literature for exegetical purposes. See: Rosenberg, "The World of Women's Torah Learning," 14; Furstenberg, "The Flourishing of Higher Jewish Learning for Women." The pluralistic and coeducational Pardes Institute, whose faculty was primarily observant Jews but featured some prominent nonobservant figures as well, opened its doors in 1973 and offered Talmud study opportunities to all its English-speaking students. See www .pardes.org.il.

57 Berman, "Forty Years Later."
58 Initially, this institution's main aim was to provide a warm and enriching religious framework for observant young women within the broader university campus; see El-Or, *Next Year I Will Know More*, 41–44.
59 Ross, "A Beit Midrash of Her Own," 315–316.
60 Berger, "The Centrality of Talmud," 331–335.
61 Brovender hired Dr. David Bernstein, a veteran American educator who had recently immigrated to Israel and was living in Jerusalem, to design and run the English-speaking gap-year program.
62 Fried, "Toanot Beit Din ve-Ha'azamat Nashim," 129. During the same period, the Religious Kibbutz movement opened a midrasha for women at Kibbutz Sde Eliyahu in the Beat Shean Valley. It was moved subsequently to Kibbutz Ein ha-Neziv and continues to service Israeli post–high school students. Talmud is taught, although it is less emphasized. See www.midrasha.co.il.
63 Zippor, "Learning Experience."
64 https://ots.org.il.
65 Bartuv and Nobolslasky, *Mah Sh'elatekh Esther ve-Tey'as.*
66 Ferziger, "Female Clergy in Male Space."
67 According to Rachel Levmore, the idea of training female religious court advocates came first from Rabbi Shlomo Riskin; see Levmore, "A View from the Other Side," 50.
68 Abramowitz, "Women Advocates Make Their Mark"; Fried, "Toanot Beit Din," 129–142; Israel-Cohen, *Between Feminism and Orthodox Judaism*, 35–36; Rosenberg, "The World of Women's Torah Learning," 26.
69 For an analysis and characterization of various styles of Talmud study that emerged in the midrashot, see Bar-El, *Ve-Talmud Torah ke-neged Kulan.*
70 El-Or, *Next Year I Will Know More*, 28.
71 Rosenberg, "The World of Women's Torah Learning," 22–25; Fuchs, "How to Create a Stay-At-Home Revolutionary: Rabbinic Discourse on Women's Education in The Haredi-Leumi Community," 121–135; Ross, "A Beit Midrash of Her Own."
72 *Ha-Kesher ha-Rav Dori*, "Sippur ha-Aliyah shel ha-Savtah Ha-Rabbanit Malka Bina."
73 Blumberg, *They Called Him Rebbe.*
74 https://biu.academia.edu.
75 Ferziger, *Beyond Sectarianism*, 157–158.
76 Hacohen, *Ari bein ha-Olamot.*

77 Ibid., 15; Isserow, "Creating New Leaders: Interview with Malke Bina, Founder and Director of MaTaN," 1; Sofer, "The Human Spirit"; Golinkin, "The Participation of Jewish Women in Public Rituals and Torah Study," 55.

78 https://www.matan.org.il/en/learn-en/beit-midrash-programs/.

79 https://www.matan.org.il/en/about-2/.

80 Greenberg, "Is Now the Time for Orthodox Woman Rabbis?," 50.

81 Isserow, "Creating New Leaders," 2.

82 Ibid.

83 www.matan.org.il.

84 Isserow, "Creating New Leaders," 3.

85 Butler, "Spirituality, Textual Study and Gender at Nishmat: A Spirited Chavruta."

86 https://nishmat.net/.

87 Bendel, "Devarim she-lo Yada'atem al Ha-Rabbanit Chana Henkin."

88 Hanau, "Rabbi Yehuda Herzl Henkin." On his grandfather, see, for example, Ferziger, "And Who Even Knows What It Is?"

89 Henkin, "Yoatzot Halachah."

90 Ibid.

91 www.yoatzot.org; Henkin, "New Conditions and New Models of Authority," 85–92.

92 www.yoatzot.org.

93 Ibid.

94 Ibid.

95 Ibid.

96 Ibid.

97 Sperber, *Rabba, Maharat, Rabbanit, Rebbetzin.*

98 www.yoatzot.org. See the discussion in Labowitz, "*Poskot* in the Palace of Torah," 292–293.

99 Avishai, "Halakhic Niddah Consultants"; Cohen, "Manhigut Datit Nashit."

100 Raucher, "Yoatzot Halacha."

101 http://www.yoatzot.org/home/; Ganzel and Zimmerman, "Women as Halakhic Professionals."

102 Zimmerman, *A Lifetime Companion to the Laws of Jewish Family Life.*

103 Henkin, "From Chaos to Repair in Women's Education and Leadership," 121.

104 www.yoatzot.org.

105 Feldman, "Halakhic Feminism or Feminist Halakha?"

106 Ferziger, "Female Clergy in Male Space."

107 Henkin and Henkin, *Nishmat ha-Bayit.* A Hebrew version appeared in 2017.

108 www.beithillel.org.il.

109 Van Elteren, "Cultural Globalization and Transnational Flows of Things American," 157.

110 Hartman, "Eulogy."

111 Moskowitz, "Long, Long Ago, When Basketball Was Kosher."

112 Gurock, *Judaism's Encounter with American Sports,* 122, 140–142.

113 Finkelman, "An Ideology for American Yeshiva Students."

114 Ariel, "Hasidism in the Age of Aquarius."

115 Hartman, "Eulogy."

116 See Rakeffet-Rothkoff, *From Washington Avenue to Washington Street*, 50–51: "I entered [the YU study hall] in 1951 . . . individuals whom I looked up to from my earliest days in the Yeshiva were David Hartman, Aharon Lichtenstein. . . . Hartman was known as 'Duvy,' and he was constantly encouraging the younger students to be more punctilious in their religious practice. . . . One day in 1953, Duvy entered the *beit ha-midrash* and very dramatically entreated us to rend our garments and sit down on the floor. When we looked at him in shock he informed us that the *Hazon Ish* had just passed away . . . the Bnei Brak sage . . . was revered throughout the Torah world. . . . We did not comply with Duvy's requests, but we certainly internalized the pain upon the loss of this eminent sage."

117 Hartman, "The Halakhic Hero: Rabbi Joseph Soloveitchik, Halakhic Man"; Goodman, *Soloveitchik's Children*; Magid, "David Hartman's Soloveitchik and the Battle for a Teachers' Legacy," 134–139.

118 Kaplan, "Rabbi Joseph B. Soloveitchik's Philosophy of Halakhah."

119 Soloveitchik, *Halakhic Man*.

120 Email correspondence from Prof. Lawrence Kaplan, June 21, 2023. Kaplan shared this story with me in 2013 and has told it publicly on numerous occasions. When preparing this chapter, I asked him to send me his recollection in writing to ensure accuracy. For an alternative perspective, see Lichtenstein, "Torah and General Culture," 284.

121 For a description of Hartman as an inspirational teacher at YU, see Sofaer, "Finding an Unlikely Home," 280–281.

122 For two accounts of these events, see Greenberg, "Yeshiva in the 1960s," 183–184; Lichtenstein, "The 60s," 375.

123 Kraut, *The Greening of American Orthodox Judaism*, 85, 92, 179.

124 Hartman, "Hesped"; Avishai, "In a Very Deep Way."

125 Eisen, "A Tribute to David Hartman."

126 www.pardes.org.il.

127 For a relatively early essay that, so to speak, "pushes the envelope" of Orthodoxy, but was deemed sufficiently "kosher" at the time to appear in the journal of the Orthodox RCA, see Hartman, "Halakhah as a Ground for Creating a Shared Spiritual Language."

128 Lorberbaum, "Beit Medrash," 57–70.

129 Eisen, "A Tribute to David Hartman."

130 Hartman, *A Heart of Many Rooms*; idem, *The God Who Hates Lies*.

131 Ellenson, "David Hartman on Judaism and the Modern Condition."

132 Lorberbaum, "Beit Medrash," 65–68.

133 Kaplan, "Back to Zechariah Frankel and Louis Jacobs"; Nagen, "Scholarship Needs Spirituality, Spirituality Needs Scholarship."

134 https://havruta-huji.co.il.

135 Werczberger and Azulay, "The Jewish Renewal Movement in Israeli Secular Society."

136 Ash, "Observant Feminism across Borders"; https://shirahadasha.org.

137 Like Brovender, Hartman had also played a role in the outreach activities of the ITRI yeshiva through funding that he raised prior to immigrating to Israel. In fact, the ITRI initiative, which later evolved into the Darchei Noam–Shappel's institutions, was originally named after Hartman's father. See the film *Torat Chaim ve-Ahavat Chesed: A Tribute to Rabbi Chaim Brovender* (2007), https://youtube.com/watch?v=tbfJCRbE66s.

138 www.hartman.org.il.

139 www.hamidrasha-israel.org.

140 https://heb.hartman.org.il.

141 Ibid.; Rosenberg and Schwartz, "Israeli Rabbis You Should Know."

142 https://zion-jerusalem.wixsite.com.

143 www.hartman.org.il.

144 https://heb.hartman.org.il.

145 Hartman, "Mikhtav Ishi me'et Nasi ha-Makhon."

146 Wistoch and Mamo Schwartz, "Rulings Devoid of Human Compassion Will Bring Orthodoxy to Its End."

147 Riskin, "The Master Teacher," 253–257.

148 Ferziger, *Beyond Sectarianism*, 71.

149 Abramson, *Circle in a Square*; Danzger, *Returning to Judaism*, 36–43; Riskin, *Listening to God*.

150 Cashman, "Riskin Remembers Marching with MLK Jr."

151 Ferziger, *Beyond Sectarianism*, 66–67, 78.

152 Riskin, *The Rebellious Wife*.

153 Kaunfer and Shanken, "An Interview with Shlomo Riskin," 10.

154 Mark, "Yakov Birnbaum's Freedom Ride," 16–17. On Stevie Wonder, see Werner, *Higher Ground*.

155 Wistoch and Mamo Schwartz, "Rulings Devoid of Human Compassion."

156 Hirschhorn, *City on a Hilltop*, 58–97; Morrison, *The Gush*; Weinberg, "Remembering Moshko, Builder of Israel."

157 www.cbs.gov.il.

158 Riskin, "Can a Leopard Change Its Spots?"

159 Mollov and Lavie, "Culture, Dialogue, and Perception Change in The Israeli-Palestinian Conflict"; Rubinstein-Shemer, "Rabbi Froman as Crisis Mediator between Israelis and Palestinians," 483.

160 Shragai, "Ha-Rav Riskin: Efshar le-haf'il Tahburah Zibburit be-Shabbat."

161 Dreyfus, "Riskin Names Female Spiritual Leader in Efrat."

162 Shapiro, "Modern Orthodoxy and Religious Truth," 143–145.

163 Tene, "Efrat's Rabbi: Same-Sex Couple Can Raise a Family."

164 Asa-el, "Middle Israel: Who's Afraid of Rabbi Riskin?"; Sarisohn, "Rabbi Riskin's Term Extended."

165 https://ots.org.il.

166 Sharon, "Rabbinical Emissary Program to Diaspora Celebrates 20 Years of Work."

167 Lipman, "Riskin Chooses Successor for His Educational Network."

168 https://tzohar-eng.org.

169 Ibid.

170 Ibid.

171 *EJPhilanthropy*, "Rabbi Dr. Kenneth Brander to Head Ohr Torah."

172 Ferziger, *Beyond Sectarianism*, 169.

173 Brander, "Ha-Askanut she-Romeset"; Klein, "Modern Orthodox Rabbi: LGBTQ+ People Can Teach at Yeshivas."

174 Kratz, "Rabbi Kenneth Brander Makes Aliyah." See also www.youtube.com/watch ?v=_hshUaeP8Kk.

CHAPTER 3. KAHANE AND CARLEBACH

1 See Magid, "Shlomo Carlebach and Meir Kahane." The author does an admirable job of noting both distinctions and similarities between the two figures. However, his ultimate aim is to show that from the perspective of Israeli politics and Zionism they shared much in common. As I have written elsewhere, the author's broader goal of demonstrating that Kahane was more reflective of normative trends within Orthodoxy than has been acknowledged leads to drawing creative connections that are thought-provoking and valuable but not sufficiently substantiated. See Ferziger, "Review of Shaul Magid, *Meir Kahane*."

2 Kahane was the counselor of Brovender in the Bnei Akiva youth movement, but Brovender never supported Kahane's later agendas.

3 Ophir (Offenbacher), *Rabbi Shlomo Carlebach*, 33–53.

4 Mayse, "Renewal and Redemption."

5 Magid, "Shlomo Carlebach and Meir Kahane," 464–465.

6 Wurtzburger, "Confronting the Challenge of the Values of Modernity," 105.

7 Lichtenstein, "Torah and General Culture," 217–292.

8 Inbari, *Messianic Religious Zionism*; Magid, *Meir Kahane*, 15–22.

9 Baumel, "Kahane in America," 317–319, 323.

10 Kelman and Magid, "The Gate to the Village."

11 Joselit, *New York's Jewish Jews*.

12 As far back as 1959, Rabbi Moshe Feinstein, the preeminent Halakhic authority in mid-twentieth-century North America, penned a responsum that addresses Carlebach's (not by name) deviations and whether they impact on the permissibility of integrating his music into wedding settings. See Moshe Feinstein, "Bi-D'var Nigunim she-asah Adam Kasher she-Ahar Zeman Nitkalkal ve-sani Shomanei im le-Nagnam al Hatunot," *Igrot Moshe—Even ha-Ezer* 1 (Bnei Brak, 1985) #96.

13 Ariel, "Hasidism in the Age of Aquarius"; Odenheimer, "On Orthodoxy: An Interview with Rabbi Shlomo Carlebach."

14 Hartman, "The Halakhic Hero"; Woolf, "Time Awareness as a Source of Spirituality."

15 Cohen, "A Holy Brother's Liberal Legacy," 505.

16 Beckerman, *When They Come For Us*, 125–128; Ferziger, "Outside the Shul"; Ophir, *Carlebach*, 264–274; Klein-Halevi, *Memoirs of a Jewish Extremist*, 77–79, 83–89, 114–120, 155–162.

17 Magid, *Meir Kahane*, 77–78.

18 Sharon, "Ben Gvir Hails Racist Kahane."

19 Inbari, *Messianic Religious Zionism*, 133–150.

20 Cohen, "A Holy Brother's Liberal Legacy," 505.

21 Magid, "Consumed by Fire"; Ophir, *Carlebach*, 205–263.

22 See, for example, the discussion of German Jews and Richard Wagner in Katz, "German Culture and the Jews," 54–59.

23 Siegelbaum, "Reb Shlomo and Me"; Torrosian, "The Legacy of Rabbi Shlomo Carlebach."

24 Margolin, "New Models of the Sacred Leader at the Beginning of Hasidism."

25 Halberstam Mandelbaum, *Holy Brother*; Ophir (Offenbacher), "Evaluating Rabbi Shlomo Carlebach's Place in Jewish History," 541.

26 Cohen, "Introduction: Shlomo Carlebach (1925–1994) and the Stories We Tell"; Husbands-Hankin, "Soul Brothers."

27 For a list of Hebrew publications, see "Shlomo Carlebach," Wikipedia Hebrew, https://he.wikipedia.org/.

28 Kahane and Mayse, "Hasidic Halakha"; Mondshine, "The Fluidity of Categories in Hasidism."

29 Mayse, "The Development of Neo-Hasidism: Part I."

30 Green and Mayse, *A New Hasidism—Roots*; Mayse, "The Development of Neo-Hasidism: Part III"; Persico, "Neo-Hasidic Revival."

31 Green and Mayse, *A New Hasidism—Branches*.

32 Ophir, "Evaluating," 545.

33 Steinhardt, "American Neo-Hasids in the Land of Israel."

34 Secunda, "Wild Things"; Turetsky, "Neo-Hasidut and American Modern Orthodoxy."

35 Fischer, "Post-Kookism and Neo-Hasidut." See the series on Hasidism and the weekly Torah portion taught by a senior staff member of YHE who was hired in 2011 in part to meet the demands of students: www.etzion.org.il.

36 https://otniel.org.

37 On the integration of spirituality and Talmudic intellectualism in contemporary Israeli yeshivot, see: Kaplan, "Back to Zechariah Frankel and Louis Jacobs?"; Nagen, "Scholarship needs Spirituality."

38 https://siach.org.il.

39 https://makor-c.org/.

40 www.matanel.org.

41 Fischer, "Radical Religious Zionism," 289–290.

42 Ariel, "Gender and Sexuality in a New Jewish Religious Movement," 73–74.

43 www.thecarlebachshul.org.

44 Ofir, *Carlebach*, 244.

45 Garb, *The Chosen Will Become Herds*.

46 Engelberg, "Modern Orthodoxy in Post-secular Times," 126–139.

47 Mark, *Mistikah ve-Shiga'on*.

48 Magid, *Hasidism on the Margin*; Brown, "Theoretical Antinomianism and the Conservative Function of Utopia; Hefter, "The Religious Phenomenology."

49 Abramovich, "A Critic from Within: Rav Shagar and the Renewal of Religious Zionism"; Jotkowitz, "The Post-Modern Theology of Rav Shagar"; Feldmann Kaye, "The Use of Hasidism."

50 See the brief discussion in Brill, "The Religious Thought of Rabbi Yehuda Amital," 11–12.

51 Ariel, "Conservative Judaism and Neo-Hasidism," 172–187; Cohen, "A Holy Brother's Liberal Legacy."

52 Ginzburg, "Kah Carlebach Patah et ha-Lev"; Katsman, "Contemporary Trends in Religious-Zionism," 154–174.

53 Imhoff, "Carlebach and the Unheard Stories," 555–560.

54 Carlebach, "My Sisters, I Hear You."

CHAPTER 4. FRAGMENTARY JUDAISM

1 Lichtenstein, *By His Light*, 180. Whenever possible, citations are from the generally more accessible republished versions of the original articles that appear in the collected volumes of Lichtenstein's work. The chapter adapts and expands upon materials in Adam S. Ferziger, "On Fragmentary Judaism: The Jewish 'Other' and the Worldview of R. Dr. Aharon Lichtenstein," *Tradition* 47, no. 4 (Winter 2015): 34–68.

2 Lichtenstein, *By His Light*, 178.

3 Lichtenstein, *Leaves of Faith 1*, 57–83.

4 Tec, *In the Lion's Den: The Life of Oswald Rufeisen*.

5 Lichtenstein, *Leaves of Faith 1*, 77–78.

6 Ferziger, *Exclusion and Hierarchy*.

7 Two English translations of the original Hebrew essay have been published: Soloveitchik, *Fate and Destiny* (1992); idem, *Kol Dodi Dofek—Listen, My Beloved Knocks* (2006).

8 Blidstein, "On the Jewish People in the Writings of Rabbi Joseph B. Soloveitchik," 31.

9 Lichtenstein, "Brother Daniel," 72.

10 Lichtenstein, *Leaves of Faith 2*, 1–32.

11 Ibid., 28.

12 Brown, *Ha-Hazon Ish*, 265–274.

13 Blidstein, "On the Jewish People," 33. It should be noted that Lichtenstein's own evaluation of Soloveitchik's approach to the non-Orthodox in *Leaves of Faith 1*, 197, minimizes their differences.

14 Lichtenstein, *Leaves of Faith 2*, 216.

15 Ibid. 221.

16 Ibid., 220.

17 Kook, *Le-Nevukhei ha-Dor*.

18 For Lichtenstein's perception of the difference between the respective approaches of Soloveitchik and Kook toward religious tolerance, see *Leaves of Faith 2*, 113: "Rabbi Kook was, philosophically, far more tolerant but, as a public figure, tolerated less; the reverse was true of the Rav [Soloveitchik]."

19 Massarik, "A Report on Intermarriage."

20 Lichtenstein, *Leaves of Faith 2*, 225–239.

21 Liebman, "Orthodoxy in American Jewish Life." See also Ferziger, "Outside the Shul."

22 Eleff, *A History of the NCSY*.

23 Danzger, *Returning to Tradition*, 36–38.

24 Lichtenstein, *Leaves of Faith 2*, 334.

25 Ibid.

26 Soloveitchik, "Message to a Rabbinic Convention," 109–114.

27 Soloveitchik, "On Seating and Sanctification," 114–118. Seth Farber has demonstrated compellingly that Soloveitchik did express appreciation for individual non-Orthodox rabbinical figures and the roles their individual synagogues played in their locales. See Farber, "Reproach, Recognition and Respect."

28 Adler et al., "Responsum on the Sabbath."

29 Lichtenstein, *Leaves of Faith 2*, 355–362.

30 Ibid., 360.

31 Ibid., 28.

32 Zaleski, "William James."

33 Lichtenstein, *Leaves of Faith 2*, 360.

34 Ellenson and Gordis, *Pledges of Jewish Allegiance*, 117–119.

35 Affirmed in a personal email communication (Jan. 1, 2015) from Dov Frimer, who was appointed to the Neeman Commission based on Lichtenstein's recommendation.

36 Wertheimer, *All Quiet on the Religious Front*, 3.

37 Bulka, *The Coming Cataclysm*, 13.

38 Lipshitz, "Recollections and Reconsiderations."

39 See, for example, Falk, "Devarim she-lo yedatem al Ha-Rav Aharon Lichtenstein."

40 Lichtenstein, "Beyond the Pale?"

41 Ibid., 214.

42 Ibid., 195.

43 Ibid., 208.

44 Ibid.

45 Ibid.

46 Ibid., 207.

47 See, for example: http://limmud.org.

48 Peled, "Still Snubbed by Chief Rabbi."

49 Lichtenstein, "Beyond the Pale," 209–210.

50 Easterman, "Ego Stands in Way of Great Leadership."

51 https://events.limmud.org.

52 The blog is the work of Dov Karoll, long-time YHE student and personal assistant to Lichtenstein. On its purpose, see http://pagesoffaith.wordpress.com.

53 Ibid.

54 Ibid.

55 Ibid.

56 Ibid.

57 Ibid.

58 For an insightful sociological analysis of LGBTQs within the Israeli religious landscape, see Avishai, *Queer Judaism*.

59 Lipman, "YU Gay Panel Broadens the Discussion, Debate."

60 Schachter et al., "Torah View of Homosexuality."

61 Broyde, "Religious Values in Secular Institutions."

62 Edelstein, "A Traditional Jewish Approach to Homosexuality."

63 Helfgot, "Rabbi Helfgot's Statement of Principles Urges Sensitivity toward Gays in Orthodoxy."

64 Bezalel, "In Israel, Modern Orthodoxy Embraces the Religious LGBTs—Partly."

65 www.beithillel.org.il.

66 Melamed, "Yahas ha-Halakhah le-Hot'im be-Mishkav Zakhar."

67 Sabato, *Mevakshei Panekha*. Citations are translated from the original Hebrew version. For the English translation, see Sabato, *Seeking his Presence*.

68 On Sabato, see Leibowitz Schmidt and Setbon, "Up Close with Rosh Yeshiva-Turned-Novelist Haim Sabato."

69 On the variant versions of the specific metaphor that Hazon Ish used and what they mean, see Brown, *Ha-Hazon Ish*, 265–274.

70 Sabato, *Mevakshei Panekha*, 142–143.

71 Ibid., 143.

72 Ibid., 144.

73 Ibid., 145.

74 Ibid. The reference to potential accusations of condescention likely reflected Lichtenstein's awareness of the comments of Amos Oz in his 1982 book *Poh ve-Sham be-Erets Yisrael*, 120, who reacted viscerally to what he considered to be the patronizing quality of Kook's identification of an inner spark of authentic religious yearning within the hearts of secular Zionists that has been covered over by their outer "shells" of heresy and secularism.

75 Ibid., 146.

76 Ibid., 148.

77 Ibid., 151–152.

78 Dahan, *The Final Redeemer*, 151–194.

79 Ibid., 152.

80 Brill, "An Ideal Rosh Yeshiva."
81 Fischer, "The Religious Humanism of Aharon Lichtenstein." See also Kolbrener, "Religion and Culture."
82 See chapter 5 herein.
83 Ibid. Lichtenstein's comments appear in *Leaves of Faith* 2, 216–217.
84 Lichtenstein, *Leaves of Faith* 1, 94–95.
85 Ibid. See similar expressions in Lichtenstein's expansive essay on the same topic, "Torah and General Culture," 252–256.
86 Gaffney, "Newman on the Common Roots of Morality and Religion."
87 Cohen, "Augustine's Doctrine of Jewish Witness Revisited."
88 Lichtenstein, "Brother Daniel," 68.

CHAPTER 5. DEMONIZATION AND THE ALTERNATIVES

1 Parts of this chapter draw upon Adam S. Ferziger, "The Role of Reform in Israeli Orthodoxy," in *Between Jewish Tradition and Modernity, Rethinking an Old Opposition: Essays in Honor of David Ellenson*, ed. Michael A. Meyer and David Myers (Detroit: Wayne University Press, 2014), 51–66; idem, "Bein Semel le-Bat Si'ah: Ha-Reformah ha-Yehudit ve-Rabbanei ha-Zionut ha-Datit," in *Ha-Tenu'ah Ha-Reformit be-Yisrael*, ed. Elazar Ben-Lulu and Ofer Schiff (Sde Boker: Makhon Ben-Gurion/Ben-Gurion University, 2022), 139–161.
2 Durkheim, *The Division of Labor in Society*, 70–110.
3 Erikson, *Wayward Puritans*, 10.
4 For a discussion of how Erikson expanded on Durkheim, see Downes and Rock, *Understanding Deviance*, 86–89.
5 Ellenson, "The Role of Reform in Selected German-Jewish Orthodox Responsa," 357–380.
6 Ibid.
7 On Sofer's approach to Reform, see, for example: Ellenson, "Traditional Reactions to Modern Jewish Reform"; Katz, "Towards a Biography of the Hatam Sofer," 403–405.
8 See Silber, "The Emergence of Ultra-Orthodoxy," 30 n. 11.
9 Moses Sofer, *Shu"t Hatam Sofer* 6 (Likutim), no. 89.
10 Katz, "Orthodoxy in Historical Perspective."
11 Ferziger, *Exclusion and Hierarchy*, 122–125.
12 Ellenson, *Rabbi Esriel Hildesheimer and the Creation of a Modern Jewish Orthodoxy*, 43–44; Silber, "The Emergence of Ultra-Orthodoxy," 30, n. 11.
13 Sarna, *American Judaism*, 193–201.
14 Wertheimer, *All Quiet on the Religious Front*, 17.
15 Ferziger, "From Demonic Deviant to Drowning Brother."
16 Schachter, "On the Matter of Masorah."
17 Don-Yehiya, "Orthodox Jewry in Israel and in North America," 159–161.
18 On early attempts at establishing Reform in 1930s Palestine, see Meyer, *Response to Modernity*, 344–345.

19   See Tabory and Lazerwitz, "Americans in the Israeli Reform and Conservative Denominations," 177–87; Meyer, *Response to Modernity*, 348–352.

20   See Meirovitch, "The Shaping of Masorti Judaism in Israel"; Tabory, "The Influence of Liberal Judaism on Israeli Religious Life," 3.

21   Israel-Shamsian, "The Israeli Religious Market and Penetration of the Conservative and Reform Movements," 56–57.

22   Edelman, "A Portion of Animosity," 219.

23   See, for example, Eisen, "Rx for Orthodox Intolerance," 92–93; Sarna, *American Judaism*, 367.

24   On Tzohar, see Ferziger, "Religion for the Secular."

25   www.beithillel.org.il.

26   Barkat, "The Reform Movement as a 'Caricature.'"

27   Nahshoni, "Ha-Ma'avak Mithamem."

28   Sela, "Ha-Rav Lior."

29   Cherlow, "Al ha-Havhanah ben Reformah le-Hithadshut."

30   Barkat, "The Reform Movement as a 'Caricature.'"

31   Roth, "Ben Hashdanut le-Hadshanut."

32   Ronen, "Rabbi Shapira: Time to Fight Neo-Reformists in Our Midst." Shapira expanded on his approach in a lecture to his students, which was transcribed and made available on the yeshiva's website: Shapira, "Me-Hashem Yatsah ha-Davar."

33   Falk, "Midrashot 'ha-kav' Yozmot Yemei iyun be-Tanakh."

34   Aviner is no less determined to rein in diversity regarding issues of modesty and sexuality. See, for example, this report on his directives regarding proper dress for prepubescent girls: Nahshoni, "Kelalei Tseniyut shel ha-Rav Aviner."

35   Henderson, *The Construction of Orthodoxy and Heresy*, 157–160.

36   Cherlow, "Reshamim ve-Lebatim mi-Shelihut be-Arzot ha-Berit."

37   Ettinger, "Tzohar Rabbis Oppose Recognition of Non-Orthodox Jewish Movements." Ironically, Dov Halbertal is also a YHE alumnus, but subsequently identified with Haredi Orthodoxy.

38   Ibid.

39   Weinberg, "The Rabbinic Race Wreckage."

40   Full disclosure: I was invited to make an academic presentation at that meeting.

41   Lubitz, *Ha-Im Lizrom im ha-Zeramim?*

42   *Serugim*, "Ha-Rav Cherlow: Azuv she-ha Rehavah ha-Reformit ba-Kotel Reikah."

43   www.makorrishon.co.il.

44   Segel, "Efshar le-Daber im Kulam."

45   Lieblich, "French Feminist Rabbi Captivates Multifaith Crowds with Musings on Mortality."

46   http://giltroy.com.

47   Aviner, "Mahloket ha-Rabanim be-Devar ha-Reformim."

48   Greenwald, "Biglal Pegishah im Reformim."

49   Klein, "Se'arat ha-Rav Melamed ve-ha-Reformim."

50   Sheleg, "Kah Hafakh Ha-Rav Melamed."

51 Ibid.
52 Melamed, *Peninei Halakhah*.
53 Ibid.
54 Pyuterkovsky, "Kerav Rav."
55 Ezra, "Ha-Mifgash shel ha-Rav Melamed im Rabah Reformit."
56 Ibid.
57 Sheleg, "Kah Hafakh Ha-Rav Melamed."
58 Pyuterkovsky, "Ha-Mikhtav Neged ha-Rav Melamed."
59 Melamed, "Ha-Rav Melamed: Lamrot ha-Peniyot Lo Etmoded al Tafkid Ha-Rav ha-Rashi." Exemplifying Yosef's Haredi credentials, in the aftermath of the October 7, 2023, Hamas massacre, strong pressure was exerted to renege on the exemption given by the government for Haredi yeshiva students from army service. Yosef responded that if such an official move was made he would encourage these young adults to leave the country. See Pfeffer, "In One Sentence, Chief Rabbi Exemplifies Haredi Arrogance towards Wartime Israel."
60 Melamed, "Ha-Rav Melamed Masbir: Lamah Hishtatafti be-Panel im Rabbah Reformit."
61 Ibid.
62 Miles and Koch, "Inviting the Stranger In."
63 https://ourcommondestiny.org.
64 Rosman, "The Pink Tank in the Room."
65 Nahshoni, "Campaign Yahadut ha-Torah."
66 Ibid.
67 *Arutz Sheva*, "Irgun Hotam Meizig."
68 *Kipah*, "Ha-Rav Yuval Cherlow: Beit ha-Mishpat ha-Elyon eino musmakh."

CHAPTER 6. BIBLICAL SCHOLARSHIP AND ORTHODOX JUDAISM

1 This chapter adapts and builds upon materials that first appeared in Adam S. Ferziger, "Fluidity and Bifurcation: Critical Biblical Scholarship and Orthodox Judaism in Israel and North America," *Modern Judaism* 39, no. 3 (Oct. 2019): 233–270.
2 Shapiro, "Is Modern Orthodoxy Moving Towards an Acceptance of Biblical Criticism?" This chapter benefitted considerably from Shapiro's pathbreaking article and the many sources he identified, as well as his talk at a panel on Orthodoxy and Biblical Studies that was held at the World Congress of Jewish Studies, Jerusalem, August 2017, at which I presented my initial findings as well.
3 Ibid., 165. Liebman expressed a similar position in "Orthodoxy in American Jewish Life," 46 n. 40.
4 On the Jacobs Affair, see, for example: Cosgrove, "Teyku," 217–237; Freedman, *Reason to Believe*; Freud-Kandel, *Louis Jacobs and the Quest for a Contemporary Jewish Theology*; Waxman, "Halakhic Change vs. Demographic Change," 58–71.
5 Greenberg, "Dr. Greenberg Discusses."

6   Greenberg, "Greenberg Clarifies."

7   Ibid.

8   Ibid.

9   Ibid.

10 Ibid.

11 Lichtenstein, "Rav Lichtenstein Writes Letter to Dr. Greenberg."

12 To be sure, isolated examples of engagement by traditionalist-oriented Jews with Biblical criticism date back earlier than the 1960s. See, for example: Levenson, *The Hebrew Bible, The Old Testament, and Historical Criticism*; Shavit and Eran, *The Hebrew Bible Reborn*; Shaw, "Orthodox Reactions to the Challenge of Biblical Criticism."

13 There are medieval Jewish exegetes as well as Orthodox ones in modern times, who understand that the last twelve verses in the Pentateuch were not written by Moses.

14 Maimonides, *Commentary on the Mishnah—Bavli Sanhedrin*, 15: 247.

15 Cherlow, "Bikoret ha-Mikra ve-Yir'at ha-Shamayim Sheli," 295 (cited and translated in Shapiro, "Is Modern Orthodoxy," 171).

16 Cherlow, *Ye-Yare le-Levav*, 246–247.

17 Hacohen, "Ha-Omnam, Ehad Hayah Yishayahu?," 86 (the translated citation appears in Frisch, "Jewish Tradition and Bible Criticism," 279).

18 For an extensive interview with Hacohen, see Horowitz, "Ko'ev et ha-Petihut."

19 An authorized biography of Navon appears at https://tikvahfund.org.

20 Navon, "Iyov lo Haya ve-lo Nivra" (cited and translated in Shapiro, "Is Modern Orthodoxy," 184).

21 Meidan, "Ahat hi ha-Emet."

22 www.herzog.ac.il.

23 For an authorized biography of Brandes prior to his appointment to head Herzog Academic College, see www.korenpub.com.

24 Brandes, "Hazal ke-Mevakrei ha-Mikra," 210.

25 On Kula, see www.beithillel.org.il.

26 Kula, *Havayah O Lo Hayah*, 171–172.

27 Cherlow, "Be-Gevul Shenei Olamot."

28 On Kugel, see Orbach, "James Kugel: Professor of Disbelief." For Gellman's approach to Biblical theology, see Gellman, *This Was from God*.

29 For Ross's approach to Bible, see Ross, "Orthodoxy and the Challenge of Biblical Criticism."

30 On Ganzel, see TheTorah.com, "An Interview with Dr. Tova Ganzel."

31 Avishai, "Halakhic *Niddah* Consultants."

32 Ganzel and Zimmerman, "Vesset ha-Guf."

33 Ganzel, "Transformation of Pentateuchal Descriptions of Idolatry."

34 Rabbi Oury Amos Cherki is a notable exception. One of the main figures in Machon Meir, the outreach yeshiva identified with Merkaz ha-Rav, his personal background is more eclectic than that of most of his colleagues. Born in Al-

geria and raised in France, he was influenced by the French Jewish theologian Rabbi Yehuda Léon Ashkenazi (Manitou) and the Jerusalem mystic Rabbi Yehudah Ashlag.

35 Shapiro, "Is Modern Orthodoxy," lists a few examples of Orthodox individuals based in the United States and United Kingdom who have put forward understandings rooted in Biblical criticism. With one exception, they are either professional academics or distinctive figures such as Rabbi Dr. Norman Solomon, who first held United Synagogue pulpits, and after he located himself within the academy published *Torah from Heaven—The Reconstruction of Faith*.

36 https://thetorah.com.

37 Ibid.

38 Jackson, "Torah min haShamayim."

39 One cofounder is Professor Marc Zvi Brettler of Duke University, whose monographs include *How to Read the Jewish Bible* and (as coauthor) *The Bible and the Believer: How to Read the Bible Critically and Religiously*. TheTorah.com editor Rabbi Dr. Zev Farber studied in American Haredi-Orthodox institutions and was ordained by the liberal-Orthodox Yeshivat Chovevei Torah. He received an MA in ancient Jewish history–Biblical period from the Hebrew University in Jerusalem and a PhD from Emory University. The other co-founder is British-born Rabbi David D. Steinberg. He has no formal connections either to the academy or to Modern Orthodoxy, but his background in outreach to nonaffiliated Jews offers insight into the activist tone of the materials. See http://thetorah.com.

40 Zev Farber, http://thetorah.com.

41 One American exception is Rabbi Dr. Eliezer Finkelman. See his contributions to TheTorah.com. A number of Orthodox rabbis educated in the UK have also published essays in TheTorah.com.

42 For an alternative analysis of TheTorah.com, see Freud-Kandel, "On Revelation, Heresy, and Mesorah—From Louis Jacobs to the TheTorah.com."

43 Regarding Orthodox Jewish Bible study and the internet as a "free zone" for non-conventional theological views, see Waxman, *Social Change and Halakhic Evolution*, 162–163. For a parallel discussion regarding Talmud study, see chapter 12.

44 www.929.org.il. Not only do Benny Lau's uncle, Tel Aviv chief rabbi and former Ashkenazi chief rabbi of Israel Yisrael Meir Lau, and the latter's son, former Ashkenazi chief rabbi of Israel David Lau, contribute articles. So does the latter's New York-based brother, the progressive Conservative rabbi Amichai Lau-Lavi, as well as numerous secular authors, scholars, and RZ colleagues.

45 See the authorized biography of Mintz at https://rabbimintz.com.

46 Sedley, "Launching in English."

47 www.929.org.il.

48 Kugel, *How to Read the Bible*.

49 Orbach, "James Kugel: Professor of Disbelief."

50 For undergraduate requirements and BRGS courses for Fall 2023, see www.yu.edu.

51 For lists of the Yeshiva College Bible and BRGS faculty members, see www.yu.edu.

52 See, for example, Bernstein, "The Orthodox Jewish Scholar and Jewish Scholarship," 20–25.

53 One faculty member, Aaron Koller, took it upon himself to expose theologically curious students and other Orthodox Jews to a broader spectrum of approaches to the historical context of the Bible. See, for example, Stone, "RAFT Hosts Discussion with Aaron Koller on Biblical Creation in the Modern World." Koller is also a contributor to TheTorah.com. To the best of my understanding, however, he has not supported perspectives from higher criticism that question issues of strong consensus.

54 Bernstein, "Why Lines Need to be Drawn (and Where)."

55 Following the typologies in Heilman, "The Many Faces of Orthodoxy: Part 1," few of the RIETS instructors are "syncretists" who "embrace the modern world." Rather, most sit somewhere between the "tolerators"—who are "entrenched in the traditional Orthodox world," but show greater understanding either to attract people to their worldview or due to the sociocultural/vocational circumstances in which they find themselves—and the "neorejectionists'"—who "with the wisdom of former—modernists . . . argue that it is not reasonable to live that way."

56 Eleff and Kastner, "Reconciling Institutional Divides." On Schachter's antagonism toward academic Jewish studies, see Landes, "Traditional Struggles," 91–97.

57 Resnick, "Shut Down the Bible Department." In 2012–13, the number of Bible course requirements were lowered, and in 2019 a new Jewish studies curriculum was put forward that further diminishes the necessity of Yeshiva College students engaging academic approaches to Bible. See Koller, "An Improved Judaic Studies."

58 For a list of the BRGS core faculty and their subspecialties, see www.yu.edu.

59 See Levy, "The State and Directions of Orthodox Bible Study," 45–46, who noted that even among those practicing Orthodox Jewish university scholars who work on the Bible, few of them explore the main areas that most non-Orthodox and non-Jewish academics concentrate upon.

60 The late talmudist Rabbi Professor Meyer Simcha Feldblum was another figure who taught initially in both frameworks, but eventually dedicated himself to the academy. See Goldberg, "Our Rosh Yeshiva," 7; Landes, "Traditional Struggles," 90. The current RIETS figure who bucks the overall trend is Rabbi Dr. Jeremy Wieder. His approach to the historicity of the Bible is summarized in Helfgot, "Torah and Historical Proof." Wieder was attacked for giving credence to a nonacceptable theological position; see, for example, "Rabbi Jeremy Wieder Claims 11 Chapters of the Torah are Mythology (contra Rabbi Moshe Meiselman)," http://jeremy-wieder-lectures.blogspot.com/.

61 On the curriculums of American Haredi yeshivot, see: Helmreich, *The World of the Yeshiva*; Ferziger, "Between Outreach and Inreach."

62 Liebman, "The Training of American Rabbis." The author critiqued all of the seminaries for focusing on theoretical study—traditionalist or academic, and not investing sufficient time in practical rabbinic preparation.

63 Lopatin, "Revelation and the Education of Modern Orthodox Rabbis."

64 www.yu.edu.

65 www.yu.2edu.

66 For an undergraduate student's experience of YU's bifurcation, see Levine, "Regarding the Building of Bridges."

67 One veteran Bible professor described it as a healthy dialectic. See Bernstein, "Where Is Our Mission? Where Is Our Raison d'Être?"

68 Sarna, "The Future of American Orthodoxy."

69 Schwartz, "Yeshiva University's New Head Plans to Bring Modern Orthodoxy into the Future"; Berman, "Religious Zionism: Moving History Forward."

70 Waxman, *Social Change and Halakhic Evolution*, 147–166, maintains that the advent of TheTorah.com was reflective of a significant overall increase during the previous decades in interest among American Modern Orthodox Jews in academic-style Bible study.

71 Avioz et al., "Prof. Joseph Fleishman: Biography."

72 On the ways *Makor Rishon* expresses core characteristics of contemporary RZ culture, see Fischer, "Two Cultures."

73 The *Da'at Mikra* Prophets and Writings series does not include critical positions that contradict directly core Orthodox theology. See Kiel, *Le-Gamro shel ha-Mifa'al ha-Parshani Da'at Mikra*, 35. See, as well, Arnovitz, *The Koren Tanakh of the Land of Israel*, which also accepts traditional dating of the Bible, while presenting individual biblical books in their geographical and cultural contexts.

74 Levy, "The State and Directions of Orthodox Bible Scholarship," 61–62, noted the greater focus of Israeli Orthodox scholars on Bible. By contrast, he wrote, "one looks in vain for sustained Bible-related publications by North American Centrists [Orthodox Jews]."

75 Waxman, *Social Change and Halakhic Evolution*, 148–166. The diversity of Israeli Orthodox theology is discussed at length in Ross, "Radical Feminism and a Theology of Jewish Autonomy."

76 Waxman, *Social Change and Halakhic Evolution*, 148–166.

77 See Gillman, "Inside or Outside? Emancipation and the Dilemmas of Conservative Judaism."

78 Tabory and Lazerwitz, "Americans in the Israeli Reform and Conservative Denominations," 335–347.

79 See the Israeli Ministry of Education protocol at http://cms.education.gov.il. See also Shinhav, "Hora'at Tanakh be-Yisrael u-ve-Hemed bi-Pherat." I thank my student Dr. Tehilla Perl for pointing me to these materials.

80 Cooperman, "Ha-Michlalah ke-Mossad Eikhuti ve-Yihudi."

81 In Migdal Oz, the first-year students spend three mornings a week studying Talmud, and one morning each concentrating on the Bible and Jewish thought. During the afternoons, classes are offered in Jewish law, Jewish thought, and the Bible. In the evenings they can choose to concentrate on either the Bible, Talmud, or Jewish Thought. See http://www.skamigdaloz.org.

82 Along with Malka Bina, Chana Henkin, Esther Lichtenstein, and Tamar Ross, who were mentioned above, other examples of influential figures in women's midrashot include: Chanah Goldinger (Dreyfuss), MA; Dr. Bryna Jocheved Levy; Malka Piotrovsky, MA; Shani Taragin, MA; Dr. Michal Tikochinsky; Dr. Yael Ziegler; and Dr. Aviva Zorenberg.

83 Feuchtwanger, "Knowledge versus Status"; Gordin, "Ha-Terumot ha-Tarbutiyot ve-ha-Hevratiyot."

84 Ross, "My Encounters with Blu Greenberg," 35–45. See also Israel-Cohen, "Between Feminism and Orthodoxy in Israel," 51–66.

85 Lichtenstein, "Rav Lichtenstein Writes Letter."

86 Lichtenstein, "Criticism and *Kitvei Kodesh*."

87 For an example that is based on a summary of his oral remarks, see Lichtenstein, "Joseph's Tears."

88 Years later, Bin-Nun wrote a doctoral dissertation at the Hebrew University in Jerusalem.

89 BIU's Bible department has a particularly high percentage of YHE Migdal Oz alumni, including: Professors Elie Assis, Joshua Berman, Yonatan Grossman, Yoseph Opher, Jonathan Jacobs, Nili Samet, and Dr. Zvi Shimon, some of whom teach as well in Herzog, or have in the past. But graduates can be found in universities and colleges throughout Israel, such as Professor Michael Segal and Dr. Shimon Gesundheit of the Hebrew University in Jerusalem's Bible department. Berman has dedicated considerable scholarship to demonstrating the shortcomings of higher Biblical criticism and cultivating academic approaches that do not undermine traditional beliefs. See: Berman, *Inconsistencies in the Torah*; idem, *Ani Maamin: Biblical Criticism, Historical Truth, and the Thirteen Principles of Faith*.

90 www.herzog.ac.il.

91 For the full range of Herzog's academic and public programs, see www.herzog.ac.il.

92 See the 2018 schedule: www.calameo.com. The second day of the program included a special panel discussion titled "How Has YHE Contributed to My Study of the Tanakh?" in which Assis from Bar-Ilan and Cherlow were among the participants.

93 On Breuer's approach, see Eckstein, "Rabbi Mordechai Breuer and Modern Orthodox Biblical Commentary." On Bin-Nun, see: Angel, "Torat Hashem Temima"; Klein-Halevi, *Like Dreamers*, 153–154, 203–204.

94 Bick, "Preface," *Torah miEtzion*, xviii.

95 Caplan, "Heker ha-Hevrah ha-Datit be-Yisrael," 226.

96 Lichtenstein, "Foreword," *Mikra and Meaning*. On Lichtenstein's approach to Bible study, see Beasely, "A Question of Character: R. Aharon Lichtenstein and the Interpretation of Biblical Texts."

97 For the most updated bibliography of his writings, see Karoll, *Torat Hesed: Bibliography of Harav Aharon Lichtenstein zt"l*.

98 Reiner, "Rabbi Aharon Lichtenstein and Academic Talmud Study."

99 On the utilization of academic approaches to Talmud within Israeli RZ yeshivot, see Kaplan, "Back to Zechariah Frankel and Louis Jacobs?"

100 Reiner, "Rabbi Aharon Lichtenstein."

101 Sabato, *Mevakshei Panekha*, 201. For a critique of Reiner's essay, see Kaplan, "An Alternate View on Rav Aharon Lichtenstein and Academic Talmud Study."

102 On Lichtenstein's ambivalent attitude toward academic study of sacred texts, see: Horowitz, "Yahasim Murkavim"; Schwartz, "Haguto shel ha-Rav Aharon Lichtenstein," 32–33; Seidler-Feller, "Rabbi Aharon Lichtenstein on the Divide between Traditional and Academic Jewish Studies"; Zuckier, "Rav Lichtenstein on Wissenschaft in His Own (Yiddish) Words."

103 Van Elteren, "Cultural Globalization and Transnational Flows of Things American," 8.

104 Nathaniel (Nati) Helfgot, a well-regarded alumnus of YHE, is probably the North American Orthodox rabbi and educator whose approach to Bible study demonstrates the closest similarities to those of the Israelis featured here, although his engagements with Biblical criticism are more nuanced and guarded than the others. See Helfgot, "Curricula, Methodologies and Values in Orthodox Tanakh Study."

CHAPTER 7. ISRAELI RELIGIOUS LEADERSHIP

1 The chapter adapts and draws upon materials in Adam S. Ferziger, "From Rabbiner Doktor to Rabbanit Doctor: Academic Education and the Evolution of Israeli Religious Leadership," in *Emet le-Ya'akov: Facing the Truths of History: Essays in Honor of Jacob J. Schacter*, ed. Zev Eleff and Shaul Seidler-Feller (Boston: Academic Studies Press, 2023), 522–544.

2 See the school's online application form, accessed Aug. 22, 2022, www.yu.edu.

3 Sales, "A World-Famous Rabbi."

4 Schorsch, "Emancipation and the Crisis of Religious Authority."

5 Ibid., 205–217.

6 Ibid.

7 A photocopy of the 1884 annual report of the Orthodox Rabbinerseminar in Berlin appears in Gottlieb, *My Opa*, 293.

8 Schorsch, "Emancipation and the Crisis of Religious Authority," 216. It should be noted that the doctoral dissertations were closer in length to contemporary master's theses. See Enders, "A Chair System in Transition," 4.

9 Maślak, "The Religious Views of Preachers in the Kraków Progressive Synagogue (Tempel)," 41–53. On negative attitudes of Eastern European rabbinical authorities

toward German-style rabbi doctors, see, for example, Etkes, *Rabbi Israel Salanter*, 304–310.

10 Kook, *Iggerot la-Re'iyyah*, 213–216; Hoffmann and Schwartz, "Early but Opposed—Supported but Late," 281 n. 48. See Shapiro, *Between the Yeshiva World and Modern Orthodoxy*, 129–134.

11 On Herzog, see: Kaye, *The Invention of Jewish Theocracy*; Radzyner, "Between Scholar and Jurist." During the mid-1930s and 1940s, a group of talented German Orthodox rabbi doctors arrived in Israel. A few of them made a considerable impact through the educational institutions that they founded and in their roles in the Religious Kibbutz and the Poalei Agudath Israel movements, but far less so in the rabbinate. Fishman, *Judaism and Modernization on the Religious Kibbutz*, 101–157; Niederland, "From Frankfurt to Jerusalem: Horev School."

12 Saks, "Rabbi Joseph B. Soloveitchik and the Israeli Chief Rabbinate."

13 One example was Rabbi Benjamin Ze'ev (Wilhelm) Benedikt, the Viennese-born figure who served for forty-five years as the official local rabbi of Haifa's Ahuza neighborhood. See Henshke, "'Met she-ein lo Menahamim." His successor in the Ahuza rabbinate is Rabbi Prof. Daniel Hershkowitz, who studied in the Mercaz Harav yeshiva, received a PhD in mathematics from the Technion in Haifa, and became a full professor at his alma mater. After a stint in politics, he served as president of Bar-Ilan University before being appointed to a high civil service post. All along, he maintained his rabbinic position. See his biography at https://mizrachi.org. Closer to the center of the country, another exception is the Tel Aviv suburb Kiryat Ono's chief rabbi, Rasson Arousi. He is one of the most powerful figures on the national council of the Chief Rabbinate. He studied in both RZ and Haredi yeshivot and received a PhD in Jewish law from Tel Aviv University and taught academic courses at the Tel Aviv University Law School and the Talmud Department of Bar-Ilan University. See his biography at www.kiryatono .muni.il. Rabbi Dr. Chaim Burgansky is the long-serving rabbi of Hoshaya, a moderate-oriented religious settlement in the Lower Galilee region, and a lecturer in the Talmud Department of Bar-Ilan University. See his biography at https://yesod.biu.ac.il.

14 Daniel Sperber, world-renowned scholar of Talmud, classics, and religious customs at Bar-Ilan University and Israel Prize laureate, was the rabbi for many years of the Yad Tamar Synagogue in the Rehavia section of Jerusalem. See Ferziger and Sperber, *The Paths of Daniel*, 5–13.

15 Rabbi Dr. Eliyahu Zini is Haifa's third well-known rabbi doctor, but he has not served within the state rabbinate system. The son of an Algerian rabbi, he grew up in Paris and studied mathematics at the University of Paris before moving to Israel in 1972. He completed his PhD at the Technion and was a close student of Benedikt. In 1980, he was appointed rabbi of the Technion synagogue, while simultaneously teaching advanced mathematics and traditional Talmud courses there. See Ringel, "The Construction and De-construction of the Ashkenazi vs. Sephardic/Mizrahi Dichotomy."

16 The roots of this institution can be found in a number of premodern and early modern geography-based frameworks, including the traditional Ashkenazic communal rabbi, the Central European *Landesrabbiner,* the French Consistoire rabbinate, the British United Synagogue chief rabbi, and the Ottoman *ḥakham bashi.* See Friedman, "Mara de-atra—mi-manhig le-pakid," 91; Schwarzfuchs, *A Concise History of the Rabbinate,* 60–63, 72–85.

17 The term "constituency" refers here to a collective to which a certain figure seeks to provide guidance or representation. See the variety of definitions in the *Oxford English Dictionary,* vol. 3, 788.

18 See, for example: Radzyner, "On the Beginning of Rabbinical Courts' Procedural Regulations"; Shochetman, *Civil Procedure in Rabbinical Courts.*

19 Schwarzfuchs, *A Concise History of the Rabbinate,* 141.

20 Ferziger, "Religion for the Secular."

21 Winer, "In Israeli First, Woman Chosen as Sole Spiritual Leader of Orthodox Community."

22 The list of Beit Hillel members and their academic credentials was provided to me in an email from Rabbi Boaz Ordman, former CEO of Beit Hillel, dated Aug. 15, 2021. The information is corroborated by the official biographies of the members posted on the Beit Hillel website (www.beithillel.org.il), with additional information regarding the vast majority of the members made available through personal publications and links on the websites of the institutions at which they work.

23 www.tzohar.org.il. Most of those in Tzohar without academic training are older members, although there are also a few prominent individuals without degrees who engage secular learning in their teaching and writing—and even lecture regularly at universities.

24 Ibid.

25 The information was collected in the spring of 2022. The main source for the charts below are the websites of the institutions themselves. I turned directly to staff members when it seemed that data was missing. That said, it is likely that there are a few individuals who possess degrees that I missed, especially among the more conservative institutions, but these are not sufficient to undermine the fundamental distinctions seen here.

26 Schorsch, "Emancipation and the Crisis of Religious Authority," 208–213.

27 In order to tap this resource, I reached out to the heads of various training programs that have emerged since the late twentieth century. I am especially thankful to Rabbi David Fine of the Barkai Center for Practical Rabbinics and Community Development and Rabbi Dr. Yehudah Altschuler, head of Bar-Ilan University's Jesselson Institute for Advanced Torah Study, for their assistance.

28 Between the years 2015 and 2021, I archived copies of calls for rabbinical applications for positions in the following locales: Alon Shvut, Binyamina, Caesarea, Givat Shmuel, Givat Ze'ev, Har Gilo, Kfar Haroeh, Leshem, Merhav Am, Neve Aliza, Ofra, Petah Tikva, Rishon LeZion, Sde Ilan, Sde Ya'akov, Tekoa, Tel Aviv, Yokne'am, and an unidentified RZ community in the north.

29 Abramovich, "The Hesder Yeshivot as Agents of Social Change," 140–142.
30 Stern and Ben-Shalom, "Soldiers and Scholars."
31 See his discussion: Nagen, "Scholarship Needs Spirituality," 116–117.
32 See her monograph: Tikochinsky, *Teach Me Thy Laws.*
33 Gradstein, "Halakhic Power Couple."
34 See her legal study: Levmore, *Min'i Einayikh mi-Dim'ah.*
35 On non-Orthodox woman rabbis and religious leaders in Israel, see Marx, "A Female Rabbi."
36 Yeshivat Drisha for women in Gush Etzion is pioneering this trend.
37 This was not a controlled study and may be deemed strong anecdotal evidence. The responses are stored on my computer hard drive and on a cloud server. I received sixteen responses to the questionnaire, twelve from men and four from women. Twelve of the respondents (nine men and three women) were Beit Hillel members. The other four were personal contacts and people who were identified through "snowball" methods of recommendation from one of the prior respondents. One male respondent was sixty-five years old and one female was sixty. The youngest respondent was thirty-six and one other was thirty-nine. The core twelve were between forty-three and fifty-four. Half of the respondents were born in Israel, six were born in the United States, one in the United Kingdom, and one in Australia.
38 Kampeas, "In a First, Israeli Government to Pay Orthodox Women to Advise on Jewish Law."
39 For a parallel argument regarding woman rabbis in the United States, see Nadell, *Women Who Would be Rabbis,* 170–214.
40 Zimmerman, *A Lifetime Companion to the Laws of Jewish Family Life.*
41 See www.yoatzot.org for the general public and www.jewishwomenshealth.org for healthcare providers.

CHAPTER 8. SYNAGOGUE AND COMBAT ZONE

1 Nadell, *Women Who Would Be Rabbis.* This chapter draws upon materials that appeared in Adam S. Ferziger, "Sanctuaries and Battlefields: Two Worlds of Judaism and Two Orthodox Feminisms," *Journal of Jewish Studies* 71, no. 2 (Autumn 2020): 397–422 (with permission of the licenser through PLSclear).
2 Irshai and Zion-Waldoks, "Modern-Orthodox Feminism in Israel between Nomos and Narrative."
3 Uzan, "From Social Norm to Legal Claim." See also Maryles Sztokman, *Orthodox Feminist Movements in Israel and the United States.*
4 Ash, "Observant Feminism across Borders."
5 Israel-Cohen, *Between Feminism and Orthodox Judaism,* 49–68. As noted in the introduction, two immigrants from the UK, Dr. Alice Shalvi and Rabbi Professor Daniel Sperber, also had profound impacts on the development of Israeli Orthodox feminism in Israel at different stages.
6 Ferziger, "Female Clergy in Male Space."

7 The ruling is available at www.rabbis.org.

8 Levinstein, *Agenda Z'vait.*

9 Blu Greenberg's *On Women and Judaism* was the first book-length attempt to articulate a forthright Orthodox feminist program.

10 Gurock, "Orthodox Judaism in the United States."

11 Linzer, "Ani li'Dodi vi'Dodi Li," 4–7; Koren, "The Bride's Voice."

12 The main opinions were summarized and analyzed by Frimer and Frimer, "Women's Prayer Services."

13 Sperber, "Congregational Dignity and Human Dignity." For an opposing view, see Frimer and Frimer, "Women, Keri"at ha-Torah, and Aliyyot." Additional sources prohibiting partnership services can be found at www.torahmusings.com.

14 Broyde and Brody, "Orthodox Women Rabbis?"; Greenberg, "Will There Be Orthodox Women Rabbis?"; Israel-Cohen, *Between Feminism and Orthodox Judaism*, 69–78; Sperber, *Rabba, Maharat, Rabbanit, Rebbetzin.*

15 http://www.rabbis.org/pdfs/Responses-of-OU-Rabbinic-Panel.pdf (henceforth cited as "OU Ruling"), 16.

16 Ferziger, "Feminism and Heresy."

17 For a range of efforts by Orthodox thinkers and scholars to define the concept of *mesorah*, see the two symposia found at www.ou.org and www.torahmusings.com.

18 "OU Ruling," 12–13.

19 Rabbi Ethan Tucker, president and *rosh yeshiva* of the egalitarian Yeshivat Hadar (based in New York with an Israel branch as well) and a highly knowledgeable adjudicator of Jewish law, received Orthodox ordination. While Hadar has many faculty and participants in its programs who identify as Orthodox, it does not formally identify with any of the major denominations and would more aptly be described as "postdenominational." See Kaunfer, *Empowered Judaism*, 129–143. The membership of the Hakhel congregation in the Baka section of Jerusalem self-identifies as Orthodox and is fully egalitarian. See Furstenberg and Shoham, "Bein 'Kehillah Meruzah' le 'Kehillah Mutredet.'"

20 Breuer, "Appointment and Succession among Yeshiva Deans," 11–16; Katz, *Tradition and Crisis*, 72–75, 141–145; Rosensweig, "The Emergence of the Professional Rabbi in Ashkenazic Jewry," 22–30; Teller, "Rabbinate."

21 Eleff, "From Teacher to Scholar to Pastor"; Friedman, "The Changing Role of the Community Rabbinate."

22 Ferziger, "Sanctuary for the Specialist."

23 Ferziger, "Female Clergy in Male Space."

24 Don-Yehiya, "Changes and Developments in Israeli Civil Religion," 189–196; Fischer, "Fundamentalist or Romantic Nationalist."

25 Fischer, "Radical Religious Zionism."

26 On Bnei-David Eli and the emergence of the Israeli Religious Zionist pre-military academies, see: Cohen, "Mitzvah be-Madim"; Lebel, "Settling the Military"; idem, "The 'Immunized Integration' of Religious-Zionists within Israeli Society"; Rosman-Stollman, *For God and Country*, 104–122.

27 https://mechinot.org.il.
28 Hadar, "The Man Behind the Controversy"; Cohen, "Mitzvah be-Madim."
29 Cohen, "Mitzvah be-Madim"; Magid, "Officers and Gentlemen?"
30 Mechinat Eli's religious approach builds upon broader Israeli notions of the connection between masculinity and military service; see Sasson-Levy, "Research on Gender and the Military in Israel."
31 Feldman, "'Point Men,'" 336–337.
32 *Serugim*, "Okef Tikshoret."
33 Levinstein, *Agenda Z'vait*.
34 www.youtube.com/watch?v=EOsQDlM8pcM.
35 www.youtube.com/watch?v=4BRdmOrzRMQ; www.youtube.com/watch?v=KUCArxDYG4o.
36 www.youtube.com/watch?v=eMrT2OvCgv4.
37 For studies published in English that address key fault lines in debates over gender and the IDF, see, for example: Harel, "Women in the Military in Israel," 1–13; Sasson-Levy, "Gender Segregation or Women's Exclusion?"; Lomsky-Feder and Sasson-Levy, *Women Soldiers and Citizenship in Israel*; Rosman-Stollman, "The Pink Tank in the Room."
38 IDF, "Mi-Nashim le-Migdar—ha-Basis ha-Tefisati."
39 Ibid.
40 Levinstein, *Agenda Z'vait*, 15.
41 Gittleman, "Female Service in the IDF."
42 Ibid.
43 Rosman-Stollman, "(Not) Becoming the Norm."
44 Avgar, "Netunim al Giyus Banot le-ZaHa"L"; "Record Number of Female Religious Soldiers," *Israel National News*, www.israelnationalnews.com. For a survey from 2024 of RZ attitudes toward serving in the IDF that was commissioned by Alumah, the organization dedicated to supporting and encouraging such service, see "Memza'ei Seker Emdot be-Noge'a le-ZaHa"L."
45 Rosman-Stollman, "Military Service as Bargaining," 1.
46 Avgar, "Netunim al Giyus Banot le-ZaHa"L."
47 See, for example: "Mechinat Tzahali Makes History with the First Halakhic Guidebook for Religious Women in the IDF," *Joint Council of Mechinot—News and Updates*, https://mechinot.org.il; Balint, "Women's Pre-army Program Reflects the Religious Debate in Israel." Full disclosure: one of my daughters studied at such an institution.
48 https://ots.org.il; Rosman-Stollman, *For God and for Country*, 123–40; idem, "Military Service as Bargaining," 75–92.
49 https://ots.org.il/.
50 Rosman-Stollman, "(Not) Becoming the Norm."
51 https://kerendanielle.org.
52 Cohen, "Politics, Alienation, and the Consolidation of Group Identity."
53 Rosman-Stollman, "Military Service as Bargaining," 18.

54 Horowitz, *Milhemet Tarbut*. The third chapter focuses on feminism and is a pre cursor to the polemical approach adopted by Levinstein.

55 Engelberg, "Religious Zionist Singles."

56 Katriel, "Review: Orna Sasson-Levy, *Gavriyut ve-Nashiyut ba-Zava ha-Yisraeli*," 198.

57 For a classic collection on the relationship between Judaism and Israeli civil life, see Deshen et al., *Israeli Judaism*.

58 Ross, "Radical Feminism and a Theology of Jewish Autonomy," 400.

59 There are, of course, North American–based exceptions that exhibit a more fluid continuum between privatized and public space. For one bold example, see Stolzenberg and Myers, *American Shtetl*.

60 Cemeteries are certainly Jewish spaces and play significant symbolic roles in defining the boundaries of Jewish group identity. Yet even for the most devout, they are only occasional venues for expressions of lived religion. The synagogue, by contrast, has evolved in the Western world into the focal Jewish collective space.

61 Wertheimer, *The American Synagogue*. To be sure, in the twentieth century the American synagogue expanded its provisions far beyond the ritual realm, and other parallel institutions such as Jewish Community Centers (JCCs) proffered parallel or alternative particularistic Jewish environments. Furthermore, for a growing number of twenty-first-century American Jews, synagogue affiliation is no longer their main Jewish portal of connection. All the same, the synagogue remains the most pristine and visible symbol of collective Judaism—with the 2018 Pittsburgh massacre, the 2019 shooting outside San Diego, and the multiple 2024 public protests offering especially strong evidence to this effect. See: Kaufman, *A Shul with a Pool*; Rebhun, *Jews and the American Religious Landscape*, 14–15.

62 Heilman, *Synagogue Life*.

63 Ferziger, "Between Catholic Israel and the K"rov Yisrael"; Marx, "Participation of Non-Jewish Family Members in BarBat-Mitzvah Ceremonies."

64 Debates regarding the status of LGBTQ Jews in Orthodox synagogues and schools have also gained traction. See Slomowitz, *Homosexuality, Transsexuality, Psychoanalysis, and Traditional Judaism*.

65 Davidman, "Accommodation and Resistance to Modernity."

66 Dolsten, "Trailblazing Hasidic Woman Elected as Brooklyn Judge."

67 Some segments of Haredi society have also demonstrated greater willingness to integrate women into public teaching roles for mixed audiences. However, this is generally in the context of special efforts to engage nonobservant audiences. See Ferziger, "Beyond Bais Yaakov."

68 Berrin, "After #MeToo."

69 Ben-Porat, *Between State and Synagogue*, 1–26; Yadgar, *Sovereign Jews*, 187–210.

70 Pink, "Founding Rabbi Retires from Yeshiva That Trains Female Religious Judges."

71 https://yashrut.org.

72 Ross, "My Encounters with Blu Greenberg." On Ross's theology, see the essays collected in Irshai and Schwartz, *A New Spirit in the Palace of Torah*.

73 Fuchs, "Innovative Ordinariness and Ritual Change in a Jerusalem Minyan." For a document that presents the worldview of this strand of Israeli feminism, see Lubitz, *Feminism Dati ke-Tikkun Olam.*

74 Rosenberg, "The World of Women's Torah Learning."

75 See links to biographies: www.nishmat.net.

76 www.yoatzot.org.

77 See links to biographies of Yeshivat Maharat alumni, current students, and staff: www.yeshivatmaharat.org.

78 Rabba Dr Anat Sharbat, formerly of the Hebrew Institute of Riverdale, for example, is an Israeli woman who completed her PhD in Talmud at Bar-Ilan University before setting out on rabbinical studies at Maharat. See www.artkibbutz.org. In the summer of 2019, she returned to Israel.

79 Van Elteren, "Cultural Globalization and Transnational Flows of Things American," 8.

80 www.noar.mod.gov.il.

81 See, for example: www.merkazherzog.org.il; https://mechinot.org.il.

82 For an example of a like-minded organization, see http://libayehudit.org.

83 *Times of Israel*, "Staff Sgt. Rose Lubin, 21."

84 Amsalem, "Ha-Lohamot Mokhihot she-be-foal."

85 See, for example, Walker, "Southern Baptists, Gender Ideology, and Female Combatants."

CHAPTER 9. "GLOCAL" RELIGIOUS PROVIDERS

1 Rosen-Zvi, "Who Is Jewish." This chapter further develops materials that appeared in Einat Libel-Hass and Adam S. Ferziger, "A Synagogue Center Grows in Tel Aviv: On Glocalization, Consumerism and Religion," *Modern Judaism* 42, no. 3 (Oct. 2022): 273–304.

2 Tabory, *The Reform Movement in Israel.*

3 Castells, *The Internet Galaxy*, 125–129.

4 On the Leo Baeck School and the Haifa Reform community, see Tabory, "Reform and Conservative Judaism in Israel," 42. See also Shaked, *From Vision to Reality.*

5 Tabory, "The Influence of Liberal Judaism on Israeli Religious Life."

6 For its institutional history, see www.beit-daniel.org.il.

7 Ilan, "The First Reform Synagogue Will Be Inaugurated."

8 Fishkoff, "Welcome to Beit Daniel."

9 Interview with Rabbi Meir Azari, May 16, 2011.

10 Bat Adam, "Both of Them Together and Each One Separately."

11 This phrase is adopted from Dvori, "A House of Judaism, a Place of Culture."

12 Kaufman, *Shul with a Pool*, xvii.

13 Scult, *The Radical American Judaism of Mordecai M. Kaplan*, 88–109.

14 Dash Moore, "A Synagogue Center Grows in Brooklyn."

15 Karp, "Overview: The Synagogue in America—A Historical Typology."

16 Orknad, "Transcending Walls in Tel Aviv."

17 Beit Daniel, "Summary of the First Year of Activity."

18 Beit Daniel, "A New Idea for Progressive Judaism in Israel."

19 *Minutes of the Marketing Committee of Beit Daniel and Ruth Daniel Residence* (Nov. 18, 2007). See also Beit Daniel newsletters, 2006–2019; booklets of seasonal activities in Beit Daniel, 2006–2013. On women as consumers of Beit Daniel's services, see Libel-Hass, "Jewish Women in Reform Settings in Israel."

20 Paz-Fuchs et al., *The Privatization of Israel.*

21 Fishkoff, *The Rebbe's Army.*

22 Interview with Rabbi Meir Azari, May 16, 2011.

23 Beit Daniel, "New Programs: Fast Forward."

24 Landau, *Beit Daniel—Cultural, Community, Education Programs*, 1–2. The Beit Daniel conversion program is analyzed in Libel-Hass and Ben-Lulu, "Are You Our Sisters?"

25 Beit Daniel, *Beit Daniel and Progressive Judaism in Tel Aviv*, 1.

26 Heiges, *Fast Facts about Beit Daniel*, 1.

27 Nesher, *Proposal to the Religious Pluralism Subcommittee of the United Jewish Communities of MetroWest—New Jersey.*

28 Ferziger, "Sanctuary for the Specialist."

29 Ferziger, "From Lubavitch to Lakewood."

30 https://reformjudaism.org.

31 Bar mitzvah family interview, Oct. 13, 2010; the parents asked not to be identified.

32 Rotem, "User-Friendly Judaism."

33 On social relationships in the internet era and creating religious congregations, see Castells, *The Rise of the Network Society*, 3; idem, *The Internet Galaxy*, 125–129.

34 Castells, *The Rise of the Network Society.*

35 Ibid.

36 Meyer, *Response to Modernity*, 369–373.

37 Ferziger, "The Lookstein Legacy"; Karp, *Jewish Continuity in America*, 61–105.

38 Carlin and Mendlovitz, "The American Rabbi," 191.

39 Interview with Rabbi Meir Azari, May 16, 2011.

40 Weber, "The Three Types of Legitimate Rule."

41 Beit Daniel, Rituals Committee protocol, Oct. 10, 1999. The protocol is in the archive of Beit Daniel and a copy is stored in the research files of Dr. Einat Libel-Hass.

42 Beit Daniel, congregant Interview, July 14, 2010; the congregant asked not to be identified.

43 Beit Daniel, Rituals Committee, May 12, 2010.

44 Beit Daniel, congregant interview, July 14, 2010; the congregant asked not to be identified.

45 Beit Daniel, informal discussion with a congregant, May 14, 2010; the congregant asked not to be identified.

46 Ferziger, *The Emergence of the Community Kollel.*

47 www.wbtla.org.
48 Interview with Rabbi Meir Azari, Oct. 26, 2010.
49 *Haaretz*, "The Movement for Progressive Judaism."
50 Halle, "Moving toward Inner-city Reform in Jaffa."
51 www.beitshmuel.co.il.
52 www.beit-daniel.org.il.
53 Ibid.
54 Beit Daniel, *"Staff Discussion 2008—Two who are One."*
55 www.beit-daniel.org.il. On Kehillat Halev, see Ben-Lulu, "Intersectionality of Traditional Jewish Ritual and Queer Pride in a Reform Congregation in Israel."
56 Meirovitch, *The Shaping of Masorti Judaism in Israel.*
57 Yadgar, *Secularism and Religion in Jewish-Israeli Politics.*
58 Sklare, *Conservative Judaism.*
59 Dorff, *Modern Conservative Judaism.*
60 Tabory, "The Israel Conservative and Reform Movements."
61 Tiferet Shalom, "How It All Started?"
62 Interview with David Lazar, Jan. 1, 2009; Tiferet Shalom, *Rabbi Search Committee.*
63 Tiferet Shalom, *Minutes of Executive Board Meetings* (Nov. 3, 1999; June 5, 2002); Tiferet Shalom, *Rabbi Search Committee—a Meeting Summary of an Interview with Rabbi David Lazar* (May 29, 2002).
64 www.kby.org.
65 Klein-Halevi, "Jewish, Observant, and Illegal in Israel."
66 Tiferet Shalom, *Rabbi Search Committee* (May 29, 2002); Tiferet Shalom, *Minutes of Executive Board Meeting* (Oct. 3, 2002).
67 Liebowitz Kalaora, *Brief of an Advertising Campaign for Tiferet Shalom Congregation*; Tiferet Shalom, *Minutes of Executive Board Meeting* (Sept. 11, 2008).
68 Tiferet Shalom, *Minutes of Executive Board Meeting* (Oct. 10, 2004; Nov. 14, 2004; Feb. 13, 2005).
69 Tiferet Shalom, *Minutes of Executive Board Meeting* (Nov. 14, 2004); interview with one of the congregation's founders (Apr. 19, 2004), who asked not to be identified. Her identity is in the files of Einat Libel-Hass; interview with David Lazar, Jan. 1, 2009.
70 Becker, *Congregations in Conflict*, 98–99.
71 Liphshiz, "Rabbi David Lazar, Too Brash for Stockholm?"
72 www.facebook.com.
73 JTA, "Reform and Conservative Synagogues Merge in New Jersey."
74 Wertheimer, *All Quiet on the Religious Front.*
75 Cohen and Eisen, *The Jew Within.*
76 Werczberger, *Jews in the Age of Authenticity.*
77 Tabory, "The Influence of Liberal Judaism on Israeli Religious Life," 183.
78 Sales, "Why You Won't Find Starbucks in Israel."
79 Ram, "Glocommodification," 15.
80 For example, see Yadgar, "A Post-secular Look at Tradition."

81 Rosner and Fuchs, *#YahadutYisraelit.*

82 Friedman, "The Changing Role of the Community Rabbinate."

83 Stern, "The Identity Crisis of the State of Israel," 272.

84 Maltz, "Number of Israelis Marrying outside Rabbinate Rising."

85 Ferziger, "Religion for the Secular."

86 https://chuppot.org.il; Fischer, "Who Is Qualified to Officiate a Halakhic Marriage?"

87 Sheleg, "Tefillat Shabbat Hilonit le-Mehadrin."

88 Yadgar, *Secularism and Religion.*

89 Weissbrod, "Shas: An Ethnic Religious Party."

90 Katz, *The Pale God,* 169–178; Yadgar, *Secularism and Religion.*

91 Cohen and Eisen, *The Jew Within,* 13–42; Roof, *Spiritual Marketplace.*

92 Wuthnow, *After Heaven.*

93 *Religion Watch,* "Praying and Networking Give Religious Right Second Wind?"

94 Caplan, "Israeli Haredi Society and the Repentance Movement"; Sharabi, "'Boundary Work' in a Religious Revival Movement."

95 Sarna, *American Judaism,* xvi, 275–276.

CHAPTER 10. FROM ANOMALY TO BESTSELLER

1 Hughes, "Jonathan Sacks: An Intellectual Portrait," 1–20; Rynhold et al., *Radical Responsibility.*

2 Sacks, *The Great Partnership.*

3 Ehrman, "The Tragedy of Rabbi Sacks." For Sacks's detailed presentation of his own personal development, see Tirosh-Samuelson, "Interview with Jonathan Sacks."

4 Ibid.

5 Email communication from Davina Wanderer-Kriel (Aug. 9, 2023).

6 www.rabbisacks.org; https://chabad.org; https://sigvsiachblog.wordpress.com. There is also a WhatsApp group called "Articles by Sacks on the Torah portion."

7 https://korenpub.co.il.

8 Email communication from Mathew Miller (July 21, 2022).

9 Ganzel, "Explicit and Implicit Polemic in Rabbi Samson Raphael Hirsch's Bible Commentary."

10 Pachter, "Davek be-Amo." See also his pamphlet, Pachter, *Zionut Datit Metunah—Manifest,* which outlines his vision for the ideological foundations for moderate RZ.

11 Cohen, "Ha-Podcast she-yakir le-Yisraelim et Ha-Rav Sacks."

12 Darman, "Ez Hayyim she-Hitagalah be-Yisrael Me'uhar Midai."

13 Pfeffer, "Or la-Yehudim: Ha-Rav Sacks ve-ha-Yahadut ha-Toranit."

14 Klein, "Ha-Rav Sacks Kavash et ha-Olam akh hitkashe lifnot le-Yisraelim be-Sefatam." For what is likely the best-known example of his verbal virtuosity, see Sacks, "How We Can Face the Future without Fear, Together," a Ted Talk that has been viewed over two million times. Note that in his public conversation with Israeli thinker Micah Goodman at the book launch of the translation of *The Great*

Partnership that took place on Nov. 13, 2013, Sacks spoke primarily in fluent, if not fluid Hebrew: https://www.youtube.com/watch?v=B16x3WLjxos.

15 Clymer, "Mishnat ha-Rav Sacks."

16 https://yonatansacks.jlm.org.il.

17 http://public.herzog.ac.il.

18 Beit-Hallahmi, "Back to the Fold: The Return to Judaism."

19 https://meirtv.com.

20 https://mechinot.org.il.

21 *Jerusalem Post*, "Herzog, Hundreds of Leaders Reflect on Legacy of Rabbi Lord Jonathan Sacks."

22 The conference included a talk (via livestream) by Harvard social scientist Robert Putnam, author of the famed 1995 essay "Bowling Alone." His oral presentation ended with very personal reflections on his relationship with Sacks: https://www .youtube.com/watch?v=c6tWeyKmg5o. In 2025, Putnam was the recipient of the the inaugural Jonathan Sacks Prize for Outstanding Achievement as a Public Intellectual, established by the Jonathan Sacks Institute at Bar-Ilan University. Full disclosure: I participated in a panel that took place after Putnam's conference talk and was a member of the prize committee.

23 Eglash, "Bar-Ilan University Moves to Establish Center."

24 Krauss, "Retreat Meyuhad be-Shem ha-Rav."

25 Schneider and Eliraz, "Miriam Peretz."

26 Glanz, "Me'orer Hashra'ah."

27 *Exodus* 12:35–36.

28 Sacks, *Ceremony and Celebration*, 167–258.

29 Ibid.

30 https://www.rabbisacks.org.

31 The main translator is Israeli journalist and poet Tsur Ehrlich; see https://library .osu.edu/.

32 Sharon, "Rabbi Sacks in Israel."

33 Miller correspondence.

34 www.rabbisacks.org.

35 Ibid.

36 Ibid.

37 See, for example: Davis, "The Reception of the Shulhan 'Arukh"; Gries, *Sifrut ha-Hanhagot*.

38 On numerous occasions, Sacks described his life-changing trip to the United States as a young Cambridge graduate at the age of twenty in 1968. There he had private meetings with both Soloveitchik and Schneerson. Sacks was later quoted as saying that "Rabbi Soloveitchik had challenged me to think. Rabbi Schneerson had challenged me to lead." See Goldman, "Jonathan Sacks, the U.K.'s Inclusive Former Chief Rabbi, Dies at 72."

39 Sacks, "The Legacy of the Lubavitcher Rebbe."

40 A search of the Sacks Trust electronic archive (www.rabbisacks.org) produces sixty-five distinct sources in which Sacks refers to Frankl by name.

41 For two views of Frankl, see: Krasovska and Mayer, *A Psychobiography of Viktor E. Frankl*; Langer, *Versions of Survival*.

42 For an example of his prior thick academic style, see Sacks, "Rabbi J.B. Soloveitchik's Early Epistemology."

43 Freud-Kandel, Ferziger, and Bayme, *Yitz Greenberg and Modern Orthodoxy*.

44 Jotkowitz, "The Radical Theology of Rabbi Jonathan Sacks"; Shapiro, "Of Books and Bans."

45 Hellinger, "Political Theology in the Thought of the 'Merkaz Ha-Rav' Yeshiva."

46 Don-Yehiya, "Messianism and Politics."

47 Mashiach, "Changes in the Understanding of Work in Religious Zionist Thought."

48 Abramovich, "The Hesder Yeshivot as Agents of Social Change."

49 Abramovich, "A Critic from Within: Rav Shagar and the Renewal of Religious Zionism"; Feldmann Kaye, *Jewish Theology for a Postmodern Age*; Sachs-Shmueli, "Shagar's Mystical Space."

50 Perez, "Rabbi Lord Jonathan Sacks' Political Thought and the State of Israel."

51 Sacks, *Morality*.

52 Tirosh-Samuelson, "Rabbi Jonathan Sacks."

53 Ibid., 5–6; Hughes, "Jonathan Sacks: An Intellectual Portrait," 2.

54 Sacks, *Tradition in an Untraditional Age*; idem, *One People*.

55 Comparing Lichtenstein and Rabinovitch, Sacks remarked, "He and the late Rabbi Aharon Lichtenstein zt"l were the *Gedolei ha-Dor*, the leaders and role models of their generation. They were very different, one scientific, the other artistic, one direct, the other oblique, one bold, the other cautious, but they were giants, intellectually, morally and spiritually. Happy the generation that is blessed by people like these." See Sacks, "My Teacher: In Memoriam."

56 Sacks had a strong personal relationship with Lamm during the course of over forty years. Three decades of correspondences between them are on file in the YU Archives. I thank head archivist Shulamith Berger for facilitating my review of these materials. For one example of the affinity of their ideas, see Sacks, "Torah Umadda: The Unwritten Chapter."

57 Sacks, "Leadership and Crisis."

58 Schapiro, "The Sabbath and the Printed Page."

59 Jackson, *Those Who Write for Immortality*, xi.

60 Hirsch, *Neunzehn Briefe über Judentum*; idem, *The Nineteen Letters*.

61 Liberles, *Religious Conflict in a Social Context*.

62 Hirsch, *The Hirsch Chumash*; idem, *Hamishah Humshei Torah*.

63 Hirsch, *Horeb*.

64 Sacks, "Without Walls."

65 Ibid.

66 Ibid.

67 Beinart, "Rabbi Jonathan Sacks Has Abdicated."

CHAPTER 11. THE DIGITAL SPHERE

1 Kirsch, "The Superbowl of Jewish Learning." This chapter draws on portions from Adam S. Ferziger, "'A Daf of Our Own': Gender, Talmud Study, and Orthodox Judaism in Digital Space," *Journal of Religion* 104, no. 4 (Fall 2024), 421–451.

2 Gradstein, "Women Celebrate Siyum HaShas in Jerusalem."

3 For a January 2021 interview with Farber that provides considerable biographical details, see https://jchatting.blogspot.com.

4 For a personal reflection of a participant, see Lockshin Bob, "The Next Women's Siyum ha-Shas." Links to video recordings of the entire event are available at https://hadran.org.il.

5 The richest academic analysis of the daf yomi phenomenon is the Hebrew article, Berlin, "Haroshet ha-Talmud."

6 Bacon, *The Politics of Tradition*. On Shapira, see 116 fn. 26.

7 Frankel, *Rabi Meir mi-Lublin*, 30.

8 Berlin, "Haroshet ha-Talmud," 122.

9 Heilman, "The Ninth Siyum Ha-Shas," 321.

10 Eleff, "The Balabatish Daf Yomi Revolution."

11 See the promotional video for the 2020 siyum: https://www.youtube.com/watch?v=Z1XvtBQW45s&t=106s.

12 Heilman, "The Ninth Siyum Shas," 316–318.

13 Berger, Jacobson, and Waxman, *Flipping Out*.

14 Stolow, *Orthodox by Design*.

15 Briggs, "Brooklyn's Talmud by Telephone."

16 Gurock, *The Men and Women of Yeshiva*, 8–43.

17 Horowitz, *Kosher USA*, 59–100.

18 www.ou.org.

19 Besser, "The People Come First."

20 https://outorah.org.

21 https://alldaf.org.

22 Ibid.

23 Ibid.

24 Finkelman, "Haredi Isolation in Changing Environments."

25 Bachrach, "10 Questions for . . . Moshe Schwed."

26 Benor, "Mensch, Bentsh, and Balagan."

27 Levine, "40,000 Participate in Daf Yomi via OU App."

28 https://alldaf.org.

29 Stefansky, "The Artscroll Interview with R' Eli Stefansky," at 23:50. See also Friedman, "The Full Story behind the 8 Minute Daf."

30 https://alldaf.org.

31 ALL DAF, "Siyum on Maseches Eruvin," https://alldaf.org.

32 Eller, "Women of the Daf."

33 Friedman, "The Family-Community Model in Haredi Society," 166–177; Shai, "Working Women/Cloistered Men."

34 In 2015 one of the leading rabbis at YU and the original instructor of the Talmud class at its Stern College for Women expressed public ambivalence about the ongoing propriety of such study. See Willig, "Trampled Laws."

35 See the video posted to YouTube of the August 2012 celebration that took place in Alon Shevut: www.youtube.com/watch?v=QkOUR2fMLPI.

36 Kurshan, *If All the Seas Were Ink*.

37 https://ilanakurshan.com.

38 www.jacquelinenicholls.com.

39 Sokol, "The Female Talmudists."

40 https://hadran.org.il.

41 Ibid.

42 www.facebook.com.

43 www.youtube.com/watch?v=RFOE3orLyh8.

44 Okun and Nimrod describe the internet as a "third space of digital religion that is hybrid in any possible sense and reinforces a lively networked religion." See "Online Ultra-Orthodox Religious Communities as a Third Space," 2825.

45 For a summary, study guide, and illustrations, see https://hadran.org.il.

46 Brooke, "Interview with Michelle Cohen Farber."

47 Written communication from Michelle Cohen Farber, Nov. 9, 2021.

48 https://hadran.org.il.

49 The Hebrew term *rabbanit* has long referred to the wife of a rabbi. However, in recent years it has also been adopted as a more formal title that connotes a female Torah scholar. Howard, "Call Her Rabbanit."

50 Megilah 23a.

51 https://hadran.org.il. On women's Torah chanting, see Sperber, "Congregational Dignity and Human Dignity."

52 www.youtube.com/watch?v=jFw6xXiHp2U.

53 Markowitz, "Rabbanit Michelle Cohen Farber Teaches the Daf at Rinat"; https://torahinmotion.org.

54 https://hadran.org.il.

55 The full citations appear at https://hadran.org.il. Personal names were omitted here out of respect for privacy.

56 Farber communication.

57 See, for example: Anzovin, "An Atheist Learns Daf Yomi"; Heilman, "With Poetry and Scholarship"; HUC-JIR, "Dr. Alyssa Gray and Rabbi Benjamin David Lead Daf Yomi Siyyum at HUC-JIR/New York."

58 Fink, "The Impact of Technology on the Study of Talmud."

59 Farber communication.

60 An FB page titled "Jewish Women Daf Yomi about Anything" is open exclusively to women and is moderated by a Reform rabbi. See www.facebook.com.

61 There is a pluralistic Hebrew-language daf yomi class that is broadcast on the FB page of the virtual *Kehillat Anan Kevodekha*, www.facebook.com.

62 For an alternative Orthodox model, see Ferziger, "Outside the Shul."

63 Troy and Wasserman, "The Talmud for Today's World."

64 www.digitalreligion.tamu.edu.

65 *Pandemic Religion: A Digital Archive*, https://pandemicreligion.org.

66 See, for example, the collection of articles in the special issue "Religion and the Internet."

67 Lövheim and Campbell, "Considering Critical Methods," 5–14.

68 Schwed, "All Daf One Year Highlight Reel."

69 The only exceptions to the standard ALL DAF configuration were the siyum events, which were livestream broadcast on the site.

70 Riches, "Review: Heidi Campbell, *Digital Creatives and the Rethinking of Religious Authority*," 352.

71 Stewart, "Text and Response in the Relationship between Online and Offline Religion," 1205.

72 Ibid.

73 Ibid.

74 Campbell, *Digital Creatives*, 121.

75 Ibid., 160.

76 Riches, "Review: Heidi Campbell," 351–352.

77 Dash Moore, "A Synagogue Center Grows in Brooklyn."

78 Stewart, "Text and Response," 1207.

79 Wimpfheimer, *The Talmud*, 232; Heilman, "The Ninth Siyum ha-Shas," 315.

80 Ibid.

81 There are a few RZ-oriented synagogues in Jerusalem that are fully egalitarian, but to date no Orthodox authority has sanctioned these services.

82 Ferziger, "Female Clergy in Male Space."

83 For a comparable phenomenon, see Morgan-Ellis, "'Like Pieces in a Puzzle': Online Sacred Harp Singing during the COVID-19 Pandemic."

84 Lieber, "A Virtual Veibershul," 632. See also Baumel-Schwartz, "Frum Surfing"; idem, "Orthodox Jewish Women as a Bridge between Israel and the Diaspora."

85 Raucher, "Yoatzot Halacha: Ruling the Internet, One Question at a Time," 66.

86 Ibid., 63. Raucher, *Conceiving Agency*, has also described the nuanced ways Haredi women assert authority in the realm of birth, intimate relations, and Jewish law.

CHAPTER 12. ZION AND BACK

1 The primary sources utilized below include Torah MiTzion (henceforth TMZ) archives, organizational literature, websites; interviews and correspondence with TMZ officials, emissaries, supporters, and students; news articles and essays written about TMZ; and personal site visits to ten North American community kol-

lels, two in Australia and one in South Africa. All interview transcripts and tapes are stored at Bar-Ilan University, Faculty of Jewish Studies, Room 37, Ramat-Gan, Israel 52900. This chapter updates and adapts aspects of Adam S. Ferziger, "Holy Land in Exile: The Torah MiTzion Movement—Toward a New Paradigm for Religious Zionism," in *Religious Zionism: Future Directions*, ed. Chaim I. Waxman (New York: Yeshiva University Press, 2008), 373–414.

2 Conversation with Robert L. Stark, Beachwood, Ohio, Sept. 6, 2003; www .torahmitzion.org.

3 Initially only couples were sent, but from 1997 single students were also integrated. See: "Site Visit by David Roth and Ze'ev Schwartz to Cleveland, November 2001," TMZ Cleveland File, TMZ Jerusalem Office, 54 King George St., Jerusalem 91710, entrance floor; interview with Rabbi Binyamin Blau, former *rosh kollel* (kollel head) of CTTK and principal of Fuchs-Mizrachi High School, Cleveland Heights, Ohio, Sept. 8, 2003.

4 Blau interview; interview with Vicky Epstein Frolich, CTTK administrator, Cleveland Heights, Ohio, Sept. 8, 2003.

5 https://torahmitzion.org.

6 Moshe Green, an American philanthropist who was active in RZ circles, gave the initial support for the TMZ organization and served as chairman until his death in 1999.

7 https://torahmitzion.org.

8 https://torahmitzion.org.

9 https://torahmitzion.org.

10 TMZ arose as part of a broader phenomenon: the emergence since the 1970s— both within the MO and Haredi sectors—of the "community kollel" as a new framework for Jewish education. See: Ferziger, *The Emergence of the Community Kollel*; idem, *Centered on Study: Typologies of the American Community Kollel*.

11 Don-Yehiya, "*Galut* in Zionist Ideology and in Israeli Society."

12 Don-Yehiya, "The Negation of the *Galut* in Religious Zionism," 129–130.

13 Don-Yehiya, "*Galut* in Zionist Ideology," 229.

14 Ibid., 253.

15 Nimni, "From *Galut* to T'futsoth," 122.

16 Don-Yehiya, "Negation," 129–130; "Shelilat ha-Galut," 229–232.

17 Quotation from his famed sermon delivered at the Merkaz ha-Rav yeshiva in Jerusalem on the Israel Independence Day that immediately preceded the War of 1967; see Kook, *Le-Netivot Yisrael* vol. 2 (cited in Don-Yehiya, "Negation," 142). See also Schwartz, *Erez ha-Mamashut ve-ha-Dimayon*, 101–127.

18 Kook, *Le-Netivot Yisrael* 1, 68 (cited in Don-Yehiya, "Negation," 143).

19 Don-Yehiya, "Negation," 145.

20 Shapiro, "The Mission of Religious Zionism," 117.

21 Kopelowitz, "Between *Mifgash* and *Shlichut*," 11–15.

22 Conforti, *Zeman Avar*, 125–126; Schweid, "Shtei Gishot la-Ra'ayon 'Shelilat ha-Golah.'"

23 Kopelowitz, "Between *Mifgash* and *Shlichut*," 13–17.

24 On Chabad and its emissaries, see, for example: Berman, "Voices of Outreach"; Fishkoff, *The Rebbe's Army*, 27–32, 111–117; Kraus, *Ha-Shevi'i*; Limonic, "The Role of Transnational Actors in the Growth of Chabad-Lubavitch."

25 For the official list and information on all the Chabad Houses, see www.chabad.org.

26 See Ferziger, *The Emergence of the Community Kollel*, 32–48.

27 https://torahmitzion.org.

28 Zohar, "Mai Kollel Zioni," 365.

29 Ibid., 367.

30 Ibid., 368–369.

31 Ibid., 367.

32 The term appears in the writings of Abraham Isaac Kook. See, for example, *Orot ha-Kodesh*, 13.

33 https://torahmitzion.org/.

34 Ibid.

35 Open letter from Moshe Gadot, recruitment coordinator, TMZ, Nov.-Dec., 2006.

36 Ibid.

37 https://torahmitzion.org.

38 Telephone discussion with Boaz Genut, former executive director of TMZ, Feb. 1, 2007.

39 The questionnaires are on file in the respective kollel site folders at the TMZ office, 54 King George St., Jerusalem 91710, entrance floor.

40 https://etzion.org.il.

41 Full disclosure: one of my sons attended YHE and served as a TMZ emissary in Sydney, Australia, in 2011.

42 See https://torahmitzion.org, which provides the following statistics regarding the numbers of emissaries they have been sent from the various yeshivot and pre-army mechinot: YHE—232; Hakotel—69; Birkat Moshe (Ma'ale Adumim)—66; Ma'a lot—60; Kiryat Shemonah—60; Or Etzion—51; Karnei Shomron—45; Otniel—44; Kerem B'Yavneh—43; Sha'alvim—43; Yerucham—41; Hispin—38; Shadmot Neriyah—31; Bnei David/Eli—30; Sderot—24; Orot Shaul—18; Hosen-Peduel—15; Akko—14; others—368.

43 Email correspondence from Ze'ev Schwartz to Leonard Matanky and Moshe Aberman (Apr. 17, 1997), TMZ Chicago File, TMZ Jerusalem Office.

44 Asscher, "The Decline in the Religious Zionist Negation of the Diaspora."

45 Klein, "Rabbi Haim Drukman."

46 Telephone interview with Rabbi Chaim Druckman, Feb. 9, 2007.

47 See, for example: Avraham, "Ha-Derekh ha-Sheleesheet," 131–140, and the responses that it provoked in the same volume, 141–158; Sheleg, "Lo Maspik le-Hitnahel."

48 https://sherut-leumi.co.il/.

49 https://torahmitzion.org.

50 Perl, "Shlihim le-khol ha-Hayyim."

51 https://ots.org.il.

52 Joffrie, "Har Etzion: Leader Asks Noam Leader to Personally Apologize to Yeshiva's Rabbis"; Lichtenstein, "Which Religious Zionism—and Which Cliff?"

53 Lichtenstein, "A Conversation with Rabbi Mosheh Lichtenstein."

54 https://www.har-el.org.

55 https://telaviv.academia.edu/HerzlHefter.

56 Hefter, "Why I Ordained Women."

57 Keats-Jaskol, "Spirituality."

58 Klein, "Pirsum Rishon: Nivhar Mahalifo shel Ha-Rav Benny Lau."

59 www.binyamin.org.il.

60 www.tzohar.org.il.

61 www.beithillel.org.il.

62 Zinger, "Secular Kfar Shmaryahu Has a Beloved Orthodox Rabbi."

63 Ibid.

64 See the photos and a description of the exhibit at www.robbinsbecher.com.

65 Ibid.

CONCLUSION

1 https://pasyn.org.

2 www.timesofisrael.com.

3 Cosgrove, "When American Jews Talk about Israel."

4 Wertheimer, *All Quiet on the Religious Front*, 25–26.

5 Wertheimer, *The New American Judaism*, 195–200.

6 Cosgrove, "When American Jews Talk about Israel."

7 Shain, *The Israeli Century*.

8 Liebman and Cohen, *Two Worlds of Judaism*.

9 Shain, *Ha-Me'ah ha-Yisraelit*, 11.

10 Della Pergola, "World Jewish Population."

11 Senor and Singer, *Start-Up Nation*.

12 Shain, *Ha-Me'ah ha-Yisra'elit*, 30.

13 Ibid.

14 Bladt et al., "Thousands of Israelis Return Home."

15 Shain, *Ha-Me'ah ha-Yisra'elit*, 16, 33–36; Abramson, "Making a Homeland, Constructing a Diaspora"; Kelner, *Tours That Bind*.

16 See, for example, www.shazur.org.

17 Pink, "Pittsburgh Jews 'Heartbroken.'"

18 Tanyos, "U.S. Sees Spike in Antisemitic Incidents."

19 Litvak, "The Islamic Republic of Iran and the Holocaust."

20 Efune, "French Philosopher Bernard-Henri Lévy Calls."

21 Finkielkraut, "In the Name of the Other."

22 Shain, *Ha-Me'ah ha-Yisraelit*, 31–33.

23 Ibid., 307.

24 Ibid., 50–51, 54.

25 Reuters, "Jewish-Led Peace Activists Protest at Statue of Liberty."

26 Niebuhr, *Moral Man and Immoral Society.*

27 Shain, *Ha-Me'ah ha-Yisra'elit,* 70–73.

28 For a brief presentation in English, see Levy-Paz, "The New (Literary) Engagement with Israel."

29 Chabon, *The Yiddish Policemen's Union.*

30 Shain, *Ha-Me'ah ha-Yisraelit,* 17.

31 Cited in ibid., 17–18.

32 Ibid., 18.

33 Kraus, *Ha-Shevi'i,* 69–76, 207–223; Heilman and Friedman, *The Rebbe,* 212–213; Morris, "The Children's Crusade," 333–343.

34 Maoz and Bekerman, "Chabad Tracks the Trekkers."

35 For the official list of permanent Chabad centers throughout the world, see www .chabad.org.

36 Lev, "Ministry to Israelis Abroad: Try Chabad for Help."

37 Berger, *The Heretical Imperative.*

38 Berger, *The Desecularization of the World.*

39 Taylor, *A Secular Age,* 4.

40 Ibid., 3.

41 Ibid., 13.

42 See, for example, Magid, *The Necessity of Exile.*

43 Kampeas, "Polls Show American Jews Approve."

44 Lidor, "The Jewishness of Some Hamas Victims Sparks Bitter Disputes over Their Burial." Palhati was buried in a walled-off area with a high fence adjacent to the main Jewish cemetery. After a public uproar, the fence was removed and the wall was lowered and covered with plantings; see Moshkovits, "Sa'arat Kevuratah shel Alina Palhati z"l."

45 Alterman, *We Are Not One*; Gordis, *We Stand Divided.* See the scores of articles collected at the Berman electronic archive: www.bjpa.org.

46 Even, "The National Significance of Israeli Demographics."

47 www.itim.org.il.

48 Rosenbaum, "A New Era in Jewish History."

49 Ferziger, "Religion for the Secular," 74–77.

50 Ibid.

51 For an illuminating discussion of ITIM's activities related to the October 2023 war, see Borschel-Dan, "What Matters Now to Rabbi Seth Farber."

52 ITIM, "ITIM: 2022 Impact Report."

53 Gross, "Religious Advocacy Group Organizes 'Love the Convert' Shabbat in U.S., Israel before Shavuot."

54 ITIM, "ITIM: 2022 Impact Report."

55 www.hartman.org.il.

56 Bitton, "Zionism as Loyalty/Ne'emanut."
57 www.thedowntownminyan.com.
58 https://www.youtube.com/watch?v=9sFDUYD9g68.
59 www.hartman.org.il.
60 Ibid.
61 Ibid.
62 Rosner and Fuchs, #YahadutYisraelit.
63 Ibid., 82.
64 Ibid., 159–170.
65 https://chuppot.org.il.
66 https://tzohar-eng.org.
67 www.habermaninstitute.org.
68 Rosner and Fuchs, #YahadutYisraelit, 154–158.
69 Engelberg, "Modern Orthodoxy in Post-secular Times"; Katsman, "New Religious-Nationalist Trends among Jewish Settlers in the Halutza Sands."
70 Zion-Waldoks, "'Family Resemblance' and Its Discontents."
71 Caspi, "Dor ha-Rezef"; Avishai, "Religious Queer People beyond Identity Conflict."
72 Jerusalem Post, "Why Are So Many of Israel's Fallen Soldiers."
73 Gurock, "Twentieth-Century American Orthodoxy's Era of Non-observance."
74 Buzaglo, "Ha-Masoratim"; Yadgar, Secularism and Religion.
75 Rosner and Fuchs, #YahadutYisraelit, 82.
76 Yehuda Kurtzer, www.facebook.com.
77 Zion, "What Kind of Religious Jew Am I?"
78 Ibid.

BIBLIOGRAPHY

Adler, Morris, Jacob Agus, and Theodore Friedman. "Responsum on the Sabbath." *Proceedings of the Rabbinical Assembly of America* XIV (1950): 112–137.

Abramovich, Shlomo. "The Hesder Yeshivot as Agents of Social Change in Religious Zionism." *Israel Studies* 25, no. 2 (2020): 138–158.

———. "A Critic from Within: Rav Shagar and the Renewal of Religious Zionism." *Studies in Judaism, Humanities, and the Social Sciences* 4, no.1 (2022): 305–318.

Abramowitz, Leah, "Women Advocates Make Their Mark." *Jewish Action* 65, vol. 2 (2004), https://d1ydyrae2d92wn.cloudfront.net [retrieved May 15, 2024].

Abramson, Edward. *A Circle in the Square: Rabbi Shlomo Riskin Reinvents the Synagogue.* Jerusalem: Urim, 2008.

Abramson, Yehonatan. "Making a Homeland, Constructing a Diaspora: The Case of Taglit-Birthright Israel." *Political Geography* 58 (May 2017): 14–23.

Alexander, Stephan, ed. *The Americanization of Europe: Culture, Diplomacy, and Anti-Americanism after 1945.* New York and Oxford: Berghahn Books, 2006.

Alterman, Eric. *We Are Not One: A History of America's Fight over Israel.* New York: Basic Books, 2022.

Amital, Yehudah. "Bino Shenot Dor va-Dor." *Alon Shevut Bogrim* 13 (2016), www.etzion.org.il [retrieved May 13, 2024].

Amsalem, Shai. "Ha-Lohamot Mokhihot she-be-foal, Anahnu Menazhot." Dec. 8, 2023, www.makorrishon.co.il [retrieved May 9, 2024].

Angel, Hayyim. "Torat Hashem Temima: The Contributions of Rav Yoel Bin-Nun to Religious Tanakh Study." *Tradition* 40, no. 3 (2007): 5–17.

Anzovin, Miriam. "An Atheist Learns Daf Yomi." Jan. 6, 2020, www.jewishboston.com [retrieved May 13, 2024].

Ariel, Ya'akov. "Hasidism in the Age of Aquarius: The House of Love and Prayer in San Francisco, 1967–1977." *Religion and American Culture* 13, no. 2 (2003): 139–165.

———. "Can Adam and Eve Reconcile?: Gender and Sexuality in a New Jewish Religious Movement." *Nova Religio* 9, no. 4 (2006): 53–78.

———. "Walking Together, Walking Apart: Conservative Judaism and Neo-Hasidism." *Jewish Culture and History* 21, 2 (2020): 172–187.

Arnovitz, David, ed. *The Koren Tanakh of the Land of Israel.* Jerusalem: Koren, 2020–2024, 5 volumes.

Aronson, Shlomo. "Israel's Security and the Holocaust: Lessons Learned, but Existential Fears Continue." *Israel Studies* 14, no. 1 (2009): 65–93.

Arutz Sheva. "Irgun Hotam Meizig: Ha-Motaziyah ha-Yehudit." Mar. 3, 2021, www.inn .co.il [retrieved May 8, 2024].

Asa-el, Amotz. "Middle Israel: Who's Afraid of Rabbi Riskin?" June 5, 2015, www.jpost .com [retrieved May 8, 2024].

Ash, Ellie. "Observant Feminism across Borders: The Transnational Origins of Partnership Minyanim." *Modern Judaism* 42, no. 2 (2022): 157–182.

Askaria. *Memza'ei Seker Emdot be-Noge'a le-ZaHa"L—Migzar ha-Dati.* Bnei Brak: Askaria, Mar. 28, 2024.

Asscher, Omri. *Reading Israel, Reading America: The Politics of Translation between Jews.* Stanford, CA: Stanford University Press, 2020.

———. "The Ben-Gurion–Blaustein 'Understanding' as an Historiographical Yardstick." *Israel Studies* 25, no. 3 (Fall 2020): 33–48.

Avgar, Ido. "Netunim al Giyus Banot le-ZaHa"L." May 22, 2017, https://fs.knesset.gov.il [retrieved May 9, 2024].

Aviner, Shlomo. "Mahloket ha-Rabanim be-Devar ha-Reformim." Nov. 15, 2020, www .srugim.co.il [retrieved May 8, 2024].

———. "Ha-Rav Aviner: Shivyon Nashim ve-Gevarim be-Veit ha-Knesset—Neo-Conservativiyut." Dec. 4, 2015, kipa.co.il [retrieved May 7, 2024].

Avioz, Michael, Omer Minka, and Yael Shemesh. "Prof. Joseph Fleishman: Biography." In *Ben Porat Yosef: Studies in the Bible and Its World,* xiii–xvii. Munster: Ugarit-Verlag, 2019.

Avishai, Bernard. "In a Very Deep Way: Remembering Rabbi David Hartman." June 12, 2017, www.thedailybeast.com [retrieved May 7, 2024].

Avishai, Orit. "Halakhic Niddah Consultants and the Orthodox Women's Movement in Israel." *Journal of Modern Jewish Studies* 7, no. 2 (2008): 195–216.

———. "Religious Queer People beyond Identity Conflict: Lessons from Orthodox LGBT Jews in Israel." *Journal for the Scientific Study of Religion* 59, no. 2 (2020): 360–378.

———. *Queer Judaism: LGBT Activism and the Remaking of Jewish Orthodoxy in Israel.* New York: New York University Press, 2023.

Avraham, Michael. "Ha-Derekh ha-Sheleesheet o: 'al Zionut Datit' le-lo Makaf." *Tzohar* 22 (Summer 2005): 131–140.

Bachrach, Rachel. "10 Questions for . . . Moshe Schwed." Aug. 12, 2020, https: //mishpacha.com [retrieved May 12, 2024].

Bacon, Gershon. *The Politics of Tradition: Agudat Yisrael in Poland, 1916–1939.* Jerusalem: Magnes, 1996.

Balint, Judy Lash. "Women's Pre-army Program Reflects the Religious Debate in Israel." Feb. 9, 2017, https://jewishstandard.timesofisrael.com [retrieved May 9, 2024].

Bar-El, Esti. *Ve-Talmud Torah ke-neged Kulan—Torah Study in Women's Batei Midrash: A Gendered Perspective.* PhD dissertation, Bar Ilan University 2009 [Hebrew].

Barkat, Amiram. "The Reform Movement as a 'Caricature.'" Dec. 11, 2005, www.haaretz .com [retrieved May 8, 2024].

Bartuv, Idit, and Anat Nobolslasky. *Mah She'elatekh Esther ve-Tey'as: Teshuvot Hilkhati-yot she-Nekhtevu al yedei Musmakhot ha-Machon le-Manhigut Hilkhatit al shem Suzy Bradesfeld*. Jerusalem: Midreshet Lindenbaum, 2014.

Bat Adam, Smadar. "Both of Them Together and Each One Separately." *Maariv* 17 (July 19, 1989) [Hebrew].

Baum, Nehami, Ofra Aran, Chaya Schwartz, and Tova Yedidaya. "Women Pursuing Higher Education in Ultra-Orthodox Society." *Journal of Social Work Education* 50, no. 1 (2014): 164–175.

Baumel, Judith Tydor. "Kahane in America: An Exercise in Right-Wing Urban Terror." *Studies in Conflict and Terrorism* 22, no. 4 (1999): 311–329. https://doi.org/10.1080/105761099265667.

———. "Frum Surfing: Orthodox Jewish Women's Internet Forums as a Historical and Cultural Phenomenon." *Journal of Jewish Identities* 29, no.1 (2009): 1–30.

———. "Orthodox Jewish Women as a Bridge between Israel and the Diaspora." In *Reconsidering Israel-Diaspora Relations*, edited by Eliezer Ben-Refael, Judit Bokser Liberant, and Yosef Gorny, 203–222. Leiden and Boston: Brill, 2014.

———. *A Very Special Life: The Bernice Chronicles—One Women's Journey through Twentieth-Century Jewish America*. Bern: Peter Lang, 2017.

Bayme, Steven. "American Orthodox Jews and the State of Israel." In *Israel and the United States: Six Decades of US-Israeli Relations*, edited by Robert Freedman, 215–231. Boulder, CO: Westview Press, 2012.

Beasely, Yaakov. "A Question of Character: R. Aharon Lichtenstein and the Interpretation of Biblical Texts." *Tradition* 47, no. 4 (2014): 126–136.

Becker, Edgell P. *Congregations in Conflict: Cultural Models of Local Religious Life*. Cambridge: Cambridge University Press, 1999.

Beckerman, Gal. *When They Come for Us, We'll Be Gone: The Epic Struggle to Save Soviet Jewry*. Boston and New York: Mariner Books, 2010.

Beinart, Peter. "Rabbi Jonathan Sacks Has Abdicated His Moral Responsibility." July 26, 2018, https://forward.com [retrieved May 12, 2024].

Beit Daniel. "A New Idea for Progressive Judaism in Israel." *Beit Daniel Newsletter* 1 (Feb.-Mar. 1992), 1–2 [Hebrew].

———. "New Programs: Fast Forward." *Beit Daniel Newsletter* 1 (Feb.-Mar. 1992), 2–3 [Hebrew].

———. *Summary of the First Year of Activity*. 1992 [Hebrew].

———. *Staff Discussion 2008—Two Who Are One*. Tel Aviv: Beit Daniel, 2008. [Hebrew].

Beit ha-Midrash le-Morim shel Yeshivat Rabbeinu Yitzhak Elhanan—Toknit Limudim 1934–36. TI course catalogue. New York, 1934–36.

Beit-Hallahmi, Benjamin. "Back to the Fold: The Return to Judaism." In *Tradition, Innovation, Conflict: Jewishness and Judaism in Contemporary Israel*, edited by Zvi Sobel and Benjamin Beit-Hallahmi, 153–172. Albany: SUNY Press, 1991.

Bendel, Netael. "Devarim she-lo Yada'atem al Ha-Rabbanit Chana Henkin." *Kipah*, June 26, 2013, *Kipah.co.il* [retrieved May 7, 2024].

Ben-Gurion, David. "Ha-Nizhiyut shel Am Yisrael." Mar. 16, 1960, www.yutorah.org [retrieved May 15, 2024].

Ben-Lulu, Elazar. "'Let Us Bless the Twilight': Intersectionality of Traditional Jewish Ritual and Queer Pride in a Reform Congregation in Israel." *Journal of Homosexuality* 68, no. 1 (2019): 23–46.

Benor, Sarah Bunin. "Mensch, Bentsh, and Balagan: Variation in the American Jewish Linguistic Repertoire." *Language & Communication* 31, no. 2 (2011): 141–154.

Ben-Porat, Guy. *Between State and Synagogue: The Secularization of Contemporary Israel*. Cambridge: Cambridge University Press, 2013.

Ben-Refael, Eliezer. "Israel-Diaspora Relations: 'Transmission Driving-Belts' of Transnationalism." In *Reconsidering Israel-Diaspora Relations*, edited by Eliezer Ben-Refael, Judit Bokser Liberant, and Yosef Gorny, 447–461. Leiden and Boston: Brill, 2014.

Berger, Michael. "The Centrality of Talmud." In *The Cambridge Guide to Jewish History, Religion, and Culture*, edited by Judith R. Baskin and Kenneth Seeskin, 311–336. New York and Cambridge: Cambridge University Press, 2012.

Berger, Peter L. *The Heretical Imperative: Contemporary Possibilities of Religious Affirmation*. Garden City, NY: Anchor Press, 1979.

———. *The Desecularization of the World: Resurgent Religion and World Politics*. Grand Rapids, MI: Ethics and Policy Center, 1999.

Berger, Shalom. "A Year of Study in an Israeli Yeshiva Program: Before and After." Doctoral dissertation, Azrieli Graduate School of Jewish Education–Yeshiva University, Jan. 1997.

Berlin, Yair. "Haroshet ha-Talmud: Mifal Daf Yomi ve-Tarbut ha-Zerikhah ha-Modernit." *Iyunim* 32 (2019): 109–136.

Berman Archive. https://bermanarchive.stanford.edu [retrieved July 26, 2024].

Berman, Ari. "Religious Zionism: Moving History Forward." *Tradition* 53, no. 3 (2021): 7–16.

Berman, Elise. "Voices of Outreach: The Construction of Identity and Maintenance of Social Ties among Chabad-Lubavitch Emissaries." *Journal for the Scientific Study of Religion* 48, no. 1 (2009): 69–85.

Berman, Joshua. *Inconsistencies in the Torah: Ancient Literary Convention and the Limits of Source Criticism*. New York and Oxford: Oxford University Press, 2017.

———. *Ani Maamin: Biblical Criticism, Historical Truth, and the Thirteen Principles of Faith*. Jerusalem: Maggid, 2020.

Berman, Saul. "Forty Years Later: The Rav's Opening Shiur at the Stern College for Women Beit Midrash." Oct. 9, 2017, https://thelehrhaus.com [retrieved May 13, 2024].

Bernstein, Louis. "Dr. Pinchos Churgin A"H on His 100th Birthday." *Jewish Press* (Dec. 2, 1994), 99.

Bernstein, Moshe J. "The Orthodox Jewish Scholar and Jewish Scholarship: Duties and Dilemmas." *Torah u-Madda Journal* 3 (1991–1992): 8–36.

———. "Why Lines Need to Be Drawn and Where." Feb. 11, 2009, www.yucommentator .com [retrieved May 8, 2024].

———. "Where Is Our Mission? Where Is Our Raison d'Être?" May 19, 2019, https: //yucommentator.org [retrieved May 8, 2024].

Berrin, Danielle. "After #MeToo, an Orthodox Rabba Confronts the Limits—and Possibilities—of Her Own Power." May 9, 2018, https://jewishjournal.com [retrieved May 9, 2024].

Besser, Yisroel. "The People Come First." Aug. 10, 2021, https://mishpacha.com [retrieved May 12, 2024].

Bezalel, Ronit. "In Israel, Modern Orthodoxy Embraces the Religious LGBTs—Partly." Sept. 22, 2016, www.timesofisrael.com [retrieved May 8, 2024].

Bick, Ezra, and Yaakov Beasely, eds. "Preface." In *Torah miEtzion*. Jerusalem: Maggid Books and Yeshivat Har-Etzion, 2011.

Bitton, Mijal. "Zionism as Loyalty/Ne'emanut." July 6, 2022, www.hartman.org.il [retrieved May 13, 2024].

Bladt, Cait, Stephanie Fasano, Ivan Pereira, and Sally Hawkins. "Thousands of Israelis Return Home to Answer Call for Military Reserve Duty." Oct. 13, 2023, https: //abcnews.go.com [retrieved May 13, 2024].

Blau, Yitzchak. "Alt-Shift." Dec. 27, 2022, https://traditiononline.org [retrieved May 15, 2024].

Blidstein, Gerald J. "On the Jewish People in the Writings of Rabbi Joseph B. Soloveitchik." *Tradition* 24, no. 3 (1989): 21–44.

Blumberg, Raphael. *They Called Him Rebbe: The Life and Good Works of Rabbi Boruch Milikowsky*. Jerusalem: Urim, 2007.

Bokster Liwerant, Judith. "Latin-American Jews—A Transnational Diaspora." In *Transnationalism: Diasporas and the Advent of a New Disorder*, edited by Eliezer Ben-Rafael and Yitzhak Sternberg, with Judit Bokser Liwerant and Yossi Gorny, 351–374. Brill: Leiden-Boston, 2009.

Borschel-Dan, Amanda. "What Matters Now to Rabbi Seth Farber: Hostages and Mixed Burials in Jewish Law." Nov. 24, 2023, www.timesofisrael.com [retrieved May 13, 2024].

Brander, Katriel (Kenny). "Ha-Askanut she-Romeset: Ha-Politika zerikhah le-hisha'er mi-huz la-Merhav ha-Hilkhati." Dec. 5, 2021, www.makorrishon.co.il [retrieved May 8, 2024].

Brandes, Yehudah. "Hazal ki-Mevakrei ha-Mikra," In *Be-Einei E-lohim ve-Adam: Ha-Adam ha-Ma'amin u-Mehkar ha-Mikra*, edited by Yehudah Brandes, Tova Ganzel, and Hayuta Deutsch, 176–211. Jerusalem: Beit Morasha, 2015.

Brettler, Marc Zvi. *How to Read the Jewish Bible*. Oxford: Oxford University Press, 2007.

Brettler, Marc Zvi, Daniel J. Harrington, and Peter Enns. *The Bible and the Believer: How to Read the Bible Critically and Religiously*. Oxford: Oxford University Press, 2013.

Breuer, Mordechai. *Modernity with Tradition: The Social History of Orthodox Jewry in Imperial Germany*. New York: Columbia, 1992.

———. "Appointment and Succession among Yeshiva Deans." *Jewish History* 13, no. 1 (1999): 11–23.

Briggs, Kenneth A. "Brooklyn's Talmud by Telephone Offers Wisdom in Daily Talks." Sept. 8, 1983, *New York Times*, section B, 1.

Brill, Alan. "An Ideal Rosh Yeshiva: *By His Light: Character and Values in the Service of God* and *Leaves of Faith* by Rav Aharon Lichtenstein." *Edah Journal* 5, no. 1 (2005), www.edah.org [retrieved May 13, 2024].

———. "Worlds Destroyed, Worlds Rebuilt: The Religious Thought of Rabbi Yehudah Amital." *Edah Journal* 5, no. 2 (2006), www.edah.org [retrieved May 13, 2024].

———. "What Is Modern in Modern Orthodoxy." In *The Road Not Taken: Yitz Greenberg and Modern Orthodox Judaism*, edited by Adam S. Ferziger, Miri Freud-Kandel, and Steven Bayme, 172–192. Boston: Academic Studies Press, 2019.

Brooke, Simon. "Interview with Michelle Cohen Farber." May 14, 2021, https://jchatting .blogspot.com [retrieved May 13, 2024].

———. "JChatting—Interviews with a Jewish Flavour," https://jchatting.blogspot.com [retrieved July 25, 2024].

Brown, Benjamin. *Ha-Hazon Ish: ha-Posek, ha-Ma'amin, u-Manhig ha-Mahapekha ha-Haredit*. Jerusalem: Magnes and Cardozo Law School of Yeshiva University, 2011.

———. "Theoretical Antinomianism and the Conservative Function of Utopia: Rabbi Mordechai Joseph of Izbica as a Case Study." *Journal of Religion* 99, no. 3 (2019): 313–340.

Brown, Michael. *The Israeli-American Connection: Its Roots in the Yishuv, 1914–1945*. Detroit: Wayne University Press, 1996.

Broyde, Michael J. "Religious Values in Secular Institutions?: Yeshiva University and the Future of Religiously Affiliated but Secularly Chartered Higher Education in America." *Journal of Law, Religion and State* 10, no. 1 (2022): 53–85.

Broyde, Michael J., and Shlomo Brody, "Orthodox Women Rabbis? Tentative Thoughts That Distinguish between the Timely and the Timeless." *Hakirah* 11 (Spring 2011): 25–58.

Bulka, Reuven P. *The Coming Cataclysm: The Orthodox-Reform Rift and the Future of the Jewish People*. Oakville, ON: Mosaic Press, 1984.

Butler, Deidre. "Spirituality, Textual Study and Gender at Nishmat: A Spirited Chavruta." *Women in Judaism: A Multidisciplinary Journal* 7, no. 1 (2010), http://wjudaism.library.utoronto.ca [retrieved May 7, 2024].

Buzaglo, Meir. "Ha-Masorati." In *Rav Tarbutiyut ba-Mivhan ha-Yisraeli*, edited by Ohad Nachtomoy, 153–162. Jerusalem: Magnes, 2003.

Campbell, Heidi. *Digital Creatives and the Rethinking of Religious Authority*. New York: Routledge, 2020.

Campbell, Heidi A., and Mia Lövheim eds. "Religion and the Internet: Considering the Online–Offline Connection." *Information, Communication & Society* 14, no. 8 (2011), 1083–1096.

———. "Considering Critical Methods and Theoretical Lenses in Digital Religion Studies," *New Media & Society* 19, no. 1 (2017), 5–14.

Canadian Jewish News. "Toronto Meetings." Mar. 12, 1963, 9.

Caplan, Kimmy. "Shorshei ha-Mizrahi be-Amerika: Ha-Rabbanut ha-Orthodoksit ha-Mehageret." *Yahadut Zmanenu* 13 (1999): 173–205.

———. "Israeli Haredi Society and the Repentance *hazarah biteshuvah* Phenomenon." *Jewish Studies Quarterly* 8 (2001): 369–398.

———. "The Internal Popular Discourse of Israeli Haredi Women." *Archives de sciences sociales des religions* 123 (July–Sept. 2003). https://doi.org/10.4000/assr.1069.

———. "Heker ha-Hevrah ha-Yehudit Datit be-Yisrael." *Megamot* 51, no. 2 (2017): 208–249.

Carlebach, Neshama. "My Sisters, I Hear You." Jan. 2, 2018, https://blogs.timesofisrael.com [retrieved May 8, 2024].

Carlin, Jerome E. and Saul H. Mendlovitz. "The American Rabbi: A Religious Specialist Responses to Loss of Authority." In *Understanding American Judaism* 1, edited by Jacob Neusner, 165–174. Eugene, OR: Wipf and Stock Publishers, 2003.

Carmy, Shalom. "Soloveitchik the Zionist." May 2018, www.firstthings.com [retrieved May 13, 2024].

Cashman, Greer Fay. "Riskin Remembers Marching with MLK Jr." Mar. 10, 2015, www.jpost.com [retrieved May 7, 2024].

Caspi, Yair. "Dor ha-Rezef." *Shalom Hartman Institute* (Aug. 30, 2018), https://heb.hartman.org.il [retrieved May 13, 2024].

Castells, Manuel. *The Rise of the Network Society*. Cambridge, MA: Blackwell, 1996.

———. *The Internet Galaxy: Reflections on the Internet, Business and Society*. Oxford: Oxford University Press, 2001.

Chabon, Michael. *The Yiddish Policemen's Union*. New York: Harper Perennial, 2007.

Cherlow, Yuval. "Al ha-Havhanah ben Reformah le-Hithadshut." *Akdamot* 7 (2000), www.bmj.org.il [retrieved May 8, 2024].

———. *Ye-Yare le-Levav*. Tel Aviv: Yediot Ahronot/Hemed Books, 2007.

———. "Bi-Gevul Shenei Olamot." Nov. 11, 2011, https://musaf-shabbat.com [retrieved May 8, 2024].

———. "Bikoret ha-Mikra ve-Yir'at ha-Shamayim Sheli: She'elah le-Rav." In *Be-Einei E-lohim ve-Adam*, edited by Yehudah Brandes, Tova Ganzel, and Hayuta Deutsch, 289–96. Jerusalem: Beit Morasha, 2015.

Churgin, Pinchos. *Vision and Legacy: Selected Papers with Essays on His Life and Work*, edited by Louis Bernstein and Raphael Yankelovitch. Ramat-Gan: BIU Press, 1987.

Clymer, Yafit. "Mishnat ha-Rav Sacks me'atgeret et ha-Yahadut ha-Yisraelit." Oct. 24, 2021, www.makorrishon.co.il [retrieved May 12, 2024].

Cohen, Asher. *Ha-Tallit ve-ha-Degel*. Jerusalem: Yad Yitzhak Ben-Zvi, 1998.

Cohen, Boaz. "Mitzvah be-Madim: ha-Sherut ha-Z'va'i ve-ha-Zibbur ha-Dati-Leumi." *Iyunim be-Tekumat Yisrael* 22 (2012): 338–347.

Cohen, Jeremy. "Augustine's Doctrine of Jewish Witness Revisited." *Journal of Religion* 89 (2009): 564–578.

Cohen, Jonathan. "Politics, Alienation, and the Consolidation of Group Identity: The Case of Synagogue Pamphlets." *Rhetoric & Public Affairs* 3, no. 2 (2000): 247–275.

Cohen, Judah M. "A Holy Brother's Liberal Legacy: Shlomo Carlebach, Reform Judaism, and Hasidic Pluralism." *American Jewish History* 100, no. 4 (2016): 485–509.

———. "Introduction: Shlomo Carlebach 1925–1994 and the Stories We Tell." *American Jewish History* 100, no. 4 (2016): ix–xiii.

Cohen, Naomi W. *The Americanization of Zionism, 1897–1948*. Hanover, NH: Brandeis University Press, 2003.

Cohen, Shimon. "Ha-Podcast she-Yakir le-Yisraelim at Ha-Rav Sacks." Nov. 13, 2022, www.inn.co.il [retrieved May 12, 2024].

Cohen, Steven, and Arnold Eisen. *The Jew Within*. Bloomington: University of Indiana Press, 2000.

Cohen, Stuart A. *Divine Service? Judaism and Israel's Armed Forces*. Farnham: Ashgate, 2013.

Cohen, Tova. "Manhigut Datit Nashit: Ha-Orthodoksiyah ha-Modernit be-Yisrael ke-Mikreh Mivḥan." *Tarbut Demokratit* 10 (2006): 251–296.

The Commentator. "Aliyah." Dec. 11, 1958, 2.

———. "Junior Trips to Israel Ended: School Policy against Leaves." Dec. 11, 1958, 1.

———. "Open Letter." Mar. 31, 1960, 1.

Conforti, Yitzhak. *Zeman Avar*. Jerusalem: Yad Ben-Zvi, 2006.

Cooperman, Yehudah. "Ha-Michlalah ke-Mossad Eikhuti ve-Yihudi." *Mikhlol* 20 (2000): 83–94.

Cosgrove, Elliot J. "Teyku: The Insoluble Contradictions in the Life and Thought of Louis Jacobs." PhD thesis, University of Chicago, 2008.

———. "When American Jews Talk about Israel, We're Really Talking about Ourselves." May 19, 2019, https://forward.com [retrieved May 13, 2024].

Cottin Pogrebin, Letti. "The Famous Israeli You've Never Heard Of." Oct. 22, 2018, www.tabletmag.com [retrieved May 13, 2024].

Dahan, Alon. *The Final Redeemer: The Messianic Doctrine of Rabbi Menachem Mendel Schneerson, the Lubavitcher Rebbe*. Tel Aviv: Contento, 2014.

Danielsen, Helge. "The American Spirit in Europe Revisited?" *Contemporary European History* 17, no. 1 (2008): 117–126.

Danzger, M. Herbert. *Returning to Judaism: The Contemporary Revival of Orthodox Judaism*. New Haven, CT: Yale University Press, 1989.

Darman, Ushi. "Ez Hayyim she-hitgalah be-Yisrael me'uhar Midai." Nov. 14, 2021, www.haaretz.co.il [retrieved May 12, 2024].

Dash Moore, Debra. "A Synagogue Center Grows in Brooklyn." In *The American Synagogue: A Sanctuary Transformed*, edited by Jack Wertheimer, 297–326. Cambridge and New York: Cambridge University Press, 1987.

Dashefsky, Arnold, and Bernard Lazerwitz. "The Role of Religious Identification in North American Migration to Israel." *Journal for the Scientific Study of Religion* 22, no. 3 (1983): 263–275.

Davidman, Lynn. "Accommodation and Resistance to Modernity: A Comparison of Two Contemporary Orthodox Jewish Groups." *Sociology of Religion* 51, no. 1 (Mar. 1990): 35–51.

Davis, Joseph. "The Reception of the Shulhan 'Arukh and the Formation of Ashkenazic Jewish Identity." *AJS Review* 26, no. 2 (2002): 251–276.

Della Pergola, Sergio. "World Jewish Population." 2017, www.jewishdatabank.org [retrieved May 13, 2024].

Deshen, Shlomo, Charles S. Liebman, and Moshe Shokeid, eds. *Israeli Judaism: The Sociology of Religion in Israel*. New Brunswick, NJ: Transaction Books, 1994.

Dolsten, Josefin. "Trailblazing Hasidic Woman Elected as Brooklyn Judge." Sept. 15, 2016, https://forward.com [retrieved May 9, 2024].

Don-Yehiya, Eliezer. "*Galut* in Zionist Ideology and in Israeli Society." In *Israel and Diaspora Jewry: Ideological and Political Perspectives*, edited by Eliezer Don-Yehiya, 219–257. Ramat Gan: BIU Press, 1991.

———. "The Negation of the *Galut* in Religious Zionism." *Modern Judaism* 12 (1992): 129–155.

———. "Orthodox Jewry in Israel and in North America." *Israel Studies* 10, no. 1 (2005): 57–87.

———. "Messianism and Politics: The Ideological Transformation of Religious Zionism." *Israel Studies* 19, no. 2 (2014): 239–263.

———. "Changes and Developments in Israeli Civil Religion: 1982–2017." *Israel Studies* 23, no. 3 (Fall 2018): 189–196.

Dorff, Elliot N. *Modern Conservative Judaism: Evolving Thought and Practice*. Lincoln: JPS/University of Nebraska Press, 2018.

Downes, David, and Paul Rock. *Understanding Deviance*. Oxford: Oxford University Press, 1982.

Dreyfus, Hannah. "Riskin Names Female Spiritual Leader in Efrat." Jan. 21, 2015, www.jta.org [retrieved May 8, 2024].

Durkheim, Emile. *The Division of Labor in Society*, translated by George Simpson. Glencoe, IL: Free Press, 1960.

Dvori, Bilha. "A House of Judaism, a Place of Culture." *Davar* (Dec. 14, 1994), 12 [Hebrew].

Easterman, Daniel. "Ego Stands in Way of Great Leadership, Chief Tells Limmud." Dec. 23, 2013, www.thejc.com [retrieved May 8, 2024].

Eckstein, Meir. "Rabbi Mordechai Breuer and Modern Orthodox Biblical Commentary." *Tradition* 33, no. 3 (1999): 6–23.

Edelman, Martin. "A Portion of Animosity: The Politics of Disenfranchisement of Religion in Israel." *Israel Studies* 5, no. 1 (2000): 204–227.

Edelstein, Avraham. "A Traditional Jewish Approach to Homosexuality." May 6, 2013, http://nleresources.com [retrieved May 8, 2024].

Efune, Dovid. "In United Nations Address, French Philosopher Bernard-Henri Lévy Calls for 'Muslim Nostra Aetate,'" Dec. 12, 2015, www.algemeiner.com [retrieved May 13, 2024].

Eglash, Ruth Marks. "Bar-Ilan University Moves to Establish Center to Advance Rabbi Jonathan Sacks' Teachings." Jan. 17, 2023, https://ejewishphilanthropy.com [retrieved May 12, 2024].

Ehrman, Hananel. "The Tragedy of Rabbi Sacks." Nov. 20, 2013, www.kipa.co.il [retrieved May 12, 2024].

Eisen, Arnold. "A Tribute to David Hartman." Feb. 11, 2013, www.jtsa.edu [retrieved May 7, 2024].

Eisen, Chaim. "Rx for Orthodox Intolerance." *Jewish Action* 58, no. 1 (1997): 92–93.

EJPhilanthropy. "Rabbi Dr. Kenneth Brander to Head Ohr Torah." Oct. 10, 2017, https://ejewishphilanthropy.com [retrieved May 8, 2024].

Eleff, Zev. *Living from Convention to Convention: A History of the NCSY, 1954–1980.* Jersey City: Ktav, 2009.

———. "From Teacher to Scholar to Pastor: The Evolving Post-war Modern Orthodox Rabbinate." *American Jewish History* 98,4 (2014): 289–313.

———. *Modern Orthodox Judaism: A Documentary History.* Philadelphia: Jewish Publication Society, 2016.

———. *Who Rules the Synagogue: Religious Authority and the Formation of American Judaism.* Oxford and New York: Oxford University Press, 2016.

———. *Authentically Orthodox.* Detroit: Wayne State University Press, 2020.

———. "The Balabatish Daf Yomi Revolution." Jan. 14, 2020, https://thelehrhaus.com [retrieved May 12, 2024].

Eleff, Zev, and Eitan Kastner. "Reconciling Institutional Divides—Rosh Kollel and YC Dean Begin Dialogue." Sept. 11, 2006, www.yucommentator.com [retrieved May 8, 2024].

Ellenson, David H. "The Role of Reform in Selected German-Jewish Orthodox Responsa: A Sociological Analysis." *Hebrew Union College Annual* 53 (1982): 357–380.

———. *Tradition in Transition: Orthodoxy, Halakhah, and the Boundaries of Modern Jewish Identity.* Lanham, MD: University Press of America, 1989.

———. *Rabbi Esriel Hildesheimer and the Creation of a Modern Jewish Orthodoxy.* Tuscaloosa: University of Alabama Press, 1990.

———. "Traditional Reactions to Modern Jewish Reform: The Paradigm of German Orthodoxy." In *History of Jewish Philosophy,* edited by Daniel Frank and Oliver Leaman, 732–758. London: Routledge, 1997.

———. "David Hartman on Judaism and the Modern Condition." *Modern Judaism* 21, no. 3 (Oct. 2001): 256–281.

———. *After Emancipation.* Cincinnati: Hebrew Union College Press, 2004.

Ellenson, David H., and Daniel Gordis. *Pledges of Jewish Allegiance: Conversion, Law, Policymaking in Nineteenth- and Twentieth-Century Orthodox Responsa.* Stanford, CA: Stanford University Press, 2012.

Eller, Sandy. "Women of the Daf." Sept. 25, 2019, https://mishpacha.com [retrieved May 13, 2024].

El-Or, Tamar. *Next Year I Will Know More: Literacy and Identity Among Young Orthodox Women in Israel*. Detroit: Wayne State University Press, 2002.

Emes Ve-Emunah. "The Amazing Story of Rav Ahron, ZTL." Feb. 7, 2006, http://haemtza.blogspot.co.il [retrieved May 13, 2024].

Enders, Jürgen. "A Chair System in Transition: Appointments, Promotions, and Gate-Keeping in German Higher Education." *Higher Education* 41 (2001): 3–25.

Engelberg, Ari. "Modern Orthodoxy in Post-secular Times: Jewish Identities on the Boundaries of Religious Zionism." *Journal of Modern Jewish Studies* 14, no. 1 (2015): 126–139.

——. "Religious Zionist Singles: Caught between 'Family Values' and 'Young Adulthood.'" *Journal for the Scientific Study of Religion* 55, no. 2 (June 2016): 349–364.

Erikson, Kai T. *Wayward Puritans: A Study in the Sociology of Deviance*. New York: John Wiley and Sons, 1966.

Etkes, Immanuel. *Rabbi Israel Salanter and the Beginning of the "Musar" Movement*. Jerusalem: Magnes Press, 1982 [Hebrew].

Ettinger, Yair. "Tzohar Rabbis Oppose Recognition of Non-Orthodox Jewish Movements." Dec. 13, 2012, www.haaretz.com [retrieved May 8, 2024].

——. *Frayed: The Disputes Unraveling Religious Zionists*. Jerusalem: Toby Press, 2023.

Even, Shmuel. "The National Significance of Israeli Demographics at the Outset of a New Decade." *Strategic Assessment—A Multidisciplinary Journal on National Security* 24, no. 3 (2021): 33–49.

Ezra, Guy. "Ha-Mifgash shel ha-Rav Melamed im Rabah Reformit: Tamuhah ve-Zorev." June 9, 2020, www.srugim.co.il [retrieved May 8, 2024].

Falk, Uri. "Midrashot 'ha-kav' Yozmot Yemei iyun be-Tanakh, ke-Kontrah li-Yimei ha-Iyun shel 'ha-Gush." June 6, 2012, www.kipa.co.il [retrieved May 8, 2024].

——. "Devarim she-lo yedatem al Ha-Rav Aharon Lichtenstein." Sept. 9, 2012, www.kipa.co.il [retrieved May 8, 2024].

Farber, Seth. "Reproach, Recognition and Respect: Rabbi Joseph B. Soloveitchik's Mid-century Attitude toward Non-Orthodox Denominations." *American Jewish History* 89, no. 2 (2001): 193–214.

——. "Rabbi Joseph B. Soloveitchik's Early Zionism." *Tradition* 52, no. 2 (2020): 127–130.

Farber, Zev. "Can Orthodox Education Survive Biblical Criticism?" Aug. 28, 2014, http://thetorah.com, [retrieved May 8, 2024].

Farbstein, Esther. *Bnot Ami mi-Telz*. Jerusalem: Mossad ha-Rav Kook, 2024.

Feinstein, Moshe. *Igrot Moshe—Even ha-Ezer* 1. Bnei Brak: NP, 1985.

Feldman, Aharon. "Halakhic Feminism or Feminist Halakha?" *Tradition* 33, no. 2 (Winter 1999): 61–79.

Feldman, Jan. "'Point Men': How Religious Women Soldiers May Restore Israel's 'Citizens' Army." *Journal of the Middle East and Africa* 8, no. 4 (2017): 325–351.

Feldmann Kaye, Miriam. *Jewish Theology for a Postmodern Age*. Liverpool: Littman Library/Liverpool University Press, 2019.

———. "The Use of Hasidism in Responding to the Challenges of Postmodernism and Technology." *Contemporary Uses and Forms of Hasidut*, edited by Shlomo Zuckier, 279–306. New York: Yeshiva University Press, 2022.

Ferziger, Adam S. "The Lookstein Legacy: An American Orthodox Rabbinical Dynasty?" *Jewish History* 13, no. 1 (1999):127–149.

———. "Between Outreach and Inreach: Redrawing the Lines of the American Orthodox Rabbinate." *Modern Judaism* 25 (2005): 237–263.

———. *Exclusion and Hierarchy: Orthodoxy, Nonobservance, and the Emergence of Modern Jewish Identity*. Philadelphia: University of Pennsylvania Press, 2005.

———. *The Emergence of the Community Kollel: A New Model for Addressing Assimilation*—Position Paper 13. Ramat-Gan: Rappaport Center for Assimilation Research—Bar-Ilan University, 2006.

———. "Religion for the Secular: The New Israeli Rabbinate." *Journal of Modern Jewish Studies* 7, no. 1 (2008): 67–90.

———. *Centered on Study: Typologies of the American Community Kollel*, Position Paper 18 Ramat-Gan: Rappaport Center for Assimilation Research—Bar-Ilan University, 2009.

———. "Feminism and Heresy: The Construction of a Jewish Metanarrative." *Journal of the American Academy of Religion* 77, no. 3 (2009): 494–546.

———. "From Demonic Deviant to Drowning Brother: Reform Judaism in the Eyes of American Orthodoxy." *Jewish Social Studies* 15, no. 3 (2009): 56–88.

———. "Between Catholic Israel and the K"rov Yisrael: Non-Jews in Conservative Synagogues 1982–2008." *Journal of Jewish Studies* 61, no. 1 (Spring 2010): 88–116.

———. "Outside the Shul: The American Soviet Jewry Movement and the Rise of Solidarity Orthodoxy, 1964–1986." *Religion and American Culture* 22, no. 1 (Winter 2012): 83–130.

———. "From Lubavitch to Lakewood: The 'Chabadization' of American Orthodoxy." *Modern Judaism* 33, no. 2 (2013): 101–124.

———. "Beyond Bais Yaakov, Orthodox Outreach and the Emergence of Haredi Women as Religious Leaders." *Journal of Modern Jewish Studies* 14, no. 1 (2015): 140–159.

———. *Beyond Sectarianism—The Realignment of American Orthodox Judaism*. Detroit: Wayne State University Press, 2015.

———. "Sanctuary for the Specialist: Gender and the Evolution of the American Orthodox Rabbinate." *Jewish Social Studies* 23, no. 3 (Spring–Summer 2018): 1–37.

———. "Female Clergy in Male Space: The Sacralization of the Orthodox Rabbinate." *Journal of Religion* 98, no. 4 (Oct. 2018): 490–516.

———. "'The Road Not Taken' and 'the One Less Traveled': The Greenberg-Lichtenstein Exchange and Contemporary Orthodoxy." In *Yitz Greenberg and Modern Orthodoxy: The Road Not Taken*, edited by Adam S. Ferziger, Miri Freud-Kandel, and Steven Bayme, 254–288. Boston: Academic Studies Press, 2019.

———. "'And Who Even Knows What It Is?' The Role of Reform in the Rulings of Rabbi Yosef Eliyahu Henkin." In *"In the Dwelling of a Sage Lie Precious Treasures"—Essays in Jewish Studies in Honor of Shnayer Z. Leiman,* edited by Yitzhak Berger and Chaim Milikowsky, 323–340. New York: Ktav, 2020.

———. "Review of Shaul Magid, *Meir Kahane: The Public Life and Political Thought of an American Jewish Radical.*" *Tradition* 55, no. 1 (2023): 144–153.

Ferziger, Adam S., and David Sperber, eds., *The Paths of Daniel: Studies in Judaism and Jewish Culture in Honor of Rabbi Professor Daniel Sperber.* Ramat Gan: BIU Press, 2017.

Feuchtwanger, Ruti. "Knowledge versus Status: Discursive Struggle in Women's Batei Midrash." *Nashim: A Journal of Jewish Women's Studies & Gender Issues* 18 (2009): 166–186.

Fink, Shmuel. "The Impact of Technology on the Study of Talmud." Dissertation, Nova Southeastern University, 2014.

Finkelman, Yoel. "Haredi Isolation in Changing Environments: A Case Study in Yeshiva Immigration." *Modern Judaism* 22, no. 1 (2002): 61–82.

———. "On the Irrelevance of Religious-Zionism." *Tradition* 39, no. 1 (2005): 21–44.

———. "An Ideology for American Yeshiva Students: The Sermons of R. Aharon Kotler, 1942–1962." *Journal of Jewish Studies* LVIII, no. 2 (Autumn 2007): 314–332.

Finkielkraut, Alain. "In the Name of the Other: Reflections on the Coming Anti-Semitism," *Azure* 18 (2004): 21–33.

Fischer, Elli. "Who Is Qualified to Officiate at a Halakhic Marriage?" Oct. 6, 2019, https://blogs.timesofisrael.com [retrieved May 12, 2024].

Fischer, Shlomo. "Fundamentalist or Romantic Nationalist: Israeli Modern Orthodoxy." In *Dynamic Jewish Belonging,* edited by Harvey Goldberg, Stuart H. Cohen, and Ezra Kopelowitz, 91–111. Oxford: Berghahn, 2011.

———. "Radical Religious Zionism: From the Collective to the Individual." In *Kabbalah and Contemporary Spiritual Revival,* edited by Boaz Huss, 285–309. Be'er Sheva: Ben-Gurion University Press, 2011.

———. "The Religious Humanism of Aharon Lichtenstein." *Tradition* 47, no. 4 (2014): 17–34.

———. "Two Orthodox Cultures: 'Centrist Orthodoxy and Religious Zionism.'" In *Reconsidering Israel-Diaspora Relations,* edited by Eliezer Ben-Refael, Judit Bokser Liberant, and Yosef Gorny, 126–168. Leiden and Boston: Brill, 2014.

———. "Post-Kookism and Neo-Hasidut." *Contemporary Uses and Forms of Hasidut,* edited by Shlomo Zuckier, 307–346. New York: Yeshiva University Press, 2022.

Fishkoff, Sue. "Welcome to Beit Daniel." *Reform Judaism* 23, no. 3 (Spring 1995): 82–84.

———. *The Rebbe's Army: Inside the World of Chabad-Lubavitch.* New York: Schocken, 2003.

Fishman, Aryei. *Judaism and Modernization on the Religious Kibbutz.* Cambridge: Cambridge University Press, 1992.

Frankel, Isser. *Rabi Meir mi-Lublin: Me'yased Yeshivat Hakhmei Lublin.* Tel Aviv: Bitan ha-Sefer, 1952.

Freedman, Harry. *Reason to Believe: The Controversial Life of Louis Jacobs.* London: Bloomsbury Continuum, 2020.

Freud-Kandel, Miri. "On Revelation, Heresy, and Mesorah—From Louis Jacobs to the TheTorah.com." *Yitz Greenberg and Modern Orthodox Judaism: The Road Not Taken*, edited by Adam S. Ferziger, Miri Freud-Kandel, and Steven Bayme, 146–171. Boston: Academic Studies Press, 2019.

———. *Louis Jacobs and the Quest for a Contemporary Jewish Theology*. Liverpool: Littman Library, 2024.

Freund, Michael. "Up Close with Rabbi Yehoshua Fass." 2008, https://jewishaction.com [retrieved May 13, 2024].

Fried, Nurit. "Toanot Beit Din ve-Ha'azamat Nashim." in *Ishah, Havah, Adam*, edited by Aviva Sharbat, 129–142. Jerusalem: Reuven Mass, 2008.

Friedman, Bentzy. "The Full Story behind the 8 Minute Daf." Jan. 1, 2020, www.theyeshivaworld.com [retrieved May 14, 2024].

Friedman, Menachem. "The Changing Role of the Community Rabbinate." *Jerusalem Quarterly* (Fall 1982): 79–99.

———. "The Family-Community Model in Haredi Society." *Studies in Contemporary Jewry* XIV (1998): 166–177.

———. "Mara de-Atra—mi-Manhig le-Pakid: Sekirah Historit-Soẓiyyologit." In *On Leadership and Leaders*, edited by Hana Amit, 85–94. Tel Aviv: Ministry of Defense, 2000.

Frimer, Aryeh A., and Dov I. Frimer. "Women's Prayer Services—Theory and Practice." *Tradition* 32, no. 2 (1998): 5–118.

———. "Women, Keri'at ha-Torah, and Aliyyot." *Tradition* 46, no. 4 (2013): special supplement, https://traditiononline.org [retrieved May 8, 2024].

Frisch, Amos. "Jewish Tradition and Bible Criticism: A Typology of Israeli Orthodox Approaches to the Question of Deutero-Isaiah." *Jewish Studies Quarterly* 19, no. 3 (2012): 259–287.

Fuchs, Ilan. "The Construction of an Ideological Curriculum: The Study of Emunah in the Har Hamor Yeshiva." *Journal of Israeli History* 35, no. 1 (2016): 75–93.

———. "How to Create a Stay-at-Home Revolutionary: Rabbinic Discourse on Women's Education in the Haredi-Leumi Community." *Nashim* 33 (Fall 2018): 121–135Fuchs, Ofira. "Innovative Ordinariness and Ritual Change in a Jerusalem Minyan." *Journal of Modern Jewish Studies* 17, no. 4 (2018): 397–415.

Furstenberg, Rochelle. "The Flourishing of Higher Jewish Learning for Women." May 1, 2000, www.jcpa.org [retrieved May 6, 2024].

Furstenberg, Yair, and Oshrat Shoham. "Bein 'Kehillah Meruzah' le 'Kehillah Mutredet.'" *De'ot* 46 (March 2010), https://toravoda.org.il [retrieved Oct. 28, 2024].

Gaffney, James. "Newman on the Common Roots of Morality and Religion." *Journal of Religious Ethics* 16, no. 1 (Spring 1988): 143–159.

Gal, Alon. *David Ben-Gurion and the American Alignment for a Jewish State*. Bloomington: Indiana University Press, 1991.

Ganin, Zvi. *An Uneasy Relationship: American Jewish Leadership and Israel, 1948–1957*. Syracuse, NY: Syracuse University Press, 2005.

Ganzel, Tova. "Explicit and Implicit Polemic in Rabbi Samson Raphael Hirsch's Bible Commentary." *Hebrew Union College Annual* (2010): 171–191.

———. "Transformation of Pentateuchal Descriptions of Idolatry." In *Transforming Visions: Transformations of Text, Tradition, and Theology in Ezekiel*, edited by William A. Tooman and Michael A. Lyons, 33–49. Eugene, OR: Pickwick Publications, 2011.

Ganzel, Tova, Yehuda Brandes, and Chayuta Deutsch, eds. *The Believer and the Modern Study of the Bible*. Boston: Academic Studies Press, 2019.

Ganzel, Tova, and Deena Rachel Zimmerman, "Vesset ha-Guf: Hebet Hilkhati ve-Refui." *Tehumin* 20 (2000): 363–376.

———. "Women as Halakhic Professionals: The Role of the Yo'atzot Halakhah." *Nashim* 22 (Fall 2011): 161–171.

Garb, Jonathan. *The Chosen Will Become Herds: Studies in Twentieth-Century Kabbalah*. New Haven, CT: Yale University Press, 2009.

Gartner, Lloyd. "Conservative Judaism and Zionism: Scholars, Preachers, and Philanthropists." In *Zionism and Religion*, edited by Samuel Almog, Jehuda Reinharz, and Anita Shapira, 204–218. Hanover, NH, and London: University Press of New England, 1998.

Gellman, Jerome Yehuda. *This Was from God: A Contemporary Theology of Torah and History*. Boston: Academic Studies Press, 2016.

Gillman, Neil. "Inside or Outside? Emancipation and the Dilemmas of Conservative Judaism." *Judaism* 38, no. 4 (1989): 408–429.

Ginzburg, Yisrael. "Kakh Carlebach Patah et ha-Lev shel Olam ha-Yeshivot." Oct. 21, 2021, www.kikar.co.il [retrieved May 8, 2024].

Glanz, Moshe. "Me'orer Hashra'ah: Mi Hayah ha-Rav Sacks Avurkha? Bikashnu me-Anshei Zibbur le-Saper." Sept. 14, 2022, www.ynet.co.il [retrieved May 12, 2024].

Goldberg, Hillel. "Rabbi Isaac Hutner: A Synoptic Interpretive Biography." *Tradition* 22, no. 4 (1987): 18–46.

Goldberg, Jacob. "Our Rosh Yeshiva." *Rabbinic Alumni Chavrusa* 6, no. 1 (Dec. 1961): 7.

Goldfinger, Rivkah. "Inyan Ishi im Daniel Tropper," Mar. 8, 2023, www.inn.co.il [retrieved May 14, 2024].

Goldman, Ari L. "Jonathan Sacks, the U.K.'s Inclusive Former Chief Rabbi, Dies at 72." Nov. 9, 2020, www.nytimes.com [retrieved May 12, 2024].

Goldman, Daniel. "Book Review—Frayed: The Disputes Unraveling Religious Zionists." *Fathom* (May 2024), https://fathomjournal.org [retrieved May 30, 2024].

Goldmintz, Jay. "The Post-High School Yeshiva Experience in Israel." *Ten Da`at* 2 (Spring 1991): 32–36.

Golinkin, David. "The Participation of Jewish Women in Public Rituals and Torah Study 1845–2010." *Nashim* 21 (Spring 2011): 46–66.

Goodman, Dennis Ross. *Soloveitchik's Children: Irving Greenberg, David Hartman, Jonathan Sacks and the Future of Jewish Theology in America*. Tuscaloosa: University of Alabama Press, 2023.

Gordin, Rachel. "Ha-Terumot ha-Tarbutiyot ve-ha-Hevratiyot im Kenisatan shel Nashim le-Sedei ha-Hinukh ha-Hilkhati." PhD dissertation, Bar-Ilan University, 2005.

Gordis, Daniel. *We Stand Divided: The Rift between American Jews and Israel.* New York: Ecco, 2019.

Gottlieb, Fred, ed. *My Opa: The Diary of a German Rabbi.* Jerusalem: Mazo Publishers, 2005.

Gradstein, Linda. "Women Celebrate Siyum HaShas in Jerusalem." Jan. 15, 2020, www.jpost.com [retrieved May 12, 2024].

———. "Halakhic Power Couple." *Jerusalem Report* (Oct. 3, 2022), 10–13.

Green, Arthur, and Ariel Evan Mayse. *A New Hasidism—Branches.* Philadelphia: JPS, 2019.

———. *A New Hasidism—Roots.* Philadelphia: JPS, 2019.

Greenberg, Blu. *On Women and Judaism: A View from Tradition.* Philadelphia: Jewish Publication Society, 1981.

———. "Will There Be Orthodox Women Rabbis?" *Judaism* 33, no. 1 (1984): 23–33.

———. "Is Now the Time for Orthodox Woman Rabbis?" *Moment* (Dec. 1993), 50–74.

Greenberg, Irving. "Dr. Greenberg Discusses Orthodoxy, YU, Viet Nam, and Sex" (interview with Hillel Goldberg). *The Commentator* (Apr. 28, 1966), 6–8.

———. "Greenberg Clarifies and Defends His Views." *The Commentator* (May 12, 1966), 8–9.

———. "Yeshiva in the 1960s." In *My Yeshiva College*, edited by Menachem Butler and Zev Nagel, 183–184. Jerusalem: Yashar, 2006.

Greenwald, Hanan. "Biglal Pegishah im Reformim: Ha-Rav Yosef Me'ayem be-Nidui al Ha-Rav Melamed." Nov. 4, 2020, www.israelhayom.co.il [retrieved May 8, 2024].

Gries, Ze'ev. *Sifrut ha-Hanhagot.* Jerusalem: Bialik Institute, 1989.

Gross, Judah Ari. "Religious Advocacy Group Organizes 'Love the Convert' Shabbat in U.S., Israel before Shavuot." May 19, 2023, https://ejewishphilanthropy.com [retrieved May 13, 2024].

Grossman, Lawrence. "Decline and Fall: Thoughts on Religious Zionism in America." In *Religious Zionism Post-Disengagement: Future Directions*, edited by Chaim I. Waxman, 31–54. New York: Yeshiva University Press, 2008.

Gurock, Jeffrey S. "Resistors and Accomodators: Varieties of Orthodox Rabbis in America, 1886–1983." *American Jewish Archives* 35 (1983): 100–187.

———. *The Men and Women of Yeshiva.* New York: Columbia University, 1988.

———. "American Orthodox Organizational Support for Zionism, 1880–1930." In *Zionism and Religion*, edited by Samuel Almog, Jehuda Reinharz, and Anita Shapira, 219–234. Hanover, NH, and London: University Press of New England, 1998.

———. "Twentieth-Century American Orthodoxy's Era of Non-observance, 1900–1960." *Torah u-Madda Journal* 9 (2000): 87–107.

———. *Judaism's Encounter with American Sports.* Bloomington: Indiana University Press, 2005.

———. "The Late Friday Night Orthodox Service: An Exercise in Religious Accommodation." *Jewish Social Studies* 12, no. 3 (Spring–Summer, 2006): 137–156.

———. *Orthodox Jews in America*. Bloomington: Indiana State University Press, 2009.

———. "Orthodox Judaism in the United States." https://jwa.org [retrieved May 8, 2024].

Haaretz. "The Movement for Progressive Judaism Obtained a Provisional Court Order against the Tel Aviv Municipality." May 2, 1978, 4 [Hebrew].

Ha-Kesher ha-Rav Dori. "Sippur ha-Aliyah shel ha-Savtah Ha-Rabbanit Malka Bina." May 6, 2016, https://ravdori.co.il [retrieved May 7, 2024].

Haretzion. "Kobetz Tanhumim," https://etzion.haretzion.org [retrieved May 15, 2024].

Hacohen, Aviad. *Ari bein ha-Olamot*. Tel Aviv: Yediot Aharonoth, 2019.

Hacohen, Aviyah. "Ha-Omnam, Ehad Hayah Yishayahu?" *Derekh Efratah* 9–10 (2000–2001): 79–88.

Hadar, Yossi. "The Man behind the Controversy." Mar. 10, 2017, www.israelhayom.co.il [retrieved May 8, 2024].

Halberstam Mandelbaum, Yitta. *Holy Brother: Inspiring Stories and Enchanted Tales about Rabbi Shlomo Carlebach*. Northvale, NJ: Jason Aronson, Inc., 1997.

Halle, Charlotte. "Moving toward Inner-City Reform in Jaffa." *Haaretz* (Oct. 25, 2002), B4. [Hebrew].

Hanau, Shira. "Rabbi Yehuda Herzl Henkin, Pioneer of Women's Leadership in Orthodoxy, Dies." Dec. 24, 2020, www.jta.org [retrieved May 7, 2024].

Harel, Ayelet. "Women in the Military in Israel." In *The Palgrave International Handbook of Israel*, edited by P. R. Kumaraswamy, 1–13. Singapore: Springer Nature Singapore, 2023.

Hartman, David. "Halakhah as a Ground for Creating a Shared Spiritual Language." *Tradition* 16 (1976): 7–40.

———. "The Halakhic Hero: Rabbi Joseph Soloveitchik, Halakhic Man." *Modern Judaism* 9, 3 (Oct. 1989): 249–273.

———. *A Heart of Many Rooms: Celebrating the Many Voices within Judaism*. Woodstock, VT: Jewish Lights, 2001.

———. *The God Who Hates Lies: Confronting and Rethinking Jewish Tradition*. Woodstock, VT: Jewish Lights, 2011.

Hartman, Tova. "Eulogy." Feb. 19, 2013, www.hartman.org.il [retrieved May 7, 2024].

Hefter, Herzl. "'In God's Hands': The Religious Phenomenology of R. Mordechai Yosef of Izbica." *Tradition* 46, no. 1 (2013): 43–64.

———. "Why I Ordained Women." July 19, 2015, https://blogs.timesofisrael.com [retrieved May 13, 2024].

Heiges, Ruth. *Fast Facts about Beit Daniel*. Tel Aviv: Beit Daniel, 2001.

Heilman, Samuel C. *Synagogue Life*. Chicago: University of Chicago Press, 1976.

———. "The Many Faces of Orthodoxy: Part 1." *Modern Judaism* 2, no. 1 (1982): 23–51.

———. "The Ninth Siyum Ha-Shas: A Case Study in Orthodox Contra-Acculturation." In *The Americanization of the Jews*, edited by Robert Seltzer and Norman S. Cohen, 311–338. New York: New York University Press, 1995.

———. *Sliding to the Right: The Contest for the Future of American Jewish Orthodoxy.* Berkeley: University of California Press, 2006.

Heilman, Samuel C., and Menachem Friedman. *The Rebbe: The Life and Afterlife of Menachem Mendel Schneerson.* Princeton, NJ: Princeton University Press, 2010.

Heilman, Uriel. "With Poetry and Scholarship, Daf Yomi Talmud Study Grows beyond Orthodox." Aug. 2, 2012, www.jta.org [retrieved May 13, 2024].

Helfgot, Nathaniel. "Curricula, Methodologies and Values in Orthodox Tanakh Study: Where They Can Help Us." *Meorot* 7, vol. 2 (2008), https://library.yctorah.org [retrieved May 8, 2024].

———. "Torah and Historical Proof." July 27, 2013, https://morethodoxy.org [retrieved May 15, 2024].

———. "Divrei ha-Rav ve-Divrei ha-Talmid ve-Divrei ha-Rav: The Impact of Rabbi Joseph B. Soloveitchik's Thought on That of R. Aharon Lichtenstein." *Tradition* 47, no. 4 (Winter 2014): 86–112.

Hellinger, Moshe. "Political Theology in the Thought of the 'Merkaz Ha-Rav' Yeshiva and Its Profound Influence on Israeli Politics and Society since 1967." *Totalitarian Movements and Political Religions* 9, vol. 4 (2008): 533–550.

Helmreich, William B. *The World of the Yeshiva.* New York and London: Free Press, 1982.

Henderson, John B. *The Construction of Orthodoxy and Heresy.* Albany: SUNY Press, 1998.

Henkin, Chana. "Yoatzot Halachah: Fortifying Tradition through Innovation." *Jewish Action* (Winter 1999): 17–18.

———. "New Conditions and New Models of Authority: The *Yoatzot Halakhah.*" In *Rabbinic and Lay Communal Authority,* edited by Susan Last Stone and Robert Hirt, 85–92. New York: Yeshiva University Press, 2003.

———. "From Chaos to Repair in Women's Education and Leadership." *Tradition* 53, no. 3 (Summer 2021): 113–122.

Henkin, Yehuda Herzl, and Chana Henkin, eds. *Nishmat ha-Bayit: Contemporary Questions on Women's Reproductive Health.* Jerusalem: Koren/Nishmat/OU Press, 2022.

Henshke, David. "'Met she-ein lo Menaḥamim:' li-Demuto shel Moreinu ve-Rabbeinu ha-Rav R. Binyamin Ze'ev Benedikt, zikhro li-berakhah." *Tzohar* 13 (2003): 1–8.

Hermann, Tamar, et al. *The National-Religious Sector in Israel 2014—Main Findings.* Jerusalem: Israel Democracy Institute, 2014.

Hirsch, Samson Raphael. *Neunzehn Briefe über Judentum.* Frankfurt am Main: Sanger, 1920.

———. *Horeb,* translated by Isidor Grunfeld. New York: Soncino Press, 1962.

———. *The Nineteen Letters,* translated by Karen Paritzky and edited by Joseph Elias. Jerusalem and New York: Feldheim Publishers, 1994.

———. *The Hirsch Chumash.* Jerusalem: Feldheim Publishers, 2002–2009.

———. *Hamishah Humshei Torah im Peirush Ha-Rav Shimshon Raphael Hirsch.* New York: Joseph Breuer Foundation, 2012–2016.

Hirschhorn, Sara Yael. *City on a Hilltop—American Jews and the Settler Movement.* Cambridge, MA: Harvard University Press, 2017.

Hoffmann, Christhard, and Daniel R. Schwartz. "Early but Opposed—Supported but Late: Two Berlin Seminaries Which Attempted to Move Abroad." *Leo Baeck Institute Yearbook* 36, no. 1 (Jan. 1991): 267–304.

Horowitz, Ariel. "Ko'ev et ha-Petihut." Sept. 5, 2015, www.makorrishon.co.il [retrieved May 8, 2024].

———. "Yahasim Murkavim." May 6, 2016, https://musaf-shabbat.com [retrieved May 8, 2024].

Horowitz, Eli. *Milhemet Tarbut*. Hevron: Me-Emek Hevron, 2007.

Horowitz, Roger. *Kosher USA*. New York: Columbia University Press, 2016.

Howard, Aaron. "Call Her Rabbanit; She's Widening the Role of Women in the Orthodox Community." Jan. 24, 2019, https://jhvonline.com [retrieved May 13, 2024].

HUC.edu. "Dr. Alyssa Gray and Rabbi Benjamin David Lead Daf Yomi Siyyum at HUC-JIR/New York." Jan. 13, 2020, http://huc.edu [retrieved May 13, 2024].

HUC-JIR. "Mission to Jerusalem." *HUC-JIR Bulletin* 12 (Mar. 3, 1960), 12–15.

Hughes, Aaron W. "Jonathan Sacks: An Intellectual Portrait." In *Jonathan Sacks: Universalizing Particularity*, edited by Hava Tirosh-Samuelson and Aaron W. Hughes, 1–20. Leiden: Brill, 2013.

Husbands-Hankin, Shonna. "Soul Brothers." *American Jewish History* 100, no. 4 (2016): 547–553.

IDF. "Mi-Nashim le-Migdar—ha-Basis ha-Tefisati." Israel: IDF, 2015.

Ilan, Shahar. "The First Reform Synagogue Will Be Inaugurated in Tel Aviv Today." *Haaretz* (Oct. 6, 1991), 2 [Hebrew].

Imhoff, Sarah. "Carlebach and the Unheard Stories." *American Jewish History* 100, no. 4 (2016): 555–560.

Inbari, Motti. *Messianic Religious Zionism Confronts Israeli Territorial Compromises*. Cambridge: Cambridge University Press, 2012.

Irshai, Ronit. "Tamar Ross: An Intellectual Portrait." In *Tamar Ross: Constructing Faith*, edited by Hava Tirosch-Samuelson and Aaron W. Hughes, 1–40. Leiden: Brill, 2016.

Irshai, Ronit, and Dov Schwartz, eds. *A New Spirit in the Palace of Torah: Jubilee Volume in Honor of Professor Tamar Ross on the Occasion of Her Eightieth Birthday*. Ramat Gan: Bar-Ilan Press, 2018.

Irshai, Ronit, and Tonya Zion-Waldoks. "Modern-Orthodox Feminism in Israel between Nomos and Narrative." *Mishpat u-Memshal* 15 (2013): 1–94.

———. *Holy Rebellion: Religious Feminism and the Transformation of Judaism and Women's Rights in Israel*. Waltham, MA.: Brandeis University Press, 2024.

Israel-Cohen, Yael. "Between Feminism and Orthodoxy in Israel." *Journal of Jewish Sociology* 50, no. 1–2 (2008): 51–66.

———. *Between Feminism and Orthodox Judaism*. Leiden: Brill, 2012.

Israelitisches Wochenblatt. "Ben-Gurion war auch in der Jeschiwah-Universität." Apr. 4, 1960, 19.

Israel National News. "Record Number of Female Religious Soldiers." Oct. 2, 2018, www.israelnationalnews.com [retrieved May 9, 2024].

Israel-Shamsian, Yael. "The Israeli Religious Market and Penetration of the Conservative and Reform Movements." MA thesis, Tel Aviv University, 2004.

Isserow, Rachelle. "Creating New Leaders: Interview with Malke Bina, Founder and Director of MaTaN." *JOFA Journal* VI, no. 1 (Winter 2006): 1–3.

ITIM. "ITIM: 2022 Impact Report." 2022, www.itim.co.il [retrieved May 15, 2024].

Jackson, Daniel. "Torah min haShamayim: Conflicts between Religious Belief and Scientific Thinking." *Conversations* 6 (2010), www.jewishideas.org [retrieved May 8, 2024].

Jackson, H. J. *Those Who Write for Immortality: Romantic Reputations and the Dream of Fame.* New Haven, CT: Yale University Press, 2015.

Joffrie, Tzvi. "Har Etzion: Leader Asks Noam Leader to Personally Apologize to Yeshiva's Rabbis." Sept. 5, 2022, www.jpost.com [retrieved May 13, 2024].

Joselit, Jenna. *New York's Jewish Jews: The Orthodox Community in the Interwar Years.* Bloomington: Indiana University Press, 1990.

Jotkowitz, Alan. "Universalism and Particularism in the Jewish Tradition: The Radical Theology of Rabbi Jonathan Sacks." *Tradition* 44, no. 3 (2011): 53–67.

———. "'And Now the Child Will Ask': The Post-modern Theology of Rav Shagar." *Tradition* 45, no. 2 (2012): 49–66.

———. "'I Am in the Middle': Rav Aharon Lichtenstein's Vision of Centrist Orthodoxy." *Hakirah* 22 (2017): 49–66.

Jerusalem Post. "Herzog, Hundreds of Leaders Reflect on Legacy of Rabbi Lord Jonathan Sacks." Sept. 18, 2022, www.jpost.com [retrieved May 12, 2024].

———. "Why Are So Many of Israel's Fallen Soldiers from Religious Zionist Camp?" Dec. 29, 2023, www.jpost.com [retrieved May 13, 2024].

Jewish Chronicle. "Rabbi Dr Nahum Eliezer Rabinovitch." June 12, 2020, www.thejc.com [retrieved May 15, 2024].

Jewish Standard. "Rabbi Helfgot's Statement of Principles Urges Sensitivity toward Gays in Orthodoxy." July 30, 2010, https://jewishstandard.timesofisrael.com [retrieved May 8, 2024].

Joint Council of Mechinot. "Mechinat Tzahali Makes History with the First Halakhic Guidebook for Religious Women in the IDF." Jan. 4, 2018, https://mechinot.org.il [retrieved May 9, 2024].

JTA. "Ben-Gurion to Visit Jewish Institutes of Higher Learning." Mar. 14, 1960, www.jta.org [retrieved May 15, 2024].

———. "Ben-Gurion Finds American Friendship Deepened; Leaves for London." Mar. 17, 1960, www.jta.org [retrieved May 15, 2024].

———. "U.S. Zionist Leaders in Counterattack on Ben-Gurion's Assault on Them." May 23, 1961, www.jta.org [retrieved May 13, 2024].

———. "Reform and Conservative Synagogues Merge in New Jersey." Sept. 11, 2015, www.jta.org [retrieved May 12, 2024].

Kahana, Maoz. "Sippur she-Sham'ati mi-Rav Yehudah Amital Hosef et ha-Sheniyut she-Hitkaymah be-Olamo." Nov. 17, 2022, www.makorrishon.co.il [retrieved May 14, 2024].

Kahana, Maoz, and Ariel Evan Mayse, "Hasidic Halakha: Reappraising the Interface of Spirit and Law." *AJS Review* 41, vol. 2 (2017): 375–408.

Kahn, Ava F. "Transnational Aspirations—The Founding of American Kibbutzim, 1940s, 1970s." In *Transnational Traditions—New Perspectives on American Jewish History*, edited by Ava F. Kahn and Adam D. Mendelsohn, 253–279. Detroit: Wayne State University Press, 2014.

Kahn, Yair, and Kalman Neuman, "A Rabbinic Exchange on the Disengagement: A Case Study in R. Aharon Lichtenstein's Approach to 'Hilkhot Tsibbur.'" *Tradition* 47, no. 4 (Winter 2014): 157–187.

Kampeas, Ron. "In a First, Israeli Government to Pay Orthodox Women to Advise on Jewish Law." June 2, 2022, www.jta.org [retrieved May 8, 2024].

———. "Polls Show American Jews Approve of Biden's Handling of Israel-Hamas War while Americans as a Whole Do Not." Nov. 16, 2023, www.jta.org [retrieved May 13, 2024].

Kaplan, Lawrence. "Rabbi Isaac Hutner's 'Daat Torah Perspective' on the Holocaust: A Critical Analysis." *Tradition* 18, no. 3 (Fall 1980): 235–248.

———. "From Cooperation to Conflict: Rabbi Professor Emanuel Rackman, Rav Joseph B. Soloveitchik, and the Evolution of American Modern Orthodoxy." *Modern Judaism* 30, no. 1 (2010): 46–68.

———. "Back to Zechariah Frankel and Louis Jacobs? On Integrating Academic Talmudic Scholarship into Israeli Religious Zionist Yeshivas and the Spectre of the Historical Development of the Halakhah." *Journal of Modern Jewish Studies* 14, no. 1 (2015): 89–108.

———. "An Alternate View on Rav Aharon Lichtenstein and Academic Talmud Study." Mar. 19, 2018, www.thelehrhaus.com [retrieved May 14, 2024].

———. "Rabbi Joseph B. Soloveitchik's Philosophy of Halakhah." *Jewish Law Annual* 7 (2021): 139–197.

Karoll, Dov. *Torat Hesed: Bibliography of Harav Aharon Lichtenstein zt"l*. Nov. 1, 2023, www.etzion.org.il [retrieved May 8, 2024].

Karp, Abraham J. *Jewish Continuity in America*. Tuscaloosa: University of Alabama Press, 1998.

———"Overview: The Synagogue in America—A Historical Typology." In *The American Synagogue: A Sanctuary Transformed*, edited by Jack Wertheimer, 1–36. Cambridge and New York: Cambridge University Press, 1987.

Katriel, Tamar. "Review: Orna Sasson-Levy, *Gavriyut ve-Nashiyut ba-Zava ha-Yisraeli*." *Sociologiah Yisraelit* 10, no. 1 (2008): 196–198.

Katz, Emily Alice. *Bringing Zion Home: Israel in American Jewish Culture, 1948–1967*. Albany: SUNY Press, 2015.

Katz, Gideon. *The Pale God: Israeli Secularism and Spinoza's Philosophy of Cult*. Boston: Academic Studies Press, 2011.

Katz, Jacob. "German Culture and the Jews." In *The Jewish Response to German Culture: From the Enlightenment to the Second World War*, edited by Jehuda Reinharz, 54–59. Waltham, MA: Brandeis University Press, 1985.

——. "Orthodoxy in Historical Perspective." In *Studies in Contemporary Jewry II*, edited by Peter H. Medding, 3–17. Bloomington: Indiana University Press, 1986.

——. *Tradition and Crisis*, translated by Bernard Dov Cooperman. Syracuse, NY: Syracuse University Press, 1993.

——. "Towards a Biography of the Hatam Sofer." In *Divine Law in Human Hands*, 403–443. Jerusalem: Magnes, 1998.

Katzman, Haim. "The Hyphen Cannot Hold: Contemporary Trends in Religious-Zionism." *Israel Studies Review* 35, no. 2 (Autumn 2020): 154–174.

——. "New Religious-Nationalist Trends among Jewish Settlers in the Halutza Sands." *International Journal of Religion* 1, no. 1 (2020): 151–165.

Kaufman, David. *A Shul with a Pool: The "Synagogue-Center" in American Jewish History*. Hanover, NH: University of New England Press, 1998.

Kaunfer, Elie. *Empowered Judaism: What Independent Minyanim Can Teach Us about Building Vibrant Jewish Communities*. Woodstock, VT: Jewish Lights Publishing, 2010.

Kaunfer, Neil, and Zev Shanken. "An Interview with Shlomo Riskin." *Response* 29 (Spring 1976): 10–14.

Kaye, Alexander. *The Invention of Jewish Theocracy: The Struggle for Legal Authority in Modern Israel*. New York: Oxford University Press, 2020.

Keats-Jaskol, Shoshana. "Spirituality: Jerusalem Rabbi Brings Process-Shul Model from Memphis, Long-Term Emissary Merges Best of US and Israeli Traditions." Dec. 28, 2017, www.jpost.com [retrieved May 13, 2024].

Kelman, Ari Y., and Shaul Magid. "The Gate to the Village: Shlomo Carlebach and the Creation of American Jewish 'Folk.'" *American Jewish History* 100, no. 4 (2016): 511–540.

Kelner, Shaul. *Tours That Bind: Diaspora, Pilgrimage, and Israeli Birthright Tourism*. New York: New York University Press, 2010.

——. *A Cold War Exodus: How American Jews Mobilized to Freed Soviet Jews*. New York: NYU Press, 2024.

Khagram, Sanjeev, and Peggy Levitt, *The Transnational Studies Reader: Intersections and Innovations*. London: Routledge, 2008.

Kiel, Yehudah. *Le-Gamro shel ha-Mifa'al ha-Parshani Da'at Mikra*. Alon Shevut: self-published, 2003.

Kipa. "Ha-Rav Yuval Cherlow: Beit ha-Mishpat ha-Elyon Eino Musmakh ve-Eino Koveyah shum Keviyah Hilkhatit Kolshehi." Mar. 1, 2021, www.kipa.co.il [retrieved May 8, 2024].

Kirsch, Adam. "The Superbowl of Jewish Learning." Jan. 3, 2020, www.wsj.com [retrieved May 12, 2024].

Klein, Abraham M. "A Great Talmudist: Rabbi Pinchas Hirschprung Interviewed." *Canadian Jewish Chronicle* (Mar. 13, 1942), 4.

Klein, Menachem. *Bar-Ilan: University between Religion and Politics*. Jerusalem: Magnes Press and Eshkol Institute, 1997 [Hebrew].

Klein, Yehonatan. "Pirsum Rishon: Nivhar Mahalifo shel Ha-Rav Benny Lau." Apr. 4, 2019, www.kipa.co.il [retrieved May 13, 2024].

Klein, Zvika "Se'arat ha-Rav Melamed ve-ha-Reformim: Mi ha-Rabanim she-lo Hatmu." Nov. 10, 2020, www.makorrishon.co.il [retrieved May 8, 2024].

———. "Ha-Rav Sacks Kavash et ha-Olam akh hitkashe lifnot le-Yisraelim be-Sefatam." Dec. 14, 2020, www.makorrishon.co.il [retrieved May 12, 2024].

———. "Rabbi Haim Drukman, Spiritual Leader of Religious Zionists, Dead at 90." Dec. 25, 2022, www.jpost.com [retrieved May 13, 2024].

———. "Modern Orthodox Rabbi: LGBTQ+ People Can Teach at Yeshivas." Mar. 12, 2023, www.jpost.com [retrieved May 8, 2024].

Klein-Halevi, Yossi. *Memoirs of a Jewish Extremist: An American Story.* New York: Little Brown, 1995.

———. "Jewish, Observant, and Illegal in Israel." *Jerusalem Report* (June 26, 1997), 12–16.

———. *Like Dreamers: The Story of the Israeli Paratroopers who Reunited Jerusalem and Divided a Nation.* New York: HarperCollins, 2013.

Kleinman, Ron. "Shitat Limud ha-Gemara ve-Shiurei 'Methodikah Talmudit' shel Ha-Rav Aharon Lichtenstein." *Tzohar* 40 (2016–17): 51–76.

Kolbrener, William. "Religion and Culture: An Ambivalent Life." In *Developing a Jewish Perspective on Culture,* edited by Yehuda Sarna, 169–186. New York: Ktav/Yeshiva University Press, 2013.

Koller, Judah. "An Improved Judaic Studies." Apr. 14, 2019, https://yucommentator.org [retrieved May 8, 2024].

Kook, Abraham Isaac. *Orot ha-Kodesh.* Jerusalem: Mossad Harav Kook, 1985.

———. *Iggerot ha-Re'iyyah.* Jerusalem: Ha-Makhon le-Hoza'at Sefarim al shem ha-Rav Zevi Yehudah, zz"l, 1986.

———. *Le-Nevukhei ha-Dor,* edited by Shahar Rahmani. Tel Aviv: Yediot Aharonot, 2014.

Kook, Zvi Yehuda. *Le-Netivot Yisrael,* vol. 2. Beit El: Beit El, 2003.

Koren, Irit. "The Bride's Voice: Religious Women Challenge the Wedding Ritual." *Nashim* 10 (2005): 29–52.

Krakowski, Moshe, Elana Riback Rand, and Suzanne Brooks. "The Role of Israel in American Haredi Life." *Modern Judaism* 41, no. 3 (Oct. 2021): 252–272.

Krasovska, Natalya, and Claude-Hélène Mayer. *A Psychobiography of Viktor E. Frankl: Using Adversity for Life Transformation.* Heidelberf: Springer International Publishing, 2021.

Kratz, Elizabeth. "Rabbi Kenneth Brander Makes Aliyah: Will Lead Ohr Torah Stone." July 25, 2018, https://jewishlink.news [retrieved May 14, 2024].

Kraus, Yitzchak. *Ha-Shevi'i.* Tel Aviv: Yedioth Aharonoth, 2007.

Krauss, Yair. "Retreat Meyuhad be-Shem ha-Rav: Koah Sacks." July 7, 2023, www.ynet.co.il [retrieved May 12, 2024].

Kraut, Benny. *The Greening of American Orthodox Judaism: Yavneh in the 1960s.* Cincinnati: HUC Press, 2011.

Krumbein, Elyakim. "From Reb Hayyim and the Rav to Shiurei Rav Aharon—The Evolution of a Tradition of Learning." In *Lomdut: The Conceptual Approach to Jewish Learning,* edited by Yosef Blau, 229–297. Jersey City: Ktav, 2006.

Kugel, James L. *How to Read the Bible: A Guide to Scripture Then and Now.* New York: Free Press, 2007.

Kuisel, Richard K. "The End of Americanization? or Reinventing a Research Field for Historians of Europe." *Journal of Modern History* 92, no. 3 (2020): 602–634.

Kula, Amit. *Havayah O Lo Hayah: Historiyah, Safah Datit, u-Demut ha-El.* Ein Zurim: Bogrei Yeshivat ha-Kibbutz ha-Dati be-Ein Zurim, 2011.

Kurshan, Ilana. *If All the Seas Were Ink: A Memoir.* New York: St. Martin's Press, 2017.

———. https://ilanakurshan.com [retrieved July 25, 2024].

Kurzweil, Avraham, Shmuel Haber, and Dov Lior. "A Rabbinic Exchange on Baruch Goldstein's Funeral." *Tradition* 28, no. 4 (Summer 1994): 59–63.

Labowitz, Gail. "*Poskot* in the Palace of Torah: A Preliminary Study of Orthodox Feminism and Halachic Process." In *Jews and Gender,* edited by Leonard J. Greenspoon, 283–311. West Lafayette, IN: Purdue University Press, 2021.

Landau, Or. *Beit Daniel—Cultural, Community, Education Programs.* Tel Aviv: Beit Daniel, 2003 [Hebrew].

Landes, David. "Traditional Struggles: Studying, Deciding, and Performing the Law at the Rabbi Isaac Elchanan Theological Seminary." Doctoral dissertation, Princeton University, 2010.

———. *Our Roshei Yeshiva: Reflections on the Lives, Thought, and Leadership of Rabbi Yehuda Amital zt"l and Rabbi Aharon Lichtenstein zt"l.* Cambridge, MA: Shikey Press, 2022.

Langer, Lawrence. *Versions of Survival: The Holocaust and the Human Spirit.* Albany: SUNY Press, 1982.

Lau, Benny. "Ha-Koteret Zekan Rabbanei ha-Zionut ha-Datit oseh lo Avel." May 7, 2020, Srugim.com.il [retrieved May 7, 2024].

Lebel, Udi. "The 'Immunized Integration' of Religious-Zionists within Israeli Society: The Pre-military Academy as an Institutional Model." *Social Identities* 22, no. 6 (2016): 642–660.

———. "Settling the Military: The Pre-military Academies Revolution and the Creation of a New Security Epistemic Community—The Militarization of Judea and Samaria." *Israel Affairs* 21, no. 3 (2015): 361–390.

Leibowitz, Shira Schmidt, and Jessica Setbon. "Up Close with Rosh Yeshiva-Turned-Novelist Haim Sabato." Fall 2006, https://jewishaction.com [retrieved May 8, 2024].

Leon, Nissim. "The Secular Origins of Mizrahi Traditionalism." *Israel Studies* 13, no. 3 (Fall 2008): 22–42.

Lev, David. "Ministry to Israelis Abroad: Try Chabad for Help." June 25, 2013, www.israelnationalnews.com [retrieved May 13, 2024].

Levenson, Jon D. *The Hebrew Bible, The Old Testament, and Historical Criticism.* Louisville, KY: Westminster/John Knox Press, 1993.

Levine, Cody. "40,000 Participate in Daf Yomi via OU App." Nov. 30, 2020, www.jpost.com [retrieved May 12, 2024].

Levine, Doron. "Regarding the Building of Bridges." Oct. 19, 2015, https://yucommentator.org [retrieved May 8, 2024].

Levinstein, Yigael. *Agenda Z'vait: Keizad Tefisat ha-Migdar Meforeret et Z'va ha-Am.* Israel: NP, Apr. 2018.

Levmore, Rachel. *Min'i Einayikh mi-Dim'ah: Heskemei Kedam-Nissu'in li-Meni'at Seiruv Get.* Jerusalem: Ariel, 2009.

———. "A View from the Other Side." *Tradition* 49, no. 1 (Spring 2016): 49–58.

Levy, B. Barry. "The State and Directions of Orthodox Bible Study." In *Modern Scholarship in the Study of Torah*, edited by Shalom Carmy, 39–80. New York: Yeshiva University Press/Ktav, 1996.

Levy-Paz, Gitit. "The New (Literary) Engagement with Israel." Dec. 12, 2018, https://blogs.timesofisrael.com [retrieved May 13, 2024].

Libel-Hass, Einat. "Jewish Women in Reform Settings in Israel: Past, Present, and Personal." *CCAR Journal* (Summer 2023): 13–22.

Libel-Hass, Einat, and Elazar Ben-Lulu. "Are You Our Sisters? Resistance, Belonging, and Recognition among Israeli Reform Jewish Female Converts." *Politics and Religion Journal* 18, no. 1 (2024): 131–157.

Liberles, Robert. *Religious Conflict in a Social Context: The Resurgence of Orthodox Judaism in Frankfurt am Main, 1838–1877.* Westport, CT, and London: Greenwood Press, 1985.

Lichtenstein, Aharon. "Brother Daniel and the Jewish Fraternity." *Judaism* 12, no. 3 (Summer 1963), 260–280.

———. "Rav Lichtenstein Writes Letter to Dr. Greenberg." *The Commentator* (June 2, 1966), 7–8.

———. "Religion and State: The Case for Interaction." *Judaism* 15, no. 4 (Fall 1966): 387–411.

———. "The State of Orthodoxy: A Symposium." *Tradition* 20, no. 1 (Spring 1982), 47–50.

———. "Jewish Values in a World of Change: The Role of Jewish Communal Service." *Journal of Jewish Communal Service* 61 (Fall 1984): 17–26.

———. "The State of K'lal Yisrael: A Symposium." *Jewish Action* 46, no. 4 (1986): 37–39.

———. "On the Murder of Prime Minister Yitzhak Rabin z"l." *Ten Da'at* 9, no. 1 (Winter 1996): 3–14.

———. "Torah and General Culture: Confluence and Conflict." In *Judaism's Encounter with Other Cultures: Rejection or Integration*, edited by Jacob J. Schacter, 220–292. Northvale, NJ: Jacob Aronson, 1997.

———. "On Aliyah: The Uniqueness of Living in Eretz Yisrael." https://etzion.org.il [retrieved March 6, 2025].

———. *By His Light: Character and Values in the Service of God*, adapted by Reuven Ziegler. Jersey City: Ktav, 2002.

———. *Leaves of Faith: The World of Jewish Learning 1.* Jersey City: Ktav, 2003.

———. *Leaves of Faith: The World of Jewish Learning 2.* Jersey City: Ktav, 2004.

———. "The 60s." In *My Yeshiva College*, edited by Menachem Butler and Zev Nagel, 374–377. Jerusalem: Yashar, 2006.

———. "My Education and Aspirations: Autobiographical Reflections of Rav Aharon Lichtenstein zt"l." *The Israel Koschitzky Virtual Beit Midrash* (2007), www.etzion.org.il [retrieved May 14, 2024].

——. "Diaspora Religious Zionism: Some Current Reflections." In *Religious Zionism Post Disengagement*, edited by Chaim I. Waxman, 3–30. New York: Yeshiva Univeristy Press/Ktav, 2008.

——. "Beyond the Pale? Reflections Regarding Contemporary Relations with Non-Orthodox Jews." In *The Relationship of Orthodox Jews with Believing Jews of Other Religious Ideologies and Non-Believing Jews*, edited by Adam Mintz, 187–223. New York: Yeshiva University Press, 2010.

——. "Criticism and *Kitvei Kodesh*." In *Rav Shalom Banaiyikh: Essays Presented to Rabbi Shalom Carmy by Friends and Students in Celebration of Forty Years of Teaching*, edited by Hayyim Angel and Yitzchak Blau, 15–32. Jersey City: Ktav, 2012.

——. "Foreword." In *Mikra and Meaning: Studies in Bible and Its Interpretation*, edited by Nethaniel Helfgot, ix–xv. Jerusalem: Maggid, 2012.

——. "Joseph's Tears," n.d., www.etzion.org.il [retrieved May 8, 2024].

——. *Pages of Faith: Exploring the Thought of HaRav Aharon Lichtenstein*, n.d., https://pagesoffaith.wordpress.com [retrieved July 25, 2024].

Lichtenstein, Mosheh. "A Conversation with Rabbi Mosheh Lichtenstein." Dec. 4, 2016, www.maalegilboa.org [retrieved May 13, 2024].

——. "Which Religious Zionism—and Which Cliff? A Response to Hillel Halkin." Jan. 18, 2023, https://jewishreviewofbooks.com [retrieved May 13, 2024].

Lidor, Canaan. "The Jewishness of Some Hamas Victims Sparks Bitter Disputes over Their Burial." Nov. 14, 2023, www.timesofisrael.com [retrieved May 13, 2024].

Lieber, Andrea. "A Virtual Veibershul: Blogging and the Blurring of Public and Private among Orthodox Jewish Women." *College English* 72, no. 6 (2010): 621–637.

Lieberman, Judith (Berlin). *Autobiography and Reflections*. Cambridge, MA: Shikey Press, 2022.

Lieblich, Julia. "French Feminist Rabbi Captivates Multifaith Crowds with Musings on Mortality." Oct. 2, 2022, www.nytimes.com [retrieved May 8, 2024].

Liebman, Charles S. "Orthodoxy in American Jewish Life." *American Jewish Yearbook* 66 (1965): 48–97.

——. "The Training of American Rabbis." *American Jewish Year Book* 69 (1968): 3–112.

——. "Diaspora Influence on Israel: The Ben-Gurion-Blaustein 'Exchange' and Its Aftermath." *Jewish Social Studies* 36, nos. 3–4 (July–Oct. 1974): 271–280.

——. "Studying Orthodox Judaism in the United States: A Review Essay." *American Jewish History* 80, no. 3 (Spring 1991): 415–424.

——. "Modern Orthodoxy in Israel." *Judaism* 47 (Fall 1998): 405–410.

Liebman, Charles S., and Steven M. Cohen. *Two Worlds of Judaism: The Israeli & American Experiences*. New Haven, CT: Yale University Press, 1990.

Liebowitz Kalaora, Shelly. *Brief of an Advertising Campaign for Tiferet Shalom Congregation*. October: NP, 2006.

Lifshitz, Cnaan. "Rabbi David Lazar, Too Brash for Stockholm?" Apr. 23, 2013, www.timesofisrael.com [retrieved May 12, 2024].

Limonic, Laura. "The Role of Transnational Actors in the Growth of Chabad-Lubavitch among Argentine Jews." *Contemporary Jewry* 41, no. 4 (2021): 843–857.

Linzer, Dov. "Ani li"Dodi vi"Dodi Li—Towards a More Balanced Wedding Ceremony." *JOFA Journal* 4, no. 2 (2003): 4–7.

Lipman, Steve. "YU Gay Panel Broadens the Discussion, Debate." Dec. 30, 2009, www.thejewishweek.com [retrieved May 8, 2024].

———. "Riskin Chooses Successor for His Educational Network." Feb. 3, 2015, https://ots.org.il [retrieved May 8, 2024].

Lipshitz, Yoni. "Recollections and Reconsiderations: Revisiting the Path of Rabbi Norman Lamm." *The Commentator* (Dec. 18, 2007), 13–14.

Litvak, Meir. "The Islamic Republic of Iran and the Holocaust: Anti-Semitism and Anti-Zionism." *Journal of Israeli History* 25, no. 1 (2006): 267–284.

Lockshin Bob, Chana. "The Next Women's Siyum ha-Shas." Jan. 15, 2020, https://thelehrhaus.com [retrieved May 12, 2024].

Lomsky-Feder, Edna, and Orna Sasson-Levy. *Women Soldiers and Citizenship in Israel: Gendered Encounters with the State.* New York: Routledge, 2018.

Lopatin, Asher. "Revelation and the Education of Modern Orthodox Rabbis." July 26, 2013, https://morethodoxy.org [retrieved May 8, 2024].

Lorberbaum, Menachem. "Beit Medrash." *Mehuyavut Yehudit Mithadeshet: Al Olamo ve-Haguto shel David Hartman* vol. 1, edited by Avi Sagi, Zvi Zohar, and Dror Yinon, 51–70. Tel Aviv: SHI/Ha-Kibbutz ha-Me'uhad, 2001.

Lövheim, Mia, and Heidi A. Campbell. "Considering Critical Methods and Theoretical Lenses in Digital Religion Studies." *New Media & Society* 19, no. 1 (2017): 5–14.

Lubitz, Rivka. *Feminism Dati ke-Tikkun Olam.* Jerusalem: Kolekh, 2019.

Lubitz, Ronen. *Ha-Im Lizrom im ha-Zeramim? Ha-Yahadut ha-Orthodoksit ve-yahasah la-Zeramim ha-Hadashim ve-le-Yehudei ha-Tefuzot.* NP: Ne'emanei Torah va-Avodah, 2021.

Lurie, Jesse Zel. "Soloveitchik, B-G, Discuss Education." *The Commentator* (Mar. 10, 1960), 1.

Luz, Ehuz. *Parallels Meet.* Philadelphia: Jewish Publication Society, 1988.

Magid, Jacob. "Officers and Gentlemen? Religious Zionist Flagship Academy Comes under Scrutiny." May 2, 2018, www.timesofisrael.com [retrieved May 8, 2024].

Magid, Shaul. *Hasidism on the Margin.* Madison: University of Wisconsin Press, 2003.

———. "'And They Created Him in Their Image': David Hartman's Soloveitchik and the Battle for a Teachers' Legacy." *Shofar* 21, no. 2 (2003): 134–139.

———. *American Post-Judaism: Identity and Renewal in a Postethnic Society.* Bloomington: Indiana University Press, 2013.

———. "Shlomo Carlebach and Meir Kahane: The Difference and Symmetry between Romantic and Materialist Politics." *American Jewish History* 100, no. 4 (Oct. 2016): 461–484.

———. "Consumed by Fire: Remembering Life in Shlomo Carlebach's Israeli Moshav, Now Engulfed in Flames." May 26, 2019, www.tabletmag.com [retrieved May 8, 2024].

———. *Meir Kahane: The Public Life and Political Thought of an American Jewish Radical.* Princeton, NJ: Princeton University Press, 2021.

——. *The Necessity of Exile*. n.l.: Ayin Press, 2023.

Maltz, Judy. "Number of Israelis Marrying outside Rabbinate Rising, Even among Orthodox Jews." June 13, 2018, www.haaretz.com [retrieved May 12, 2024].

Maoz, Darya, and Zvi Bekerman. "Chabad Tracks the Trekkers: Jewish Education in India." *Journal of Jewish Education* 75, no. 2 (2009): 173–193.

Marcus, Shmuel. "The Indomitable Spirit of Rabbi Ahron Soloveichik." 2001, https://jewishaction.com [retrieved May 14, 2024].

Margolin, Ron. "New Models of the Sacred Leader at the Beginning of Hasidism." In *Saints and Role Models in Judaism and Christianity*, edited by Marcel Poorthuis and Joshua J. Schwartz, 377–391. Leiden: Brill, 2004.

Mark, Jonathan. "Yakov Birnbaum's Freedom Ride." *Jewish Week* (Apr. 30, 2004), 16–17.

Mark, Zvi. *Mistikah ve-Shiga'on bi-Yezirat Rabbi Nahman mi-Breslov*. Jerusalem and Tel Aviv: SHI/Am 'Oved, 2003.

Markowitz, Pearl. "Rabbanit Michelle Cohen Farber Teaches the Daf at Rinat." Feb. 27, 2020, https://jewishlink.news [retrieved May 13, 2024].

Marx, Dalia. "A Female Rabbi Is Like an Orange on the Passover Plate—Women and the Rabbinate: Challenges and Horizons." In *Rabbi-Pastor-Priest: Their Roles and Profiles Through the Ages*, edited by Walter Homolka and Heinz-Gunther Schotler, 219–240. Berlin: Walter de Gruyter, 2013.

——. "Participation of Non-Jewish Family Members in BarBat-Mitzvah Ceremonies in the American Reform Movement: Boundaries or Inclusion." In *Becoming Jewish: New Jews and Emerging Jewish Communities in Globalized Jewish World*, edited by Tudor Parfitt and Nethanel Fisher, 354–369. Newcastle upon Tyne: Cambridge Scholars Publishing, 2016.

Maryles Sztokman, Elana. *Orthodox Feminist Movements in Israel and the United States: Community Struggle versus State Struggle*. Ramat Gan: Argov Center for the Study of Israel and the Jewish People, 2014.

Mashiach, Amir. "Changes in the Understanding of Work in Religious Zionist Thought: Rabbi T.I. Thau as a Case Study." *Religions* 9, no. 10 (2018), www.mdpi.com [retrieved May 12, 2024].

Maślak, Alicja. "The Religious Views of Preachers in the Kraków Progressive Synagogue Tempel in the Nineteenth Century." *Gal Ed* 25 (2017): 41–53.

Massarik, Fred. "A Report on Intermarriage." 1972, www.jewishdatabank.org [retrieved May 8, 2024].

Mayse, Ariel Evan. "The Development of Neo-Hasidism: Echoes and Repercussions, Part I: Introduction, Hillel Zeitlin, and Martin Buber." Dec. 19, 2018, https://thelehrhaus.com [retrieved May 8, 2024].

——. "The Development of Neo-Hasidism: Echoes and Repercussions, Part III: Shlomo Carlebach and Zalman Schachter-Shalomi." Jan. 23, 2019, https://thelehrhaus.com [retrieved May 8, 2024].

——. "Renewal and Redemption: Spirituality, Law, and Religious Praxis in the Writings of Rabbi Zalman Schachter-Shalomi." *Journal of Religion*, 101, no. 4 (2021): 455–504.

Meidan, Yaakov. "Ahat hi ha-Emet." *Alon Shevut* 161 (2002), www.asif.co.il [retrieved May 8, 2024].

Meirovitch, Harvey W. *The Shaping of Masorti Judaism in Israel*. Ramat Gan: Argov Center–Bar-Ilan University, 1999.

Melamed, Eliezer. "Ha-Rav Melamed Masbir: Lamah Hishtatafti be-Panel im Rabbah Reformit." Nov. 6, 2020, www.inn.co.il [retrieved May 8, 2024].

———. "Ha-Rav Melamed: Lamrot ha-Peniyot Lo Etmoded al Tafkid Ha-Rav ha-Rashi." Nov. 25, 2020, www.inn.co.il [retrieved May 8, 2024].

———. *Peninei Halakhah* [20 volumes]. Har Bracha: Yeshivat Har Bracha, 2002–2023.

Merriam-Webster. *Merriam-Webster Dictionary*, www.merriam-webster.com [retrieved July 26, 2024].

Meyer, Michael A. *Response to Modernity: A History of the Reform Movement in Judaism*. Detroit: Wayne State University Press, 1995.

Miles, Sam, and Regan Koch. "Inviting the Stranger In: Intimacy, Digital Technology and New Geographies of Encounter." *Progress in Human Geography* (Oct. 9, 2020), https://doi.org/10.1177%2F0309132520961881.

Miller, Peter N. "Meeting Again and Again: Reading Pinkhos Churgin's Essay Seventy-Five Years Later." In *Rav Hesed: Essays in Honor of Rabbi Dr. Haskel Lookstein*, vol. 2, edited by Rafael Medoff, 61–74. New York: Ktav, 2009.

Mintz, Adam. https://rabbimintz.com [retrieved July 26, 2024].

Mirsky, Yehudah. *Rav Kook: A Mystic in a Time of Revolution*. New Haven, CT: Yale University Press, 2013.

———. "The New Heavens in the New World: The Religious Hebraism of Samuel K. Mirsky." In *The Paths of Daniel: Studies in Judaism and Jewish Culture in Honor of Rabbi Professor Daniel Sperber*, edited by Adam S. Ferziger and David Sperber, 101–128. Ramat Gan: BIU Press, 2017.

Mittelman, Tonya. "Women in the Torah World in the Thought of Rabbi Aharon Lichtenstein." *Tradition* 52, no. 1 (2020): 67–80.

Mollov, Ben, and Chaim Lavie. "Culture, Dialogue, and Perception Change in the Israeli-Palestinian Conflict." *International Journal of Conflict Management* 12, no. 1 (2001): 69–87.

Mondshine, Yehoshua. "The Fluidity of Categories in Hasidism: *Avera Lishma* in the Teachings of R. Zvi Elimelekh of Dynow." In *Hasidism Reappraised*, edited by Ada Rapoport-Albert, 301–320. London: Valentine Mitchell, 1996.

Morgan-Ellis, Esther M. "'Like Pieces in a Puzzle': Online Sacred Harp Singing during the COVID-19 Pandemic." *Frontiers in Psychology* 12 (2021), www.frontiersin.org [retrieved May 13, 2024].

Morris, Bonnie J. "The Children's Crusade: The Tzivos Hashem Youth Movement as an Aspect of Hasidic Identity." *Judaism* 40, no. 3 (1991): 333–343.

Morrison, David. *The Gush*. Jerusalem: Gefen, 2003.

Moshkovits, Yisrael. "Sa'arat Kevuratah shel Alina Palhati z"l: Geder ha-Matekhet be-Veit ha-Almin Hussar." Nov. 16, 2023, www.ynet.co.il [retrieved May 13, 2024].

Moskowitz, Ira. "Long, Long Ago, When Basketball Was Kosher." May 19, 2006, www
.haaretz.com [retrieved May 6, 2024].

Nadell, Pamela. *Women Who Would be Rabbis*. Boston, MA: Beacon Press, 1998.

Nadler, Allan. "Maimonides in Ma'ale Adumim." Summer 2018, https:
//jewishreviewofbooks.com [retrieved May 15, 2024].

Nagen, Yakov. "Scholarship Needs Spirituality, Spirituality Needs Scholarship: Challenges for Emerging Talmudic Methodologies." *Torah u-Madda Journal* 16 (2012–
2013): 101–133.

Nahshoni, Kobi. "Ha-Ma'avak Mithamem: Ha-im Rabbanei Tzohar lo Yukhlu le-
Haten." July 7, 2007, www.ynet.co.il [retrieved May 8, 2024].

———. "Kelale Tseniyut shel ha-Rav Aviner: Kakh Tilbeshi mi-Gil Shalosh." Dec. 30,
2012, www.ynet.co.il [retrieved May 8, 2024].

———. "Campaign Yahadut ha-Torah: Ha-Mitgairim ha-Reformim hushvu le-
Kelavim." Mar. 3, 2021, www.ynet.co.il [retrieved May 8, 2024].

Navon, Chaim. "Iyov lo Haya ve-lo Nivra: Al Mikra ve-Historia." *Alon Shevut* 159
(2001), www.asif.co.il [retrieved May 8, 2024].

Nesher, Ila. *Proposal to the Religious Pluralism Subcommittee of the United Jewish Communities of MetroWest—New Jersey*. Tel Aviv: Beit Daniel, 2007.

Niebuhr, Reinhold. *Moral Man and Immoral Society*. New York: Charles Scribner's
Sons, 1934.

Nicholls, Jaqueline. www.jacquelinenicholls.com [retrieved July 25, 2024].

Niederland, Doron. "From Frankfurt to Jerusalem: Horev School—A Special Approach in the Israeli Religious School System." *Zutot* 4, no. 1 (June 2004): 142–152.

Nimni, Ephraim, ed. *The Challenge of Post Zionism*. London: Zed Books, 2003.

Odenheimer, Micha. "On Orthodoxy: An Interview with Rabbi Shlomo Carlebach."
Gnosis 16 (1990): 46–49.

Okun, Sarit, and Galit Nimrod. "Online Ultra-Orthodox Religious Communities as
a Third Space: A Netnographic Study." *International Journal of Communication* 11
(2017): 2825–2841.

Ophir (Offenbacher), Natan. *Rabbi Shlomo Carlebach: Life, Mission, and Legacy*. Jerusalem and New York: Urim Publications, 2014.

———. "Evaluating Rabbi Shlomo Carlebach's Place in Jewish History." *American Jewish History* 100, no. 4 (2016): 541–546.

Orbach, Michael. "James Kugel: Professor of Disbelief." Mar. 4, 2014, www.momentmag
.com [retrieved May 8, 2024].

Orknad, Robert. "Transcending Walls in Tel Aviv." 2012, https://issuu.com [retrieved
May 9, 2024].

The Oxford English Dictionary. Oxford and New York: Oxford University Press, 1998.

Oxford University Press. *Oxford English Dictionary*, www.oed.com [retrieved July
26, 2024].

Oz, Amos. *Poh ve-Sham be-Erets Yisrael*. Tel Aviv: Am Oved, 1982.

Pachter, Ido. "Hitpathutah shel ha-Orthodoksiyah ha-Modernit be-Amerika: Dega-
mim ve-Shitot." PhD dissertation, BIU, 2016.

———. "Yahadut shel Emet: Kavim le-Demuto shel Ha-Rav Nahum Rabinovitch." May 16, 2018, www.makorrishon.co.il [retrieved June 5, 2024].

———. "Davek be-Amo: Ha-Rav Yonatan Sacks hayah ha-Rav ha-Rashi shel ha-Yahadut." Nov. 11, 2020, www.makorrishon.co.il [retrieved May 12, 2024].

———. *Zionut Datit Metunah—Manifest Ra'ayoni.* Petah Tikvah: Ne'emanei Torah va-Avodah, 2023.

Pandemic Religion: A Digital Archive. https://pandemicreligion.org [retrieved May 15, 2024].

Paz-Fuchs, Amir, Ronen Mandelkern, and Itzhak Galnoor, eds. *The Privatization of Israel: The Withdrawal of State Responsibility.* New York: Palgrave Macmillan, 2018.

Peled, Daniella. "Still Snubbed by Chief Rabbi, Limmud U.K. Kicks Off Annual Conference." Dec. 23, 2012, www.haaretz.com [retrieved May 8, 2024].

Perez, Nahshon. "Rabbi Lord Jonathan Sacks' Political Thought and the State of Israel." *Israel Affairs* 29, no. 3 (2023): 700–715.

Perl, Noam. "Shlihim le-khol ha-Hayyim." Jan. 1, 2010, www.ynet.co.il.

Persico, Tomer. "Neo-Hasidic Revival: Expressivist Uses of Traditional Lore." *Modern Judaism* 34, no. 3 (2014): 287–308.

Persky, Charles. "Plainclothesmen, Cops Keep Ben-Gurion's Party Intact." *The Commentator* (Mar. 31, 1960), 3.

Pfeffer, Anshel. "In One Sentence, Chief Rabbi Exemplifies Haredi Arrogance towards Wartime Israel." Mar. 10, 2024, www.haaretz.com [retrieved May 8, 2024].

Pfeffer, Yehoshua. "Or la-Yehudim: Ha-Rav Sacks ve-ha-Yahadut ha-Toranit." Nov. 15, 2020, iyun.org.il [retrieved May 12, 2024].

Pianko, Noam. *Zionism and the Roads Not Taken: Rawidowicz, Kaplan, and Kohn.* Bloomington: Indiana University Press, 2010.

Pink, Aiden. "Founding Rabbi Retires from Yeshiva That Trains Female Religious Judges." Oct. 4, 2017, https://forward.com [retrieved May 9, 2024].

———. "Pittsburgh Jews 'Heartbroken' After Poway Synagogue Shooting Six Months Later." Apr. 27, 2019, https://forward.com [retrieved May 13, 2024].

Putnam, Robert. "Bowling Alone: America's Declining Social Capital." *Journal of Democracy* 6, no. 1 (1995): 65–78.

Pyuterkovsky, Shlomo. "Ha-Mikhtav Neged ha-Rav Melamed: Hemshekh ha-Pegi'ah ha-Haredit ba-Rabbanut ha-Rashit." Nov. 8, 2020, www.makorrishon.co.il [retrieved May 8, 2024].

———. "Kerav Rav: Ha-Se'arah Sviv ha-Pegishah im ha-Rabah ha-Reformit." Nov. 18, 2020, www.makorrishon.co.il [retrieved May 8, 2024].

Rabinovitch, Nahum. Yad Peshutah. Ma'ale Adumim: Ma'aliyot. 1987-2011 (21 volumes)
———. *Shu"t Siah Nahum.* Ma'ale Adumim: Ma'aliyot, 2008.

Radzyner, Amihai. "Between Scholar and Jurist: The Controversy over the Research of Jewish Law Using Comparative Methods at the Early Time of the Field." *Journal of Law and Religion* 23, no. 1 (2007–2008): 189–248.

———. "On the Beginning of Rabbinical Courts' Procedural Regulations: 'Sidrei Ha-Mishpatim,' 1921." *Bar-Ilan Law Studies* 25 (2009): 37–75 [Hebrew].

Rakeffet-Rothkoff, Aaron. *From Washington Avenue to Washington Street*. Jerusalem: Gefen/OU Press, 2011.

Ram, Uri. "Glocommodification: How the Global Consumes the Local—McDonald's in Israel." *Current Sociology* 52 (2004): 11–31.

Raucher, Michal. "Yoatzot Halacha—Ruling the Internet, One Question at a Time." In *Digital Religion*, edited by Heidi A. Campbell, 57–73. New York: Routledge, 2017.

———. *Conceiving Agency: Reproductive Authority among Haredi Women*. Bloomington: Indiana University Press, 2020.

Rebhun, Uzi. *Jews and the American Religious Landscape*. New York: Columbia University Press, 2016.

Rebhun, Uzi, and Lilach Lev Ari. *American Israelis: Migration, Transnationalism, and Diasporic Identity*. Leiden: Brill, 2013.

Reichner, Elyashiv. *By Faith Alone: The Story of Rabbi Yehuda Amital*, translated by Elli Fischer. Jerusalem: Koren, 2011.

Reiner, Rami. "Rabbi Aharon Lichtenstein and Academic Talmud Study." Feb. 1, 2018, www.thelehrhaus.com [retrieved May 8, 2024].

Reisinger, Morgan Elizabeth. *Historical Assessment of the Transformation of Kibbutzim of Israel's Southern Arava*. Worcester, MA: Worcester Polytechnic Institute, 2019. https://digitalcommons.wpi.edu [retrieved May 16, 2024].

Religion Watch. "Praying and Networking Give Religious Right Second Wind?" *Religion Watch* 32, no. 11 (2017), www.religionwatch.com [retrieved May 16, 2024].

Remennick, Larissa. "Transnational Lifestyles among Russian Israelis: A Follow-Up Study." *Global Networks* 13, no. 4 (Oct. 2013): 478–497.

Resnick, Elliot. "Shut Down the Bible Department." Mar. 21, 2013, www.kolhamevaser.com [retrieved May 8, 2024].

Reuters. "Jewish-Led Peace Activists Protest at Statue of Liberty to Demand Gaza Ceasefire." Nov. 7, 2023, www.reuters.com [retrieved May 13, 2024].

Riches, Tanya. "Review: Heidi Campbell, *Digital Creatives and the Rethinking of Religious Authority*." *Journal of Religion, Media and Digital Culture* 10 (2021): 350–355.

Ringel, Joseph. "The Construction and De-construction of the Ashkenazi vs. Sephardic/Mizrahi Dichotomy in Israeli Culture: Rabbi Eliyahou Zini vs. Rabbi Ovadia Yosef." *Israel Studies* 21, no. 2 (Summer 2016): 182–205.

Riskin, Shlomo (Steven). "B-G Stresses Study in Israel to Overflow Crowd at YU." *The Commentator* (Mar. 31, 1960), 1.

———. *The Rebellious Wife, the Agunah, and the Right of Women to Initiate Divorce in Jewish Law, a Halachic Solution*. New York: Ktav, 1989.

———. "Can a Leopard Change Its Spots?" *Sh'ma Journal* 26 (Sept. 29, 1995): 3–5.

———. "The Master Teacher." In *My Yeshiva College*, edited by Menachem Butler and Zev Nagel, 253–257. Jerusalem: Yashar, 2006.

———. *Listening to God: Inspirational Stories for my Granchildren*. Jerusalem: Koren/Maggid, 2011.

Robbins, Andrea, and Max Becher. *Andrea Robbins and Max Becher*, www.robbinsbecher.com [retrieved July 25, 2024].

Robinson, Ira. "A Portrait of the Rabbi as a Young Man: Rabbi Pinchas Hirschprung's Memoir of His Escape from Europe to Canada." *Canadian Jewish Studies* 27 (2019): 37–47.

Ronen, Gil. "Rabbi Shapira: Fight Neo-Reform Movement." May 7, 2009, www.israelnationalnews.com [retrieved May 8, 2024].

Roof, Wade Clark. *Spiritual Marketplace: Baby Boomers and the Remaking of American Religion*. Princeton, NJ: Princeton University Press, 1999.

Rosenbaum, Alan. "A New Era in Jewish History." Mar. 16, 2017, www.jpost.com [retrieved May 13, 2024].

Rosenberg, Yair, and Yedidya Schwartz. "Israeli Rabbis You Should Know." Oct. 6, 2016, www.tabletmag.com [retrieved May 7, 2024].

Rosensweig, Bernard. "The Emergence of the Professional Rabbi in Ashkenazic Jewry." *Tradition* 11, no. 3 (1970): 22–30.

Rosensweig, Yoni. "My Rebbe—Rav Nachum Eliezer Rabinovitch." May 14, 2020, https://thelehrhaus.com [retrieved May 16, 2024].

Rosen-Zvi, Yishai. "Who Is Jewish: The Less-Known Sides of Reform Judaism." Nov. 11, 2014, www.haaretz.co.il [retrieved May 9, 2024].

Rosman-Stollman, Elisheva. *For God and Country? Religious Student-Soldiers in the Israel Defense Forces*. Austin: University of Texas Press, 2014.

———. "Not Becoming the Norm: Military Service by Religious Israeli Women as a Process of Social Legitimation." *Israel Studies Review* 33, no. 1 (Mar. 2018): 42–60.

———. "Military Service as Bargaining: The Case of Religious Women Soldiers in Israel." *Politics, Religion & Ideology* 19, no. 2 (Mar. 2018): 158–175.

———. "The Pink Tank in the Room: The Role of Religious Considerations in the Discussion of Women's Combat Service—The Case of the Israel Defense Forces." *Religions* 11, no. 11 (2020), www.mdpi.com [retrieved May 8, 2024].

Rosner, Shmuel, and Camil Fuchs. *#Yahadut Yisraelit: Diyukan shel Mahapekhah Tarbutit*. Shoham: Kinneret, Zemurah, Dvir, 2018.

———. *#Israeli Judaism: Portrait of a Cultural Revolution*. Jerusalem: Jewish People Policy Institute, 2019.

Ross, Tamar. *Expanding the Palace of Torah: Orthodoxy and Feminism*. Waltham, MA: Brandeis University Press, 2004.

———. "A Beit Midrash of Her Own: Women's Contribution to the Study and Knowledge of Torah." In *Study and Knowledge in Jewish Thought*, edited by Howard Kreisel, 309–357. Beersheva: Ben-Gurion University of the Negev Press, 2006.

———. *Armon ha-Torah mi-Ma'alah—Al Orthodoksiyah ve-Feminism*. Tel Aviv: Am Oved, 2007.

———. "My Encounters with Blu Greenberg as a Reflection of the Odyssey of Orthodox Feminism." In *You Arose, a Mother in Israel: A Festschrift in Honor of Blu Greenberg*, edited by Devorah Zlochower, 35–45. New York: JOFA, 2017.

———. "Orthodoxy and the Challenge of Biblical Criticism: Reflections on the Importance of Asking the Right Question." In *The Believer and the Modern Study of the Bible*, edited by Tova Ganzel, Yehuda Brandes, and Chayuta Deutsch, 263–287. Boston: Academic Studies Press, 2019.

Rotem, Tamar. "User-Friendly Judaism." *Haaretz* (Sept. 16, 1999), 3B.

Roth, Meir. "Ben Hashdanut le-Hadshanut." *Akdamot* 8 (2000), www.bmj.org.il [retrieved May 8, 2024].

Rozen, Yisrael. "Bli Galgal Rezervi shel ha-Hevre ha-Zioniim tisha'aru Teku'im." Oct. 10, 2011, www.srugim.co.il [retrieved May 7, 2024].

Rubinstein-Shemer, Nesya. "'Because of Your Beard I Can Talk to You': Rabbi Froman as Crisis Mediator between Israelis and Palestinians." *Religions* 14, no. 4 (2023), https://doi.org/10.3390/rel14040483 [retrieved May 7, 2024].

Rynhold, Daniel, Michael J. Harris, and Tamra Wright, eds. *Radical Responsibility Celebrating the Thought of Chief Rabbi Lord Jonathan Sacks.* London: London School of Jewish Studies, 2012.

Sabato, Haim. *Mevakshei Panekha: Sihot in Ha-Rav Aharon Lichtenstein.* Tel Aviv: Yedioth Ahronoth, 2011.

———. *Seeking His Presence: Conversations with Rabbi Aharon Lichtenstein.* Tel Aviv: Yedioth Books, 2021.

Sachar, Abram L. *Brandeis University—A Host at Last,* revised edition. Hanover, NH: Brandeis University Press, 1995.

Sachs, Jeffrey D. *The Ages of Globalization—Geography, Technology, and Institutions.* New York: Columbia University Press, 2019.

Sachs-Shmueli, Leore. "Shagar's Mystical Space: Moving between the Languages of Kabbalah, Hasidism, and Rav Kook." *Religions* 13, no. 1 (2021), www.mdpi.com [retrieved May 12, 2024].

Sacks, Jonathan. "Rabbi J.B. Soloveitchik's Early Epistemology: A Review of *The Halakhic Mind.*" *Tradition* 23, no. 3 (1988): 75–87.

———. "Torah Umadda: The Unwritten Chapter." *Tradition* 53, no. 3 (1990): 192–205.

———. *Tradition in an Untraditional Age.* London: Vallentine. Mitchell, 1990.

———. *One People?: Tradition, Modernity, and Jewish Unity.* London: Littman Library, 1993.

———. "Leadership and Crisis." In *Hazon Nachum: Studies in Jewish Law, Thought, and History Presented to Dr. Norman Lamm on the Occasion of his Seventieth Birthday,* edited by Yaakov Elman and Jeffrey S. Gurock, 3–10. New York: New York University Press, 1997.

———. "Without Walls." 2008, www.rabbisacks.org [retrieved May 12, 2024].

———. *The Great Partnership: Science, Religion, and the Search for Meaning.* New York: Schocken, 2012.

———. *Ceremony and Celebration.* Jerusalem: Koren/Magid, 2017.

———. "How We Can Face the Future without Fear, Together." Apr. 2017, www.ted.com [retrieved May 12, 2024].

———. "The Legacy of the Lubavitcher Rebbe." July 4, 2019, www.rabbisacks.org [retrieved May 12, 2024].

———. *Morality: Restoring the Common Good in Divided Times.* London: Hodder and Stoughton, 2020.

———. "My Teacher: In Memoriam." *Covenant and Conversation* (July 18, 2020), www .rabbisacks.org [retrieved May 16, 2024].

———. www.rabbisacks.org [retrieved July 26, 2024].

Saks, Jeffrey. "Rabbi Joseph B. Soloveitchik and the Israeli Chief Rabbinate: Biographical Notes 1959–60." *Bekhol Derakhekha Daehu* (2006): 45–67.

———. "Rabbi Soloveitchik Meets Rav Kook." *Tradition* 39, no. 3 (Fall 2006): 90–97.

Sales, Ben. "Why You Won't Find Starbucks in Israel." Oct. 11, 2015, www.haaretz.com [retrieved May 12, 2024].

———. "A World-Famous Rabbi, a Popular Assistant and a Succession Crisis: Inside the Rupture at Park East Synagogue." Oct. 27, 2021, www.jta.org [retrieved May 8, 2024].

Salmon, Yosef. "The Mizrachi Movement in America: A Belated but Sturdy Offshoot." *American Jewish Archives* 48 (1996): 161–175.

———. *Religious Zionism—First Encounters*. Jerusalem: Magnes, 2001.

Sarisohn, Hannah. "Rabbi Riskin's Term Extended after Rabbinate Had Thrown Doubt on His Continued Tenure." June 30, 2015, www.jpost.com [retrieved May 8, 2024].

Sarna, Jonathan. "The Debate over Mixed Seating in the American Synagogue." In *The American Synagogue: A Sanctuary Transformed*, edited by Jack Wertheimer, 363–394. New York: Cambridge University Press, 1987.

———. "Converts to Zionism in the American Reform Movement." In *Zionism and Religion*, edited by Samuel Almog, Jehuda Reinharz, and Anita Shapira, 188–203. Hanover, NH, and London: University Press of New England, 1998.

———. "The Future of American Orthodoxy." Feb. 1, 2001, http://shma.com [retrieved May 8, 2024].

———. *American Judaism*. New Haven, CT: Yale University Press, 2004.

———. "Reviewed Works: *An Uneasy Relationship: American Jewish Leadership and Israel, 1948–1957* by Zvi Ganin; *The Struggle for Soviet Jewry in American Politics: Israel versus the American Jewish Establishment* by Fred Lazin; *From Exodus to Freedom: A History of the Soviet Jewry Movement* by Stuart Altshuler." *Israel Studies* 11, no. 3 (Fall 2006): 168–173.

Sasson, Theodore. *The New American Zionism*. New York: New York University Press, 2014.

Sasson-Levy, Orna. "Research on Gender and the Military in Israel." *Israeli Studies Review* 26, no. 2 (Winter 2011): 73–98.

———. "Gender Segregation or Women's Exclusion? The Military as a Case Study." In *Civil–Military Relations in Israel: Essays in Honor of Stuart A. Cohen*, edited by Elisheva Rosman-Stollman and Aharon Kampinsky, 147–171. Lanham, MD: Lexington Books, 2014.

Schachter, Herschel Zvi. "On the Matter of Masorah." 2003, www.torahweb.org [retrieved May 8, 2024].

Schachter, Herschel Zvi, Mordechai Willig, Michael Rosenzweig, and Mayer Twersky. "Torah View of Homosexuality." 2010, www.torahweb.org [retrieved May 8, 2024].

Schapiro, Danielle. "The Sabbath and the Printed Page." June 6, 2023, www.wsj.com [retrieved May 12, 2024].

Schiff, Alvin. "The Development of Israel Study Programs." 2003, www.bjpa.org [retrieved May 16, 2024].

Schneider, Anat, and Esti Eliraz. "Miriam Peretz: Queen of Hearts and Mother of Boys," May 3, 2022, www.israeltoday.co.il [retrieved May 12, 2024].

Schorsch, Ismar. "Emancipation and the Crisis of Religious Authority: The Emergence of the Modern Rabbinate." In *Revolution and Evolution: 1848 in German-Jewish History*, edited by Werner E. Mosse, Arnold Paucker, and Reinhard Rürup, 205–247. Tübingen: J. C. B. Mohr P. Siebeck, 1981.

Schwartz, Dov. *Erez ha-Mamashut ve-ha-Dimayon*. Tel Aviv: Am Oved, 1997.

———. *Faith at the Crossroads: A Theological Profile of Religious Zionism*. Leiden: Brill, 2002.

———. *Religious Zionism: History and Ideology*. Boston: Academic Studies Press, 2008.

———. "Bein Orthodoksiyah Modernit le-Zionut Datit: Behinah Mehudeshet." *Yisrael* 14 (2014): 223–230.

———. "Haguto shel ha-Rav Lichtenstein: Tadmit u-Meziut." *Da'at* 76 (2014): 7–57.

Schwartz, Yaakov. "Yeshiva University's New Head Plans to Bring Modern Orthodoxy into the Future." Oct. 19, 2017, www.timesofisrael.com [retrieved May 8, 2024].

Schwarzfuchs, Simon. *A Concise History of the Rabbinate*. Oxford and Cambridge, MA: B. Blackwell, 1993.

Schwed, Moshe. "All Daf One Year Highlight Reel." Jan. 2021, https://alldaf.org [retrieved May 13, 2024].

Schweid, Eliezer. "Shtei Gishot la-Ra'ayon 'Shelilat ha-Golah' ba-Ideologiyah ha-Zionit." *Ha-Zionut: Me'assef* 9 (1984): 21–44.

Scult, Mel. *The Radical American Judaism of Mordecai M. Kaplan*. Bloomington: Indiana University Press, 2015.

Secunda, Shai. "Wild Things: The New Neo-Hasidism and Modern Orthodoxy." Winter 2022, https://jewishreviewofbooks.com [retrieved May 8, 2024].

Sedley, David. "Launching in English, Chapter-a-Day Project Looks to Bring Bible Back to the Masses." July 15, 2018, www.timesofisrael.com [retrieved May 8, 2024].

Segal, Hagai. "Efshar le-Daber im Kulam." June 11, 2020, www.makorrishon.co.il [retrieved May 8, 2024].

Segev, Zohar. "American Zionists' Place in Israel after Statehood: From Involved Partners to Outside Supporters." *American Jewish History* 93, no. 3 (Sept. 2007): 277–302.

Seidler-Feller, Shaul. "Rabbi Aharon Lichtenstein on the Divide between Traditional and Academic Jewish Studies." Mar. 27, 2018, http://seforim.blogspot.co.il [retrieved May 8, 2024].

Sela, Neta. "Ha-Rav Lior: Kol Maga im ha-Reformim Asur Hilkhatit." Oct. 24, 2006, www.ynet.co.il [retrieved May 8, 2024].

Senor, Dan, and Saul Singer, *Start-Up Nation*. New York: Twelve Books, 2009.

Shafran Gittleman, Idit. "Female Service in the IDF: The Challenge of an 'Integrated' Army." Feb. 2, 2018, www.lawfareblog.com [retrieved May 8, 2024].

Shai, Don. "Working Women/Cloistered Men: A Family Development Approach to Marriage Arrangements among Ultra-Orthodox Jews." *Journal of Comparative Family Studies* 33, no. 1 (2002), 97–115.

Shain, Yossi. *Ha-Me'ah ha-Yisraelit ve-ha-Yisraelizaziyah shel ha-Yahadut.* Tel Aviv: Yedioth Aharonoth, 2019.

———. *The Israeli Century.* Brentwood, TN: Wicked Son, 2021.

Shaked, Saar. *Form Vision to Reality: Judaism, Study and Leadership in the Leo Baeck Educational Center.* Haifa: Leo Baeck Educational Center, 2006 [Hebrew].

Shalev, Alon. "Major Themes in the Biography and Thought of Rabbi Isaac Hutner." MA thesis, Ben-Gurion University, 2013 [Hebrew].

Shalvi, Alice. *Never a Native.* London: Halban Publishers, 2019.

Shapira, Anita. *Ben-Gurion: Father of Modern Israel.* New Haven, CT: Yale University Press, 2014.

Shapira, Haim-Moshe. "The Mission of Religious Zionism." In *Religious Zionism: An Anthology,* edited by Yosef Tirosh, 111–120. Jerusalem: Torah Department/WZO, 1975.

Shapira, Yehoshua. "Me-Hashem Yatsah ha-Davar, al ha-Neo-Reformah." 2009, www .yrg.org.il [retrieved May 8, 2024].

Shapiro, David H. *From Philanthropy to Activism: The Political Transformation of American Zionism in the Holocaust Years, 1933–1945.* Oxford: Pergamon, 1993.

Shapiro, Marc B. *Between the Yeshiva World and Modern Orthodoxy: The Life and Works of Rabbi Jehiel Jacob Weinberg, 1884–1966.* London: Littman Library of Jewish Civilization, 1999.

———. "Of Books and Bans." *Edah Journal* 3, no. 2 (2003): 1–16.

———. *The Limits of Orthodox Theology.* Oxford and Portland, OR: Littman Library, 2004.

———. *Saul Lieberman and the Orthodox.* Scranton, PA: University of Scranton Press, 2006.

———. "Is Modern Orthodoxy Moving towards an Acceptance of Biblical Criticism?" *Modern Judaism* 37, no. 2 (2017): 165–193.

———. "Modern Orthodoxy and Religious Truth." In *Yitz Greenberg and Modern Orthodoxy,* edited by Adam S. Ferziger, Miri Freud-Kandel, and Steven Bayme, 129–146. Boston: Academic Studies Press, 2019.

Sharabi, Asaf. "'Boundary Work' in a Religious Revival Movement: The Case of the 'Teshuvah Movement' in Israel." *Ethnography* 14, no. 2 (2013): 233–254.

Sharon, Jeremy. "Rabbi Sacks in Israel to Promote Idea of Compatibility of Science and Religion." Nov. 10, 2013, www.jpost.com [retrieved May 12, 2024].

———. "Rabbinical Emissary Program to Diaspora Celebrates 20 Years of Work." May 16, 2019, www.jpost.com [retrieved May 8, 2024].

———. "Ben Gvir Hails Racist Kahane, Is Booed for Saying He Doesn't Want to Expel All Arabs." Nov. 10, 2022, www.timesofisrael.com [retrieved May 8, 2024].

Shavit, Yaakov, and Mordechai Eran. *The Hebrew Bible Reborn: From Hebrew Scripture to the Book of Books*. Berlin: Walter de Gruyter, 2007.

Shaw, Steven. "Orthodox Reactions to the Challenge of Biblical Criticism." *Tradition* 10, no. 3 (Spring 1969): 61–85.

Sheinman, Zvi. "Ha-Rav Cherlow: Medinat Yisrael Zerikhah le-ha-kir ba-Reformim." Dec. 11, 2012, www.srugim.co.il [retrieved May 8, 2024].

Sheleg, Yair. *Ha-Dati'im ha-Hadashim*. Jerusalem: Keter, 2000.

———. *Hashpa'at ha-Aliyah mi-Zefon America al ha-Hayyim ha-Orthodoksim be-Yisrael*. Ramat-Gan: Merkaz Argov/Bar-Ilan University Press, 2000.

———. "Lo Maspik le-Hitnahel, Zarikh gam le-Hithazek." Sept. 10, 2003, www.haaretz.co.il [retrieved May 13, 2024].

———. "Mufkarim." May 31, 2007, www.haaretz.co.il [retrieved May 7, 2024].

———. "Tefillat Shabbat Hilonit le-Mehadrin." June 11, 2011, www.haaretz.co.il [retrieved May 12, 2024].

———, ed. *Mi-Mashgiah Kashrut le-Nahag ha-Keter: Ha-Zionut ha-Datit ve-ha Hevrah ha-Yisraelit*. Jerusalem: Israel Democratic Institute, 2019.

———. *Ha-Hardal"im*. Jerusalem: Israel Democratic Institute, 2020.

———. "Kah Hafakh Ha-Rav Melamed le-Demut ha-Toranit ha-Mashpiah ba-Zionut ha-Datit." June 24, 2020, www.makorrishon.co.il [retrieved May 8, 2024].

———. *Ha-Hut ha-Meshulash: Kizur Toldot ha-Zionut ha-Datit*. Modi'in: Kinneret, Zmora, Dvir, 2024 [digital version].

Sherzer, Adi. "Exporting Israel to the Diaspora: The Attempt to Make Israel's Independence Day into a Worldwide Jewish Holiday." *Israel Studies* 25, no. 1 (2019): 174–197.

Shiff, Ofer. "Mabat Aher al ha-Americanizaziah shel ha-Zionut." *Iyunim be-Tekumat Yisrael* 10 (2000): 180–206.

———. *The Downfall of Abba Hillel Silver and the Foundation of Israel*. Syracuse, NY: Syracuse University Press, 2014.

———. "Early American Zionist Responses to the Israeli Demand for *Aliya*." *Modern Judaism* 38, no. 1 (2018): 96–119.

Shiff, Ofer, Adi Sherzer, and Talia Gorodess. "The Ben-Gurion–Blaustein Exchange: Ben-Gurion's Perspective between an Ideological Capitulation and a Strategic Alliance." *Israel Studies* 25, no. 3 (2020): 15–32.

Shimoni, Gideon. "Theory and Practice of Shlilat Hagalut Reconsidered." In *The Age of Zionism*, edited by Anita Shapira, Jehuda Reinharz, and Jay Harris, 45–64. Jerusalem: Merkaz Shazar, 2000 [Hebrew].

Shinhav, Shmuel. "Hora'at Tanakh be-Yisrael u-ve-Hemed bi-Pherat." 2011, www.daat.ac.il [retrieved May 8, 2024].

Shochetman, Eliav. *Civil Procedure in Rabbinical Courts*. Jerusalem: E. S. Sidrei Mishpat, 2011 [Hebrew].

Shragai, Nadav. "Ha-Rav Riskin: Efshar le-haf'il Tahburah Zibburit be-Shabbat." Jan. 23, 2018, www.srugim.co.il [retrieved May 8, 2024].

Shurin, Aharon Ben Zion. *Bein Yehudei Arzot ha-Berit*. Jerusalem: Mossad ha-Rav Kook, 1981.

Siegelbaum, Chana Bracha. "Reb Shlomo and Me." Nov. 2, 2015, www.berotbatayin.org [retrieved Nov 2, 2024].

Silberstein, David. "Personal Autonomy in the Thought of R. Nachum Eliezer Rabinovitch." *The Lehrhaus* (June 8, 2020), https://thelehrhaus.com.

Sklare, Marshall. *Conservative Judaism: An American Religious Movement.* New York: Free Press, 1955.

Slomowitz, Alan, ed. *Homosexuality, Transsexuality, Psychoanalysis, and Traditional Judaism.* New York: Routledge, 2019.

Sofaer, Abraham. "Finding an Unlikely Home." In *My Yeshiva College*, edited by Menachem Butler and Zev Nagel, 280–281. Jerusalem: Yashar, 2006.

Sofer, Barbara. "The Human Spirit: Being Malka Bina." Oct. 2, 2014, www.jpost.com [retrieved May 6, 2024].

Sokol, Sam. "The Female Talmudists." Oct. 7, 2012, www.jpost.com [retrieved May 13, 2024].

Solomon, Norman. *Torah from Heaven—The Reconstruction of Faith.* Liverpool: Littman Library, 2012.

Soloveitchik, Joseph B. "Message to a Rabbinic Convention." In *The Sanctity of the Synagogue*, edited by Baruch Litvin, 109–114. New York: Spero Foundation, 1959.

———. "On Seating and Sanctification." In *The Sanctity of the Synagogue*, 114–118.

———. *Halakhic Man*, translated by Lawrence Kaplan. Philadelphia: JPS, 1983.

———. *Fate and Destiny: From the Holocaust to the State of Israel*, translated by Lawrence Kaplan. Hoboken, NJ: Ktav, 1992.

———. *Covenant, Community and Commitment: Selected Letters and Communications*, edited by Nathaniel Helfgot. New York: Toras Horav/Ktav, 2005.

———. *Kol Dodi Dofek: Listen, My Beloved Knocks*, translated by David Z. Gordon. New York: Ktav, 2006.

Sperber, Daniel. "Congregational Dignity and Human Dignity: Women and Public Torah Reading." In *Women and Men in Communal Prayer: Halakhic Perspectives*, edited by Howard Trachtman, 27–205. New York: JOFA, 2010.

———. *Rabba, Maharat, Rabbanit, Rebbetzin: Women with Leadership Authority According to Halachah.* Jerusalem: Urim Publications–Maharat, 2020.

Serugim. "Okef Tikshoret: 100,000 Hovrot shel ha-Rav Levinstein." Apr. 1, 2018, www.srugim.co.il [retrieved May 8, 2024].

———. "Ha-Rav Cherlow: Azuv she-ha Rehavah ha-Reformit ba-Kotel Reikah." July 20, 2023, www.srugim.co.il [retrieved May 8, 2024].

Stefansky, Eli. "The Artscroll Interview with R' Eli Stefansky—'A Deeper Look.'" Oct. 4, 2021, www.youtube.com/watch?v=XuDIatPdlZw [retrieved May 13, 2024].

Steinhardt, Joan. "American Neo-Hasids in the Land of Israel." *Nova Religio: The Journal of Alternative and Emergent Religions* 13, no. 4 (2010): 22–42.

Stern, Nehemia, and Uzi Ben-Shalom. "Soldiers and Scholars: Ritual Dilemmas among National Religious Combat Soldiers in the Israel Defense Forces." *Journal of Contemporary Ethnography* 49, no. 3 (2020): 345–370.

Stern, Yedidya Z. "The Identity Crisis of the State of Israel." *Democratic Culture* 14 (2012): 257–272 [Hebrew].

Stewart, Anna Rose. "Text and Response in the Relationship between Online and Offline Religion." *Information, Communication & Society* 14, no. 8 (2011): 1204–1218.

Stitskin, Leon D., ed. *Studies in Judaica: in Honor of Dr. Samuel Belkin as Scholar and Educator*. New York: Ktav, 1974.

Stolow, Jeremy. "Transnationalism and the New Religio-politics: Reflections on a Jewish Orthodox Case." *Theory, Culture, and Society* 21, no. 2 (2004): 109–137.

Stolzenberg, Nomi M., and David N. Myers, *American Shtetl: The Making of Kiryas Joel, a Hasidic Village in Upstate New York*. Princeton, NJ: Princeton University Press, 2022.

Stone, Yakov. "RAFT Hosts Discussion with Aaron Koller on Biblical Creation in the Modern World." Sept. 29, 2016, https://yucommentator.org [retrieved May 8, 2024].

Tabory, Ephraim. "Reform and Conservative Judaism in Israel: A Social and Religious Profile." *American Jewish Year Book* 83 (1983): 41–61.

———. "The Influence of Liberal Judaism on Israeli Religious Life." *Israel Studies* 5, no. 1 (2000): 183–203.

———. *The Reform Movement in Israel: Achievements and Chances*. Ramat Gan: Bar Ilan University, 2000 [Hebrew].

———. "The Israel Conservative and Reform Movements and the Market for Liberal Judaism." In *Jews in Israel: Contemporary Social and Cultural Patterns*, edited by Uzi Rebhun and Chaim I. Waxman, 285–314. Waltham, MA: UPNE, 2004.

———. "Americans in the Israeli Reform and Conservative Denominations." In *Israeli Judaism: The Sociology of Religion in Israel*, edited by Shlomo Deshen, Charles S. Liebman, and Moshe Shokeid, 335–347. New Brunswick, NJ: Transaction Books, 1994.

Tabory, Ephraim, and Bernard Lazerwitz. "Americans in the Israeli Reform and Conservative Denominations: Religiosity under an Ethnic Shield?" *Review of Religious Research* 24, no. 3 (1983): 177–187.

Tal, David. "David Ben-Gurion's Teleological Westernism." *Journal of Modern Jewish Studies* 10, no. 3 (2011): 351–364.

Tanyos, Faris. "U.S. Sees Spike in Antisemitic Incidents since Beginning of Israel-Hamas War, Anti-Defamation League Says." Oct. 25, 2023, www.cbsnews.com [retrieved May 13, 2024].

Taylor, Charles. *A Secular Age*. Cambridge, MA: Belknap Press of Harvard University Press, 2007.

Taylor, Derek. *Defenders of the Faith: The History of Jews' College and the London School of Jewish Studies*. Elstree: Vallentine Mitchell, 2016.

Tec, Nechama. *In the Lion's Den: The Life of Oswald Rufeisen*. Oxford: Oxford University Press, 2008.

Teller, Adam. "Rabbinate: The Rabbinate before 1800." In *YIVO Encyclopedia of Jews in Eastern Europe*, edited by Gershon Hundert. New York: YIVO. 2010, www.yivoencyclopedia.org [retrieved May 8, 2024].

Tene, Elad. "Efrat's Rabbi: Same-Sex Couple Can Raise a Family." Jan. 1, 2009, www.ynet.com [retrieved May 8, 2024].

TheTorah.com. "An Interview with Dr. Tova Ganzel." Aug. 4, 2015. https://thetorah.com [retrieved May 8, 2024].

Tiferet Shalom. "How It All Started?" www.tiferetshalom.org.il [retrieved May 15, 2024].

Times of Israel. "Staff Sgt. Rose Lubin, 21: Fought Hamas in South, Fell in Jerusalem." Nov. 13, 2023, www.timesofisrael.com [retrieved May 9, 2024].

Torat Chaim ve-Ahavat Chesed: A Tribute to Rabbi Chaim Brovender. 2007, https://youtube .com/watch?v=tbfJCRbE66s [retrieved March 6, 2025].

Tikochinsky, Michal. *Teach Me Thy Laws: The Beginning of Legal Scholarship in the "Minhat Hinnukh" and Its Author Rabbi Yosef Baavad.* Jerusalem: Nevo, 2020 [Hebrew].

Tirosh-Samuelson, Hava. "Rabbi Jonathan Sacks: Religious Pluralism and the Partnership of Religion and Science." *Kulturní studia/Cultural Studies* 20, no. 1 (2023): 3–24.

Torrosian, Ronn. "The Legacy of Rabbi Shlomo Carlebach." May 20, 2015, www .algemeiner.com [retrieved May 8, 2024].

Troy, Gil. http://giltroy.com [retrieved July 25, 2024].

Troy, Tevi, and Noam Wasserman. "The Talmud for Today's World." Sept. 14, 2023, www.firstthings.com [retrieved May 13, 2024].

Turetsky, Yehuda. "The Year in Israel Has Changed: Neo-Hasidut and American Modern Orthodoxy." In *Contemporary Uses and Forms of Hasidut*, edited by Shlomo Zuckier, 347–370. New York: Yeshiva University Press, 2022.

Tzahor, Zeev. "David Ben-Gurion's Attitude toward the Diaspora." *Judaism* 32, no. 1 (Winter 1983): 9–22.

Uzan, Elad. "From Social Norm to Legal Claim: How American Orthodox Feminism Changed Orthodoxy in Israel." *Modern Judaism* 36, no. 2 (2016): 144–162.

Van Elteren, Mel. *Americanism and Americanization: A Critical History of Domestic and Global Influence.* Jefferson, NC, and London: McFarland, 2006.

———. "Cultural Globalization and Transnational Flows of Things American: The Systemic Dimension of Globalization." *IntechOpen* (Aug. 1, 2011), www.intechopen .com [retrieved May 13, 2024].

Walker, Andrew T. "Southern Baptists, Gender Ideology, and Female Combatants." Oct. 5, 2016, https://providencemag.com [retrieved May 9, 2024].

Waxman, Chaim I. "The Centrality of Israel in American Jewish Life: A Sociological Analysis." *Judaism* 25, no. 2 (Spring 1976): 175–187.

———. *American Aliyah: Portrait of an Innovative Migration Movement.* Detroit: Wayne University State Press, 1989.

———. "In the End Is It Ideology?: Religio-cultural and Structural Factors in American Aliya." *Contemporary Jewry* 16 (1995): 50–67.

———. "A Brief History of Year in Israel Programs." In *Flipping Out: Myth or Fact: The Impact of the "Year in Israel,"* edited by Shalom Z. Berger, Daniel Jacobson, and Chaim I. Waxman, 160–163. Jerusalem: Yashar Books, 2007.

———, ed. *Religious Zionism Post Disengagement: Future Directions.* New York: Yeshiva University Press, 2008.

———. "Halakhic Change vs. Demographic Change: American Orthodoxy, British Orthodoxy, and the Plight of Louis Jacobs." *Journal of Modern Jewish Studies* 14, no. 1 (2015): 58–71.

———. *Social Change and Halakhic Evolution in American Orthodoxy*. Liverpool: Littman Library, 2017.

———. "Review: *We Stand Divided: The Rift between American Jews and Israel* by Daniel Gordis." *Israel Journal of Foreign Affairs* 14, no. 2 (2020): 323–326.

———. "Looking Backward: Modern Orthodoxy in the Year 2000." 2022, https://traditiononline.org [retrieved May 8, 2024].

Waxman, Dov. *Trouble in the Tribe: The American Jewish Conflict over Israel*. Princeton, NJ, and Oxford: Princeton University Press, 2016.

Weber, Max. "The Three Types of Legitimate Rule." *Berkeley Publications in Society and Institutions* 4, no. 1 (1958): 1–11.

Weinberg, David M. "The Rabbinic Race Wreckage." Apr. 25, 2013, www.jpost.com [retrieved May 8, 2024].

———. "Remembering Moshko, Builder of Israel—Opinion." Feb. 18, 2021, www.jpost.com [retrieved May 7, 2024].

Weissbrod, Lilly. "Shas: An Ethnic Religious Party." *Israel Affairs* 9, no. 4 (2003): 79–104.

Werczberger, Rachel. *Jews in the Age of Authenticity*. New York: Peter Lang, 2017.

Werczberger, Rachel, and Na'ama Azulay. "The Jewish Renewal Movement in Israeli Secular Society." *Contemporary Jewry* 31 (2011): 107–128.

Werner, Craig. *Higher Ground: Stevie Wonder, Aretha Franklin, Curtis Mayfield, and the Rise and Fall of American Soul*. New York: Crown Archetype, 2007.

Wertheimer, Jack, ed. *The American Synagogue—A Sanctuary Transformed*. Cambridge: Cambridge University Press, 1987.

———. *All Quiet on the Religious Front: Jewish Unity, Denominationalism, and Postdenominationalism in the United States*. New York: American Jewish Committee, 2005.

———. *The New American Judaism*. Princeton, NJ: Princeton University Press, 2018.

Wieder, Jeremy. "Rabbi Jeremy Wieder Claims 11 Chapters of the Torah Are Mythology contra Rabbi Moshe Meiselman." June 12, 2011, http://jeremy-wieder-lectures.blogspot.com [retrieved May 8, 2024].

Wiesel, Eliezer (Elie). "Yomo ha-Yehudi shel Ben-Gurion." *Yedioth Aharonoth* (Mar. 17, 1960), 2.

Willig, Mordechai. "Trampled Laws." 2015, www.torahweb.org [retrieved May 15, 2024].

Wimpfheimer, Barry Scott. *The Talmud: A Biography*. Princeton, NJ: Princeton University Press, 2018.

Winer, Stuart. "In Israeli First, Woman Chosen as Sole Spiritual Leader of Orthodox Community." Apr. 29, 2021, www.timesofisrael.com [retrieved May 16, 2024].

Wistoch, Moshe, and Adi Mamo Schwartz. "Rulings Devoid of Human Compassion Will Bring Orthodoxy to Its End." Mar. 30, 2018, https://ots.org.il [retrieved May 7, 2024].

Wolf, Daniel. "'Hiddush' within the Beit Midrash: R. Aharon Lichtenstein's Approach to Lomdus as an Adaptive Improvement to the Brisker Derekh." Tradition 47, no. 4 (Winter 2014): 113–125.

Woolf, Jeffrey R. "Time Awareness as a Source of Spirituality in the Thought of Rabbi Joseph B. Soloveitchik." Modern Judaism 32, no. 1 (2012): 54–75.

Wurtzburger, Walter. "Confronting the Challenge of the Values of Modernity." Torah U-Madda Journal 1 (1989): 104–112.

Wuthnow, Robert. After Heaven: Spirituality in America since the 1950s. Berkeley: University of California Press, 1998.

Yadgar, Ya'akov. Secularism and Religion in Jewish-Israeli Politics: Traditionists and Modernity. Abingdon: Routledge, 2010.

———. "A Post-secular Look at Tradition: Toward a Definition of Traditionalism." Telos-New York 156 (2011): 77–98.

———. Sovereign Jews: Israel, Zionism, and Judaism. Albany: SUNY Press, 2017.

Yanklowitz, Shmuly. "The Growing Legacy of Rabbi Chaim Brovender." Oct. 27, 2013, https://blogs.timesofisrael.com [retrieved May 6, 2024].

Yeshivat Har Etzion, Israel Koschitzky Torat Har Etzion. https://etzion.org.il [retrieved July 25, 2024].

Zaleski, Carol. "William James: The Varieties of Religious Experience 1902." First Things (Mar. 2000), www.firstthings.com [retrieved May 8, 2024].

Zameret, Zvi, and Moshe Tlamim, "Ben-Gurion's Private Beliefs and Public Policy." Israel Studies 4, no. 2 (Fall 1999): 64–89.

Ziegler, Reuven, and Yehudah Mirsky. "Torah and Humanity in a Time of Rebirth: Rav Yehuda Amital as Educator and Thinker." In Torah and Western Thought; Intellectual Portraits of Orthodoxy and Modernity, edited by Meir Y. Soloveichik, Stuart W. Halpern, and Shlomo Zuckier, 179–218. New Milford, CT, and Jerusalem: Maggid Books, 2015.

Zimmerman, Deena R. A Lifetime Companion to the Laws of Jewish Family Life. Jerusalem and New York: Urim Publications, 2005.

Zinger, Vered. "Secular Kfar Shmaryahu Has a Beloved Orthodox Rabbi: What Is the Secret of His Success?" Mar. 21, 2023, www.haaretz.co.il [retrieved May 13, 2024].

Zion, Mishael. "What Kind of Religious Jew Am I? The Rachel and Jon Kind." Sept. 8, 2024, www.timesofisrael.com [retrieved Dec. 2, 2024].

Zion-Waldoks, Tanya. "'Family Resemblance' and Its Discontents: Towards the Study of Orthodoxy's Politics of Belonging and Lived Orthodoxies in Israel." AJS Review 46, no. 1 (2022): 12–37.

Zippor, Amichai. "Learning Experience." July 5, 2007, www.jpost.com [retrieved May 6, 2024].

Zohar, Haim. "Mai Kollel Zioni." In Me'ah Shenot Hinukh Zioni-Dati, edited by Shlomoh Raz, 365–372. Jerusalem: Histadrut ha-Mizrachi/Ha-Poel ha-Mizrachi/Ha-Merkaz ha-Olami, 2006.

Zuckier, Shlomo. "Rav Lichtenstein on Wissenschaft in His Own Yiddish Words." Mar. 26, 2018, www.thelehrhaus.com [retrieved May 8, 2024].

Zuckier, Shlomo, and Shalom Carmy, "An Introductory Biographical Sketch of R. Aharon Lichtenstein." *Tradition* 47, no. 4 (2015): 6–16.

LIST OF ORGANIZATIONS AND WEBSITES

929 Organization—www.929.org.il

ALL DAF—https://alldaf.org

Bar-Ilan University: Basic Jewish Studies—https://yesod.biu.ac.il

Beit Daniel Institute—www.beit-daniel.org.il

Beit Hillel: Attentive Spiritual Leadership—www.beithillel.org.il

Beit Shmuel (Jerusalem)—www.beitshmuel.co.il

Binyamin Regional Council—www.binyamin.org.il

Chabad—www.chabad.org

Gesher Organization—www.gesherusa.org

Giyur K'Halacha—www.giyur.org.il

Haberman Institute for Jewish Studies—www.habermaninstitute.org

Hadran: Talmud Study for Women—https://hadran.org.il

Haredi Research Group—https://www.harediresearchgroup.org.

Havruta: Beit Midrash for Students of the Hebrew University

Havurat Tel Aviv—www.havurattelaviv.org

Herzog Center for Jewish Identity—www.merkazherzog.org

Herzog College—www.herzog.ac.il

Israel Central Bureau of Statistics—www.cbs.gov.il

Israel Ministry of Education—http://cms.education.gov.il

ITIM: The Jewish Life Advocacy Center—Itim.org.il

JChatting: Interviews with a Jewish Flavour—https://jchatting.blogspot.com

Jewish Theological Seminary Library—https://www.jtsa.edu/library

Jewish Voice for Peace—www.jewishvoice.org

Jewish Women's Health (Nishmat)—www.jewishwomenshealth.org

Joint Council of Pre-Army Academies (mechinot)—https://mechinot.org.il

Jonathan Sacks School, Jerusalem—https://yonatansacks.jlm.org.il

Jonathan Sacks - The Rabbi Sacks Legacy—www.rabbisacks.org

Kiryat Ono Municipal Council—www.kiryatono.muni.il

Koren Publishers—https://korenpub.com

Limmud: Jewish Learning Festivals—https://limmud.org

Machon Meir Institute/Yeshiva—https://meirtv.com

Makor Rishon Weekly Newspaper—www.makorrishon.co.il

Masa Israel—www.masaisrael.org

Matan: The Sadie Rennert Women's Institute for Torah Studies—www.matan.org.il

Matanel Foundation—https://www.matanel.org

Merkaz Liba for Israeli Public Policy—https://libayehudit.org

Midreshet Danielle—https://kerendanielle.org

Midreshet Ein HaNatziv www.midrasha.co.il
Migdal Oz Beit Midrash—www.skamigdaloz.org
Mizrachi: Religious Zionist Movement—https://mizrachi.org
Ne'emanei Torah va-Avoda Organization—https://toravoda.org.il
Nefesh b'Nefesh Organization—www.nbn.org.il
Nishmat: The Jeanie Schottenstein Center for Advanced Torah Study for Women—https://nishmat.net
Nishmat's Golda Koschitzky Center for Yoatzot Halacha—www.yoatzot.org
Ohio State University Libraries—https://library.osu.edu
Ohr Torah Stone—https://ots.org.il
Or Hamidbar: Spiritual Judaism in the Desert—https://orhamidbar.org
Orthodox Union (OU)—https://outorah.org
Pardes Institute—www.pardes.org.il
Park Avenue Synagogue—https://pasyn.org
Rabbinic Council of America (RCA)—www.rabbis.org
ReformJudaism.org—https://reformjudaism.org
Shalom Hartman Institute—www.hartman.org.il
Shazur/Interwoven Organization—www.shazur.org
Shira Hadasha Congregation (Jerusalem)—https://shirahadasha.org
The Carlebach Shul (New York)—www.thecarlebachshul.org
The Downtown Minyan (New York)—www.thedowntownminyan.com
Tikvah Fund—https://tikvahfund.org
TMZ/Torah MiTzion Organization—https://torahmitzion.org
Tzohar Organization—www.tzohar.org.il
Yeshiva University—www.yu.edu
Yeshivat Chovevei Torah (YCT)—https://yctorah.org
Yeshivat Kerem B'Yavneh—www.kby.org
Yeshivat Ma'alot—https://yesmalot.co.il
Yeshivat Maharat—www.yeshivatmaharat.org
Yeshivat Otniel—https://otniel.org
Yeshivat Siach—https://siach.org.il
Yeshivat Har Etzion (YHE)—www.etzion.org.il
www.rabbisacks.org
Zion—An Eretz Yisraeli Community in Jerusalem—www.new-kehilat-zion-eng.com

INDEX

Page numbers in italics indicate Figures and Tables.

ABOUT THE AUTHOR

ADAM S. FERZIGER is Professor and Head of the Rabbi Samson Raphael Hirsch Chair for Research of the *Torah im Derekh* Movement in the Israel and Golda Koschitzky Department of Jewish History and Contemporary Jewry, Bar-Ilan University, and co-convener of the annual Oxford Summer Institute on Modern and Contemporary Judaism, University of Oxford. He has published over sixty peer-reviewed articles, and written and edited eight books, including *Exclusion and Hierarchy* (2005) and *Beyond Sectarianism*, which was honored with a National Jewish Book Award in 2016.